NUMBER	EQUATION	PAGE
(6.4)	$$s = \sqrt{\frac{\Sigma(X - \bar{X})^2}{N}}$$	129
(7.1)	$$z = \frac{X - \bar{X}}{s} = \frac{X - \mu}{\sigma}$$	146
(8.2)	$$\lambda = \frac{\Sigma \text{ maximum frequency } (X) - \text{maximum frequency } (Y)}{N - \text{maximum frequency } (Y)}$$	180
(8.3)	$$G = \frac{C - D}{C + D}$$	185
(8.4)	$$d_{yx} = \frac{C - D}{C + D + T_y}$$	189
(8.5)	$$\text{tau-}b = \frac{C - D}{\sqrt{(C + D + T_y)(C + D + T_x)}}$$	191
(9.1)	$$r = \frac{\Sigma(X - \bar{X})(Y - \bar{Y})}{\sqrt{[\Sigma(X - \bar{X})^2][\Sigma(Y - \bar{Y})^2]}}$$	202
(9.2)	$$r = \frac{N \Sigma XY - (\Sigma X)(\Sigma Y)}{\sqrt{[N \Sigma X^2 - (\Sigma X)^2][N \Sigma Y^2 - (\Sigma Y)^2]}}$$	203
(9.4)	$$r_s = 1 - \frac{6 \Sigma D^2}{N(N^2 - 1)}$$	215
(10.1)	$$Y' = a + b_y X$$	230
(10.3)	$$b_y = \frac{\Sigma(X - \bar{X})(Y - \bar{Y})}{\Sigma(X - \bar{X})^2}$$	232
(10.4)	$$b_y = r \frac{s_y}{s_x}$$	232
(10.5)	$$b_y = \frac{N(\Sigma XY) - (\Sigma X)(\Sigma Y)}{N(\Sigma X^2) - (\Sigma X)^2}$$	232
(10.6)	$$a = \bar{Y} - b_y \bar{X}$$	233

Fundamentals of Social Statistics

Fundamentals of Social Statistics

Second Edition

Kirk W. Elifson
Georgia State University

Richard P. Runyon and Audrey Haber

McGraw-Hill, Inc.
New York   St. Louis   San Francisco   Auckland   Bogotá
Caracas   Lisbon   London   Madrid   Mexico City   Milan
Montreal   New Delhi   San Juan   Singapore
Sydney   Tokyo   Toronto

FUNDAMENTALS OF SOCIAL STATISTICS

Printed and bound by Book-mart Press, Inc.

6 7 8 9 10 BKM BKM 9 9 8 7 6 5 4

ISBN 0-07-557292-3

This book was set in Serif by Ruttle, Shaw & Wetherill, Inc.
The editors were Philip A. Butcher, Betrand W. Lummus,
and Eleanor Castellano;
the designer was Chuck Carson;
the production supervisor was Birgit Garlasco.
Cover photograph by Masahiro Sano, courtesy of The Stock Market.

Library of Congress Cataloging-in-Publication Data

Elifson, Kirk W., (date).
    Fundamentals of social statistics / Kirk W. Elifson, Richard P.
Runyon, and Audrey Haber. —2nd ed.
      p.   cm.
    Includes bibliographical references.
    ISBN 0-07-557292-3. —ISBN 0-07-019460-2 (instructor's manual)
    1. Social sciences—Statistical methods.   2. Statistics.
I. Runyon, Richard P.   II. Haber, Audrey.   III. Title.
HA29.E482   1990
519.5—dc20   89-13055

Contents

Preface   xi

1   Introduction

1   The Definition of Statistical Analysis   2

1.1   What Is Statistics?   3
1.2   Definitions of Terms Commonly Used in Statistics   7
1.3   Descriptive Statistics   10
1.4   Inferential Statistics   12
1.5   The Goals of Research   13
1.6   A Word to the Student   15
     Summary   16
     Terms to Remember   17
     Exercises   18

2   Basic Mathematical Concepts   22

2.1   Introduction   23
2.2   Summation Rules   24
2.3   Types of Numbers and Scales   27
2.4   Continuous and Discrete Variables   33
2.5   Rounding   35
2.6   Ratios   37
2.7   Proportions, Percentages, and Rates   38
     Summary   43
     Terms to Remember   43
     Exercises   44

2   Descriptive Statistics

3   Frequency Distributions and Graphing Techniques   54

3.1   Grouping of Data   54
3.2   Cumulative Frequency and Cumulative Percentage Distributions   55
3.3   Graphing Techniques   59
3.4   Misuse of Graphing Techniques   61
3.5   Nominally Scaled Variables   62
3.6   Ordinally Scaled Variables   63
3.7   Interval- and Ratio-Scaled Variables   63
3.8   Forms of Frequency Curves   69

3.9 Other Graphic Representations   72
Summary   73
Terms to Remember   74
Exercises   75

4 Percentiles   82

4.1 Introduction   83
4.2 Cumulative Percentiles and Percentile Rank   84
4.3 Percentile Rank and Reference Group   90
4.4 Centiles, Deciles, and Quartiles   90
Summary   92
Terms to Remember   92
Exercises   93

5 Measures of Central Tendency   96

5.1 Introduction   97
5.2 The Arithmetic Mean $(\bar{X})$ 99
5.3 The Median (Md_n) 107
5.4 The Mode (M_o) 109
5.5 Comparison of Mean, Median, and Mode   110
5.6 The Mean, Median, Mode, and Skewness   114
Summary   115
Terms to Remember   116
Exercises   116

6 Measures of Dispersion   122

6.1 Introduction   123
6.2 The Range   124
6.3 The Interquartile Range   125
6.4 The Mean Deviation   125
6.5 The Variance (s^2) and Standard Deviation (s) 128
6.6 Interpretation of the Standard Deviation   134
Summary   134
Terms to Remember   135
Exercises   136

7 The Standard Deviation and the Standard Normal Distribution   142

7.1 Introduction   143
7.2 The Concept of Standard Scores   143
7.3 The Standard Normal Distribution   148
7.4 Characteristics of the Standard Normal Distribution   148
7.5 Transforming Raw Scores to z Scores   150
7.6 Illustrative Problems   152
7.7 The Standard Deviation as an Estimate of Error and Precision   158
7.8 Interpreting the Standard Deviation   159

	Summary	160
	Terms to Remember	160
	Exercises	160

8 An Introduction to Contingency Tables   166

8.1	Introduction	167
8.2	Dependent and Independent Variables	167
8.3	The Bivariate Contingency Table	168
8.4	Percentaging Contingency Tables	170
8.5	Existence, Direction, and Strength of a Relationship	172
8.6	Introduction to Measures of Association for Contingency Tables	177
8.7	Nominal Measures of Association: Lambda	178
8.8	Ordinal Measures of Association	182
8.9	Goodman and Kruskal's Gamma	184
8.10	Somer's d	189
8.11	Kendall's tau-b	190
	Summary	191
	Terms to Remember	192
	Exercises	193

9 Correlation   198

9.1	The Concept of Correlation	199
9.2	Calculation of Pearson's r	201
9.3	Pearson's r and z Scores	204
9.4	The Correlation Matrix	206
9.5	Interpreting Correlation Coefficients	208
9.6	Spearman's Rho (r_s)	214
	Summary	216
	Terms to Remember	216
	Exercises	217

10 Regression and Prediction   224

10.1	Introduction to Prediction	225
10.2	Linear Regression	228
10.3	Residual Variance and Standard Error of Estimate	238
10.4	Explained and Unexplained Variation	240
10.5	Correlation and Causation	243
	Summary	245
	Terms to Remember	246
	Exercises	246

11 Multivariate Data Analysis   253

11.1	Introduction	254
11.2	The Multivariate Contingency Table	255
11.3	Partial Correlation	258

11.4   Multiple Regression Analysis   264
Summary   272
Terms to Remember   273
Exercises   274

3 Inferential Statistics: Parametric Tests of Significance

12 Probability   282

12.1   An Introduction to Probability   283
12.2   The Concept of Randomness   285
12.3   Approaches to Probability   288
12.4   Formal Properties of Probability   290
12.5   Probability and Continuous Variables   302
12.6   Probability and the Normal-Curve Model   303
12.7   One- and Two-Tailed p Values   305
Summary   308
Terms to Remember   309
Exercises   310

13 Introduction to Statistical Inference   318

13.1   Why Sample?   319
13.2   The Concept of Sampling Distributions   320
13.3   Testing Statistical Hypotheses: Level of Significance   324
13.4   Testing Statistical Hypotheses: Null Hypothesis and
Alternative Hypothesis   327
13.5   Testing Statistical Hypotheses: The Two Types of Error   330
13.6   A Final Word of Caution   336
Summary   336
Terms to Remember   337
Exercises   338

14 Statistical Inference and Continuous Variables   342

14.1   Introduction   343
14.2   Sampling Distribution of the Mean   346
14.3   Testing Statistical Hypotheses: Population Mean and
Standard Deviation Known   350
14.4   Estimation of Parameters: Point Estimation   355
14.5   Testing Statistical Hypotheses with Unknown Parameters:
Student's t 358
14.6   Estimation of Parameters: Interval Estimation   363
14.7   Confidence Intervals and Confidence Limits   365
14.8   Test of Significance for Pearson's r: One Sample Case   370
14.9   Test of Significance for Goodman's and Kruskal's Gamma   374
Summary   375
Terms to Remember   375
Exercises   376

15 An Introduction to the Analysis of Variance 382

15.1	Multigroup Comparisons	383
15.2	The Concept of Sums of Squares	385
15.3	Obtaining Variance Estimates	389
15.4	Fundamental Concepts of Analysis of Variance	391
15.5	Assumptions Underlying Analysis of Variance	391
15.6	An Example Involving Three Groups	392
15.7	The Interpretation of F	394
	Summary	396
	Terms to Remember	396
	Exercises	397

4 Inferential Statistics: Nonparametric Tests of Significance

16 Statistical Inference with Categorical Variables: Chi Square and Related Measures 404

16.1	Introduction	405
16.2	The χ^2 One-Variable Case	407
16.3	The χ^2 Test of the Independence of Variables	410
16.4	Limitations in the Use of χ^2	413
16.5	Nominal Measures of Association Based on χ^2	416
	Summary	419
	Terms to Remember	420
	Exercises	420

17 Statistical Inference: Ordinally Scaled Variables 426

17.1	Introduction	427
17.2	Mann-Whitney U-Test	428
17.3	Nonparametric Tests Involving Correlated Samples	433
17.4	The Sign Test	433
17.5	Wilcoxon Matched-Pairs Signed-Rank Test	436
	Summary	438
	Terms to Remember	438
	Exercises	439

5 Appendixes

A	Review of Basic Mathematics	444
B	Glossary of Symbols	454
C	Tables	461
D	Glossary of Terms	506
E	References	519

6 Answers to Selected Exercises 528

Index	567

Preface

While an undergraduate, I enrolled in the first of many statistics courses. At that time the course frequently left me and my classmates confused and floundering to the extent that we learned little about statistics; however, I was unable to express the faults I found with the assigned text. The book lacked interesting and relevant examples, omitted computational steps, introduced but did not define new concepts, and seldom presented the relevance or logic of the techniques it purported to teach. I was frequently juggling numbers that were not placed into a meaningful context rather than engaging in any real problem solving.

My first experience with statistics would have been far more pleasant had the instructor assigned a book that was less vulnerable to these criticisms. One of my primary reasons for writing this book was to create a text that is not deficient in these areas. Often, I have found that my experience as a statistics professor has been shaped by my initial statistics course. When a textbook presents the subject clearly, logically, and completely—not in abstract terms, but through concrete examples—students understand better and enjoy the material more. Students *can* learn statistics and have a satisfying experience, provided the material is presented appropriately. I hope that you find this text far more useful than the one I first used.

This book is the second edition of a major revision of the best-selling behavioral science statistics textbook, *Fundamentals of Behavioral Statistics,* by Richard P. Runyon and Audrey Haber. Their book is now in the sixth edition and has been used by over one-quarter of a million students. Rewriting one of the most widely acclaimed behavioral science textbooks for use by social scientists was a challenge I could not resist. I was asked to preserve the strength of the book that had made it such a success with students, professors, and practitioners, yet write a text that would meet the specific needs of those in sociology and the related areas of criminology, family and urban studies, political science, and social welfare.

Student and faculty response to the first edition has been very satisfying. This current edition features a broader emphasis on the interpretation of data. To illustrate, Case Examples have been prominently displayed throughout the text. These examples are excerpted from a rich and varied selection of contemporary research in the social sciences. With each of these Case Examples, raw data are presented and analyzed in terms of the topics featured in a given chapter. Later, they are subjected to more advanced analyses. The effect of these Case Examples is to bring cohesion to statistical topics that are often perceived as separate and discrete. Statistics in Action, another new feature, presents a recently published article or other research including design, research goals, and raw data. The boxed examples demonstrate statistical analysis at a level appropriate to student understanding, then offer additional data for analysis followed by solutions. The same study is often repeated later in the text with more advanced analyses, so students can observe the continuity and connectedness of statistical analysis.

The chapter on probability has undergone considerable revision, including the addition of tree and Venn diagrams, as well as conditional and joint probabilities. A new chapter, "Statistical Inference with Ordinally Scaled Variables," has been added. It discusses such topics as the Mann–Whitney U-test, nonparametric tests involving correlated samples, the sign test, and the Wilcoxon matched-pairs signed-rank test. A new section on goals of statistical research has been added in Chapter 1, Kendall's tau-b has been added to Chapter 8, and approximately 20 percent of the exercises at the end of each chapter are new.

Features of the Book

A number of important features have been included in this text. Key terms appear in boldface, and terms that require emphasis have been italicized. Visual devices, such as charts, figures, and graphs are also incorporated to ensure minimum understanding by the student. New equations are discussed fully rather than mechanically applied, and ample examples are initially provided to ensure comprehension.

Each chapter begins with a content listing to provide the student with an overview of the included material and ends with a glossary of key terms and chapter summary. A student workbook has been designed to provide review practice and feedback for the student. The workbook incorporates a programmed review of terms, symbols, and concepts; selected computational exercises for application purposes; and test questions. A software statistics disk for IBM microcomputers is available for students to learn statistical concepts by calculating basic statistical measures.

The Appendix includes a review of basic mathematics, a glossary of symbols keyed to the first page on which the symbols appear, and a complete set of tables accompanied by explicit directions for their use. Other features of the book are a master glossary of key terms, a chronological listing (inside the front and back covers of the text) of the most frequently used equations, and a comprehensive index.

Acknowledgments

I owe a debt of gratitude to the many colleagues and professors who have taught me statistics. From my students I have also learned much about statistics and how it should be taught.

Several persons at McGraw-Hill were particularly helpful. Bertrand W. Lummus encouraged and supported me throughout the development of the second edition. Phillip Butcher served as the book's editor as it was being completed. Eleanor Castellano ably coordinated the book's editing and production, and Elaine Honig copyedited the manuscript.

Good reviewers are invaluable to an author. The following persons read all or part of the manuscript and offered valuable suggestions: Esther Heffernan, Edgewood College; James F. Iaccino, Illinois Benedictine College; Tai Shick Kang, SUNY–Buffalo; Edward Nelson, California State University–Fresno; and J. D. Robson, University of Arkansas at Little Rock.

Finally, I wish to thank Claire for her invaluable support and Kristin and Shelley, my daughters, for their love and unfailing interest in the project.

Kirk W. Elifson

Fundamentals of Social Statistics

1

Introduction

chapter

The Definition of Statistical Analysis

1   The Definition of Statistical Analysis
2   Basic Mathematical Concepts

chapter **1**

The Definition of Statistical Analysis

1.1 What Is Statistics?
1.2 Definitions of Terms Commonly Used in Statistics
1.3 Descriptive Statistics
1.4 Inferential Statistics
1.5 The Goals of Research
1.6 A Word to the Student

1.1 What Is Statistics?

Think for a moment of the thousands of incredibly complex things you do during the course of a day. You are absolutely unique. No one else possesses your physical features, your intellectual makeup, your personality characteristics, and your value system. Yet, like billions of others of your species, you are among the most finely tuned and enormously sophisticated statistical instruments ever devised by natural forces. Every moment of your life provides testimony to your ability to receive and process a variety of information and then to use this information instantly to determine possible courses of action.

To illustrate, imagine you are driving in heavy traffic. You are continuously observing the road conditions, noting the speed of cars in front of you compared to your own speed, the position and rate of approach of vehicles to your rear, and the presence of automobiles in the oncoming lane. If you are an alert driver, you are constantly summarizing this information—usually without words or even awareness.

Imagine next that, without warning, the driver of the car in front of you suddenly jams on the brakes. In an instant you must act upon this prior information. You must brake the car, turn left, turn right, or pray. Your brain instantly considers alternative courses of action: If you jam on the brakes, what is the possibility that you will stop in time? Is the car behind you far enough away to avoid a rear-end collision? Can you avoid an accident by turning into the left lane or onto the right shoulder? Most of the time your decision is correct. Consequently, most of us live to a ripe old age.

BOX 1.1

Acquired Immunodeficiency Syndrome (AIDS) in Europe

Statistics is one of the most widely used tools in the behavioral, social, medical, and physical sciences. Statistical information is collected on virtually every aspect of life and death. The resulting data are then subjected to various levels of statistical processing, inferences are drawn, and decisions are made that directly and indirectly affect our daily lives.

Often, observations are made at varying times to permit the comparison of changes over time. The records of these observations are then analyzed and the

results are summarized visually in graphic form. The data summarized in the following graph (Figure 1.1) show the number of cases and the number of deaths ascribed to acquired immunodeficiency syndrome (AIDS) in 21 European countries from 1981 through the first 6 months of 1985 [MMWR, **35**(3), 1986]. The graph leaves little to the imagination. It shows a progressive increase over time in both the number of new cases and the number of deaths from previously diagnosed cases.

Table 1.1 shows the risk groups that

Figure 1.1   Acquired immunodeficiency syndrome cases and deaths, by 6-month period of diagnosis—21 European countries, January 1, 1981 to June 30, 1985.

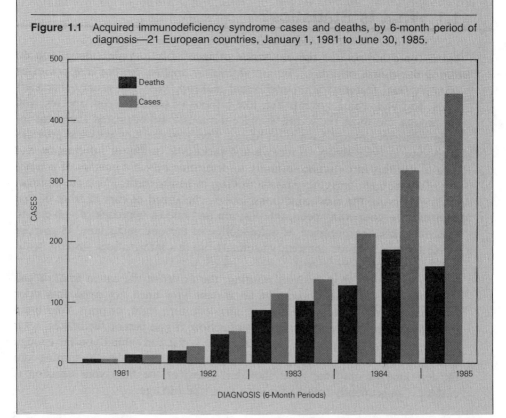

are identified according to the country of origin. Among native Europeans, the overwhelming majority of victims are either homosexual or bisexual. Known risk factors have been identified as any practices that involve the sharing of body fluids with individuals infected with AIDS. These include sexual intercourse, the shared use of intravenous drug paraphernalia, and blood transfusions if the donor blood contains the AIDS virus. Note that the majority of AIDS victims from the Caribbean Islands and Africa do not appear to be among risk groups that are known to be highest in Europe and the United States—homosexual and bisexual males. Rather, among African nationals AIDS appears to be more common among heterosexuals than homosexuals (124 out of 157 are males and females presumed to be heterosexual, whereas only 11 out of 157 were identified as homosexual or bisexual). The same appears to be true of Caribbean nationals (only 4 out of 39 were identified as homosexual or bisexual).

As of this writing, there is neither a vaccine nor a cure for AIDS, nor does any breakthrough appear imminent. For the present, prevention appears to be the only available option in the efforts to stem the tide in the spread of AIDS. Large-scale educational efforts—enlisting the active participation of medical, social, and mental health professionals—are underway to convince those at greatest risk to modify many aspects of their sexual behavior [MMWR, 35(10), 1986].

Source: From Centers for Disease Control (1986) "Acquired Immunodeficiency Syndrome—Europe", *Morbidity and Mortality Weekly Report,* 35, 35–46.

Table 1.1   Acquired immunodeficiency syndrome cases, by patient risk group and geographic origin—21 European countries, through September 30, 1985

Patient risk group	Origin				Total	
	Europe	Caribbean Islands	Africa	Other	No.	(%)
1. Male homosexual or bisexual	1,031	4	11	39	1,085	(69)
2. IV drug abuser	90	—	—	—	90	(6)
3. Hemophilia patient	52	—	—	1	53	(3)
4. Transfusion recipient (without other risk factors)	30	—	5	—	35	(2)
5. 1- and 2-associated*	21	—	1	2	24	(2)
6. No known risk factor						
Male	59	24	81	3	167	(11)
Female	31	10	43	—	84	(5)
7. Unknown	16	1	16	2	35	(2)
Total	1,330 (85%)	39 (2%)	157 (10%)	47 (3%)	1,573	(100)

*Individuals were IV drug users and either homosexual or bisexual.

In this situation, as in many others during the course of a lifetime, you have accurately assessed the possibilities and taken the right course of action. And you make such decisions thousands of times each and every day of your life. For this reason you should regard yourself as a mechanism for making statistical decisions. In this sense you are already a statistician.

In daily living our statistical functioning is usually informal and loosely structured. Consider the times you have contemplated the *likelihood* of someone you are attracted to, but do not know well, rejecting your invitation to have lunch. We *behave* statistically, although we may be totally unaware of the formal laws of probability, which will be presented in Chapter 12.

In this course we will attempt to provide you with some of the procedures for collecting and analyzing data, and making decisions or inferences based on these analyses. Since we will frequently be building upon your prior experiences, you will often feel that you have made a similar analysis before: "Why, I have been calculating averages almost all my life—whenever I determine my test average in a course or the mileage my car gets," and "I compute range whenever I figure how much my time varies on my favorite two-mile jog." If you constantly draw upon your previous knowledge and relate course materials to what is familiar in daily life, statistics need not, and should not, be the bugaboo it is often painted to be.

What, then, is statistics all about? To many people statistics is merely a collection of numerical facts that are expressed in terms of a summarizing statement such as: "Seven out of ten doctors prescribe the pain reliever that is contained in Product X," or "During his current hitting streak, Wade Boggs hit safely in 20 of his last 45 times at bat," or "During the 4th of July weekend, 1986, more than 6 million New Yorkers and visitors participated in the centennial celebration of the unveiling of the Statue of Liberty."

However, this is not the way statistics is defined by scientists. Rather, **statistics** is a method for dealing with data and involves the organization and analysis of numerical facts or observations that are collected in accordance with a systematic plan. The plan for collecting data is called the **research design**. Broadly speaking, the design of a particular study is structured to provide answers to specific questions. In the study of AIDS in Europe (Box 1.1), for example, some of the following questions were raised: Is AIDS increasing in the European community? If so, what is the rate of increase? Can we identify specific groups at risk for contracting AIDS? To answer these questions, the design required the collection of information from each of 21 different countries on new cases and deaths from AIDS over an extended period of time and involved the classification of cases by country of origin, sexual orientation, IV drug abuse, transfusion history, and gender.

A distinction may be made between the two functions of the statistical method: **descriptive** statistical techniques and **inferential** or **inductive** statistical techniques.

The major concern of descriptive statistics is to present information in a convenient, usable, and understandable form. Inferential statistics, on the other hand, is concerned with generalizing this information or, more specifically, with making inferences about populations that are based on samples taken from those populations.

In describing the functions of statistics, we have already presented certain terms with which you may or may not be familiar. Before elaborating on the differences between descriptive and inductive statistics, we define certain terms you need to learn that will be employed repeatedly throughout the text.

1.2 Definitions of Terms Commonly Used in Statistics

Variable Any characteristic of a person, group, or environment that can vary *or* denote a difference. Thus, weight, occupational prestige, sex, political ideology, pollution count, group cohesion, and race are all variables since they can vary or denote a difference. A variable is contrasted with a constant, the value of which never changes (e.g., pi, which is equal to 3.14). Note that sex would be a constant in a study of only male delinquents and that a male–female comparison would not be possible.

Data Numbers or measurements that are collected as a result of observations, interviews, and so on. They may be head counts such as the number or percentage of individuals stating a preference for a Republican presidential candidate; or they may be scores, as on a job satisfaction scale. Note that *data* is the plural form of *datum*. So you would say, "The data *are* available to anyone who wishes to see them or the data *show* that capital punishment is not a deterrent."

Population A complete set of individuals, objects, or measurements having some common observable characteristic. We might focus, for example, on a population of Jews over 65 living in Los Angeles or handicapped students attending UCLA or Korean entrepreneurs in "Koreatown." We can distinguish between a **finite population** and an **infinite population**. All babies born in a particular year would constitute a finite population for it would be possible to compile a list of their names. Thus, a population is finite if a specific number of elements can be enumerated. Most populations studied by social scientists are finite. Other examples of finite populations would include all four-year colleges in the United States or all voluntary associations in Milwaukee. An infinite population cannot be listed and is necessarily theoretical in nature. It would be impossible, for example, to compile a complete list of *all* babies regardless of when they were born or will be born.

Element A single member of a population. Thus, if a population consists of all the presently divorced males in a particular county, each divorced male constitutes an element. Or, if all the child abuse cases coming to the attention of a municipal court constitutes a population, each case would be an element.

Parameter   Any characteristic of a *population* that is measurable, for example, the proportion of registered Democrats among Americans of voting age. A parameter is only measurable in a finite population; however, later in the text you will learn procedures that allow for an estimation of a parameter in either a finite or infinite population. In this text we follow the practice of employing Greek letters (e.g., μ, σ) to represent population parameters. You will learn, for example, that if μ (pronounced "mu") equals 42, we are referring to an average for an entire population, and if σ (pronounced "sigma") equals 3.1, we are referring to a measure of variability for an entire population.

Sample   A subset or part of a population. For example, the newly elected members of the United States House of Representatives constitute a sample of the population of all the current members of the House of Representatives. All of the participants in a senior citizen center would constitute a sample of the senior citizens in the community. A sample could be drawn from the population of all female students in a college or from the population of all social work majors with a grade point average of at least 3.00.

Random sample*   Sample in which all elements have an equal chance of being selected. This requires that all of the elements can be identified or listed. It would be possible, for example, to draw a random sample of prison inmates in the Pontiac State Penitentiary since a complete list of the inmates is available. The sample of senior citizens mentioned earlier would not be random. It would be possible, however, to draw a random sample from the senior citizen center participants if a complete list were available. Random sampling permits inferences about characteristics of the population from which the sample is selected.

It should be noted that random sampling is not an end in itself, merely a means to an end. The goal is that the sample accurately reflect all of the characteristics of the population from which it was drawn. Random sampling is only one way to achieve this goal.

Statistic   A number that describes a characteristic of a sample. Commonly, we use a statistic that is calculated from a sample in order to estimate a population parameter; for example, a sample of Americans of voting age is used to estimate the proportion of Democrats in the entire population of voters. We will use italic letters (e.g., $\overline{X}$, s) to represent sample statistics. For example, if an author specifies that $\overline{X}$ (the mean of the X scores) equals 4.12, you know immediately that the referent is a sample and not a population. If you read that

---

* Simple random sampling is more precisely defined in Section 12.2 as selecting samples in such a way that each sample of a given size has precisely the same probability of being selected.

the mean age of a sample of male prostitutes in Portland is 22.4, you would know that $\overline{X} = 22.4$.

It should be noted that for every statistic that describes some aspect of a sample there is a corresponding parameter that describes the same aspect of a population. Thus, for the statistic "mean of a sample" there is a parameter "mean of the population." We will employ italic letters (e.g., $\overline{X}$ sample mean) to represent sample statistics. Therefore, by looking at statistical notation, we can distinguish between samples and population.

Example　Imagine that a public opinion polling firm has been contracted to conduct a study for a U.S. senator from Wisconsin concerning the percentage of the state's registered voters who approve of nuclear power as an energy source. As part of the polling process, 750 individuals are randomly selected from the voter registration lists and carefully interviewed. The 750 people selected are *elements*, and all of the elements selected constitute the *random sample*.

The *variable* of interest is the registered voters' attitude toward nuclear power (not everyone will feel the same way and the answers will vary). The *data* consist of all of the responses to the question asked of each person included in the sample. When the data are analyzed according to certain rules to yield summary statements such as the percentage who favor the use of nuclear power as an energy source, the resulting numerical value (in this case a percentage) is a *statistic*. The *population* we are interested in generalizing about is all of the state's registered voters. The "true" percentage favoring nuclear power among all of the state's registered voters constitutes a *parameter* (see Figure 1.2). Note that it is highly unlikely that the parameter will ever be known, since finding it would require interviewing every registered voter in the state. Since this is usually not feasible for economic and other reasons, it is rare that an exhaustive study of populations in public opinion polling is undertaken. Consequently, parameters are rarely known; but, as we will see, they are commonly estimated from sample statistics.

A carefully selected sample can provide a very accurate description of the population from which it was drawn. Excellent samples are surprisingly small relative to the population. For example, a properly drawn national sample of 3000 adults can provide extremely accurate information about the U.S. adult population. The logic will become clear once you have studied *sampling distributions* in Chapter 13.

It is, of course, possible to define a very small population by narrowing the definition of "common observable characteristic" to something like "all students attending their Sociology 201 class at Knox College today." In this event, calculating a parameter (such as the class average on the examination given today) would pose no difficulty. For such small populations there is no reason to select samples and to calculate sample statistics.

From the point of view of the instructor observations on the students in

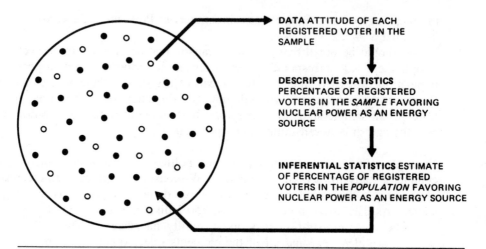

Figure 1.2   A *random sample* is selected from some population. The hollow and solid dots represent all registered voters in Wisconsin. The hollow dots represent the sample. *Data* are collected and summarized, using descriptive statistics. In *inferential statistics*, we attempt to estimate one or more population *parameters* (e.g., the percentage of all registered voters in Wisconsin favoring nuclear power as an energy source).

Sociology 201 at Knox College may be of supreme importance. However, such limited populations would be of little theoretical interest. In the real workaday world the social scientist is usually interested in making statements having general validity over a wider set of people (or elements), and thus must *estimate* the (population) parameter. This estimate is based on the statistic that is calculated on the sample. Thus, we might use the observations on the students at Knox College as a basis for estimating parameters of the larger population.

Let us return to the two functions of statistical analysis for a closer look.

1.3 Descriptive Statistics

When social scientists conduct a study, they usually collect a great deal of information or data about the problem at hand. The data may take a variety of forms: the number of medical schools in each state, the SAT scores of a group of college students, or the number of completed questionnaires from a research project. In their original form, as collected, these data are usually a confusing hodgepodge of scores, frequency counts, etc. In performing the descriptive function, the statistician employs rules and procedures for presenting information about a variable or the relationship between variables in a more usable and meaningful form.

Rules are also followed when calculating various *statistics* from masses of raw data. Imagine that a team of social scientists administered a questionnaire concerning drug usage and attitudes to a group of high school students. What are some of the things they might do with the resulting information?

1. They might rearrange the scores and group them in various ways in order to be able to see at a glance an overall picture of the data (Chapter 3, "Frequency Distributions and Graphing Techniques"). For example, how many of the students use drugs regularly? How many have never used drugs? Which drugs are used most frequently? What is the age distribution of the students? What percentage of the students are Jewish? How do the students' attitudes toward drugs vary? What is the extent of multiple drug use?

2. They might construct tables, graphs, and figures to permit visualization of the results (Section 3.3, "Graphing Techniques," in Chapter 3). A pie chart might summarize the drugs most frequently used by the students, whereas a trend chart would provide a concise picture of the extent of drug use by year in school.

3. They might convert raw scores to other types of scores that are more useful for specific purposes. Thus, these scores could be used to rank the students, compare a student with the class average, etc. Other types of conversion will also be described in the text (Chapter 4, "Percentiles," and Chapter 7, "The Standard Deviation and the Normal Distribution").

4. They might calculate averages, to learn something about the typical attitudes of the students (Chapter 5, "Measures of Central Tendency"). What is the mean age when the students first used marijuana? What is the most frequently held attitude toward the legalization of marijuana?

5. Using the average as a reference point, they might describe the spread of scores about this central point. Statistics that measure this spread of scores are known as measures of variability or measures of dispersion (Chapter 6, "Measures of Dispersion"). Are the attitudes held by the freshmen more or less homogeneous than the seniors' attitudes? Are males more likely to be polydrug users than are females?

6. They may obtain a relationship between two different variables. Statistics are available for describing the relationship between two variables. The statistics for describing the extent of the relationship are referred to as measures of association.

Such statistics are extremely useful to the social scientist. For example, it might be important to determine the relationship between the number of books in the home and classroom grades or that between students' attitudes toward drugs and the extent to which they reported having committed delinquent acts. Once these relationships are known, the social scientist may use information from one variable to predict another (Chapter 8, "An Introduction to Contingency Tables,'' Chapter 9, ''Correlation,'' and Chapter 10, ''Regression and Prediction'').

1.4 Inferential Statistics

As a social scientist your task is not nearly over when you have completed the descriptive function. In fact, you are often nearer to the beginning than to the end of the task. The reason for this is clear when we consider that the purpose of the research is often to explore hypotheses of a general nature, rather than simply to compare limited samples.

Imagine that you are a sociologist who is interested in determining the effectiveness of a videotape lecture approach versus the usual procedure of the professor delivering lectures in person. Consequently, you design a study involving two conditions: *experimental* and *control*. The question you wish to answer is which approach (videotape teaching versus the in-person lecture approach) results in better student performance on a final sociology examination. The students in the experimental group view videotapes of the lectures attended by the control group. The students in the control group serve as a basis for comparison and are taught using the usual lecture approach. After all students have been tested, you might find that ''on the average'' the experimental group that viewed the videotapes did not perform as well on the final examination as did the control group. In other words, the average of the experimental group on the final examination was lower than that of the control group. You then ask the question, ''Can I conclude that the teaching technique produced the difference between the two groups?'' To answer this question, it is not sufficient to rely solely upon *descriptive statistics*.

''After all,'' you reason, ''even if both techniques worked, it is highly unlikely that the two groups' final examination averages would have been *identical*. *Some* difference would have been observed.'' The operation of chance factors such as the time at which the classes are scheduled is certain to produce some differences in the final examination scores between the two groups. The critical question, from the point of view of inferential statistics, becomes: Is the difference between groups great enough to rule out chance factors in the experiment as a sufficient explanation? Stated another way, if you were to repeat the experiment, would you be able to predict with confidence that the same differences (i.e., the control group would consistently perform better than the experimental group) would systematically occur? Ultimately, we wish to infer to the population from which the study participants were drawn. Thus, we want to use the results of this experiment to reach conclusions about which technique would be best in similar sociology courses.

As you can see, *inference* is used much in the same way you would use logical reasoning when talking with friends. This notation of logical reasoning is sometimes employed to establish community standards in pornography litigation. Because the tolerance for pornography differs greatly from community to community, a survey of residents is often conducted to determine what sorts of sexually explicit activities should be available commercially. A well-drawn sample survey of 600 Milwaukee adults could be used by prosecution or defense lawyers in a pornography case to conclude that Milwaukee adults hold a particular attitude. If 78% of those interviewed believed that nude nightclubs should not be allowed, the prosecutors would seek to convince the jury members that the sample survey results allow for the inference that basically the same attitude is held by the population of Milwaukee's adult residents.* In this instance the sample was used to infer to the population from which it was drawn.

As soon as you raise these questions, you move into the area of statistical analysis known as *inferential* (or *inductive*) statistics. As you will see, much of this text is devoted to procedures that the researcher uses to arrive at conclusions extending beyond the sample statistics themselves.

1.5 The Goals of Research

Social scientists engage in a rich variety of different activities in diverse settings that involve the collection and analysis of numerical observations or data. These activities are generally subsumed under the label "research." The goals of these research activities may be classified into three broad categories: information gathering, describing relationships, and establishing causality. It should be noted that these goals are not mutually exclusive. All three are common components of many research efforts.

1.5.1 Information Gathering

The focus of many statistical activities is to provide accurate information about some aspect of our professional activities that arouses our interest. For example, we may wish to know if the proportion of women entering the field of sociology is changing over the years or the average starting salary of recent Ph.D.s accepting positions at academic institutions or the proportion of criminal justice departments requiring statistics courses for their majors.

In these information gathering activities the emphasis is to provide accurate descriptions of the situations studied. The information is considered valuable in its own right. Thus, there may not be any effort to relate the data to other events or situations. For example, we may make no attempt to answer the question, why are the starting salaries of new Ph.D.s in academia X dollars?

---

* Making inferences of this nature is specifically addressed in Section 14.7.2.

1.5.2 Describing Relationships

In the course of conducting research we often obtain measurements on two or more variables from each respondent, and we wish to know whether or not the variables go together or covary. Does academic performance vary in relation to SAT scores? Is there a relationship between environment and aggressiveness as some researchers have claimed? Does our ability to recall childhood experiences relate to the pleasantness/unpleasantness associated with these experiences at the time they occurred?

Studies of this sort are referred to as correlational. They attempt to determine whether or not two variables are related (i.e., correlated—think of them as co-related) or vary together and, if so, to measure the direction and strength of the relationship. To illustrate, if we have measurements on two variables for each individual, we may raise such questions as: As the values of one variable increase (e.g., SAT scores), do the paired measures on the second variable also increase (e.g., academic performance)? Or are increases in one variable (e.g., age) associated with decreases in a second variable (e.g., income)? Or does there not appear to be any detectable relationship between the two variables (e.g., health status and frequency of eating pizza).

It is important to note that correlations between naturally occurring variables such as income, gender, racial/ethnic backgrounds, or life satisfaction do not, as such, permit us to claim that changes in one variable *cause* changes in a second variable. They merely establish whether or not the two variables vary together. Many serious misinterpretations of data have occurred because people have ignored this fact. Thus, at various times in our history as a nation members of various minority groups (e.g., blacks, Italians, Poles, Jews, etc.) have labored under the label of inferiority because their low positions on the educational and socioeconomic ladders have been attributed to their racial and/or ethnic backgrounds. The point is that these groups differed from each other in many ways other than their ethnic/racial backgrounds—for example, command of the English language, educational and economic opportunities, and lifestyles—to name a few. To focus on a single characteristic (such as ethnic background) that distinguished each of these groups from the majority and to attribute their social and economic position to this characteristic is to ignore the wealth of other ways in which they differ.

1.5.3 Establishing Causality

One of the paramount goals of any science is to go beyond statements of relationships (e.g., If the value of A is high, then the value of B is also high) to those of causality (e.g., increases in the values of A *cause* the value of B to increase also). In spite of hundreds of years of speculating, thinking, and writing about causality, it remains a somewhat elusive term. Not all scientists agree on the procedures for establishing cause-effect relationships. Indeed, some even doubt its feasibility while others question its necessity. However, the vast majority of scientists appear to agree that a statement such as "*A* causes *B*" is among the most powerful that a scientist can make and should be at the core of scientific inquiry.

Social scientists generally assume that three criteria must be met before causality can be established. First, the two variables must covary. Let's consider an example involving personal income and health care. If we conduct a study and find that the more affluent respondents tend to receive better and more frequent health care than do the poorer respondents, then we can conclude that there is some relationship between the two variables for our study participants. Second, the time-order in which the variables occur must be consistent. In this particular example we assume that health care is dependent on one's financial situation. If we find that in the vast majority of instances that changes in the respondents' incomes were followed by anticipated changes in their health care, we have established that the time-order of the variables is consistent with our assertion of causality. Third, and most difficult for social scientists, other possible explanations for the relationship we have observed must be eliminated. Perhaps the relationship is a function of a variable we did not consider. The poorer study participants may have been in excellent health and therefore did not need to seek health care. We will say much more on this third criteria for establishing causality later in Chapter 10.

1.6 A Word to the Student

The study of statistics need not and should not become a series of progressive exercises in calculated tedium. If it is approached with the proper frame of mind, statistics can be one of the most exciting fields of study; it has applications in virtually all areas of human endeavor and cuts across countless fields of study. H. G. Wells, the nineteenth-century prophet, remarked, "Statistical thinking will one day be as necessary for efficient citizenship as the ability to read and write." Keep this thought constantly in mind. The course will be much more interesting and profitable to you if you develop the habit of "thinking statistically."

A common misconception held by lay persons is that statistics is merely a rather sophisticated method for fabricating lies or falsifying our descriptions of reality. We do not deny that some unscrupulous individuals employ statistics for just such purposes. However, such uses of statistics are anathema to the social scientist who is dedicated to the establishment of truth. From time to time we make references to various techniques that are used for lying with statistics. The purpose, though, is not to instruct you in these techniques but to make you aware of the various *misuses* of statistical analyses so that you do not inadvertently "tell a lie," and you may be aware when others do.

When you see statistical information being exhibited, develop a healthy attitude of skepticism. Ask pertinent questions. When a national magazine sends a physically fit reporter to ten different diet doctors and he or she receives an unneeded prescription from each, do not jump to the conclusion that all diet doctors are frauds. Do not say, "After all, ten out of ten is a rather high proportion" and dismiss further inquiry at this point. Ask how the reporter obtained the sample. Was it drawn at random, or is it possible that the doctors were selected purposely on the basis of prior information indicating they were rather careless in their professional practices? Question constantly, but reserve judgment until you have the answers.

Watch commercials on television; read newspaper advertisements. When the pitchman claims, "Dodoes are more effective," ask, "More effective than what? What is the evidence?"

There is also something you can do to maximize the benefits derived from the course. You should set aside a separate section of your notebook to keep permanent records of your solutions to exercises. You will find that these solutions will provide an invaluable useful review of statistical procedures. For some of you their use will long outlive the completion of this course. Of more immediate concern, however, it will be necessary to refer back to these solutions as you explore more advanced statistical techniques. Your notebook will reflect an important fact of statistical life: Researchers do not simply collect data, conduct a single statistical analysis of the data, and then share their results with others in the form of a published paper. Rather, they typically subject the same set of data to many levels of statistical analysis. It is hoped that this course will reflect the continuity among the various phases of ongoing research: Research design, descriptive and inferential data processing, and the ensuing conclusions are part of an organic whole. Something fundamental is lost if they are treated like discrete, independent elements of a jigsaw puzzle. To impart a flavor of real-world research, we will follow a number of research studies through all phases of their development, from their conception to a statement of conclusions that appear to be supported by the statistical facts.

Summary

In this chapter we saw that many people regard statistics merely as a collection of numerical facts. Scientists, however, stress the use of statistics as a method or tool concerned with the collection, organization, and analysis of numerical facts.

A distinction is made between two functions of the statistical methods, descriptive and inferential statistical analyses. The former is concerned with the organization and presentation of data in a convenient, usable, and communicable form. The latter is addressed to the problem of making broader generalizations or inferences from sample data to populations.

We also looked at the goals of research, which included gathering information, describing relationships, and establishing causality. We noted the important role of a systematic plan (the design of the study) in accomplishing these goals.

A number of terms commonly employed in statistical analysis were defined.

Finally, it was pointed out that statistics is frequently employed for the purpose of "telling lies." Such practices are inimical to the goal of establishing a factual basis for our conclusions and statistically based decisions. However, you should be aware of the techniques for telling statistical lies, so that you do not inadvertently "tell one" yourself or fail to recognize one when someone else does.

New terms or concepts that have been introduced in a chapter will be listed at the end of each chapter. Some of these terms will be more precisely defined in other chapters and consequently may appear again.

Terms to Remember

Data   Numbers or measurements that are collected as a result of observations, interviews, etc.

Descriptive statistics   Procedures used to organize and present data in a convenient, usable summary form.

Element   A single member of a population.

Finite population   A population whose elements or members can be listed.

Inferential or inductive statistics   Procedures used to arrive at broader generalizations or inferences from sample data to populations.

Infinite population   A population whose elements or members cannot be listed.

Parameter   Any characteristic of a finite population that can be estimated and is measurable or of an infinite population that can be estimated.

Population   A complete set of individuals, objects, or measurements having some common observable characteristic.

Random sample   A sample in which all elements have an equal chance of being selected.

Research design   The plan for collecting data.

Sample   A subset or part of a population.

Statistic   A number that describes a characteristic of a sample.

Statistics   A collection of numerical facts expressed in summarizing statements; method of dealing with data: a tool for collecting, organizing, and analyzing numerical facts or observations that are collected in accordance with a systematic plan.

Variable   Any characteristic of a person, group, or environment that can vary or denotes a difference.

Exercises

1. In your own words, describe what you understand the study of statistics to be. Compare your definition to the one provided in the book.

2. Indicate whether each of the following represents a variable, a constant, or both depending on the usage:

    a) Number of days in the month of August.

    b) The number of labor strikes per year in the United States since 1975.

    c) The murder rate in Peoria last year.

    d) Scores obtained on a 100-item multiple-choice examination.

    e) Maximum score possible on a 100-item multiple-choice examination.

    f) Age of freshmen entering college.

    g) Percentage of people in the United States who tried marijuana in 1989.

    h) Amount of money spent per year by students.

    i) Number of counties in Texas.

3. In the example cited in Section 1.2, imagine that the survey results indicated that, overall, 57% of the senator's constituents favored nuclear power as an energy source.

    a) May we assume that if the respondents were reinterviewed 6 months later the percentage favoring would remain the same?

    b) What factors might have caused a shift in attitudes?

4. Bring in newspaper articles citing recent survey or poll results. In how many articles is the method of sampling mentioned? Do the articles reveal where the financial support for the surveys came from? Why is this information important? Why is it so commonly not revealed?

5. List four populations and indicate why they are finite or infinite.

6. When surveying small populations (e.g., school superintendents in Rhode Island), social scientists frequently study all of the elements rather than draw a sample. Can you think of any other populations with few elements?

7. We wish to generalize from a sample to the:

    a) data   **c)** statistic

    b) population   **d)** variable

8. What is the difference between descriptive and inferential statistics?

9.   **a)** How could you determine the average welfare payment received by recipients in your state?

    b) Would you have to contact each person?

    c) Identify the population.

    d) Would the average in this example be a statistic or a parameter? Why?

10. Professor Normal Yetman of the University of Kansas has concerned himself with possible economic discrimination against black athletes by the media.* He has analyzed their opportunities to appear on commercials, make guest appearances, and obtain off-season jobs. Two of the findings follow:

    a) In 351 commercials associated with New York sporting events in the autumn of 1966, black athletes appeared in only 2.

    b) An analysis of media advertising opportunities for athletes on a professional football team in 1971 revealed that 8 of 11 whites had an opportunity in contrast to only 2 of 13 black athletes.

Indicate whether these two examples provide:

    a) parameters   **c)** descriptive statistics

    b) data   **d)** inferential statistics

11. List five social science variables and briefly discuss how they might be measured.

12. Differentiate between the following pairs of words:

    a) sample–population

    b) statistic–parameter

    c) inferential statistics–descriptive statistics

    d) experimental group–control group

    e) finite population–infinite population

---

* *Source:* Gary Lehman, Associated Press sportswriter, August 22, 1975.

13. You have interviewed 42 students attending a nearby university. Carefully consider how you might define the population from which the sample was drawn.

    (*Hint:* For example, were graduate students and part-time students sampled?)

14. Under what conditions might you poll the entire student body referred to in Exercise 13?

15. In some urban areas nearly 50% of all residential telephone numbers are unlisted.

    a) What types of persons would you expect to be underrepresented in a telephone survey in which the sample was drawn using the current telephone directory?

    b) Can you think of a procedure that might result in a more representative sample of all residential telephone numbers?

16. What would constitute the element in the following examples?

    a) Ten federal prison wardens were polled concerning the best method for transporting dangerous convicts.

    b) The safety records of ten federal prisons were compared.

    c) Per capita educational expenditures of all Tennessee counties were contrasted.

    d) Over 240 female students were interviewed concerning their attitude toward drinking.

17. Would it be possible to list all adults residing in Detroit on January 1, 1989? Why or why not?

18. Which of the following examples involve descriptive statistics and which involve inferential statistics?

    a) The grade point average of the sociology majors at Cleveland State is 3.04.

    b) Recent surveys indicate that 76% of adult Americans favor prayer in public schools.

    c) Cocaine usage was reported by 8% of the high school seniors at Lamar High School.

    d) Fourteen dentists committed suicide last year in Texas.

    e) A sample survey revealed that about 13% of U.S. adults are illiterate.

19. Football telecasters frequently point to tables like the following and offer

comments such as, "Here are the half-time statistics. They really tell the story of this game!"

	Team A	Team B
First downs	6	10
Passes attempted	12	8
Passes completed	7	4
Yards passing	62	30
Yards running	78	104
Total yards	140	134
Turnovers	2	1
Time of possession	12′04″	17′56″

Are these numbers in fact statistics? If not, what are they?

20. Indicate whether each of the following constitutes a statistic, data, or inference from statistics.

    a) A sample of 250 wage earners in Carlthorp City yielded a per-capita income of $14,460.

    b) Based on a random sample of 250 wage earners in Carlthorp City, it is believed that the average income of all wage earners in this city is about $14,500.

    c) The slug from a .22 rifle traveled 1 mile.

    d) My tuition payment this year was $4580.

    e) The number of people viewing Monday night's television special was 23,500,000.

chapter 2

Basic Mathematical Concepts

2.1 Introduction
2.2 Summation Rules
2.3 Types of Numbers and Scales
2.4 Continuous and Discrete Variables
2.5 Rounding
2.6 Ratios
2.7 Proportions, Percentages, and Rates

2.1 Introduction

"I'm not much good at math. How can I possibly pass a statistics course?" We have heard these words from the lips of countless undergraduate students. For many, this is probably a concern stemming from prior discouraging experiences with mathematics. A brief glance through the pages of this text may only serve to increase this anxiety, since many of the equations appear rather complicated and may seem impossible to master. Therefore, it is most important to set the record straight right at the beginning of the course.

You do not have to be a mathematical genius to master the statistical principles in this text. The degree of mathematical sophistication necessary for a firm grasp of the fundamentals of statistics is often exaggerated. As a matter of actual fact, statistics requires a good deal of arithmetic computation, sound logic, and a willingness to stay with a point until it is mastered. To paraphrase Carlyle, success in statistics requires an infinite capacity for taking pains. Beyond this modest requirement, little is needed but the mastery of several algebraic and arithmetic procedures that most students learned early in their high school careers. In this chapter we review the grammar of mathematical notations, discuss several types of numerical scales, and adopt certain conventions for rounding numbers.

If you wish to brush up on basic mathematics, Appendix A contains a review of all the math necessary to master this text.

2.2 Summation Rules

Throughout the textbook you will be learning new mathematical symbols. For the most part we will define these symbols when they first appear. However, there are four notations that will appear so frequently that their separate treatment at this time is justified. These notations are X, Y, N, and the uppercase Greek letter Σ (pronounced "sigma").

While defining these symbols and demonstrating their use, we will also review the grammar of mathematical notation. It is not surprising that many students become so involved in the numerous mathematical formulas and symbols that they fail to realize that mathematics has its nouns, adjectives, verbs, and adverbs.

Mathematical nouns   In mathematics we commonly use symbols to stand for quantities. The notation we use most commonly in statistics to represent quantity (or a score) is X, although we will occasionally use Y. In addition, X and Y are used to identify variables; for example, if age and educational attainment are two variables in a study, X might be used to represent age and Y to represent educational attainment. Another frequently used noun is the symbol N, which represents the number of scores or measurements with which we are dealing. Thus, if we have ten scores

$$N = 10$$

Mathematical adjectives   When we want to modify a mathematical noun, we commonly use subscripts that indicate a specific score in a series and identify it more precisely. Thus, if we have a series of scores or quantities, we may represent them as X_1 (refers to the first X score and is read as "X sub 1"), X_2, X_3, X_4, etc. We will frequently encounter X_i, in which the subscript may take on any value that we want.

Mathematical verbs   Notations that direct the reader to do something have the same characteristics as verbs in the spoken language. One of the most important verbs is the symbol already alluded to as Σ. This notation directs us to sum all quantities or scores following the symbol. Thus

$$\sum(X_1, X_2, X_3, X_4, X_5) = X_1 + X_2 + X_3 + X_4 + X_5$$

indicates that we should add together all of these quantities from X_1 through X_5. Thus, if $X_1 = 1$, $X_2 = 3$, $X_3 = 5$, $X_4 = 7$, and $X_5 = 9$, the five quantities would sum to 25. Other verbs we will encounter frequently are $\sqrt{}$, directing us to find the square root, and exponents* (X^a), which tell us to raise a quantity

---

* An exponent indicates how many times a number is to be multiplied by itself.

to the indicated power. For example, X^2, where $X = 2$, can be rewritten 2^2 or 2×2, both of which equal 4. In mathematics, mathematical verbs are commonly referred to as *operators*.

Mathematical adverbs These are notations that, as in spoken language, modify the verbs. We will frequently find that the summation signs are modified by adverbial notations. Let us imagine we want to indicate the following quantities are to be added:

$$X_1 + X_2 + X_3 + X_4 + X_5 + \cdots + X_N$$

Symbolically, we would represent these operations as follows:

$$\sum_{i=1}^{N} X_i$$

The notations above and below the summation sign indicate that i takes on the successive values from 1, 2, 3, 4, 5, up to N. Stated verbally, the notation reads: We should sum all quantities of X starting with $i = 1$ (i.e., X_1) and proceeding through to $i = N$ (i.e., X_N).

The following shorthand version excludes the notations above and below the summation sign and is often used when all of the quantities from 1 to N are to be added. It is equivalent to the complete version:

$$\sum X = \sum_{i=1}^{N} X_i = X_1 + X_2 + X_3 + X_4 + X_5 + \cdots + X_N$$

Sometimes this form of notation may direct us to add only selected quantities; thus

$$\sum_{i=2}^{5} X_i = X_2 + X_3 + X_4 + X_5$$

Stated verbally, the notation reads: We should sum all quantities of X starting with $i = 2$ (i.e., X_2) and proceeding through to $i = 5$ (i.e., X_5). The shorthand version would not allow us to convey this information.

Example If $N = 4$ and $X_1 = 2$, $X_2 = 3$, $X_3 = 4$, and $X_4 = 5$, then let us evaluate:

a) $\displaystyle\sum_{i=1}^{N} X_i$ b) $\displaystyle\sum_{i=2}^{N} X_i$ c) $\displaystyle\sum X_i^2$

Solution

a) $\sum\limits_{i=1}^{N} X_i = X_1 + X_2 + X_3 + X_4 = 2 + 3 + 4 + 5 = 14$

b) $\sum\limits_{i=2}^{N} X_i = X_2 + X_3 + X_4 = 3 + 4 + 5 = 12$

c) In this case note that

$$\sum X_i^2 = \sum_{i=1}^{N} X_i^2$$

and therefore

$$\sum X_i^2 = X_1^2 + X_2^2 + X_3^2 + X_4^2 = 2^2 + 3^2 + 4^2 + 5^2$$
$$= 4 + 9 + 16 + 25 = 54$$

Finally, note the difference between the following two pairs of summations:

a) $\sum\limits_{i=1}^{N} X_i^2 \quad$ and $\quad \left(\sum\limits_{i=1}^{N} X_i \right)^2$

Thus, if $X_1 = 2$, $X_2 = 3$, and $X_3 = 4$ then

$$\sum_{i=1}^{N} X_i^2 = X_1^2 + X_2^2 + X_3^2 \quad \text{and} \quad \left(\sum_{i=1}^{N} X_i \right)^2 = (X_1 + X_2 + X_3)^2$$
$$= 2^2 + 3^2 + 4^2 \qquad\qquad\qquad = (2 + 3 + 4)^2$$
$$= 4 + 9 + 16 \qquad\qquad\qquad\quad = (9)^2$$
$$= 29 \qquad\qquad\qquad\qquad\quad = 81$$

b) $\left(\sum X \right)\left(\sum Y \right) \neq \sum XY$

Thus, if $X_1 = 5$, $X_2 = 10$, $X_3 = 15$ and $Y_1 = 2$, $Y_2 = 4$, $Y_3 = 6$ then

$$\left(\sum X \right)\left(\sum Y \right) = (X_1 + X_2 + X_3)(Y_1 + Y_2 + Y_3)$$
$$= (5 + 10 + 15)(2 + 4 + 6)$$
$$= (30)(12)$$
$$= 360$$

and $\displaystyle\sum XY = X_1Y_1 + X_2Y_2 + X_3Y_3$

$$= 5(2) + 10(4) + 15(6)$$

$$= 10 + 40 + 90$$

$$= 140$$

2.3 Types of Numbers and Scales

Cultural anthropologists, psychologists, and sociologists have repeatedly called attention to the common human tendency to explore the world that is remote from our experiences long before we have investigated that which is closest to us. So, while we probe distant stars and describe with great accuracy their apparent movements and relationships, we virtually ignore the very substance that gave us life: air (which we inhale and exhale over four hundred million times a year). In our experience a similar pattern exists in relation to the student's familiarity with numbers and concepts of them.

In our numerically oriented Western civilization, student Cory uses numbers long before he is expected to calculate the batting averages of the latest baseball hero. Nevertheless, ask him to define a number, or to describe the ways in which numbers are employed, and you will likely be met with an expression of bewilderment. "I have never thought about it before," he will frequently reply. After a few minutes of soul searching and deliberation, he will probably reply that numbers are symbols denoting amounts of things that can be added, subtracted, multiplied, and divided. These are all familiar arithmetic concepts, but do they exhaust all possible uses of numbers? At the risk of reducing our student to utter confusion, you may ask: "Is the symbol 7 on a baseball player's uniform such a number? What about your home address? Channel 2 on your television set? Do these numbers indicate amounts of things? Can they reasonably be added, subtracted, multiplied, or divided? Can you multiply the number on any football player's back by any other number and obtain a meaningful value?" A careful analysis of our use of numbers in everyday life reveals a very interesting fact: Most of the numbers we use do not have the mathematical properties we usually give to them; that is, they cannot be meaningfully added, subtracted, multiplied, and divided. A few examples are the serial number of a home appliance, a zip code number, a telephone number, a home address, an automobile registration number, and the catalog numbers on a book in the library.

The important point is that numbers are used in a variety of ways to achieve many different ends. Much of the time these ends do not include the representation of an amount or a quantity. In fact, there are two different ways in which numbers are used:

1. To name (**nominal numbers**) and
2. To represent position in a series (**ordinal numbers**).

Measurement is the assignment of numbers to objects or events according to sets of predetermined (or arbitrary) rules. The different levels of measurement that we will discuss represent different levels of numerical information contained in a set of observations (data), such as: a series of house numbers, the order of finish in a horse race, a set of I.Q. scores, or the price per share of various stocks. The type of scale obtained depends on the kinds of mathematical operations that can be legitimately performed on the numbers. In the social sciences we encounter measurements at every level.

It should be noted that there are other schema for classifying numbers and the ways they are used. We use the nominal–ordinal classification because it best handles the types of data we obtain in the social sciences. As you will see, we count, we place in relative position, and we obtain numerical scores. It should also be noted that the assignment to categories is not always clear-cut or unambiguous. There are times when even experts cannot agree. To illustrate: Is the number in your street address nominal or ordinal? The answer depends on your need. For certain purposes it can be considered nominal, such as when used as a *name* of a dwelling. At other times it can be considered ordinal, since the numbers place your house in a position relative to other houses on the block. Thus, 08 may be to the left of 12 and to the right of 04.

The fundamental requirements of observation and measurement are acknowledged by all the physical and social sciences as well as by any modern-day corporation interested in improving its competitive position. The things that we observe are often referred to as **variables.** Any particular observation is called the **value of the variable**. Let us look at two examples.

If we are studying the number of days of hospitalization among different kinds of patients, our variable is the number of days in the hospital. Thus, if a patient spends 8 1/2 days in the hospital, the value of the variable is 8.50.

If we are interested in determining whether or not an employer discriminates on the basis of racial background, the racial classification of the employees is our variable. This variable may have several values, such as black, black Hispanic, white, and white Hispanic.

2.3.1 Nominal Scales

Four basic levels of measurement scales are utilized by social and physical scientists. These include the nominal scale, the ordinal scale, the interval scale, and the ratio scale. Each type of scale has unique characteristics, and as we will see later, implications for the type of statistical procedures that can be used with it.

Nominal scales do not involve highly complex measurement, but rather involve rules for placing individuals or objects into categories. The categories must (1) be homogeneous, (2) be mutually exclusive,* and (3) make no assumption about ordered relationships between categories.

---

* We refer to categories as *mutually exclusive* because it is impossible for a person's score to belong to more than one category.

Consider a study of anti-Semitism. Let's classify the respondents into one of two categories: Jewish and non-Jewish. Such a dichotomy would satisfy each of the three classification rules for a nominal scale. All of the respondents in the Jewish category are *homogeneous* (similar) in terms of the variable religious identification in that only Jewish respondents are included. The respondents in the non-Jewish category are also homogeneous. The categories we have chosen are *mutually exclusive* since no respondent can be placed into both categories; that is, a person is either Jewish or non-Jewish. Finally, we can make no assumptions about the ordered relationships between categories, only that the individuals in the Jewish category *differ* from those in the non-Jewish category in terms of their religious identification. Our data would consist of the number of individuals in each of these two categories. Note that we do not think of the variable religious affiliation as representing an ordered series of values, such as height, prestige, or speed. A person that is female does not have more of the variable sex than one that is male.

Observations of unordered variables constitute the lowest level of measurement because they are the least mathematically versatile of the four levels of measurement scales and are referred to as nominal scale of measurement. We may assign numerical values to represent the various classes in a nominal scale but these numbers function only as category labels. If we wished to compare female and male responses to a question concerning parenting and were using a computer to analyze our results, we might assign a number to each category of the variable. Thus, male may be assigned a zero and female a one. Our data would consist of the number of observations in each of these two classes. Note that we do not think of this variable as representing an ordered series of values, such as height, weight, speed, etc. A person that is female does not have any more of the variable, sex, than one that is male.

If we wished to classify persons in terms of their present marital status we might number the categories for convenience, but the numbers would only serve to identify the class. Here we have assigned numbers as we would names and it would be meaningless to add or subtract them. For example, (1) married, (2) divorced, (3) separated, (4) single, and (5) widowed. Other examples of nominal level variables include sex, religious affiliation, race, blood type, and astrological sign.

The data used with nominal scales consist of frequency counts or tabulations of the number of occurrences in each class of the variable under study. In the aforementioned anti-Semitism study our frequency counts of Jewish and non-Jewish respondents would comprise our data. Such data are often referred to interchangeably as *frequency data, nominal data,* or *categorical data.*

2.3.2 Ordinal Scales

When we move into the next higher level of measurement, we encounter variables in which the categories *do* represent a rank-ordered series of relationships. Thus, the categories in **ordinal scales** are not only homogeneous and mutually exclusive, but they stand in some kind of *relation* to one another. More specifically, the relationships are expressed in terms of the algebra of inequalities: *a* is less than *b* ($a < b$) or *a* is greater than *b* ($a > b$). In Figure 2.1 we see that *B* and *C* are higher than *A*, but we cannot say how much higher because we do not know the distance between *A*, *B*, and *C* since the values are measured on an ordinal scale. We cannot even be sure if the distance *AB* is greater than, equal to, or less than the distance *BC*.

Types of relationships encountered in an ordinal scale are: greater, poorer, healthier, more prejudiced, more feminine, more prestigious, etc. The numerals employed in connection with ordinal scales indicate only position in an ordered series and not how much of a difference exists between successive positions on the scale. (See Case Example 2.1.) We can rank order the following educational degrees from higher to lower [e.g., (1) doctorate, (2) master's degree, (3) bachelor's degree], but we cannot say that the Ph.D. is twice as high as the bachelor's degree or that a particular difference exists between categories.

Examples of ordinal scaling include rank ordering: the leading causes of death among the elderly, academic departments in a college according to their prestige, baseball teams according to their league standing, officer candidates in terms of their leadership qualities, and potential candidates for political office according to their name recognition with the people. Note that the ranks are assigned according to the ordering of individuals within the class. Thus, the most popular candidate may receive the rank of 1, the next most popular may receive the rank of 2, etc., down to the least popular candidate. It does not, in fact, make any difference whether or not we give the best known candidate the highest numerical rank or the lowest, *so long as we are consistent in placing the individuals accurately with respect to their relative position in the ordered series.*

It is important to realize that many social scientists believe all of the attitude scales employed in the social sciences are ordinal level scales. When you and others are asked, for example, to respond to a question with Likert-type response categories [e.g., (1) strongly disagree, (2) disagree, (3) agree, and (4) strongly agree], the responses are ordinal in nature. Consider course evaluations and the following statement: "My professor is well prepared for class." If a friend in the class responds "(1) strongly disagree" and you respond "(3) agree," we can only conclude that you ranked the professor more favorably on this question than did your friend. We cannot claim that your rating of "3" or "agree" indicates that you rated the professor three times as high as your friend did since she rated the professor "1" or "strongly disagree."

Figure 2.1   Relationship of three points on an ordinal scale.

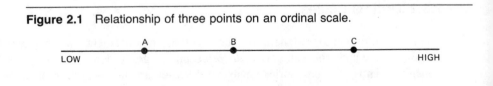

Help Is Where You Find It

Offering advice is not the exclusive province of people specifically trained to give such help. Members of some occupational categories are necessarily involved in interpersonal relationships with their clients, often involving intimate revelations by the clients and attempts to render verbal assistance by the help-giver. One aspect of this study dealt with the response strategies of four different occupational groups (hairdressers, lawyers, supervisors, and bartenders) when clients sought help and advice concerning personal problems. The various strategies employed by members of each of these groups were rank ordered in an ordinal scale from most frequent to least frequent. Table 2.1 shows ordinal ranking of 11 different strategies among hairdressers and bartenders.

Table 2.1 reveals some interesting differences as well as similarities in the help-giving strategies of these two professions. Both rate offering support, trying to be lighthearted, and just listening high on their hierarchy of response strategies. The most notable disagreement involves telling the clients to count their blessings. Hairdressers are more inclined to adopt this strategy than bartenders.

Table 2.1 Ordinal position of response strategies of hairdressers and bartenders when clients seek advice and counsel. A rank of 1 corresponds to the most frequently used strategy and 11 to the least frequently used strategy

Strategy	Hairdressers	Bartenders
Offer support and sympathy	1	3
Try to be lighthearted	2	2
Just listen	3	1
Present alternatives	4	4
Tell person to count blessings	5	10
Share personal experiences	6	5
Try not to get involved	7	6
Give advice	8	7
Ask questions	9	9
Try to get person to talk to someone else	10	11
Try to change topic	11	8

Source: Based on Emory L. Cowen's (1982), "Help Is Where You Find It," *American Psychologist*, **37**(4), 385–395.

We will be looking at these data again in Chapter 9 when we obtain the correlation between the rankings of response strategies of these two occupational groups.

Again, the numbers associated with the categories only indicate their ordered relationship, not how much of a difference exists between the categories. It should be noted, however, that consensus in this area is not complete.

2.3.3 Interval and Ratio Scales

Finally, the highest level of measurement in science is achieved with scales employing numbers (**interval** and **ratio scales**). The numerical values associated with these scales permit the use of mathematical operations such as adding, subtracting, multiplying, and dividing. In interval and ratio scales, equal differences between points on any part of the scale are equal. The only difference between the two scales stems from the fact that the interval scale employs an arbitrary zero point, whereas the ratio scale employs a true zero point. Consequently, only the ratio scale permits us to make statements concerning the ratios of numbers in the scale; for example, 4 feet are to 2 feet are to 1 foot. A good example of the difference between an interval and a ratio scale is a person's height as measured from a table top (interval) versus height as measured from the floor.

With both interval and ratio scales we can state exact differences between categories. This property or characteristic is particularly valuable because many statistical procedures can only be used with interval or ratio measures. Most statisticians consider the often used variables age, education, and income as ratio variables because each has a true zero point. The first two, age and education, have a true zero point of zero years. We can say that if a wife has completed 14 years of formal education and her husband 7 years, she has had twice as much formal education as he has. We cannot, of course, assume that she has twice as much knowledge because knowledge cannot be measured in standard units. Additionally, four concepts you will study later in this chapter—proportions, percentages, rates, and ratios—are all ratio measures. I.Q., however, which has no true zero point (it is not possible to say someone has no intelligence) is an interval measure.

Some statisticians enjoy pointing out that common social science variables such as income and education can be conceived of as only ordinal level measures in some instances. They might ask, for example, "Does a $1000 raise mean the same thing to an individual whose annual income exceeds $100,000 as it does to someone whose annual income is $15,000?" Or, "Is the one-unit difference between 8 and 9 years of formal education really equivalent to the one-unit difference between 18 and 19 years of formal education?" The argument being made is that the *meaning* of the $1000 or 1 additional year of formal education differs in these examples. While the implications of these examples are interesting to consider, we will treat variables such as these as ratio measures. Also, apart from the difference in the nature of the zero point, interval and ratio scales have the same mathematical properties and will be treated alike throughout the text.

It should be clear that one of the most sought after goals of the social scientist is to achieve measurements that are at least interval in nature. Indeed, interval scaling is assumed for most of the statistical tests reported in this book. However, although it is debatable that many of our scales achieve interval measurement, most social scientists are willing to make the assumption that they do.

One of the characteristics of higher-order scales is that they can readily be transformed into lower-order scales. Thus, the outcome of a 1-mile foot race may be expressed as time scores (ratio scale), for example, 3:56, 3:58, and 4:02. The time scores may then be transformed into an ordinal scale, for example, first-, second-, and third-place finishers. However, the reverse transformation is not possible. If we know only the order of finishing a race, for example, we cannot express the outcome in terms of a ratio scale (time scores). Although it is permissible to transform scores from higher-level to lower-level scales, it is not usually recommended since information is lost in the transformation. For example, risk-taking behavior might be scored from 0 to 10 depending on the number of ten "risky" activities (e.g., driving over 100 miles per hour, skydiving, unprotected intercourse with a person having active genital herpes, etc.) in which a person has engaged. We could convert this interval–level measure into an ordinal-level measure by reclassifying everyone into three categories—(1) Nonrisk taker, (2) moderate risk taker, (3) high risk taker—but we would lost information about the respondents. Table 2.2 provides a summary of measurement scales.

2.4 Continuous and Discrete Variables

Imagine that you are given the problem of trying to determine the number of children per American family. Your scale of measurement would start with zero (no children) and would proceed, by *increments of 1* to perhaps 15 or 20. Note that, in moving from one value on the scale to the next, we proceed by *whole numbers* rather than by fractional amounts. Thus, a family has either 0, 1, 2, or more children. In spite of the statistical abstraction that the American

Table 2.2 Summary of measurement scales

	Characteristics	Permissible Mathematical Manipulations
Nominal	Categories homogeneous, mutually exclusive, and no assumption made about ordered relationships between categories.	Enumerating the number of cases per category and counting the relative category sizes.
Ordinal	All of the above plus the categories can be rank-ordered.	All of the above plus rank-ordering the categories.
Interval	All of the above plus exact differences between categories may be specified and an arbitrary zero point is assumed.	All of the above plus addition, subtraction, multiplication, and division.
Ratio	All of the above with the exception that a true zero point is assumed.	All of the above.

family averages 1 3/4 children, we do not know a single couple that has achieved this marvelous state of family planning.

Such variables are referred to as **discrete** or **discontinuous variables**, and they have equality of *counting units* as their basic characteristic. Thus, if we are studying the number of children in a family, each child is equal with respect to providing one counting unit. Mathematical operations such as adding, subtracting, multiplying, and dividing are permissible with discrete variables. We can say that a family with four children has twice as many children as one with two children. Observations of discrete variables are always exact so long as the counting procedures are accurate. Examples of discrete variables are group size, the number of males in a class, the number of work stoppages in Illinois, and the number of welfare recipients in a county.

You should not assume from this discussion that discrete variables necessarily involve *only* whole numbers. However, most of the discontinuous variables used by social scientists are expressed in terms of whole numbers. For example, a political scientist tabulates the number of people who voted for a particular candidate, or a sociologist tabulates the number of kindergarten children from family units of different sizes. In each of these examples we are clearly dealing with values that proceed by whole numbers.

In contrast, a **continuous variable** is one in which there are an unlimited number of *possible* values between *any two adjacent values*. Thus, if the variable is height measured in inches, then 4 inches and 5 inches would be two adjacent values of the scale. However, there can be an infinite number of intermediate values, such as 4.5 inches or 4.7 inches. If the variable is height measured in tenths of inches, then 4.5 inches and 4.6 inches are two adjacent values of the scale, but there can *still* be an infinite number of intermediate values such as 4.53 inches or 4.59 inches.

A variable which may take on an unlimited (infinite) number of intermediate values is referred to as a *continuous* variable. It is important to note that, although our measurement of discrete variables may be exact, our measure of continuous variables is always approximate. If we were measuring the attitudes of Philadelphians toward their police, for example, we would find a wide variety of attitudes ranging from "very positive" to "very negative" because no two people can have *exactly* the same attitude (Figure 2.2). Other social science examples of continuous variables include measures of achievement motivation, political activism, religiosity, and income.

Let's consider one additional point. Continuous variables are often expressed as whole numbers and therefore appear to be discontinuous. Thus, you may say that you are 5 feet, 8 inches tall and weigh 150 pounds. However, the decision to express heights to the nearest inch and weights to the nearest pound was yours. You could just as easily have expressed height to the nearest fraction of an inch and weight to the nearest ounce. You do not have such a choice when reporting such things as the number of children in a family. These *must* occur as whole numbers.

Figure 2.2 depicts the difference between continuous and discrete variables.

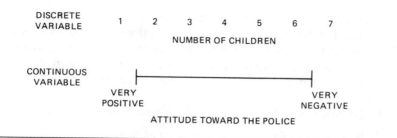

Figure 2.2 Discrete and continuous variables.

2.4.1 Continuous Variables, Errors of Measurement, and True Limits of Numbers

In our preceding discussion we pointed out that continuously distributed variables can take on an unlimited number of intermediate values. Therefore, we can never specify the exact value for any particular measurement, since it is possible that a more sensitive measuring instrument can slightly increase the accuracy of our measurements. For this reason we stated that numerical values of continuously distributed variables are always approximate. However, it is possible to specify the limits within which the true value falls; for example, the **true limits** of a value of a continuous variable are equal to that number plus or minus one-half of the unit of measurement.

Let us look at a few examples. You have a bathroom scale, which is calibrated in terms of pounds. When you step on the scale, the pointer will usually be a little above or below a pound marker. However, you report your weight to the nearest pound. Thus, if the pointer were approximately three-quarters of the distance between 212 and 213 pounds, you would report your weight as 213 pounds. It would be understood that the true limit of your weight, assuming an accurate scale, falls between 212.5 and 213.5 pounds. If, on the other hand, you are measuring the weight of whales, you would probably have a fairly gross unit of measurement, say, 100 pounds. Thus, if you reported the weight of a whale as 32,000 pounds, you would mean that the whale weighed between 31,950 pounds and 32,050 pounds. If the scale were calibrated in terms of 1000 pounds, the true limits of the whale's weight would be between 31,500 pounds and 32,500 pounds.

2.5 Rounding

Imagine we have obtained some data that, in the course of conducting our statistical analysis, require that we divide one number into another. There will be innumerable occasions in this course when you will be required to perform this arithmetic operation. In most cases the answer will be a value that extends to an endless number of decimal places. For example, if we were to express the fraction 1/3 in decimal form, the result would be $0.33333+$. It is obvious that we cannot extend this series of numbers *ad infinitum*. We must terminate at some point and assign a value to the last number in the series that best reflects the remainder. When we do this, two types of problems arise:

1. To how many decimal places do we carry the final answer?

2. How do we decide on the last number in the series?

The answer to the first question is usually given in terms of the number of significant figures. For simplicity and convenience we adopt the following policy with respect to rounding:

> In obtaining the final answer, we should round to two more places than were in the original data. We should not round the intermediate steps.*

Thus, if the original data were in whole-numbered units, we would round our answer to the second decimal. If in tenths, we would round to the third decimal, and so forth.

Once we have decided the number of places to carry our final figures, we are still left with the problem of representing the last digit. Fortunately, the rule governing the determination of the last digit is perfectly simple and explicit. Rule I: If the remainder beyond that digit is greater than 5, increase the digit to the next higher number. If the remainder beyond that digit is less than 5, allow that digit to remain as it is. Let's look at a few illustrations. In each case we will round to the second decimal place:

$$6.546 \quad \text{becomes} \quad 6.55$$
$$6.543 \quad \text{becomes} \quad 6.54$$
$$1.967 \quad \text{becomes} \quad 1.97$$
$$1.534 \quad \text{becomes} \quad 1.53$$

You may ask, "In these illustrations what happens if the digit at the third decimal place is 5?" You should first determine whether or not the digit is exactly 5. If it is 5 plus the slightest remainder, Rule I holds and you must add one to the digit at the second decimal place. If it is almost, but not quite 5, the digit at the second decimal place remains the same. If it is *exactly 5, with no remainder*, then Rule II applies: Round the digit at the second decimal

---

* Since many of you will be using calculators, you should be aware of minor differences that may occur in the final answer. These differences may be attributed to the fact that different calculators will carry the intermediate steps to a different number of decimal places. Thus, a calculator that carries the intermediate steps to 4 places will probably produce a slightly different final answer than one that carries to 14 places.

place to the *nearest even number*. If this digit is already even, then it is not changed. If it is odd, then *add* 1 to this digit to make it even. As you review the rules you should see that their purpose is to eliminate bias in either direction over the long run. Let's look at several illustrations in which we round to the second decimal place:

6.545001	becomes	6.55	Why?
6.545000	becomes	6.54	Why?
1.9652	becomes	1.97	Why?
0.00500	becomes	0.00	Why?
0.01500	becomes	0.02	Why?
16.89501	becomes	16.90	Why?

2.6 Ratios

One of the several ratios commonly used by social scientists is the *sex ratio* or the number of males per 100 females. We find that sex ratios vary between cities, rural-urban areas, and age groups. A city such as Washington, D.C., has a relatively low sex ratio due to the large number of clerical and secretarial positions associated with governmental affairs, whereas Anchorage, Alaska, which is a frontier city, is characterized by a very high sex ratio because of the high concentration of males in the work force. A ratio results from dividing the number of cases in one category by the number of cases in another category, and in the case of the sex ratio the quantities are multiplied by 100 to eliminate the decimal. Let's compute the sex ratio for the United States in 1984 when there were approximately 114.76 million males and 121.39 million females:*

$$\text{sex ratio} = \frac{\text{number of males}}{\text{number of females}} \times 100$$
$$\text{sex ratio} = \frac{114.8 \text{ million males}}{121.4 \text{ million females}} \times 100$$
$$= 94.6$$

We interpret our computed sex ratio as 94.6 males per 100 females. If we calculated the sex ratio by age group, we would observe the trend evident in the accompanying table. Can you explain why there are so few males per 100 females among the 65+ age group? A total of 11,301,000 males and 16,741,000 females were 65+ in 1984. Verify the age-specific sex ratio of 67.5 for the 65+ age group.

---

* U.S. Bureau of the Census. The values have been rounded.

Age-specific sex ratio

	Sex Ratio
Under 14	104.8
14–24	102.2
24–44	97.9
45–64	91.4
65+	67.5
All ages	94.5

Another ratio used by social scientists is the *dependency ratio*, which indicates the number of individuals per 100 younger than 15 or older than 64 relative to those between the ages of 15 and 64. High dependency ratios characterize developing nations. Why? In Vietnam the population totaled 62.2 million persons in 1987, of which 24.9 million or 40% were less than 15 and 2.5 million or 4% were over 64 years old. The dependency ratio in Vietnam is approximately 78.7, whereas this figure for the United States is 51.5:*

$$\frac{\text{dependency}}{\text{ratio}} = \frac{\text{persons younger than 15 or older than 64}}{\text{persons 15 to 64}} \times 100$$

$$\frac{\text{dependency}}{\text{ratio for}} = \frac{24.9 \text{ million} + 2.5 \text{ million}}{34.8 \text{ million}} \times 100$$
Vietnam

$$= 78.7$$

A more common use of ratios involves comparing one quantity to another. Nonwhites in the United States constituted approximately 35.2 million persons in 1984 and whites 201.0 million, for a total of approximately 236.2 million persons. We can express the ratio of nonwhites to whites as 35.2:201.0 or 1:5.7. We will see that ratios provide the basis for proportions, percentages, and rates in that all are based on the relationship between two categories or quantities.

2.7 Proportions, Percentages, and Rates

A **proportion** is calculated by dividing the quantity in one category by the total of all the categories. In 1983, the most frequent cause of death among persons aged 15 to 24 was accidents. During that year 19,263 persons died

---

* Adapted from the 1987 World Population Data Sheet of the Population Reference Bureau, Inc. In industrial nations, the numerator is frequently adjusted to persons younger than 21 because few enter the work force at age 15, as is common in developing nations. The ratio for the United States is based on the same equation as the Vietnam figure for comparative purposes.

following an accident (automobile, household, etc.), and a total of 32,080 in this age group died from the five leading causes of death (see Table 2.3). Given this information, we can calculate that the proportion of accidental deaths out of the total number of deaths in 1983 attributable to the five leading causes for the 15 to 24 age group equaled 0.600 by dividing 19,263 by 32,080 using Eq. (2.1).

$$\text{proportion } (p) = \frac{f}{N} \tag{2.1}$$

$$p = \frac{19,263}{32,080} = 0.600$$

where f = frequency, the number of cases in any category
N = the number of cases in all categories

Proportions can range in value from 0 (if there are no cases in a category) to 1.000 (if a category contains all the cases). Note also in Table 2.3 that the proportions associated with the five categories total 0.999 because they are mutually exclusive and exhaustive; hence, the categories constitute a nominal level of measurement.

A proportion can be converted to a **percentage** when multiplied by 100 as shown in Eq. (2.2):

$$\text{percentage } (\%) = \left(\frac{f}{N}\right) \times 100 \tag{2.2}$$

Box 2.1 provides an additional example of percentages based on national interviews.

Consider Table 2.3. We can convert the proportion of deaths associated with suicide to a percentage by multiplying the proportion 0.146 by 100, and the proportion associated with accidents can also be converted to a percentage when multiplied by 100. Hence, 14.6% died from suicide, and 60.0% from an accident, or a total of 74.6% of the deaths reported in Table 2.3 resulted

Table 2.3 Five leading causes of death in 1983 among persons 15 to 24 years of age (both sexes)

	Number	Proportion	Percentage
Accidents	19,263	0.600	60.0
Homicide	4,856	0.151	15.1
Suicide	4,690	0.146	14.6
Malignancies	2,226	0.069	6.9
Heart disease	1,045	0.033	3.8
Total	32,080	0.999*	99.9*

*Do not total 1.000 and 100.0 due to rounding.
Source: Centers for Disease Control, Homicide Surveillance: High-Risk Racial and Ethnic Groups—Blacks and Hispanics, 1970 to 1983. Atlanta: Centers for Disease Control, November 1986.

from these two causes. If we added the 15.1% who were victims of homicide, the 6.9% who died of malignancies, and the 3.3% who died of heart disease, we could account for 99.9% of the 32,080 deaths.

We are frequently concerned with *percentage change*. While you probably have been calculating percentage change for many years, a brief review is worthwhile. Two time periods are involved when calculating percentage change. Consider how we might calculate the percentage of population increase in a small village in Wisconsin from the 1970 to 1980 census. If the population totaled 1000 in 1970 and increased to 1710 in 1980, how do we determine the percentage increase? Our first time period is 1970 and the second 1980. Using the information and the following procedure, we can now calculate the percentage change:

$$\frac{\text{percentage}}{\text{change}} = \frac{\text{(quantity at time 2)} - \text{(quantity at time 1)}}{\text{(quantity at time 1)}} \times 100 \qquad (2.3)$$

$$\frac{\text{percentage}}{\text{change}} = \frac{(1710 - 1000)}{1000} \times 100$$

$$= \frac{710}{1000} \times 100$$

$$= 0.71 \times 100 = 71\%$$

The procedure works equally well if the percentage change is negative. If the population of our fictitious village declined from 1000 in 1970 to 900 in 1980, we would anticipate negative growth:

$$\frac{\text{percentage}}{\text{change}} = \frac{(900 - 1000)}{1000} \times 100$$

$$= \frac{-100}{1000} \times 100 = -10\%$$

The population decline is 10%. Also see Case Example 2.2.

Note that it is very important that you not disregard the minus sign in the numerator. The denominator will always constitute your base and is the quantity at time 1. Another way of looking at the concept of percentage change is to remember that we are interested in changes from our base (in this case the population in 1970). If the quantity at time 2 is less than the base (time 1), we know that the percentage change is negative. Consider another example. Suppose you earned $15,000 in 1988 and the next year received a major promotion that included an annual salary of $30,000. Your salary has doubled and the percentage increase is 100%. Demonstrate this to yourself.

We have seen the value of proportions and percentages; however, one more related value, the **rate**, allows us to examine our data in another way.

BOX 2.1

Victimization by Violent Crime: Income and Race

Income level	Race White (%)	Race Black (%)
Under $3,000	6.26	5.57
$3,000–7,499	4.12	5.18
$7,500–9,999	3.67	4.06
$10,000–14,999	3.53	4.12
$15,000–24,999	2.87	3.04
$25,000 & above	2.50	2.74

The accompanying table shows the percentage of victimization by violent crime (rape, robbery, or assault) during 1982, broken down in terms of race and income level. The data are based on interviews of about 60,000 households and represent 128,000 occupants of age 12 and over. Note that, with the exception of the lowest income category, a greater percentage of blacks are victims of crime within each income level. Note also that there appears to be an inverse relationship between income level and victimization rate: the higher the income level is, the lower the rate of victimization is. This relationship appears to hold for both blacks and whites.

Much of the data collected in the behavioral and social sciences consist of head counts—the number of people falling in one category as opposed to another category. We commonly use percentages or proportions to summarize such data. Various agencies of the criminal justice system rely heavily on the "head count" technique to summarize data on crimes and victims of crimes.

Source: Langan, P. A. and Innes, C. A. (1985), "The Risk of Violent Crime," Bureau of Justice Statistics Special Report, NCJ-97119.

For example, it allows us to determine the number of deaths by each cause for a given number of persons. We know that 60.0% of the deaths attributable to the five leading causes in the 15 to 24 age group were caused by accidents (Table 2.3). We *do not* know how many deaths per 100,000 persons in the 15 to 24 age group, for example, were caused by accidents. Or, put another way, if you are between 15 and 24 years of age, is it very likely you will die in an accident? A total of approximately 40,550,000 persons were between the ages of 15 and 24 in 1983. We know that 19,263 died of accidents; therefore, we can calculate the percentage in this age group that died of an accident. You should find that the proportion of deaths attributable to accidents is approximately 0.000475, the percentage is 0.0475 (resulted from multiplying the proportion by 100), and the rate per 100,000 is 47.50 (resulted from multiplying the proportion by 100,000).

Rates are always reported for a specific number of cases, normally per 100, per 1000, or per 100,000. The birthrate can be calculated in a variety of ways including rate of live births per 1000 population, rate per 1000 women of child-bearing age (normally 15 to 44), or what is termed an *age-specific* birthrate. So be sure you know how a rate is calculated. The age-specific

CASE EXAMPLE 2.2

Crime Rates and Percentage Change

Table 2.4 provides a summary of violent and property crime in the United States during the period from 1980 to 1984. The overall trends indicate that crime has decreased during this time period as is evident from tracing the rate per 100,000 over the five years or by examining the percentage change values. The standardized rate per 100,000 persons ensures that the figures are independent of population growth. Verify the total percent change for all crimes of -15.4 from 1980 to 1984 by using Eq. (2.3).

Table 2.4 Crimes and crime rates, by type: 1980 to 1984

		Violent Crime					Property Crime			
Item and Year	Total	Total	Mur-der*	Forci-ble rape	Rob-bery	Aggra-vated assault	Total	Bur-glary	Lar-ceny—theft	Motor vehi-cle theft
Rate per 100,000 inhabitants:										
1980	5,950	597	10.2	36.8	251	299	5,353	1,684	3,167	502
1981	5,858	594	9.8	36.0	259	290	5,264	1,650	3,140	475
1982	5,604	571	9.1	34.0	239	289	5,033	1,489	3,085	459
1983	5,175	538	8.3	33.7	217	279	4,637	1,338	2,869	431
1984	5,031	539	7.9	35.7	205	290	4,492	1,264	2,791	437
Percent change, rate per 100,000 inhabitants:										
1980–1984	−15.4	−9.6	−22.5	−3.0	−18.2	−2.8	−16.1	−25.0	−11.9	−13.0
1983–1984	−2.8	.3	−4.8	5.9	−5.1	3.9	−3.1	−5.5	−2.7	1.5

Source: U.S. Federal Bureau of Investigation, *Crime in the United States,* annual.
* Includes nonnegligent manslaughter.

birthrate is the rate of live births per 1000 women in specific age categories. In 1983 the age-specific birthrate for women 15 to 19 years was 51.7, for women 20 to 24 it was 108.3, for women 25 to 29 it was 108.7, for women 30 to 34 it dropped to 64.6, and for women 35 to 39 it was only 22.1.* The importance of the age-specific birthrate is that we can determine which age groups are having disproportionate numbers of children.

Formally, a **rate** is a ratio of the occurrences in a group category to the total number of elements in the group with which we are concerned.

$$\text{rate} = \frac{\text{number of occurrences in a group category}}{\text{total number of elements in the group}}$$

* *Source:* U.S. National Center for Health Statistics, *Vital Statistics of the United States,* annual.

This ratio is then multiplied by a given number (normally 100, 1000, or 100,000) to determine the rate per a given number of persons or events. If you were told that the burglary rate per 100,000 population in San Diego is 1600, you would know immediately that the rate was calculated by forming a ratio of the number of burglaries in San Diego to the total number of persons in San Diego and multiplying by 100,000 (to give the rate per 100,000).

Summary

In this chapter we pointed out that advanced knowledge of mathematics is not a prerequisite for success in this course. A sound background in high school mathematics plus steady application to assignments should be sufficient to permit mastery of the fundamental concepts put forth in this text.

To aid the student who may not have had recent contact with mathematics, we have attempted to review some of the basic concepts of mathematics. Included in this review are (1) the grammar of mathematical notations; (2) types of numbers; (3) types of numerical scales; (4) continuous and discrete scales; (5) rounding; and (6) ratios, proportions, percentages, and rates. Students requiring a more thorough review of mathematics may refer to Appendix A.

Terms to Remember

Continuous variables Variables which can assume an unlimited number of intermediate values.

Discrete variables (Discontinuous variables) Variables which have equality of counting units.

Interval scale A scale in which exact distances can be known between categories. The zero point in this scale is arbitrary, and arithmetic operations are permitted.

Measurement The assignment of numbers to objects or events according to sets of predetermined (or arbitrary) rules.

Nominal numbers Numbers used to name.

Nominal scale Scales in which the categories are homogeneous, mutually exclusive, and unordered.

Ordinal numbers Numbers used to represent position or order in a series.

Ordinal scale A scale in which the classes can be rank-ordered, that is, expressed in terms of the algebra of inequalities (e.g., $a < b$ or $a > b$).

Percentage A proportion that has been multiplied by 100.

Proportion   A value calculated by dividing the quantity in one category by the total of all of the components.

Rate   A ratio of the occurrences in a group category to the total number of elements in the group with which we are concerned.

Ratio   The number of cases in one category divided by the number of cases in another category.

Ratio scale   The same as interval scale, except that there is a true zero point.

True limits of a number   The true limits of a value of a continuous variable are equal to that number plus or minus one-half of the unit of measurement.

Variable   Any characteristic of a person, group, or environment that can vary or denote a difference.

Exercises

The following exercises are based on this chapter and Appendix A.

1. Determine the square roots of the following numbers to two decimal places?
   a) 160   **b)** 16   **c)** 1.60   **d)** 0.16   **e)** 0.016

2. Find a when $b = 10$, $c = 4$, and $a + b + c = 19$.

3. Find y when $N = 4$ and $20 + N = y + 2$.

4. Find ΣX when $N = 20$, $\bar{X} = 60$, where $\bar{X} = \Sigma X/N$.

5. Find N when $\bar{X} = 90$, $\Sigma X = 360$, where $\bar{X} = \Sigma X/N$.

6. Find N when

   $$\Sigma(X - \bar{X})^2 = 640, \qquad s^2 = 16, \qquad \text{where} \qquad s^2 = \frac{\Sigma(X - \bar{X})^2}{N}$$

7. Find s^2 when

   $$\Sigma(X - \bar{X})^2 = 240, \qquad N = 12, \qquad \text{where} \qquad s^2 = \frac{\Sigma(X - \bar{X})^2}{N}$$

8. Determine the value of the following expressions in which $X_1 = 4$, $X_2 = 5$, $X_3 = 7$, $X_4 = 9$, $X_5 = 10$, $X_6 = 11$, $X_7 = 14$.

   a) $\displaystyle\sum_{i=1}^{4} X_i =$ **b)** $\displaystyle\sum_{i=1}^{7} X_i =$ **c)** $\displaystyle\sum_{i=3}^{6} X_i =$

   d) $\displaystyle\sum_{i=2}^{5} X_i =$ **e)** $\displaystyle\sum_{i=1}^{N} X_i =$ **f)** $\displaystyle\sum_{i=4}^{N} X_i =$

9. Express the following in summation notation:

a) $X_1 + X_2 + X_3$ b) $X_1 + X_2 + \cdots + X_N$

c) $X_3^2 + X_4^2 + X_5^2 + X_6^2$ d) $X_4^2 + X_5^2 + \cdots + X_N^2$

10. Using the values of X_i given in Exercise 8, show that

$$\sum_{i=1}^{N} X_i^2 \neq \left(\sum_{i=1}^{N} X_i \right)^2$$

11. Indicate the level of measurement for the following studies:

    a) The name recognition of several political candidates was coded into the following categories:
      1) recognize the name
      2) do not recognize the name

    b) Respondents in a community standards survey were asked to classify sexually explicit material as:
      1) very obscene
      2) obscene
      3) not obscene at all

    c) The respondents in "11(b)" were also asked if the government should:
      1) ban the material
      2) protect the material

    d) A sample of middle-aged men was asked to rank-order their three biggest fears of growing older.

    e) The percentage of population loss or gain over the past 10 years was calculated by state.

12. The following questions were included in a recent series of student surveys. Indicate the level of measure for each question.

    a) How satisfied are you with your life?
      1) very satisfied
      2) satisfied
      3) neither satisfied nor unsatisfied
      4) unsatisfied
      5) very unsatisfied

    b) What type of job do you expect to obtain when you graduate?
      _____

    c) Of your five closest friends, how many are men? _____

    d) Estimate what percent of your study time is spent effectively.
      _____

    e) What is your current grade point average? _____

f) Have you ever belonged to a:
1) labor union _____yes _____no
2) church or synagogue _____yes _____no
3) social club _____yes _____no

g) What is your race, or ethnic background?
1) Hispanic
2) white, other than Hispanic
3) black, other than Hispanic
4) Oriental
5) American Indian
6) other (specify _____)

13. Indicate if the following scales are continuous or discrete:

a) family size

b) political party preference

c) attractiveness

d) racial tolerance

14. State the true limits of the following numbers?
a) 0   **b)** 0.5   **c)** 1.0   **d)** 0.49   **e)** -5 **f)** -4.5

15. Round the following numbers to the second decimal place:
a) 99.99500   **b)** 46.40501
c) 2.96500   **d)** 0.00501
e) 16.46500   **f)** 1.05499
g) 86.2139   **h)** 10.0050

16. There are 18 males and 21 females in your social welfare class. What is the ratio of males to females?

17. **a)** Calculate the ratio of male to female homicide rates for the following years.
b) Also, calculate the male–female ratio for whites and for blacks.

Homicide Victims

| | White | | Black | | |
Year	Male	Female	Male	Female	Total
1980	10,381	3,177	8,385	1,898	23,841
1981	9,941	3,125	8,312	1,825	23,203
1982	9,260	2,179	7,730	1,743	21,912

Source: U.S. Center for Health Statistics, *Vital Statistics of the United States,* annual.

18. New York State had a total of approximately 8,339,000 males and 9,219,000 females in 1980. What was the sex ratio? (*Source:* U.S. Bureau of the Census, *Census of Population: 1980,* I.)

19. In 1987 Japan had a total population of 122.2 million persons of whom 22% were younger than 15 and 10% were over 64. What was the dependency ratio and how would you interpret your answer? (*Source:* Adapted from 1987 World Population Data Sheet of the Population Reference Bureau, Inc.)

20. Determine the proportion and percentage of the population in the Baltimore Metropolitan Statistical Area that is contained in each of the following areas (population estimated as of July 1, 1984):

Anne Arundel County	389,000
Baltimore County	673,000
Carroll County	105,000
Harford County	151,000
Howard County	136,000
Queen Anne's County	28,000
Baltimore City	764,000

Source: *Statistical Abstract of the United States,* 1986, p. 870.

21. Examine the accompanying table and calculate the women's earnings as a percentage of men's earnings. Determine the percentage change of women's and men's earnings from 1960 to 1975.

Median annual earnings of year-round full-time workers 14 years and over by sex, 1960 to 1975

Year	Annual Earnings (Dollars)	
	Women	*Men*
1960	3,293	5,417
1965	3,823	6,375
1970	5,323	8,966
1975	7,504	12,758

Source: U.S. Department of Labor, Bureau of Labor Statistics, *U.S. Working Women: A Data Book,* 1977.

22. It has often been speculated that Californians cope with earthquake hazards by avoidance—simply not thinking about them. Professor Ralph H. Turner, a sociologist and the director of UCLA's Institute for Social Science Research, has collected data that bear on this common belief. Here are the data collected on a number of survey questions concerned with media coverage of earthquake-related information.

Find the proportion and percentage of individuals responding in each category to each of the questions raised in the survey.

Do the responses appear to support the common view that Californians avoid thinking about earthquakes?

a) Do the media provide too little, too much, or sufficient coverage about what to do if an earthquake strikes?

b) How about the news media's coverage on preparations for an earthquake?

	Number Responding
Too little	386
About right	103
Too much	8
No opinion	3

	Number Responding
Too little	357
About right	121
Too much	14
No opinion	8

c) Do the media provide sufficient information about what the government is doing to prepare for an earthquake?

d) How about the attention the media pay to nonscientific earthquake predictions?

	Number Responding
Too little	413
About right	67
Too much	10
No opinion	10

	Number Responding
Too little	126
About right	142
Too much	215
No opinion	17

23. The local chapter of the John Birch Society lost 25 members from the previous year, and membership now totals 38. What is the percentage change?

24. An interviewer completed 150 interviews this month. How many interviews must be completed next month for a 25% increase?

25. In 1965 a total of 2,857,000 persons were on active military duty, as compared to 2,138,000 in 1984. (*Source:* U.S. Department of Defense, *Selected Manpower Statistics*, annual.) Assuming these estimated numbers are exact:

   a) Calculate the percentage change from 1965 to 1984.

   b) The number of military personnel in 1984 is what percentage of the number in 1965?

26. Examine the accompanying table and calculate the percentage change for each of the categories from January 1974 to December 1978.

Supplemental security income for the aged, blind, and disabled: Number of persons receiving federally administered payments and total amount, 1974 and 1978

	Number of Persons				Amount of Payments
Period	Total	Aged	Blind	Disabled	Total
January 1974	3,215,632	1,865,109	72,390	1,278,133	$365,149,000
December 1978	4,216,925	1,967,900	77,135	2,171,890	546,567,000

Source: Social Security Administration, Social Security Bulletin, May 1979, 42(5).

27. The world's population and estimated population are shown here. Calculate the rate of growth in percent for each of the five-year time periods (e.g., 1960–1965, 1965–1970, etc.).

World Midyear Population	(millions)
1960	3,049
1965	3,358
1970	3,721
1975	4,103
1980	4,473
1985	4,865
1990	5,271
1995	5,708
2000	6,159

Source: U.S. Bureau of the Census, World Population 1985 and unpublished data. Statistical Abstract of the United States, 1986.

28. The accompanying table shows the number of male and female victims of homicide between the years 1978 and 1982:

Year	Number of Male Victims of Homicide	Number of Female Victims of Homicide
1978	15,838	4,594
1979	17,628	4,922
1980	19,088	5,190
1981	18,572	5,074
1982	17,315	5,043
Total	88,441	24,823

a) Of the total number of male homicide victims during the years 1978 through 1982, find the percentage for each year.

b) Of the total number of female homicide victims during the years 1978 through 1982, find the percentage for each year.

c) Of the total number of homicide victims in 1982, find the percentage that was male.

d) Of the total number of homicide victims in the 1978 to 1982 period, find the percentage that was female.

29. Using the figures shown in the accompanying table, answer the following questions:

   a) Of all the students majoring in each academic area, what percentage is female?

   b) Considering only the males, what percentages are found in each academic area?

   c) Considering only the females, what percentages are found in each academic area?

   d) Of all students majoring in the five areas, what percentage is male? What percentage is female?

	Males	Females
Business administration	400	100
Education	50	150
Humanities	150	200
Science	250	100
Social science	200	200

30. Following is a list showing the number of births in the United States (expressed in thousands) between 1950 and 1980. Calculate the percentage of males and females for each year.

Year	Males	Females
1950	1824	1731
1955	2074	1974
1960	2180	2078
1965	1927	1833
1970	1915	1816
1975	1613	1531
1980	1853	1760

Source: U.S. National Center for Health Statistics, *Vital Statistics of the United States,* annual.

31. The suicide rates per 100,000 population in 1981 are shown here for selected countries, by sex and age group. Discuss the differences by age, sex, and country and consider the possible reasons for the varying rates.

Country	Male					Female				
	Total	15–24 Yr	25–44 Yr	45–64 Yr	65 Yr & Over	Total	15–24 Yr	25–44 Yr	45–64 Yr	65 Yr & Over
U.S.	18.0	19.7	24.5	23.7	33.5	5.7	4.6	8.0	9.4	6.0
Austria	42.1	33.6	49.5	60.4	81.6	14.5	6.8	13.3	21.3	28.2
Ireland	8.6	9.7	12.3	11.4	19.0	2.9	1.8	4.4	6.0	4.0
France	28.5	14.6	30.6	42.0	73.9	11.1	5.0	11.0	16.0	23.6

Source: World Health Organization, World Health Statistics, annual.

32. If there were 192 homicides in the Atlanta (Georgia) Standard Metropolitan Statistical Area (SMSA), and the SMSA population totaled 1,902,000, what is the homicide rate per 1000 persons?

33. The total number of lawyers practicing in 1980 for selected states are shown below along with the 1980 population. Calculate the population per lawyer and the rate per 1000 persons.

State	Population in 1980	Total Lawyers in 1980
Alaska	402,000	1,355
Arkansas	2,286,000	3,188
California	23,668,000	64,840
District of Columbia	638,000	25,465
Georgia	5,463,000	11,087
Illinois	11,427,000	32,421
New York	17,558,000	62,745

Source: American Bar Foundation, Chicago, Ill., The Lawyer Statistical Report: A Statistical Profile of the U.S. Legal Profession in the 1980s, 1985.

2
Descriptive Statistics

3 Frequency Distributions and Graphing
      Techniques
4 Percentiles
5 Measures of Central Tendency
6 Measures of Dispersion
7 The Standard Deviation and the Standard
      Normal Distribution
8 An Introduction to Contingency Tables
9 Correlation
10 Regression and Prediction
11 Multivariate Data Analysis

chapter **3**

Frequency Distributions and Graphing Techniques

3.1 Grouping of Data
3.2 Cumulative Frequency and Cumulative Percentage
    Distributions
3.3 Graphing Techniques
3.4 Misuse of Graphing Techniques
3.5 Nominally Scaled Variables
3.6 Ordinally Scaled Variables
3.7 Interval- and Ratio-Scaled Variables
3.8 Forms of Frequency Curves
3.9 Other Graphic Representations

3.1 Grouping of Data

Imagine that you conducted a survey for the State Recreation Division assessing visitor use of a state park. Your job was to distribute the questionnaires to the drivers of cars entering the park during a 2-week period and to collect the completed questionnaires as the cars exited the park gate. Prior to a complete analysis of the 25 questions that were included on the questionnaires, your boss wants to get a sense of the visitors' ages. Because you collected forms from over 2000 cars, it is obvious that you cannot examine all of them in a short period of time, so you pull at **random** (i.e., in such a way that each sample of a given size in a population has an equal chance of being selected) 75 completed questionnaires.

Altogether, the questionnaires returned by the drivers of the 75 cars sampled indicate that the cars contained a total of 110 occupants. You write down the ages of the 110 occupants with the results listed in Table 3.1.

As you glance over the data in Table 3.1, it becomes clear that your boss will not be able to make heads or tails out of them unless you organize them in some systematic fashion. It occurs to you to list all of the scores from the lowest to the highest and then place a slash mark alongside each age every time it occurs (Table 3.2). The number of slash marks, then, represents the frequency of occurrence of each age, and f is the symbol for frequency.

By doing this, you have constructed an **ungrouped frequency distribution** of scores. Note that in the present example the ages are widely spread

Table 3.1   Ages of 110 park visitors selected at random

40	8	15	29	58	42	49	24	56	5
48	35	33	52	17	35	38	41	42	47
11	22	66	40	34	65	23	49	30	34
16	57	52	53	15	25	31	45	49	51
52	74	47	39	57	48	53	36	48	40
64	13	37	44	44	33	30	26	37	53
21	25	0	60	69	40	52	40	62	44
33	47	24	19	46	52	40	33	73	47
39	27	43	21	23	26	44	39	26	35
69	38	61	37	50	12	25	43	71	42
45	43	35	63	29	65	3	50	45	53

out, a number of ages have a frequency of zero, and there is no visually clear indication of a pattern. Under these circumstances it is customary for most researchers to *group* the scores into what are referred to as class intervals and then obtain a frequency distribution of grouped scores.

3.1.1 Grouping into Class Intervals

Grouping into class intervals involves "collapsing the scale" and assigning scores to **mutually exclusive** and **exhaustive*** classes where the classes are defined in terms of the grouping intervals used. The reasons for grouping are threefold: (1) Unless computers are available, it is uneconomical and unwieldy to deal with a large number of cases spread out over many scores. (2) Some of the scores have such low frequency counts associated with them that we are not justified in maintaining these scores as separate and distinct entities. (3) Categories provide a concise and meaningful summary of the data.

On the negative side is, of course, the fact that grouping inevitably results in the loss of information. For example, individual scores lose their identity when we group into class intervals, and some small errors in statistics based on grouped scores are unavoidable.

The question now becomes, "On what basis do we decide upon the grouping intervals we will use?" Obviously, the interval selected must not be so large that we lose the information provided by our original measurement. For example, if we were to divide the previously collected ages into two classes, those below 36 and those 36 and above, practically all the information about the original ages would be lost. On the other hand, the class intervals should not be so small that the purposes served by grouping are defeated. In answer to our question, there is, unfortunately, no general solution that can be applied to all data. Much of the time the choice of the number of class intervals

---

* We refer to the classes as *mutually exclusive* because it is impossible for a person's score to belong to more than one class. *Exhaustive* means that all scores can be placed within the established categories.

Table 3.2   Ungrouped frequency distribution of ages of 110 park visitors selected at random

X	f	X	f	X	f	X	f
0*	/	21	//	42	///	63	/
1	0	22	/	43	///	64	/
2	0	23	//	44	////	65	//
3	/	24	//	45	///	66	/
4	0	25	///	46	/	67	0
5	/	26	///	47	////	68	0
6	0	27	/	48	///	69	//
7	0	28	0	49	///	70	0
8	/	29	//	50	//	71	/
9	0	30	//	51	/	72	0
10	0	31	/	52	/////	73	/
11	/	32	0	53	////	74	/
12	/	33	////	54	0		
13	/	34	//	55	0		
14	0	35	////	56	/		
15	//	36	/	57	//		
16	/	37	///	58	/		
17	/	38	//	59	0		
18	0	39	///	60	/		
19	/	40	//////	61	/		
20	0	41	/	62	/		

* Less than 1 year old.

must represent a judgment based on a consideration of how the data will be utilized. Some variables such as age and educational attainment lend themselves to categorization quite well. For example, high school and college graduation provide meaningful "cutting points."

Often the desired interval size determines the number of class intervals that will be used. Let's assume we will present the data in 5-year age intervals; an examination of the raw scores reveals that 15 class categories will include all of the respondents who range in age from less than 1 to 74.

Once we have decided on an appropriate number of class intervals for a set of data, the procedures for assigning scores to class intervals are quite straightforward. Although several different techniques may be used, we will use only one for the sake of consistency. The procedures are as follows:

Procedure for establishing class intervals

Step 1. Find the difference between the highest and the lowest score values contained in the original data. Add 1 to obtain the total number of scores or potential scores. In the present example this result is $(74 - 0) + 1 = 75$.

Step 2. Divide this figure by the number of class intervals that will provide the best summary of the data to obtain the number of scores or potential scores in each class interval. Ten to 15 intervals will be adequate in most instances. If the resulting value is not a whole number (and it usually is not), we prefer to round to the nearest odd number so that a whole number will be at the middle of the class interval. However, this practice is far from universal and you would not be wrong if you rounded to the *nearest number*. In the present example we use 15 intervals, therefore, the number of scores for each class interval is 75/15, or 5. We designate the width of the class interval by the symbol i. In the example, $i = 5$.

Step 3. Take the lowest score in the original data (0 in the present example) as the minimum value in the lowest class interval. Add to this $i = 1$ to obtain the maximum score of the lowest class interval. Thus, the lowest class interval of the data is $0 - 4$, because $(0 + i - 1 = 0 + 5 - 1 = 4)$.

Step 4. The next higher class interval begins at the integer following the maximum score of the lower class interval. In the present example the next integer is 5. Follow the same procedures as in step 3 to obtain the maximum score of the second class interval. Follow these procedures for each successive higher class interval until all of the scores are included in their appropriate class intervals. Every score must fall in one, and only one, interval.

Step 5. Assign each obtained score to the class interval within which it is included. The **grouped frequency distribution** appearing in Table 3.3 was obtained by using these procedures.

You will note that by grouping you have obtained an immediate picture of the distribution of ages of park visitors. For example, you know that the ages of visitors ranged from an infant less than 1 year old to someone 74 years old. Also, the majority of park visitors in your sample are adults, with a clustering of frequencies in the class intervals between the ages of 33 and 53. It is also apparent that the number of scores in the extremes tends to taper off. Thus, we have achieved one of our objectives in grouping: to provide an economical and manageable array of scores.

If we chose to use ten categories, we would divide 75 (see Step 1) by 10 and find the width of i to be 7.5. Rounding to the nearest odd number (Step 2) would give us an i equal to 7. To obtain the maximum score of the lowest class interval (Step 3), we would add $(0 + i - 1 = 0 + 7 - 1 = 6)$. Step 4 would lead us to establish the following intervals:

0–6	43–49
7–13	50–56
14–20	57–63
21–27	64–70
28–35	71–77
36–42	

Table 3.3   Grouped frequency distribution of ages based upon data appearing in Table 3.2

Class Interval	f	Class Interval	f	Class Interval	f
0–4	2	25–29	9	50–54	12
5–9	2	30–34	9	55–59	4
10–14	3	35–39	13	60–64	5
15–19	5	40–44	17	65–69	5
20–24	7	45–49	14	70–74	3
				$N = 110$	

Note that rounding to the nearest odd number in Step 2 resulted in 11 rather than 10 categories.

One word of caution: Most scores with which the social scientist deals are expressed as whole numbers rather than as decimals. This is why our examples involve whole numbers. However, scores are occasionally expressed in decimal form. The simplest procedure is to treat the scores as if the decimals did not exist; in other words, treat each score as a whole number. The decimals can then be reinserted at the final step. If in the preceding example the highest score had been 7.4 and the lowest 0.0, the calculations would have been exactly the same. At the last step, however, the highest interval would have been changed to 7.0 and 7.4 and the lowest to 0.0 to 0.4, with corresponding changes in between. The width of the class interval would have been 0.5.

3.1.2 The True Limits of a Class Interval

In our prior discussion of the true limits of a number (Section 2.4.1) we pointed out that the true value of a number is equal to its apparent value plus or minus one-half of the unit of measurement. The unit of measurement in Table 3.3 is 1, therefore, we will add and subtract $1/2 = 0.5$ from the lower and upper real limit of each category. Thus, although we write the limits of the highest class interval as 70 to 74, the true limits of the interval are 69.5 ($70 - 0.5$) to 74.5 ($74 + 0.5$) (i.e., the lower real limit of 70 and the upper real limit of 74, respectively). Later, when calculating certain statistics for grouped data, we will make use of the *true limits* of the class interval.

3.2 Cumulative Frequency and Cumulative Percentage Distributions

It is often desirable to rearrange the data from a frequency distribution into a **cumulative frequency distribution,** which is a distribution that shows the cumulative frequency *below* the upper real limit of the corresponding class interval. Besides aiding in the interpretation of the frequency distribution, a cumulative frequency distribution is of great value in obtaining the median and the various percentile ranks of scores, as we will see in Chapter 4.

The cumulative frequency distribution is obtained in the following manner. Looking at the data in Table 3.4, you will note that the entries in the column labeled f indicate the frequency of park visitors falling within each class interval. Each entry within the cumulative frequency column indicates the number of all cases or frequencies *less than the upper real limit* of that interval. Thus, in the third class interval from the top in Table 3.4 the entry 7 in the cumulative frequency column indicates that a total of 7 visitors in your park visitor sample of 110 persons were younger than 14.5, the upper real limit of the interval 10 to 14. The entries in the cumulative frequency distribution are obtained by the simple process of successive addition of the entries in the frequency column. The value of 19 in the cumulative frequency column corresponding to the age interval 20 to 24 was obtained by adding $2 + 2 + 3 + 5 + 7 = 19$. Note that the bottom entry in the cumulative frequency column is always equal to N, or in this instance, 110. If you fail to obtain this result, you know that you have made an error in cumulating frequencies and should check your work.

The **cumulative proportion distribution** column, also shown in Table 3.4, is obtained by dividing each entry in the cumulative f column by N. When each **cumulative proportion** is multiplied by 100, we obtain a **cumulative percentage distribution.** Note that the bottom entry in the cumulative pro-

Table 3.4   Grouped frequency distribution and cumulative frequency distribution based on data appearing in Table 3.3. $N = 110$

Class Interval	f	Proportion	%	Cumulative f	Cumulative Proportion	Cumulative %
0–4	2	0.0182	1.82	2	0.0182	1.82
5–9	2	0.0182	1.82	4	0.0364	3.64
10–14	3	0.0273	2.73	7	0.0637	6.37
15–19	5	0.0455	4.55	12	0.1092	10.92
20–24	7	0.0636	6.36	19	0.1728	17.28
25–29	9	0.0818	8.18	28	0.2546	25.46
30–34	9	0.0818	8.18	37	0.3364	33.64
35–39	13	0.1182	11.82	50	0.4546	45.46
40–44	17	0.1545	15.45	67	0.6091	60.91
45–49	14	0.1273	12.73	81	0.7364	73.64
50–54	12	0.1091	10.91	93	0.8455	84.55
55–59	4	0.0364	3.64	97	0.8819	88.19
60–64	5	0.0455	4.55	102	0.9274	92.74
65–69	5	0.0455	4.55	107	0.9729	97.29
70–74	3	0.0273	2.73	110	1.0002*	100.02*

* Do not add to 1.0000 and 100.00 due to rounding.

portion column must equal 1.00 and the **cumulative percentage** (%) column must equal 100% since all of the cases have been included.

We are now able to confirm our earlier observation that the majority of the park visitors were adults. Consider the cumulative % column, for example, where we see that only 17% of the visitors were younger than 24.5 years of age, the upper real limit of 24. The % column clearly shows that the 40 to 44 age category included the largest percentage of visitors.

We should note that psychologists, educators, and other behavioral scientists typically use cumulative frequency and cumulative percentage tables in which the class intervals are presented from high to low. Sociologists and other social scientists normally present class intervals from low to high as in Table 3.4. Both approaches are equally valid.

3.3 Graphing Techniques

We have just examined some of the procedures involved in making sense out of a mass of unorganized data. As we pointed out, your work is usually just beginning when you have constructed frequency distributions of data. The next step, commonly, is to present the data in pictorial form so that the reader may easily determine the essential features of a frequency distribution and compare one with another if desired. Such pictures, called graphs, should *not* be thought of as substitutes for statistical treatment of data, but rather, as *visual aids* for thinking about and discussing statistical problems.

3.4 Misuse of Graphing Techniques

As you may be aware, graphs that present data incorrectly can mislead the reader. For example, in Figure 3.1, the vertical (*Y*-axis or **ordinate**) and horizontal (*X*-axis or **abscissa**) have been lengthened to produce two distinctly different impressions.

It will be noted that Figure 3.1(a) tends to exaggerate the difference in frequency counts among the three classes, whereas Figure 3.1(b) tends to minimize these differences. The problem involves selection of scale units to represent the horizontal (*X*) and vertical (*Y*) axes. Clearly, the choice of these units is arbitrary, and the decision to make the *Y*-axis twice the length of the *X*-axis is just as correct as the opposite representation. It is clear that in order to avoid problems we need to present the data in a straightforward manner.

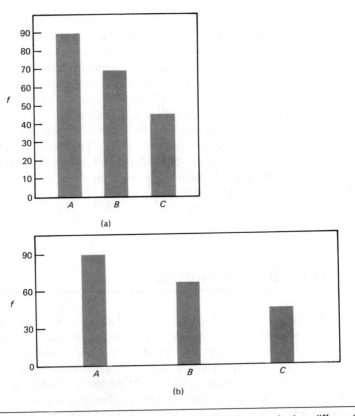

Figure 3.1 Bar graphs representing the same data but producing different impressions by varying the relative lengths of the *Y*-axis and the *X*-axis.

3.5 Nominally Scaled Variables

The **bar graph,** illustrated in Figure 3.2, is a graphic device used to represent data that are either nominally or ordinally scaled. A vertical bar is drawn* for each category, in which the *height* of the bar represents the number of members of that class. If we arbitrarily set the width of each bar at one unit, the *area* of each bar may be used to represent the frequency for that category. Thus, the total area of all of the bars is equal to *N* or 100%.

In preparing frequency distributions of nominally scaled variables, you must keep two things in mind:

---

* Bar graphs are sometimes drawn horizontally (this has an advantage in cases where the number of cases (or classes) is large and the list may occupy a full page in length). Nevertheless the vertical array (as shown in Figure 3.2) is more often used (and more easily understood at sight) because of its adaptability to a histogram or a frequency curve (see Figures 3.4 and 3.6).

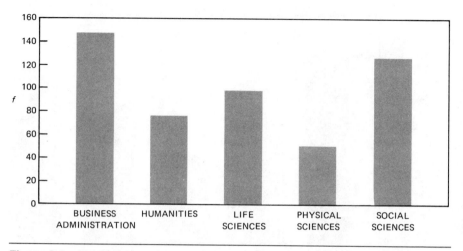

Figure 3.2 Number of students enrolled in introductory sociology courses who are majoring in the various academic fields (hypothetical data).

1. No order is assumed to underlie nominally scaled variables. Thus, the various categories can be represented along the horizontal axis (X-axis) in any order you choose. We prefer to arrange the categories alphabetically to eliminate any possibility of personal factors entering into the decision.

2. The bars should be separated rather than contiguous, so that any implication of continuity among the categories is avoided.

3.6 Ordinally Scaled Variables

You will recall that the scale values of ordinal scales carry the implication of an ordering that is expressible in terms of the algebra of inequalities (greater than, less than). In terms of our preceding discussion, ordinally scaled variables should be treated in the same way as nominally scaled variables, except that the categories should be placed in their naturally occurring order along the horizontal (X) axis. Figure 3.3 illustrates the use of the bar graph with an ordinally scaled variable.

3.7 Interval- and Ratio-Scaled Variables

3.7.1 Histogram

As discussed earlier, interval- and ratio-scaled variables differ from ordinally scaled variables in one important way; that is, equal differences in scale values

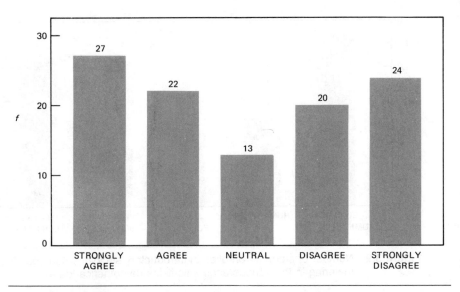

Figure 3.3   Distribution of 106 physicians' responses to the question, "Should venereal disease treatment be made available to minors without the knowledge of their parents?" (hypothetical data).

are equal. This means that we permit the vertical bars to touch one another in graphic representations of interval- and ratio-scaled frequency distributions. Such a graph is referred to as a **histogram,** and it replaces the bar graph used with nominal and ordinal variables. Figure 3.4 illustrates the use of the histogram with a discretely distributed ratio-scaled variable.

Figure 3.4   Frequency distribution of the number of children per family among 389 families surveyed in a small suburban community (hypothetical data).

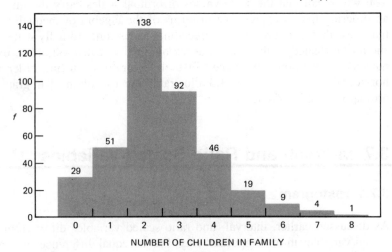

We noted previously (Section 3.5) that frequency may be represented by either the area of a bar or its height. However, there are many graphic applications in which the height of the bar, or the ordinate, may give misleading information concerning frequency. Consider Figure 3.5, which shows the data grouped into *unequal* class intervals and the resulting histogram. The widths of the bars in Figure 3.5 have been drawn proportional to the size of the class intervals, and the heights of the bars indicate the relative frequency within each age category. Thus, the 30- to 40-year-old category is represented by a bar 2½ times wider than the 14- to 15-year-old category. In this instance the area under each bar does not reflect the frequency of cases, and confusion is sure to result. In general, it is advisable to construct histograms using equal intervals whenever we are dealing with variables in which an underlying continuity may be assumed.

3.7.2 Frequency Curve (Frequency Polygon)

We can readily convert the histogram into another commonly used form of graphic representation, the **frequency curve,** by joining the midponts of the bars with straight lines. However, it is not necessary to construct a histogram

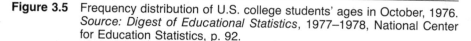

Figure 3.5 Frequency distribution of U.S. college students' ages in October, 1976. *Source: Digest of Educational Statistics,* 1977–1978, National Center for Education Statistics, p. 92.

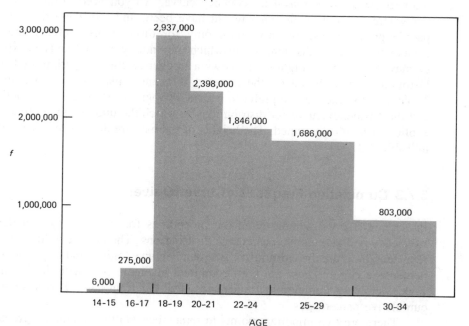

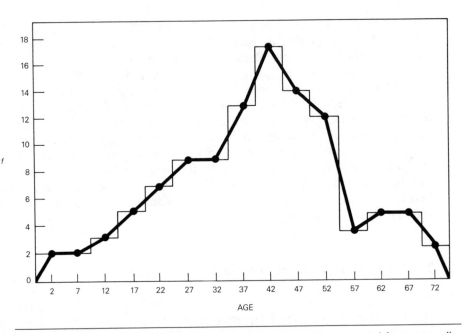

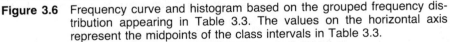

Figure 3.6 Frequency curve and histogram based on the grouped frequency distribution appearing in Table 3.3. The values on the horizontal axis represent the midpoints of the class intervals in Table 3.3.

prior to the construction of a frequency curve. All you need to do is place a dot where the tops of the bars would have been, and join these dots. Some people prefer to use the histogram only for discrete distributions and the frequency curve for distributions in which the underlying continuity is explicit or may be assumed. Figure 3.6 shows a frequency curve superimposed on a histogram that is based on the grouped frequency distribution appearing in Table 3.3. In practice, we prefer to use the histogram for discrete distributions and the frequency curve for distributions in which the underlying continuity is explicit or may be assumed. The heights of the bars are determined by the data in Table 3.3.

3.7.3 Cumulative Frequency Curve (Ogive)

In Section 3.2 we demonstrated the procedures for constructing cumulative frequency and cumulative percentage distributions. The corresponding graphic representations are the **cumulative frequency curve (ogive)** and the cumulative percentage curve. These are both combined in Figure 3.7, with the left-hand Y-axis showing cumulative frequencies and the right-hand Y-axis showing cumulative percentages.

There are two important points to remember: (1) the cumulative frequen-

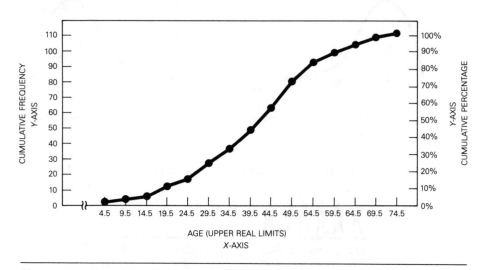

Figure 3.7 Cumulative frequency and cumulative percentage curve based on cumulative frequency and cumulative percentage distributions appearing in Table 3.4.

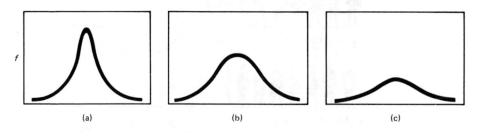

Figure 3.8 Three forms of bell-shaped distributions: (a) leptokurtic, (b) mesokurtic, and (c) platykurtic.

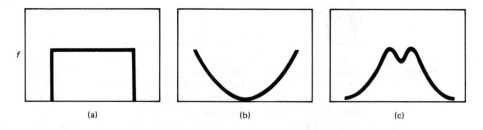

Figure 3.9 Illustrations of three nonnormal symmetrical frequency curves.

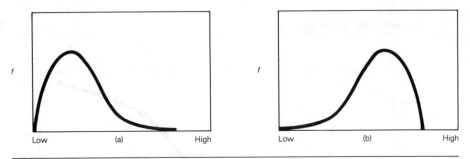

Figure 3.10 Illustrations of skewed frequency curves (scores increase from left to right).

FOR EVERY 10 PUPILS IN THE 5th GRADE IN FALL 1968.

9.8 ENTERED THE 9th GRADE IN FALL 1972.

8.7 ENTERED THE 11th GRADE IN FALL 1974.

7.5 GRADUATED FROM HIGH SCHOOL IN 1976.

4.7 ENTERED COLLEGE IN FALL 1976.

2.4 WERE LIKELY TO EARN BACHELOR'S DEGREES IN 1980.

Figure 3.11 Estimated retention rates, fifth grade through college graduation: United States, 1968–1980. *Sources:* U.S. Department of Health, Education, and Welfare, National Center for Education Statistics, *Biennial Survey of Education in the United States; Statistics of State School Systems; Fall Statistics of Public Elementary and Secondary Day Schools;* and unpublished data.

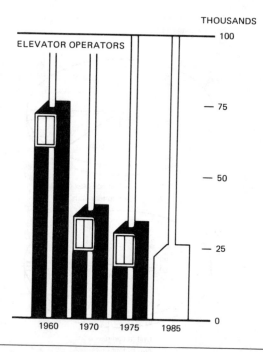

Figure 3.12 Number of elevator operators, actual and projected for given years. *Sources:* 1960–1970 Decennial Census, Bureau of the Census; 1970–1985, Bureau of Labor Statistics. Data for 1970 and 1985 are unpublished; data for 1975 are in *Employment and Earnings,* January 1976, p. 11, as cited in Bureau of Labor Statistics Bulletin 1979.

cies are plotted against the *upper real limit* of each interval and (2) the maximum value on the Y-axis in the cumulative frequency curve is N, and in the cumulative percentage curve it is 100%.

3.8 Forms of Frequency Curves

Frequency curves may take on an unlimited number of different shapes. However, many of the statistical procedures discussed in the text assume a particular form of distribution: namely, the bell-shaped **normal curve.**

In Figure 3.8 several forms of bell-shaped distributions are shown. Curve (a), which is characterized by a piling up of scores in the center of the distribution, is referred to as a **leptokurtic distribution.** In curve (c), in which the opposite condition prevails, the distribution is referred to as **platykurtic.** And finally, curve (b) takes on the form of a bell-shaped normal curve and is referred to as a **mesokurtic distribution.**

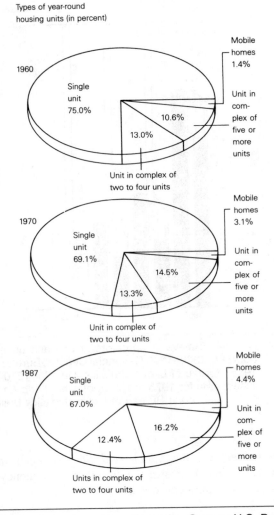

Types of year-round
housing units (in percent)

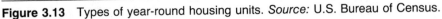

Figure 3.13 Types of year-round housing units. *Source:* U.S. Bureau of Census.

The normal curve is referred to as a symmetrical distribution, since if it is folded in half, the two sides will coincide.* Not all symmetrical curves are bell shaped, however. Three different nonnormal symmetrical curves are shown in Figure 3.9.

Certain distributions have been given names, for example, that in Figure 3.9(a) is called a *rectangular* distribution and that in Figure 3.9(b) a U-

---

* A theoretical bell-shaped curve called a standard normal distribution will be discussed in Chapter 7.

distribution. Incidentally, the distribution appearing in Figure 3.9(c) is found when a variable has a high concentration of frequencies around two separate values or if the frequency distributions of two different populations are represented in a single graph.* For example, a frequency distribution of average adult male and female earnings might yield a curve similar to Figure 3.9(c) because the average annual income of males is considerably higher than that of females. Hence, the two peaks would reflect the income differential between males and females.

When a distribution is not asymmetrical and "tails" off at one end, it is said to be **skewed.** If we say that a distribution is **positively skewed** or skewed to the right, we mean the distribution has relatively fewer frequencies at the high end of the horizontal axis. If, on the other hand, we say that a distribution is **negatively skewed** or skewed to the left, we mean there are relatively fewer frequencies at the low end of the horizontal axis. Figure 3.10(a) is positively skewed, and Figure 3.10(b) is negatively skewed.

It is not always possible to determine by inspection whether or not a distribution is skewed. Consider the frequency curve and histogram we plotted in Figure 3.6 for the sample of park visitors. Would you say that the curve is skewed to the left or right? Of course, in this instance it is rather difficult to be certain. There is a precise mathematical method for determining both direction and magnitude of skew. It is beyond the scope of this book to go into a detailed discussion of this topic.

---

* This is sometimes called a bimodal distribution.

Figure 3.14   U.S. population–projections to 2050. *Source:* U.S. Bureau of the Census, Current Population Reports, series p-25.

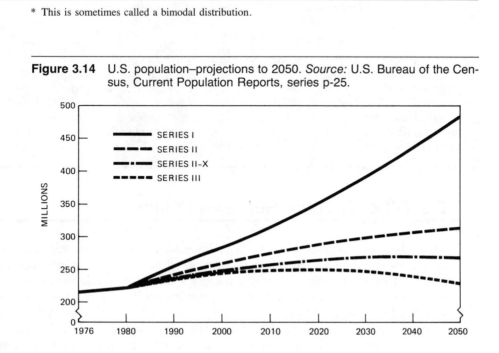

BOX 3.1

New AIDS Cases in the United States by Year

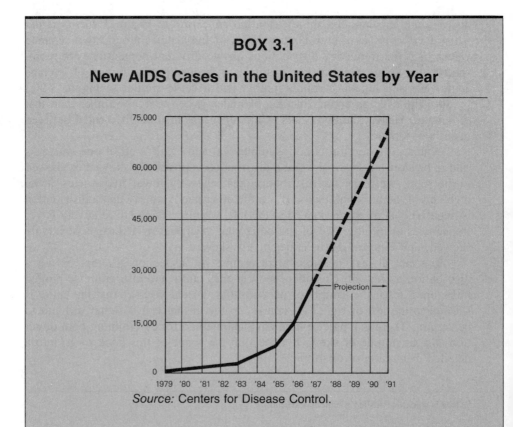

Source: Centers for Disease Control.

The number of new AIDS (acquired immune deficiency syndrome) cases is projected to increase dramatically each year in the United States. By 1991 it is expected that the cumulative total will exceed 270,000 cases. The trend chart shows that the disease spreads very rap- idly. Those primarily affected at the present time include homosexual or bi- sexual men, intravenous drug users who share needles, sexual partners of those having the antibody, and hemophiliacs who must frequently receive blood transfusions.

3.9 Other Graphic Representations

Throughout this chapter we have been discussing graphic representations of frequency distributions. However, other types of data are frequently collected by social scientists. We will briefly discuss a few graphic representations of such data. A frequently used graphic representation is the *pictograph* as rep- resented by Figures 3.11 and 3.12. Figure 3.11 clearly presents the attrition of students from the formal educational system. This adaptation of a bar graph allows the reader to see at a glance that considerable attrition occurs between the fifth grade and graduation from college. Indeed, of 10 students who were in the fifth grade in 1968, only 2.4 were likely to earn a college degree in 1980. Figure 3.12 depicts the declining numbers of elevator operators needed in the United States. In 1985 the projection was that only 25,000 persons will be employed as elevator operators due to the increased number of automatic elevators and a decline in the manual models.

The *pie chart* (see Figure 3.13) involved dividing the "pie" or circle into its component parts to represent the distribution of a nominal level variable. A protractor is used to divide the 360 degrees in a circle into percentages to reflect the actual distribution of the variable. For example, single unit housing constitutes 67.0% of the housing in 1987, and the corresponding segment of the pie must be 241.2 degrees since 1% equals 3.6 degrees ($360/100 = 3.6$ and $67.0 \times 3.6 = 241.2$).

Finally, an example of a *trend chart* is provided by the U.S. population projections in Figure 3.14. The four series have been determined by altering the three components of population change—births, deaths, and net immigration. Series II, II-x, and III are considered the most realistic projections, with Series I assuming an extremely high birthrate in the future. Box 3.1 provides an example of a trend chart based upon the AIDS epidemic.

Summary

This chapter was concerned with the techniques used in making sense out of a mass of data. We demonstrated the construction of frequency distributions of scores and presented various graphing techniques. When the scores are widely spread out, many have a frequency of zero. It is customary to group scores into class intervals. The resulting distribution is referred to as a grouped frequency distribution.

The basis for arriving at a decision concerning which grouping units to use and which procedures to follow to construct a grouped frequency distribution were discussed and demonstrated. It was seen that the true limits of a class interval are obtained in the same way as the true limits of a score. The procedures for converting a frequency distribution into a cumulative frequency distribution, a cumulative proportion distribution, and a cumulative percentage distribution were demonstrated.

We also reviewed the various graphing techniques used in the social sciences. The basic purpose of graphical representation is to provide visual aids for considering and discussing statistical problems. The primary objective is to present data in a clear, unambiguous fashion so that the reader may determine at a glance the relationships that we want to portray.

We discussed devices that mislead the unsophisticated reader. The use of the bar graph with nominally and ordinally scaled variables, and the use of the histogram and the frequency curve with continuous and discontinuous ratio- or interval-scaled variables were covered. Various forms of normally distributed data, non-bell-shaped symmetrical distributions, and asymmetrical or skewed distributions were presented. Finally, we discussed and demonstrated several graphic representations of data, other than frequency distributions, commonly used in the social sciences.

Terms to Remember

Abscissa (*X*-axis)   Horizontal axis of a graph.

Bar graph   A form of graph that uses bars to indicate the frequency of occurrence of observations within each nominal or ordinal category.

Cumulative frequency   The number of cases (frequencies) at and below a given point.

Cumulative frequency curve (ogive)   A curve that shows the number of cases below the upper real limit of an interval.

Cumulative frequency distribution   A distribution that shows the cumulative frequency below the upper real limit of the corresponding class interval.

Cumulative percentage   The percentge of cases (frequencies) at and below a given point.

Cumulative percentage distribution   A distribution that shows the cumulative percentage below the upper real limit of the corresponding class interval.

Cumulative proportion   The proportion of cases (frequencies) at and below a given point.

Cumulative proportion distribution   A distribution that shows the cumulative proportion below the upper real limit of the corresponding class interval.

Exhaustive   A grouped frequency distribution is said to be exhaustive when all possible scores can be placed within the established categories.

Frequency curve (Frequency polygon)   A form of graph, representing a frequency distribution, in which a continuous line is used to indicate the frequency of the corresponding scores.

Grouped frequency distribution   A frequency distribution in which the values of the variable have been grouped into class intervals.

Histogram   A form of bar graph used with interval- or ratio-scaled frequency distribution.

Leptokurtic distribution   A bell-shaped distribution characterized by a piling up of scores in the center of the distribution.

Mesokurtic distribution   Bell-shaped distribution; "ideal" form of normal curve.

Mutually exclusive   Events A and B are said to be mutually exclusive if both cannot occur simultaneously.

Negatively skewed distribution   A distribution that has relatively fewer frequencies at the low end of the horizontal axis.

Normal curve   A frequency curve with a characteristic bell-shaped form.

Ogive   A cumulative frequency curve that shows the number of cases below the upper real limit of an interval.

Ordinate (Y-axis)   The vertical axis of a graph.

Platykurtic distribution   A frequency distribution characterized by a flattening in the central position.

Positively skewed distribution   A distribution that has relatively fewer frequencies at the high end of the horizontal axis.

Random sampling   A method of selecting samples so that each sample of a given size in a population has an equal chance of being selected.

Skewed distribution   A distribution that departs from symmetry and tails off at one end.

Ungrouped frequency distribution   An ungrouped frequency distribution shows the number of times each score occurs when the values of a variable are arranged in order according to their magnitudes.

Exercises

1. Give the true limits, the width of interval, and the midpoints for each of the following class intervals:

   a) 8–12   **b)** 6–7   **c)** 0–2

   d) 5–14   **e)** (-8)–(-2) **f)** 2.5–3.5

   g) 1.50–1.75   **h)** (-3)–$(+3)$

2. For each of the following sets of measurements, state (Assume $i = 15$):

    a) The best width of class interval (i).

    b) The apparent limits of the lowest interval.

    c) The true limits of that interval.

    d) The midpoint of that interval.

       i) 0 to 106   **ii)** 29 to 41   **iii)** 18 to 48

       iv) -30 to $+30$ **v)** 0.30 to 0.47   **vi)** 0.206 to 0.293

3. Given the following list of scores in a statistics examination, use $i = 5$ for the class intervals and:

    a) Set up a frequency distribution.

    b) List the true limits and midpoint of each interval.

    c) Prepare a cumulative frequency distribution.

    d) Prepare a cumulative percentage distribution.

Scores on a Statistics Examination									
63	88	79	92	86	87	83	78	40	67
68	76	46	81	92	77	84	76	70	66
77	75	98	81	82	81	87	78	70	60
94	79	52	82	77	81	77	70	74	61

4. Using the data in Exercise 3, set up frequency distributions with the following:

    Discuss the advantages and the disadvantages of employing these widths.

    a) $i = 1$ (ungrouped frequency distribution)   **b)** $i = 3$

    c) $i = 10$ **d)** $i = 20$

5. The case loads for social workers vary greatly. The accompanying table lists the number of clients to whom 40 social workers have been assigned (Assume $i = 5$):

    a) Construct a grouped frequency distribution.

    b) List the true limits of each interval.

    c) Describe the distribution in words.

68	57	68	79	92	86	87	83	78	67
84	92	63	46	81	92	77	84	86	52
51	46	77	98	81	82	81	87	42	85
90	37	94	52	82	77	81	77	94	49

6. Several entries in a frequency distribution of children's ages are 1 to 5, 6 to 10, 11 to 15.

    a) What is the width of the interval?

    b) What are the lower and upper real limits of each of these three intervals?

    c) What are the midpoints of each interval?

7. Discuss the value of constructing a grouped frequency distribution from a set of ungrouped scores. Can you think of a situation when you would not want to group a set of data? Why?

8. Construct a grouped frequency distribution using 5 to 9 as the lowest class interval, for the following scores on a job satisfaction scale. List the width and real limits of the highest class interval. If high scores indicate high satisfaction and it is possible to score as low as 0 or as high as 75, how would you characterize this distribution of scores?

67	63	64	57	56	55	53	53	54	54
45	45	46	47	37	23	34	44	27	44
45	34	34	15	23	43	16	44	36	36
35	37	24	24	14	43	37	27	36	26
25	36	26	5	44	13	33	33	17	33

9. Do Exercise 8 again, using 3 to 7 as the lowest class interval. Compare the resulting frequency distribution with those of Exercises 8, 10, and 11.

10. Repeat Exercise 8, using 4 to 5 as the lowest class. Compare the results with those of Exercises 8, 9, and 11.

11. Repeat Exercise 8, using 0 to 9 as the lowest class. Compare the results with those of Exercises 8, 9, and 10.

12. Give an example of a variable that would have a distribution that would be characterized as:

    a) Normal.   **b)** U-shaped.

    c) Positively skewed.   **d)** Negatively skewed.

    e) Rectangular.

13. Given the following frequency distribution of the number of previous arrests for 50 inmates at a state prison, draw a histogram, a frequency curve, and a cumulative frequency curve (ogive).

Class Interval	f	Class Interval	f
0–2	0	15–17	3
3–5	17	18–20	1
6–8	15	21–23	1
9–11	8	24–26	0
12–14	4	27–29	1

14. Given the information in the accompanying table, draw a bar graph and discuss the reasons that might contribute to the variation in the percentages.

Percentage of employed women in each occupation group with year-round full-time jobs in 1975

Occupational Group	Percentage Who Worked Year Round, Full Time
Professional-technical	52.0
Managerial-administrative, except farm	64.5
Sales	25.8
Clerical	49.6
Craft	43.1
Operatives, except transport	38.7
Transport equipment operatives	17.4
Nonfarm laborers	32.7
Service, except private household	26.5
Private household	13.1
Farm	25.3

Source: Bureau of Labor Statistics, *U.S. Working Women: A Data Book,* 1977.

15. Given the accompanying table, draw three histograms and compare the results for the three columns of data. Which do you believe more accurately portrays the real picture?

Estimated number of illegitimate live births and illegitimacy rates and ratios: Selected years, 1940–1980

Year	Number	Rate per 1000 Unmarried Women Aged 14 to 44 Years	Ratio per 1000 Total Live Births
1980	665,700	29.4	184.3
1970	398,700	26.4	106.9
1960	224,300	21.6	52.7
1950	141,600	14.1	39.8
1940	89,500	7.1	37.9

Source: U.S. National Center for Health Statistics, *Vital Statistics of the United States,* annual.

16. Describe the types of distributions you would expect if you were to graph each of the following:

   a) Annual incomes of U.S. families.

   b) The heights of adult U.S. males.

   c) The heights of adult U.S. females.

   d) The heights of U.S. males and females combined in one graph.

17. Construct a bar graph to present the data in the accompanying table. (*Hint:* Consider superimposing the black population figures on the total figures.) Also, construct a trend chart that summarizes the relationship between the black and total population since 1790.

Total resident population in the United
States for selected years: 1790–1980

	Millions of Persons	
Year	*Total*	*Black*
1790	3.9	0.8
1860	31.4	4.4
1870	39.8	5.4
1890	62.9	7.5
1900	76.2	8.8
1910	92.2	9.8
1920	106.0	10.5
1930	123.2	11.9
1940	132.2	12.9
1950	151.3	15.0
1960	179.3	18.9
1970	203.2	22.6
1975	212.6	24.4
1980	226.5	26.7

Source: Bureau of the Census, *The Social and Economic Status of the Black Population in the United States: An Historical View, 1790–1978,* Series P-23, No. 80 and Current Population Reports.

18. Construct a trend chart for the accompanying food stamp data. Has the number of participants increased more rapidly than the total retail value or the cost to participants? Construct a cumulative frequency distribution for the total retail value column.

Federal Food Stamp Program: 1961–1978

Year (Ending June 30)	Participants (1000)	Value of Stamps Issued	
		Total retail value (million $)	Cost to participants (million $)
1961	50	1	
1962	141	35	22
1963	358	50	31
1964	360	73	44
1965	633	85	53
1966	1,218	174	109
1967	1,832	296	190
1968	2,402	452	279
1969	3,222	603	374
1970	6,457	1,090	540
1971	10,549	2,713	1,190
1972	11,594	3,309	1,512
1973	12,107	3,884	1,753
1974	13,524	4,727	2,009
1975	19,197	7,266	2,880
1976	17,982	8,700	3,373
1977	16,097	8,340	3,282
1978	15,248	8,280	3,141

Source: U.S. Department of Agriculture, Food and Nutrition Service, *Agricultural Statistics,* as cited in U.S. Bureau of the Census, *Statistical Abstract of the United States: 1979,* Table 30.

19. Using the following data, construct a pie chart for 1974 and 1984. Contrast the differences in words.

Attendance figures for selected spectator sports, 1974 and 1984

Sports	Attendance (in thousands)	
	1974	1984
Major league baseball	30,026	45,262
Professional basketball	9,204	11,110
Professional football	10,675	14,053
Horse racing	75,800	74,076
Greyhound racing	16,274	22,076

Source: U.S. Department of Commerce, *Social Indicators.*

20. Figures on birthrates are usually given in terms of the number of births per thousand in the population. This table shows the birthrate data at the end of each decade since the turn of the century, rounded to the nearest whole number.

   a) Plot these data on a trend chart.

   b) Is any general trend in birthrate discernible?

Year	Number of Births Per 1000 Population
1900	32
1910	30
1920	28
1930	21
1940	19
1950	24
1960	24
1970	18
1980	16

Source: U.S. National Center for Health Statistics, *Vital Statistics of the United States,* annual.

21. Construct a trend chart for the number of work stoppages and for the number of workers involved. What trends are apparent to you?

Year	Number of Work Stoppages	Workers Involved (1000)
1950	424	1698
1955	363	2055
1960	222	896
1965	268	999
1970	381	2468
1975	235	965
1980	187	795
1985	54	324

Source: U.S. Bureau of Labor Statistics, *Current Wage Developments,* monthly.

22. Using the following data, construct two pie charts to show the age composition of the U.S. Senate and House of Representatives in 1985.

Congress	Age in Years					
	Under 40	*40–49*	*50–59*	*60–69*	*70–79*	*80 & Over*
U.S. Senate	4	27	38	25	4	2
House of Representatives	71	155	131	59	17	2

Source: Congressional Directory, biennial.

chapter **4**

Percentiles

4.1 Introduction
4.2 Cumulative Percentiles and Percentile Rank
4.3 Percentile Rank and Reference Group
4.4 Centiles, Deciles, and Quartiles

4.1 Introduction

A declining birthrate and an increasing life span have resulted in major changes in the age composition of the U.S. population during the past century. Suppose someone told you that in 1985 approximately 24.7 million people in the United States were 65 years of age or older. What would be your reaction? Would you decide that the elderly are not nearly so numerous as you thought? Or that the United States is fast becoming a nation of elderly? You should conclude that you do not have enough information to offer a knowledgeable comment.

It should be clear that by itself a figure such as 24.7 million is not very meaningful. It takes on much more meaning when it can be compared to the total population and to the population of other age categories. If you were told that 89% of the U.S. population was 65 or less years old, you would have a frame of reference for interpreting the information. You would know the **percentile rank** of the 65-year-old persons. The percentile rank of a score, then, represents the percent of cases in a distribution that had scores (in this case, ages) at or *lower* (younger) *than the one cited*. Thus, to say that an age of 65 has a percentile rank of 89 indicates that 89% of the population is 65 or less.

Consider one more example before we continue. Suppose you took the Advanced Graduate Record Examination in Sociology and received a score of 510. By itself the score would not mean much, but assume that a score of 510 put you at the 51st percentile. Now you know that 51% of the persons who took the examination on the same day received an equal or lower score than you and 49% received a higher score. Knowing the percentile rank of a score allows you to compare it with other scores.

4.2 Cumulative Percentiles and Percentile Rank

4.2.1 Obtaining the Percentile Rank of Scores from a Cumulative Percentage Graph

In Chapter 3 we learned how to construct cumulative frequency and cumulative percentage distributions. If we were to graph a cumulative percentage distribution, we could read the percentile ranks directly from the graph. Note that the reverse is also true; that is, given a percentile rank, we could read the corresponding scores. Figure 4.1 displays a graphic form of the cumulative percentage distribution presented in Table 4.1. Box 4.1 provides an additional example of a cumulative percentage graph.

To illustrate, imagine that we wanted to determine the percentile rank of 60-year-old persons. We locate 60 along the horizontal axis and construct a perpendicular at that point so that it intercepts the curve. From that point on the curve we read directly across on the scale to the left and see that the percentile rank is approximately 85. On the other hand, if we wanted to know

Figure 4.1 Graphic representation of a cumulative percentage distribution (age composition of the U.S. population in 1985). Persons over 85 have been excluded. (*Note:* The cumulative percentage corresponding to a given score is the same as the percentile rank of that score.) *Source:* U.S. Bureau of the Census.

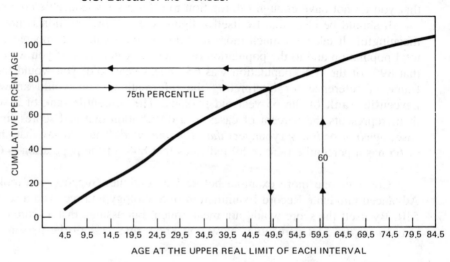

Table 4.1 Grouped frequency distribution and cumulative frequency distribution of the age composition of the United States in 1985

Age Interval	f (in Millions)	%	Cumulative f (in Millions)	Cumulative %
0–4	18.8	8.2	18.8	8.2
5–9	16.3	7.1	35.1	15.3
10–14	16.6	7.2	51.7	22.5
15–19	18.0	7.8	69.7	30.3
20–24	20.5	8.9	90.2	39.2
25–29	20.6	8.9	110.8	48.1
30–34	19.3	8.4	130.1	56.5
35–39	17.3	7.5	147.4	64.0
40–44	14.1	6.1	161.5	70.1
45–49	11.5	5.0	173.0	75.1
50–54	10.9	4.7	183.9	79.8
55–59	11.1	4.8	195.0	84.6
60–64	10.6	4.6	205.6	89.2
65–69	9.2	4.0	214.8	93.2
70–74	7.3	3.2	222.1	96.4
75–79	5.1	2.2	227.2	98.6
80–84	3.1	1.4	230.3	100.0

Note: Excludes the 2,588,000 persons over 85 years of age because the 85+ age category as reported by the U.S. Bureau of the Census does not have an upper limit and would not be comparable.

the score at a given **percentile**, we could reverse the procedure. For example, what is the score at the 75th percentile? We locate the 75th percentile on the vertical axis and read directly to the right until we meet the curve; at this point we construct a line perpendicular to the horizontal axis and read the value on the scale of scores. In the present example it can be seen that the age at the 75th percentile is approximately 49.

4.2.2 Obtaining the Percentile Rank of Scores Directly

We are often called upon to determine the percentile rank of scores without the assistance of a cumulative percentage curve, or with greater precision than is possible with a graphical representation.

Using the grouped frequency distribution found in Table 4.1, let's determine directly the percentile rank of an age of 60, which we previously approximated by the use of the cumulative percentage curve. The first thing we should note is that an age of 60 falls within the interval 60 to 64. The total cumulative frequency below that interval is 195 million. Since a percentile rank of a score is defined symbolically as

$$\text{percentile rank} = \frac{\text{cum} f}{N} \times 100 \qquad (4.1)$$

BOX 4.1

The Stress of the Beginning

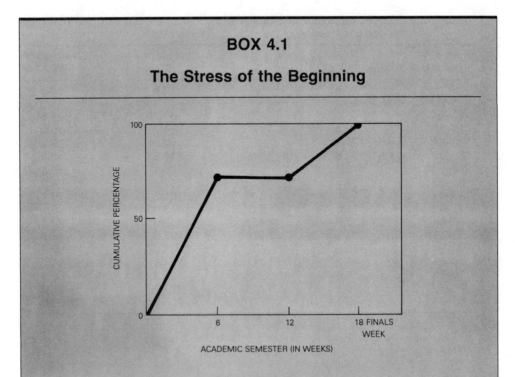

ACADEMIC SEMESTER (IN WEEKS)

It has frequently been maintained that suicides among college students result from the stresses of final examinations. A long-term study at the University of California, Berkeley, investigated various factors related to student suicides. The figure above shows that the percentage of suicides was greatest in the opening weeks of the semester, leveled off at mid-semester, and showed a mod-erate increase during the last third of the semester. Thus, contrary to popular opinion, the period of greatest danger appears to be the beginning, rather than the end of the semester.

Source: Seiden, R. H. (1966). "Campus Tragedy: A Story of Student Suicide," *Journal of Abnormal Psychology,* **71,** 389–399, Copyright © by the American Psychological Association, Reprinted by permission.

it is necessary to find the precise cumulative frequency corresponding to an age of 60. It is clear that the cumulative frequency corresponding to an age of 60 lies somewhere between 195 million and 205.6 million, the cumulative frequencies at both extremes of the interval. We must now establish the exact cumulative frequency of an age of 60 within the interval 60 to 64. In doing this, we are actually trying to determine the proportion of distance that we must move into the interval in order to find the number of cases included up to an age of 60.

An age of 60 is 0.5 years above the lower real limit of the interval (i.e., $60 - 59.5 = 0.5$). Since there are 5 ages within the interval (60, 61, 62, 63, and 64), 60 years of age is 0.5/5 of the distance through the interval. We now make a very important assumption: *that the cases or frequencies within a particular interval are evenly distributed throughout that interval.* Since there are 10.6 million cases within the interval, we may now calculate that an age of 60 is $(0.5/5) \times 10.6$, or the 1.06-millionth case within the interval. In other words, the frequency 1.06 million corresponds to 60 years of age. We already know from Table 4.1 that in 1985, 195.0 million persons were younger than 60 years of age or will be less than the lower real limit of the interval 60 to 64. Adding the two together $(195 + 1.06)$, we find that an age of 60 has a cumulative frequency of 196.06 million. Substituting 196.06 into Eq. (4.1), we obtain

$$\text{percentile rank of 60 years of age} = \frac{196.06}{230.3} \times 100 = 85.13$$

You will note that our answer, when rounded to the nearest percentile, agrees with the approximation obtained by the use of the graphical representation of a cumulative percentage distribution (Figure 4.1).

Equation (4.2) presents a generalized equation for calculating the percentile rank of a given score.

$$\text{percentile rank} = \frac{\text{cum} f_{\text{ll}} + \left(\dfrac{X - X_{\text{ll}}}{i} \right)(f_i)}{N} \times 100 \qquad (4.2)$$

where

$\text{cum} f_{\text{ll}}$ = cumulative frequency at the lower real limit
$\qquad\qquad$ of the interval containing X
X = given score
X_{ll} = score at lower real limit of interval containing X
i = width of interval
f_i = number of cases within the interval containing X

Let's calculate the percentile rank of 60 years of age using Eq. (4.2), where

$$\text{cum} f_{\text{ll}} = 195$$
$$X = 60$$
$$X_{\text{ll}} = 59.5$$
$$i = 5$$
$$f_i = 10.6$$
$$N = 230.3$$

Now the percentile rank can be calculated in the following manner:

$$\text{percentile rank} = \frac{195 + \left(\dfrac{60 - 59.5}{5}\right)(10.6)}{230.3} \times 100$$

$$= \frac{195 + 0.1(10.6)}{230.3} \times 100$$

$$= \frac{196.06}{230.3} \times 100$$

$$= 85.13$$

4.2.3 Finding the Score Corresponding to a Given Percentile Rank

What if you want to know the age above and below the 50 percentile in 1985?

To obtain the answer, we must work in the reverse direction, from the cumulative frequency scale to the scale of ages. We first must determine the cumulative frequency corresponding to the 50th percentile (which we will later refer to as the median of a distribution). Once we know the cumulative frequency, we will locate the interval that contains the cumulative frequency and then establish the age in question. Here is how we calculate the answer. It follows algebraically from Eq. (4.1) that

$$\text{cum} f = \frac{\text{percentile rank}}{100} \times N \qquad (4.3)$$

Since we are interested in an age at the 50th percentile and N is 230.3 million, the cumulative frequency of a score at the 50th percentile is

$$\text{cum} f = \frac{50 \times 230.3}{100} = 115.15 \text{ or } 115.2 \text{ million}$$

Referring to Table 4.1, we see that the frequency 115.2 million is in the age interval with the real limits of 29.5 to 34.5. It is 4.4 million frequencies into the interval since the cum f at the lower real limit of the interval is 110.8 million, which is 4.4 million less than 115.2. There are 19.3 million persons in the interval. Thus, the frequency 115.2 million is 4.4/19.3 of the way through an interval with a lower real limit of 29.5 and an upper real limit of 34.5. In other words, it is 4.4/19.3 of the way through the 5 ages in the interval. Expressed in age units, (4.4/19.3) × 5 or 0.228 × 5 = 1.14. By adding 1.14 to 29.5, we obtain the age at the 50th percentile, which is 30.64.

For students desiring a generalized method for determining scores (ages) corresponding to a given percentile, Eq. (4.4) should be helpful:

$$\text{Score at a given percentile} = X_{\text{ll}} + \frac{i\,(\text{cum}f - \text{cum}f_{\text{ll}})}{f_i} \qquad (4.4)$$

where

X_{ll} = score at lower real limit of the interval containing cum f
i = width of the interval
cum f = cumulative frequency of the score
cum f_{ll} = cumulative frequency at the lower real limit of the interval containing cum f
f_i = number of cases within the interval containing cum f

To illustrate the use of the equation, consider an example with which we are already familiar. What age is at the 85.13th percentile? First, by using Eq. (4.3), we obtain

$$\text{cum} f = \frac{85.13 \times 230.3}{100} = 196.05^* \text{ million}$$

If you refer to Table 4.1, you will see that our calculated cum f of 196.05 million is reasonable, given the 85.13th percentile. Try to get in the habit of ensuring that your answers are correct.

The age at the lower real limit of the interval containing the frequency 196.05 million is 59.5; i is 5; cum f to the lower real limit of the interval is 195.0; and the number of cases within the interval is 10.6 million. Substituting these values into equation (4.4), we obtain

$$\text{age at 85.13th percentile} = 59.5 + \frac{5(196.05 - 195.0)}{10.6}$$

$$= 59.5 + 0.5 = 60 \text{ years of age}$$

Note that this is the age from which we previously obtained the percentile rank 85.13 and that this equation illustrates, incidentally, a good procedure for checking the accuracy of your calculations. In other words, whenever you find the percentile rank of a score (age, etc.), you may take that answer and determine the score corresponding to that percentile value. You should obtain the original score. Similarly, whenever you obtain a score corresponding to a

---

* Differs slightly from 196.06 calculated earlier due to rounding.

given percentile rank, you may take that answer and determine the percentile rank of that score. You should always come back to the original percentile rank. Failure to do so indicates that you have made an error. It is preferable to repeat the solution without reference to your prior answer rather than attempt to find the mistake in your prior solution. Such errors are frequently of the proofreader type, defy detection, are time consuming to locate, and are highly frustrating.

4.3 Percentile Rank and Reference Group

Just as a score is meaningless in the abstract, so is a percentile rank. A percentile rank must always be expressed in relation to some reference group. Thus, if a friend claims that he obtained a percentile rank of 93 in a test of mathematical aptitude, you might not be terribly impressed if the reference group were made up of individuals who completed only the eighth grade. On the other hand, if the reference group consisted of individuals holding doctorate degrees in mathematics, your reaction would unquestionably be quite different.

Separate norms are frequently published for many standardized tests. Table 4.2 shows the raw score equivalents for selected percentile points on several advanced tests of the Graduate Record Examination. Note that a person scoring 500 would obtain a percentile rank of 63 on the Advanced Test in Sociology, but only have a percentile rank of 42 on the Advanced Test in History.

4.4 Centiles, Deciles, and Quartiles

Occasionally you will encounter the terms centile, decile, and quartile. All refer to a specific division of the scale of percentile ranks. A scale of percentile ranks is comprised of 100 units. A **centile** is equivalent to a percentile and is a percentage rank that divides a distribution into 100 equal parts. The 13th centile is specified as C_{13} and is equivalent to the 13th percentile. A **decile** is a percentage rank that divides a distribution into 10 equal parts. The 9th decile (specified as D_9) is equivalent to the 90th centile (percentile). The 1st decile is the 10th centile, etc. You should convince yourself that there are 9 deciles in any scale of percentile ranks. Why are there not 10?

A **quartile** is a percentile rank that divides a distribution into 4 equal parts. There are 3 quartiles in any scale of percentile ranks and they include the 1st quartile (Q_1), which is equivalent to the 25th centile, the 2nd quartile (Q_2), which is equivalent to the 50th centile or 5th decile, and the 3rd quartile (Q_3), which is equivalent to the 75th centile. Figure 4.2 shows the relationship among centiles, deciles, and quartiles.

Table 4.2 Subject tests interpretive data for total scores: 1981–1984—percentile ranks used on score reports percent of examinees scoring lower than selected scaled scores*

Scaled Score	Education	French	History	Political Science	Psychology	Sociology	Scaled Score
980							980
960							960
940							940
920							920
900							900
880							880
860							860
840							840
820							820
800							800
780							780
760					99		760
740					99		740
720		99	99		97	99	720
700		98	99		95	99	700
680		96	98		92	99	680
660	99	94	96	99	88	98	660
640	98	90	94	98	83	96	640
620	96	86	90	97	77	95	620
600	93	82	86	94	71	92	600
580	90	76	80	90	63	89	580
560	85	69	73	85	56	87	560
540	79	61	65	79	48	83	540
520	73	52	55	72	40	78	520
500	65	44	46	64	33	73	500
480	57	35	35	56	26	66	480
460	49	27	26	46	20	60	460
440	40	20	17	38	15	53	440
420	32	14	11	30	11	46	420
400	25	9	6	23	7	38	400
380	18	6	2	17	5	30	380
360	13	3	1	12	3	24	360
340	9	2		8	2	18	340
320	6	1		5	1	14	320
300	4			3		9	300
280	2			1		6	280
260	1					3	260
240						1	240
Number of examinees	14,238	1,567	7,131	6,415	43,939	4,152	Number of examinees
Percent women†	72	74	34	31	64	50	Percent women†
Percent men†	28	26	66	68	36	50	Percent men†
Mean	458	512	509	462	539	434	Mean
Standard deviation	90	88	77	85	96	106	Standard deviation

* Based on the performance of examinees tested between October 1, 1981, and September 30, 1984.
† In some cases, percent women plus percent men is less than 100 percent because some examinees do not indicate their gender.

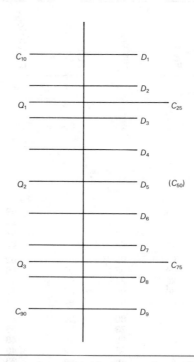

Figure 4.2 Comparison of centiles, deciles, and quartiles.

Summary

In this chapter we saw that, by itself, a score is meaningless unless it is compared to a standard base or scale. Scores are often converted into units of the percentile rank scale in order to provide a readily understandable basis for their interpretation and comparison.

We saw that percentile ranks of scores and scores corresponding to a given percentile may be approximated from a cumulative percentage graph. Direct computational methods were demonstrated to permit a more precise location of the percentile rank of a score and the score corresponding to a given percentile. A percentile rank was shown to be meaningless in the abstract. It must always be expressed in relation to some reference group. A distribution can be divided into centiles, deciles, and quartiles, as discussed.

Terms to Remember

Centile   A percentage rank that divides a distribution in 100 equal parts. Same as a percentile.

Decile   A percentage rank that divides a distribution into 10 equal parts.

Percentile rank   Number that represents the percentage of cases in a distribution that had scores at or lower than the one cited.

Percentiles   Numbers that divide a distribution into 100 equal parts. Same as a centile.

Quartile   A percentage rank that divides a distribution into 4 equal parts.

Exercises

1. Estimate the percentile rank of the following ages, using Figure 4.1.

    a) 1   **b)** 12   **c)** 34

2. Calculate the percentile rank of the ages in Exercise 1, using Table 4.1.

3. Estimate the ages corresponding to the following percentiles, using Figure 4.1.

    a) 25   **b)** 50

4. Calculate the ages corresponding to the percentiles in Exercise 3, using Table 4.1.

5. If your parents told you that they had just read in the newspaper that overall the public high school students in your county were at the 42nd percentile in a standardized reading test, how might you clearly explain the meaning of the test results to them?

6. Refer to Exercise 13 in Chapter 3.

    a) What is the percentile rank of an inmate who has been arrested six times?

    b) How many times would an inmate have to have been arrested to be at the 1st quartile? The 3rd quartile? The 2nd quartile?

7. A researcher administered a religious knowledge test to 36 persons, and their scores are presented here.

    a) Which specific scores would be above the 3rd quartile?

    b) What score is at the 50th percentile?

    c) The 50th centile?

    d) The 9th decile?

Use $i = 3$ and assume that the lowest class interval is 0–2.

9	6	8	10
2	2	5	0
7	1	4	2
5	8	0	1
6	7	10	1
2	4	9	7
3	3	9	6
4	6	4	4
0	2	1	4

8. The following questions are based on Table 4.2.

a) John H. proudly proclaims that he obtained a "higher" percentile ranking than his friend, Howard. Investigation of the fact reveals that his score on the test was actually lower. Must it be concluded that John H. was lying, or is some other explanation possible?

b) Jean obtained a percentile rank of 56 on the political science test. What was her score? What score would she have had to obtain to achieve the same percentile rank on the psychology test?

c) The Department of Sociology at Anomie University uses the Advanced Graduate Record Examination in Sociology as an element of the admissions procedure. No applicant obtaining a percentile rank below 73 is considered for admission, regardless of other qualifications. Thus, the 73rd percentile might be called a cutoff point. What score constitutes the cutoff point for this distribution?

d) The Department of Political Science uses the 72nd percentile as a cutoff point. Lee obtained a raw score of 500. What are his chances of being considered for admission?

9. Using the frequency distribution in Table 3.4, calculate the percentile ranks of the following ages:

a) 30   **b)** 34   **c)** 51   **d)** 73

10. For Table 3.4, what age is at the

a) 10th percentile?   **b)** 5th decile?

c) 64th centile?   **d)** 99th percentile?

11. Given the frequency distribution you constructed for the social worker's case load in Exercise 5, Chapter 3, how many clients would a caseworker need to be placed in the

a) 1st quartile?   **b)** 3rd quartile?

12. Given the accompanying table, (a) calculate the percentile rank for the following size families:

i) 3   **ii)** 5   **iii)** 7

(b) In what way does this table violate the standard procedure outlined in Chapter 3 for constructing frequency distributions?

Size of U.S. families of Spanish origin in 1977	
Size	**Number (in Thousands)**
2	662
3	636
4	625
5	408
6	218
7 or more persons	216

Source: U.S. Bureau of the Census, Persons of Spanish Origin in the United States: March 1978, *Current Population Reports,* Series P-20, No. 339, U.S. Government Printing Office, Washington, D.C., 1979.

13. Given Exercise 12, what size family lies at the 5th decile? The 2nd quartile? The 3rd quartile?

14. Calculate the percentage, cumulative frequency, and cumulative percentage for these ungrouped frequency data. What is the percentile rank of the eighth graders, the eleventh graders?

Grade	Public Elementary and Secondary Enrollment in 1983 (1000)
Kindergarten	2,751
First	3,079
Second	2,780
Third	2,772
Fourth	2,759
Fifth	2,798
Sixth	2,930
Seventh	3,249
Eighth	3,225
Ninth	3,331
Tenth	3,104
Eleventh	2,862
Twelfth	2,680
Total	38,320

Source: U.S. National Center for Education Statistics, *Digest of Education Statistics,* annual.

chapter **5**

Measures of Central Tendency

5.1 Introduction
5.2 The Arithmetic Mean ($\bar{X}$)
5.3 The Median (Md_n)
5.4 The Mode (M_o)
5.5 Comparison of Mean, Median, and Mode
5.6 The Mean, Median, Mode, and Skewness

5.1 Introduction

The ambiguity in the use of the term *average* causes confusion among lay people and perhaps leads to their suspicion that statistics is more of an art than a science (see Box 5.1). Unions and management speak of average salaries and frequently cite numerical values that are in sharp disagreement with each other; television programs and commercials are said to be prepared with the "average viewer" in mind; politicians are deeply concerned about the views of the average American voter; the average family size is frequently given as a fractional value, a statistical abstraction that is ridiculous; the term *average* is commonly used as a synonym for the term *normal;* the TV weather reporter tells us we had an average day or that rainfall for the month is above or below average. Indeed, the term *average* has so many popular meanings that many statisticians prefer to drop it from the technical vocabulary and refer, instead, to **measures of central tendency.** We define a measure of central tendency as an *index of central location used in the description of frequency distributions.* Since the center of a distribution may be defined in different ways, there are a number of different measures of central tendency. In this chapter we concern ourselves with three of the most frequently used measures of central tendency: the mean, the median, and the mode.

BOX 5.1

The Ambiguity of "Average"

**Annual Salaries of
XYZ Company
(in Dollars)**

30,000
24,000
14,000
10,000 ◄——— Mean
 9,000
 9,000
 9,000
 7,000 ◄——— Median
 6,000
 6,000
 6,000
 5,000 ⎤
 5,000 ⎬◄——— Mode
 5,000 ⎟
 5,000 ⎦

The term "average" is frequently used by mass media, labor unions, corporations, hucksters, politicians, and students to describe scores or numerical values in the central part of a distribution. Unfortunately, there are three different measures of central tendency, which, for a given distribution, may deviate substantially from one another. This disparity often gives rise to heated disagreements among individuals who focus their attention upon one or another

measure of central tendency. Many people are confused by all this bickering and the endless citation of conflicting statistics. They may conclude, in dismay, "Statistics are meaningless. You can do anything you want with them."

In the accompanying table we show an array of annual salaries of a hypothetical small business that employs 15 individuals, including the president and the vice-president. The company has recently gone on strike. The leader of the strike cites the poor wages—pointing to the most frequently occurring wage (the mode). "The average salary is five thousand dollars," shouts the leader, in a controlled rage. Management, looking at the arithmetic average (mean) of all the salaries, replies with righteous indignation, "Nonsense! The average salary is ten thousand dollars." A mediator, looking at exactly the same data but concentrating on the middle salary (the median), expostulates contemptuously, "Balderdash! Both of you are wrong. The average salary is seven thousand dollars."

Thus doth statistics make liars of us all!

5.1.1 Describing Frequency Distributions

Throughout the first four chapters of the book, we dealt with organizing data into a meaningful and useful form. We want to go beyond that to describe our data so that meaningful statements can be made about them. A frequency distribution represents an organization of data, but it does not, in itself, permit us to make statements either describing the distribution or comparing two or more distributions.

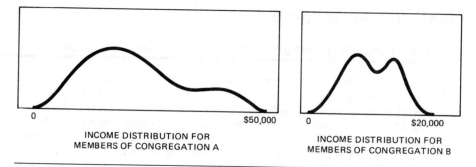

INCOME DISTRIBUTION FOR
MEMBERS OF CONGREGATION A

INCOME DISTRIBUTION FOR
MEMBERS OF CONGREGATION B

Figure 5.1   Hypothetical income distributions of two church congregations.

Frequency distributions can be characterized by three different features: (1) Frequency data have a characteristic *form* or shape, as you learned in Section 3.8 where we discussed the forms of frequency data, including symmetrical and skewed distributions. (2) Frequency data cluster around a *central value* that lies between the two extreme values of the variable under study. This feature is the topic of this chapter. (3) Frequency data can be characterized by their degree of *dispersion,* spread, or variability about the central value. This last topic is discussed in Chapter 6.

Given these three features about a particular distribution, the social scientist can clearly convey to others the characteristics of a particular distribution. For example, the income distributions of the members of two church congregations might be summarized graphically as shown in Figure 5.1. The two distributions in Figure 5.1 differ with respect to form, a central value, and variability. In this and the following chapter you will learn how to reduce considerable data to a few summary values. Being able to locate a single point of central tendency, particularly when combined with a summary description of the dispersion of scores about that point, can be very useful. While there is much to be gained by these summary values, the danger of course is that you lose considerable information that was available when the data were in their original form.

5.2 The Arithmetic Mean $\bar{X}$)

5.2.1 Methods of Calculation

You are already familiar with the arithmetic **mean,** for whenever you obtain an "average" of grades by summing the grades and dividing by the number of grades, you are calculating the arithmetic mean. In short, *the mean is the*

Statistics in Action 5.1

Emotional Contrast and Mood: Calculating the Mean

January 28, 1986 is a day that will remain etched in the memory of many witnesses to the tragic events of that day. Following many days of frustrating delays in the launch of *Challenger* with seven astronauts aboard, the shuttle soared skyward in an apparently perfect launch. The successful launch was greeted with great joy throughout the nation, including numerous classrooms where children and teachers cheered for the first teacher in space. A little more than a minute into the flight, joy was suddenly transformed into horror as the shuttle was demolished by a massive blast. In the days afterward, many observers reported feelings of great sadness and depression. Is it possible that the sharp contrast in emotions (from joy to horror in a matter of moments) contributed to the emotional aftermath of this tragedy?

Long before the events of this day, a team of researchers at the University of Manchester, England, had been investigating the effects of intense prior emotions on our subsequent emotional reactions to situations that evoke contrasting emotional states. Is horror more unpleasant when it is preceded by humor? Is humor funnier when preceded by horror?

The following ratings of unpleasantness were obtained on ten male subjects when five televised scenes of horror were preceded by six humorous scenes and on ten other male subjects for whom the horror scenes were not preceded by humorous scenes. The higher the score was, the greater was the reported unpleasantness.*

Horror Preceded by Humor	Horror First
36	29
31	34
36	27
20	33
41	10
34	28
32	26
34	31
32	30
33	35
$\Sigma X = 329$	$\Sigma X = 283$
$\overline{X} = 32.9$	$\overline{X} = 28.3$

a) The following ratings of unpleasantness were obtained on ten female subjects when horror was preceded by humor and on ten other female subjects for whom horror was not preceded by humor. The higher the score was, the greater was the reported unpleasantness. Calculate the mean for each condition.

b) Prepare a graph showing the means of the males and females under each condition.

Horror Preceded by Humor	Horror First
42	30
26	33
40	37
31	32
37	30
37	31
43	45
43	36
44	38
41	38

c) Do the results of the study appear to support the contrast hypothesis? That is, emotionally contrasting experiences tend to exaggerate the extent of the emotional swing.

ANSWERS

a) $\Sigma X = 384,$　　　　$\overline{X} = 38.4,$　　　　$\Sigma X = 350,$　　　　$\overline{X} = 35.0$

b)

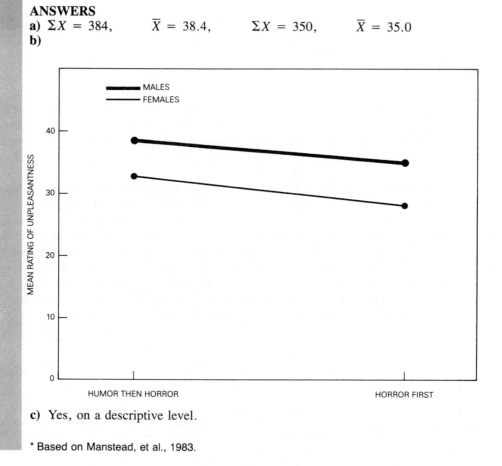

c) Yes, on a descriptive level.

* Based on Manstead, et al., 1983.

sum of the scores or values of a varible divided by the number of scores. Stated in algebraic form:

$$\overline{X} = \frac{X_1 + X_2 + \cdots + X_N}{N} = \frac{\Sigma X}{N} = \frac{\text{sum of scores}}{\text{number of scores}} \qquad (5.1)$$

where

X = a raw score in a set of scores
$\overline{X}$ = the mean and is referred to as X bar*
N = the number of scores
Σ = sigma and directs us to sum all of the scores

Note that we are using the shorthand version of $\overline{X}$ here. It is not necessary to include the subscript i because we are summing all of the X values.

The following equations show the procedure for computing the arithmetic mean of the scores 7, 28, 11, 25, and 10.

$$X_1 = 7, X_2 = 28, X_3 = 11, X_4 = 25, \text{ and } X_5 = 10$$

$$\overline{X} = \frac{7 + 28 + 11 + 25 + 10}{5} = 16.2$$

The mean serves as a summary value for the distribution of the five scores. Note that interval-level data are required before you can calculate the mean because both addition and division of the scores are required. However, social scientists often compute the mean on ordinal-level data. Statistics in Action 5.1 provides further examples of calculating the mean.

Obtaining the mean from an ungrouped frequency distribution You will recall that we constructed a frequency distribution as a means of eliminating the constant repetition of scores that occur with varying frequency, in order to permit a single entry in the frequency column to represent the number of times a given score occurs. Thus, in Table 5.1 we know from column f that the score of 8 occurred six times. In calculating the mean, then, it is not necessary to add 8 six times since we may multiply the score by its frequency and obtain the same value of 48. Since each score is multiplied by its corresponding frequency prior to summing, we may represent the mean for frequency distributions as follows:

$$\overline{X} = \frac{\Sigma fX}{N} \qquad (5.2)$$

---

* In Section 1.2 we indicated that italic letters would be used to represent sample statistics and Greek letters to represent population parameters. The Greek letter μ will be used to represent the population mean.

Table 5.1 Computational procedures for calculating the mean with ungrouped frequency distributions

X	f	fX	
4	2	8	
5	2	10	$\bar{X} = \dfrac{\Sigma fX}{N}$
6	3	18	
7	4	28	
8	6	48	$\bar{X} = \dfrac{232}{29}$
9	4	36	
10	5	50	
11	2	22	$\bar{X} = 8.00$
12	1	12	
	$N = 29$	$\Sigma fX = 232$	

Obtaining the mean from a grouped frequency distribution, raw score method The calculation of the mean from a grouped frequency distribution involves essentially the same procedures that are used with ungrouped frequency distributions. To start, the midpoint of each interval is used to represent *all scores within that interval*. Thus, the assumption is made that the scores in an interval are evenly distributed. The midpoint of each interval (X_m) is multiplied by its corresponding frequency, and the product is summed and divided by N. If you encountered a distribution such as in Exercise 12, Chapter 4, where an interval was not closed, it would be impossible to determine the midpoint and hence you could not calculate the mean. The procedures used to calculate the mean from a grouped frequency distribution are demonstrated in Table 5.2 using Eq. (5.3).

$$\bar{X} = \frac{\Sigma f X_m}{N} \qquad (5.3)$$

5.2.2 Properties of the Arithmetic Mean

One of the most important properties of the mean requires that you understand the concept of deviation. A **deviation** is the distance and direction of a score from a reference point that is normally the mean. A deviation is positive when the score is larger than the mean and negative when the score is less than the mean.

The first important property of the mean is that it is the point in a distribution of measurements or scores about which the sum of the deviations are equal to zero. In other words, if we were to subtract the mean from each score and add the resulting deviations from the mean, this sum would equal zero. Symbolically

$$\sum (X - \bar{X}) = 0$$

Table 5.2 Computational procedures for calculating the mean from a grouped frequency distribution

1 Class Interval	2 Frequency f	3 Midpoint X_m	4 Frequency Multiplied by the Midpoint fX_m	
75–79	3	77	231	
80–84	4	82	328	
85–89	8	87	696	
90–94	10	92	920	
95–99	15	97	1455	$\bar{X} = \dfrac{\Sigma fX_m}{N}$
100–104	20	102	2040	
105–109	15	107	1605	
110–114	10	112	1120	$= \dfrac{10{,}195}{100}$
115–119	8	117	936	
120–124	5	122	610	
125–129	2	127	254	$= 101.95$
$N = 100$			$\Sigma fX_m = 10{,}195$	

Therefore, the mean is the value that balances all of the scores on either side of it. You may wish to think of it as a center of gravity. In this sense the mean is analogous to the fulcrum of a seesaw. In playing on seesaws, you may have noticed that it is possible for a small individual to balance a heavy individual if the latter moves closer to the fulcrum. Thus, if you wanted to balance a younger brother or sister (presumably lighter than you) on a seesaw, you would move yourself toward the center of the board. The arithmetic mean of the values $X_1 = 2$, $X_2 = 3$, $X_3 = 4$, $X_4 = 5$, $X_5 = 6$ is 4. Substituting these values into the symbolic equation above, we find that the sum of the deviations of these five values from their mean of 4 equals 0 as follows:

$$(2 - 4) + (3 - 4) + (4 - 4) + (5 - 4) + (6 - 4) =$$
$$(-2) + (-1) + (0) + (+1) + (+2) = 0$$

A second important property of the mean is that *the mean is very sensitive to extreme values when these are not dispersed evenly on both sides of it.* Observe the two **arrays** of scores in Table 5.3. An *array is an arrangement of data according to their magnitude from the smallest to the largest value.* Note that all of the scores in both distributions are the same except for the very large score of 33 in column X_2. This one extreme score is sufficient to double the size of the mean. Thus, when a distribution is markedly skewed, the mean provides a misleading estimate of central tendency, whereas the median better reflects the central region of that distribution. Annual income is a commonly studied variable in which the median is preferred over the mean, since the distribution is distinctly skewed in the direction of high incomes. The incomes of multimillionaires exert a much stronger upward pull on the mean

Table 5.3 Comparison of the means of two arrays of scores, one of which contains an extreme value

Group 1 Score, X_1	Group 2 Score, X_2
2	2
3	3
5	5
7	7
8	33
$\Sigma X_1 = 25$	$\Sigma X_2 = 50$
$\overline{X}_1 = 5.00$	$\overline{X}_2 = 10.00$

than the incomes of paupers exert on a downward pull. Income does not go below zero, but there is no similar restraint on the upper end of the scale.

The sensitivity of the mean to extreme scores is a characteristic that has important implications governing our use of it. These implications will be discussed in Section 5.5, in which we compare the three measures of central tendency.

A third important property of the mean is that the **sum of squares** *of deviations from the arithmetic mean is less than the sum of squares of deviations about any other score or potential score*. To illustrate this property of the mean, Table 5.4 shows the squares and the sum of squares when deviations are taken from the mean and various other scores in a distribution. It can be seen that the sum of squares is smallest in column 4, when deviations are taken from the mean. This property of the mean provides us with another definition: *The mean is that measure of central tendency that makes the sum of squared deviations around it minimal*. The method of locating the mean by finding the minimum sum of squares is referred to as the **least-squares property of the mean.** The least-squares property of the mean is of considerable value in statistics, particularly when it is applied to curve fitting.

Table 5.4 The squares and sum of squares of deviations taken from various scores in a distribution

1 X	2 $(X-2)^2$	3 $(X-3)^2$	4 $(X-\overline{X})^2$	5 $(X-5)^2$	6 $(X-6)^2$
2	0	1	4	9	16
3	1	0	1	4	9
4	4	1	0	1	4
5	9	4	1	0	1
6	16	9	4	1	0
Totals	30	15	10	15	30

$N = 5$

$\overline{X} = 4$

A fourth important property of the mean is that it is the most stable or reliable measure of central tendency. Let's say that we draw 25 separate random samples of 500 persons who are registered voters in New York State (it is possible that a few persons will be selected in more than one of the samples). If we computed the mean, the median, and the modal age for each of the 25 samples, we would find that in most instances the mean would show less fluctuation than either the median or mode. That is, the frequency distribution for the 25 mean ages would be more compact (show less variability) than would either the frequency distribution of the 25 median ages or the 25 modal ages. The reason that stability or reliability is particularly important stems from our effort to infer from a sample to the population. We learned in Chapter 1 that the population parameter is frequently unknown, but that we can calculate sample statistics. Thus, the sample is a convenient way to estimate population characteristics or parameters. Normally, it is not possible to draw more than one sample, so, because of its stability, we tend to use the sample mean as the best single estimate of its corresponding population parameter.

Each of these four properties of the arithmetic mean will be considered further in future chapters.

5.2.3 The Weighted Mean

Imagine that four classes in introductory sociology obtained the following mean scores on the final examination: 75, 78, 72, and 80. Could you sum these four means together and divide by 4, to obtain an overall mean for all four classes? This could be done *only if* the N in each class is identical. What if, as a matter of fact, the mean of 75 is based on an N of 30, the second mean is based on 40 observations, the third on $N = 25$, and the fourth on $N = 50$?

The total sum of scores may be obtained by multiplying each mean by its respective N and summing.

Thus

$$\sum (N \cdot \overline{X}) = 30(75) + 40(78) + 25(72) + 50(80)$$

$$= 11,170$$

The **weighted mean,** $\overline{X}_w$, can be expressed as the sum of the mean of each group multiplied by its respective weight (the N in each group) divided by the sum of the weights (i.e., $\Sigma w = \Sigma N_i = N$).

$$\overline{X}_w = \frac{\Sigma(w \cdot \overline{X})}{\Sigma w} = \frac{\Sigma(N_i \cdot \overline{X})}{N} \tag{5.4}$$

$$\overline{X}_w = \frac{30(75) + 40(78) + 25(72) + 50(80)}{145}$$

$$= \frac{11,170}{145} = 77.03$$

Your grade point average is calculated by using the weighted mean. Exercise 17 at the end of the chapter is such an example.

5.3 The Median (Md_n)

The **median** is defined as *that score or potential score in a distribution of scores, above and below which one-half of the frequencies fall*. If this definition sounds vaguely familiar to you, it is not by accident. The median is merely a special case of a percentile rank. Indeed, the median is the score at the 50th percentile.

Consider the following array of scores: 5, 19, 37, 39, 45. Note that the scores must be arranged in order of magnitude and that N is an odd number. Thus, computing the median requires ordinal-level data. A score of 37 is the median, since two scores fall above it and two scores fall below it.* If N is an *even* number, the median is the arithmetic mean of the two middle values. The two middle values in the array of scores 8, 26, 35, 43, 47, 73 are 35 and 43. The arithmetic mean of these two values is (35 + 43)/2, or 39. Therefore, the median is 39. Equation (5.5) provides a generalized rule for computing the median position. It should be clear at this point that the median is a positional measure that requires data measured on either an ordinal or interval scale.

$$\text{median case number} = \frac{N + 1}{2} \qquad (5.5)$$

In the first example with five values the median case number would be 3 and the score of 37 is the median. When N is even, as in the case of the second example, the median case number is 3.5, hence we take the arithmetic mean of the 3rd and 4th values as we did in the example. Again, we find the median to be 39.

5.3.1 The Median of a Grouped Frequency Distribution

The generalized procedures discussed in Chapter 4 for determining the score at various percentile ranks may be applied to the calculation of the median.

---

* When working with an array of numbers where N is odd, the definition of the median does not quite hold; that is, in the preceding example in which the median is 37, two scores lie below it and two above it, as opposed to one-half of N. Consider the score of 37 as falling one-half on either side of the median.

The median of a grouped frequency distribution may be computed by using a modification of Eq. (4.4) as shown in Eq. (5.6).

$$\text{median} = X_{ll} + i\,\frac{(N/2) - \text{cum}\,f_{ll}}{f_i} \tag{5.6}$$

where

X_{ll} = score at lower real limit of the interval containing the median

i = width of the interval

$\text{cum}\,f_{ll}$ = cumulative frequency at the lower real limit of the interval containing the median

f_i = number of cases within the interval containing the median

N = total number of cases in the frequency distribution

Applied to the data appearing in Table 4.1 (Section 4.2.2), the median becomes

$$\text{median} = 29.5 + 5\,\frac{(230.3/2) - 110.8}{19.3}$$

$$= 29.5 + 5\,\frac{(115.2 - 110.8)}{19.3}$$

$$= 29.5 + 1.14 = 30.64$$

where $X_{ll} = 29.5$, $i = 5$, $\text{cum}\,f_{ll} = 110.8$, $f_i = 19.3$, $N = 230.3$. We are assuming that the scores within an interval are evenly distributed.

5.3.2 A Special Case

Occasionally the middle score in an array of scores is tied with other scores. How do we specify the median when we encounter tied scores?

Consider the following array of 20 scores: 2, 3, 3, 4, 5, 7, 7, 8, 8, 8, 8, 9, 10, 12, 14, 15, 17, 19, 19, 20. The easiest procedure is to convert the array to an ungrouped frequency distribution and apply Eq. (5.6). However, the i in the numerator may be eliminated since it is equal to 1.

$$\text{median} = X_{ll} + \frac{(N/2 - \text{cum} f_{ll})}{f_i} \qquad (5.7)$$

$$= 7.5 + \frac{(20/2 - 7)}{4}$$

$$= 7.5 + \frac{3}{4} = 8.25$$

X	f	cum f	X	f	cum f
2	1	1	12	1	14
3	2	3	13	0	14
4	1	4	14	1	15
5	1	5	15	1	16
6	0	5	16	0	16
7	2	7	17	1	17
8	4	11	18	0	17
9	1	12	19	2	19
10	1	13	20	1	20
11	0	13			

5.3.3 A Characteristic of the Median

An important characteristic of the median is its *insensitivity* to extreme scores. Consider the following set of scores: 2, 5, 8, 11, 48. The median is 8. This is true in spite of the fact that the set contains one extreme score of 48. Had the 48 been a score of 97, the median would *remain the same*. This characteristic of the median makes it valuable for describing central tendency in certain types of distributions in which the *mean* is an unacceptable measure of central tendency due to its sensitivity to extreme scores. This point will be further elaborated in Section 5.5 when the uses of the three measures of central tendency are discussed.

5.4 The Mode (M_o)

Of all measures of central tendency, the **mode** is the most easily determined since it is obtained by inspection rather than by computation. *The mode is the score that occurs with greatest frequency.* For grouped data the mode is designated as the midpoint of the interval containing the highest frequency count. In Table 5.2 the mode is a score of 102 since it is the midpoint of the interval (100–104) containing the greatest frequency.

If the data in Table 5.2 were represented as a frequency curve (polygon) or as a histogram, the mode would also be 102. The mode of a frequency curve is the highest value on the curve. In a histogram the mode is represented by the midpoint of the tallest column.

The mode can be determined for nominal-, ordinal-, or interval-level data, and therefore is the most versatile of the three measures of central tendency discussed in this chapter. Consider a study in which the respondents were classified by their religious affiliation in the following manner: Protestant, 47%; Catholic, 42%; and Jewish, 11%. The modal category would be Protestant. Note that the mode is located in the category with the plurality of cases. A majority of cases, that is, over 50%, is not required.

The mode, from a statistical perspective, is also the most probable value. If the names of all of the respondents classified by religious affiliation were placed in a large container, the name drawn first would most probably be that of a Protestant simply because Protestants are most numerous in this particular study.

In some distributions, such as Figure 3.9(c), there are two high points that produce the appearance of two humps, as on a camel's back. Such distributions are referred to as being *bimodal*. A distribution with more than two humps is referred to as being multimodal. Figure 3.9(a) depicts a distribution with no mode.

5.5 Comparison of Mean, Median, and Mode

We have seen that the mean is a measure of central tendency in which the *sum* of the deviations on one side equals the sum of the deviations on the other side. The median divides a frequency distribution into two equal parts so that the *number* of scores below the median equals the *number* of scores above the median. The mode is the score that occurs with the greatest frequency.

In general, the arithmetic mean is the preferred statistic for representing central tendency because of several desirable properties. To begin with, the mean is a member of a mathematical system, which permits its use in more advanced statistical analyses because it is based on interval-level data. It is the preferred measure of central tendency if the distribution of scores is not skewed. We have used deviations from the mean to demonstrate two of its most important characteristics; that is, the sum of deviations is zero and the sum of squares is minimal. Deviations of scores from the mean provide valuable information about any distribution. We will be making frequent use of deviation scores throughout the remainder of the text. In contrast, deviation scores from the median and the corresponding squared deviations have only limited applications to more advanced statistical considerations.

As previously noted, one important function of inferential statistics is to provide estimates of parameters. If we take a number of different samples from a symmetrical population with a single mode and wish to estimate the population mean from these samples, the mean would be a better estimator than the median. The size of the error of any given estimate using the mean of the sample is likely to be less than an estimate using the sample median due to the stability of the mean which was discussed in Section 5.2.

On the other hand, there are certain situations in which the median is preferred as the measure of central tendency. When the distribution is symmetrical, the mean, the median, and the mode are identical. Under these circumstances the mean should be used. However, as we have seen, when the distribution is markedly skewed, the mean, which is analogous to a center of gravity, will provide a misleading estimate of central tendency because under these circumstances it is not a central score. The mean for group 2 in Table 5.3 is 10, even though four of the five scores are less than this value. Annual family income is a commonly studied variable in which the median is preferred over the mean since the distribution of this variable is distinctly skewed in the direction of high salaries, with the result that the mean overestimates the income obtained by most families. You will find upon examination of most census information that the median is used more frequently than the mean or mode because the median is less sensitive to extreme values such as are encountered with age, educational attainment, and income distributions. Computation of the median requires that the data be measured at the ordinal level or higher.

The mode is used far less than the mean and median in the social sciences. It is particularly appropriate whenever a quick, rough estimate of central tendency is desired. The mode, however, is very versatile in that it can be used with all levels of measurement.

5.5.1 Indeterminant Values

There are a number of different occasions when values of the variable are indeterminate. The highest class (and sometimes the lowest) in many summaries of health and age-related statistics do not include either an upper or lower boundary. If age is the variable of interest, the highest class may be 80 and above; if income is the variable, the lowest class may be under $2,500 and the highest class may be $50,000 and over. Since we are unable to specify the limits of these classes, we cannot ascertain the midpoint. Consequently, a mean cannot be calculated. (See Statistics in Action 5.2.)

The inability, on occasion, to specify a value of a variable can also have important implications for the study of the environment. Many electronic and chemical tests for toxic substances in the environment (such as groundwater and air) are unable to detect quantities below certain values. It is not that these substances do not exist at these lower values but that the test procedures are simply unable to find them. To illustrate, if a given substance is measured in parts per million per cubic meter and the available technology cannot measure amounts less than 50 parts per million, then samples containing 49, 48, 47, and fewer parts per million would not be detected. If there are many of these undetected values and they are all recorded as zero, the mean would be an inappropriate statistic since all of the recorded zeros would draw the mean toward them. The resulting sample mean could seriously underestimate the actual amount of the toxic substance in the environment studied. Under these circumstances the median might provide a better estimate of central tendency since it would be unaffected by the spurious zeros—unless, of course, the majority of the readings are in the undetectable range.

Statistics in Action 5.2

AIDS in Europe, Classified by Age and Gender: Calculating Measures of Central Tendency with Open-Ended Classes

Statistical information concerned with disease and matters of life and death (vital statistics) are often presented in the form of age-related grouped frequency distributions. The class widths may or may not be equal and the highest age class is commonly open-ended. These features are exemplified in Table 5.5, where the four lowest classes have a width of 5, the next four have a width of 10, and the upper limit of the highest class is left undefined. The use of unequal widths and open-ended classes can be justified: We may wish to have a more precise look at certain age categories and there may be too few cases in the higher age brackets to warrant separate classes. However, these procedures complicate the calculation of measures of central tendency. When a class is open-ended, we cannot locate the midpoint of the class. Consequently, the mean cannot be ascertained. But we can obtain the median and the percentile rank of any age except for those included in the open-ended class. We need only pay particular attention to each class width when calculating either the median and percentile ranks of scores or finding the score corresponding to a specific percentile rank.

Note that Table 5.5 is an example in which the class values are presented from high to low.

a) If you wish to compare graphically the male and female distributions of the ages at which AIDS is diagnosed, what type of distribution would be most appropriate and why?
b) Based on your answer to (a), construct the graph that permits the visual comparison of AIDS cases by age category. Do there appear to be differences in the ages at which AIDS is diagnosed in males and females?
c) Prepare cumulative frequency and cumulative percentage distributions for males alone, females alone, and males and females combined.
d) What is the median age at which AIDS is first diagnosed in males? females?
e) What is the mean age at which AIDS is first diagnosed in males? females?

Table 5.5 AIDS cases by age and gender—
21 European countries through
September 30, 1985

Age Group (Real Limits)	Males	Females
60 & above	21	4
50–60	103	9
40–50	375	12
30–40	622	36
20–30	277	57
15–20	8	0
10–15	3	0
5–10	3	1
0–5	15	14
	$N = 1427$	$N = 133$

ANSWERS

a) Grouped percentage distributions because of the enormous difference in the number of males versus females infected (almost 11 to 1).

b)

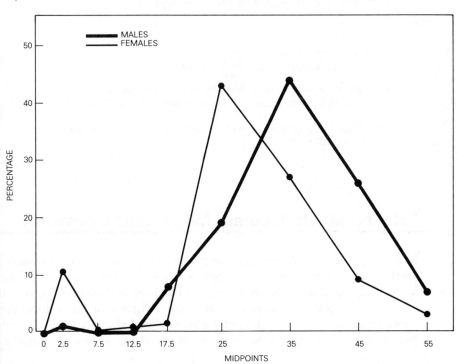

Diagnosed cases of AIDS appear to peak in the 20s in females and in the 30s in males.

c)

Age Group (Real Limits)	Males			Females			Combined		
	f	cum f	cum %	f	cum f	cum %	f	cum f	cum %
60 & above	21	1427	100.00	4	133	100.00	25	1560	100.00
50–60	103	1406	98.53	9	129	96.99	112	1535	98.40
40–50	375	1303	91.31	12	120	90.23	387	1423	91.22
30–40	622	928	65.03	36	108	81.20	658	1036	66.41
20–30	277	306	21.44	57	72	54.14	334	378	24.23
15–20	8	29	2.03	0	15	11.28	8	44	2.82
10–15	3	21	1.47	0	15	11.28	3	36	2.31
5–10	3	18	1.26	1	15	11.28	4	33	2.12
0–5	15	15	1.05	14	14	10.53	29	29	1.86
	$N = 1427$			$N = 133$			$N = 1560$		

d) The cumulative frequency of the score is 713.5.

$N = 1427$
$i = 10$
score at lower limit $= 30$
score units within class $= 6.55145$

The score at the 50th percentile equals 36.5515 for males.

The cumulative frequency of the score is 66.5.

$N = 133$
$i = 10$
score at lower limit $= 20$
score units within class $= 9.03509$

The score at the 50th percentile equals 29.0351 for females.

e) Neither mean can be calculated because the highest class is open-ended.

Source: From ''Acquired Immunodeficiency syndrome—Europe,'' *Morbidity and Mortality Weekly Report* (1986), **35**(3), 35–46.

5.6 The Mean, Median, Mode, and Skewness

In Chapter 3 we demonstrated several forms of skewed distributions. We pointed out, however, that skew cannot always be determined by inspection. If you understand the differences between the mean and the median, you should be able to suggest a method for determining whether or not a distribution is skewed and, if so, the direction of the skew. The basic fact to keep in mind is that the mean is pulled in the direction of the skew, whereas the median and

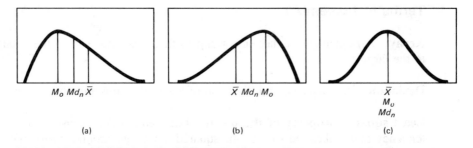

Figure 5.2 The relationship among the mean, median, and mode in (a) positively skewed, (b) negatively skewed, and (c) symmetrical distributions.

mode, unaffected by extreme scores, are not. When the mean is higher than the median, the distribution may be said to be positively skewed; when the mean is lower than the median, the distribution is negatively skewed. Figure 5.2 demonstrates the relationship among the mean, the median, and the mode in positively skewed, negatively skewed, and symmetrical distributions.

Summary

In this chapter we discussed, demonstrated the calculation of, and compared three indices of central tendency that are frequently used to describe frequency distributions: the mean, the median, and the mode.

We saw that the mean may be defined variously as the sum of scores divided by the number of scores, the point in a distribution that makes the summed deviations equal to zero, or the point in the distribution that makes the sum of the squared deviations minimal. The median divides the distribution in half, so that the number of scores below the median equals the number of scores above it. Finally, the mode is defined as the most frequently occurring score. We demonstrated the method for obtaining the weighted mean of a set of means when each of the individual means is based on a different N.

Because of special properties it possesses, the mean is the most frequently used measure of central tendency. However, because of the mean's sensitivity to extreme scores that are not balanced on both sides of the distribution, the median is usually the measure of choice when distributions are markedly skewed. The mode is rarely used in the social sciences.

Finally, we demonstrated the relationship among the mean, the median, and the mode in positively skewed, negatively skewed, and symmetrical distributions.

Terms to Remember

Array   Arrangement of data according to their magnitude from the smallest to the largest value.

Deviation   The distance and direction of a score from a reference point.

Least squares property of the mean   The mean is that measure of central tendency that makes the sum of the squared deviations around it minimal.

Mean   Sum of the scores or values of a variable divided by their number.

Measure of central tendency   Index of central location used in the description of frequency distributions.

Median   Score in a distribution of scores, above and below which one-half of the frequencies fall.

Mode   Score that occurs with the greatest frequency.

Sum of squares   Deviations from the mean, squared and summed.

Weighted mean   Sum of the mean of each group multiplied by its respective weight (the N in each group), divided by the sum of the weights (total N).

Exercises

1. Find the mean, the median, and the mode for each of the following sets of measurements. Show that $\Sigma(X - \overline{X}) = 0$.

   a) 10, 8, 6, 0, 8, 3, 2, 5, 8, 0

   b) 1, 3, 3, 5, 5, 5, 7, 7, 9

   c) 119, 5, 4, 4, 4, 3, 1, 0

2. In which of the sets of data in Exercise 1 is the mean a poor measure of central tendency? Why?

3. Which measure(s) of central tendency can be computed for Figure 3.3 in Chapter 3? Why? Which measure(s) should not be computed? Why?

4. You have calculated measures of central tendency on family income and expressed your data in dollars. You decide to recompute after you have

multiplied all the dollars by 100 to convert them to cents. How will this affect the measures of central tendency?

5. Calculate the measures of central tendency for the data in Table 3.3 in Chapter 3.

6. In Exercise 1(c), if the score of 119 were changed to a score of 19, how would the various measures of central tendency be affected?

7. On the basis of the following measures of central tendency, indicate whether or not there is evidence of skew and, if so, its direction:

    a) $\overline{X} = 56$,   median $= 62$,   mode $= 68$

    b) $\overline{X} = 68$,   median $= 62$,   mode $= 56$

    c) $\overline{X} = 62$,   median $= 62$,   mode $= 62$

    d) $\overline{X} = 62$,   median $= 62$,   mode $= 30$, mode $= 94$

8. What is the nature of the distributions in Exercises 7(c) and (d)?

9. Calculate the mean of the following array of scores: 3, 4, 5, 5, 6, 7:

    a) Add a constant, say, 2, to each score. Recalculate the mean. Generalize: What is the effect on the mean of adding a constant to all scores?

    b) Subtract the same constant from each score. Recalculate the mean. Generalize: What is the effect on the mean of subtracting a constant from all scores?

    c) Square all the scores. Recalculate the mean. Generalize: What is the effect on the mean of squaring all the scores?

    d) Multiply each score by a constant, say, 2. Recalculate the mean. Generalize: What is the effect on the mean of multiplying each score by a constant?

    e) Divide each score by two. Recalculate the mean. Generalize: What is the effect on the mean of dividing each score by a constant?

10. What is the mean, median, and mode for Figure 3.4 in Chapter 3? How is each affected by the skew of the distribution?

11. If we know that the mean and median of a set of scores are equal, what can we say about the form of the distribution?

12. Given the information in the following table, calculate the appropriate measures of central tendency.

Immigration to the United States,
1821–1980

Period	Number (in Thousands)
1821–1830	152
1831–1840	599
1841–1850	1713
1851–1860	2598
1861–1870	2315
1871–1880	2812
1881–1890	5247
1891–1900	3688
1901–1910	8795
1911–1920	5736
1921–1930	4107
1931–1940	528
1941–1950	1035
1951–1960	2515
1961–1970	3322
1971–1980	4493

Total 49,655

Source: U.S. Immigration and Naturalization Service, *Annual Report.* Immigrants are nonresident aliens (i.e., non-U.S. citizens) admitted to the United States for permanent residence.

13. In a departmental final exam the following mean grades were obtained for classes of 25, 40, 30, 45, 50, and 20 students: 72.5, 68.4, 75.0, 71.3, 70.6, and 78.1:

    a) What is the total mean over all sections of the course?

    b) Draw a line graph showing the size of the class along the X-axis and the corresponding means along the Y-axis. Does there appear to be a relationship between class size and mean grades on the final exam?

14. On the basis of examination performance an instructor identifies the following groups of students:

    a) Those with a percentile rank of 90 or higher.

    b) Those with a percentile rank of 10 or less.

    c) Those with percentile ranks between 40 and 49.

    d) Those with percentile ranks between 51 and 60.

    Which group would the instructor work with if he or she wished to raise the *median* performance of the total group? Which group if he or she wished to raise the *mean* performance of the total group?

15. Which of the measures of central tendency is most affected by the degree of skew in the distribution? Explain.

16. Given the information in the following table, calculate the mean, median, and mode for marriages and divorces:

Marriages and divorces in the United States

Year	Marriages (1000s)	Divorces (1000s)
1965	1800	479
1966	1857	499
1967	1927	523
1968	2069	584
1969	2145	639
1970	2159	708
1971	2190	773
1972	2282	845
1973	2284	915
1974	2230	977
1975	2153	1036
1976	2155	1083
1977	2178	1091
1978	2243	1122
1979	2331	1181
1980	2390	1189
1981	2422	1213
1982	2456	1170

Source: U.S. National Center for Health Statistics. *Vital Statistics of the United States*, annual.

17. A student compiled the following academic record in college. What is her overall grade point average if $A = 4, B = 3, C = 2, D = 1, F = 0$?

Credit Hours	Grade
40	A
55	B
15	C
10	D
0	F

18. While backpacking on the Appalachian Trail, you encounter 20 hikers and note the number of days they have been out. Given the following data, demonstrate that the sum of deviations about the mean equals zero:

5	1	15	9
4	42	19	9
39	6	22	8
14	18	14	1
12	14	8	19

19. A review of the files for 35 juvenile offenders presently held in a county detention home reveals that the majority have been arrested previously. Compute the mean, median, and modal number of arrests for the juvenile offenders:

Number of Previous Arrests	f
0	3
1	4
2	6
3	9
4	6
5	2
6	3
7	2
	N = 35

20. Surveys are typically pretested to identify procedural, sampling, and wording problems. A telephone interview was pretested using ten respondents in a recent statewide survey of attitudes toward pornography:

   a) Calculate the appropriate measures of central tendency for the following three variables. (*Hint:* Note the level of measurement for each of the variables.)

   b) Do you see any problem with the frequency distribution of these variables that might require modifying the questionnaire or interview procedure?

Respondent	Age	Sex	Attitude toward Pornography*
1	32	M	19
2	43	F	24
3	21	F	11
4	19	F	30
5	76	F	50
6	50	F	42
7	40	M	17
8	26	F	33
9	21	F	24
10	63	F	47

*Scores may range from 10 to 50 with a high score indicating opposition to pornography.

21. Calculate the mean number of workers involved per work stoppage for each year represented in Exercise 21 in Chapter 3. Describe the trend which you have observed.

22. Calculate the median for the data in Table 5.2. (*Hint:* Construct a cumulative frequency or a cumulative percentage column to locate the class interval containing the median.)

23. In Section 5.5 we stated that the mean is usually *more reliable* than the median, i.e., less subject to fluctuations. Suppose we conduct an experiment consisting of 30 tosses of three dice, obtaining the following results:

6, 6, 2	5, 4, 3	4, 3, 2	2, 1, 1	6, 5, 3	6, 5, 4
4, 1, 1	4, 4, 3	6, 4, 1	5, 4, 3	5, 1, 1	6, 2, 1
6, 5, 5	6, 6, 4	6, 4, 2	5, 4, 4	6, 5, 2	5, 4, 3
6, 4, 3	5, 3, 2	5, 1, 1	4, 3, 1	6, 3, 3	5, 4, 1
4, 2, 1	6, 3, 3	6, 5, 4	4, 2, 2	6, 6, 5	6, 3, 1

a) Calculate the 30 means and 30 medians.

b) Starting with the real limits of the lower interval 0.5–1.5, group the means and medians into separate frequency distributions.

c) Draw histograms for the two distributions. Do they support the contention that the mean is a more stable estimator of central tendency? Explain.

d) Assume that we place the means and means into two separate hats and draw one at random from each. V   ıs the likelihood that
   i) a statistic greater than 5.5 would be obtained?
   ii) a statistic less than 1.5 would be obtained?
   iii) a statistic greater than 5.5 or less than 1.5 would be obtained?

chapter **6**

Measures of
Dispersion

6.1 Introduction
6.2 The Range
6.3 The Interquartile Range
6.4 The Mean Deviation
6.5 The Variance (s^2) and Standard Deviation (s)
6.6 Interpretation of the Standard Deviation

6.1 Introduction

In the introduction to Chapter 4 we saw that a score by itself is meaningless. A score takes on meaning only when it is compared with other scores or other statistics. If we know the mean of the distribution of a given variable, we can determine whether a particular score is higher or lower than the mean. But how much higher or lower? It is clear at this point that a measure of central tendency such as the mean provides only a limited amount of information. To describe a distribution more fully, or to interpret a score more fully, additional information is required concerning the **dispersion** of scores about our measure of central tendency.

Consider Figure 6.1. In both examples of frequency curves the mean of the distribution is exactly the same. However, note the difference in the interpretations of a score of 128. In Figure 6.1(a), because the scores are widely dispersed about the mean, a score of 128 may be considered only moderately high. Quite a few individuals in the distribution scored above 128, as indicated by the area to the right of 128. In Figure 6.1(b), on the other hand, the scores are compactly distributed about the same mean. This is a more *homogeneous* distribution. Consequently, the score of 128 is now virtually at the top of the distribution and it may therefore be considered a very high score.

In interpreting individual scores, we must find a companion to the mean or the median. This companion must in some way express the degree of

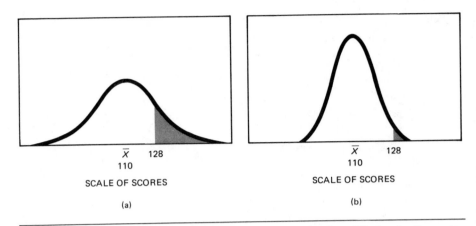

Figure 6.1   Two frequency curves with identical means but differing in dispersion or variability.

dispersion of scores about the measure of central tendency. We will discuss five such measures of dispersion or variability: the **range,** the **interquartile range,** the **mean deviation,** the **variance,** and the **standard deviation.** Of the five, we will find the standard deviation to be our most useful measure of dispersion in both descriptive and inferential statistics. In advanced inferential statistics, as in analysis of variance (Chapter 15), the variance will become a most useful measure of variability.

6.2 The Range

When we calculated the various measures of central tendency, we located a *single point* along the scale of scores and identified it as the mean, the median, or the mode. When our interest shifts to measures of dispersion, however, we must look for an index of variability that indicates the *distance* along the scale of scores.

One of the first measures of distance that comes to mind is the **range.** The range is by far the simplest and the most straightforward measure of dispersion. It is the scale distance between the largest and smallest score.* In a recent study conducted by one of the authors the youngest respondent was 28 years old and the oldest was 90. Thus, the range was 90 − 28 or 62.

Although the range is meaningful, it is of little use because of its marked instability, particularly when the range is based on a small sample. Note that if there is one extreme score in a distribution, the dispersion of scores will

---

* Sometimes the range is computed by subtracting the lowest score from the highest score and adding 1.

appear to be large when, in fact, the removal of that score may reveal an otherwise compact distribution. Several years ago a resident of an institution for retarded persons was found to have an I.Q. score in the 140s. Imagine the erroneous impression that would result if the scores for the residents varied from 20 to 140 and the range was reported to be 120! Stated another way, the range reflects only the two most extreme scores in a distribution, and the remaining scores are ignored.

6.3 The Interquartile Range

In order to overcome the instability of the range as a measure of dispersion, we sometimes calculate the interquartile range. The interquartile range is calculated by subtracting the score at the 25th percentile (referred to as the first quartile or Q_1) from the score at the 75th percentile (the third quartile or Q_3).

$$\text{interquartile range} = Q_3 - Q_1 \qquad (6.1)$$

This measure of score variation is more meaningful than the range because it is not based on two extreme scores. Rather, it reflects the middle 50% of the scores. It does, however, have two shortcomings: (1) Like the range, it does not by itself permit the precise interpretation of a score within a distribution, and (2) like the median, it does not enter into any of the higher mathematical relationships that are basic to inferential statistics. Figure 6.2 provides a comparison of the range and interquartile range. Statistics in Action 6.1 includes an example of the interquartile range.

6.4 The Mean Deviation

In Chapter 5 we pointed out that when we are dealing with data that are characterized by a bell-shaped distribution, the mean is our most useful measure of central tendency. We calculated the mean by adding together all of the scores and dividing them by N. If we carried these procedures one step further, we could subtract the mean from each score, sum the differences (deviations from the mean), and thereby obtain an estimate of the amount of deviation from the mean. By dividing by N, we would have a measure that would be analogous to the arithmetic mean except that it would represent the dispersion of scores from the arithmetic mean.

If you think for a moment about the characteristics of the mean, which we discussed in the preceding chapter, you will encounter one serious difficulty. The sum of the deviations of all scores from the mean must add up to zero. If we defined the mean deviation (also referred to as the **average deviation**) as

Statistics in Action 6.1

Reduction in Inequalities

Sociologists have long observed that great inequality in educational attainment can contribute to social tensions in much the same way as excessive income inequality, by fostering elitism, class differences, and political instability. Indeed at one time a college education was a mark of rank and social standing, as well as of acquired knowledge and skill. The situation in 1940 was not near this extreme, as some able children from poor families had been attending colleges for some time. Still, the lack of even a high school diploma by many was striking and the relative number going to college was small. The growth in attainment that was to take place would change this situation. It would bring with it a decrease in the amount of inequality in educational attainment.

The table shows the distribution of the population 25 years old and over by years of school completed for 1940 and 1982, along with measures of the amount of variance or inequality in the distribution. Because there is a practical upper limit on the amount of formal education an individual can obtain, we expect that as more and more people attain higher levels, the closer together they would become. However, it is important to measure the degree to which this is happening so that judgments can be made about how important the reductions are and comparisons can be made in different places and times.

Measures of absolute inequality (standard deviation, interquartile range) are essentially based on the absolute difference in years of attainment between individuals. As the table shows, both measures declined significantly. The interquartile range shows that the range of attainment across the middle 50 percent of the population was 5.7 years of schooling in 1940 but only 3.5 years in 1982. The standard deviation declined over the same period from 3.8 to 3.4 years.

Years of school completed by persons 25 years old and over and measures of dispersion: 1940 and 1982

1940	Less than 5 years	5 to 7 years	8 years	9 to 11 years	12 years	13 to 15 years	16 years and over
Percentage distribution	13.7	29.1	17.5	15.1	14.3	5.5	4.6
Median (years) 8.4
Standard deviation (years). 3.8
Interquartile range (years). 5.7

1982	Less than 5 years	5 to 7 years	8 years	9 to 11 years	12 years	13 to 15 years	16 years and over
Percentage distribution	3.0	5.6	7.1	13.3	37.9	15.3	17.7
Median (years) 12.6
Standard deviation (years). 3.4
Interquartile range (years) 3.5

Source: U.S. Bureau of the Census, Special Demographic Analysis, CDS-85-1, Education in the United States: 1940–1983, U.S. Government Printing Office, Washington, D.C., 1985. Portions of the text originally appeared on pp. 4–5 of the report.

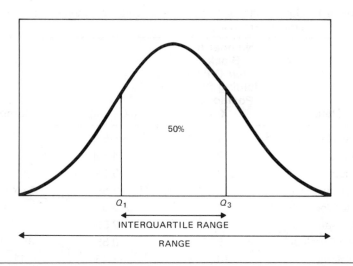

Figure 6.2 Comparison of range and interquartile range for a hypothetical distribution.

this sum divided by N, the mean deviation would always have to be zero. You will recall in Chapter 5 that we used the fact that $\Sigma(X - \overline{X}) = 0$ to arrive at one of several definitions of the mean.

Now if we were to add all of the deviations *without regard to sign* and divide by N, we would still have a measure reflecting the mean deviation from the arithmetic mean. The resulting statistic would be based on the absolute value of the deviations. The **absolute value of a number** is the value of a number without regard to sign. The absolute value of a positive number or of zero is the number itself. The absolute value of a negative number can be found by changing the sign to a positive one. Thus, the absolute value of $+3$ *or* -3 is 3. The symbol for an absolute value is $|\ \ |$. Thus, $|-3| = 3$ and $|+3| = 3$.

The calculation of the mean deviation (MD) is shown in Table 6.1. The data in Tables 6.1 through 6.4 were compiled by the Joint Center for Political Studies in Washington, D.C. and include the number of black officials in 11 southern states holding elected state positions in July 1977.*

As a basis for comparison of the dispersion of several distributions, the mean deviation has some value. For example, the greater the mean deviation is, the greater the dispersion of scores is. However, for interpreting scores within a distribution, the mean deviation is less useful since there is no precise mathematical relationship between the mean deviation, as such, and the location of scores within a distribution.

You may wonder why we have bothered to demonstrate the mean deviation

---

* These figures do not include black officials holding congressional, regional, city, county, or other elected positions.

Table 6.1 Computational procedures for calculating the mean deviation from an array of scores

State	Number of Black Elected Officials Holding State Positions* X	$(\lvert X - \bar{X}\rvert)$	Computation
West Virginia	1	$\lvert -5.55\rvert$	
Virginia	2	$\lvert -4.55\rvert$	
Florida	3	$\lvert -3.55\rvert$	
Kentucky	3	$\lvert -3.55\rvert$	$MD = \dfrac{\Sigma(\lvert X - \bar{X}\rvert)^{\dagger}}{N}$ (6.2)
Mississippi	4	$\lvert -2.55\rvert$	
Arkansas	4	$\lvert -2.55\rvert$	
North Carolina	6	$\lvert -0.55\rvert$	$MD = \dfrac{45.65}{11} = 4.15$
Louisiana	10	$\lvert +3.45\rvert$	
Tennessee	11	$\lvert +4.45\rvert$	
South Carolina	13	$\lvert +6.45\rvert$	
Alabama	15	$\lvert +8.45\rvert$	

$$\Sigma X = 72 \quad \Sigma(\lvert X - \bar{X}\rvert) = 45.65 \qquad N = 11$$

$$\bar{X} = \frac{\Sigma X}{N} = \frac{72}{11} = 6.55$$

*Source: The Social and Economic Status of the Black Population in the United States: An Historical View, 1790–1978. Current Population Reports, Special Studies Series P-23, No. 80, Table 132. Reproduced by permission. Copyright by Joint Center for Political Studies, Washington, D.C. All rights reserved.

$\dagger$ For scores arranged in the form of a frequency distribution, the following equation for the mean deviation should be used:

$$MD = \Sigma f(\lvert X - \bar{X}\rvert)/N$$

when it is of so little use in statistical analysis. As you will see, the standard deviation and the variance, which have great value in statistical analysis, are very closely related to the mean deviation.

6.5 The Variance (s^2) and Standard Deviation (s)*

After looking at Table 6.1, you might pose this question: "We had to treat the values in column $(X - \bar{X})$ as absolute numbers because their sum was equal

---

* Italic letters will be used to represent sample statistics, and Greek letters to represent population parameters; for example, σ^2 represents the population variance and σ represents the population standard deviation. The problem of estimating population parameters from sample values will be discussed in Chapter 14.

to zero. Why could we not square each $(X - \bar{X})$ and then add the squared deviations? In this way we would legitimately rid ourselves of the minus signs, while still preserving the information that is inherent in these deviation scores."

The answer: We could, if by so doing, we arrived at a statistic of greater value in judging dispersion than those we have already discussed. It is fortunate that the standard deviation, based on the squaring of these deviation scores, is of considerable value in three different respects. (1) The standard deviation reflects dispersion of scores, so that the dispersion of different distributions may be compared by using the standard deviation (s). (2) The standard deviation permits the precise interpretation of scores within a distribution. (3) The standard deviation, like the mean, is a member of a *mathematical system,* which permits its use in more advanced statistical considerations. We will use measures based on s when we advance into inferential statistics, and will have more to say about the interpretive aspects of s after we have shown how it is calculated.

6.5.1 Calculation of Variance and Standard Deviation, Mean Deviation Method, with Ungrouped Scores

The **variance** is defined verbally as *the sum of the squared deviations from the mean divided by N.* Symbolically, it is represented as

$$s^2 = \frac{\Sigma(X - \bar{X})^2}{N} \qquad (6.3)*$$

The **standard deviation** is the *square root* of the variance and is defined as

$$s = \sqrt{\frac{\Sigma(X - \bar{X})^2}{N}} \qquad (6.4)$$

The computational procedures for calculating the standard deviation, utilizing the mean deviation method, are shown in Table 6.2.

You will recall from Section 5.2.2 that the sum of the $(X - \bar{X})^2$ column [i.e., $\Sigma(X - \bar{X})^2$] is known as the **sum of squares** and that this sum is minimal when deviations are taken about the mean. From this point on in the text we will encounter the sum of squares with regularity. It will take on a number of different forms, depending on the procedures that we elect for calculating it. However, it is important to remember that, whatever the form, the sum of squares represents the *sum of the squared deviations from the mean.*

The mean deviation method was shown to help you conceptually understand that the standard deviation is based on the deviation of scores from the

---

* The important distinction between biased $\Sigma(X - \bar{X})^2/N$ and unbiased $\Sigma(X - \bar{X})^2/(N - 1)$ estimates of the population variance will be discussed in Chapter 14.

Table 6.2 Computational procedure for calculating s, mean deviation method, from an array of scores

State	Number of Black Elected Officials Holding State Positions*	$(X - \bar{X})$	$(X - \bar{X})^2$	Steps
West Virginia	1	−5.55	30.80†	1. Count the num-
Virginia	2	−4.55	20.70	ber of scores to
Florida	3	−3.55	12.60	obtain N.
Kentucky	3	−3.55	12.60	$N = 11$
Mississippi	4	−2.55	6.50	2. Sum the scores
Arkansas	4	−2.55	6.50	in the X column
North Carolina	6	−0.55	0.30	to obtain X.
Louisiana	10	+3.45	11.90	$\Sigma X = 72$
Tennessee	11	+4.45	19.80	3. Find the mean.
South Carolina	13	+6.45	41.60	$\dfrac{\Sigma X}{N} = \dfrac{72}{11} = 6.55$
Alabama	15	+8.45	71.40	

$\Sigma X = 72 \quad \Sigma(X - \bar{X}) = -0.05‡ \quad \Sigma(X - \bar{X})^2 = 234.70$

$N = 11$
$\bar{X} = 6.55$

4. Compute the deviation of each X value from the mean and place it in $(X - \bar{X})$ column.

5. Square each value in the $(X - \bar{X})$ column and place it in the $(X - \bar{X})^2$ column.

6. Sum the squared deviations. $\Sigma(X - \bar{X})^2 = 234.70$

7. Substitute the values found in Steps 1 and 6 in the equation for s and solve.

$$s = \sqrt{\frac{\Sigma(X - \bar{X})^2}{N}}$$

$$= \sqrt{\frac{234.70}{11}}$$

$$= \sqrt{21.34}$$

$$= 4.62$$

*Source: The Social and Economic Status of the Black Population in the United States: An Historical View, 1970–1978. Current Population Reports, Special Studies Series P-23, No. 80, Table 132. Reproduced by permission. Copyright by Joint Center for Political Studies, Washington, D.C. All rights reserved.
† A comparison of the values in the $(X - \bar{X})$ column with those in the $(X - \bar{X})^2$ column demonstrates that the standard deviation weights extreme departures from the mean more heavily than does the mean deviation.
‡ Does not equal 0 due to rounding.

Table 6.3 Computational procedures for calculating the standard deviation and variance, raw score method, from an array of scores

State	Number Of Black Elected Officials Holding State Positions* X	X^2	Steps
West Virginia	1	1	1. Count the number of scores to obtain N. $N = 11$.
Virginia	2	4	
Florida	3	9	2. Sum the scores in the X column to obtain ΣX. $\Sigma X = 72$.
Kentucky	3	9	
Mississippi	4	16	3. Find the mean. $\Sigma X/N = 72/11 = 6.55$.
Arkansas	4	16	
North Carolina	6	36	4. Square each score and place it in the adjacent column.
Louisiana	10	100	
Tennessee	11	121	5. Sum the X^2 column to obtain $\Sigma X^2 = 706$.
South Carolina	13	169	
Alabama	15	225	6. Substitute the values found in Steps 3 and 5 in the equation for s and solve:

$N = 11$ $\Sigma X = 72$ $\Sigma X^2 = 706$

$\bar{X} = 6.55$

$$s = \sqrt{\frac{\Sigma X^2}{N} - (\bar{X})^2}$$

$$= \sqrt{\frac{706}{11} - 6.55^2}$$

$$= \sqrt{64.18 - 42.90}$$

$$= \sqrt{21.28} = 4.61$$

Also

$$s^2 = \frac{\Sigma X^2}{N} - (\bar{X})^2$$

$$= \frac{706}{11} - 42.90$$

$$= 64.18 - 42.90 = 21.28$$

*Source: The Social and Economic Status of the Black Population in the United States: An Historical View, 1790–1978. Current Population Reports, Special Studies Series P-23, No. 80, Table 132. Reproduced by permission. Copyright by Joint Center for Political Studies, Washington, D.C. All rights reserved.

mean. The mean deviation Eq. (6.4) is extremely unwieldy for use in calculation, particularly when the mean is a fractional value, which is usually the case.

6.5.2 Calculation of Standard Deviation, Raw Score Method with Ungrouped Scores

Equation (6.5) is the computational or raw score equation we use for s. It is mathematically equivalent to the mean deviation Eq. (6.4) used to compute s.

$$s = \sqrt{\frac{\Sigma X^2}{N} - (\bar{X})^2} \qquad (6.5)$$

You will note that the result using Eq. (6.5) agrees almost exactly with the answer we obtained by the mean deviation Eq. (6.4) in Table 6.2. Table 6.3 summarizes the computational procedure that is used to calculate s with Eq. (6.5).

6.5.3 Calculation of Standard Deviation, Raw Score Method, from an Ungrouped Frequency Distribution

If we take the data in Table 6.2 and arrange them into an ungrouped frequency distribution, we obtain the accompanying table.

X	f
1	1
2	1
3	2
4	2
6	1
10	1
11	1
13	1
15	1

To calculate s, square each score and multiply by its corresponding frequency. Sum these products to obtain ΣfX^2. Place this value in Eq. (6.6):

$$s = \sqrt{\frac{\Sigma fX^2}{N} - (\bar{X})^2} \qquad (6.6)$$

Table 6.4 summarizes the procedure for obtaining the standard deviation from an ungrouped frequency distribution using Eq. (6.6).

6.5.4 Errors to Watch For

In calculating the standard deviation using the raw score method, students commonly confuse the similar-appearing terms ΣX^2 (or ΣfX^2) and $(\Sigma X)^2$ (or $[\Sigma fX]^2$). It is important to remember that the former represents the sum of the

Table 6.4 Procedures for calculating the standard deviation of scores from an ungrouped frequency distribution

X*	f	fX	X²	fX²	Computation
1	1	1	1	1	$s = \sqrt{\dfrac{\Sigma fX^2}{N} - (\bar{X})^2}$
2	1	2	4	4	
3	2	6	9	18	
4	2	8	16	32	
6	1	6	36	36	$= \sqrt{\dfrac{706}{11} - 6.55^2}$
10	1	10	100	100	
11	1	11	121	121	$= \sqrt{64.18 - 42.90}$
13	1	13	169	169	
15	1	15	225	225	$= \sqrt{21.28} = 4.61$
	$N = 11$	$\Sigma fX = 72$		$\Sigma fX^2 = 706$	$\bar{X} = 6.55$

* *Source: The Social and Economic Status of the Black Population in the United States: An Historical View, 1790–1978. Current Population Reports, Special Studies Series P-23, No. 80, Table 132. Reproduced by permission. Copyright by Joint Center for Political Studies, Washington, D.C. All rights reserved.*

squares of each of the individual scores, whereas the latter represents the square of the sum of the scores. For example:

$$\text{Given: } X_1 = 2, X_2 = 3, X_3 = 4, X_4 = 5, X_5 = 6$$

$$\Sigma X^2 = 2^2 + 3^2 + 4^2 + 5^2 + 6^2 = 90$$

$$(\Sigma X)^2 = (2 + 3 + 4 + 5 + 6)^2 = 20^2 = 400$$

$$\Sigma X^2 \neq (\Sigma X)^{2*}$$

By definition, it is impossible to obtain a negative sum of squares or a negative standard deviation. In the event that you obtain a negative value under the square root sign, you have probably confused ΣX^2 and $(\Sigma X)^2$.

A rule of thumb for estimating the standard deviation is that the ratio of the range to the standard deviation is rarely smaller than 2 or greater than 6. Generally, you will find that the more scores (larger the sample) you are dealing with, the larger the ratio is. In our preceding example the ratio was 14/4.62 = 3.03. Had our sample been considerably larger, the ratio would have been closer to 6. This will become clearer after learning about the normal distribution in the next chapter. If you obtain a standard deviation that yields a ratio greater than 6 or smaller than 2 relative to the range, you have almost certainly made an error.

* Does not equal ($\neq$).

6.6 Interpretation of the Standard Deviation

You may have noticed that the size of the standard deviation is related to the variability in the scores. The more homogeneous the scores are, the smaller the standard deviation is, and, conversely, the more heterogeneous the scores are, the larger the standard deviation is. The means are equal in Arrays A and B in the accompanying table, yet there is considerable difference in the variability of the scores, and therefore in the size of the standard deviations. You should also note that extreme scores have a disproportionate effect on the standard deviation since we square the raw deviations from the mean. Examine the impact of the raw score 9 in Array B, for example, on the $(X - \bar{X})^2$ column. These points are best illustrated by the mean deviation method of computation.

A complete understanding of the meaning of the standard deviation requires a knowledge of the relationship between the standard deviation and the normal distribution. In order to be able to interpret the standard deviations that are calculated in this chapter, we need to explore the relationship among the raw scores, the standard deviation, and the normal distribution. This material is presented in the following chapter.

Array A			Array B		
X	$X - \bar{X}$	$(X - \bar{X})^2$	X	$X - \bar{X}$	$(X - \bar{X})^2$
4	0	0	2	-2	4
4	0	0	2	-2	4
4	0	0	3	-1	1
4	0	0	4	0	0
4	0	0	9	$+5$	25
$\Sigma X = 20$	$\Sigma(X - \bar{X}) = 0$	$\Sigma(X - \bar{X})^2 = 0$	$\Sigma X = 20$	$\Sigma(X - \bar{X}) = 0$	$\Sigma(X - \bar{X})^2 = 34$
$\bar{X} = 4$			$\bar{X} = 4$		
$N = 5$			$N = 5$		
		$s = \sqrt{0/5} = 0$		$s = \sqrt{34/5} = 2.6$	

Summary

We have seen that to describe a distribution of scores fully, we require more than a measure of central tendency. We must be able to describe how these scores are dispersed about central tendency. In this connection we discussed five measures of dispersion: the range, the interquartile range, the mean deviation, the standard deviation, and the variance. The summary procedure for calculating the variance and standard deviation from a grouped frequency distribution is presented in Table 6.5.

Table 6.5 Summary procedures: Calculating the variance and standard deviation from a grouped frequency distribution

1 Class Interval	2 f	3 Midpoint of Interval X_m	4 fX_m	5 fX_m^2	Steps
0–2	1	1	1	1	1. Sum the f column to ob-
3–5	4	4	16	64	tain $N = 63$.
6–8	9	7	63	441	2. Prepare column 3,
9–11	10	10	100	1,000	showing the midpoint of
12–14	16	13	208	2,704	each interval.
15–17	11	16	176	2,816	3. Multiply the f in each in-
18–20	8	19	152	2,888	terval by the score at
21–23	3	22	66	1,452	the midpoint of its corre-
24–26	1	25	25	625	sponding interval. Val-

$N = 63$ $\Sigma fX_m = 807$ $\Sigma fX_m^2 = 11{,}991$

ues in column 2 are multiplied by corresponding values in column 3. Place in column 4.

4. Sum column 4 to obtain ΣfX_m.
5. Divide ΣfX_m by N to obtain $\bar X$. Thus $\bar X = 807/63 = 12.81$.
6. Multiply values in column 4 by corresponding values in column 3 to obtain fX_m^2. Sum this column to obtain $\Sigma fX_m^2 = 11{,}991$.
7. Substitute the values in Steps 1, 5 and 6 in the equation for s^2:

$$s^2 = \frac{\Sigma fX_m^2}{N} - (\bar X)^2$$

$$= \frac{11{,}991}{63} - (12.81)^2$$

$$= 190.33 - 164.10$$

$$= 26.23.$$

Then

$$s = \sqrt{26.23}$$

$$= 5.12.$$

Terms to Remember

Absolute value of a number The value of a number without regard to sign.

Dispersion The spread or variability of scores about the measure of central tendency.

Interquartile range   A measure of variability obtained by subtracting the score at the 1st quartile from the score at the 3rd quartile.

Mean deviation (average deviation)   Sum of the deviation of each score from the mean, without regard to sign, divided by the number of scores.

Range   Measure of dispersion; the scale distance between the largest and the smallest score.

Standard deviation   Measure of dispersion defined as the square root of the sum of the squared deviations from the mean, divided by N. Also can be defined as the square root of the variance.

Sum of squares   Deviations from the mean, squared and then summed.

Variance   Sum of the squared deviations from the mean, divided by N.

Exercises

1. Calculate s^2 and s for the following array of scores: 3, 4, 5, 5, 6, 7.

   a) Add a constant, say, 2, to each score. Recalculate s^2 and s. Would the results be any different if you had added a larger constant, say, 200?
   Generalize: What is the effect on s and s^2 of adding a constant to an array of scores? Does the variability increase as we increase the magnitude of the scores?

   b) Multiply each score by a constant, say, 2. Recalculate s and s^2.
   Generalize: What is the effect on s and s^2 of multiplying each score by a constant?

2. The following table lists the average sentence and number of months served by first-time federal prisoners for a variety of offenses. Calculate the standard deviation for both columns and discuss:

Average sentence and time served by prisoners released from federal institutions for the first time: 1965 to 1984

Offense	Average Sentence (Months)	Average Time Served (Months)
Counterfeiting	32.4	14.9
Drug Laws	44.8	19.5
Embezzlement	22.1	12.0
Forgery	29.7	12.6
Income Tax	18.8	10.8
Kidnapping	209.4	73.8
Robbery	136.8	46.8
White Slave Traffic	82.0	37.2

Source: U.S. Bureau of Prisons, *Statistical Report,* annual.

3. Why is it necessary to supplement measures of central tendency with measures of dispersion to describe a distribution completely?

4. The list that follows presents the greatest distance (in miles) 15 children have ever traveled from their homes. Calculate the mean, standard deviation, and the variance. What are the advantages of each?

1000	100	400
600	3000	700
250	600	1100
400	1000	1300
500	50	200

5. What is the nature of a distribution if $s = 0$?

6. Calculate the standard deviations for the following sets of measurements:

   a) 10, 8, 6, 0, 8, 3, 2, 2, 8, 0   b) 1, 3, 3, 5, 5, 5, 7, 7, 9

   c) 20, 1, 2, 5, 4, 4, 4, 0   d) 5, 5, 5, 5, 5, 5, 5, 5, 5, 5

7. Why is the standard deviation in Exercise 6(c) so large? Describe the effect of extreme scores on s.

8. Determine the range for the sets of measurements in Exercise 6. For which of these is the range a misleading index of variability and why?

9. For the following table, find the standard deviation for females and for males. Which sex is more homogeneous in its number of physician visits per year?

Average number of physician visits by age and sex (hypothetical data)

Age	Males	Females
Under 5	5.8	6.5
5–9	3.2	4.2
10–14	4.4	4.6
15–19	4.8	5.4
20–24	5.1	6.0
25–29	5.3	5.7
30–34	5.2	5.4

10. For the following grouped frequency distribution, find (a) the standard deviation and (b) the variance (hypothetical data).

Number of self-reported delinquent acts

Delinquent Acts	f
0–2	13
3–5	6
6–8	3
9–11	2
12–14	4
15–17	2
	$N = 30$

11. Find (a) the standard deviation and (b) the variance for the following distribution. Which measure do you believe best reflects the distribution and why?

In how many political campaigns have you worked ten or more hours (hypothetical data)?

Number of Campaigns	f
1	22
2	15
3	11
4	9
5	4
6	2
7	1
8	1
	$N = 65$

12. Find the (a) mean, (b) standard deviation, and (c) range for each major in the following table. Which discipline has been most stable? Least stable? (*Hint:* Use the mean deviation method to ensure your calculator can accommodate the values.)

Earned Bachelor's Degrees in the United States

	Political Science	History	Sociology
1969–1970	26,000	43,000	30,000
1970–1971	27,000	45,000	33,000
1971–1972	28,000	44,000	35,000
1972–1973	30,000	41,000	35,000
1973–1974	31,000	37,000	35,000
1974–1975	29,000	31,000	32,000
1975–1976	28,000	28,000	28,000

Source: U.S. Department of Health, Education, and Welfare, National Center for Education Statistics, reports on *Earned Degrees Conferred.* (Figures have been rounded to the nearest thousand.)

13. Compute the interquartile range and the mean deviation for the following scores:

$$18, 2, 4, 6, 10, 7, 9, 11, 14, 8, 3, 16, 20, 22, 24, 25$$

14. Three classes of math students took a test and received the following scores:

Class I	Class II	Class III
$\bar{X} = 72$	$\bar{X} = 74$	$\bar{X} = 70$
$s = 2.1$	$s = 5.6$	$s = 4.0$

Which class had the most variability on its test score? Which class had the least?

15. Recall that in Chapter 1 a comparison of in-person lecture versus videotape lecture approaches was discussed. The control and experimental group final examination scores are presented below:

Control Group	Experimental Group
$\bar{X} = 79$	$\bar{X} = 68$
$s = 2.6$	$s = 4.6$
$N = 27$	$N = 25$

Which teaching technique appears to be most successful? Is it possible that some individual students fared better with the videotape (experimental) approach?

16. The outside appearances of homes in four neighborhoods were rated by a team of real estate appraisers. The ratings, which ranged from 0 (low) to 100 (high), reflected the expected resale value of the homes.

A random sample of ten ratings from each of the neighborhoods is presented below. Which of the neighborhoods is most homogeneous? Which is most heterogeneous? Which neighborhood is most affluent? The least affluent?

A	B	C	D
37	96	24	22
42	78	36	16
40	84	17	9
32	69	49	14
35	88	56	20
36	84	17	6
39	92	59	8
29	90	32	20
31	8C	66	19
42	71	19	14

17. Calculate the range, mean, standard deviation, and variance for the Appalachian Trail data in Chapter 5, Exercise 18.

18. Calculate the standard deviation and variance for the data in Table 5.2.

19. The annual accumulation of snow and ice pellets for selected cities is shown below. Calculate the standard deviation for the ten cities. Recompute the standard deviation excluding Juneau, Alaska, and describe the change in your answer. Finally, exclude Atlanta and recompute for the other nine cities. Describe how extreme scores affect the standard deviation.

Annual snow and ice pellet accumulation
(in inches)

Juneau	102.8	St. Louis	19.8
Omaha	31.0	Atlanta	1.9
Wilmington	20.9	Chicago	40.3
Washington	17.0	Louisville	17.5
Denver	50.0	New York	28.7

Source: U.S. National Oceanic and Atmospheric Administration, Comparative Climatic Data, annual as cited in the Statistical Abstract of the United States, 1986, Table No. 373.

20. In the study described in Statistics in Action 5.1, the rating of unpleasantness of humor was obtained on male and female subjects when humorous scenes alone were shown (humor first) or when humorous scenes were preceded by five scenes of horror (1 minute excerpts from the movie *Halloween*).

The following table presents the pleasantness ratings made by the four groups of subjects (the lower the score was, the greater was the pleasantness).

Humor First		Humor Preceded by Horror	
Male	**Female**	**Male**	**Female**
17	9	17	10
24	12	11	15
13	20	25	14
13	18	20	7
24	23	6	10
18	18	10	13
21	21	6	6
28	32	31	6
12	12	8	11
9	12	17	14

Source: Based on data from Manstead et al., 1983.

a) Calculate the mean, median, range, variance, and standard deviation for each of the four groups.

b) Combine the male and female scores in humor first and find the mean, median, range, variance, and standard deviation.

c) Combine the male and female scores in humor preceded by horror and find the mean, median, range, variance, and standard deviation. Are the means consistent with the emotional contrast hypothesis that would predict lower scores when humor is preceded by horror?

d) Determine the measure of skew for each of the groups in (a).

21. Refer to Exercise 20. We have noted that the range, variance, and standard deviation are all measures of the dispersion or variability of scores in a distribution. For each of the four groups in Exercise 20(a):

a) Plot the values of the range on the X-axis and the values of the corresponding standard deviation on the Y-axis.

b) Do low values of the range appear to be associated with low values of the standard deviation?

c) In the absence of knowledge of the standard deviation, does it appear that the range can provide information on the relative dispersion of different distributions?

chapter **7**

The Standard Deviation and the Standard Normal Distribution

7.1 Introduction

7.2 The Concept of Standard Scores

7.3 The Standard Normal Distribution

7.4 Characteristics of the Standard Normal Distribution

7.5 Transforming Raw Scores to z Scores

7.6 Illustrative Problems

7.7 The Standard Deviation as an Estimate of Error and Precision

7.8 Interpreting the Standard Deviation

7.1 Introduction

We have emphasized previously that scores are generally meaningless by themselves. To take on meaning they must be compared to the distribution of scores from some reference group. Indeed, the scores derived from any index or scale become more meaningful when they are compared to some reference group of objects or persons. If we learned there were 491 violent crimes in San Antonio and 1475 violent crimes in Cleveland during a comparable time period, we would not be able to determine which city had the highest rate of violence until we knew the population of each city during the same time period. Simply noting that there is approximately a 1 to 3 ratio in actual numbers of violent acts between the two cities would prove misleading. We would need to calculate rates for a comparable number of persons, for example, a rate per 100,000 population for each city, before we could make a valid comparison.

7.2 The Concept of Standard Scores

In interpreting a single score, we want to place it in some position with respect to a collection of scores from a reference group. In Chapter 4 you learned to place a score by determining its percentile rank. Recall that the percentile rank of a score tells the percentage of scores that are of lower-scale value. Another

BOX 7.1

So You Want to Interpret a Test Score?

As we previously noted, a score in and of itself is meaningless. In this chapter, we see that the z-score transformation provides a precise means of interpreting any value of a variable when the scores are normally distributed. The following excerpt from *Winning with Statistics* illustrates the use of the z-score transformation in the interpretation of test scores on standard psychological and educational tests.

Here are the step-by-step procedures for taking all of the mystery out of the interpretation of test scores on standard tests.

1. Determine the mean and the standard deviation of the test. Sometimes different means and standard deviations are given for different age groups. Be sure to find these two measures for the age group in which you are interested.

2. Transform the score you are interested in interpreting to a z-score using the following equation:

$$z = \frac{\text{Score} - \text{Mean}}{\text{Standard deviation}}$$

If you are interested in interpreting a score of 40 and you know that the mean and standard deviation are 30 and 9, respectively, you would have

$$z = \frac{40 - 30}{9} = \frac{10}{9} = 1.1$$

3. Look up a positive value of 1.1 under column B of the accompanying table. Here we find an entry of 86. This means that 86 percent of a comparison group with which this score is being compared obtained scores lower than 86. Only 14 percent (column C) scored higher.

There it is. It's as easy as that.

Percent of Scores Above and Below a Given z-Score

A	B	C
z	Percent of Cases Below	Percent of Cases Above
−2.2	1	99
−2.1	2	98
−2.0	2	98
−1.9	3	97
−1.8	4	96
−1.7	4	96
−1.6	5	95
−1.5	7	93
−1.4	8	92
−1.3	9	91
−1.2	12	88
−1.1	14	86
−1.0	16	84
−0.9	18	82

Percent of Scores Above and Below a Given z-Score (continued)

A	B	C
z	Percent of Cases Below	Percent of Cases Above
−0.8	21	79
−0.7	24	76
−0.6	27	73
−0.5	31	69
−0.4	34	66
−0.3	38	62
−0.2	42	58
−0.1	46	54
0.00	50	50
0.1	54	46
0.2	58	42
0.3	62	38
0.4	66	34
0.5	69	31
0.6	73	27
0.7	76	24
0.8	79	21
0.9	82	18
1.0	84	16
1.1	86	14
1.2	88	12
1.3	91	9
1.4	92	8
1.5	93	7
1.6	95	5
1.7	96	4
1.8	96	4
1.9	97	3
2.0	98	2
2.1	98	2
2.2	99	1

Source: Excerpted from R. P. Runyon, *Winning with Statistics*. Reading, Mass.: Addison-Wesley, 1977.

approach for interpretation of a single score might be to view it with reference to some central point, such as the mean. Thus, a score of 20 in a distribution with a mean of 23 might be reported as −3 because it is 3 units less than the mean, as can be seen in Figure 7.1. We can also express this deviation score as a **standard score** in terms of standard deviation units. If the standard deviation of a set of scores is 1.5 (i.e., one standard deviation is 1.5), a score of 20 would be two standard deviations below the mean of 23 since the absolute difference between 20 and 23 is −3. Dividing −3 by our standard deviation

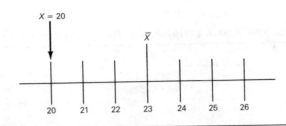

Figure 7.1   Example showing the relationship of the raw score to the mean.

of 1.5 yields -2, which is the number of standard deviations that the raw score of 20 is below the mean.

This process of dividing the deviation of a score from the mean by the standard deviation is known as the transformation of a raw score to a z score. Symbolically, z is defined as

$$z = \frac{X - \overline{X}^*}{s} = \frac{X - \mu}{\sigma} \tag{7.1}$$

where

$$\mu = \text{the population mean}$$
$$\sigma = \text{the population standard deviation}$$

Thus, in the preceding example where $\overline{X} = 23$, $s = 1.5$, and $X = 20$, we can confirm the z score equivalent of $X = 20$ using Eq. (7.1).

$$z = \frac{X - \overline{X}}{s}$$

$$z = \frac{20 - 23}{1.5}$$

$$z = -2.0$$

A z score represents the *deviation of a specific score from the mean expressed in standard deviation units*. For example, if the z score value of a raw score is $+2.1$, we know that the raw score lies 2.1 standard deviations to the right of the mean. A positive z score indicates the raw score is greater than the mean, a negative z score indicates the raw score is less than the mean, and a z score of zero indicates the raw score equals the mean.

---

* It is sometimes useful to go from a z score to a raw score: $X = zs + \overline{X}$, or $X = z\sigma + \mu$.

In order to appreciate fully the value of transforming z scores, let's summarize three of their most important properties.*

1. The sum of the z scores is zero.

2. The mean of the z scores is zero.

3. The standard deviation and the variance of z scores are one.

Thus, if we computed the z scores for all the raw scores in a bell-shaped frequency distribution using Eq. (7.1), we would find that the z scores would sum to zero, their mean would be zero, and their standard deviation and variance would be one.

What is the value of transforming a raw score to a z score? The conversion to z scores always yields a mean of 0 and a standard deviation of 1, but it does not "normalize" a nonnormal distribution. However, if the *population of scores*

---

* A complete mathematical explanation of several z score properties is provided here for those interested:

1. The sum of the z scores is zero. Symbolically stated:

$$\Sigma z = 0$$

2. The mean of z scores is zero. Thus

$$z = \frac{\Sigma z}{N} = 0$$

3. The sum of the squared z scores equals N. Thus

$$\Sigma z^2 = N$$

This characteristic may be demonstrated mathematically:

$$\Sigma z^2 = \frac{\Sigma(X - \bar{X})^2}{s^2} = \frac{1}{s^2} \cdot \Sigma(X - \bar{X})^2$$

$$= \frac{N}{\Sigma(X - \bar{X})^2} \cdot \Sigma(X - \bar{X})^2$$

$$= N$$

4. The standard deviation and the variance of z scores are one. Thus

$$s_z = s_z^2 = 1$$

To demonstrate, we have

$$s_z^2 = \frac{\Sigma(z - \bar{z})^2}{N}$$

Since $\bar{z} = 0$, then

$$s_z^2 = \frac{\Sigma z^2}{N}$$

Since $\Sigma z^2 = N$, then

$$s_z^2 = \frac{N}{N} = 1$$

on a given variable is normal, we may express any score as a percentile rank by locating our z in the standard normal distribution. In addition, since z scores represent abstract numbers, as opposed to the concrete values of the original scores (inches, years of education, income, etc.), we may compare an individual's position on one variable with his or her position on a second. To understand these two important characteristics of z scores, we must make reference to the standard normal distribution.

7.3 The Standard Normal Distribution

The **standard normal distribution** is a theoretical model that is based on the mathematical equation in the footnote.* There is a family of curves that may be called normal. A normal curve's exact shape is determined by its population mean (μ) and its population standard deviation (σ). Each unique combination of a normally distributed population's μ and σ yields a unique normally distributed curve. Students sometimes have the mistaken impression that the shape of all normal curves is as regular as the coat hangers one particular dry cleaner might use. This is not the case. While all coat hangers share some basic characteristics, we all know that there are several variations of their characteristic shape. Normal curves also vary; for example, some are flatter than others and some more peaked. All normal curves do, however, share the characteristics summarized in Section 7.4.

7.4 Characteristics of the Standard Normal Distribution

All standard normal distributions have a μ of 0, a σ of 1, and a total area equal to 1.00. They are also symmetrical. If you folded Figure 7.2 along a

---

* It will be recalled that the Greek letters μ and σ represent the population mean and the standard deviation, respectively. The equation of the normal curve is

$$Y = \frac{Ni}{\sigma\sqrt{2\pi}} e^{\dfrac{-(X - \mu)^2}{2\sigma^2}}$$

where

Y = the frequency at a given value of X
σ = the standard deviation of the distribution
π = a constant equaling approximately 3.1416
e = approximately 2.7183
N = total frequency of the distribution
μ = the mean of the distribution
i = the width of the interval
X = any score in the distribution

It should be clear that there is a family of curves that may be called normal. By setting $Ni = 1$, a distribution is generated in which $\mu = 0$ and total area under the curve equals 1.

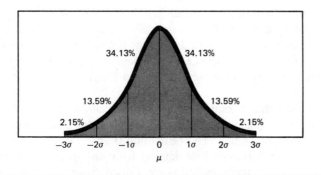

Figure 7.2 Areas between selected points under the normal curve.

line that would connect the point where the horizontal axis equals 0 and the highest point on the curve, two mirror images would result. A normal curve is sometimes referred to as a bell-shaped curve in that the mean, median, and modal values are equal and both sides of the curve slope gently away from its highest point.

The normal distribution is a mathematical abstraction that is not found in the real world. It consists of a family of distributions in which the curves approach but never touch the horizontal axis. This is another way of saying that no matter how distant a given value of the variable is from the central concentration, there are other values, both negative and positive, that are more distant. In contrast, empirical distributions have upper and lower limits beyond which no real measurements are found. If we are measuring height, weight, and age of humans, for example, we will find no real-world negative values for these variables (such as -50 pounds, -4 years of age), nor will there be any real observations beyond some upper limit (e.g., According to the Guinness Book of Records, the heaviest person on record weighs 1400 pounds, give or take a few).

There is also a fixed proportion of cases between a vertical line, or ordinate, erected at any one point on the horizontal axis and an ordinate erected at any other point. Taking a few reference points along the normal curve, we can make the following statements.

1. Between the mean and 1 standard deviation above the mean is found 34.13% of all the cases. Similarly, 34.13% of all the cases fall between the mean and 1 standard deviation below the mean. Stated in another way, 34.13% of the *area* under the curve is found between the mean and 1 standard deviation above the mean, and 34.13% of the *area* falls between the mean and 1 standard deviation below the mean.

2. Between the mean and 2 standard deviations above the mean is found 47.72% of all the cases. Since the normal curve is symmetrical, 47.72% of the area also falls between the mean and 2 standard deviations below the mean.

3. Finally, between the mean and 3 standard deviations above the mean is found 49.87% of all the cases. Similarly, 49.87% of the cases fall between the mean and 3 standard deviations below the mean. Thus, 99.74% (49.87% + 49.87%) of all the cases fall between ±3 standard deviations. You can verify this by summing the areas in Figure 7.2.

We see that a total of 6 standard deviation units (±3 standard deviations from the mean) account for nearly 100% of the cases, and hence nearly 100% of the range of values. The remaining 0.26% (100% − 99.74%) of the cases lie beyond ±3 standard deviations from the mean. This leads us to another characteristic of the standard normal distribution: It is comprised of an infinite number of cases since the curve never closes.

7.5 Transforming Raw Scores to z Scores

Many variables in the real world such as the weight of a large number of persons, their attitudes toward the military, or their scores on a standardized examination approximate a normal distribution. As a result, we can use our theoretical distribution, the standard normal distribution, as a basis for comparison. To make such a comparison, we must first transform the scores of the normally distributed variable to z scores. We are, in effect, creating a new variable with $\mu = 0$ and $\sigma = 1$, which is expressed in units of the standard normal curve. These units are referred to as standard deviation units or z scores. Figure 7.3 clarifies the relationships among raw scores on a standardized examination, z scores, and percentile ranks of a normally distributed variable. It assumes that $\mu = 500$ and $\sigma = 100$.

The mean of the raw scores in Figure 7.3 is 500 and the corresponding mean of the standard normal distribution is 0. A raw score of 600 is one standard deviation to the right of the mean of 500 since one standard deviation equaled 100. The z score of $+1$, which is equivalent to 600 in raw units, is also located one standard deviation to the right of its z score mean of 0. The following calculations provide further clarification. Applying Eq. (7.1), we have

if $X = 500$, $\mu = 500$, and $\sigma = 100$

$$\text{then} \quad z = \frac{X - \mu}{\sigma} = \frac{500 - 500}{100} = 0$$

if $X = 600$, $\mu = 500$, and $\sigma = 100$

$$\text{then} \quad z = \frac{X - \mu}{\sigma} = \frac{600 - 500}{100} = +1$$

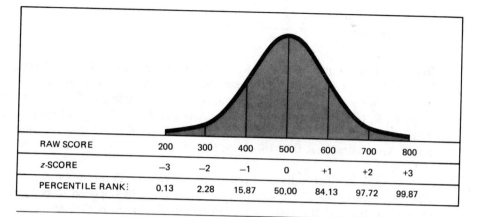

RAW SCORE	200	300	400	500	600	700	800
z-SCORE	−3	−2	−1	0	+1	+2	+3
PERCENTILE RANK	0.13	2.28	15.87	50.00	84.13	97.72	99.87

Figure 7.3 Relationships among raw scores, z scores, and percentile ranks of a normally distributed variable in which μ = 500 and σ = 100.

You should carefully note that these relationships apply *only to scores from normally distributed populations*. When scores are from a population that is skewed (e.g., the per capita income in the United States) rather than normally distributed, the standard normal distribution may not be used as a model for the data and z scores should not be computed. Transforming the raw scores to standard scores does not in any way alter the form of the original distribution nor does it, as we just saw, alter the relationship between the raw scores. The only change is to convert the mean to 0 and the standard deviation to 1. If the original distribution of scores is nonnormal, the *distribution* of z scores will be nonnormal. In other words, our transformation to z's will *not* convert a nonnormal distribution to a normal distribution.

7.5.1 Finding the Area between Given Scores

Up to this point, we have confined our discussion of area under the standard normal curve to selected points. As a matter of fact, however, it is possible to determine the percent of areas between *any* two points by making use of the tabled values of the area under the normal curve (see Table A in Appendix C). You have learned to convert a raw distribution of scores into a standard normal distribution so that you can use Table A, which was developed by a statistician who computed the area between the mean and every possible z score from 0 to 4.00. The left-hand column in Table A headed by z represents the deviation from the mean expressed in standard deviation units. *By referring to the body of the table, we can determine the proportion of total area between a given score and the mean (column B) and the area beyond a given score (column C).*

Thus, if a woman had a score of 24.65 on a normally distributed variable with μ = 16 and σ = 5, her z score would be +1.73 using Eq. (7.1).

$$z = \frac{X - \mu}{\sigma} = \frac{24.65 - 16}{5} = +1.73$$

Referring to column B in Table A, we find that 0.4582 or 45.82%* of the area lies between her score and the mean. Since 50% of the area also falls below the mean in a symmetrical distribution, we may conclude that 50% + 45.82%, or 95.82%, of all the area falls below a score of 24.65. Note that we can now translate this score into a percentile rank of 95.82. Referring to column C in Table A, we find that 0.0418 or 4.18% of the area lies beyond a z score of +1.73.

Suppose another individual obtained a score of 7.35 on the same normally distributed variable. His z score would be −1.73, as opposed to her z score of +1.73, because the raw scores (24.65 and 7.35) are both 8.65 units from the mean of 16. Using Eq. (7.1), we obtain

$$z = \frac{7.35 - 16}{5} = -1.73$$

Since the normal curve is symmetrical, only the areas corresponding to the positive z values are given in Table A. The proportion of cases between a negative z value and the mean will equal the proportion of cases between a positive z value of equal value and the mean. Thus, the area between the mean and a z of −1.73 is also equal to 0.4582 or 45.82% of the total area. The percentile rank of a score below the mean may be obtained by subtracting 45.82% either from 50% or directly from column C. In either case the percentile rank of a score of 7.35 is 4.18 because 4.18% of the scores were equal to or less than 7.35.

Before we consider some further uses of the normal curve, recall that one of its characteristics is that it contains an infinite number of cases. If you look at the value in column C associated with $z = 4.00$, you will find that the proportion of cases beyond $z = 4.00$ is 0.00003. The area beyond $z = 5.00$ is 0.0000003 (not shown in Table A), and indeed, there will always be cases regardless of how far we move to the left or right of the mean in this theoretical curve. Most social science texts do not show the area beyond 4 or 5 standard deviations; however, the precision of physics, for example, requires measurement up to ±10 to 15 standard deviations from the mean!

7.6 Illustrative Problems

Let us examine several sample problems in which we assume that the mean of the general population, μ, is equal to 100 on a standardized test, and the

---

* The areas under the normal curve are expressed as proportions of area. To convert to percentage of area, multiply by 100 or move the decimal two places to the right.

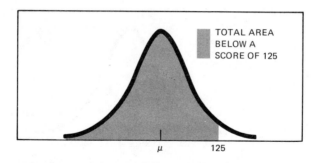

Figure 7.4   Proportion of area below a score of 125 in a normal distribution with $\mu = 100$ and $\sigma = 16$.

standard deviation, σ, is 16. It is assumed that the variable is normally distributed.

Problem 7.1

Mary Jones obtains a score of 125 on a state law board examination. What percent of cases falls between her score and the mean? What is her percentile rank in the general population?

At the outset, it is always wise to construct a crude diagram representing the relationships in question. Thus, in the present example the diagram would appear as shown in Figure 7.4. To find the value of z corresponding to $X = 125$, we subtract the population mean from 125 and divide by 16. Thus, using Eq. (7.1), we obtain

$$z = \frac{125 - 100}{16} = 1.56$$

Looking up 1.56 in column A (Table A), we find the value 0.4406 to the right in column B, which tells us that 44.06% of the area falls between the mean and 1.56 standard deviations above the mean. Mary Jones's percentile rank is, therefore, $50 + 44.06$ or 94.06.

Problem 7.2

John Doe scores 93 on a test. What is his percentile rank in the general population (Figure 7.5)?

$$z = \frac{93 - 100}{16} = -0.44$$

The minus sign indicates that the score is below the mean. Looking up 0.44 in column A, we find the value 0.3300 in column C, which tells us that 33.00% of the cases falls below his score. Thus, his percentile rank is 33.00.

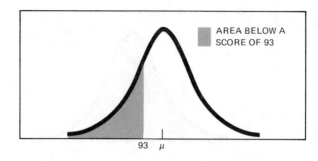

Figure 7.5 Proportion of area below a score of 93 in a normal distribution with $\mu = 100$ and $\sigma = 16$.

Problem 7.3

What proportion of the area falls between a score of 88 and a score of 120 (Figure 7.6)?

Note that to answer this question we do *not* subtract 88 from 120 and divide by σ. The areas in the normal probability curve are designated in relation to the mean as a fixed point of reference. We must, therefore, separately calculate the area between the mean and a score of 88 and the area between the mean and a score of 120. We then add the two areas to answer our problem.

Find the z corresponding to $X = 88$:

$$z = \frac{88 - 100}{16} = -0.75$$

Find the z corresponding to $X = 120$:

$$z = \frac{120 - 100}{16} = 1.25$$

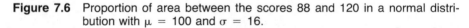

Figure 7.6 Proportion of area between the scores 88 and 120 in a normal distribution with $\mu = 100$ and $\sigma = 16$.

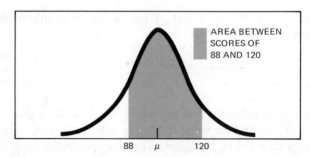

Find the required areas by referring to column A and column B (Table A):

Area between the mean and $z = -0.75$ is 0.2734

Area between the mean and $z = 1.25$ is 0.3944

Add the two areas together.
Thus, the proportion of the area between 88 and 120 = 0.6678 or 66.78%.

Problem 7.4

What percent of the area falls between a score of 123 and 135 (Figure 7.7)?

Again, we cannot obtain the answer directly; we must find the area between the mean and a score of 123 and subtract this from the area between the mean and a score of 135.

Find the z corresponding to $X = 135$:

$$z = \frac{135 - 100}{16} = 2.19$$

Find the z corresponding to $X = 123$:

$$z = \frac{123 - 100}{16} = 1.44$$

Find the required areas by referring to column A and column B:

Area between the mean and $z = 2.19$ is 0.4857 or 48.57%

Area between the mean and $z = 1.44$ is 0.4251 or 42.51%

Figure 7.7 Percent of area between the scores 123 and 135 in a normal distribution with $\mu = 100$ and $\sigma = 16$.

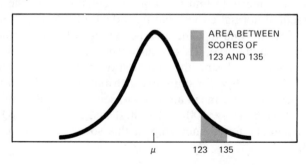

Subtract to obtain the area between 123 and 135. The result is

$$48.57 - 42.51 = 6.06\%$$

Problem 7.5

We stated earlier that our transformation to z scores permits us to compare an individual's position on one variable with his or her position on another variable. Let's illustrate this important use of z scores.

On a standard aptitude test John G. obtained a score of 245 on the verbal portion and 175 on the mathematics portion. The means and the standard deviations of each of these normally distributed tests are as follows: Verbal, $\mu = 220$, $\sigma = 50$; Math, $\mu = 150$, $\sigma = 25$. On which test did John score higher? We need to compare John's z score on each test. Thus

$$\text{verbal } z = \frac{245 - 220}{50} \qquad \text{math } z = \frac{175 - 150}{25}$$

$$= 0.50 \qquad\qquad = 1.00$$

We may conclude, therefore, that John scored higher on the math portion because his math score was one full standard deviation ($z = 1.00$) above the mean of the math portion, whereas his verbal score was only one-half of a standard deviation ($z = 0.50$) above the mean of the verbal portion. We can also express these scores as percentile ranks by using Table A. John's percentile rank is 84.13 on the math test and only 69.15 on the verbal test.

Problem 7.6

In each of the preceding problems, we knew the mean, standard deviation, and the value of the variable for which we wanted the corresponding percentage of area. There are numerous occasions when we are given the desired percentage of area and wish to know the value of the variable that yields that percentage. To illustrate, imagine that you wish to join a highly selective intellectual society that requires members to be in the upper 2% of the population in intelligence. The IQ test used for selection has a mean of 100 and a standard deviation of 16.

The first step is to find the value of z that cuts off the upper 2% of area in the standard normal curve, that is, 0.0200 of the area. Referring to column C in Table A, we find that the area beyond a z of 2.05 excludes 2.02% of the area in the normal curve. This is sufficiently close so that we'll use this value in our calculations. Using the equation $X = z\sigma + \mu$ when parameters are known or $X = zs + \bar{X}$ for normally distributed variables in which the sample standard deviation and mean are known (see footnote Section 7.2, p. 146), we find $X = 2.05 \times 16 + 100 = 132.8$. Thus, a minimum IQ of 133 would be needed to qualify for membership in this society. See Box 7.2 for a further example.

BOX 7.2

Designing Seat Size in Commercial Carriers: For Comfort or Profit?

Are you one of those rather wide-of-beam travelers who must gird your spirits for the next commercial airline flight (or take a trip on an intracity or intercity bus) because the seat width always seems to be about 2 inches shy of your comfort zone? Although measuring beam widths may not seem to be the most significant human enterprise, fortunes may be won or lost by common carriers by a seemingly minor shift in the width of the passenger seats. To illustrate, if a given aircraft has 50 rows, 4 across, it can accommodate a maximum load of 200 passengers. However, if it can trim a few inches from each seat and a few more from the aisle, one more seat per row can be added, bringing the passenger capacity up to 250. That is a 25% increase $[(250 - 200)/200 \times 100 = 25\%]$ in seating capacity!

Let's assume that the beam width of airline passengers (including elbows) is normally distributed with a mean of 20 inches and a standard deviation of 2. Cheapflight Airlines finds that by reducing each seat by 3 inches and the aisle by 5 inches, it can accommodate five seats to a row. By doing so, it can reduce ticket fares considerably and increase the number of flights running at or near capacity.

Taking the opposite tack, Broadbeam Airlines decides to emphasize passenger comfort in its advertising campaign. By trimming 8 inches off the aisle, it can increase the seat width to 22 inches. However, its passenger capacity remains 200. Broadbeam justifies its higher fares in terms of its luxurious seating.

What percentage of the passengers in each airline will find the seat width comfortable?

Broadbeam Airlines: $z = (22 - 20)/2 = 1.00$. Presumably, all passengers with a $z \leq 1.00$ will luxuriate in posterior comfort. This comes to a generous 84.13% (50% + 34.13%).

Cheapflight Airlines: $z = (17 - 20)/2 = -1.5$. Only passengers with a $z \leq -1.50$ will find the seating capacity adequate. Referring to Table A, we find that the area beyond z is 0.0668. Thus, only about 7% of Cheapflight's passengers will emerge from the flight without severely pinched posteriors. About 93% will be at their wits' end.

Now, suppose another airline wanted to join the battle of the beams and base their advertising pitch on the claim that 97.5% of its passengers could sit in total comfort. How wide would the seats have to be to justify this claim?

Notice that the problem here is the same as in Problem 7.6. We are given the desired percentage of area and would like to know the value of the variable that yields this percentage. The first step is to find the value of z that excludes 0.0250 (2.5%) of the area. Referring to column C in Table A, we find that the area beyond a z of 1.96 equals 0.0250. Using the equation $X = z\sigma + \mu$, we find $X = 1.96 \times 2 + 20 = 23.92$. In other words, the seats would have to be about 24 inches wide.

7.7 The Standard Deviation as an Estimate of Error and Precision

In the absence of any specific information, what is our best single basis for predicting a score that is obtained by any given individual? If the data are drawn from a normally distributed population, we find that the mean (or *any* measure of central tendency) is our best single predictor. The more compactly our scores are distributed about the mean, the smaller our errors will be in prediction, on the average. Conversely, the greater the spread or dispersion of scores about the mean is, the greater will be our errors in prediction, on the average, when we use the mean to estimate or predict scores. Since the standard deviation reflects the dispersion of scores, it becomes, in a sense, an estimate of error. For the same reasons the standard deviation is also a measure of precision. If two distributions have the same mean but different degrees of dispersion, the one with the smaller standard deviation provides more precise measures (i.e., measures closer to the mean), on the average.

To illustrate, imagine we are comparing two artillery units, Battery A and Battery B. A zero score means the shell was on target; a positive score means the shell went beyond the target, and a negative score indicates that it fell short of the target. Table 7.1 summarizes the results.

Although both batteries achieved the same mean, it is clear that more of the shells of Battery B landed close to the target than did the shells of Battery A. In other words, the firing of Battery B was more precise. This greater precision is reflected in the lower standard deviation of Battery B.

Table 7.1 Hypothetical scores made by two artillery batteries when firing at designated target

Distance from Target (in meters)	Frequency	
	Battery A	Battery B
200	2	0
150	4	1
100	5	5
50	7	10
0	9	13
−50	7	10
−100	5	5
−150	4	1
−200	2	0
	$\overline{X} = 0$	$\overline{X} = 0$
	$s = 102.74$	$s = 65.83^*$

* Note that, although the mean accuracy of both batteries was identical, the shelling of Battery B showed less dispersion or scattering.

7.8 Interpreting the Standard Deviation

In Chapter 6 we noted that an interpretation of the standard deviation is dependent on an understanding of the normal distribution. Imagine two random samples, A and B, from a normally distributed population with a mean age of 40. A total of 100 persons are included in sample A and 100 persons in sample B. We find that the ages of the persons in the two samples are distributed as shown in Figure 7.8.

While both curves have a mean of 40, it is apparent that sample A exhibits more variability than sample B, as shown by their frequency curves and respective standard deviations of 14.0 and 11.7. But we can say much more about the two distributions in Figure 7.8. For instance, we know from Table A that 68.26 (2 × 34.13) percent of the persons in sample A are between the ages of 26 and 54 since these values are −1 and +1 standard deviation units from the mean (40 + 14 = 54; 40 − 14 = 26 since s_A = 14.0). Recall that when we state that s_A = 14.0, we are saying that *one* standard deviation in sample A equals 14.0. By adding and subtracting one standard deviation (in this case it is 14.0 for sample A) to and from the mean of 40, we immediately know the ages equivalent to z = +1 and z = −1 since z scores are measured in standard deviation units. If you are interested in knowing the raw scores that are ±2 standard deviations from the mean, move 28 (2 × 14.0) units to the right and left of the mean. Hence, the ages 12 and 68 are 2 standard deviations from the mean in sample A. Their z score equivalents are −2 and +2. Looking at Table A you will find that 95.44 (2 × 47.72) percent of the persons in sample A are between the ages of 12 and 68.

For comparative purposes, consider sample B with its standard deviation

Figure 7.8 Two frequency curves with identical means but different standard deviations.

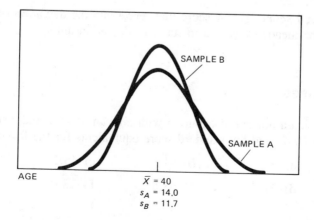

SAMPLE B

SAMPLE A

AGE

$\bar{X}$ = 40
s_A = 14.0
s_B = 11.7

of 11.7. The ages equivalent to $z = \pm 1$ can be calculated by adding 11.7 to the mean of 40 and subtracting 11.7 from the mean.

$$40 + 11.7 = 51.7$$

$$40 - 11.7 = 28.3$$

Whereas in sample A we found that the ages corresponding to $z = \pm 1$ were 26 and 54, we find that for sample B the ages are 28.3 and 51.7. This finding supports our earlier contention that sample B is more homogeneous (shows less variability) than sample A.

Summary

In this chapter we demonstrated the value of the standard deviation for comparison of the dispersion of scores in different distributions of a variable, the interpretation of a score with respect to a single distribution, and the comparison of scores on two or more variables. We showed how to convert raw scores into units of the standard normal curve (transformation to z scores). Various characteristics of the standard normal curve were explained. A series of problems demonstrated the various applications of the conversion of normally distributed variables to z scores and z scores to raw scores.

We considered the standard deviation as an estimate of error and as an estimate of precision. Finally, we discussed the standard deviation as an interpretive tool.

Terms to Remember

Standard normal distribution   A frequency distribution that has a mean of 0, a standard deviation of 1, and a total area equal to 1.00.

Standard score (z)   A score that represents the deviation of a specific score from the mean, expressed in standard deviation units.

Exercises

1. Given a normal distribution with a mean of 45.2 and a standard deviation of 10.4, find the standard score equivalents for the following scores:

   a) 55   b) 41   c) 45.2

   d) 31.5   e) 68.4   f) 18.9

2. Find the proportion of area under the normal curve between the mean and the following *z* scores:

a) −2.05   **b)** −1.90   **c)** −0.25

d) +0.40   **e)** +1.65   **f)** +1.96

3. Find the proportion of area under the normal curve beyond *z*:

a) −2.05   **b)** −1.90   **c)** −0.25

d) +0.40   **e)** +1.65   **f)** +1.96

4. Given a normal distribution based on 1000 cases with a mean of 50 and a standard deviation of 10, find:

a) The proportion of area and the number of cases *between* the mean and the following scores:

60   70   45   25

b) The proportion of area and the number of cases *above* the following scores:

60   70   45   25   50

c) The proportion of area and the number of cases *between* the following scores:

60–70   25–60   45–70   25–45

5. Below are student Spiegel's scores, the mean, and the standard deviation on each of three tests given to 3000 students.

Test	μ	σ	Spiegel's Score
Arithmetic	47.2	4.8	53
Verbal comprehension	64.6	8.3	71
Geography	75.4	11.7	72

a) Convert each of Spiegel's test scores to standard scores.

b) On which test did Spiegel do the best? On which was he the worst?

c) Spiegel's score in arithmetic was surpassed by how many students? his score in verbal comprehension? in geography?

d) What assumption must be made in order to answer the preceding question?

e) Spiegel's friend Sue had a *z* score of −1.1 on the geography test. What was her raw score?

6. On a normally distributed mathematics aptitude test, for females

$$\mu = 60, \qquad \sigma = 10$$

and for males

$$\mu = 64, \qquad \sigma = 8.$$

    a) Arthur obtained a score of 62. What is his percentile rank relative to the male and female scores?

    b) Helen's percentile rank is 73 relative to the female scores. What is her percentile rank relative to the male scores?

    c) In comparison with other students of their own sex, who did better, Arthur or Helen?

7. If frequency curves were constructed for each of the following, which do you feel would approximate a normal curve?

    a) Heights of a large representative sample of adult American males.

    b) Means of a large number of samples with a fixed N (say, $N = 100$) drawn from a normally distributed population of scores.

    c) Weights, in ounces, of ears of corn selected randomly from a cornfield.

    d) Annual income, in dollars, of the breadwinner of a large number of American families selected at random.

    e) Weight, in ounces, of all fish caught in a popular fishing resort in a season.

8. In a normal distribution with $\mu = 72$ and $\sigma = 12$:

    a) What is the score at the 25th percentile?

    b) What is the score at the 75th percentile?

    c) What is the score at the 9th decile?

    d) Find the percent of cases scoring above 80.

    e) Find the percent of cases scoring below 66.

    f) Between what scores do the middle 50% of all cases lie?

9. Answer Exercise 8(a) through (f), for:

    a) $\mu = 72$ and $\sigma = 8$

    b) $\mu = 72$ and $\sigma = 4$

    c) $\mu = 72$ and $\sigma = 2$

10. Given the following information, determine whether Larry did better on Test I or Test II. On which test did Mindy do better?

	Test I	Test II
μ	500	24
σ	40	1.4
Larry's scores	550	26
Mindy's scores	600	25

11. Are all sets of z scores normally distributed? Why or why not?

12. You have just completed interviewing 75 ministers. Initial calculations indicate that the number of years of formal education they have completed is normally distributed with a mean of 13.4 and a standard deviation of 3.0.

    a) How many years of education must a minister have completed to be in the top decile? (*Hint:* Find z at the 90th percentile.)

    b) How many years of education must a minister have completed to be 1 standard deviation above the mean?

    c) Approximately how many ministers will be within ± 2 z scores of the mean?

    d) Interpret the standard deviation for this problem. What does it tell you.

13. Your roommate has just received the results of her Graduate Record Examination in the mail. The mean of the verbal section was 510, the standard deviation 102, and the scores were normally distributed. Her reported score was 640, but the computer did not print her percentile rank. She has never had a statistics course and needs your assistance to calculate her percentile rank and help her understand the meaning of her score. State your explanation briefly. Feel free to use visual examples to supplement your answer.

14. Several of your friends also took the Graduate Record Examination discussed in Exercise 13. Compute the z score and the percentile rank for each of the following scores:

Recall that

$$\overline{X} = 510 \quad \text{and} \quad s = 102$$

X	z Score	Percentile Rank
270		
780		
500		
410		
565		

15. **a)** Which of the scores in Exercise 14 would place your friends in the top 10% of those who took the test?

b) The upper quartile?

c) Above the median?

d) In the lowest quartile?

e) What percent of the area under the curve lies between the lowest and highest score?

f) Compute the two scores that lie equidistant from the mean and include 95% of the area under the curve.

16. Calculate the z score for each of the following:

a) A score of 36 on a police sergeant's promotion examination, given a mean of 25 and a standard deviation of 3.1.

b) An IQ of 110 given a mean of 100 and a standard deviation of 15.

c) A height of 6'5" in the National Basketball Association, given a mean of 6'6" and a standard deviation of 5 inches. (*Hint:* Convert to inches.)

d) A job satisfaction score of 59, given a mean of 75 and a standard deviation of 10.

17. Common colds normally require 7 to 10 days for complete remission. A friend who is a health food advocate read that sucking on a zinc gluconate tablet three times a day is supposed to reduce the recovery time. She knows you are taking a statistics course and needs your help analyzing the following data she has collected from friends who used zinc tablets to recover quickly from a cold. They reported the following number of days to recover completely:

6	7	6
4	4	3
7	5	5
5	5	7
8	6	9
3	8	4
2	5	5
6	4	6

Assume the data approximate a normal curve.

a) Compute the mean and standard deviation.

b) Do the zinc tablets appear to work?

c) How many recovery days place the patient at the 25th percentile?

d) Again, assuming a normal curve, what proportion required 4 days or less? What proportion required 7 or more days?

18. Is there more than one normal distribution?

19. In what sense can the standard deviation be regarded as a measure of precision?

20. Refer to Box 7.2. The values of μ and σ were given for the populations and included both males and females. Suppose the mean beam is 18 for females, 22 for males with $\sigma = 2$ for both populations.

a) What percentage of males and females flying Cheapflight will be comfortable?

b) What percentage of males and females flying Broadbeam will be comfortable?

21. How wide would the seats have to be in order to achieve the comfort zone for 90.32% of the (a) females? (b) males?

chapter **8**

An Introduction to Contingency Tables

8.1 Introduction

8.2 Dependent and Independent Variables

8.3 The Bivariate Contingency Table

8.4 Percentaging Contingency Tables

8.5 Existence, Direction, and Strength of a Relationship

8.6 Introduction to Measures of Association for Contingency Tables

8.7 Nominal Measures of Association: Lambda

8.8 Ordinal Measures of Association

8.9 Goodman and Kruskal's Gamma

8.10 Somer's *d*

8.11 Kendall's tau-*b*

8.1 Introduction

In Chapters 3 to 7 we have considered one variable at a time, focusing on the frequency distribution, percentiles, measures of central tendency, and measures of dispersion. We now turn to examining the statistical relationship between two variables.

Social scientists have a primary interest in determining the extent to which variables are related in order to understand and predict behavior. Consider the following examples: In what manner is the variable years of educational attainment related to annual income? Are additional years of education a wise investment in terms of a person's potential earning power? Is a person's choice of leisure activities determined by his or her social class? To what extent is group cohesiveness a function of work group size? Is interest in politics related to a woman's parents' political involvement? To what extent is the "welfare experience" shared by two or more generations within a family?

8.2 Dependent and Independent Variables

All of the questions can be answered by analyzing two variables simultaneously. A *bivariate* or two-variable analysis normally involves specifying a dependent and an independent variable. The **dependent variable** (symbolized by Y) is

167

the variable that is being predicted or explained. It is dependent on the **independent variable** (symbolized by X) which is the predictor variable. In an experimental context the dependent variable is referred to as the criterion variable and the independent variable as the experimental or treatment variable. In the videotape instructional example outlined in Chapter 1 the instruction technique (lecture versus videotape of the lecture) would be the independent or experimental variable (X) and the students' test scores would be the dependent or criterion variable (Y).

Consider the relationship between marital status and employment status of American women. Until relatively recently, it was fairly easy to predict the likelihood of a woman holding a job if we knew her marital status, as married women seldom worked outside the home. Such a relationship can be diagramed as shown in Figure 8.1.

Marital status is the independent or predictor variable and employment status is the dependent variable or the variable we wish to predict. The arrow indicates that marital status hypothetically exerts an influence on employment status. Whether a variable is designated the independent variable or the dependent variable is determined by its usage. Marital status could be a dependent variable if we wished to predict it from one's age. Or employment status could be used to predict an adult's self-esteem, in which case it would be the independent variable and self-esteem the dependent variable. The point is that a variable must be placed into a framework or research situation before it can be designated as either independent or dependent.

8.3 The Bivariate Contingency Table

In Chapter 3 you learned about frequency distributions. We will now return to that topic as we begin to consider the relationship between two variables. The U.S. Department of Labor conducted a national study of employment patterns among American women.* Using hypothetical data from that study, let us consider the relationship between employment status and marital status, which was diagramed in Figure 8.1. The frequency distributions for these variables are presented in Table 8.1.

The percentages of cases within each category reflect the responses of the actual national sample; however, the distributions presented are based on only 200 hypothetical responses in order to simplify the presentation. The frequency distribution was constructed following a personal interview with each of our 200 hypothetical respondents. A portion of this information is presented with the frequency distributions. At the time of the interview 98 (49%) of the 200 women were employed and 102 (51%) were not. Table 8.1 also shows that 35 respondents were never married, 125 are married, 15 are divorced, and 25 are

---

* U.S. Department of Labor, *U.S. Working Women.*

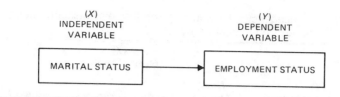

Figure 8.1 Relationship between marital status and employment status.

widowed. Table 8.1 does not conveniently tell us the marital status of the 98 employed women nor of the 102 women not employed. We wish to know if a woman's marital status (the independent variable) might serve as a useful predictor of her employment status (the dependent variable).

Several other variables could have been considered as predictors of employment status, including the woman's financial needs, educational attainment, the number of children in her home, etc.; however, here we seek only a partial understanding of why some women work and others do not by examining only the relationship between employment status and marital status. The simultaneous use of two or more predictor variables is discussed in Chapter 11.

Table 8.2 presents a bivariate distribution of the two variables. The 21 women in the upper left-hand cell of Table 8.2 have never been married *and* are presently employed. We also can say that the 21 of the 35 never married respondents are employed and 14 are not employed. Had the tabulations of the individual respondents in Table 8.1 been shown in their entirety, we would be able to identify the 21 women whose pattern of responses was "employed–

Table 8.1 Tabulations and frequency distributions for employment status and marital status

Respondent	Employment Status	Marital Status
1	Employed	Divorced
2	Not Employed	Never Married
3	Not Employed	Married
⋮	⋮	⋮
200	Employed	Married

Employment Status	Frequency	%	Marital Status	Frequency	%
Employed	(98)	49.0	Never married	(35)	17.5
Not Employed	(102)	51.0	Married	(125)	62.5
Total	(200)	100.0	Divorced	(15)	7.5
			Widowed	(25)	12.5
			Total	(200)	100.0

Table 8.2 Contingency table summarizing the relationship between employment status and marital status

	(X) Marital Status				
(Y) **Employment Status**	*Never* *Married*	*Married*	*Divorced*	*Widowed*	Total
Employed	21	60	11	6	98
Not Employed	14	65	4	19	102
Total	35	125	15	25	$N = 200$

never married.'' We now have available the **conditional distribution** of the two variables, and we can examine the distribution of the categories of one variable under the differing conditions or categories of another.

Table 8.2 has been presented in the manner generally used by social scientists. Normally, the independent variable (X) is the column variable and is placed at the top of the table; the dependent variable (Y) is the row variable and is placed to the left of the table. However, this convention is not followed by all social scientists, and it is important that you carefully examine tables to avoid misinterpretation. The boxes or cells contain the cell frequencies (e.g., 21, 60, 11, 6, etc.) and/or the cell percentages. The column and row totals of the contingency table are referred to as *marginals*. A **contingency table** shows the joint distribution of two variables. There are as many column marginals as there are categories of the variable placed at the top of the table, and their values are the column totals (35, 125, 15, and 25). The row marginals are the row totals (98 and 102). Marginals provide a convenient summary of the distribution of cases for each of the variables. In fact, you have probably noticed that the marginals in Table 8.2 are equivalent to the frequency distributions in Table 8.1.

Table 8.2 is a 2 × 4 table (read ''2 by 4 table'') because there are two rows and four columns. Tables can have any number of rows and columns, depending on the number of categories of the variables.

8.4 Percentaging Contingency Tables

Contingency tables can be percentaged in three ways, depending on the base (denominator) that is used.* Table 8.3 illustrates the three ways of percentaging a table.

The most common way of percentaging a table (assuming that the inde-

---

* In Chapter 2 you learned that a proportion is calculated by dividing a quantity in one category by the total of all the categories, and that a proportion can be converted to a percentage when multiplied by 100.

Table 8.3 Three ways of percentaging a contingency table

Original table

(X)
Marital Status

(Y) Employment Status	Never Married	Married	Divorced	Widowed	Total
Employed	21	60	11	6	98
Not Employed	14	65	4	19	102
Total	35	125	15	25	N = 200

(a) Percentaging down using column marginals as the base

(X)
Marital Status

(Y) Employment Status	Never Married	Married	Divorced	Widowed
Employed	60.0%	48.0%	73.3%	24.0%
Not Employed	40.0%	52.0%	26.7%	76.0%
Total	100.0%	100.0%	100.0%	100.0%

(b) Percentaging across using the row marginals as the base

(X)
Marital Status

(Y) Employment Status	Never Married	Married	Divorced	Widowed	Total
Employed	21.4%	61.2%	11.2%	6.1%	99.9%*
Not Employed	13.7%	63.7%	3.9%	18.6%	99.9%*

* Does not add to 100.0% due to rounding.

(c) Percentaging on the total using the total number of cases as the base

(X)
Marital Status

(Y) Employment Status	Never Married	Married	Divorced	Widowed	Total
Employed	10.5%	30.0%	5.5%	3.0%	
Not Employed	7.0%	32.5%	2.0%	9.5%	
Total					100.0%

pendent variable is the column variable) is that of *percentaging down* as in Table 8.3(a) where you see that the percentages in each of the marital status columns total 100%. For example, 60% and 40% in the never married column total 100%. We typically percentage down because we are normally interested in assessing the effect of the independent variable on the dependent variable. When we percentage down, the column marginals (35, 125, 15, and 25) become the base (the denominator) with which the percentages are calculated. Focusing again on the upper left-hand cell, we can calculate that 60.0% of the never married respondents are employed by dividing 21 by 35, which is the column marginal for the never married respondents. *Percentaging down* is also referred to as *percentaging on the independent variable* when the independent variable is the column variable. Percentaging down allows us to determine the effect of the independent variable by comparing across the percentages within a row, that is, by comparing people in different categories of the independent variable. In Table 8.3(a) we see, by comparing across the employed row, that 60.0% of the never married respondents are employed, 48.0% of the married respondents are employed, as are 73.0% of the divorced respondents and 24.0% of the widowed respondents. Thus we see that the overall relationship between the two variables is consistent with what we might assume logically.

   Percentaging across, as illustrated in Table 8.3(b), means that the row marginals are used as the base and that the percentages in both of the employment status rows total 100%. We see that 21.4% of the employed respondents have never married, whereas 13.7% of those respondents who are not employed have never married. Rather than percentaging down and comparing across as we did in Table 8.3(a), we now are percentaging across and comparing up and down. One value of percentaging across in Table 8.3(b) is that a profile of the employed versus the not employed respondents can be established in terms of their marital status. Such a usage does *not* provide us with any indication of the extent to which the independent variable affects the dependent variable.

   A third method of percentaging uses the total number of cases as the base; therefore, the sum of all the cell percentages is 100%. Percentaging on the total (200) as in Table 8.3(c) offers yet another interpretation of the data. The 10.5% figure in the upper left-hand cell indicates that 10.5% or 21 of the 200 respondents have never married *and* are employed. The joint percentage distribution that results from percentaging on the total, like the second method, also does *not* allow for determining the influence of the independent variable on the dependent variable and is rarely presented; however, it is an appropriate method of percentaging in certain instances. (See Statistics in Action 8.1.)

8.5 Existence, Direction, and Strength of a Relationship

We are now ready to consider whether two variables are statistically related and, if so, in what manner. Table 8.4 illustrates five unique relationships between family income and marital satisfaction. Family income is the independent variable because it is used to predict marital satisfaction, the dependent variable.

Labeling the categories of ordinal or interval scale variables normally follows a standard convention.* The lowest category of the independent variable (the column variable) is placed at the left, and the highest category of the independent variable is placed at the right. When labeling the dependent variable (the row variable), the highest category is placed at the top and the lowest category at the bottom.† You are cautioned that this convention is not followed by all social scientists; therefore, you should carefully examine all tables before interpreting the data.

Comparison of the conditional distribution of the two variables determines whether a relationship exists between the variables. In Table 8.4(a), for instance, all the conditional relationships are identical in that 60% of the low-income marriages are characterized as highly satisfying, as are 60% of the high-income marriages. There is also no difference when we compare percentages across the low marital satisfaction row, and therefore knowing a couple's income does not help us predict their marital satisfaction. Stated another way, income and marital satisfaction are unrelated in Table 8.4(a). The difference in these percentages (0% in both instances), which was calculated by comparing the percentages within the categories of the dependent variable between the two extreme categories of the independent variable, is referred to as the **percentage difference** or **epsilon (ε).** A relationship is said to exist between two variables when one or more of the epsilons are not equal to 0.

Table 8.4(b) has also been percentaged down due to the placement of the independent variable. Comparing the percentages across the high category of marital satisfaction, we note a 20% percentage difference. Forty percent of the low-income marriages versus 60% of the high-income marriages reportedly are highly satisfying: Thus, epsilon equals 20. The reverse is true upon comparing the percentages across the low category of marital satisfaction where we see that a larger percentage (60%) of the low-income marriages are characterized by low marital satisfaction than are high-income marriages (40%), and therefore epsilon equals 20. We can conclude that income has a moderate **positive relationship** with marital satisfaction. Higher-income couples are more likely to report higher marital satisfaction than are lower-income couples.

Relationships between two variables can either be positive or negative. A positive relationship is one in which high scores on one variable tend to be associated with high scores on the other variable, and conversely, low scores on one variable tend to be associated with low scores on the other variable. Naturally, we cannot specify the direction of a relationship when one or both

---

* This placement of the categories of a nominal-level variable in a contingency table is determined by the user's personal preference because the categories are not ordered.

† This placement of the variables and variable categories corresponds to other statistical graphs including the scatter diagrams presented in Chapters 9 and 10.

Statistics in Action 8.1

Curiosity Is Dangerous to More than Cats: Finding Column, Row, and Total Percentages

Take the problem of the seemingly insatiable curiosity of children. Their explorations of the worlds of sight, smell, sound, and touch often get them into serious difficulties. Look at the following table. Here we find a summary of a study conducted on 950 children who had ingested products containing hydrocarbons (Anas et al., 1981). From the results, we can learn what dangerous hydrocarbons are most commonly ingested by children and how often hospitalization is required. Armed with such knowledge, community agencies can often undertake educational and preventive programs that are targeted on both careless adults and offending substances.

By looking across the "Hospitalized" row, we see that furniture polish is the most frequent offender, followed by gasoline, lighter fluid, and paint thinner. Reading across the "Nonhospitalized" row, we see that most cases (800) do not require hospitalization.

Frequency of children hospitalized and not hospitalized following ingestion of substances containing hydrocarbons

Outcome	Substance Ingested							
	Cleaning Fluids	Furniture Polish	Gasoline	Kerosene	Lighter Fluid	Paint Thinner	Other	Total
Hospitalized	6	48	28	12	23	23	10	150
Nonhospitalized	24	312	128	72	112	88	64	800

$N = 950$

Prepare tables showing:

a) The column percentages (percentage on the independent variable).

b) The row percentages.

c) The total percentages.

d) Looking at the raw data, identify the substance that accounted for the largest number of hospitalization cases. Which accounted for the least number?

e) Looking at Table (a) in the answers, identify the substance that is most likely to result in hospitalization. Which substance is least likely to result in hospitalization?

f) Looking at Table (b) in the answers, which substance accounted for the greatest percentage of total hospitalizations? Which accounted for the least?

g) On the basis of the consideration of all ways of calculating percentages, which substances appear to be most important to "keep out of the reach of children"?

ANSWERS
Table (a) Column percentages

Outcome	Cleaning Fluids	Furniture Polish	Gasoline	Kerosene	Lighter Fluid	Paint Thinner	Other
Hospitalized	20	13	18	14	17	21	14
Nonhospitalized	80	87	82	86	83	79	86
	100%	100%	100%	100%	100%	100%	100%

Table (b) Row percentages

Outcome	Cleaning Fluids	Furniture Polish	Gasoline	Kerosene	Lighter Fluid	Paint Thinner	Other	Total
Hospitalized	4	32	19	8	15	15	7	100%
Nonhospitalized	3	39	16	9	14	11	8	100%

Table (c) Total percentages

Outcome	Cleaning Fluids	Furniture Polish	Gasoline	Kerosene	Lighter Fluid	Paint Thinner	Other	Total
Hospitalized	1	5	3	1	2	2	1	
Nonhospitalized	3	33	13	8	12	9	7	
								100%

d) Furniture polish produces the greatest number of hospitalizations and cleaning fluids produce the least. Looking only at the raw data, we might be tempted to assert that furniture polish is the most dangerous substance and cleaning fluid is the least.

e) Paint thinner is most likely to result in hospitalization (21% of the time) and furniture polish is least likely (13% of the time).

f) When we compute the row percentages, we find that ingesting furniture polish leads to the greatest percentage of hospitalizations and cleaning fluids leads to the least.

g) From the point of view of accessibility, it is apparent that many children have easy access to furniture polishes. Table (c) reveals that 38% (5 + 33) of all cases involved furniture polishes. However, Table (a) shows that furniture polishes produced a relatively low rate of hospitalization among children ingesting these products (13%). Paint thinner is both fairly accessible [11% of all cases—see Table (c)] and leads to the highest rate of hospitalization [21%—see Table (a)]. Table (c) indicates that cleaning fluids are least accessible (4% of all ingestions), but lead to a 20% hospitalization rate [see Table (a)]. So, you see, there is no simple answer except "All those substances are potentially dangerous—some because of the sheer numbers of children who ingest them and others because of their inherent danger once ingested."

Table 8.4   Illustration of five types of relationships in contingency tables

(a) No relationship

	(X) Family Income	
(Y) Marital Satisfaction	Low	High
High	60%	60%
Low	40%	40%
Total	100%	100%

(b) Positive relationship

	(X) Family Income	
(Y) Marital Satisfaction	Low	High
High	40%	60%
Low	60%	40%
Total	100%	100%

(c) Negative relationship

	(X) Family Income	
(Y) Marital Satisfaction	Low	High
High	60%	40%
Low	40%	60%
Total	100%	100%

(d) Perfect positive relationship

	(X) Family Income	
(Y) Marital Satisfaction	Low	High
High	0%	100%
Low	100%	0%
Total	100%	100%

(e) Perfect negative relationship

	(X) Family Income	
(Y) Marital Satisfaction	Low	High
High	100%	0%
Low	0%	100%
Total	100%	100%

of the variables are nominal level, as in Table 8.2. If the variables are not measured at the ordinal level, we can only speak of the existence and strength of a relationship.

Table 8.4(c) provides an example of a **negative relationship.** Variables are said to be negatively related when high scores on one variable tend to be accompanied by low scores on the other. Conversely, low scores on one variable tend to be associated with high scores on the other. We see in Table 8.4(c) that high-income marriages tend to be less satisfying than low-income marriages. The variables have a moderate, negative relationship.

The strength of a relationship can range from nonexistent to perfect. A *nonexistent relationship* is one in which knowledge of the independent variable does not improve our prediction of the dependent variable or when the variables are unrelated, as in Table 8.4(a). A **perfect relationship** is one in which knowledge of the independent variable allows a perfect prediction of the dependent variable or vice versa. Table 8.4(d) presents a **perfect positive relationship** between family income and marital satisfaction and Table 8.4(e) shows a **perfect negative relationship.**

8.6 Introduction to Measures of Association for Contingency Tables

Several measures of association appropriate for contingency tables are presented in the remainder of this chapter, none of which requires that we make assumptions about the population distribution. Those measures that have been developed specifically for nominal-level data provide a measure of the strength of the relationship. The measures for ordinal-level or interval-level data include both a measure of the strength and the direction of the relationship.

All of the measures are either symmetric or asymmetric. **Symmetric measures of association** make no distinction between the independent and dependent variable. Symmetric measures provide a single summary value of mutual or two-way association. If we wished to establish the relationship between two items in a job satisfaction scale, a symmetric measure of association would be appropriate. We would be interested only in determining the relationship between the two items, neither of which would be classified as independent or dependent.

An **asymmetric measure of association** is a summary value of one-way association and requires that the independent and dependent variables be specified. Two summary values are available when an asymmetric statistic is calculated: one value results from designating the row variable as independent, and a second value results from designating the column variable as independent.* An ordinal-level asymmetric measure of association would be an appropriate measure to use if the column variable were income and the row variable were wealth. In this special instance you might wish to examine the relationship between these variables, first assuming that income has a causal effect upon wealth, and second assuming that wealth has a causal effect upon income. A summary statistic could be computed for each of these two relationships.

---

* Unless noted otherwise, we will assume that X designates the independent variable and that it is the column variable.

8.7 Nominal Measures of Association: Lambda

Computing percentage differences, or epsilon (ϵ), for data in contingency form is only one way of determining the existence of a relationship between two variables. In addition, social scientists are interested in the degree to which a variable is helpful in predicting an attitude or behavior as measured by a second variable. **Lambda (λ)** is a statistic used to evaluate the usefulness of one variable in predicting another. It helps answer the question: Do we merely need to know the marginal values of the dependent variable in order to predict, or does it help to partition the dependent variable into categories of the independent variable?

Lambda is a measure of association for nominal-level variables, based on the logic of **proportional reduction in error,** known as **PRE.*** It is useful for any size table. While computational procedures are available for asymmetrical and symmetrical lambda, only asymmetrical lambda will be presented.†

Let's consider the logic of PRE measures in general and lambda specifically using the data first presented in Table 8.2, repeated here as Table 8.5.

If you knew that 102 women in a sample of 200 women were not employed and you were asked to predict or guess the employment status of the 200 women in the sample without knowledge of their marital status, you would guess that none of them is employed, given the row marginals. Such a strategy would result in your correctly predicting 102 of the 200 women in the sample because 102 are not employed. You would have incorrectly predicted the employment status of 98 women. Therefore, your guess of "not employed" would result in a slightly reduced number of errors.

If, on the other hand, you were asked to predict employment status while knowing marital status, you could make more refined guesses. If you knew a woman had been divorced *or* had never married, you would no longer want to guess "not employed" because the majority of women in *both* marital status categories are employed.

In order to analyze the usefulness of the partitioning of the data, social scientists calculate lambda, which expresses the relationship between the errors produced with the first type of guess and the errors produced with the second type of guess. To formalize this logic, statisticians refer to the predictions from tables as being based on one of two rules. Both rules govern procedures aimed at reducing the error in predictions. Rule I for lambda assumes no knowledge about the independent variable.

---

* Lambda can be computed using ordinal- or interval-level data; however, lambda ignores ranks and intervals, and information would be lost. Lambda or another appropriate statistic such as phi, Cramer's V, or the contingency coefficient (which are presented in Chapter 16) must be computed whenever *any* of the variables are measured at the nominal level.

† Symmetrical lambda measures the mutual influence of two variables on each other.

Table 8.5 Employment status by marital status

(Y) Employment Status	Never Married	Married	Divorced	Widowed	Total
	(X) Marital Status				
Employed	21	60	11	6	98
Not Employed	14	65	4	19	102
Total	35	125	15	25	N = 200

Rule I: Predict the modal category of the dependent variable.*

In essence, we only use the row marginals of the dependent variable to make our prediction.

Given additional information about our sample of women, we should be able to improve our prediction of their employment status. The data in Table 8.5 indicate, for example, that the women's employment status is related to their marital status. Now let us predict employment status given information about the respondent's marital status, which is the independent variable. We now use *Rule II for lambda,* which assumes knowledge of the independent variable.

Rule II: Predict the within-category mode of the independent variable.

Now we would predict that all of the never married respondents are employed, since the within-category mode of the never married group is the employed category of the dependent variable. Rule II requires that we predict all of the married respondents are not employed, all of the divorced respondents are employed, and all of the widowed respondents are not employed.

Let's see how many errors in prediction we would make if we used Rule II. We would have correctly predicted the employment status of 21 out of the 35 never married respondents (therefore, 14 errors in prediction), 65 of the 125 married respondents (60 errors), 11 of the 15 divorced respondents (4 errors), and 19 of the 25 widowed respondents (6 errors). We have made a total of 84 prediction errors (14 + 60 + 4 + 6) given the respondents' marital status (using Rule II), compared to 98 prediction errors *without* knowledge of the respondents' marital status (using Rule I). Thus, we have reduced our prediction errors by 14 (98 − 84 = 14) now that we have information on the independent variable. Lambda can be calculated using the following equation, which is based on shifting from Rule I to Rule II once knowledge of the independent variable is available:

---

* The mode of a category was defined in Chapter 5 as the score that occurs with the greatest frequency.

$$\lambda = \frac{(\text{errors using Rule I}) - (\text{errors using Rule II})}{\text{errors using Rule I}} \qquad (8.1)*$$

Substituting into Eq. (8.1), we find that lambda equals 0.14.

$$\lambda = \frac{98 - 84}{98} = \frac{14}{98} = 0.14$$

While lambda is easily calculated using Eq. (8.1) in a table with few rows and cells, this is not the case with a larger table, and a computational equation is available for these purposes:

$$\lambda = \frac{\Sigma \text{ maximum frequency } (X) - \text{maximum frequency } (Y)}{N - \text{maximum frequency } (Y)} \qquad (8.2)$$

where

maximum frequency (X) = the within-category mode for each category of the independent variable

maximum frequency (Y) = the modal frequency of the dependent variable, and

N = sample size

In words, Eq. (8.2) can be read:

$$\text{lambda} = \frac{\begin{array}{c}\text{sum of the within-category}\\ \text{modes of the independent}\\ \text{variable}\end{array} - \begin{array}{c}\text{modal frequency of}\\ \text{the dependent variable}\end{array}}{\text{sample size} - \begin{array}{c}\text{modal frequency of}\\ \text{the dependent variable}\end{array}}$$

Applying Eq. (8.2) to the data in Table 8.5, we obtain

$$\lambda = \frac{(21 + 65 + 11 + 19) - 102}{200 - 102}$$

$$= \frac{14}{98}$$

$$= 0.14$$

---

* Equation (8.1) assumes Y is the dependent variable. Under these circumstances lambda is frequently written λ_{yx} with the first subscript designating the dependent variable. Subscript variables, for example, x and y, will appear in lowercase italics throughout this text.

8.7.1 Interpretation of Lambda

The value of lambda is determined by the proportional reduction in error when predicting the dependent variable on shifting from prediction Rule I to prediction Rule II. Formally stated, the prediction rules for lambda are:

Rule I: Predict the modal category of the dependent variable.

Rule II: Predict the within-category mode of the independent variable.

Lambda measures the strength of the relationship and ranges from 0 when the variables are not related to 1 when they are perfectly related. If lambda equals 0, knowledge of the independent variable is of no value when predicting the dependent variable, and we cannot predict any better when shifting from Rule I to Rule II than we can by using only Rule I. When lambda equals 1, knowledge of the independent variable allows you to predict the dependent variable perfectly.

A lambda of 0.14 indicates a weak relationship between marital status and employment status. Multiplying by 100 allows us to state that we have reduced the number of prediction errors by 14% when moving from Rule I to Rule II. Rule I resulted in an error rate of 98/200 or 49%, and Rule II resulted in an error rate of 84/200 or 42%. Shifting from Rule I to Rule II reduced the rate 7% (49% − 42% = 7%) which is the *absolute* reduction in error. To calculate *proportional* reduction in error, we divide the 7% absolute reduction in error by the original error rate of 49%, yielding a lambda of 0.14.

8.7.2 Limitations of Lambda

In spite of lambda's strengths, which include use with nominal-level data, no assumptions concerning the distribution of the variables (a normal distribution is not necessary), and use with any size table, lambda does have two limitations. The first is that lambda has no sign and hence gives us no indication of the direction of the relationship, a limitation that stems from its use with nominal-level data. The second limitation results from the prediction rules on which lambda is based. Lambda equals 0 whenever *all* the within-category modes of the independent variable occur in the row containing the modal category of the dependent variable. In Table 8.6 lambda equals 0, yet it is clear that the variables are related as there is a 23.2% (85.7% − 62.5% = 23.2%) percentage difference between males and females who desire to have children, an 8.9% percentage difference between males and females who have no desire for children, and a 14.3% percentage difference between the undecided males and females. For males *and* females, the within-category modes of the independent variable (60 and 50) are *both* located in the row containing the modal

Table 8.6 Desire to have children by sex of respondent (hypothetical study of college students)

(Y) Desire to Have Children?	(X) Sex of Respondent Male	Female	Total
Yes	85.7 (60)	62.5 (50)*	110
No	8.6 (6)	17.5 (14)	20
Undecided	5.7 (4)	20.0 (16)	20
Total	100.0 (70)	100.0 (80)	N = 150

Using Eq. (8.2), we have

$$\lambda = \frac{\Sigma \text{ maximum frequency } (X) - \text{maximum frequency } (Y)}{N - \text{maximum frequency } (Y)}$$

$$= \frac{(60 + 50) - 110}{150 - 110}$$

$$= 0$$

category of the dependent variable; therefore, shifting from Rule I to Rule II will result in no reduction in prediction error; and lambda equals 0.

  While we have found that lambda equals 0, it is apparent that a relationship does exist between sex and desire to have children. As was noted in Section 8.5, we can only conclude that there is no relationship between two variables if the percentage differences between categories of the independent variable are zero.

8.8 Ordinal Measures of Association[†]

Measures of association for contingency tables using ordinal-level (or interval-level) data are based on the logic of **pair-by-pair comparison.** We will present

---

* While a variety of conventions are available, we prefer that when cell percentages *and* frequencies are presented in a contingency table, the frequencies should be placed in parentheses. Contingency tables will be routinely percentaged on the independent variable unless stated otherwise.

[†] Gamma, Somer's *d*, and Kendall's tau-*b* can be used with interval-level data.

Goodman and Kruskal's gamma, Somer's *d*, and Kendall's tau-*b*, three of the measures most frequently used by social scientists as ordinal measures of association.

8.8.1 The Logic of Pair-by-Pair Comparison

Each case in a contingency table can theoretically be paired with every other case in the table. Table 8.7 contains four cases, *A*, *B*, *C*, and *D*, which can form six distinct pairs. Upon pairing cases *A* and *B* in Table 8.7, we see that case *A* is lower on variable *X* than is case *B* (*A*'s *X* value is young and *B*'s is middle-aged), but *A* is higher on *Y* than is case *B*. Table 8.8 presents a summary of the relationships between all pairs of cases.

A **discordant pair** is one in which the two cases are ranked in the opposite order on both variables. A **concordant pair** is one in which the two cases are ranked in the same order on both variables. A **tied pair** is one in which the two cases are ranked similarly on one or both of the variables. To the extent

Table 8.7 Income by age

(Y) Income	(X) Age		
	Young	Middle-Aged	Old
High	A		D
Medium		B	
Low			C

Table 8.8 Pairs of cases in Table 8.7

Pair	Summary	Relationship
AB	A lower on X than is B A higher on Y than is B	Discordant
AC	A lower on X than is C A higher on Y than is C	Discordant
AD	A lower on X than is D A and D tied on Y	Tied on Y
BC	B lower on X than is C B higher on Y than is C	Discordant
BD	B lower on X than is D B lower on Y than is D	Concordant
CD	C and D tied on X C lower on Y than is D	Tied on X

Table 8.9 Concordant and discordant patterns in contingency tables

(a)					(b)			

(Y) Income	(X) Age — Young	(X) Age — Middle-aged	(X) Age — Old
High	20	6	2
Moderate	5	30	2
Low	1	4	10

Discordant pairs predominate. Relationship is *negative*.

(Y) Income	(X) Age — Young	(X) Age — Middle-aged	(X) Age — Old
High	1	6	10
Moderate	5	30	2
Low	20	4	2

Concordant pairs predominate. Relationship is *positive*.

that a pattern emerges in which discordant pairs predominate, the relationship between the variables is negative as shown in Table 8.9(a). A situation in which concordant pairs predominate and which is characterized by a positive relationship is shown in Table 8.9(b).

The diagonals have been shaded to highlight the predominant pattern in the tables. In Table 8.9(a) you will note that low scores on X *tend* to be paired with high scores on Y and vice versa. Gamma, Somer's d, and Kendall's tau-b are sensitive to patterns such as these, and their values reflect the extent to which concordant or discordant pairs predominate. If gamma, Somer's d, or Kendall's tau-b were calculated for Table 8.9(b), we would anticipate a positive relationship since the majority of cases lie on the positive diagonal; that is, low scores on X tend to be paired with low scores on Y, and high scores on X tend to be paired with high scores on Y.

8.9 Goodman and Kruskal's Gamma

Gamma (G)* is a symmetric measure of association for ordinal-level or interval-level data. No specification of which variable is independent and which is dependent is therefore necessary, and only one value of gamma is possible. Gamma ranges from −1 to +1, has a proportional reduction in error (PRE) interpretation, and is based on the logic of pair-by-pair comparison. Furthermore, gamma can be calculated for any size table.[†]

---

* Most social scientists symbolize gamma by G, although some prefer the lowercase Greek letter (γ).

[†] Yule's Q is a special case of gamma that was developed specifically for 2 × 2 tables. The values of G and Q are equivalent for 2 × 2 tables and are subject to the same interpretation and limitations. Social scientists generally prefer gamma because it can be used with any size contingency table containing ordinal-level or interval-level data.

The equation for computing gamma compares the number of concordant pairs (C) to the number of discordant pairs (D). Gamma ignores ties, a weakness we will address later. The computation of gamma for Table 8.7 is shown below Eq. (8.3). Note that the sign of gamma in this instance is negative because discordant pairs outnumber concordant pairs 3 to 1.

$$G = \frac{C - D}{C + D} \qquad (8.3)$$

where

$$C = \text{number of concordant pairs, and}$$

$$D = \text{number of discordant pairs}$$

$$G = \frac{1 - 3}{1 + 3} = \frac{-2}{4} = \frac{-1}{2} = -0.5$$

8.9.1 Calculating Concordant and Discordant Pairs in Contingency Tables

Determining the number of concordant and discordant pairs for contingency tables with many cases is more complicated than the previous example, which included only four cases. The data in Table 8.10 are hypothetical results of a study of the relationship between political liberalism and year in college for a sample of college students.

Concordant pairs The cells in Table 8.10 have been labeled with letters to facilitate the discussion. The lowest category of the independent variable, year in college, is freshman, and the highest category is senior. The not liberal

Table 8.10 Political liberalism by year in college

(Y) Political Liberalism	(X) Year in College				Total
	Freshman	Sophomore	Junior	Senior	
Very Liberal	a 2	b 3	c 7	d 10	22
Moderately Liberal	e 8	f 12	g 9	h 7	36
Not Liberal	i 10	j 5	k 4	l 3	22
Total	20	20	20	20	N = 80

category of the dependent variable is scored low, and the very liberal category scored high. The scores in Table 8.10, with obvious exceptions, tend to follow the *positive diagonal* connecting cells i and d.* We anticipate a positive relationship between X and Y due to the patterning of cases that are concentrated in cells i, f, g, and d. The positive diagonal in any contingency table connects the low-low cells of the dependent and independent variable (not liberal and freshman, therefore, cell i in Table 8.10) with the high-high cells of the dependent and independent variable (very liberal and senior, therefore, cell d in Table 8.10). The negative diagonal always connects the low-high cells of the dependent and independent variable (not liberal and senior, therefore, cell l in Table 8.10) with the high-low cells of the dependent and independent variables (very liberal and freshman, therefore, cell a in Table 8.10).

The first step in identifying the concordant pairs in any contingency table is to locate the cell on the positive diagonal that represents a low score on X and Y. The procedure we will follow for computing gamma assumes that the table is laid out in the standard manner described in Section 8.5. In this example we must therefore begin at cell i. The cases that are concordant with the cases in cell i lie in those cells to the right and above cell i.[†] Cells concordant with cell i are cells b, c, d, f, g, and h because the cases in these cells are higher on both variables than the cases in cell i. The cells contain 3, 7, 10, 12, 9, and 7 cases, respectively, for a total of 48 cases. We can calculate the number of concordant *pairs* we have identified so far by multiplying the number of cases in cell i by the total number of cases in those cells above and to the right of cell i; therefore, we have identified 10 × 48 or 480 concordant pairs. We continue this procedure until we have counted all concordant pairs.

Our focal cell now is cell j because we must systematically move across the row, then up to the next row and across, etc., until we have identified all concordant pairs. We note that only cells c, d, g, and h are above and to the right of cell j. The cases in these four cells are concordant with the cases in cell j because all of the cases are higher on both variables than are the cases in cell j. A total of 33 cases (7 + 10 + 9 + 7) lie in these cells. Multiplying by the 5 cases in cell j, we now have identified 165 (5 × 33) additional concordant pairs. Continuing, we see that the 4 cases in cell k form concordant pairs with the cases in cells d and h for 68 (4 × 17) concordant pairs. The 8 cases in cell e are concordant with those in cells b, c, and d, and the 12 cases in cell f are concordant with the cases in cells c and d. Finally, the 9 cases in cell g are concordant with the cases in cell d. The calculations to determine the number of concordant pairs are summarized in Table 8.11.

---

* Table 8.9(a) is characterized by a negative diagonal.

[†] The initial focal cell for computing concordant pairs could have been cell d, which lies at the opposite end of the positive diagonal. If we began with cell d, we would locate cells to the left and below cell d because they are concordant with cell d. Hence either cell i or d could have been chosen as the starting point.

Table 8.11   Calculation of concordant pairs

Focal Cell	Paired Cells	Calculation of Concordant Pairs	
i	*b, c, d, f, g, h*	$10(3 + 7 + 10 + 12 + 9 + 7) =$	480
j	*c, d, g, h*	$5(7 + 10 + 9 + 7) =$	165
k	*d, h*	$4(10 + 7) =$	68
e	*b, c, d*	$8(3 + 7 + 10) =$	160
f	*c, d*	$12(7 + 10) =$	204
g	*d*	$9(10) =$	90
		Total concordant pairs $=$	1167

Discordant pairs   Identifying the discordant pairs of cases involves a procedure similar to identifying the concordant pairs. Our focal cell lies on the *negative diagonal* that runs from cell *a* to cell *l* in Table 8.10. We begin with cell *a* and work down the diagonal locating those cells that contain cases whose value is less than the cases in cell *a* on both the independent and dependent variable. Therefore, cells *f, g, h, j, k,* and *l,* all of which lie below and to the right of cell *a,* contain cases discordant with those in cell *a*.* We then move systematically across and down to identify the remaining focal cells, which include cells *b, c, e, f,* and *g*. The calculations necessary to determine the discordant pairs are presented in Table 8.12.

We have found that concordant pairs predominate and can now calculate gamma, making use of Eq. (8.3).

$$G = \frac{C - D}{C + D} = \frac{1167 - 426}{1167 + 426} = +0.465$$

---

* The discordant pairs could also be calculated by beginning with cell *l,* which is located at the opposite end of the negative diagonal, and locating cells above and to the left. The choice of either starting point is a matter of personal preference.

Table 8.12   Calculation of discordant pairs

Focal Cell	Paired Cells	Calculation of Discordant Pairs	
a	*f, g, h, j, k, l*	$2(12 + 9 + 7 + 5 + 4 + 3) =$	80
b	*g, h, k, l*	$3(9 + 7 + 4 + 3) =$	69
c	*h, l*	$7(7 + 3) =$	70
e	*j, k, l*	$8(5 + 4 + 3) =$	96
f	*k, l*	$12(4 + 3) =$	84
g	*l*	$9(3) =$	27
		Total discordant pairs $=$	426

8.9.2 Interpreting Gamma

Gamma ranges from -1.00 when there is a perfect negative relationship between the variables (all untied pairs are discordant) to $+1.00$ where there is a perfect positive relationship (all untied pairs are concordant).* When the variables are unrelated, gamma equals 0 because there are an equal number of concordant and discordant pairs.

The gamma of $+0.465$ indicates a moderate, positive relationship between year in school and political liberalism, or in other words, the seniors at the college we surveyed are more politically liberal than are the freshmen. Our data of course do not allow us to know if the observed relationship is due to the liberalizing effect of a college education or if natural aging by four years would have the same liberalizing effect. Because gamma has a PRE interpretation, we can also say that using knowledge of the independent variable (year in college) to predict the order of the cases on the dependent variable (political liberalism), we have reduced our errors by 46.5%. However, because gamma is a symmetric measure of association, we can also say that, given knowledge of the dependent variable, we can reduce our errors by 46.5% when predicting the independent variable.

The procedure for determining the statistical significance of gamma is presented in Section 14.9.

8.9.3 Limitations of Gamma

Gamma ignores tied pairs, and hence a gamma value may reflect far less than all the possible pairs. There are $N(N - 1)/2$ or 3160 possible pairs of cases in Table 8.10. Of these pairs, 1593 (426 + 1167) are discordant *or* concordant. Tied pairs total 1567 (3160 − 1593), and therefore nearly 50% of all the possible pairs have been ignored in the calculation of gamma. As a result, gamma tends to overstate the actual relationship. Indeed, it is possible for gamma to equal -1 or $+1$ when all but one pair of cases is tied! Somer's d and Kendall's tau-b overcome the problem, and are discussed in the following sections.

Gamma, along with all other ordinal-level statistics, can only detect a straight-line relationship between the variables. If a horseshoe-shaped curve best described the relationship between the variables, for example, the value of gamma would be very low. Naturally you must learn to identify situations such as this in which a nonlinear[†] relationship exists, and not compute gamma.

---

* Recall that a tied pair is one in which two cases are ranked similarly on one or both of the variables.

[†] *Nonlinear* (or curvilinear) means not characterized by a straight line.

In spite of these drawbacks, gamma is the most frequently used measure of association for ordinal-level and interval-level data in contingency form.

8.10 Somer's d

Somer's d is an asymmetrical measure of association for ordinal-level data that incorporates tied ranks. It is similar to gamma in that it is based on pair-by-pair comparison. Two values of d (d_{yx} where Y is the dependent variable and d_{xy} in which X is treated as the dependent variable) are possible; however, here we will assume Y is dependent. The computational equation requires that we determine the number of concordant pairs (C); the number of discordant pairs (D); and T_y, which is the number of pairs with different X values, but with the same Y value. Thus the cases in cell a are tied with those in cells b, c, and d because all are ranked very liberal on Y yet are in differing years in college. The computational procedure for Somer's d (with Y dependent) is presented in Eq. (8.4):

$$d_{yx} = \frac{C - D}{C + D + T_y} \qquad (8.4)$$

where

T_y = pairs with different X values but with the same Y values
C = number of concordant pairs, and
D = number of discordant pairs

The logic of including ties on the dependent variable when calculating a measure of association for contingency data is that a tie on the dependent variable given differing X values suggests that X exerts no influence on Y.* Rather than ignoring ties as does gamma, Somer's d, which is a more conservative measure, includes ties on the dependent variable to ensure a more accurate reflection of the true strength of association. Somer's d must always be less than or equal to gamma when calculated for the same contingency table due to the inclusion of the T_y term in the denominator. While Somer's d does not have a direct PRE interpretation, it has become very popular with social

---

* Somer's d_{yx} ignores ties on the independent variable. If we wished to compute d_{xy} where X is dependent, the T_y term in Eq. (8.4) would be replaced by T_x, which includes pairs with different Y values but which share the same X value. For example, cell a is tied with cells e and i because all are freshmen, yet they are ranked differently on political liberalism. Ties on X will be discussed in the next section.

Table 8.13 Computation of d_{yx} for the data in Table 8.10

	(X) Year in College				
(Y) **Political** **Liberalism**	Freshman	Sophomore	Junior	Senior	Total
Very Liberal	*a* 2	*b* 3	*c* 7	*d* 10	22
Moderately Liberal	*e* 8	*f* 12	*g* 9	*h* 7	36
Not Liberal	*i* 10	*j* 5	*k* 4	*l* 3	22
Total	20	20	20	20	N = 80

scientists in the past decade. Somer's d_{yx} has been calculated for the data in Table 8.10 (repeated here as Table 8.13).

$$d_{yx} = \frac{C - D}{C + D + T_y}$$

$$\left. \begin{array}{l} C = 1167 \\ D = 426 \end{array} \right\} \text{(From Section 8.9.1)}$$

$$\begin{aligned} T_y &= 2(3 + 7 + 10) + 3(7 + 10) + 7(10) \\ &+ 8(12 + 9 + 7) + 12(9 + 7) + 9(7) \\ &+ 10(5 + 4 + 3) + 5(4 + 3) + 4(3) \\ &= 807 \end{aligned}$$

Using Eq. (8.4), we obtain

$$d_{yx} = \frac{1167 - 426}{1167 + 426 + 807} = +0.309$$

You will note that this value is considerably less than the gamma of $+0.465$ that we computed for the same set of data. Somer's d ranges from -1 (perfect negative relationship) to $+1$ (perfect positive relationship) and assumes a linear or straight-line relationship between the variables. A Somer's d_{yx} of $+0.309$ indicates a weak to moderately positive relationship between year in school and political liberalism when year in school serves as the independent variable.

8.11 Kendall's tau-*b* (τ_b)

Kendall's tau-*b* differs from Somer's d in that its computation involves pairs of cases that are tied on both X and Y. It is a symmetrical measure of association for ordinal-level data whose maximum value of ± 1 is possible in a square table (the number of rows equal the number of columns, i.e., $r = c$). Equation (8.5) for tau-b is

$$\text{tau-}b = \frac{C - D}{\sqrt{(C + D + T_y)(C + D + T_x)}} \qquad (8.5)$$

To compute tau-b, we must determine C, D, T_y, and T_x where T_x equals the number of pairs tied on X, but with different Y values. Using Table 8.13 as an illustration, we see that the cases in cell a are tied on X with cases in cells e and i and the cases in cell e are tied on X with the cases in cell i. Likewise, the cases in cell b are tied on X with the cases in cells f and j and the cases in cell f are tied with the cases in j. The procedure for determining ties on X, but not on Y is as follows:

$$
\begin{aligned}
T_x = {} & 2(8 + 10) + 8(10) \\
& + 3(12 + 5) + 12(5) \\
& + 7(9 + 4) + 9(4) \\
& + 10(7 + 3) + 7(3) = 475
\end{aligned}
$$

Substituting the known values of C, D, and T_y from below Table 8.13 allows us to compute tau-b:

$$
\begin{aligned}
\text{tau-}b &= \frac{1167 - 426}{\sqrt{(1167 + 426 + 807)(1167 + 426 + 475)}} \\[2mm]
&= \frac{741}{\sqrt{(2400)(2068)}} \\[2mm]
&= \frac{741}{2227.8} \\[2mm]
&= +0.333
\end{aligned}
$$

A tau-b of $+0.333$ indicates a positive relationship between political liberalism and year in school. Tau-b is a symmetric statistic, and therefore we can say that our errors in prediction for either variable can be reduced by 33.3% given information about the order of pairs on the other variable. Table 8.13 is rectangular, therefore, the maximum value for tau-b is less than ± 1. Its value may never be larger than gamma due to the incorporation of tied cases in the computation. In this particular instance gamma would be a more appropriate ordinal-level statistic since $r \neq c$ in Table 8.13.

Summary

In this chapter we have learned about the presentation and interpretation of contingency tables. We have also discussed four distribution-free measures of association appropriate for nominal- or ordinal-level data.

Lambda is a measure of association for nominal data based on the logic of proportional reduction in error. Lambda can serve as either a symmetric or asymmetric measure. The value of lambda ranges from 0 to 1, and it can be used with tables of any dimension. Lambda equals 0 when the distribution of cases on the dependent variable is extremely skewed.

Gamma, Somer's d, and tau-b are measures of association for ordinal data based on the logic of pair-by-pair comparison. Gamma and tau-b are symmetric measures of association with a PRE interpretation, whereas Somer's d is an asymmetric measure and does not have a PRE interpretation. While gamma ignores ties, Somer's d and tau-b are more conservative measures that incorporate tied ranks on the dependent variable. Somer's d_{yx} incorporates ties on the dependent variable Y and tau-b's computation involves ties on X and Y. Gamma and Somer's d range from -1 to $+1$, can be used with tables of any dimension, and assume the variables are linearly related. The maximum value for tau-b is less than ± 1 when $r \neq c$.

Terms to Remember

Asymmetric measure of association   A measure of the one-way effect of one variable upon another.

Concordant pair   Two cases are ranked similarly on two variables.

Conditional distribution   The distribution of the categories of one variable under the differing conditions or categories of another.

Contingency table   A table showing the joint distribution of two variables.

Dependent variable   The variable that is being predicted. Also referred to as the criterion variable.

Discordant pair   Two cases are ranked in the opposite order on two variables.

Epsilon (ϵ)   The percentage difference within a category of the dependent variable between the two extreme categories of the independent variable.

Gamma (G)   A symmetric measure of association for ordinal-level data based on pair-by-pair comparison with a PRE interpretation.

Independent variable   The predictor variable. Referred to as the experimental variable in an experiment.

Kendall's tau-b   A symmetric measure of association for ordinal-level data.

Lambda (λ)   An asymmetric or symmetric measure of association for nominal-level data.

Marginals   The column and row totals of a contingency table.

Negative relationship High scores on one variable tend to be associated with low scores on the other, and conversely, low scores on one variable tend to be associated with high scores on the other variable.

Pair-by-pair comparison An approach to prediction for ordinal-level data in contingency form.

Percentage difference Differences in percentages normally measured between the two extreme categories of the independent variable within a category of the dependent variable. Also referred to as epsilon (ϵ).

Perfect relationship A relationship in which knowledge of the independent variable allows a perfect prediction of the dependent variable or vice versa.

Positive relationship High scores on one variable tend to be associated with high scores on the other variable, and conversely, low scores on one variable tend to be associated with low scores on the other variable.

Proportional reduction in error (PRE) A ratio of the prediction errors without information about the independent variable to the prediction errors having information about the independent variable.

Somer's d An asymmetrical measure of association for ordinal-level data that incorporates tied ranks.

Symmetric measure of association A measure of the mutual association between two variables.

Tied pair Two cases are ranked similarly on one or both of two variables.

Exercises

1. Percentage the following table down, across, and on the total. Interpret the data for each of the ways you have percentaged.

	High School Grade Point Average		
Drug Use	Low	Moderate	High
High	0	5	15
Moderate	15	10	10
Low	10	5	5

$N = 75$

2. Identify and defend your choice of independent and dependent variables for the table in Exercise 1. Which direction would you percentage, given your selection?

3. Discuss the existence, direction, and strength of a relationship for the data in Exercise 1 by examining the percentages and distribution of cases. Calculate an appropriate measure of association, defend your choice, and interpret the results.

4. Compute lambda. Interpret your answer.

(Y) Educational Attainment	(X) Religious Affiliation		
	Protestant	Catholic	Jewish
College	10	15	15
High School	10	20	10

N = 80

5. Compute gamma, Somer's *d*, and tau-*b*. Compare and interpret your answers.

(Y) Perceived Health	(X) Social Isolation		
	Low	Moderate	High
Excellent	10	4	3
Average	5	6	7
Poor	2	4	9

N = 50

6. Over 5 million adults in the United States reported that they wanted a job, yet were not seeking employment. Assuming that sex is the independent variable and that reason for not seeking work is the dependent variable, percentage the following table and compute an appropriate measure of association. Interpret the results.

(Y) Reason For Not Seeking Work	(X) Sex	
	Male	Female
In School	693	681
Ill or Disabled	326	394
Keeping House	32	1226
Think Cannot Get a Job	305	540
Total	1356	2841

N = 4197
(In thousands)

Source: U.S. Bureau of Labor Statistics, *Employment and Earnings,* monthly.

7. Using a contingency table of your choice for illustrative purposes, discuss the logic underlying proportional reduction in error. Discuss the logic of pair-by-pair comparison using a different example.

8. For the following research situations construct a hypothetical table and select an appropriate measure of association:

  a) You have conducted a health survey and wish to examine the relationship between the number of close friends a person has and whether or not the respondent has seriously considered suicide.

  b) You wish to explore the relationship between the length of time U.S. senators have served in the Senate and the region of the country in which their home state is located.

  c) You wish to determine if lower-income persons are more likely to be the victim of a street assault than are upper-income persons.

9. A weakness of gamma is that it overstates the actual relationship between variables when there are ties in the data. Why is this the case, and how do Somer's *d* and tau-*b* avoid this weakness?

10. Interracially married couples in the United States totaled approximately 319,000 in 1970, 421,000 in 1977, and 762,000 in 1984. The following table indicates the racial composition of interracial marriages by year. Percentage the table, and discuss the relationship between year and racial composition of the marital pair.

Racial Composition of Marriage Partners	Year		
	1970	*1977*	*1984*
Husband black, wife white	41	95	111
Wife black, husband white	24	30	64
Husband black, wife other	8	20	17
Wife black, husband other*	4	2	6
Husband white, wife other*	139	177	340
Wife white, husband other*	94	97	224
Total	310	421	762
	(In thousands)		

Source: U.S. Bureau of the Census.

* "Other" indicates spouse is neither black nor white but is Oriental or another unspecified racial category.

11. Discuss the strengths and weaknesses of lambda, tau-*b*, gamma, and Somer's *d*.

12. A study was conducted to examine the possible precipitating influences or causes of a person having a religious experience. Calculate lambda for the following table and interpret your results.

(Y) Religious Experience?	(X) Possible Precipitator			
	Death of a Loved One	Romantic Breakup of a Relationship	Loss of a Job	Severe Physical Pain
Yes	10	10	5	15
No	10	40	10	10

$N = 110$

13. Construct a table with ordinal-level variables in which there is a strong relationship between two variables, but because it is not linear, that is, it does not follow either the positive or negative diagonal, gamma, tau-b, and Somer's d will not accurately reflect the strong pattern that is evident. Calculate gamma, tau-b, or Somer's d and discuss. (*Hint:* Choose two variables that have several categories to allow for the demonstration of a nonlinear relationship.)

14. Construct tables in which:

    a) Lambda = 1, lambda = 0.

    b) Tau-b = 1, tau-b = 0.

    c) Gamma = 1, gamma = 0.

    d) Somer's d = 1, Somer's d = 0.

15. a) Compute lambda for this table.

    b) Interpret your answer.

    c) Interpret the percentages.

(Y) Attitude Toward Labor Unions	(X) Region of Orientation		Total
	Non-South	South	
Prounion	66.7 (40)	37.5 (15)	(55)
Antiunion	33.3 (20)	62.5 (25)	(45)
Total	100.0 (60)	100.0 (40)	$N = 100$

16. The following table summarizes the relationship between the use of cocaine and condoms among female prostitutes. Assuming use of cocaine is the independent variable, (a) percentage down, (b) compute gamma, Somer's *d*, and tau-*b*, and (c) discuss.

Use of Condoms	Use of Cocaine		
	Never	*Sometimes*	*Frequently*
Always	25	10	1
Sometimes	15	10	9
Never	4	6	20

N = 100

17. Many companies have reduced the size of work groups to promote group cohesion. Assuming work group size is the independent variable, (a) percentage down, (b) compute gamma, Somer's *d*, and tau-*b*, and (c) discuss the relationship shown in the following table.

Group Cohesion	Size of Work Group		
	3–6	*7–10*	*11–14*
High	52	70	28
Moderate	22	75	12
Low	13	60	40

N = 372

chapter **9**

Correlation

9.1 The Concept of Correlation
9.2 Calculation of Pearson's *r*
9.3 Pearson's *r* and *z* Scores
9.4 The Correlation Matrix
9.5 Interpreting Correlation Coefficients
9.6 Spearman's Rho (r_s)

9.1 The Concept of Correlation

We are frequently interested in determining the relationship between two interval- or ratio-scaled variables. For example, college admissions personnel are very concerned with the relationship between SAT scores and performance at college. Do students who score high on the SAT also perform well in college? Conversely, do high school students who score low on the SAT perform poorly in college? Is there a relationship between socioeconomic status and recidivism in crime? Is a spouse's power in a marriage related to his or her earnings? What is the relationship between the size of a law firm and beginning salaries for new members? In order to express the extent to which two variables are related, we need to compute a measure of association called a **correlation coefficient.** There are many types of measures of association, several of which were presented in Chapter 8.

The decision as to which measure of association to use with a specific set of data depends on such factors as (1) the type of scale or measurement in which each variable is expressed (nominal, ordinal, interval, or ratio), (2) the nature of the underlying distribution (continuous or discrete), and (3) the characteristics of the distribution of scores (linear or nonlinear). Table 9.1 summarizes the measures of association that are included in this text. The level of measurement indicated is a minimal requirement. Lambda and the other nominal-level measures, for example, can be calculated if one of the variables is measured at the nominal level and the other is measured at the ordinal level.

Table 9.1 A summary of measures of association presented in this text

Scale	Symbol	Used with	Chapter
Nominal	λ (lambda)	Two nominal-level variables.	8
	ϕ (phi coefficient)	Two dichotomous variables.	16
	C (contingency coefficient)	Two nominal-level variables with equal rows and columns.	16
	V (Cramer's V)	Two nominal-level variables.	16
Ordinal	G (Goodman and Kruskal's gamma)	Two ordinal-level variables.	8
	d (Somer's d)	Two ordinal-level variables.	8
	tau-b (Kendall's tau-b)	Two ordinal-level variables.	8
	r_s (Spearman's rho)	Two ordinal-level variables. If one variable is ordinal level and one is interval level, both must be expressed as ranks prior to calculating r_s.	9
Interval/Ratio	r (Pearson's correlation coefficient)	Two interval- and/or ratio-level variables.	9
	R (multiple correlation coefficient)	Three or more interval- and/or ratio-level variables.	11

The Pearson correlation coefficient (r) (also referred to as **Pearson's r,** the *Pearson product-moment correlation coefficient,* and r) will be discussed in this chapter. Pearson's r is a measure of the linear or straight-line relationship between two interval-level variables. It is a symmetric statistic.

The form of the relationship between two interval- or ratio-level variables can be presented visually in a *scatter diagram* (also referred to as a *scattergram* or *scatterplot*). A **scatter diagram** is a graphic device used to visually summarize the relationship between two variables. The X-axis is traditionally the horizontal axis and represents the independent variable. The vertical axis normally represents Y, the dependent variable.* The axes are drawn perpendicular to each other, approximately equal in length and marked to accommodate the full range of scores. Each coordinate represents two values: a score on the X variable and a score on the Y variable. Figure 9.1 displays the relationship between the desired number of children and the actual number of children reported by six hypothetical couples. Couple A preferred two children and have two children; therefore, their coordinate has been located at the point at which X and Y both equal 2. The scatter diagram allows for a visual inspection of the relationship between the two variables, and it is evident that three of the couples (B, D, and E) do not have the number of children that they desired. The Pearson correlation coefficient (r) for the data in Figure 9.1 equals $+0.21$.

---

* As with all statistical conventions, they are not always followed; therefore, always determine the independent and dependent variable before interpreting the data.

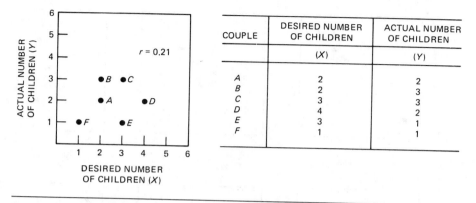

Figure 9.1 Scatter diagram showing the relationship between the desired and actual number of children for six couples (hypothetical data).

Let's consider the meaning of this value along with the correlation coefficients below the scatter diagrams in Figure 9.2.

The values of the Pearson correlation coefficient vary between $+1.00$ [see Fig. 9.2(a)] and -1.00 [see Fig. 9.2(f)]. Both extremes represent perfect relationships between variables, and 0.00 represents the absence of a relationship [see Fig. 9.2(d)]. The *size* of the correlation coefficient indicates the strength of the relationship. The closer the points in the scatter diagram approach the form of a straight line, the stronger the relationship between X and Y. We ignore the sign of the coefficient when interpreting the strength of a relationship; hence the relationships in Figures 9.2(a) and (f) are equally strong in spite of their opposite signs.

The direction of a relationship is indicated by the *sign* of the correlation coefficient. A **positive relationship** (or direct relationship) indicates that high scores on one variable tend to be associated with high scores on a second variable, and conversely, low scores on one variable tend to be associated with low scores on the second variable [see Figs. 9.2(a), (b), and (c)]. A **negative relationship** (also referred to as an *inverse or indirect relationship*) indicates that low scores on one variable tend to be associated with high scores on a second variable. Conversely, high scores on one variable tend to be associated with low scores on the second variable [see Figs. 9.2(e) and 9.2(f)].

9.2 Calculation of Pearson's *r*

9.2.1 Mean Deviation Method

The mean deviation method for calculating Pearson's *r* is not often used by social scientists because it involves more time and effort than other computa-

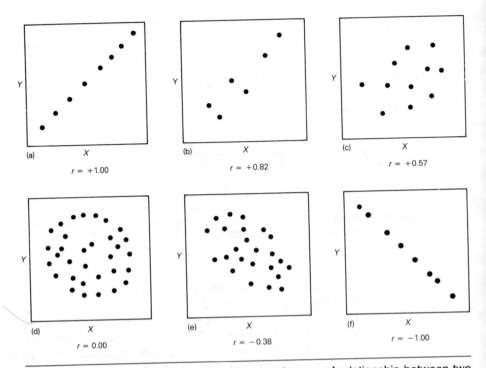

Figure 9.2 Scatter diagrams showing various degrees of relationship between two variables.

tional techniques. It is being presented here primarily because it sheds further light on the characteristics of Pearson's r. However, with small samples, it is as convenient a computational equation as any, unless a calculator is available. The mean deviation computational equation for r is

$$r = \frac{\Sigma(X - \bar{X})(Y - \bar{Y})}{\sqrt{[\Sigma(X - \bar{X})^2][\Sigma(Y - \bar{Y})^2]}} \tag{9.1}$$

Equation (9.1) provides a conceptual understanding of the Pearson correlation coefficient. The numerator of the equation is the **covariation** of X and Y or the extent to which X and Y vary together. It is the numerator that determines the *sign* of the correlation coefficient. A positive r results from high values of X tending to be paired with high values of Y, and conversely, low values of X tending to be paired with low values of Y. Substitute the values from Figure 9.1 into the numerator of Eq. (9.1) to ensure that you understand covariation and how it determines the sign of r. Also note that the covariation has an unrestricted upper range and that, by itself, it is not a good measure of association.

The denominator is always positive because the values are squared. It consists of the square root of the product of the standard deviation of X and Y

ole 9.2 Computational procedures for r using the mean deviation method (hypothetical data)

pon-ent	Mother's Education X	$(X - \bar{X})$	$(X - \bar{X})^2$	Daughter's Education Y	$(Y - \bar{Y})$	$(Y - \bar{Y})^2$	$(X - \bar{X})(Y - \bar{Y})$
A	1	-6	36	7	-6	36	36
B	3	-4	16	4	-9	81	36
C	5	-2	4	13	0	0	0
D	7	0	0	16	3	9	0
E	9	2	4	10	-3	9	-6
F	11	4	16	22	9	81	36
G	13	6	36	19	6	36	36

$$\bar{X} = 7 \qquad \Sigma(X - \bar{X})^2 = 112 \qquad \bar{Y} = 13 \qquad \Sigma(Y - \bar{Y})^2 = 252 \qquad \Sigma(X - \bar{X})(Y - \bar{Y}) = 138$$

$$r = \frac{\Sigma(X - \bar{X})(Y - \bar{Y})}{\sqrt{[\Sigma(X - \bar{X})^2][\Sigma(Y - \bar{Y})^2]}} = \frac{138}{\sqrt{(112)(252)}} = \frac{138}{168.00} = 0.82$$

since, in the more complex version of the equation on which Eq. (9.1) is based, both the numerator and denominator are divided by N. Thus, it is the denominator that restricts the range of r to ± 1 and results in r being independent of the measurement units of X and Y. The data in Table 9.2, which summarize educational attainment scores for seven female respondents and for their mothers, will be used to illustrate the mean deviation method for computing r.

The computational procedures for the mean deviation method should be familiar to you. The symbols $\Sigma(X - \bar{X})^2$ and $\Sigma(Y - \bar{Y})^2$ were used to compute standard deviation in Chapter 6. In fact, in calculating r only one step has been added, that of obtaining the sum of cross-products $\Sigma(X - \bar{X})(Y - \bar{Y})$, which was identified earlier as the covariation of X and Y. This is obtained by multiplying the deviation of each individual's score from the mean of the X variable by its corresponding deviation on the Y variable and then summing all of the cross-products. Notice that if maximum deviations in X had lined up with maximum deviations in Y and so on down through the array, $\Sigma(X - \bar{X})(Y - \bar{Y})$ would have been equal to 168.00, which is the same as the value of the denominator, and would have produced a correlation of 1.00. In this instance we found the correlation between the mother's and daughter's education to be 0.82.

9.2.2 Raw Score Method

In calculating Pearson's r by the raw score method, we use Eq. (9.2):

$$r = \frac{N \Sigma XY - (\Sigma X)(\Sigma Y)}{\sqrt{[N \Sigma X^2 - (\Sigma X)^2][N \Sigma Y^2 - (\Sigma Y)^2]}} \tag{9.2}$$

The procedure for calculating r by the raw score method is summarized in Table 9.3. Note that we calculate all of the quantities separately and substitute them into the equation. Here you find exactly the same coefficient ($r = 0.82$) as you did using the mean deviation method. As with the mean deviation method, all of the procedures are familiar to you. The quantity ΣXY is obtained by multiplying each X value by its corresponding Y and then summing these products. Also, be sure to make the distinction between ΣX^2 and $(\Sigma X)^2$ as well as between ΣY^2 and $(\Sigma Y)^2$.

9.3 Pearson's *r* and *z* Scores*

The Pearson correlation coefficient can also be computed using z scores and, furthermore, z scores provide an intuitive interpretation that the raw score method is unable to offer. A high positive Pearson's r indicates that each individual obtains approximately the same z score on both variables. In a *perfect* positive correlation ($r = +1.00$) each individual obtains exactly the same z score on both variables.

With a high negative r, each individual obtains approximately the same z score on both variables, but the z scores are opposite in sign.

Remembering that the z score represents a measure of relative position in standard deviation units on a given variable (i.e., a high positive z represents a high score relative to the remainder of the distribution, and a high negative z represents a low score relative to the remainder of the distribution), we may now generalize the meaning of Pearson's r.

Pearson's r represents the extent to which the same individuals, events, etc., occupy the same relative position on two variables.

In order to explore the fundamental characteristics of the Pearson correlation coefficient, let's slightly modify the mother's and daughter's educational attainment scores example to demonstrate a perfect positive correlation. In Table 9.4 we find the educational attainment scores for the seven pairs of mothers and daughters on the two variables, X and Y, where X represents the educational attainment of the mother and Y represents the educational attainment of the daughter.

The scale values of X and Y do not need to be the same for the calculation of r. In this example we see that X ranges from 1 through 13, whereas Y ranged from 4 through 22. This independence of r from specific scale values, which was initially noted in Section 9.2.1, permits us to investigate the relationships among an unlimited variety of variables. If we measure, for example, a person's yearly income in dollars *or* hundreds of dollars and separately correlate both

---

* z scores were initially discussed in Section 7.2.

Table 9.3 Computational procedures for r using the raw score method (hypothetical data)

Respon- dent	Mother's Education X	X²	Daughter's Education Y	Y²	XY
A	1	1	7	49	7
B	3	9	4	16	12
C	5	25	13	169	65
D	7	49	16	256	112
E	9	81	10	100	90
F	11	121	22	484	242
G	13	169	19	361	247

$N = 7$ $\Sigma X = 49$ $\Sigma X^2 = 455$ $\Sigma Y = 91$ $\Sigma Y^2 = 1435$ $\Sigma XY = 775$
$\overline{X} = 7$ $\overline{Y} = 13$

$$r = \frac{N \Sigma XY - (\Sigma X)(\Sigma Y)}{\sqrt{[N \Sigma X^2 - (\Sigma X)^2][N \Sigma Y^2 - (\Sigma Y)^2]}}$$

$$= \frac{7(775) - (49)(91)}{\sqrt{[7(455) - (49)^2][7(1435) - (91)^2]}}$$

$$= \frac{5425 - 4459}{\sqrt{[3185 - 2401][10{,}045 - 8281]}}$$

$$= \frac{966}{\sqrt{[784][1764]}}$$

$$= \frac{966}{1176}$$

$$= 0.82$$

Table 9.4 Raw scores and corresponding z scores for seven pairs of mothers and daughters on two variables (hypothetical data)

Respon- ent	Mother's Education X	X − X̄	(X − X̄)²	z_x	Daughter's Education Y	Y − Ȳ	(Y − Ȳ)²	z_y	$z_x z_y$
A	1	−6	36	−1.5	4	−9	81	−1.5	2.25
B	3	−4	16	−1.0	7	−6	36	−1.0	1.00
C	5	−2	4	−0.5	10	−3	9	−0.5	0.25
D	7	0	0	0.0	13	0	0	0.0	0.00
E	9	2	4	0.5	16	3	9	0.5	0.25
F	11	4	16	1.0	19	6	36	1.0	1.00
G	13	6	36	1.5	22	9	81	1.5	2.25

$\Sigma X = 49$ $\Sigma (X - \overline{X})^2 = 112$ $\Sigma Y = 91$ $\Sigma (Y - \overline{Y})^2 = 252$ $\Sigma z_x z_y = 7.00$
$\overline{X} = 7$ $s_x = \sqrt{\dfrac{112}{7}} = 4.00$ $\overline{Y} = 13$ $s_y = \sqrt{\dfrac{252}{7}} = 6.00$

measures of income with a second variable such as occupational status, the resulting correlation between income and status will be the same regardless of which income measure we use.

The z scores of each respondent on each variable are identical in the event of a perfect positive correlation. Had we reversed the order of either variable, that is, paired 1 with 22, paired 3 with 19, etc., the z scores would still be identical, but would be opposite in sign. In this latter case the correlation would be a maximum *negative* ($r = -1.00$).

If we multiply the paired z scores and then sum the results, we will obtain maximum values only when the correlation is 1.00. Indeed, as the correlation approaches zero, the sum of the products of the paired z scores also approaches zero. Note that when the correlation is perfect, the sum of the products of the paired z scores is equal to N, where N equals the number of pairs. These facts lead to an equation for r using z scores that is algebraically equivalent to Eqs. (9.1) and (9.2).

$$r = \frac{\Sigma(z_x z_y)}{N} \qquad (9.3)$$

Thus for Table 9.4

$$r = \frac{7.00}{7} = 1.00$$

We suggest that you take the data in Table 9.1 and calculate r, using Eq. (9.3). You will arrive at a far more thorough understanding of r in this way.

Equation (9.3) is unwieldy because it requires calculation of separate z's for each score of each individual. Imagine the task of calculating r when N exceeds 50 cases, as it often does. For this reason computational Eq. (9.2) is normally used.

9.4 The Correlation Matrix

Researchers frequently present a **correlation matrix,** which is a summary of the statistical relationships between all possible pairs of variables. Table 9.5 presents the Pearson correlation coefficients for all of the possible relationships among five variables for 420 hypothetical respondents. Computation of the coefficients required that five measures, that is, one for each of the five variables in Table 9.5, be available for all of the respondents. The diagonal of a correlation matrix represents the correlation of a variable with itself; therefore, all of the values on the diagonal are 1.00. Each row in the matrix represents the correlation of a specific variable with other variables, as does each column.

Table 9.5 Pearson correlation coefficients among five variables ($N = 420$)
(hypothetical data)

	1	2	3	4	5
1. Age	1.00				
2. Occupational status	0.02	1.00			
3. Income	−0.19	0.33	1.00		
4. Education	−0.23	0.50	0.40	1.00	
5. Attitude toward federal funding of abortion (negative scored low)	−0.47	0.01	−0.19	0.14	1.00

The variable age, for example, is presented in row 1 and in column 1. If you wish to know the relationship between age and education, read down the age column until you come to the education row where you find $r = -0.23$. Notice that the scoring procedure for the attitude toward the federal funding for abortion variable has been stated explicitly to avoid misunderstanding. In this case we see that a person who is opposed to federal funding for abortion would receive a low score and a pro-federal funding person would receive a high score. Since it would be possible to score this item in the opposite manner (i.e., negative attitude scored high), it is always important to specify the scoring procedure in a potentially ambiguous situation such as this. If the scoring of the abortion item were reversed, all of the signs of the correlation coefficients associated with the abortion variable would also be reversed. The hypothetical example below shows the effect of scoring variable 5 in two ways.

	1. Age	5a. Attitude toward abortion (negative attitude scored low) (Range = 0 to 10)	5b. Attitude toward abortion (negative attitude scored high) (Range = 0 to 10)
Sue advocates the use of federal funds for abortion (positive attitude)	30	10	0
Tom is neutral	42	5	5
Jim opposes the use of federal funds (negative attitude)	50	0	10

Correlating age with variable 5a (equivalent to variable 5 in Table 9.5) would result in a negative correlation whereas correlating age with variable 5b would result in a positive correlation. In either instance the interpretation would be the same. The younger the respondent is, the more likely he or she believes federal funds should be used to fund abortions.

Some social scientists prefer to display the correlation coefficients below the diagonal as shown in Table 9.5 and others prefer above the diagonal.* Either approach is equally appropriate because the coefficients above and below the diagonal are a mirror image of each other. Hence you will seldom see a matrix with coefficients above and below the diagonal (referred to as a *square matrix*).

9.5 Interpreting Correlation Coefficients

The correlation between age and attitude toward the federal funding of abortion in Table 9.5 is -0.47, which may also be written $r_{15} = -0.47$ where the subscripts 1 and 5 refer to the variables as numbered in Table 9.5. The negative coefficient indicates that there is a negative, inverse, or indirect relationship between the variables. Younger respondents tend to favor federal funding of abortion, and conversely, older respondents tend to be opposed to federal funding of abortion. Although there is no established rule that specifies what constitutes a weak, moderate, or strong relationship, these very general guidelines may be useful: a weak relationship, $r = \pm 0.01$ to ± 0.30; a moderate relationship, $r = \pm 0.31$ to ± 0.70; and a strong relationship, $r = \pm 0.71$ to ± 0.99. A perfect relationship is ± 1.00, and no relationship is indicated when $r = 0$.

Students frequently ask how large a coefficient must be before it is respectable. The magnitude and sign of a coefficient should be interpreted relative to previous inquiries whenever possible. The correlation between occupational status and educational attainment for a national sample of adult males normally falls between 0.50 and 0.60.[†] If an investigator found a marked departure from these values when studying similar variables, he or she would closely examine the computational procedures and data for errors.

Those social scientists who investigate the relationship between attitudes and behaviors, on the other hand, routinely expect the relationship to be weaker, generally between 0.20 and 0.40. Thus, previous studies can serve as guidelines in interpreting the relationship you choose to investigate.

When low correlations are found, one is strongly tempted to conclude that there is little or no relationship between the two variables under study. However, it must be remembered that r reflects only the *linear* relationship between two variables. The failure to find evidence of a relationship may be due to one of three possibilities: (1) The variables are, in fact, unrelated, (2) the range of values on one or both of the variables is restricted, or (3) the variables are not

---

* Table 11.5 in Chapter 11 presents a correlation matrix in which the coefficients are displayed above the diagonal.

[†] The sign of a coefficient is frequently omitted when it is positive.

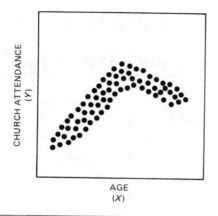

Figure 9.3 Scatter diagram of two variables that are related in a nonlinear fashion (hypothetical data).

related linearly.* In the latter instance Pearson's r would not be an appropriate measure of the degree of relationship between the variables because it assumes a linear relationship.

To illustrate, if we were plotting the relationship between age and church attendance, we might obtain a scatter diagram like that shown in Figure 9.3. It is usually possible to determine whether there is a substantial departure from a straight-line relationship by examining the scatter diagram. If the distribution of points in the scatter diagram is egg shaped or elliptical, without the decided bending that occurs in Figure 9.3, it may safely be assumed that the relationship is linear. Any small departures from linearity will not greatly influence the size of the correlation coefficient. On the other hand, where there is marked curvilinearity, as in Figure 9.3, a curvilinear coefficient of correlation would better reflect the relationship between the two variables under investigation. Although it is beyond the scope of this text to investigate nonlinear coefficients of correlation, you should be aware of this possibility and, as a matter of course, should construct a scatter diagram prior to calculating Pearson's r. Case Example 9.1 provides additional examples of curvilinear relationships.

The assumption of linearity of relationship is the most important requirement to justify the use of Pearson's r as a measure of relationship between two variables. Pearson's r need not be calculated only with normally distributed variables, particularly when the sample size exceeds 50. So long as the distributions of the two variables are unimodal and relatively symmetrical, Pearson's r may legitimately be computed.

Another situation giving rise to artificially low correlation coefficients results from restricting the range of values of one or both of the variables. For

---

* A fourth possibility, that of a third variable suppressing the relationship, will not be discussed.

CASE EXAMPLE 9.1

Craning and Gawking at Nothing

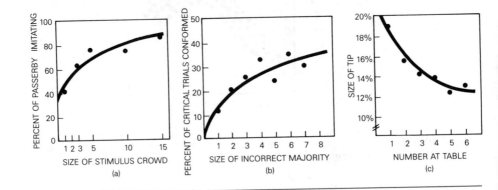

Figure 9.4 Several studies showing curvilinear relationships among variables. (a) Data from S. Milgram, L. Bickman, and L. Berkowitz (1969), "Note on the Drawing Power of Crowds," *Journal of Personality and Social Psychology,* **13**, 79–82; (b) Data from H. B. Gerard, R. A. Wilhelmy, and E. S. Conolley (1968), "Conformity and Group Size," *Journal of Personality and Social Psychology,* **8**, 79–82; (c) Data from S. Freeman, M. R. Walker, R. Borden, and B. Latané (1975), "Diffusion of Responsibility and Restaurant Tipping. Cheaper by the Bunch," *Personality and Social Psychology Bulletin,* **1**, 584–587.

Bibb Latané proposed a theory of social impact that specifies the effect of other persons on an individual. Basing these conclusions on many different avenues of social research, the author states ". . . when other people are the source of impact and the individual is the target, impact should be a multiplicative function of the strength, immediacy, and number of other people." He presents considerable evidence that the relationship between impact and the number of people is not linear. In fact, the impact of each additional person added to the group is less than the impact of the preceding individual. This produces a curvilinear relationship between the number of people and social impact.

Have you ever been on a crowded city street and seen people craning and gawking at some nonexistent event? Figure 9.4(a) shows that as the size of the crowd increases, the percent of passersby who imitate craning and gawking behavior increases. Figure 9.4(b) shows that, similarly, in an Asch type of study in which confederates gave incorrect answers to a length-of-line judging task, conformity increased with the size of the incorrect majority. Finally, in Figure 9.4(c) the size of the tip, in percent of total, decreases with the number of people seated at the table. Note that all describe curvilinear relationships between the independent variable (the number of people involved) and the dependent measure.

Source: Based on Bibb Latané (1981), ''The Psychology of Social Impact,'' *American Psychologist,* **36**(4), 342-356.

example, if we were interested in the relationship between age and height for children from 3 to 16 years of age, we would undoubtedly obtain a rather high correlation coefficient between these two variables. However, suppose that we were to restrict the range of one of our variables? What effect would this have on the size of the coefficient? Consider that same relationship between age and height, but only for those children between the ages of 9 and 10. We would probably end up with a low coefficient.

You will note that the overall relationship illustrated in Figure 9.5 indicates a moderately strong negative relationship between age and life satisfaction ($r = -0.67$), but when we focus only on those respondents 40 years of age and less ($r = -0.51$) or those over 40 ($r = -0.38$), we see that the relationship is attenuated or weakened. **Restriction of range** (sometimes referred to as *truncated range*) can normally be attributed to one of two causes: (1) a group of respondents might be inadvertently excluded from the study and (2) the respondents might be naturally homogeneous with respect to a particular variable. The exclusion of potential respondents can occur, for example, when home interviews are conducted only during daylight hours. Such a procedure results in interviewing very few respondents in the work force and hence introduces the possibility of a restricted range in the respondents' ages. Note the reduced age variation to the left and right of the vertical line in Figure 9.5.

The second contributing factor, that of a naturally homogeneous group of respondents, is not uncommon in social science research, for much of this research is conducted in colleges and universities where respondents have been

Figure 9.5 Scatter diagram illustrating high correlation over entire range of both variables ($r = -.67$) but lower correlation when the range is restricted above or below 40 years of age (hypothetical data).

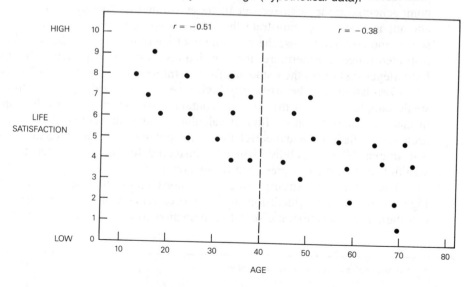

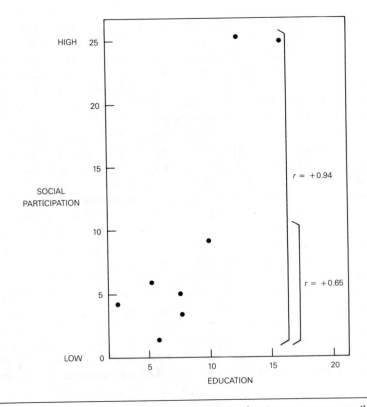

Figure 9.6   Scatter diagram illustrating the effect of extreme scores on the correlation coefficient (hypothetical data).

preselected for attitude and related variables. Thus, they represent a fairly homogeneous group with respect to these variables. Consequently, when an attempt is made to demonstrate the relationship between variables like SAT scores and college grades, the resulting coefficient may be low because of the restricted range. Furthermore, the correlations would be expected to be lower for colleges that select their students from within a narrow range of SAT scores.

Correlations can be artificially high when we are dealing with extremely small samples or when the data set contains extreme scores.* In the former instance the correlation coefficient calculated using the sample data may not accurately reflect the actual correlation in the population from which the sample was drawn. This possibility will be considered further in Chapter 12. The significance test for r is presented in Section 14.8.

The impact of extreme scores on a correlation coefficient is shown in Figure 9.6 where the inclusion of the two extreme scores inflates the initial correlation of education and social participation from $r = 0.65$ to $r = 0.94$.

---

* Also referred to as *deviant cases* or *outliers*.

Help Is Where You Find It!

We previously examined some of the data in Cowen's report when we discussed ordinal scales of measurement (Case Example 2.1). Table 9.6 presents the rankings of four different occupational groups in terms of how frequently they use various help-giving strategies when engaged with clients. We want to learn the extent to which they agree or disagree in their use of the 11 different strategies.

Table 9.6 Ordinal position of response strategies of four different occupations when clients seek advice and counsel. A rank of 1 corresponds to the most frequently used strategy and 11 to the least frequently used strategy

Strategy	Hairdressers	Bartenders	Lawyers	Supervisors
Offer support and sympathy	1	3	1	1.5
Try to be lighthearted	2	2	8	8
Just listen	3	1	5	1.5
Present alternatives	4	4	4	4
Tell person to count blessings	5	10	7	9
Share personal experiences	6	5	6	5
Try not to get involved	7	6	9.5	10
Give advice	8	7	3	7
Ask questions	9	9	2	3
Try to get person to talk to someone else	10	11	9.5	6
Try to change topic	11	8	11	11

Table 9.7 Ordinal position of response strategies of two different occupations when clients seek advice and counsel. A rank of 1 corresponds to the most frequently used strategy and 11 to the least frequently used strategy

Strategy	Hairdressers	Bartenders	Difference	Difference Squared
Offer support and sympathy	1	3	−2	4
Try to be lighthearted	2	2	0	0
Just listen	3	1	2	4
Present alternatives	4	4	0	0
Tell person to count blessings	5	10	−5	25
Share personal experiences	6	5	1	1
Try not to get involved	7	6	1	1
Give advice	8	7	1	1
Ask questions	9	9	0	0
Try to get person to talk to someone else	10	11	−1	1
Try to change topic	11	8	3	9
				$\Sigma\, D^2 = 46$

Table 9.8 Intercorrelations among four occupational groups on strategies for help-giving to clients

	Hairdressers	Bartenders	Lawyers	Supervisors
Hairdressers	1.00	0.79	0.43	0.46
Bartenders	—	1.00	0.30	0.43
Lawyers	—	—	1.00	0.78
Supervisors	—	—	—	1.00

We must now find all possible intercorrelations among the four occupational groups. All told, six different correlations must be calculated: hairdressers versus bartenders, lawyers, and supervisors (three comparisons), bartenders versus lawyers and supervisors (two comparisons), and lawyers versus supervisors (one comparison). We'll show the calculation of r_S only for hairdressers versus bartenders (Table 9.7) and will summarize all their intercorrelations in Table 9.8.

The Spearman rank correlation for these data is

$$r_s = 1 - \frac{6(46)}{1320}$$

$$= 0.79$$

Table 9.8 shows the Spearman rank intercorrelations among all four occupational groups in terms of their help-giving strategies displayed in a correlation matrix.

Examination of Table 9.8 reveals that hairdressers and bartenders intercorrelate more highly than either does with lawyers and supervisors. The r_s of 0.79 is the highest of the six intercorrelations. Moreover, lawyers and supervisors intercorrelated higher with each other than they do with hairdressers and bartenders.

Source: Based on Emory L. Cowen (1982), "Help Is Where You Find It," *American Psychologist,* **37**(4), 285–395.

9.6 Spearman's Rho (r_S)

The second measure of correlation we discuss, r_s, is computed for ranked data on two variables. Imagine you are a sociologist, and after long years of observation you have developed a strong suspicion that the social class of husbands and wives prior to marriage is very similar. In an effort to test your idea you obtain a measure of the social class background for a sample of 15 couples. You are now able to use the social class measure to rank the wives from highest to lowest relative to the other wives, and you can rank the husbands in the same manner as shown in Table 9.9. For example, the wife who was ranked first would have had the highest social class score of the 15

Table 9.9 Computational procedures for calculating r_s from ranked variables (hypothetical data)

Wife's Rank (X)	Husband's Rank (Y)	D	D²	
1	4	−3	9	$r_s = 1 - \dfrac{6\,\Sigma D^2}{N(N^2 - 1)}$
2	2	0	0	
3	9	−6	36	
4	1	3	9	$= 1 - \dfrac{6(204)}{15(224)}$
5	7	−2	4	
6	10	−4	16	
7	8	−1	1	$= 1 - \dfrac{1224}{3360}$
8	13	−5	25	
9	5	4	16	
10	3	7	49	$= 1 - 0.36$
11	11	0	0	
12	6	6	36	$= 0.64$
13	12	1	1	
14	15	−1	1	
15	14	1	1	
		$\Sigma D = 0$	$\Sigma D^2 = 204$	

wives who were ranked. Her husband's social class score would have been the fourth highest among the men since he was ranked fourth.

Spearman's rho requires that you obtain the differences in the ranks, square each difference, sum the squared differences, and substitute the resulting values into Eq. (9.4).

$$r_s = 1 - \frac{6\Sigma D^2}{N(N^2 - 1)} \qquad (9.4)$$

where

$$D = \text{rank } X - \text{rank } Y, \text{ and}$$
$$N = \text{the number of ranked pairs}$$

As a matter of course, ΣD should be obtained even though it is not used in any of the calculations. It constitutes a useful check on the accuracy of your calculations up to this point since ΣD must equal zero. Case Example 9.2 provides a further discussion of r_s.

If you obtain any value other than zero, you should recheck your original ranks and the subsequent subtractions.

The value of r_s will equal $+1.00$ when the two sets of ranks are in perfect agreement, -1.00 when the two sets of ranks are in perfect disagreement, and 0 when there is no agreement, that is, the pairs are random; hence r_s is a measure of the extent to which the two sets of ranks are in agreement or disagreement. The computations in Table 9.9 in which r_s was found to equal 0.64 indicate that there is considerable difference in the social class rankings prior to marriage of our sample of 15 wives and their husbands.

Occasionally, upon converting scores to ranks, you will find two or more tied scores. In this event, assign the mean of the tied ranks to each of the tied scores. The next score in the array receives the rank normally assigned to it. Thus, the ranks of the scores 128, 122, 115, 115, 115, 107, 103 would be 1, 2, 4, 4, 4, 6, 7, and the ranks of the scores 128, 122, 115, 115, 107, 103 would be 1, 2, 3.5, 3.5, 5, 6.

When there are tied ranks on either or both the X and the Y variables, the Spearman equation yields an inflated value, particularly when the number of tied ranks is high. The Pearson's r equation should be applied to the ranked data when there are numerous ties. The significance test for r_s is presented in Section 14.8.3.

Summary

In this chapter we discussed the concept of correlation and demonstrated the calculation of the Pearson correlation coefficient (r) using the mean deviation, raw score, and z score computational procedures. The scatter diagram was presented as an interpretive and summary device.

Correlation is concerned with determining the extent to which two variables are related or tend to vary together. The quantitative expression of the extent of the relationship is given in terms of the magnitude of the correlation coefficient. Correlation coefficients vary between values of -1.00 and $+1.00$; both extremes represent perfect relationships. A coefficient of zero indicates the absence of a relationship between two variables. The correlation matrix is used to summarize the correlations between all possible variable pairs.

Pearson's r is appropriate only for variables that are linearly related. Several situations that can contribute to artificially low or high correlations were discussed.

Spearman's rho (r_s) is a measure of association for ordinal data that provides a measure of the extent to which two sets of ranks are in agreement or disagreement. The value of r_s will equal $+1.00$ when the two sets of rankings are in perfect agreement and -1.00 when the two sets of rankings are in perfect disagreement.

Terms to Remember

Correlation coefficient   A measure that expresses the extent to which two variables are related.

Correlation matrix   A summary of the statistical relationships among all possible pairs of variables.

Covariation The extent to which two variables vary together.

Negative relationship Variables are said to be negatively related when high scores on one variable tend to be associated with low scores on the other variable. Conversely, low scores on one variable tend to be associated with high scores on the other.

Pearson's _r_ (product-moment correlation coefficient) A correlation coefficient used with interval- or ratio-scaled variables.

Positive relationship Variables are said to be positively related when high scores on one variable tend to be associated with high scores on the other. Conversely, low scores on one variable tend to be associated with low scores on the other.

Restricted range A truncated range on one or both variables, resulting in a deceptively low correlation between these variables.

Scatter diagram A graphic device used to summarize visually the relationship between two variables.

Spearman's rho (r_s) A measure of association for ordinal-level data that provides a measure of the extent to which two sets of ranks are in agreement or disagreement.

Exercises

1. You have hypothesized that membership growth in large city churches is positively associated with distance from the central business district (CBD). Compute _r_ for the following data set of 20 churches and determine if the data support your hypothesis.

Church	% Growth in Past Year	Distance from CBD (In Miles)	Church	% Growth in Past Year	Distance from CBD (in Miles)
1	14	6	11	3	0
2	8	3	12	1	6
3	9	21	13	14	12
4	2	0	14	6	3
5	4	3	15	2	1
6	0	4	16	4	7
7	15	9	17	7	4
8	22	9	18	8	2
9	7	4	19	11	9
10	9	3	20	6	7

2. Using distance from the CBD as the independent variable and percentage of growth in the past year as the dependent variable, construct a scattergram for the data in Exercise 1. Does the relationship appear to be reasonably linear?

3.   a) Calculate the correlation between fear of crime (great fear scored high) and age.

    b) Reverse the scoring for fear of crime and recompute r. Assume fear of crime scores can theoretically vary between 1 and 15; therefore, 1 becomes 15, etc.

Age	Fear of Crime
22	2
35	7
47	6
56	14
72	13

4. Explain in *your own words* the meaning of correlation.

5. In each of the following examples identify a potential problem in the interpretation of the results of a correlational analysis.

    a) The relationship between age and frequency of drinking for an adolescent sample between the ages of 13 and 18.

    b) The correlation between aptitude and grades for honor students at a university.

    c) The relationship between vocabulary and reading speed among children in a "culturally deprived" community.

6. For a group of 50 individuals $\Sigma z_x z_y$ is 41.3. What is the correlation between the two variables?

7. The following scores were made by five students on two tests. Calculate the Pearson r (using $r = \Sigma z_x z_y / N$). Convert to ranks and calculate r_s.

Student	Text X	Text Y
A	5	1
B	5	3
C	5	5
D	5	7
E	5	9

Generalize: What is the effect of tied ranks on r_s?

8. Set up a data set demonstrating that gum disease is negatively related to the use of dental floss. Assume $N = 10$. Calculate r for your data.

9. Which correlation coefficient below indicates the strongest relationship? The weakest relationship? A negative relationship?

    a) -0.89 **b)** $+0.32$ **c)** $+0.58$

10. Calculate r for all pairs of the following variables and construct a correlation matrix.

1. Age	2. Education	3. Income	4. Family Size
40	8	$ 7,000	6
32	17	$46,000	4
21	16	$33,000	3
36	14	$30,000	3
51	12	$31,000	5

11. A study focusing on political activism among black ministers reported that the Pearson r between age and an "attitude toward the police" scale (negative scored low) was -0.14. Interpret this finding. Church size and the minister's education were correlated $+0.41$. What does this finding tell you and how might it be interpreted? (*Source:* William M. Berenson, Kirk W. Elifson, and Tandy Tollerson III, Preachers in politics: Political activism among the black ministry, *Journal of Black Studies,* Volume 6, June 1976, pp. 373–392).

12. The following data show scores on advanced sections of the Graduate Record Examination and college grade point averages. What is the relationship between these two variables?

GRE Scores	Grade Point Averages	GRE Scores	Grade Point Averages
440	1.57	528	2.08
448	1.83	550	2.15
455	2.05	582	3.44
460	1.14	569	3.05
473	2.73	585	3.19
485	1.65	593	3.42
489	2.02	620	3.87
500	2.98	650	3.00
512	1.79	690	3.12
518	2.63		

13. Explain the difference between $r = -0.76$ and $r = +0.76$.

14. Construct a scatter diagram for each of the following four sets of data.

a)		b)		c)		d)	
X	Y	X	Y	X	Y	X	Y
1.5	0.5	0.5	5.0	0.5	0.5	0.5	1.0
1.0	0.5	0.5	4.5	1.0	1.0	0.5	2.5
1.0	2.0	1.0	3.5	1.0	1.5	0.5	4.5
1.5	1.5	1.5	4.0	1.5	2.5	1.0	3.5
1.5	2.0	1.5	2.5	1.5	3.5	1.5	1.0
2.0	2.0	2.0	3.0	2.0	2.5	1.5	2.5
2.5	2.5	2.5	2.0	2.0	3.5	1.5	4.0
2.5	3.2	2.5	3.5	2.5	4.5	2.0	1.0
3.0	2.5	3.0	2.5	3.0	3.5	3.0	2.0
3.0	3.5	3.0	2.0	3.5	3.0	3.0	3.5
3.5	3.5	3.5	2.0	3.5	2.5	3.0	4.5
3.5	4.5	3.5	2.5	3.5	2.0	3.5	1.0
4.0	3.5	4.0	1.5	4.0	2.5	3.5	1.0
4.0	4.5	4.0	0.7	4.0	2.0	3.5	3.5
4.5	4.5	5.0	0.5	4.5	1.0	4.0	3.5
5.0	5.0			5.0	1.0	4.0	4.5
				5.0	0.5	4.5	2.5
						4.5	1.0

15. By inspecting the scatter diagrams for the data in Exercise 14, determine which one represents:

a) A curvilinear relation between X and Y.

b) A positive correlation between X and Y.

c) Little or no relation between X and Y.

d) A negative correlation between X and Y.

16. Discuss the following correlation matrix, which is based on interviews with 275 lawyers (hypothetical data).

	1	2	3	4
1. Size of law firm	1.00			
2. Salary	0.40	1.00		
3. Age	−0.11	0.67	1.00	
4. Education	0.03	0.00	0.07	1.00

17. The following data show the scores obtained by a group of 20 students on a college entrance examination and a verbal comprehension test. Prepare a scatter diagram and calculate a Pearson's r for these data.

Student	College Entrance Exam (X)	Verbal Compre-hension Test (Y)	Student	College Entrance Exam (X)	Verbal Compre-hension Test (Y)
A	52	49	K	64	53
B	49	49	L	28	17
C	26	17	M	49	40
D	28	34	N	43	41
E	63	52	O	30	15
F	44	41	P	65	50
G	70	45	Q	35	28
H	32	32	R	60	55
I	49	29	S	49	37
J	51	49	T	66	50

18. Outreach workers have identified seven neighborhoods that have the greatest predominance of intravenous drug users. The estimated number of drug users by neighborhood is shown below along with the area's median household income. Convert the data to ranks and compute r_s.

Neighborhood	Number of Drug Users	Median Income
A	75	$ 9,000
B	20	20,000
C	0	27,000
D	110	6,200
E	40	14,000
F	200	7,500
G	60	12,000

19. Two consulting agencies have independently ranked ten counties in terms of the quality of their public schools. Compute r_s to determine the extent to which the two sets of rankings correspond.

County	Rank of Schools by Agency A	Rank of Schools by Agency B
A	1	1
B	4	2
C	3	3
D	2	4
E	7	6
F	5	7
G	6	5
H	8	9
I	9	10
J	10	8

20. The data in the following table represent scores obtained by ten students on a statistics examination, and their final grade point average. Prepare a scatter diagram and calculate Pearson's r for these data.

Student	Score on Statistics Exam, X	Grade Point Average, Y	Student	Score on Statistics Exam, X	Grade Point Average, Y
A	90	2.50	F	70	1.00
B	85	2.00	G	70	1.00
C	80	2.50	H	60	0.50
D	75	2.00	I	60	0.50
E	70	1.50	J	50	0.50

21. A sociological study involved the rating of teachers. In order to determine the reliability of the ratings, the ranks given by two different observers were tabulated. Are the ratings reliable? Explain your answer.

Teacher	Rank by Observer A	Rank by Observer B	Teacher	Rank by Observer A	Rank by Observer B
A	12	15	I	6	5
B	2	1	J	9	9
C	3	7	K	7	6
D	1	4	L	10	12
E	4	2	M	15	13
F	5	3	N	8	8
G	14	11	O	13	14
H	11	10	P	16	16

22. Twenty-five high school students were randomly selected from public high schools in the Boston area and asked to report anonymously the number of rock concerts they attended during the past year and the average number of days per week that they smoke marijuana. Given the accompanying data, compute r and interpret your answer. What does it tell you?

Number of Rock Concerts Attended	Days per Week Marijuana Smoked	Number of Rock Concerts Attended	Days per Week Marijuana Smoked
4	2	4	2
7	4	4	2
0	0	3	0
1	2	11	7
6	3	14	6
2	1	6	3
2	0	3	0
3	1	1	2
2	4	4	5
3	3	0	0
2	1	1	1
0	0	3	1
		0	1

23. What effect does departure from linearity have on Pearson's *r*?

24. How does the range of scores sampled affect the size of the correlation coefficient?

25. What is the effect of reversing the scoring of a variable included in a correlation matrix?

26. How well do you remember the names of the seven dwarfs from Disney's animated classic *Snow White and the Seven Dwarfs?* The following table shows the order in which they were recalled, the percent of subjects recalling the names of each of them, and the percent who correctly identified them in a recognition task.

Dwarf	Order of Recall	Recalled %	Recognized %
Sleepy	1	86	91
Dopey	2	81	95
Grumpy	3	75	86
Sneezy	4	78	93
Doc	5	58	80
Happy	6	62	70
Bashful	7	38	84

Source: Based on Meyer and Hildebrand, 1984.

a) What is the measure of relationship appropriate for these data?

b) Prepare a correlation matrix showing the intercorrelations of these three variables.

chapter 10

Regression and Prediction

10.1 Introduction to Prediction
10.2 Linear Regression
10.3 Residual Variance and Standard Error of Estimate
10.4 Explained and Unexplained Variation
10.5 Correlation and Causation

10.1 Introduction to Prediction

Is length of courtship a good predictor of marital success? What role does sexual compatibility play in a successful marriage? Knowing a person's employment record, what can we say about the likelihood of her receiving a promotion? Knowing a student's mathematics aptitude score, can we estimate how well he will do in a statistics course?

Let's look at an example. Suppose we are trying to predict student Jones's score on the final exam. If the only information available was that the class mean on the final was 75 ($\overline{Y} = 75$), the best guess we could make is that he would obtain a score of 75 on the final.* However, far more information is usually available; for example, Mr. Jones obtained a score of 62 on the midterm examination. How can we use this information to make a better prediction about his performance on the final exam? If we know that the class mean on the midterm examination was 70 ($\overline{X} = 70$), we could reason that since he scored below the mean on the midterm, he would probably score below the mean on the final. At this point we appear to be closing in on a more accurate prediction of his performance. How might we further improve the accuracy of

---

* See Section 5.2.2, in which we demonstrated that the sum of the deviations from the mean is zero and that the sum of squares of deviations from the arithmetic mean is less than the sum of squares of deviations about any other score or potential score.

BOX 10.1

The Heavyweight Champions of Gas-Guzzling

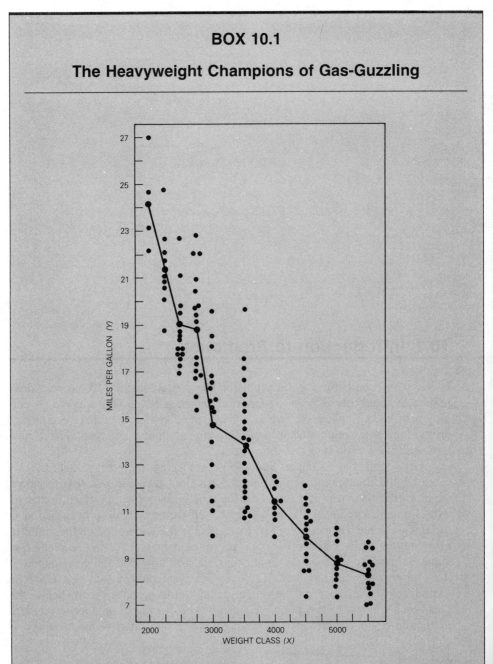

One of the benefits of correlated data is that mathematicians have worked out ways of predicting values of one variable from knowledge of the values of a correlated variable. The method is *regression analysis*.

The following, adapted from *Winning with Statistics,* shows how correlated data may be used to guide decision making when you are purchasing the latest dream machine.

Living with Regression Analysis

The beauty of correlated data, particularly when the relationship is high, as in the case of weight of auto and miles per gallon, is that mathematicians have worked out ways of predicting values on one variable from knowledge of the values of a correlated variable. The method is known as *regression analysis*. Please don't let the term throw you. We can arrive at a pretty fair comprehension of regression without stumbling about in the arcane caverns of mathematics.

Take a look at the accompanying figure. It shows a scatter diagram of weight of automobile and miles per gallon. Note that I have drawn a line connecting the mean miles per gallon at each weight of car. The resulting line is a pretty good *approximation* to what mathematicians call the regression line for predicting Y-values (miles per gallon) from knowledge of X-values (auto weight). For purposes of discussion, we'll treat that line as if it were the regression line. In mathematical shorthand, it is called the line of regression of Y on X. But that is not important. What is important is that when the relationship between X and Y is high, we can use the regression line

to predict Y-values from known X-values, achieving startling degrees of accuracy.

Let's see how this works. Let us say that you are considering buying one of two cars. Brand A is flaming red and weighs 3200 pounds when equipped. The second, brand B, is a metallic gold and weighs 2400 pounds. You can make your best guess about the overall performance of brand A by looking at [the figure] and drawing a vertical line at 3200 pounds until it intersects the regression line. Now look left to find the corresponding value for miles per gallon. Your best guess, then, is that the 3200-pound car will average somewhere around 15 miles per gallon. Repeat the same procedure for brand B, drawing a vertical line at 2400 pounds. That comes to about 20 miles per gallon, an improved fuel performance of about 33 percent, using 15 mpg as the base.

So there it is. Regression analysis can be relevant to your daily living. Indeed, although you may not be aware of it, you have probably provided a numerical value in more than one regression equation in your lifetime, if you have ever applied for college admission, taken a series of tests for job placement, or filled out a life insurance application.

Source: Excerpted from R. P. Runyon, *Winning with Statistics*. Reading, Mass.: Addison-Wesley, 1977.

our prediction? Simply knowing that he scored below the mean on the midterm does not give us a clear picture of his relative standing on this exam. If, however, we know the standard deviation on the midterm, we could express his score in terms of his relative position, that is, his z score. Let's imagine that the standard deviation on the midterm was 4 ($s_x = 4$). Since he scored 2 standard deviations below the mean ($z_x = -2.00$), would we be justified in guessing that he would score 2 standard deviations below the mean on the final ($zy = -2.00$)? That is, if $s_y = 8$, would you predict a score of 59 on the final? No! You will note that an important piece of information is missing: the correlation between the midterm and the final. You may recall from our discussion of correlation* that Pearson's r represents the extent to which the same individuals or events occupy the same relative position on two variables. Thus we are justified in predicting a score of exactly 59 on the final only when the correlation between the midterm and the final exam is perfect (i.e., when $r = +1.00$). Suppose that the correlation is equal to zero. Then it should certainly be obvious that we are not justified in predicting a score of 59; rather, we are once again back to our original prediction of 75 (i.e., $\bar{Y}$).

In summary, when $r = 0$, our best prediction is 75 ($\bar{Y}$); when $r = +1.00$, our best prediction is 59 ($z_y = z_x$). It should be clear that predictions from intermediate values of r will fall somewhere between 59 and 75.[†]

An important advantage of a correlational analysis, then, stems from its application to problems involving predictions from one variable to another. (See Box 10.1.) Sociologists, educators, political scientists, and economists are constantly being called upon to make predictions. To provide an adequate explanation of r and to illustrate its specific applications, we need to proceed with an analysis of linear regression.

10.2 Linear Regression

To simplify our discussion, let's start with an example of two variables that are usually perfectly or almost perfectly related: monthly salary and annual income. In Table 10.1 we have listed the monthly income of eight employees of a small welfare office. These data are shown graphically in Figure 10.1. It is customary to refer to the horizontal axis as the X-axis and to the vertical axis as the Y-axis. If one variable occurs earlier in time (or before) the other, the earlier one (or the independent variable) is represented on the X-axis. It will be noted that all salaries are represented on a straight line extending diagonally from the lower left-hand corner to the upper right-hand corner.

10.2.1 Equation for Linear Relationships

The equation relating monthly salary to annual income may be represented as

$$Y' = 12X$$

where the prime mark on Y indicates Y is being predicted.

---

* See Section 9.2.
† We are assuming that the correlation is positive. If the correlation were -1.00, our best prediction would be a score of 91, that is, $z_y = -z_x$.

Table 10.1 Monthly salaries and annual income of eight employees of a welfare office (hypothetical data)

Employee	Monthly Salary	Annual Income
A	1600	19,200
B	1700	20,400
C	1725	20,700
D	1750	21,000
E	1800	21,600
F	1850	22,200
G	1900	22,800
H	1975	23,700

You may substitute any value of X (the independent variable) into the equation and obtain the value of Y (the dependent variable) directly. For example, if another employee's monthly salary were $2000, her annual income would be

$$Y' = 12(2000) = 24,000$$

Let's add one more factor to this linear relationship. Suppose all of the employees received a $500 raise. The equation would now read

$$Y' = 500 + 12X$$

Figure 10.1 Monthly salaries and annual income of eight employees of a welfare office.

ANNUAL INCOME IN DOLLARS (Y)

MONTHLY SALARY IN DOLLARS (X)

Thinking back to your high school days of algebra, you will probably recognize this equation as a special case of the general equation for a straight line, that is

$$Y' = a + b_yX \qquad (10.1)$$

in which Y and X represent variables that change from individual to individual, and a and b_y represent constants for a particular set of data. More specifically, b_y represents the *slope of a line* relating values of Y to values of X. Thus, Y is the dependent variable and X is the independent variable. This is referred to as the *regression of Y on X*. In the present example the slope of the line is 12, which means that Y changes by a factor of 12 for each unit change in X. The letter a represents the value of Y when $X = 0$ and is referred to as the Y-*intercept* or the point at which the line crosses the Y-axis.

Equation (10.1) may be regarded as a method for predicting Y from known values of X. When the correlation is 1.00 (as in the present case), the predictions are perfect.

In Figure 10.1 the line, if extended, would intersect the Y-axis at $Y = 0$; therefore, $a = 0$. Figure 10.2(a) presents one example in which the Y-intercept is positive ($a = +1.0$) and Figure 10.2(b) contains another in which the Y-intercept is negative ($a = -2.5$).

The slope can also be negative. Figure 10.3(a) depicts a negative slope, for example, because as X increases, Y decreases or as X decreases, Y increases. Figure 10.3(b) shows a positive slope because X and Y vary in the same direction (they are both increasing or decreasing). Figure 10.3(c) has a slope equaling 0. As X varies, Y remains constant. Note that the regression line parallels the X-axis and a equals the mean of Y because the regression line will cross the Y-axis at $\overline{Y}$.

Figure 10.2   Regression lines showing positive and negative Y-intercepts.

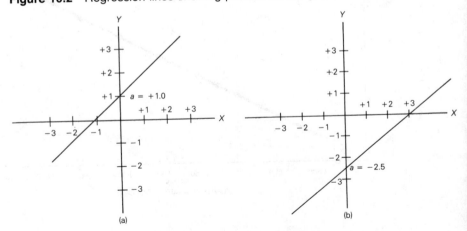

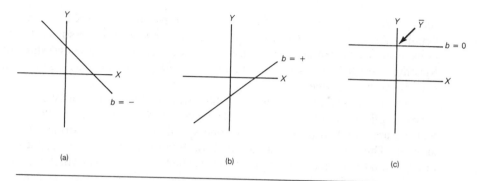

Figure 10.3 Regression lines showing three contrasting slopes.

The slope is frequently defined as the ratio of the change in Y to the change in X:

$$b_y = \frac{\text{change in } Y}{\text{change in } X} = \frac{\Delta Y}{\Delta X} = \frac{Y_2 - Y_1}{X_2 - X_1} \qquad (10.2)$$

Using any two coordinates on the line, we can quickly calculate the slope. The following section presents several ways of computing the slope. Looking at Table 10.1 and Figure 10.1, we can arbitrarily use employee A's monthly salary and annual income as our X_1 and Y_1 values and employee C's monthly salary and annual income as our X_2 and Y_2 values since the coordinates for employees A and C lie on the line. We can arbitrarily choose any two coordinates on the line because the slope is constant and unchanging for any given linear regression example. Substituting into Eq. (10.2), we confirm that the slope is 12:

$$b_y = \frac{Y_c - Y_a}{X_c - X_a} = \frac{20{,}700 - 19{,}200}{1725 - 1600} = \frac{1500}{125} = 12$$

Thus we could say that if X increases $100, Y will increase $1200. The rate of change is 12 to 1 (Y to X), and hence the slope is 12.

10.2.2 Predicting Y from Knowledge of X

In social science research the correlations we obtain are almost never perfect. Therefore, we must find a straight line that *best fits* or describes our data and make predictions from that line. But what do we mean by "best fit"? When discussing the mean and the standard deviation, we defined the mean as that point in a distribution that makes the sum of squared deviations from it minimal, that is, less than the sum of squared deviations about any other score or potential score. When applying this principle to correlation and regression, we are defining the *best-fitting straight line* as the line that makes the squared deviations around it minimal. This straight line is referred to as a **regression line.** Synonyms for the regression line include the line of best fit, least squares line, and the prediction line.

The term *prediction,* as used in statistics, does not necessarily carry with it any implication about the future. The term *predict* simply refers to the fact that we are using information about one variable to obtain information about another. Thus, if we know a woman's occupational status, we may use this information to predict how much education she has completed (which we would assume preceded her having been hired for the job).

At this point we will highlight a new symbol you recently encountered: Y'.* This may be read as "Y prime," "the predicted Y," or "estimated Y." We use this symbol with the regression line or the regression equation to estimate or predict a score on one variable from a known score on another variable.

Returning to the equation for a straight line, we are faced with the problem of determining b and a for a particular set of data so that Y' may be obtained. One equation for obtaining the slope of the line relating Y to X, which is known as the line of regression of Y on X, is the mean deviation equation:

$$b_y = \frac{\Sigma(X - \bar{X})(Y - \bar{Y})}{\Sigma(X - \bar{X})^2} \qquad (10.3)$$

You may have noticed that the numerator for this equation and for the mean deviation computational Eq. (9.1) for r are identical. The numerator in Eq. (9.1) determined the sign of r, and the numerator of Eq. (10.3) also determines the sign of b. It follows that the sign of r will always be the same as the sign of b for a given data set. Equation (10.3) is mathematically equivalent to Eq. (10.4), which clearly shows the relationship between r and b where b is equal to r times the ratio of the standard deviation of Y and the standard deviation of X. Hence, r equals b only when the standard deviations of X and Y are equal:

$$b_y = r\frac{s_y}{s_x} \qquad (10.4)$$

Equations (10.3) and (10.4) are mathematically equivalent to Eq. (10.5), which is the raw score computational equation preferred by many social scientists. You will note that it is very similar to the raw score Eq. (9.2) used to compute r:

$$b_y = \frac{N(\Sigma XY) - (\Sigma X)(\Sigma Y)}{N(\Sigma X^2) - (\Sigma X)^2} \qquad (10.5)$$

---

* The symbol $\hat{Y}$ (read "Y cap"), an alternative symbol that also designates the predicted Y, is preferred by some social scientists.

The constant a is given by Eq. (10.6):

$$a = \bar{Y} - b_y\bar{X} \qquad (10.6)$$

10.2.3 An Illustrative Regression Problem

We now can use Eq. (10.1) to predict Y. Let's solve a sample problem using the data introduced in Section 10.1.

Mr. Jones, you will recall, scored 62 on the midterm examination. What is our prediction concerning his score on the final examination? The following table lists the relevant statistics.

Midterm (X Variable)	Final (Y Variable)
$\bar{X} = 70$	$\bar{Y} = 75$
$S_x = 4$	$S_y = 8$
$X = 62$	
$r = 0.60$	

We can use Eq. (10.1) to predict Mr. Jones's score on the final examination in the following manner. Using Eq. (10.4), we can calculate b_y:

$$b_y = r\frac{S_y}{S_x} = 0.60\frac{8}{4} = 1.20$$

We see that $b = 1.20$ or that, as X increases one unit on the X-axis, Y increases 1.20 units on the Y-axis. Now we can calculate a, or our Y-intercept, using Eq. (10.6):

$$a = \bar{Y} - b_y\bar{X} = 75 - (1.20)70 = -9$$

We now know that $a = -9$ or that the regression line crosses the Y-axis at the value $Y = -9$. Using the values we have just calculated for b and a and his score of 62 on the midterm, we can now use Eq. (10.1) to predict Mr. Jones's score on the final exam:

$$Y' = a + b_yX = -9 + 1.20(62) = 65.40$$

Our prediction is that Mr. Jones will receive a score of 65.40 on the final examination. This example should begin to convey to you the interrelatedness of the various approaches to calculating a and b and predicting Y.

A reasonable question at this point is, "Since we know $\bar{Y}$ and s_y in the preceding problem, we presumably have all the observed data at hand. Therefore, why do we wish to predict Y from X?'' It should be pointed out that the purpose of this example was to acquaint you with a prediction equation. In actual practice, however, correlational techniques are most commonly used to make predictions about future samples where Y is unknown.

For example, let's suppose that you are a demographer and over a period of years have accumulated much information concerning the relationship between the state of the economy and average family size. You find that it is now possible to use economic information (the independent variable, X) to predict average family size (the dependent variable, Y), and then use this information to establish population projections.

Since we discussed the relationship between Pearson's r and z scores in Chapter 9, it should be apparent that the prediction equation may be expressed in terms of z scores. Mathematically, it can be shown that

$$z_{y'} = rz_x \qquad\qquad (10.7)$$

where $z_{y'} = Y'$ (the predicted final exam score) is expressed in terms of a z score.

Mr. Jones's score of 62 on the midterm can be expressed as a $z = -2.00$, since it is two standard deviations to the left of the mean, and we know the correlation between the midterm and final exam scores is 0.60. Thus, $z_{y'} = 0.60(-2.00) = -1.20$.

10.2.4 The Mean Deviation and Raw Score Computational Procedures for Linear Regression

Table 10.2 illustrates the mean deviation method of computation to provide you with a conceptual understanding of regression analysis. The computational procedures and the figures will be familiar to you as they were used to compute r in Table 9.2. We find b to equal 1.232, which indicates that as X increases one unit, Y increases 1.232 units. The regression line intersects the Y-axis at 4.38 since $a = 4.38$. These two values, a and b, determine the regression line and also provide us with a general prediction equation for these data. For example, using Eq. (10.1), we can predict respondent C's educational attainment knowing only her mother's educational attainment (5 years of formal education) in the following manner. Because

$$Y' = 4.38 + 1.232X$$
$$Y'_c = 4.38 + 1.232(5)$$
$$Y'_c = 10.54$$

Our prediction is that respondent C has completed 10.54 years of education; however, we know she has actually completed 13 years, or 2.46 more years than we predicted (see Table 10.2).

Table 10.2 Computational procedures for linear regression using the mean deviation method (hypothetical data)

Respondent	Mother's Education X	$(X - \bar{X})$	$(X - \bar{X})^2$	Daughter's Education Y	$(Y - \bar{Y})$	$(X - \bar{X})(Y - \bar{Y})$
A	1	−6	36	7	−6	36
B	3	−4	16	4	−9	36
C	5	−2	4	13	0	0
D	7	0	0	16	3	0
E	9	2	4	10	−3	−6
F	11	4	16	22	9	36
G	13	6	36	19	6	36

$N = 7$ $\Sigma X = 49$ $\Sigma(X - \bar{X})^2 = 112$ $\Sigma Y = 91$ $\Sigma(X - \bar{X})(Y - \bar{Y}) = 138$

$\bar{X} = 7$ $\bar{Y} = 13$

Using Eq. (10.3), we obtain

$$b_y = \frac{\Sigma(X - \bar{X})(Y - \bar{Y})}{\Sigma(X - \bar{X})^2} = \frac{138}{112} = 1.232$$

Using Eq. (10.6), we have

$$a = \bar{Y} - b_y(\bar{X}) = 13 - 1.232(7) = 4.38$$

Since

$$Y' = a + b_y X$$
$$Y' = 4.38 + 1.232X$$

Also

$$r = 0.82 \text{ (see Table 9.2)}.$$

Table 10.3 illustrates raw score computational Eq. (10.5). The raw score procedure provides us with the same results as did the mean deviation method presented in Table 10.2. Note that the correlation coefficient is positive ($r = +0.82$), as is the sign of the slope ($b = +1.232$).

10.2.5 Constructing a Regression Line

Let's return to the problem of constructing a regression line for predicting scores on the Y variables. As we have already pointed out, the regression line seldom passes through all the paired scores. It will, in fact, pass among the paired scores in such a way as to minimize the squared deviations between the regression line (the predicted scores) and the obtained scores. Earlier we pointed out that the mean is the point in a distribution that makes the sum of the squared deviations around it minimal. The regression line is analogous to the mean since, as we will demonstrate, the sum of deviations of scores around the regression line is zero and the sum of squares of these deviations is minimal. Some students find it helpful to think of the regression line as a "generalization" of the data.

Table 10.3 Raw score procedure for linear regression (hypothetical data)

Respon- dent	Mother's Education X	X^2	Daughter's Education Y	Y^2	XY
A	1	1	7	49	7
B	3	9	4	16	12
C	5	25	13	169	65
D	7	49	16	256	112
E	9	81	10	100	90
F	11	121	22	484	242
G	13	169	19	361	247

$$N = 7 \quad \Sigma X = 49 \qquad \Sigma X^2 = 455 \quad \Sigma Y = 91 \qquad \Sigma Y^2 = 1435 \quad \Sigma XY = 775$$
$$\overline{X} = 7 \qquad\qquad\qquad \overline{Y} = 13$$

Using Eq. (10.5), we have

$$b_y = \frac{N(\Sigma XY) - (\Sigma X)(\Sigma Y)}{N(\Sigma X^2) - (\Sigma X)^2}$$

$$= \frac{7(775) - (49)(91)}{7(455) - (49)^2}$$

$$= \frac{5425 - 4459}{3185 - 2401}$$

$$= \frac{966}{784}$$

$$b_y = 1.232$$

Also, using Eq. (10.6), we get

$$a = \overline{Y} - b_y\overline{X}$$
$$a = 13 - 1.232(7)$$
$$a = 4.38$$

Using Eq. (10.1), we obtain

$$Y' = a + b_y X$$
$$Y' = 4.38 + 1.232X$$

Also

$$r = 0.82 \text{ (see Table 9.2)}$$

The regression line always crosses the coordinate $(\overline{X}, \overline{Y})$; therefore, a convenient method of constructing our regression line involves locating the Y-intercept (a) on the Y-axis (in this instance, $a = 4.38$) and the coordinate determined by the means of X and Y. Connecting this coordinate with the Y-intercept determines the regression line that must pass through the coordinate determined by the means of X and Y.

It is helpful to remember that the closer the data points (coordinates) are to the line, the larger is the magnitude of r. When $r = 1.00$, all of the data

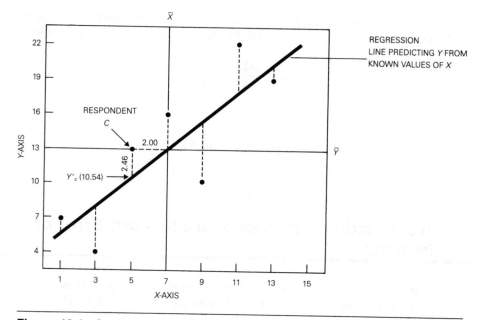

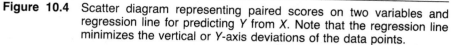

Figure 10.4 Scatter diagram representing paired scores on two variables and regression line for predicting Y from X. Note that the regression line minimizes the vertical or Y-axis deviations of the data points.

points will lie on the line, and the predicted Y values will equal the actual Y values.

The coordinate for respondent C has been highlighted in Figure 10.4 to help you further understand prediction. Recall that in the previous section we predicted that respondent C would complete 10.54 years of education, given that her mother had completed the fifth grade. By examining Figure 10.4, you should see that the predicted Y value (Y′) lies on the line predicting Y from known values of X.* Indeed, the regression line is also referred to as the *prediction line*. Projecting a perpendicular line from any point on the X-axis (assuming we are predicting Y from known values of X) to the prediction line allows us to determine the approximate predicted Y value for the corresponding X value from which the perpendicular line originated. As is shown in Figure 10.4, the predicted Y value of 10.54 years (see Section 10.2.4), given that X equals 5 years, is 2.46 years lower than the actual Y value (13) for respondent C. That is, respondent C completed 2.46 more years of education than we expected, given her mother's education.

The small triangle in Figure 10.4 confirms the slope that we calculated

---

* Occasionally we wish to predict X from known values of Y.

earlier for the data in Tables 10.2 and 10.3. You should see that as X increases 2.00 units, Y increases 2.46 units. Substituting into Eq. (10.2), we obtain

$$b_y = \frac{\Delta Y}{\Delta X} = \frac{2.46}{2.00} = 1.23$$

or

$$b_y = \frac{Y_2 - Y_1}{X_2 - X_1} = \frac{13 - 10.54}{7 - 5} = \frac{2.46}{2} = 1.23$$

10.3 Residual Variance and Standard Error of Estimate

Figure 10.5 shows a series of scatter diagrams (reproduced from Fig. 10.4) and the regression line for predicting Y from known values of X. The regression

Figure 10.5 Scatter diagram of paired scores on two variables, regression line for predicting Y values from known values of X, and the mean of the distribution of Y scores ($\overline{Y}$): $r = 0.82$ (from data in Table 10.4). (a) Deviations of scores ($Y - \overline{Y}$) from the mean of Y, total variation. (b) Deviations of predicted scores ($Y' - \overline{Y}$) from the mean of Y, explained variation. (c) Deviations of scores ($Y - Y'$) from the regression line, unexplained variation.

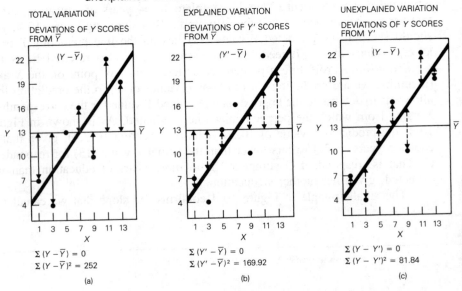

Table 10.4 Computational procedures for total, explained, and unexplained variation (data from Table 10.2)

Respon-dent	X	Y	Y'	$(Y - \bar{Y})$	$(Y - \bar{Y})^2$	$(Y' - \bar{Y})$	$(Y' - \bar{Y})^2$	$(Y - Y')$	$(Y - Y')^2$
A	1	7	5.61	−6	36	−7.39	54.61	1.39	1.93
B	3	4	8.07	−9	81	−4.93	24.30	−4.07	16.56
C	5	13	10.54	0	0	−2.46	6.05	2.46	6.05
D	7	16	13.00	3	9	0	0	3.00	9.00
E	9	10	15.46	−3	9	2.46	6.05	−5.46	29.81
F	11	22	17.93	9	81	4.93	24.30	4.07	16.56
G	13	19	20.39	6	36	7.39	54.61	−1.39	1.93
	$\bar{X} = 7$	$\bar{Y} = 13$			$\Sigma(Y - \bar{Y})^2 = 252$		$\Sigma(Y' - \bar{Y})^2 = 169.92^*$		$\Sigma(Y - Y')^2 = 81.84^*$

* Do not add to 252 due to rounding (169.92 + 81.84 ≠ 252).

line represents our best basis for predicting Y scores from known values of X. As we can see, not all of the Y values fall on the regression line. However, if the correlation had been 1.00, all the Y scores (the years of education completed by the seven respondents) would have fallen exactly on the regression line. The deviations $(Y - Y')$ in Figure 10.5(c) and Table 10.4 represent our errors in prediction. The $(Y - Y')$ column in Table 10.4 shows the errors in prediction for each of the seven respondents. Earlier we calculated respondent C's predicted Y score (Y') to be 10.54. Substituting this value and the actual Y score for her, we can calculate the size *and* direction of the error in prediction.

$$Y_{\text{respondent } C} - Y'_{\text{respondent } C} = 13 - 10.54 = +2.46$$

The value +2.46 tells us that the coordinate for respondent C lies 2.46 years above the regression line. The size and direction of the error in prediction (referred to as a **residual**) for the remaining six respondents is shown in the $(Y - Y')$ column of Table 10.4. Note that there will be as many residuals as cases (respondents, etc.), although a residual will equal 0 if an obtained Y score lies on the prediction line, i.e., $Y_i = Y_i'$.

Note the similarity of $Y - Y'$ (the deviation of the Y scores from the predicted scores, which always lie on the regression line) to $Y - \bar{Y}$ (the deviation of Y scores from $\bar{Y}$); the algebraic sum of the deviations around the regression line is equal to zero. Earlier, we saw that the algebraic sum of the deviations around the mean is also equal to zero.

You will recall that in calculating the variance (s^2) we squared the deviations from the mean, summed, and divided by N. The square root of the variance was the standard deviation. Now, if we were to square and sum the deviations of the scores from the regression line, $\Sigma(Y - Y')^2$, we would have a basis for calculating another variance and standard deviation. The variance around the regression line is known as the **residual variance** and is defined as

$$s^2_{\text{est } y} = \frac{\Sigma(Y - Y')^2}{N} \tag{10.8}$$

The standard deviation around the regression line (referred to as the **standard error of estimate**) is the square root of the residual variance. The standard error of estimate provides a measure of how well the regression equation predicts Y, given information about X. Thus

$$s_{\text{est } y} = \sqrt{\frac{\Sigma(Y - Y')^2}{N}} \tag{10.9}$$

Fortunately, there is a simplified method for calculating $s_{\text{est } y}$.

$$s_{\text{est } y} = s_y\sqrt{1 - r^2}* \tag{10.10}$$

You will note that when $r = \pm 1.00$, $s_{\text{est } y} = 0$, which means that there are no deviations from the regression line, and therefore no errors in prediction. On the other hand, when $r = 0$, the errors of prediction are maximal for that given distribution, that is, $s_{\text{est } y} = s_y$.

With the data in Table 10.3, the following statistics were calculated:

$$\overline{X} = 7 \qquad\qquad \overline{Y} = 13$$
$$s_x = 4.32 \qquad\qquad s_y = 6.48$$
$$r = 0.82$$

Using Eq. (10.10), we obtain

$$s_{\text{est } y} = 6.48\sqrt{1 - 0.82^2}$$
$$= 6.48(0.5724)$$
$$= 3.71$$

As we have already indicated, the standard error of estimate has properties that are similar to those of the standard deviation. The smaller the standard error of estimate is, the less dispersed the scores are around the regression line.

10.4 Explained and Unexplained Variation[†]

If we look again at Figure 10.5, we can see that there are three separate sums of squares that can be calculated from the data. These are:

1. Variation of scores around the sample mean [Fig. 10.5(a)]. This variation is given by $\Sigma(Y - \overline{Y})^2$ and is referred to as the **total variation** or the **total**

---

* The values of $\sqrt{1 - r^2}$ may be obtained directly from Table G. Thus for $r = 0.82$ we have $\sqrt{1 - r^2} = 0.5724$.

[†] Although analysis of variance is not covered until Chapter 15, much of the material in this section will serve as an introduction to some of the basic concepts of analysis of variance.

sum of squares (TSS). It is basic to the determination of the variance and the standard deviation of the sample. The total sum of squares is a measure of the variation in the Y scores.

2. Variation of scores around the regression line (or predicted scores) [Fig. 10.5(c)]. This variation is given by $\Sigma(Y - Y')^2$ and is referred to as **unexplained variation** or **residual sum of squares (RSS).** The reason for this choice of terminology should be clear. If the correlation between two variables is ± 1.00, all of the scores fall on the regression line. Consequently, we have in effect explained *all* of the variation in Y terms of the variation in X. In other words, in the event of a perfect relationship, there is no unexplained variation. However, normally the correlation is less than perfect, and many of the scores will not fall right on the regression line, as we have seen. The deviations of these scores from the regression line represent variation that is not accounted for by the correlation between two variables. Hence, the term *unexplained variation* is used.

3. Variation of predicted scores about the mean of the distribution [Fig. 10.5(b)]. This variation is given by $\Sigma(Y' - \overline{Y})^2$ and is referred to as **explained variation** or **regression sum of squares (RegSS).** The reason for this terminology should be clear from our discussion in the preceding paragraph and our prior reference to predicted deviation (Section 10.3). You will recall our previous observation that the greater the correlation is, the greater the predicted deviation is from the sample mean. It further follows that the greater the predicted deviation is, the greater the explained variation is. When the predicted deviation is maximum, the correlation is perfect, and 100% of the variation of the scores around the sample mean is explained.

It can be shown mathematically that the total variation consists of two components that may be added together. These two components represent unexplained variation and explained variation, respectively. Thus

$$\Sigma(Y - \overline{Y})^2 = \Sigma(Y - Y')^2 + \Sigma(Y' - \overline{Y})^2 \qquad (10.11)$$
$$\text{Total} \qquad \text{Unexplained} \quad \text{Explained}$$
$$\text{variation} \qquad \text{variation} \qquad \text{variation}$$

These calculations are shown in Figure 10.5. You will note that the sum of the explained variation (169.92) and the unexplained variation (81.84) is equal to the total variation. The slight discrepancy found in this example is due to rounding r to 0.82 prior to calculating the predicted scores.

Now, when $r = 0.00$, then $\Sigma(Y' - \overline{Y})^2 = 0.00$. (Why? See Section 10.2.) Consequently, the total variation is equal to the unexplained variation. Stated another way, when $r = 0$, all variation is unexplained. On the other hand, when $r = 1.00$, then $\Sigma(Y - Y')^2 = 0.00$, since all of the scores are on the regression line. Under these circumstances the total variation equals the explained variation. In other words, all variation is explained when $r = 1.00$.

The ratio of the explained variation to the total variation is referred to as the **coefficient of determination** and is symbolized by r^2. The equation for the coefficient of determination is

$$r^2 = \frac{\text{explained variation}}{\text{total variation}} = \frac{\Sigma(Y' - \bar{Y})^2}{\Sigma(Y - \bar{Y})^2} \qquad (10.12)$$

Referring to Figure 10.5, we see that the proportion of explained variation to total variation is

$$r^2 = \frac{169.92}{252} = 0.67$$

It can be seen that the coefficient of determination indicates the proportion of total variation that is explained in terms of the magnitude of the correlation coefficient. When $r = 0$, the coefficient of determination, r^2, equals 0. When $r = 0.5$, the coefficient of determination is 0.25. In other words, 25% of the total variation is accounted for. Finally, when $r = 1.00$, then $r^2 = 1.00$ and all variation is accounted for or explained. In the preceding example 67% of the variation in Y has been explained by X.

Figure 10.6 depicts graphically the proportion of variation in one variable that is accounted for by the variation in another variable when r takes on different values.

We have previously shown that the coefficient of determination, r^2, is equal to 0.67 for the data summarized in Figure 10.5. Note that the square root of this number (i.e., $\sqrt{0.67}$) equals 0.82—which is r for these data.

Since r^2 represents the proportion of variation accounted for, $(1 - r^2)$ represents the proportion of variation that is *not* explained in terms of the correlation between X and Y. This concept is known as the **coefficient of nondetermination** and is symbolized by k^2. Thus, k^2 represents the proportion of variation in Y that must be explained by variables other than X.

In summary, the relationship between k^2 and r^2 is

$$k^2 = 1 - r^2 \qquad (10.13)$$

or

$$k^2 + r^2 = 1 \qquad (10.14)$$

For the data in Figure 10.5, k^2 may be obtained directly:

$$k^2 = \frac{\text{unexplained variation}}{\text{total variation}} = \frac{81.84}{252} = 0.33$$

or, by use of Eq. (10.13):

$$k^2 = 1 - r^2 = 1 - 0.67 = 0.33$$

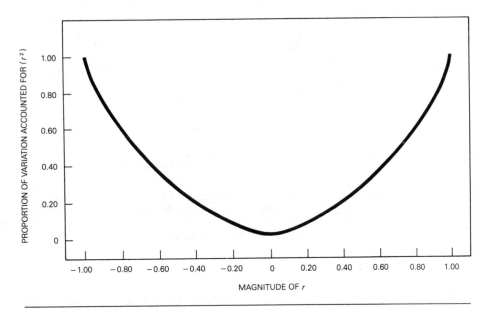

PROPORTION OF VARIATION ACCOUNTED FOR (r^2)

MAGNITUDE OF r

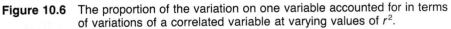

Figure 10.6 The proportion of the variation on one variable accounted for in terms of variations of a correlated variable at varying values of r^2.

10.5 Correlation and Causation

You have seen that when two variables are related, it is possible to predict one from your knowledge of the other. This relationship between correlation and prediction often leads to a serious error in reasoning; that is, the relationship between two variables frequently carries with it the implication that one has caused the other. This is especially true when there is a temporal relationship between the variables in question, that is, when one precedes the other in time. What is often overlooked is the fact that the variables may not be causally connected in any way, but that they may vary together by virtue of a common link with a third variable. Thus, if you are a bird watcher, you may note that as the number of birds increases in the spring, the grass becomes progressively greener (see Fig. 10.7). However, recognizing that the extended number of hours and the increasing warmth of the sun is a third factor influencing both of these variables, you are not likely to conclude that the birds cause the grass to turn green, or vice versa. However, there are many occasions, particularly in the social sciences, when it is not so easy to identify the third factor.

Suppose that you have demonstrated that there is a high positive correlation between the number of hours students spend studying for an exam and their subsequent grades on that exam. You may be tempted to conclude that the number of hours of study causes grades to vary. This seems to be a perfectly

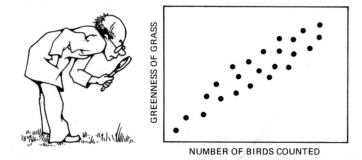

Figure 10.7   Note that when the census count of birds is low, the grass is not very green. When there are many birds, the grass is very green. Therefore, the number of birds determines how green the grass will become. What is wrong with this conclusion?

reasonable conclusion, and is probably in close agreement with what your parents and instructors have been telling you for years. Let's look closer at the implications of a causal relationship. On the assumption that a greater number of hours of study causes grades to increase, we would be led to expect that *any* student who devotes more time to study is guaranteed a high grade and that one who spends less time on studying is going to receive a low grade. This is not necessarily the case. We have overlooked the fact that it might be that the better student (by virtue of higher intelligence, stronger motivation, better study habits, etc.) who devotes more time to study performs better simply because he or she has a greater capacity to do so.

What we are saying is that correlational studies simply do not permit inferences of causation. Correlation is a *necessary* but not a *sufficient* condition to establish a causal relationship between two variables.

Huff's book* includes an excellent chapter devoted to the confusion of correlation with causation. He refers to faulty causal inferences from correlational data as the **post hoc fallacy.** The following excerpt illustrates a common example of the post hoc fallacy.

> Reams of pages of figures have been collected to show the value in dollars of a college education, and stacks of pamphlets have been published to bring these figures—and conclusions more or less based on them—to the attention of potential students. I am not quarreling with the intention. I am in favor of education myself, particularly if it

---

* Reprinted from D. Huff and I. Geis, *How to Lie with Statistics*, New York: W. W. Norton & Co., Inc., 1954, with permission.

includes a course in elementary statistics. Now these figures have pretty conclusively demonstrated that people who have gone to college make more money than people who have not. The exceptions are numerous, of course, but the tendency is strong and clear.

The only thing wrong is that along with the figures and facts goes a totally unwarranted conclusion. This is the *post hoc* fallacy at its best. It says that these figures show that if *you* (your son, your daughter) attend college you will probably earn more money than if you decide to spend the next four years in some other manner. This unwarranted conclusion has for its basis the equally unwarranted assumption that since college-trained folks make more money, they make it because they went to college. Actually we don't know but that these are the people who would have made more money even if they had *not* gone to college. There are a couple of things that indicate rather strongly that this is so. Colleges get a disproportionate number of two groups of kids—the bright and the rich. The bright might show good earning power without college knowledge. And as for the rich ones—well money breeds money in several obvious ways. Few sons of rich men are found in low-income brackets whether they go to college or not.

Summary

Let's briefly review what we have learned in this chapter. We have seen that it is possible to "fit" a straight line to a bivariate distribution of scores for predicting Y scores from known X values.

We saw that when the correlation is perfect, all of the scores fall on the regression line. Thus, there is no error in prediction. The lower the degree of relationship is, the greater the dispersion of scores is around the regression line, and the greater the errors of prediction are. Finally, when $r = 0$, the mean of the sample provides our best predictor for a given variable.

The regression line was shown to be analogous to the mean: The summed deviations around it are zero and the sum of squares are minimal. The standard error of estimate was shown to be analogous to the standard deviation.

We saw that three separate sums of squares, reflecting variability, may be calculated from correlational data. Variation about the mean of the distribution for each variable: This variation is referred to as the *total variation* or *total sum of squares*. Variation of each score about the regression line: This variation is known as *unexplained variation* or *residual sum of squares*. Variation of each predicted score about the mean of the distribution for each variable: This variation is known as *explained variation* or *regression sum of squares*. We saw that the sum of the explained variation and the unexplained variation is equal to the total variation.

Finally, we saw that the ratio of the explained variation to the total variation provides us with the proportion of the total variation that is explained. The term applied to this proportion is *coefficient of determination*.

Terms to Remember

Coefficient of determination (r^2)   The ratio of the explained variation to the total variation.

Coefficient of nondetermination (k^2)   Proportion of variation not explained in terms of the correlation between the two variables.

Explained variation   The variation of predicted scores about the mean of the distribution. Same as the regression sum of squares.

Post hoc fallacy   Faulty causal inferences from correlational data.

Regression line (line of "best fit")   A straight line that makes the squared deviations around it minimal.

Regression sum of squares   The variation of predicted scores about the mean of the distribution. Same as the explained variation.

Residual   The size and direction of the error in prediction or the vertical distance from the observed data coordinate to the regression line.

Residual sum of squares   The variation of scores around the regression line. Same as the unexplained variation.

Residual variance   The variance around the regression line.

Standard error of estimate   The standard deviation of scores around the regression line.

Total sum of squares   The variation of scores around the sample mean. Same as the total variation.

Total variation   The variation of scores around the sample mean. Same as the total sum of squares.

Unexplained variation   The variation of scores around the regression line. Same as the residual sum of squares.

Exercises

1. Find the equation of the regression line for the following data.

X	1	2	3	4	5
Y	5	3	4	2	1

2. Using the data in Exercise 1, construct a scattergram and draw the regression line. (*Hint:* The regression line always passes through the coordinate formed by $\overline{X}$ and $\overline{Y}$.)

3. Using the data in Exercise 1, calculate the total sum of squares, the residual sum of squares, the regression sum of squares, r and r^2. Using Eq. (9.1) or (9.2), confirm your answer for r^2.

4. Using the data in Exercise 1, compute the residuals and the predicted Y values.

5. Assuming that TSS $= 100$, RSS $= 75$, and RegSS $= 25$, discuss the concepts of explained and unexplained variance. Compute the coefficients of determination and nondetermination and discuss.

6. In a study concerned with the relationship between two variables, X and Y, the following was obtained.

$$\overline{X} = 119 \qquad\qquad \overline{Y} = 1.30$$
$$s_x = 10 \qquad\qquad s_y = 0.55$$
$$r = 0.70$$
$$N = 100$$

a) Sally B. obtained a score of 130 on the X variable. Predict her score on the Y variable.

b) A score of 128 on the Y variable was predicted for Bill B. What was his score on the X variable?

c) Determine the standard error of estimate of Y. Interpret your answer.

7. A study was undertaken to find the relationship between family stability and performance in college. The following results were obtained.

Family Stability	College Average
$\overline{X} = 49$	$\overline{Y} = 1.35$
$s_x = 12$	$s_y = 0.50$
$r = 0.36$	
$N = 60$	

a) Norma obtained a score of 65 on the X variable. What is your prediction of her score on the Y variable?

b) Determine the standard error of estimate of Y. Interpret your answer.

c) What proportion of the total variation in Y is accounted for by the X variable?

8. Assume that $\overline{X} = 30$, $s_x = 5$; $\overline{Y} = 45$, $s_y = 8$. Draw a separate graph showing the regression line for the following values of r.

    a) 0.00   **b)** 0.20   **c)** 0.40

    d) 0.60   **e)** 0.80   **f)** 1.00

9. For the following data (assume enrollment is the independent variable):

    a) Calculate a and b_y. Interpret your answer; that is, what does it tell you?

    b) Plot the data and draw the regression line.

    c) Calculate r and r^2. Interpret your answer.

Public elementary and secondary schools enrollment and expenditures data for selected U.S. cities, 1978*

City	Enrollment (1000) 1978	Total Expenditures (Million $'s) 1978
Baltimore, Md.	152	310
Boston, Mass.	77	261
Chicago, Ill.	511	1285
Cleveland, Ohio	115	292
Dallas, Tex.	135	259
Detroit, Mich.	238	459
Houston, Tex.	207	378
Indianapolis, Ind.	78	117
Los Angeles, Calif.	587	1335
Memphis, Tenn.	116	150
Milwaukee, Wis.	101	227
New Orleans, La.	91	139
New York, N.Y.	1046	2522
Philadelphia, Pa.	254	575
Phoenix, Ariz.	184	281
St. Louis, Mo.	78	144
San Antonio, Tex.	64	98
San Diego, Calif.	119	270
San Francisco, Calif.	65	176
Washington, D.C.	120	293

* *Source:* U.S. National Center for Education Statistics, *Statistics of Public Elementary and Secondary Day Schools,* annual.

10. For the following data (assume percentage registering is the independent variable):

    a) Calculate a, b_y, and r.

    b) Interpret your answers.

Percent reported registered to vote and percent voting, 1968–1986*

Year	Percentage of U.S. Adults Reporting They Registered to Vote	Percentage of U.S. Adults Reporting They Voted
1968	74.3	67.8
1972	72.3	63.0
1974	62.2	44.7
1976	66.7	59.2
1978	62.6	45.9
1980	66.9	59.2
1982	64.1	48.5
1984	68.3	59.9
1986	64.3	46.0

* *Source:* U.S. Bureau of the Census, Current Population Reports, series P-20, No. 344, and earlier reports.

11. Assume that students take two tests for entrance into the college of their choice. Both are normally distributed tests. The college-entrance examination has a mean of 47.63 and a standard deviation of 13.82. The verbal comprehension test has a mean equal to 39.15 and a standard deviation equal to 12.35. The correlation between the two tests equals 0.85.

   a) Estelle obtained a score of 40 on her college entrance examination. Predict her score on the verbal comprehension test.

   b) Howard obtained a score of 40 on the verbal comprehension test. Predict his score on the college entrance examination.

12. For the following data (assume size of work group is the independent variable):

   a) What is your prediction of the measure of group cohesiveness for a work group numbering 15?

   b) What percent of the total variation in Y is explained by X?

Group	Size of Work Group	Measure of Group Cohesiveness (Low Value Indicates a Cohesive Work Group)
A	10	1
B	18	4
C	4	2
D	20	5
E	12	3
F	13	3
G	11	4

13. On the basis of the obtained data (below), an experimenter asserts that the older a child is, the fewer irrelevant responses he or she makes in an experimental situation.

    a) Determine whether this conclusion is valid.

    b) Mindy, age 13, enters the experimental situation. What is the most probable number of irrelevant responses the experimenter would predict for Mindy?

Age	Number of Irrelevant Responses	Age	Number of Irrelevant Responses
2	11	7	12
3	12	9	8
4	10	9	7
4	13	10	3
5	11	11	6
5	9	11	5
6	10	12	5
7	7		

14. Review the magazine section of your Sunday newspaper, monthly magazines, television, and radio advertisements for examples of the post hoc fallacy.

15. In a recent study Thornton (1977) explored the relationship of marital happiness to the frequency of sexual intercourse and to the frequency of arguments. Twenty-eight married couples volunteered to monitor their daily frequency of sexual intercourse and arguments for 35 consecutive days, and then they indicated their perceived marital happiness using a 7-point scale ranging from very unhappy (1) to perfectly happy (7). Some of Thornton's results are summarized here.

	Marital Happiness	Sexual Intercourse	Arguments
Mean	5.32	13.46	6.15
s	1.66	7.32	4.19

Correlation between happiness and arguments = $-.740$
Correlation between happiness and intercourse = $.705$

    a) How happy would you predict a couple to be who reported having ten arguments during the 35-day study period?

    b) How happy would you predict a couple to be who reported having sexual intercourse one time each day during the 35-day study period?

    c) A couple reporting that they are very unhappy (rating = 1.0) are most likely engaging in sexual intercourse how often?

d) What is the standard error of estimate for marital happiness when frequency of sexual intercourse is the predictor? What is the standard error of estimate when frequency of arguments is the predictor?

e) What proportion of the variability in ratings of marital happiness is accounted for by frequency of sexual intercourse? What proportion is accounted for by frequency of arguments?

f) What is the coefficient of nondetermination when marital happiness is predicted from frequency of sexual intercourse? What is the coefficient of nondetermination when marital happiness is predicted from frequency of arguments?

16. The per capita gross national product (GNP) is widely recognized as an estimate of the living standard of a nation. It has been claimed that per capita energy consumption is, in turn, a good predictor of per capita GNP. The accompanying table shows the GNP (expressed in dollars per capita) and the per capita energy consumption (expressed in millions of BTUs per capita) of various nations.

a) Construct a scatter diagram from the accompanying data.

b) Determine the correlation between GNP and energy expenditures.

c) Construct the regression line for predicting per capita GNP from per capita energy consumption.

d) The following nations were not represented in the original sample. Their per capita energy expenditures were Chile, 21; Ireland, 49; Belgium, 88. Calculate the predicted per capita GNP for each country. Compare the predicted values with the actual values which are, respectively, 400; 630; 1400.

Country	Energy Consumption (in Millions of BTUs)	GNP (Dollars)
India	3.4	55
Ghana	3.0	270
Portugal	7.7	240
Colombia	12.0	290
Greece	12.0	390
Mexico	23.0	310
Japan	30.3	550
USSR	69.0	800
Netherlands	75.0	1100
France	58.0	1390
Norway	67.0	1330
West Germany	90.0	1410
Australia	88.0	1525
United Kingdom	113.0	1400
Canada	131.0	1900
United States	180.0	2900

17.	X	3	4	5	6	7	8	9	10	11
	Y	4	3	5	6	8	7	9	9	11

a) Determine the correlation for the accompanying scores.

b) Given this correlation, and the computed mean for Y, predict the value of Y' for each X.

c) Calculate $\Sigma(Y - \bar{Y})^2$.

d) Calculate the unexplained variance.

e) Calculate the explained variance.

f) Calculate the coefficient of determination. Show that the square root of that value equals r.

18. A manager of a political campaign found a correlation of 0.70 between the number of people at a party and the loaves of bread consumed.

Number of People	Number of Loaves
$\bar{X} = 50$	$\bar{Y} = 5$
$s_x = 15$	$s_y = 1.2$

a) For a party of 60 people, calculate the predicted number of loaves needed.

b) For a party of 35, calculate the predicted number of loaves needed.

c) What is the $s_{est\ y}$? Interpret your answer.

chapter 11

Multivariate
Data Analysis

11.1 Introduction
11.2 The Multivariate Contingency Table
11.3 Partial Correlation
11.4 Multiple Regression Analysis

11.1 Introduction

In the previous chapters we have examined univariate and bivariate statistical techniques. Often, however, the complexity of social science issues requires that several variables be analyzed simultaneously. When this is the case, we utilize **multivariate statistical techniques,** which allow us to determine the nature of the relationships between three or more variables.

When the relationship between marital status and employment status was considered in Chapter 8 (An Introduction to Contingency Tables), we concluded that a weak relationship existed between the two variables. That is, knowing a woman's marital status improved our ability to predict her employment status. In the process of establishing that a relationship existed, however, we ignored other variables that might have been useful in determining why some of the women in the sample chose to work and others did not. What if we had divided our sample into two groups: those women who need to work for financial reasons and those who do not? It is very likely that introducing a third variable, in this instance the financial necessity of working, into the analysis would allow us to understand more fully the employment status of the women in our sample. Indeed, it is possible that a major reason for women working is the need for additional income. A fourth variable, the presence or absence of young children in the home, might also help clarify the complex reasons that determine whether or not a woman chooses to work outside the home.

In Chapter 9 (Correlation) you learned to assess the direction and strength of the relationship between two interval-level variables. Although it is valuable to know the correlation between two variables, you were later warned in Chapter 10 not to equate correlation with causation, as a third variable might be responsible for the observed bivariate correlation.

You also may have concluded after studying Chapter 10 (Regression and Prediction) that using a single independent variable to predict a dependent variable was far too simplistic an approach given the complexity of human attitudes and behavior. Age by itself, for example, can be used as an independent variable to predict a person's life satisfaction. However, if several other independent variables, such as an individual's economic and health status, were used jointly with the individual's age, we would expect to improve our prediction of life satisfaction.

All of these examples require the use of multivariate data analysis. The multivariate techniques presented in this chapter are extensions of what you have learned in Chapters 8, 9, and 10. They include the topics of multivariate contingency table analysis, partial correlation analysis, and multiple regression and correlation analysis. You may wish to briefly review those chapters prior to reading this chapter.

11.2 The Multivariate Contingency Table

Table 11.1 shows the relationship between high school seniors' plans to attend college and their parents' level of educational attainment. The table has been percentaged down, and comparisons made across the table reveal a positive relationship between parental educational attainment and seniors' plans to attend college (gamma = 0.443). Therefore, the more formal education the parent has completed, the more likely the student has plans to attend college following graduation from high school.

Before we can conclude that parental educational attainment is a key determinant of plans to attend college, we must consider the possibility that the relationship is due to a third variable. Perhaps the relationship between the initial two variables differs by sex. We can assess the effect of sex on college plans by analyzing the female and male respondents separately, as shown in Tables 11.1(b) and (c). Note that the distribution of cases in Table 11.1(a) would result if we combined Tables 11.1(b) and (c). For example, totaling the 347,000 cases in the upper right cell of Table 11.1(b) and the 362,000 cases in the upper right cell of Table 11.1(c) would result in the 709,000 cases in the upper right cell of Table 11.1(a).

The relationship between parental educational attainment and college plans of female seniors is presented in Table 11.1(b), and male seniors are included in Table 11.1(c). Tables 11.1(b) and (c) are referred to as **conditional tables** or **partial tables** because they summarize the relationship between two variables for subgroups, categories, or conditions of one or more other variables. The variable sex in this instance is referred to as a **control or test variable**

Table 11.1 College plans by educational attainment for head of family

(a) For females and males

(X)
Educational Attainment for Head of Family

(Y) College Plans	Elementary	High School	College	Total
Plan to attend	31.6 (149)	42.4 (714)	71.4 (709)	(1572)
May attend	28.9 (136)	28.2 (475)	17.7 (176)	(787)
Will not attend	39.5 (186)	29.4 (495)	10.9 (108)	(789)
Total	100.0 (471)	100.0 (1684)	100.0 (993)	N = 3148

Gamma = +0.443

(b) For females

Females (Z)
Educational Attainment for Head of Family (X)

(Y) College Plans	Elementary	High School	College	Total
Plan to attend	34.7 (70)	45.7 (391)	75.6 (347)	(808)
May attend	26.7 (54)	24.8 (212)	15.7 (72)	(338)
Will not attend	38.6 (78)	29.5 (252)	8.7 (40)	(370)
Total	100.0 (202)	100.0 (855)	100.0 (459)	N = 1516

Gamma = +0.468

(c) For males

Males (Z)
Educational Attainment for Head of Family (X)

(Y) College Plans	Elementary	High School	College	Total
Plan to attend	29.4 (79)	39.0 (323)	67.8 (362)	(764)
May attend	30.5 (82)	31.7 (263)	19.5 (104)	(449)
Will not attend	40.1 (108)	29.3 (243)	12.7 (68)	(419)
Total	100.0 (269)	100.0 (829)	100.0 (534)	N = 1632

Gamma = +0.425

Numbers in thousands. Reported in Current Population Reports, "College Plans of High School Seniors," Series P-20, No. 299.

and is designated by the letter Z. **Statistical elaboration** refers to the introduction of a control or test variable into an analysis to determine if a two-variable relationship remains the same or varies under the different categories or conditions of the control or test variable.

We are seeking to understand the bivariate relationship better by examining it under a variety of conditions. Although introducing a control variable cannot establish causation, if the bivariate relationship remains strong with the introduction of a theoretically relevant control variable(s), we are more confident that the relationship is possibly causal.*

Tables 11.1(b) and (c) are also referred to as first-order conditional tables. The **order of a conditional table** is determined by the number of control or test variables that have been introduced. A zero-order table [like Table 11.1(a)] includes no control variables; a first-order conditional table [like Table 11.1(b) or (c)] includes one control variable; and a second-order conditional table contains two control variables employed simultaneously, etc.

The effect of sex, our control variable, has been physically removed in Table 11.1(b), which contains only females and in Table 11.1(c), which contains only males. Thus, both tables are homogeneous in terms of the test variable. Put another way, sex has been controlled or held constant. This was not the case in Table 11.1(a), which contained both females and males.

Controlling for the effects of sex has had a very minor influence on the bivariate relationship in Table 11.1(a). While the relationship between parental educational attainment and college plans is slightly stronger for females than males (gamma = 0.468 versus 0.425), the difference between the gammas is slight. Furthermore, a comparison of the percentages in Table 11.1(a) with those in Tables 11.1(b) and (c), as well as a comparison of the partial tables, supports the finding that controlling for the effects of sex had little impact.

We do see some differences as we compare the percentages in the three tables, however, the trends across rows are quite similar. For example, compare the percentages across the three rows labeled "Plan to attend" in Tables 11.1(a), 11.1(b), 11.1(c); then compare the three "May attend" rows; and finally, the three "Will not attend" rows.

Perhaps at this point you have asked yourself why sex was chosen as a control variable. Several other variables might have proven equally as important or more important than sex. The choice is based on logic and the theoretical context of the variables being investigated. Another potential test variable that could have an effect on the relationship between parental educational attainment and college plans of high school seniors is the student's academic aptitude. Studies have shown that lower socioeconomic students with a high academic

---

* The following three criteria must be met to establish causality: (1) The two variables must be correlated or statistically related, (2) the independent variable must precede the dependent variable in time (i.e., must occur prior to the dependent variable), and (3) the bivariate relationship must not be due to the effect of a third variable (i.e., alternative explanations of the bivariate relationship must be eliminated by introducing control variables).

aptitude are more likely to attend college than lower socioeconomic students with a low academic aptitude. Aptitude seems to have an influence independent of family economic and educational background. If we controlled for aptitude using an interval measure of a standardized test, it would be necessary to establish "cutting points." Dividing the scores into low, medium, and high categories would result in three, first-order partial tables, one for each category.

Controlling for an ordinal- or interval-level variable reduces but does not eliminate the influence of a test variable. For example, family income could be trichotomized into the following three categories: (1) less than $10,000, (2) $10,000–$20,000, and (3) over $20,000; yet within each of the categories, considerable variation remains. Family income cannot be held constant in the sense that all of the cases in a partial table are homogeneous with respect to the test variable, as was the case when we controlled for sex and analyzed males and females separately.

The variation within categories of an ordinally or intervally measured test variable can be *reduced* by increasing the number of categories; however, there may not be a sufficient number of cases for all the cells that would result; and also, too many cells can make the data very difficult to interpret. A 3 × 3 bivariate table and a test variable with three categories would result in three first-order partial tables, each containing 9 cells for a total of 27 cells (3 × 9 = 27).

11.3 Partial Correlation

11.3.1 Introduction

A study of black ministers in Nashville, Tennessee, was conducted, from which a model of their political involvement was developed.* Two demographic variables, the minister's age and years of formal education, were moderately correlated with civic participation (CP), a variable based on a combination of such activities as having worked in political campaigns, telephoned a state or local official about a community problem, contributed money to support a political campaign, etc. On the basis of the bivariate correlations (age with CP, $r = -0.30$ and education with CP, $r = 0.49$), the authors concluded that both age and education were important determinants of the minister's civic participation (the dependent variable).

Model A describes the expected relationships among the three variables. Education is shown as an **intervening variable** linking age and civic participation.

MODEL A   AGE ⟶ EDUCATION ⟶ CIVIC PARTICIPATION

---

* William M. Berenson, Kirk W. Elifson, and Tandy Tollerson III, Preachers in politics: A study of political activism among the black ministry, *Journal of Black Studies* 6, June 1976, pp. 373–383.

Two other models were considered. Model B assumes that age and civic participation are **spuriously related** due to their relationship with education, and in model C age serves as an intervening variable.* Neither model B or C was considered plausible due to the unlikely causal ordering of education and age.

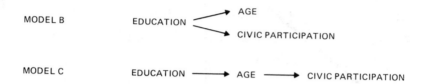

To test model A, we calculated a partial correlation coefficient before proceeding with a test of the overall model. A **partial correlation coefficient** is a measure of the linear relationship between two interval-level variables, controlling for one or more other variables.[†] In this instance the partial correlation coefficient between age and civic participation, controlling for educational attainment, was −0.04, suggesting that education was an intervening variable causally linking age and civic participation.

11.3.2 The Logic of the Partial Correlation Coefficient

Technically, the partial correlation of variables X and Y controlling for variable Z is the correlation of the residuals of the regressions of X on Z and Y on Z. In other words, you can think of the control variable (Z) serving as an independent variable to predict X and Y in two separate regression analyses. Two sets of residuals are computed in the process.[‡] The first set of residuals represents the variation in X not explained by Z, and the second set of residuals represents the variation in Y not explained by Z. The partial correlation coefficient between X and Y controlling for Z can be computed by correlating these two sets of residuals.

Partial correlation coefficients can be computed using the computational

---

* A *spurious relationship* is said to exist when the zero-order relationship between an independent and dependent variable disappears or becomes significantly weaker with the introduction of a control or test variable. The variables are spuriously related because their relationship is due to the causal influence of the test variable on the variables.

[†] Many social scientists routinely use ordinal-level variables that are evenly distributed and have five or more categories with interval statistical techniques. Violating the assumption of interval-level data given these restrictions does not have a marked impact on the outcome (Labovitz, 1970). As Blalock has noted, ". . . if one becomes too much of a purist with respect to measurement criteria, there may be an equally dangerous tendency to throw away information that is not completely satisfactory" (1979, p. 444). Henkel (1975) offers an opposing argument.

[‡] A *residual* was defined in Chapter 10 as the size and direction of the error in prediction or the distance from an observed data coordinate to the regression line.

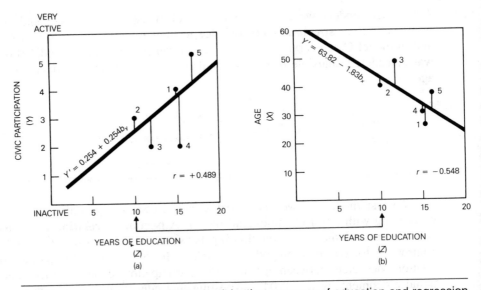

Figure 11.1 Regression of civic participation on years of education and regression of age on years of education.

equation presented in the following section; however, a thorough understanding requires that one conceptual example be presented in which the logic of correlating two sets of residuals is developed. The partial correlation between age and civic participation, controlling for education, will serve as an illustration. Figure 11.1 is based on the scores presented in Table 11.2 of the five hypothetical male black ministers. Civic participation and age have been individually regressed on education, which serves as the control variable.

The *statistical control* procedure used in partial correlation analysis differs from the *physical control* procedure used with multivariate contingency tables in Section 11.2. Statistical control involves an adjustment process rather than placing the respondents into categories or subgroups as is the case when physical controls are used. Minister 2 has been arbitrarily highlighted in Figure 11.1(a) and (b). In Figure 11.1(a) the coordinate for minister 2 lies above the regression line, indicating that he scored higher on civic participation that was predicted given his 10 years of formal education. By the same token in Figure 11.1(b), the coordinate for minister 2 lies below the regression line, indicating that he is younger than was predicted given his 10 years of formal education.

The positive residual for minister 2 in Figure 11.1(a) indicates the extent to which his civic participation score is independent of (unexplained by) his education score. The negative residual shown in Figure 11.1(b) for minister 2 indicates the extent to which his age is independent of (unexplained by) his education score. The actual values of these two residuals ($+0.71$ and -3.57) are presented in Table 11.2.

Note in Figures 11.1(a) and (b) that both residuals for minister 2 are based

Table 11.2 Raw scores, predicted scores, and residuals for five black ministers

Black Minister	Age (X)	Civic Participation (Y)	Years of Education (Z)	Y' with Z Independent	X' with Z Independent	Y − Y'	X − X'
1	28	4	15	3.56	36.44	+0.44	−8.44
2	42	3	10	2.29	45.57	+0.71	−3.57
3	50	2	12	2.79	41.92	−0.79	+8.08
4	34	2	15	3.56	36.44	−1.56	−2.44
5	41	5	16	3.81	34.62	+1.19	+6.38

on the same education score (10 years in this instance); hence, education has been controlled or held constant. This is also true of the four other ministers, and therefore the residuals or deviations from the regression line shown in Figures 11.1(a) and (b) reflect the variation in civic participation and age that cannot be accounted for by education.

Table 11.2 includes the five ministers' ages, civic participation scores, and years of formal education, along with the predicted values for age (X') and civic participation (Y') when they were regressed independently on edu-

Table 11.3 Computational procedures for the partial correlation coefficient using residuals

Black Minister	Regression Residual for Civic Participation with Education Independent Y − Y'	Regression Residual for Age with Education Independent X − X'	$(Y − Y')^2$	$(X − X')^2$	$(X − X') \cdot (Y − Y')$
1	+0.44	−8.44	0.19	71.23	−3.71
2	+0.71	−3.57	0.50	12.74	−2.53
3	−0.79	+8.08	0.62	65.29	−6.38
4	−1.56	−2.44	2.43	5.95	+3.81
5	+1.19	+6.38	1.42	40.70	+7.59
$N = 5$	$\Sigma = -0.01^*$	$\Sigma = 0.01^*$	$\Sigma = 5.16$	$\Sigma = 195.91$	$\Sigma = -1.22$

$$r = \frac{N\Sigma XY - (\Sigma X)(\Sigma Y)}{\sqrt{[N\Sigma X^2 - (\Sigma X)^2][N\Sigma Y^2 - (\Sigma Y)^2]}} \qquad (9.2)$$

$$= \frac{5(-1.22) - (0.01)(0.01)}{\sqrt{[5(195.91) - (0.01)^2][5(5.16) - (0.01)^2]}}$$

$$= \frac{6.10}{\sqrt{25{,}272.39}}$$

$$= -0.04$$

Note: When substituting into Eq. (9.2), $X − X' = X$ and $Y − Y' = Y$.
* Does not sum to zero due to rounding.

Table 11.4 Zero-order correlation matrix

	X	Y	Z
(X) Age	1.00		
(Y) Civic participation	−0.30	1.00	
(Z) Education	−0.55	0.49	1.00

cation (Z), the control variable. The actual values of the residuals shown in Figure 11.1 are also provided. These residual values are used with Eq. (9.2) in Table 11.3 to compute the partial correlation coefficient between age and civic participation controlling for education.

11.3.3 The Computational Equation

Now that you fully understand the logic of partial correlation coefficients, computational Eq. (11.1) is the preferable means of computing first-order partial correlation coefficients.* Equation (11.1) requires that all of the relevant zero-order correlation coefficients be known, as shown in Table 11.4. It is not necessary to calculate the residuals to determine the partial correlation coefficient. Recall from Section 9.1 that the size of a correlation coefficient directly reflects the goodness of fit of the regression line to the coordinates, and therefore provides us with an explicit description of the residuals.

$$r_{XY.Z} = \frac{r_{XY} - r_{XZ}r_{YZ}}{\sqrt{(1 - r_{XZ}^2)(1 - r_{YZ}^2)}} \qquad (11.1)$$

where

X = the independent variable

Y = the dependent variable, and

Z = the control variable

The partial correlation coefficient between X and Y controlling for Z is symbolized by $r_{XY.Z}$ (read "r sub XY dot Z"). The numerator of Eq. (11.1) provides for a measure of the variation that variables X and Y share in common, less the product of the variation that X and Y share with Z, the control variable. The denominator involves taking the square root of the product of the variation in X and Y that is not explained by Z. Partial correlation coefficients can range from −1.00 to +1.00 and, when squared, are a measure of the percent of

---

* Computational equations for higher-order partial correlation coefficients will not be discussed in this text. The **order of a partial correlation coefficient** indicates the number of control or test variables. The interested reader should consult Blalock, 1979.

variation two variables have in common after controlling for the effects of a third (or third and fourth, etc.) variable. Squaring a partial correlation coefficient of -0.04 tells us that X and Y have less than 1% of their variance in common after Z has been controlled. Entering the correlation coefficients from Table 11.4 into Eq. (11.1) yields

$$r_{XY.Z} = \frac{-0.30 - (-0.55)(0.49)}{\sqrt{(1 - (-0.55)^2)(1 - 0.49^2)}}$$

$$= \frac{-0.03}{\sqrt{0.53}}$$

$$= -0.04$$

This is the same value that was computed earlier. Comparison of the partial correlation coefficient (-0.04) with the zero-order correlation coefficient between age and civic participation $(r = -0.30)$ suggests that education causally links age and civic participation.

Unfortunately, partial correlation coefficients cannot help us distinguish between a spurious relationship and one in which the control variable acts as an intervening variable as shown in the accompanying figure. Based on the logic developed in Section 11.3.1, the spurious interpretation appears to be far less plausible than an intervening variable interpretation.

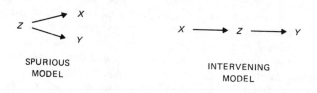

SPURIOUS
MODEL

INTERVENING
MODEL

11.3.4 A Final Word

A partial correlation coefficient can also be defined as a weighted average of the zero-order correlation between two variables within categories of the control variable. To the extent that zero-order association between two variables is generally uniform across all categories of the control variable, a partial correlation coefficient can be a useful tool. However, when the association is not uniform within all categories of the control variable, the partial correlation coefficient is a misleading measure. A partial correlation coefficient of approximately zero could result, for instance, from two variables having a positive relationship below the median of the control variable and a negative relationship above the median. In the event that the relationship between X and Y is not uniform across all categories of the control variable, a multivariate contingency table should be used rather than partial correlation coefficients. (See Box 11.1.)

BOX 11.1

The Concept of Interaction

Two variables are said to *interact* when their association is not uniform across all categories of a third variable. Consider the example in Section 11.3.2 in which we computed the partial correlation coefficient between age and civic participation controlling for education. Assume we had a large hypothetical sample (say, $N = 300$) and we divided the ministers into three categories based on their educational attainment (e.g., 0–7, 8–12, 13 + years). If we computed a zero-order correlation coefficient for each of the three subsamples we have created, we might get results such as:

Age by Civic Participation Controlling for Education

Less than 8 years	8–12 years	13 or more years
$r = -0.26$	$r = +0.02$	$r = +0.32$

These results would indicate that interaction was present because the relationship between age and civic participation differs across the categories of educational attainment. If there was a consistent relationship across categories, or if there was consistently little or no relationship across categories, we would conclude there was no interaction. These results would indicate that a partial correlation coefficient would be inappropriate and misleading.

You should see that the same principles discussed here can be applied to multivariate contingency tables. If the measures of association for the partial or conditional tables are not consistent across the categories of a third variable, we can also say that we have interaction.*

* Interaction can be defined in several other ways including:
  (1) Two variables are said to interact when the effect of one variable on another is contingent upon the presence of a third variable,

  and
  (2) Interaction is the joint effect of two or more independent variables on a dependent variable, independent of the separate effects of the independent variables.

11.4 Multiple Regression Analysis

11.4.1 Introduction

Multiple regression analysis is a logical extension of simple regression, which was discussed in Chapter 10. The basic concepts are very similar. Differences stem from multiple regression's use of two or more independent variables as predictors of a dependent variable; simple regression involves only one independent and one dependent variable. Several predictor variables used jointly can potentially account for considerably more variation in a dependent variable than can a single predictor variable.

A multiple regression equation with two independent variables is written in the following manner:

$$Y' = a + b_1X_1 + b_2X_2 \qquad (11.2)$$

where

Y' = the predicted value of the dependent variable*

a = the Y-intercept

b_1 = the slope associated with the first independent variable (X_1), and

b_2 = the slope associated with the second independent variable (X_2)

The slopes are interpreted in the following manner: b_1 represents the units of change in Y given one unit increase in X_1, holding X_2 constant; and b_2 represents the units of change in Y given one unit increase in X_2, holding X_1 constant.

11.4.2 Visual Presentation of Multiple Regression Analysis

A visual presentation of multiple regression analysis with one dependent variable and two independent variables is shown in Figure 11.2.

Visualize, with the aid of three pencils, some tape, a flat piece of cardboard, and Figure 11.2, how the X_1-, X_2-, and Y-axes can be arranged to construct a three-dimensional model. Place two of the pencils on a flat surface such that the erasers touch, and the pencils form an angle similar to that shown between the X_1- and X_2-axes. Extend the third pencil, which represents the Y-axis, vertically from the intersection of the first two pencils. The pencils can be taped together in this position. To locate a hypothetical coordinate such as $X_1 = 1$, $X_2 = 2$, and $Y = 4$, begin at the intersection of the three axes, move one unit (say, 1/4 inch) out on the X_1-axis, and mark the distance. Move two units out on the X_2-axis, and mark the distance. Now extend vertical lines from the one-unit value on the X_1-axis and the two-unit value on the X_2-axis in the direction that allows them to intersect. Finally, move up four units relative to the Y-axis from this point of intersection, and the coordinate $X_1 = 1$, $X_2 = 2$, and $Y = 4$ has been established. Once all of the coordinates have been located, you will have created a three-dimensional figure with a ''cloud'' of points in space formed by the coordinates.

---

* Some texts use a ''hat'' symbol (e.g., $\hat{Y}$) to designate a predicted value.

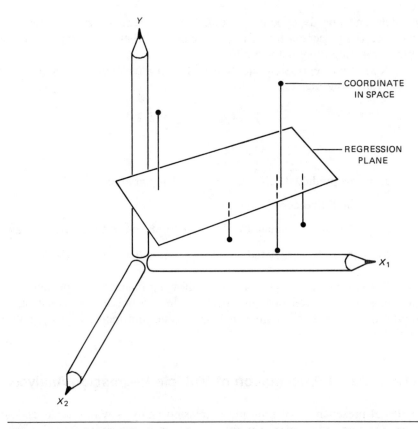

Figure 11.2 A three-dimensional portrayal of multiple regression analysis.

A regression *line* of best fit relative to the coordinates in space would not be appropriate in this instance; however, a regression *plane* can be fitted to the points. A cardboard backing to a notepad can serve as the plane, as shown in Figure 11.2. Those coordinates that lie above the plane have positive residuals, and those that lie below the plane have negative residuals. Two slopes are required to know how to tilt the plane relative to the X_1- and X_2-axes, and a is the point at which the plane crosses the Y-axes.

11.4.3 Multiple Regression: An Example

In the preceding discussion of partial correlation coefficients civic participation among black ministers was the dependent variable, age the independent variable, and education the control variable. It was determined that education acted as an intervening variable linking age and civic participation.

Multiple regression analysis allows us to use two or more interval-level or ratio-level variables simultaneously as predictors of an interval-level dependent variable. Equation (11.3) is based on a multiple regression analysis of the data in Table 11.2. Civic participation (Y) is the dependent variable, whereas age (X_1) and education (X_2) are the independent variables. The computation involved in multiple regression analysis is far too tedious and time-consuming for inclusion. While a computer was used to compute Eq. (11.3), the following example will allow you to understand the basic concepts of multiple regression:

$$Y' = 0.175 - 0.007X_1 + 0.242X_2 \qquad (11.3)$$

Equation (11.3) can be rewritten in words as

$$\begin{array}{c}\text{a minister's}\\ \text{predicted}\\ \text{civic}\\ \text{participation}\\ \text{score}\end{array} = 0.175 - 0.007 \left(\begin{array}{c}\text{the}\\ \text{minister's}\\ \text{age}\end{array}\right) + 0.242 \left(\begin{array}{c}\text{the}\\ \text{minister's}\\ \text{education}\end{array}\right)$$

The value of a, which is 0.175, indicates that the regression plane intersects the Y-axis at 0.175. The **multiple regression coefficient*** associated with X_1 (age) indicates that Y' (civic participation) decreases 0.007 Y units with each one-year increase in X_1 (age), holding X_2 (education) constant. Similarly, the multiple regression coefficient associated with X_2 (education) indicates that Y' increases 0.242 Y units for each additional year of formal education holding X_1 (age) constant. As was true of simple regression coefficients, the sign associated with a multiple regression coefficient must always be the same as the sign of the zero-order correlation of the independent variable with the dependent variable.† For example, age is correlated -0.30 with civic participation (see Table 11.4), and the sign of the coefficient for age in Eq. (11.3) is also negative.

Given Eq. (11.3), we can predict the civic participation scores of the five ministers. From Table 11.2 we see that the first minister is 28 years old and has completed 15 years of formal education. Substituting into Eq. (11.3) we obtain

$$Y' = 0.175 - 0.007(28) + 0.242(15) = 3.61$$

Therefore, the predicted civic participation score for the first minister is 3.61, whereas his actual score was 4 (see Table 11.2). The difference between the actual (Y_1) and predicted score (Y_1') yields the residual of $+0.39$ for the first

---

* Multiple regression coefficients are also referred to as partial regression coefficients, unstandardized partial regression coefficients, and unstandardized multiple regression coefficients.

† If the zero-order correlation coefficients between two or more variables in a multiple regression equation are close to 0.00, the signs may not be the same.

minister $(Y_1 - Y_1' = 4 - 3.61 = 0.39)$, hence his coordinate lies $0.39\ Y$ units above the regression plane. As was the case with simple regression, the five residuals (one for each minister) will sum to 0.

Equation (11.3) does not allow us to assess the *relative* importance of the independent variables in predicting civic participation, because the coefficients are based on different measurement units. Thus, an examination of unstandardized regression coefficients such as in Eq. (11.3) cannot reveal which predictor variables are of the greatest importance. Unlike r, which is independent of the measurement units of the variables involved (Section 9.2.1), b is not independent of measurement units in either a simple or multiple regression context.

Computer programs for multiple regression analysis routinely calculate unstandardized regression coefficients based on the raw data [Eq. (11.3)] and the standardized regression coefficients based on standard scores.* The following standardized regression equation for the five ministers is mathematically equivalent to the unstandardized Eq. (11.3), if one converts the raw X_1, X_2, and Y scores to z scores and substitutes these standardized scores into the equation:

$$Y' = -0.043X_1 + 0.465X_2$$

Note that there is no Y-intercept in a standardized regression equation. The means of all the variables are 0 when they are standardized; therefore, because the regression plane must pass through the coordinate $(\overline{X}_1, \overline{X}_2, \overline{Y})$ or $(0, 0, 0)$, the Y-intercept (a) always equals 0 in a standardized regression equation.

With standardized regression coefficients it is possible to assess the *relative* importance of the independent variables. The values (ignoring the signs) of the standardized regression coefficients are directly comparable, and because they are expressed in standardized units, it is evident that education (X_2) is the strongest predictor. The standardized coefficient associated with X_1 is interpreted in the following manner: Y' decreases 0.043 standard deviation units with each one standard deviation increase in X_1, holding X_2 constant. The standardized regression coefficient associated with X_2 indicates that Y' increases 0.465 standard deviation units with each one standard deviation increase in X_2, holding X_1 constant. Standaridzed regression coefficients are symbolized by the Greek letter β (beta).[†]

The relationship between the standardized and unstandardized coefficients is shown in Eq. (11.4):

$$\beta_{yx_1 \cdot x_2} = b_{yx_1 \cdot x_2} \left(\frac{S_{x_1}}{S_y} \right) \qquad (11.4)$$

---

* The concept of standard scores was discussed in Section 7.2.

† Standardized regression coefficients are also referred to as *beta weights* and *standardized path coefficients*. These coefficients are based on sample data.

Statistics In Action 11.1

Zero-Order Correlation, Multiple Regression, and Multiple Correlation Analysis of a Delinquency Scale

Scholars continue to search for explanations of why adolescents engage in delinquent acts. Tables 11.5 and 11.6 summarize the results of an Atlanta area study of self-reported delinquency among a sample of 600 adolescents.[*] A delinquency scale served as the dependent variable and was measured by combining 20 items that were weighted according to their seriousness (e.g., hurt someone badly, steal something valued at more than $50, set fire to something, run away from home, hit a parent, intentionally damage school property, and take part in a gang fight). A computer was required to calculate the values in the tables.

The relationship of the independent (predictor) variables with each other and delinquency is shown in Table 11.5. We have also included the means and standard deviations for each of the variables. A guide for interpreting the correlations is included under each variable. Thus, the correlation between variable 1, "friends smoke marijuana," and variable 2, "parent's attitudes toward friends" ($r = -0.28$), tells us that those students who reported that their friends smoke marijuana also tend to have parents who do not approve of their friends. A

[*] Kirk W. Elifson, David M. Petersen, and C. Kirk Hadaway, Religiosity and Delinquency: A Contextual Analysis. *Criminology* 21, November 1983, pp. 505–527.

Table 11.5 Zero-order correlations, means, and standard deviations (N = 498)

Variable	Mean	Standard Deviation	1	2	3	4	5	6	7	8
1. Friends smoke marijuana ("All" = low)	3.69	1.09	1.00	−.28	.01	.25	−.17	.34	.25	−.31
2. Parent's attitudes toward friends (approve = low)	4.55	1.36		1.00	−.11	−.24	.30	−.27	−.27	.26
3. Sex (male = low)	1.49	0.51			1.00	.17	.00	.01	.10	−.15
4. High school grade average (A = 10)	6.89	2.09				1.00	−.06	.10	.16	−.22
5. Closeness to mother (close = low)	2.97	1.12					1.00	−.16	−.17	.19
6. Obey all parent's rules ("No" = low)	3.45	1.27						1.00	.28	−.21
7. Importance of religion (unimportant = low)	2.55	1.21							1.00	−.14
8. Weighted delinquency scale (not delinquent = low)	9.54	10.73								1.00

dichotomous variable such as variable 3, "sex," can also be included in a correlation analysis. The correlation between sex and delinquency ($r = -0.15$) indicates that males are slightly more likely to have reported committing delinquent acts than are females. Had you not known that males were scored low (0 in this analysis), and thus females were scored high (1 in this analysis), you would not have been able to interpret the correlation. Sex can be treated as an interval variable because the distance between being male (0) and female (1) is consistently 1.

Table 11.6 provides the results of the multiple regression analysis of the variables. The unstandardized and standardized regression coefficients are included along with the standard error of b (a measure of the extent to which the unstandardized regression coefficients would vary if a new sample were drawn and the data were reanalyzed) and the F-ratio (a measure which is discussed in conjunction with the analysis of variance that indicates the statistical significance of the regression coefficients, that is, the likelihood that the value of the coefficients in Table 11.6 reflect the relationships in the population from which the sample was drawn). The asterisks indicate that all of the variables with the exception of "importance of religion" are statistically significant predictors of "delinquency."

Looking at the standardized regression coefficients, that allow us to determine the relative importance of the predictors, we can see that whether or not one's "friends smoke marijuana" is the best predictor ($\beta = -0.20$). The predictor variables are presented in terms of their relative importance as can be seen by the size of the standardized regression coefficients. What parents think of their child's friends, closeness to one's mother, sex, and high school grade point average are important independent variables. Males are more likely to be delinquent than females and poorer students more likely to be delinquent than good students. The importance of religion to the adolescent was clearly unimportant as a predictor.

The seven predictor variables accounted for 17% of the variance in the delinquency scale ($R = 0.42$ and $R^2 = 0.17$).

Table 11.6 Regression analysis of the weighted delinquency scale

Independent Variable	Zero-Order Correlation	Unstandardized Regression Coefficient (b)	Standard Error of b	Standardized Regression Coefficient (β)	F-Ratio
Friends smoke marijuana	−0.31	−2.01	0.45	−0.20	19.8*
Parent's attitudes toward friends	+0.26	+0.93	0.37	+0.12	6.4*
Sex	−0.15	−2.46	0.88	−0.12	7.8*
High school grade point average	−0.22	−0.55	0.23	−0.11	6.0*
Closeness to mother	+0.19	+1.00	0.42	+0.10	5.8*
Obey all parent's rules	−0.21	−0.74	0.38	−0.09	3.7*
Importance of religion	−0.14	−0.11	0.39	+0.01	0.1
Y-intercept		2.11			

$R = 0.42$
$R^2 = 0.17$

*$p < .001$

The subscript $yx_1.x_2$ indicates that Y is the dependent variable, X_1 is the independent variable for which the standardized regression coefficient is being computed, and the second independent variable (X_2) has been statistically controlled.

In words:

$$\begin{array}{c} \text{standardized regression} \\ \text{coefficient for } X_1 \\ \text{controlling} \\ \text{for } X_2 \end{array} = \begin{array}{c} \text{unstandardized} \\ \text{coefficient for} \\ X_1 \text{ controlling} \\ \text{for } X_2 \end{array} \left(\frac{\text{standard deviation of } X_1}{\text{standard deviation of } Y} \right)$$

The unstandardized coefficient associated with X_1 in Eq. (11.3) is -0.007, the standard deviation of X_1 is 8.37, and the standard deviation of Y is 1.30. Therefore, substituting into Eq. (11.4), we have

$$\beta_{yx_1.x_2} = -0.007 \left(\frac{8.37}{1.30} \right)$$

$$= -0.045*$$

Thus, it is possible to convert an unstandardized equation into the standardized form if the standard deviations of the independent and dependent variables are known. Both standardized and unstandardized coefficients are included in Statistics in Action 11.1.

11.4.4 The Multiple Correlation Coefficient

The **multiple correlation coefficient (R)** is a measure of the linear relationship between a dependent variable and the combined effects of two or more independent variables. It is symbolized by a capital R to differentiate it from r, the zero-order correlation coefficient, which was discussed in Chapter 9. As was true of r, squaring R yields a far more interpretable measure. R^2, or the **coefficient of multiple determination,** indicates the proportion of total variation in a dependent variable that is explained jointly by two or more independent variables. For the black minister example, $R = 0.49$ and $R^2 = 0.24$; thus, 24% of the variation in civic participation has been explained by age and education, and 76% ($100\% - 24\% = 76\%$) of the variation has not been explained.[†]

Figure 11.3 presents the concept of the coefficient of multiple determination diagrammatically. The shaded area designated by letters a, c, and d in Figure 11.3 represents the total variation in Y explained jointly by X_1 and X_2.

---

* Differs slightly from -0.043 computed earlier due to rounding.

[†] The unexplained variation is sometimes referred to as the *coefficient of nondetermination* and is symbolized by $1 - R^2$ or k^2.

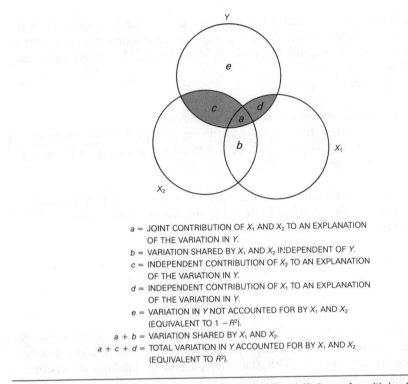

a = JOINT CONTRIBUTION OF X_1 AND X_2 TO AN EXPLANATION
    OF THE VARIATION IN Y.
b = VARIATION SHARED BY X_1 AND X_2 INDEPENDENT OF Y.
c = INDEPENDENT CONTRIBUTION OF X_2 TO AN EXPLANATION
    OF THE VARIATION IN Y.
d = INDEPENDENT CONTRIBUTION OF X_1 TO AN EXPLANATION
    OF THE VARIATION IN Y.
e = VARIATION IN Y NOT ACCOUNTED FOR BY X_1 AND X_2
    (EQUIVALENT TO $1 - R^2$).
a + b = VARIATION SHARED BY X_1 AND X_2.
a + c + d = TOTAL VARIATION IN Y ACCOUNTED FOR BY X_1 AND X_2
    (EQUIVALENT TO R^2).

Figure 11.3 A diagrammatic presentation of the coefficient of multiple determination.

Area c represents the independent contribution of X_2 to an explanation of the variation in Y and area d represents the independent contribution of X_1. Area a represents the joint contribution of X_1 and X_2. The total area represented by areas a and b indicates the variation shared by X_1 and X_2. Area e indicates the variation in Y that has not been accounted for by the two independent variables, X_1 and X_2.

Unfortunately, there is no way to partition the variation in Y that was explained by X_1 and the variation that was explained by X_2 unless X_1 and X_2 are unrelated. In this example X_1 and X_2 are statistically associated as shown by their intersection (areas a and b), and it is impossible to know what proportion of the variation in Y, which is indicated by area a, is attributable to X_1 and what proportion is attributable to X_2.

Summary

In this chapter we have learned about multivariate statistical techniques including multivariate contingency tables, partial correlation analysis, multiple regression analysis, and multiple correlation analysis. All of these techniques involve examining the relationship among three or more variables simultaneously.

Multivariate contingency tables allow us statistically to elaborate the relationship between two variables by introducing a control variable.

Partial correlation analysis provides us with a measure of the linear relationship between two interval-level variables having statistically controlled for one or more other interval-level variables. The concept of statistical control was presented, as was the computational procedure. The partial correlation coefficient should not be used when the zero-order association between two variables is not uniform across all categories of the control variable.

Multiple regression analysis allows us to use two or more interval-level variables simultaneously as predictors of an interval-level dependent variable. The interpretation and relationship of unstandardized and standardized multiple regression coefficients was presented. The interpretation and use of multiple regression coefficients was also discussed.

Terms to Remember

Coefficient of multiple determination (R^2)   A measure of the proportion of total variation in a dependent variable that is explained jointly by two or more independent variables.

Conditional table   A contingency table that summarizes the relationship between two variables for categories or conditions of one or more other variables. Same as a partial table.

Control variable   A variable whose subgroups or categories are used in a conditional table to examine the relationship between two variables. Same as a test variable.

Interaction   Two variables are said to interact when their association is not uniform across all categories of a third variable.

Intervening variable   A variable that causally links two other variables.

Multiple correlation coefficient (R)   A measure of the linear relationship between a dependent variable and the combined effects of two or more independent variables.

Multiple regression coefficient   A measure of the influence of an independent variable on a dependent variable when the effects of all other independent variables in the multiple regression equation have been held constant.

Multivariate statistical technique   A statistical technique used to determine the nature of the relationships among three or more variables.

Order of a conditional table   The order of a table is the number of control or test variables that are included.

Order of a partial correlation coefficient The order of a partial correlation coefficient indicates the number of control or test variables.

Partial correlation coefficient A measure of the linear relationship between two interval-level variables controlling for one or more other interval-level variables.

Partial table A contingency table that summarizes the relationship between two variables for categories or conditions of one or more other variables. Same as a conditional table.

Spurious relationship Exists when the zero-order relationship between an independent and dependent variable disappears or becomes significantly weaker with the introduction of a control variable.

Statistical elaboration The process of introducing a control variable to determine whether a bivariate relationship remains the same or varies under the different categories or conditions of the control variable.

Test variable A variable whose subgroups or categories are used in a conditional table to examine the relationship between two variables. Same as a control variable.

Exercises

1. Discuss the advantages of using multivariate statistical procedures rather than bivariate statistical procedures.

2. Differentiate between physical control as used with multivariate contingency tables and statistical control as used with partial correlation analysis.

3. Given the following bivariate contingency table, introduce a control variable (e.g., education or another variable of your choice) and manipulate the data to show its influence on the relationship of age and attitude toward socialized medicine.

(Y) Favor Socialized Medicine?	(X) Age Young	(X) Age Old	Total
Yes	34.7 (51)	63.6 (82)	(133)
No	65.3 (96)	36.4 (47)	(143)
Total	100.0 (147)	100.0 (129)	N = 276

4. The following table presents data obtained from a sample of college students. Based on the data, answer the following questions.

a) Identify the independent, dependent, and control variables that are included in this table.

b) Without doing any statistical operations beyond examining the percentages and numbers in the cells of the table, give an interpretation about the relationship between the variables in the table (what does this table tell us?) and describe the effect of the control variable.

c) Reconstruct or "collapse" this three-variable table into a two-variable table in a way that would allow you to examine the simple relationship between age and political orientation, and indicate whether it appears that young or old students are more conservative (again, it is not necessary to do any statistical operation other than simple examination of percentages and numbers of cases).

Political Orientation	Young Level in School		Old Level in School		
	Under-graduate	*Graduate*	*Under-graduate*	*Graduate*	
Liberal	75.0 (30)	25.0 (15)	60.0 (30)	50.0 (25)	
Conservative	25.0 (10)	75.0 (45)	40.0 (20)	50.0 (25)	
Total	100.0 (40)	100.0 (60)	100.0 (50)	100.0 (50)	N = 200

5. The data in Table A show the relationship between the length of prison sentence (in months) received by defendants charged with violations of the Federal Drug Abuse Prevention and Control Act during a 2 year period. Table B shows the relationship between the length of sentence and year by the type of substance involved. Percentage the tables and discuss the influence of the control variable.

Table A

Sentence in Months	Time Period		Total
	Year 1	*Year 2*	
1–12	1404	885	2289
13–35	811	623	1434
36–59	1143	956	2099
60+	1310	1141	2451
Total	4668	3605	N = 8273

Table B

Sentence in Months	Marijuana		Narcotics		Controlled Substances (Prescribed Drugs)	
	Year 1	Year 2	Year 1	Year 2	Year 1	Year 2
1–12	466	241	757	412	181	232
13–35	281	158	410	328	120	137
36–59	274	245	749	518	120	193
60+	183	139	1022	739	105	263
Total	1204	783	2938	1997	526	825
	N = 1987		N = 4935		N = 1351	

Source: Administrative Office of the U.S. Courts.

6. You are studying the relationship among church attendance, self-reported delinquent acts, and drug usage among a sample of high school students. Given the following correlation matrix, compute the first-order partial correlation coefficient between church attendance and reported delinquent acts controlling for drug usage. Interpret the results.

	1.	2.	3.
1. Self-reported delinquent acts	1.00		
2. Church attendance	−0.32	1.00	
3. Drug usage	+0.41	−0.17	1.00

7. Explain why technically the partial correlation of variables X and Y controlling for variable Z is the correlation of the residuals of the regressions of X on Z and Y on Z.

8. Why should a partial correlation coefficient not be computed when the association between two variables is not uniform across all categories of the control variable?

9. If $r_{xz} = +0.80$, $r_{xz} = +0.61$, and $r_{yz} = +0.43$, compute $r_{xy \cdot z}$.

10. Income (X_1) and seniority (X_2) have been used as predictors of job satisfaction (Y) for a sample of municipal employees. Given the following regression equation, interpret the Y-intercept and the regression coefficients associated with income and seniority.

$$Y' = 1.1 + 0.35X_1 + 0.12X_2$$

11. Is the equation in Exercise 10 in standardized or unstandardized form? How can you tell?

12. Given the scores for five of the employees included in the study summarized in Exercise 10, compute the predicted Y scores and the residuals for each of the five employees.

	X_1	X_2	Y
Employee 1	10	2	6
2	15	3	5
3	9	6	7
4	21	9	9
5	46	15	21

13. Assume that the following table contains the results of regression analyses of data from a national sample survey of 11th grade black and white students. The purpose of the analysis is to see what factors account for students' performance levels on math achievement tests (the dependent variable). The independent variables are (1) the student's cumulative grade average, (2) the student's family socioeconomic status (SES), (3) the student's reading ability test score, (4) the percentage of the student's class that is white, and (5) a measure of the teaching ability of the student's math teacher. Using the standardized regression coefficients and other statistics in the table, answer the following questions.

Independent Variables	White Students	Black Students
1. Cumulative grade average	0.10	0.24
2. Family SES	0.42	0.49
3. Reading test score	0.39	0.05
4. % white in class	0.37	-0.19
5. Teacher's ability	0.17	0.34
Multiple correlation coefficient (R)	0.72	0.38
Coefficient of multiple determination (R^2)	0.52	0.14

a) For which group, blacks or whites, does the regression model using these five variables do a better job in predicting or explaining math achievement scores? How do you know that?

b) Of the variables listed, which one seems to be the most important contributing factor to the math test achievement score? Which are the least important factors in this analysis?

c) In multiple regression analysis, what is the meaning or interpretation of standardized regression coefficients such as those in the table? How would you interpret the fact that for white students the standardized regression coefficient of teacher's ability is 0.17 and for black students it is 0.34. That is, what do these coefficients tell us?

14. The following questions refer to Statistics in Action 11.1.

   a) Write the unstandardized and standardized regression equations.

   b) Interpret the meaning of the unstandardized and standardized equations associated with grade point average.

   c) What does the Y-intercept tell us in this instance? Why is there no Y-intercept for the standardized equation?

   d) What is the dependent variable? How many independent variables are included in Table 11.6 and what are they?

   e) What proportion of the variation in the dependent variable has been explained by the independent variables? What percentage of the variation has been explained? What proportion of the variation in the dependent variable has not been explained?

   f) Which independent variable is the best predictor of delinquency? Which is the poorest?

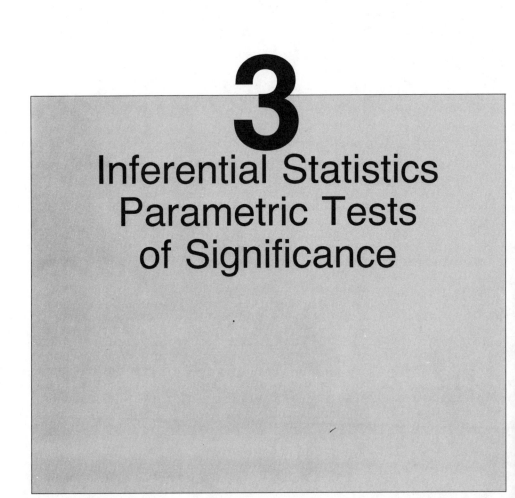

3

Inferential Statistics
Parametric Tests
of Significance

12 Probability
13 Introduction to Statistical Inference
14 Statistical Inference and Continuous Variables
15 An Introduction to the Analysis of Variance

chapter **12**

Probability

12.1 An Introduction to Probability

12.2 The Concept of Randomness

12.3 Approaches to Probability

12.4 Formal Properties of Probability

12.5 Probability and Continuous Variables

12.6 Probability and the Normal-Curve Model

12.7 One- and Two-Tailed *p* Values

12.1 An Introduction to Probability

In the past few chapters we have been primarily concerned with the presentation of techniques employed by statisticians and scientists to describe and present data. Statisticians and scientists study *some* people and/or events but they want their conclusions to hold for other people and/or events that they have *not* specifically tested. In other words, they want to generalize their results to an entire population even though they specifically examined only a small sample.

Most national opinion polls are based on samples of less than 3000 respondents and yet the results can be used to infer accurately how the adult population feels about the issues under consideration. Often you will read that a given percentage of those polled (e.g., 42%) favor a solution or hold a particular opinion and the results are accurate within ±3 percentage points. As you will learn in Chapter 14, this means that if the entire population were interviewed, the actual percentage holding the opinion has a high probability of falling somewhere between 39% and 45%.

Probability is not so unfamiliar as many would think. Indeed, in everyday life you are constantly called upon to make probability judgments, although you may not recognize them as such. For example, suppose that, for various reasons, you are unprepared for today's class. You seriously consider not attending class. What are the factors that will influence your decision? Obviously, one consideration would be the likelihood that the instructor will discover you are not prepared. If the risk is high, you decide not to attend class; if low, then you will attend.

BOX 12.1

The Gambler's Fallacy

Probability theory is the foundation stone of inferential statistics. Without it, our interpretation of data would progress little beyond sheer guesswork. Considering its importance, it is surprising that mistaken notions about probability pervade the thinking of many people. One is the "Gambler's Fallacy," illustrated in this excerpt from *Winning with Statistics*.

I'm Overdue for a Run of Luck

Famous last words! This one takes many forms and invades many fields. The gambler is tossing coins and loses four in a row. Reasoning that five losses in a row is exceedingly rare ($p = 0.031$, odds against $= 31.25:1$), he decides to increase the ante. "I'm due for a win," he proclaims confidently. Your favorite baseball player has gone 0 for 4. When he comes to bat for the fifth time, you exude confidence: "he's due for a hit." The opposing quarterback has just completed six consecutive passes against your team. You breathe a sigh of relief: "The next is bound to be incomplete or intercepted."

Although these examples are not all exactly the same, they have one thing in common—the belief that events have memories. It is as if the gambler is reasoning, "The coin will remember that it came up heads four times in a row and will try to balance out the 'law of averages' by coming up tails on the next toss." This is sheer nonsense. So long as the coin is "honest," it is just as likely to come up heads as tails on the next toss or on any toss, for that matter. We speak of this condition as *independence*—the outcome of one trial has no effect on later trials. This is just another way of denying that coins or dice or cards or roulette wheels have memories.

It is somewhat different when dealing with activities involving behavior. Although a bat and ball have no memory, "turns at bat" are not always independent, particularly if they are against a pitcher of Tom Seaver's caliber. And your football team could have seven passes completed against it because of its porous defense. Nevertheless, it is incorrect to cite the "law of averages" as the reason for expecting something different on the next trial. The law of averages has no enforcement agency behind it, nor is there a Supreme Court to oversee the constitutionality of its "decisions." Indeed, the only thing it has in common with jurisprudence is its impartiality.

Source: Excerpted from R. P. Runyon, *Winning with Statistics*, Reading, Mass.: Addison-Wesley, 1977.

Let's look at this example in slightly different terms. There are two alternative possibilities:

Event *A:*   Your lack of preparation *will* be detected.
Event *B:*   Your lack of preparation *will not* be detected.

There is uncertainty in this situation because more than one alternative is possible. Your decision whether or not to attend class will depend on the degree of assurance you associate with each of these alternatives. Thus, if you are fairly certain that the first alternative will prevail, you will decide not to attend class.

Suppose that your instructor frequently calls upon students to participate in class discussion. In fact, you have noted that most of the students are called upon in any given class session. This is an example of a situation in which the first alternative is likely. Stated another way, the probability of event A is higher than the probability of event B. Thus, you decide not to attend class. Although you have not used any formal probability laws in this example, you have actually made a judgment based on an *intuitive* use of probability.

As social scientists we concern ourselves with such questions as the probability that a prisoner will commit another crime after being released from prison, or the probability that a particular candidate will win an election.

You may have noted that many of the questions raised in the exercises earlier in the book began with, "What is the likelihood that . . .?" These questions were in preparation for the formal discussion of probability occurring in the present and subsequent chapters. However, before discussing the elements of probability, we should understand one of the most important concepts in inferential statistics—randomness.

12.2 The Concept of Randomness

You will recall that when discussing the role of inferential statistics in Chapter 1, we pointed out the fact that population parameters are rarely known or knowable. It is for this reason that we are usually forced to draw samples from a given population and estimate the parameters from the sample statistics. We want to select these samples in such a way that they are representative of the populations from which they are drawn. One way to achieve representativeness is to employ simple **random sampling:** *selecting samples in such a way that each sample of a given size has precisely the same probability of being selected,* or, alternatively, *selecting the events in the sample such that each event is equally likely to be selected in a sample of a given size.*

Consider selecting samples of $N = 2$ from a population of five numbers: 0, 1, 2, 3, 4. If, for any reason, any number is more likely to be drawn than any other number, each sample would *not* have an equal likelihood of being drawn. For example, if for any reason the number 3 were twice as likely to be drawn as any other number, there would be a preponderance of samples containing the value 3. Such sampling procedures are referred to as being **biased.** When we are interested in learning the characteristics of the general population for a given variable, we should not select our sample from automobile registration lists or at random on a street corner in New York City. The dangers of generalizing to a population from such biased samples should be clear to you. Unless the condition of randomness is met, we may never know to what population we should generalize our results.

Moreover, the statistical tests presented in this text require **independent** random sampling. Two events are said to be independent if the selection of one has no effect upon the probability of selecting the other event. We can most readily grasp independence in terms of games of chance, assuming they are played honestly. Knowledge of the results of one toss of a coin, one throw of a die, one spin of the roulette wheel, or one selection of a card from a well-shuffled deck (assuming replacement of the card after each selection) will not aid us in our predictions of future outcomes.

When we are involved in conducting an experiment, we must concern ourselves with introducing randomness at two junctures of the study: *selecting* our subjects at random from the population of interest, and *assigning* these subjects at random to the experimental conditions.

It is beyond the scope of this text to delve deeply into sampling procedures, since that topic is a full course by itself. However, consider how we achieve randomness when drawing a sample from a population. Let's suppose we wish to select 25 persons randomly from a population totaling 300. One method to achieve randomness would be to place the names of each of the 300 persons in the population on a folded slip of paper. After shuffling the slips of paper and placing them in a container, we could reach into the container and draw 25 names.

An alternative method would be to use the table of random digits (Table M in Appendix C). Since the digits in this table have already been randomized by a computer, the effect of shuffling has been achieved. We assign each of our 300 persons comprising the population a number from 001 to 300. We may start with any row or column of digits in Table M. For example, if we start with the first row and choose consecutive sets of three digits, we obtain the following numbers: 100, 973, 253, 376, 520, 135, and so on. If any number over 300 or any repeated number appears, we disregard it and continue until we have chosen 25 "usable" numbers, which represent the 25 people that will constitute our sample.

Most present-day computers have a function that generates random digits. If you have access to a computer, you will save much time by letting the computer do the selecting for you. This randomization function is at the heart of the many games that computers play.

The reason for the paramount importance of random procedures will become clear in this chapter and the next. Fundamentally, it is based on a fascinating fact of inferential statistics: *Each event may not be predictable when taken alone, but collections of random events can take on predictable forms.* The binomial distribution, which we will discuss at greater length in Section 13.3, illustrates this fact. If we were to take, say, 20 unbiased coins and toss them into the air, we could not predict accurately the proportion that would land "heads." However, if we were to toss these 20 coins a great many times, record the number turning up heads on each trial, and construct a frequency distribution of outcomes in which the horizontal axis varies between no heads and all heads, the plot would take on a characteristic and predictable form known as the *binomial distribution* (see Fig. 12.1). By employing the binomial model, we would be able to predict with considerable accuracy over a large number of trials the percentage of the time various outcomes will occur. What is perhaps more fascinating is the fact that the distribution of outcomes of this two-category variable more and more closely approximates the normal curve as N (the number of tosses of a single coin or the number of coins tossed at one time) becomes larger. Indeed, with large Ns we may use the normal curve to describe the probability of various outcomes of a binomial variable.

The same reasoning is true with respect to the normal-curve model. In the absence of any specific information, we might not be able to predict a person's status with respect to a given trait (intelligence, height, weight, etc.). However, as we already know, frequency distributions of scores on these traits commonly take the form of the normal curve. Thus, we may predict the proportion of individuals scoring between specified score limits.

What is perhaps of more importance, from the point of view of inferential

Figure 12.1 Probabilities of obtaining varying numbers of heads (from 0 to 20) on repeated tosses of an "honest" coin. Note how closely the histogram resembles the normal curve.

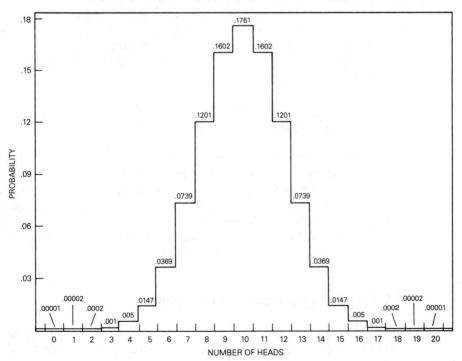

statistics, is the fact that distributions of sample statistics ($\overline{X}$, s, median, etc.), based on random sampling from a population, also take on highly predictable forms. Chapter 13 deals with the concept of **sampling distributions,** which are theoretical probability distributions of a statistic that would result from drawing all possible samples of a given size from some population.

With this brief introduction to the concept of randomness, you are prepared to look at probability theory.

12.3 Approaches to Probability

Probability may be regarded as a theory that is concerned with the possible outcomes of a study. It must be possible to list every outcome that can occur, and we must be able to state the expected relative frequencies of these outcomes. It is the method of assigning relative frequencies to each of the possible outcomes that distinguishes the classical from the empirical approach to probability theory.

12.3.1 Classical Approach to Probability

The theory of probability has always been closely associated with games of chance. For example, suppose we want to know the probability that a single card selected from a 52-card deck will be an ace of spades. There are 52 possible outcomes. We assume an ideal situation in which we expect that each outcome is equally likely to occur. Thus, the probability of selecting an ace of spades is one out of 52 or 1/52. This kind of reasoning has led to the following classical definition of probability:

$$p(A) = \frac{\text{number of outcomes in which event } A \text{ occurs}}{\text{total number of outcomes } (A \text{ occurs } + A \text{ does not occur})} \qquad (12.1)$$

It should be noted that probability is defined as a proportion (p). The most important point in the classical definition of probability is the assumption of an *ideal* situation in which the composition of the population is known; that is, the total number of possible outcomes (N) is known. In this example the total number of possible outcomes was 52 (all cards in the deck), and each outcome was assumed to have an equal likelihood of occurrence. Thus, p (ace of spades) = 1/52; p (king of hearts) = 1/52, and so on.

12.3.2 Empirical Approach to Probability

Although it is usually easy to assign expected relative frequencies to the possible outcomes of games of chance, we cannot do this for most real life situations. In actual situations expected relative frequencies are assigned on the basis of empirical findings. Thus, we may not know the exact proportion of students in a university who have worked in a political campaign, but we may conduct a simple random sample of students in the university and estimate the proportion who have worked in a campaign. Once we have arrived at an estimate, we can use classical probability theory to answer questions such as, What is the probability that in a sample of ten students, drawn at random from the student body, three or more will have worked in a political campaign?

If in a simple random sample of 100 students we found that 30 had worked in a campaign, we could estimate that the proportion of experienced campaigners in the university was 0.30, using Eq. (12.1):

$$p(\text{campaigners}) = \frac{30}{100} = 0.30$$

Thus, the probability is 0.30 that a student in the university will have campaigned previously. (*Note:* This represents an *empirical* probability; that is, the expected relative frequency was assigned on the basis of empirical findings.)

Although we use an idealized model in our forthcoming discussion about the properties of probability, we can apply the same principles to many practical problems.

Take the gender of an about-to-be-born child. What is the probability that it will be a girl? On the surface the answer would appear to be easy. Hypothetically, the birth of a boy or girl would appear to be equally likely, 0.50 in both cases. However, such is not the case. In the United States the proportion

Table 12.1 Proportion of male births, by race, in United States over 12-year period, 1970–1981

Year	White	Black
1970	0.5143	0.5076
1971	0.5136	0.5069
1972	0.5139	0.5059
1973	0.5138	0.5068
1974	0.5143	0.5074
1975	0.5143	0.5074
1976	0.5141	0.5067
1977	0.5141	0.5064
1978	0.5141	0.5069
1979	0.5138	0.5072
1980	0.5141	0.5072
1981	0.5138	0.5067
Mean	0.5140	0.5069
Standard deviation	0.0001	0.0004

of annual male births has been exceptionally stable for many years—0.5140 for whites and 0.5069 for blacks (see Table 12.1).

A gambler who made his livelihood on taking bets on the gender of children about to be born could do quite well, over the long run, by giving even odds that the child will be a boy. If he bet only on white babies, on every 10,000 bets, the gambler could expect to win, on the average, 5140 times and lose 4860 times.

The fundamental feature of empirical probabilities is that they are based on actual measurements rather than on theoretical proportions. As a matter of fact, there is usually little or no basis for assigning theoretical probabilities to most of the situations confronted by the student of behavior: for example, the probability that a person will require treatment for a disorder at some time in his or her life, the probability that a convicted felon will return to crime, or the probability that a child will be born with a congenital defect. Probabilities such as these must be obtained empirically and are always subject to revision in the light of additional data.

12.3.3 Subjective Approaches to Probability

There are many occasions when we lack the objective data for estimating probabilities. Nevertheless, we may have strong feelings that we term "a hunch," "common sense," or an intuition. Someone working on a suicide "hot line" may say, "I can't tell you precisely why I feel this way, but I believe that the caller is at high risk for suicide." We should not dismiss these subjective probabilities out-of-hand. Even though subjective probabilities cannot, by their very nature, be documented and substantiated, they may nevertheless arise from a lifetime of observation and assessment of subtle cues. Indeed, it is likely that any important decision we have made in life includes subjective probabilities as a basic ingredient. For this reason we accept the notion of subjective probabilities. Once made, we expect them to follow the same rules as probabilities obtained by either the classical or the empirical approach.

12.4 Formal Properties of Probability

12.4.1 Probabilities Vary Between 0 and 1.00

From the classical definition of probability, p is always between 0 and 1, inclusively. If an event is certain to occur, its probability is 1; if it is certain not to occur, its probability is 0. For example, the probability of drawing the ace of spades from an ordinary deck of 52 playing cards is 1/52. The probability of drawing a red ace of spades is zero because the ace of spades is never red. However, the probability of drawing a card with *some* marking on it is $p =$

1. Thus, for any given event, say, A, $0 \leq p(A) \leq 1.00$, in which the symbol $\leq$ means "less than or equal to."

12.4.2 Expressing Probability

In addition to expressing probability as a proportion, several other ways are often used. It is sometimes convenient to express probability as a *percentage* or as the *number of chances* in 100.

To illustrate: If the probability of an event is 0.05, we expect this event to occur 5% of the time, or *the chances that this event will occur* are 5 in 100. This same probability may be expressed by saying that the odds are 95 to 5 *against* the event occurring, or 19 to 1 against it.

When expressing probability as the *odds against* the occurrence of an event, we use Eq. (12.2):

$$\text{odds against event } A \qquad\qquad (12.2)$$
$$= (\text{total no. of outcomes} - \text{no. of times event } A \text{ occurs})$$
$$to \text{ no. of times event } A \text{ occurs}$$

Thus, if $p(A) = 0.01$, the *odds against* the occurrence of event A are 99 to 1.

12.4.3 The Addition Rule

When we know the possible outcomes of an experiment, it is possible to identify any number of different events for purposes of probability analysis. To illustrate, we may raise such questions as

1. What is the probability of obtaining one event *or* another, for example, drawing a queen *or* a club from a deck of playing cards?

2. What is the probability of obtaining two events simultaneously, for example, selecting a queen *and* a club from a deck of playing cards?

To answer the first question, we must make use of the **addition rule;** and for the second, we use the **multiplication rule.** We examine the addition rule in this section and the multiplication rule in Section 12.4.4.

When Events Are Not Mutually Exclusive*

Suppose that, in an effort to obtain data on current reasons for seeking professional help, a questionnaire was sent out to administrators at various mental

---

* Recall from Chapter 2 that two events would not be mutually exclusive if they *can* occur simultaneously.

health clinics throughout the country. One part of the questionnaire dealt with the abuse of drugs and alcohol among those receiving care at the clinics. The results of the questionnaires showed that out of 5900 patients, 354 abused alcohol and 236 abused drugs; of these (the abusers of alcohol and drugs) 118 abused both. Let us define Event *A* as the abuse of alcohol and Event *B* as the abuse of drugs.

Based on the replies, we can estimate the probability of each event from the sample:

$$p(A) = \frac{354}{5900} = 0.06$$

$$p(B) = \frac{236}{5900} = 0.04$$

Now, if we wished to know the probability that a given patient was either an alcohol or drug abuser, we might be tempted to add together the number of patients abusing alcohol and the number abusing drugs, divide by *n* to obtain $p(A \text{ or } B) = (354 + 236)/5900 = 0.10$. However, this probability does not take into account the 118 people who are counted twice—once as alcohol abusers and once as drug abusers. In other words, the two categories are not mutually exclusive. This is shown as the overlapping area in the Venn diagram in Figure 12.2.

To determine the probability of event *A* or event *B*, we must subtract the 118 cases that overlap both categories. This leads to the general case of the addition rule. It is called the general case because it applies equally to mutually exclusive and nonmutually exclusive categories:

$$p(A \text{ or } B) = p(A) + p(B) - p(A \text{ and } B) \qquad (12.3)$$

Figure 12.2   Venn diagram showing that the two categories, alcohol abuse and drug abuse, are not mutually exclusive. To obtain *p(A or B)*, we must subtract out the area of overlap.

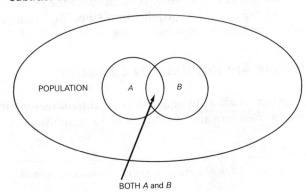

BOTH *A* and *B*

where $p(A$ and $B)$ represents the probability associated with the overlapping events.

In the present example $p(A$ or $B) = 354/5900 + 236/5900 - 118/5900 = 0.08$. Thus, according to this survey, the probability is 0.08 that a given individual seeking help at a mental health clinic is either an alcohol or a drug abuser (or both).

Overlapping categories is also characteristic of many games of chance, for example, roulette or cards. To illustrate, if we want to know the probability of selecting either a heart (to fill a flush) or a jack (to fill a straight), we must take into account the fact that the jack of hearts overlaps both events. If we let Event A equal the probability of a heart, $p(A) = 13/52$. The probability of Event B (a jack) is 4/52. However, the probability of both occurring (a jack of hearts) is 1/52. Therefore, $p(A$ or $B) = 13/52 + 4/52 - 1/52 = 16/52 = 0.31$.

Mutually Exclusive Events

By definition, when events are mutually exclusive, there is no overlapping of the categories. Since both Event A and Event B cannot occur together, the probability of Event A and Event B is 0; that is, $p(A$ and $B) = 0$.

Therefore, if the events A and B are **mutually exclusive** (i.e., if both events *cannot* occur simultaneously), the last term disappears (reduces to zero). Thus, the addition rule with mutually exclusive events becomes

$$p(A \text{ or } B) = p(A) + p(B) \qquad (12.4)$$

Furthermore, the addition rule for mutually exclusive events (12.4) can be rewritten to include more than two events. For example,

$$P(A \text{ or } B \text{ or } C) = p(A) + p(B) + p(C)$$

Consider a population comprised of 30% Catholics, 25% Methodists, 40% Baptists, and 5% Lutherans. What is the probability of getting a Catholic or a Methodist or a Baptist in a single draw?

$$\frac{30}{100} + \frac{25}{100} + \frac{40}{100} = \frac{95}{100} = 0.95$$

To illustrate further, in Exercise 12 of Chapter 4, we presented census figures on the size of U.S. families of Spanish origin. These figures are reproduced in Table 12.2.

What is the probability that a given family of Spanish origin has either two or three members? Using Eq. (12.4), we find $p(2 \text{ or } 3) = p(2) + p(3) = 0.239 + 0.230 = 0.469$.

Table 12.2 Size of U.S. families of Spanish origin

Size	Number (in thousands)	p
2	662	0.239
3	636	0.230
4	625	0.226
5	408	0.148
6	218	0.079
7 or more persons	216	0.078

Source: U.S. Bureau of Census, *Current Population Reports,* Series P-20, no. 339, U.S. Government Printing Office.

What is the probability that such a family will number 6 or more? $p(6$ or 7 or more) $= 0.079 + 0.078 = 0.157$.

Equation (12.4) can be extended to include any number of mutually exclusive events. Thus

$$p(A \text{ or } B \text{ or } \ldots Z) = p(A) + p(B) + \cdots + p(Z)$$

In Chapters 13 and 16 we will be dealing with problems based on *dichotomous,* yes/no, or *two-category* variables, in which the events in question are not only mutually exclusive, but are also **exhaustive.** For example, if women constitute 52% of the population in a given city and men constitute 48% of the population, what is the probability of drawing a woman and a man in one draw? Not only is it impossible to obtain both events simultaneously (i.e., they are mutually exclusive), but there is *no possible outcome other than a woman or a man.* In the case of mutually exclusive and exhaustive events, we arrive at the very useful formulation:

$$p(A) + p(B) = 1.00 \tag{12.5}$$

In treating dichotomous populations, we commonly use the two symbols P and Q to represent, respectively, the probability of the occurrence of an event and the probability of the nonoccurrence of an event. Thus, if we are flipping a single coin, we can let P represent the probability of occurrence of a head and Q the probability of the nonoccurrence of a head (i.e., the occurrence of a tail). Note that Q represents not-P ($\overline{P}$). These considerations lead to three useful formulations:

$$P + Q = 1.00 \tag{12.6}$$

$$P = 1.00 - Q \tag{12.7}$$

$$Q = 1.00 - P \tag{12.8}$$

when the events are *mutually exclusive and exhaustive.*

12.4.4 The Multiplication Rule

In the preceding section we were concerned with determining the probability of obtaining one event or another based on a *single* draw (or trial) from a population. In statistical inference we are often faced with the problem of ascertaining the probability of the **joint or successive occurrence** of two or more events when *more* than one draw or trial is involved. For example, what is the probability that we will draw a diamond and a heart on two successive draws from a deck of playing cards?

Much research has been done on the effects of physical attractiveness on various aspects of our behavior. In a field study by Benson et al.* the objective was to ascertain whether favoritism for the physically attractive generalizes to behavioral helping responses. Graduate school applications, complete with mailing address, envelope, and stamps were "inadvertently" left in a number of telephone booths at a busy metropolitan airport. Pictures of the applicant were prominently displayed, some chosen to be physically attractive and others to be unattractive. Thus, physical attractiveness was the independent variable. The dependent response was whether or not the subject engaged in helping behavior, defined as "mailing the application or taking the envelope to one of the airport ticket counters."

Based on the results of the study by Benson et al., what is the probability that five out of five male subjects will engage in helping behavior (mailing the envelope containing the application or delivering it to an airport ticket counter)? Often our question will take on a somewhat modified form. If we assume an attractive female applicant, what is the probability that five out of five male subjects will engage in helping behavior? This last question is concerned with conditional probabilities. In this case we are asking if the probability of obtaining helping behavior is conditional on the attractiveness of the applicant. In this section we examine joint, marginal, and conditional probabilities as well as the multiplication rule for independent and nonindependent events.

Joint, Marginal, and Conditional Probabilities

To illustrate joint, marginal, and conditional probabilities, let's return to the data presented in Table 12.3.

If we divide each of the cell frequencies and the marginal (row and column) totals by n, we obtain a joint probability Table (12.4). Note that the table provides direct answers to such questions as "What is the probability that help was provided to an attractive applicant?" "For the total sample, what

---

* *Source:* Based on Peter L. Benson, Stuart A. Karabenick, and Richard M. Lerner (1976), "Pretty Pleases: The Effects of Physical Attractiveness, Race, and Sex on Receiving Help," *Journal of Experimental Social Psychology,* **12**, 409–415.

Table 12.3 Number helping when applicant is attractive or unattractive female (whites and blacks combined) and subject is male

Helping Response	Characteristics of Target		Row Totals
	Attractive	Unattractive	
Helped	52	35	87
Did not help	62	71	133
Column totals	114	106	220

is the probability that help was not provided?'' ''What is the probability that help was not provided to an unattractive applicant?''

Joint probabilities Each cell in Table 12.4 shows the joint probability associated with the column and row variables. For example, the joint probability that the applicant was both attractive (Event A) and helped (Event B) is

$$p(A \text{ and } B) = \frac{52}{220} = 0.236$$

However, the joint probability of an applicant being unattractive (Event $\overline{A}$) and helped (Event B) is

$$p(\overline{A} \text{ and } B) = \frac{35}{220} = 0.159$$

Also, the joint probability of an applicant being attractive (Event A) and not helped (Event $\overline{B}$) is

$$p(A \text{ and } \overline{B}) = \frac{62}{220} = 0.282$$

Marginal probabilities Note that each marginal probability represents a simple probability of an event and is *not* conditional on other events. For this reason marginal probabilities are also referred to as unconditional probabilities.

Table 12.4 Joint probability table of helping behavior when applicant was either attractive or unattractive*

Helping Response	Attractive (A)	Unattractive ($\overline{A}$)	Marginal Probability
Helped (B)	0.236 (52/220)	0.159 (35/220)	0.395 (87/220)
Did not help ($\overline{B}$)	0.282 (62/220)	0.323 (71/220)	0.605 (133/220)
Marginal probability	0.518 (114/220)	0.482 (106/220)	1.000 (220/220)

* Cell and marginal frequencies divided by total sample size are shown in parentheses.

Thus, in Table 12.4, the right-hand or row marginals show the simple probability of a person being helped or not helped without regard to whether or not she is attractive. Thus, the unconditional probability of being helped is 0.395, whereas the unconditional probability of not being helped is 0.605.

Similarly, the column marginals show the probability that the applicant was attractive (0.518) or unattractive (0.482) whether or not she was helped.

Conditional probabilities When the information we have about events is limited to the marginal probabilities, our best predictions concerning the probability of a given event is similarly restricted to these marginal probabilities. Thus, if we know only that a male entered the phone booth that contained a "lost" job application, our best estimate of the probability that he will help is 0.395 and that he will not help is 0.605. But what if we are given some additional information, such as "The applicant was attractive." Notice that the sample space is now limited to attractive applicants, rather than to all applicants, since we now have more information than we had before. Will this information permit us to "fine tune" our assessment of the probability that the male entering the phone booth will engage in helping behavior? The answer is "Yes" if helping behavior is conditional on the attractiveness of the applicant.

To illustrate, Table 12.4 provides three probabilities for each helping response—the marginal probability that help will be provided, the joint probability that the applicant is attractive and helped, and the joint probability that the applicant is attractive and not helped. Now suppose we know in advance that the applicant is attractive. Will this additional information provide a basis for a better assessment of the probability that she will be helped? Let's see.

To find the **conditional probability** that the applicant will receive help, we divide the joint probability that she is attractive and helped $p(A \text{ and } B)$ by the marginal probability that she is attractive $p(A)$. Thus, in the present example

$$p(B|A) = \frac{p(A \text{ and } B)}{p(A)} = \frac{0.236}{0.518}$$

$$= 0.456$$

where $p(B|A)$ is the conditional probability of Event B given that Event A has occurred. Similarly

$$p(A|B) = \frac{p(A \text{ and } B)}{p(B)}$$

where $p(A|B)$ is the conditional probability of Event A given that Event B has occurred.

Note that knowing only the marginal probability, we would have assessed the applicant's chance of being helped as 0.395. Knowing that she is attractive permitted us to raise our assessment of the probability to 0.456.

Let's look at one additional example. Knowing that an applicant is unattractive, what is our assessment of the probability of her not being helped, that is, of $p(\overline{B}|\overline{A})$?

$$p(\overline{B}|\overline{A}) = \frac{p(\overline{A} \text{ and } \overline{B})}{p(\overline{A})} = \frac{0.323}{0.482}$$

$$= 0.670$$

Using only the marginal probabilities, we would have estimated the probability of any applicant not being helped as 0.605. Taking into account our knowledge of her unattractiveness, we were able to increase the probability assessment to 0.67.

Table 12.5 summarizes the conditional probabilities derived from Table 12.4.

Note that the conditional probabilities shown in the two columns at the right relate to the probability of the applicant being attractive (A) and unattractive ($\overline{A}$) when the status of helping is known. Thus, we see that the probability of not being attractive when help has not been received $p(\overline{A}|\overline{B})$ is 0.534.

Similarly, the two rows at the bottom of the table show the probabilities of the applicant receiving help (B) or not receiving help ($\overline{B}$) when the status of her attractiveness is known. Thus, the probability that an attractive person receives help $p(B|A)$ is 0.456.

The Multiplication Rule for Independent Events

Consider the following conceptual experiment. You toss a single coin into the air and a head appears. Assuming an ideal coin, the probability of a head is 1/2 and the probability of a tail is 1/2. Now toss the coin a second time. Does the outcome of the first toss in any way affect the outcome of the second toss? If it does not, the two outcomes are said to be **independent.** Since we have

Table 12.5 Joint and conditional probability table of helping behavior when the applicant was either attractive or unattractive. The conditional probabilities are calculated by dividing the joint probabilities within each cell by its marginal probability

Helping Response	Attractive (A)	Unattractive ($\overline{A}$)	Marginal Probability	Conditional Probability
Helped (B)	0.236	0.159	0.395	$p(A|B)$ $p(\overline{A}|B)$ 0.597 0.403
Did not help ($\overline{B}$)	0.282	0.323	0.605	$p(A|\overline{B})$ $p(\overline{A}|\overline{B})$ 0.466 0.534
Marginal probability	0.518 $p(B|A)$ 0.456 $p(\overline{B}|A)$ 0.544	0.482 $p(B|\overline{A})$ 0.330 $p(\overline{B}|\overline{A})$ 0.670	1.000	

assumed an ideal coin (i.e., it is balanced, will not stand on end, is not motivated to change its behavior, etc.), we may assume that the two outcomes are independent so that the probability of obtaining a head remains 1/2 as does the probability of obtaining a tail. When outcomes or events are independent, the multiplication rule states:

The probability of the simultaneous or successive occurrence of two events is the product of the separate probabilities of each event.

In symbolic form:

$$p(A \text{ and } B) = p(A)p(B) \tag{12.9}$$

Suppose we toss a single coin on three successive occasions. What is the probability of obtaining the event "all heads"? To obtain this event, all three *outcomes must be a head. Thus*

$$p(H, H, \text{ and } H) = p(H)p(H)p(H)$$

$$= \left(\frac{1}{2}\right)\left(\frac{1}{2}\right)\left(\frac{1}{2}\right)$$

$$= \frac{1}{8} \quad \text{or} \quad 0.125$$

Sampling with replacement is an example of independent events. Suppose that we draw a single card from a deck of playing cards and obtain a king of hearts. The probability of this outcome is $1/52 = 0.019$. If we return the card to the deck, shuffle the cards well and make a second selection, what is the probability of selecting the king of hearts again? It remains 1/52. When sampling with replacement, what is the probability of selecting the king of hearts twice in succession? Using the multiplication rule for independent events, we obtain $p(KH \text{ and } KH) = (1/52)(1/52) = 1/2704$ or 0.00037.

The Multiplication Rule for Nonindependent (Dependent) Events

The multiplication rule for dependent events can most readily be grasped by contrasting sampling with replacement with sampling without replacement. Imagine we were to make two successive draws from a deck of playing cards. What is the probability that we obtain two kings?

If we use sampling with replacement, the two events are independent. Since the probability of selecting a king is 4/52, the probability of drawing two consecutive kings $p(K \text{ and } K)$ is $(4/52)(4/52) = 0.0059$.

However, if we use sampling without replacement, the events are not independent. If we select a king on the first draw, there will be only three kings left in a deck containing 51 cards. In other words, the results of the first draw influence the possible consequences of the second draw. In fact, the conditional probability of selecting a king on the second draw assuming that a king has been selected on the first draw $p(K|K)$ is $3/51 = 0.059$.

For **nonindependent** or dependent events, the multiplication rule becomes

Given two events A and B, the probability of obtaining both A and B jointly is the product of the probability of obtaining one of these events times the conditional probability of obtaining one event, given that the other event has occurred.

Stated symbolically

$$p(A \text{ and } B) = p(A)p(B|A) = p(B)p(A|B) \qquad (12.10)$$

In the present example the probability of selecting a king on the first draw $p(K)$ is equal to 4/52. The probability of selecting a king on the second draw, given a king drawn on the first is 3/51. Thus, when using sampling without replacement, the probability of selecting two consecutive kings is

$$p(K \text{ and } K) = p(K)p(K|K)$$

$$= \left(\frac{4}{52}\right)\left(\frac{3}{51}\right)$$

$$= 0.0045$$

Figure 12.3 Tree diagram of the statistical experiment involving two draws, without replacement, from a deck of playing cards. The event of interest is the probability of selecting two consecutive kings.

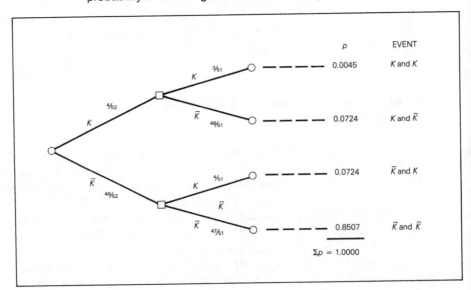

Figure 12.3 is a tree diagram of this statistical experiment that illustrates the calculation of the probability of all possible events.

Note that we can calculate the probability of each event by successively multiplying the probability associated with each branch by the probability associated with connecting branches. Thus, the probability of selecting two kings is found by multiplying the probabilities of the two K branches (4/52) (3/51). Similarly, the two $\bar{K}$ branches provide the basis for calculating the selection of two nonkings on successive draws.

Figure 12.4 shows the tree diagram for calculating the conditional probabilities of the study concerned with physical attractiveness of the target and the helping behavior by the subjects.

A second example of the multiplication rule for nonindependent (dependent) events involves a contingency table. Given the following population in which the relationship between attitude toward busing for integration purposes and race is summarized, what is the probability of drawing a nonwhite person who favors busing?

	Race		
Attitude Toward Busing	*Nonwhite*	*White*	Total
Favor	200	300	500
Oppose	50	450	500
Total	250	750	1000

Figure 12.4 Tree diagram used to calculate the probability of various conditional events relating to physical attractiveness of the target and helping behavior by the subjects.

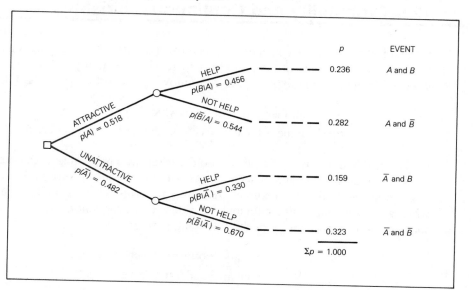

Event A is the probability of drawing a nonwhite person, and event B is the probability of drawing a person who favors busing. The probability of event A occurring is 0.25 because 250 of the 1000 persons are nonwhite, and the probability of event B occurring is 0.5 because 500 of the 1000 persons in the population favor busing. We also need to know the probability of B given A or A given B. The probability of A given B is 0.4 because 500 persons favor busing and 200 of these persons are nonwhite. The probability of B given A is 0.8 because 250 persons are nonwhite and, of these persons, 200 favor busing. Therefore, applying Eq. (12.10), we can solve the problem in one of two ways:

$$p(A \text{ and } B) = p(A)p(B|A) = (0.25)(0.8) = 0.2$$

But we also know that

$$p(A \text{ and } B) = p(B)p(A|B)$$

Therefore

$$p(A \text{ and } B) = (0.5)(0.4) = 0.2$$

Our answers agree and can be confirmed by locating the "favor-nonwhite" cell in the contingency table. Two hundred of the 1000 persons in the population are nonwhite and favor busing; therefore, they constitute 20% or 0.2 of the population and we have confirmed our answer.

12.5 Probability and Continuous Variables

Up to this point we have considered probability in terms of the expected relative frequency of an event. In fact, as you will recall, probability was defined in terms of frequency and expressed as the following proportion [Eq. (12.1)]:

$$p(A) = \frac{\text{number of outcomes in which event } A \text{ occurs}}{\text{total number of outcomes (A occurs + A does not occur)}}$$

However, this definition presents a problem when we are dealing with continuous variables such as age or income. As we pointed out in Section 3.7.1, it is generally advisable to represent frequency in terms of areas under a curve when we are dealing with continuous variables. Thus, for continuous variables, we may express probability as the following proportion:

$$p = \frac{\text{area under portions of a curve}}{\text{total area under the curve}} \qquad (12.11)$$

Since the total area in a probability distribution is equal to 1.00, we define *p* as the proportion of total area under portions of a curve.

Chapters 13 through 16 use the standard normal curve as the probability model. Let's examine the probability-area relationship in terms of this model.

12.6 Probability and the Normal-Curve Model

In Section 7.4 we stated that the standard normal distribution has a mean of 0, a standard deviation of 1, and a total area that is equal to 1.00. We saw that when scores on a normally distributed variable are transformed into *z* scores, we are, in effect, expressing these scores in units of the standard normal curve. This permits us to express the difference between any two scores as proportions of total area under the curve. Thus, we may establish probability values in terms of these proportions, as in Eq. (12.11). Let us look at several examples that illustrate the application of probability concepts to the normal-curve model.

12.6.1 Illustrative Problems*

For all problems, assume $\mu = 100$ and $\sigma = 16$.

Problem 12.1

What is the probability of selecting at *random,* from the general population, a person with an aptitude score of at least 132? The answer to this question is given by the proportion of area under the curve above a score of 132 (Fig. 12.5).

First, we must find the *z* score corresponding to $X = 132$.

$$z = \frac{132 - 100}{16} = 2.00$$

In column C of Table A in Appendix C, we find that 0.0228 of the area lies at or beyond a *z* of 2.00. Therefore, the probability of selecting, at random, a person with a score of at least 132 is 0.0228.

Problem 12.2

What is the probability of selecting, at random, an individual with a score of at least 92?

---

* See Section 7.6.

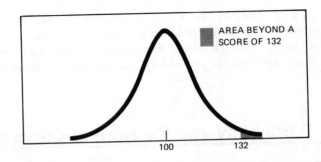

AREA BEYOND A
SCORE OF 132

100   132

Figure 12.5 Proportion of area above a score of 132 in a normal distribution with $\mu = 100$ and $\sigma = 16$.

We are dealing with two mutually exclusive and exhaustive areas under the curve. The area under the curve above a score of 92 is P; the area below a score of 92 is Q. In solving our problem, we may therefore apply Eq. (12.7):

$$P = 1.00 - Q$$

By expressing a score of 92 in terms of its corresponding z, we may obtain the proportion of area below $X = 92$ (i.e., Q) directly from column C (Table A).

The z score corresponding to $X = 92$ is

$$z = \frac{92 - 100}{16} = -0.50$$

The proportion of area below a z of -0.50 is 0.3085. Therefore, the probability of selecting, at random, an individual with a score of at least 92 becomes

$$P = 1.00 - 0.3085 = 0.6915$$

Figure 12.6 illustrates this relationship.

Problem 12.3

Let's look at an example involving the multiplication law. Given that sampling with replacement is used, what is the probability of drawing, at random, three individuals with scores equaling or exceeding 124? For this problem, we again assume that $\mu = 100$ and $\sigma = 16$.

The z score corresponding to $X = 124$ is

$$z = \frac{124 - 100}{16} = 1.5$$

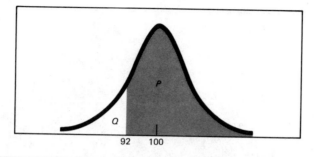

Figure 12.6 Proportion of area above (*P*) and below (*Q*) a score of 92 in a normal distribution with μ = 100 and σ = 16.

In column C (Table A), we find that 0.0668 of the area lies at or beyond $X = 124$. Therefore

$$p(A, B, C) = p(A \text{ and } B \text{ and } C) = p(A) \times p(B) \times p(C)$$

$$= (0.0668)(0.0668)(0.0668)$$

$$= 0.0003$$

12.7 One- and Two-Tailed *p* Values

In the first problem we posed the question, "What is the probability of selecting a person with a score as high as 132?" We answered the question by examining only one tail of the distribution, namely, scores as high as or higher than 132. For this reason we refer to the probability value that we obtained as being a **one-tailed *p* value.**

In statistics and research the following question is frequently asked, "What is the probability of obtaining a score (or statistic) this *deviant* from the mean? . . . or a score (or statistic) this *rare* . . . or a result this *unusual*?" Clearly, when the frequency distribution of scores is symmetrical, a score of 68 or lower is every bit as deviant from a mean of 100 as is a score of 132. That is, both are two standard deviation units away from the mean (assuming $\sigma = 16$). When we express the probability value, taking into account both tails of the distribution, we refer to the *p* value as being **two-tailed.** In symmetrical distributions *two-tailed p values* may be obtained merely by doubling the one-tailed probability value. Thus, in the preceding problem the probability of selecting a person with a score as rare or unusual as 132 is 2 × 0.0228 = 0.0456.

We may illustrate the distinction between one- and two-tailed *p* values by referring to the sampling experiment we have used throughout the text. Figure 12.7 shows a probability histogram based on Table 12.6. Recall that this

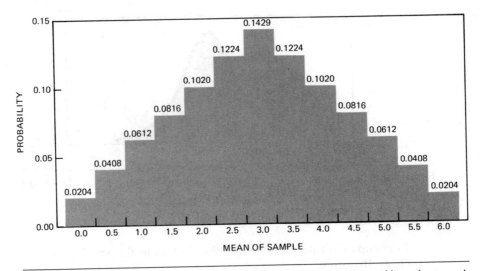

Figure 12.7 Probability histogram of means based on selecting, with replacement, samples of $N = 2$ from a population of seven numbers.

Table 12.6 Frequency and probability distribution of means of samples of size $N = 2$, drawn with replacement from a population of seven scores (0, 1, 2, 3, 4, 5, 6)

$\overline{X}$	f	$p(\overline{X})$
6.0	1	0.0204
5.5	2	0.0408
5.0	3	0.0612
4.5	4	0.0816
4.0	5	0.1020
3.5	6	0.1224
3.0	7	0.1429
2.5	6	0.1224
2.0	5	0.1020
1.5	4	0.0816
1.0	3	0.0612
0.5	2	0.0408
0.0	1	0.0204
	$N_x = 49$*	$\Sigma\, p(\overline{X}) = 0.9997$†

* We use N_x to refer to the total number of means obtained in our sampling experiment and to distinguish it from N, which is the number of scores on which each mean is based. In this sampling experiment $N_x = 49$.

† $\Sigma p(\overline{X})$ should equal 1.000. The discrepancy of 0.0003 represents rounding.

distribution was obtained by selecting, with replacement, all possible samples of $N = 2$ from a population of seven scores.

If we ask, "What is the probability of obtaining a mean equal to zero?" we need refer only to the left tail of the probability histogram in order to find the answer of 0.0204. However, if we ask, "What is the probability of obtaining as deviant an outcome as a sample mean equal to zero?" we would have to look at both the left and the right tails. Since a mean of 6 is equally deviant from the mean of the distribution, we use the addition rule to obtain the two-tailed value:

$$p(\overline{X} = 0 \text{ or } \overline{X} = 6)$$
$$= p\,(\overline{X} = 0) \text{ and } p(\overline{X} = 6)$$
$$= 0.0204 + 0.0204 = 0.0408$$

Let's look at two additional examples.

Example 1 What is the probability of obtaining a mean as low as 0.5 (i.e., a mean of 0.5 or lower)?

We find the probability of obtaining a mean of 0.5 and a mean of 0.0 (the only mean lower than 0.5), and add these probabilities together to obtain the one-tailed p value:

$$p(\overline{X} \le 0.5) = p(\overline{X} = 0.5) + p(\overline{X} = 0.0)$$
$$= 0.0408 + 0.0204 = 0.0612$$

Example 2 What is the probability of obtaining a mean as deviant from the distribution mean as a sample mean of 0.5?

The answer to this question calls for a two-tailed p value obtained by applying the addition rule to

$$p(\overline{X} = 0.5) + p(\overline{X} = 0.0) + p(\overline{X} = 5.5) + p(\overline{X} = 6.0)$$

However, since the distribution is symmetrical and means of 5.5 and 6.0 are equally as deviant as 0.5 and 0.0, respectively, we need only double the p value obtained in example 1:

$$p(0.5 \ge \overline{X} \ge 5.5) = 2(0.0612)$$
$$= 0.1224$$

Incidentally, the left-hand member of this expression is read: *The probability of a mean equal to or less than 0.5 or equal to or greater than 5.5.*

The distinction between one- and two-tailed probability values takes on added significance as we progress into inferential statistics.

Summary

In this chapter we discussed the importance of the concept of randomness in inferential statistics. Randomness refers to selecting the events in the sample such that each event is equally likely to be selected in a sample of a given size. Independent random sampling refers to the fact that the selection of one event has no effect on the probability of selecting another event. Although the individual events are unpredictable, collections of random events take on characteristic and predictable forms. The normal curve was cited in this regard.

The theory of probability is concerned with the outcomes of studies. We can distinguish between probabilities established by assuming *idealized* relative frequencies and those established empirically by determining relative frequencies. Probability was defined as

$$p(A) = \frac{\text{number of outcomes in which } A \text{ occurs}}{\text{total number of outcomes}}$$

The formal properties of probability were also discussed.

Probabilities vary between 0 and 1.00.

The addition rule is as follows: If A and B are two events, the probability of obtaining either of them is equal to the probability of A plus the probability of B minus the probability of their joint occurrence. Thus

$$p(A \text{ or } B) = p(A) + p(B) - p(A \text{ and } B)$$

If events A and B are *mutually exclusive,* the addition rule becomes

$$p(A \text{ or } B) = p(A) + p(B)$$

If the two events are *mutually exclusive and exhaustive,* we obtain

$$p(A) + p(B) = 1.00$$

Allowing P to represent the probability of occurrence and Q to represent the probability of nonoccurrence, we find that three additional useful formulations for mutually exclusive and exhaustive events are

$$P + Q = 1.00, \quad P = 1.00 - Q, \quad Q = 1.00 - P$$

The multiplication rule varies for independent and dependent events. *When events are independent* and when sampling with replacement, the selection on one trial is *independent* of the selection on another trial. Given two events, A and B, the probability of obtaining both A and B in successive trials is the product of the probability of obtaining one of these events times the probability of obtaining the second of these events:

$$p(A \text{ and } B) = p(A)p(B)$$

When events are nonindependent and when sampling without replacement, the selection of one event affects the probability of selecting each remaining event, so they are *dependent*. Thus, given two events, A and B, the probability of obtaining both A and B jointly or successively is the product of the probability of obtaining one of the events times the conditional probability of obtaining one event, given that the other event has occurred. Symbolically

$$p(A \text{ and } B) = p(A)p(B|A) = p(B)p(A|B)$$

We discussed the application of probability theory to continuously distributed variables. Probability is expressed in terms of the proportion of area under a curve. Hence

$$p = \frac{\text{area under portions of a curve}}{\text{total area under a curve}}$$

We saw how we may use z scores and the standard normal curve to establish various probabilities for normally distributed variables.

Finally, we distinguished between one- and two-tailed probability values.

Terms to Remember

Addition rule   If A and B are mutually exclusive events, the probability of obtaining *either of them* is equal to the probability of A plus the probability of B. Symbolically

$$p(A \text{ or } B) = p(A) + p(B)$$

Bias   In sampling, when selections favor certain events or certain collections of events.

Conditional probability   The probability of an event given that another event has occurred. Represented symbolically as $p(A|B)$, the probability of A given that B has occurred.

Exhaustive   Two or more events are said to be exhaustive if they exhaust all possible outcomes. Symbolically

$$p(A \text{ or } B \text{ or } \ldots) = 1.00$$

Independence The condition that exists when the occurrence of a given event will not affect the probability of the occurrence of another event. Symbolically

$$p(A|B) = p(A) \quad \text{and} \quad p(B|A) = p(B)$$

Joint (or successive) occurrence The occurrence of two events simultaneously. Such events cannot be mutually exclusive.

Multiplication rule Given two events A and B, the probability of obtaining both A and B jointly is the product of the probability of obtaining one of these events times the conditional probability of obtaining one event, given that the other event has occurred. Symbolically

$$p(A \text{ and } B) = p(A)p(B|A) = p(B)p(A|B)$$

Mutually exclusive Events A and B are said to be mutually exclusive if both cannot occur simultaneously. Symbolically, for mutually exclusive events

$$p(A \text{ and } B) = 0.00$$

Nonindependence The condition that exists when the occurrence of a given event affects the probability of the occurrence of another event.

One-tailed p values Probability values obtained by examining only one tail of the distribution.

Probability A theory concerned with possible outcomes of studies. Symbolically

$$p(A) = \frac{\text{number of outcomes in which } A \text{ occurs}}{\text{total number of outcomes}}$$

Random sampling Samples are selected in such a way that each sample of a given size has precisely the same probability of being selected.

Sampling distribution A theoretical probability distribution of a statistic that would result from drawing all possible samples of a given size from some population.

Two-tailed p values Probability values that take into account both tails of the distribution.

Exercises

1. Imagine that we have a population of the following four scores: 0, 3, 6, and 9.

a) Construct a probability distribution and histogram of all possible means when sampling with replacement, $N = 2$.

b) Construct a probability histogram of all possible means when sampling with replacement, $N = 3$. (*Hint:* The table for finding the means follows. The values appearing in the cells represent the means of the three draws.)

First draw		0				3				6				9			
Second draw		0	3	6	9	0	3	6	9	0	3	6	9	0	3	6	9
Third draw	0	0	1	2	3	1	2	3	4	2	3	4	5	3	4	5	6
	3	1	2	3	4	2	3	4	5	3	4	5	6	4	5	6	7
	6	2	3	4	5	3	4	5	6	4	5	6	7	5	6	7	8
	9	3	4	5	6	4	5	6	7	5	6	7	8	6	7	8	9

2. The original population of the four scores in Exercise 1 was rectangular (they all had the same associated frequency of 1). Compare the probability distributions in 1(a) and 1(b) and attempt to form a generalization about the form and the dispersion of the distribution of sample means as we increase the sample size.

3. Answer the following questions based on the probability histograms obtained in Exercise 1.

a) Drawing a single sample of $N = 2$, what is the probability of obtaining a mean equal to zero? Contrast this result with the probability of randomly selecting a mean equal to zero when $N = 3$.

b) For each distribution, determine the probability of selecting a sample with a mean as rare or as unusual as 9.

c) From each probability histogram, determine the probability of selecting a sample with a mean as low as 3.

d) From each probability histogram, determine the probability of selecting a sample mean as deviant from the population mean as a mean of 3.

4. For the probability distribution of $N = 2$ [Exercise 1(a)], find

a) $p(\overline{X} < 6)$ b) $p(\overline{X} \geq 7.5)$ c) $p(\overline{X} = 4.5)$

5. For the probability distribution of $N = 3$ [Exercise 1(b)], find

a) $p(3 \leq \overline{X} \leq 6)$ b) $p(4 \leq \overline{X} \leq 5)$ c) $p(\overline{X} = 2 \text{ or } \overline{X} = 8)$

6. Let's now imagine a different type of sampling experiment. You have selected all possible samples of $N = 2$ from a population of scores and obtained the following means: 1, 2, 2, 3, 3, 3, 4, 4, 5. You now place paper slips in a hat with these means written on them. You select one mean, record it, and replace it in the hat. You select a second mean, *subtract* it from the first, and then replace it in the hat. The table for describing all possible *differences between means* of $N = 2$ follows.

		First Draw of Mean								
		1	2	2	3	3	3	4	4	5
Second draw of mean	1	0	1	1	2	2	2	3	3	4
	2	−1	0	0	1	1	1	2	2	3
	2	−1	0	0	1	1	1	2	2	3
	3	−2	−1	−1	0	0	0	1	1	2
	3	−2	−1	−1	0	0	0	1	1	2
	3	−2	−1	−1	0	0	0	1	1	2
	4	−3	−2	−2	−1	−1	−1	0	0	1
	4	−3	−2	−2	−1	−1	−1	0	0	1
	5	−4	−3	−3	−2	−2	−2	−1	−1	0

a) Construct a frequency distribution of differences between means.

b) Construct a probability distribution of differences between means.

c) Find the mean and the standard deviation of the differences between means.

7. Based on the responses to Exercise 6, answer the following questions. Drawing two samples at random and with replacement from the population of means, and subtracting the second mean from the first, what is the probability that you will select

a) A difference between means equal to zero?

b) A difference between means equal to or less than 1 *or* equal to or greater than −1? (*Note:* −2, −3, −4 are all less than −1.)

c) A difference between means equal to −4?

d) A difference between means as rare or as deviant as −4?

e) A difference between means equal to or greater than 3?

f) A difference between means equal to or less than −3?

g) A difference between means as rare or as unusual as −3?

h) A difference between means equal to or less than 2 or equal to or greater than −2?

8. List all the possible outcomes of a coin that is tossed three times. Calculate the probability of

  a) 3 heads **b)** 3 tails

  c) 2 heads and 1 tail **d)** at least 2 heads

9. A card is drawn at random from a deck of 52 playing cards. What is the probability that

  a) It will be the ace of spades?

  b) It will be an ace?

  c) It will be an ace or a face card?

  d) It will be a spade or a face card?

10. Express the probabilities in Exercises 8 and 9 in terms of *odds against*.

11. In a single throw of two dice, what is the probability that

  a) A 7 will appear?

  b) A doublet (two of the same number) will appear?

  c) A doublet or an 8 will appear?

  d) An even number will appear?

12. On a slot machine (commonly referred to as a "one-armed bandit") there are three reels with five different fruits plus a star on each reel. After inserting a coin and pulling the handle, the player sees that the three reels revolve independently several times before stopping. What is the probability that

  a) Three lemons will appear?

  b) Any three of a kind will appear?

  c) Two lemons and a star will appear?

  d) Two lemons and any other fruit will appear?

  e) No star will appear?

13. Three cards are drawn at random (without replacement) from a deck of 52 cards. What is the probability that

  a) All three will be hearts?

  b) None of the three cards will be hearts?

  c) All three will be face cards?

14. Calculate the probabilities in Exercise 13 if each card is replaced after it is drawn.

15. A well-known test of intelligence is constructed so as to have normally distributed scores with a mean of 100 and a standard deviation of 16.

   a) What is the probability that someone picked at random will have an I.Q. of 122 or higher?

   b) There are I.Q.'s so *high* that the probability is 0.05 that such I.Q.'s would occur in a random sample of people. Those I.Q.'s are beyond what value?

   c) There are I.Q.'s so *extreme* that the probability is 0.05 that such I.Q.'s would occur in a random sample of people. Those I.Q.'s are beyond what values?

   d) The next time you shop you will undoubtedly see someone who is a complete stranger to you. What is the probability that his I.Q. will be between 90 and 110?

   e) What is the probability of selecting two people at random
      i) with I.Q.'s of 122 or higher?
      ii) with I.Q.'s between 90 and 110?
      iii) one with an I.Q. of 122 or higher, the other with an I.Q. between 90 and 110?

   f) What is the probability that on leaving your class, the first student you meet will have an I.Q. below 120? Can you answer this question on the basis of the information provided previously? If not, why not?

16. Which of the following selection techniques will result in random samples? Explain your answers.

   a) *Population:* Viewers of a given television program. *Sampling technique:* On a given night, interviewing every fifth person in the studio audience.

   b) *Population:* A homemade pie. *Sampling technique:* A wedge selected from any portion of the pie.

   c) *Population:* All the students in a suburban high school. *Sampling technique:* Selecting one student sent to you by each homeroom teacher.

17. The proportion of people who are Baptist in a particular city is 0.20. What is the probability that

   a) A given individual, selected at random, will be a Baptist?

   b) Two out of two individuals will be Baptists?

   c) A given individual will *not* be a Baptist?

   d) Two out of two individuals will *not* be Baptists?

18. A bag contains six blue marbles, four red marbles, and two green marbles. If you select a single marble at random from the bag, what is the probability that it will be

    a) Red?   **b)** Blue?   **c)** Green?   **d)** White?

19. Selecting *without* replacement from the bag described in Exercise 18, what is the probability that

    a) Three out of three will be blue?

    b) Two out of two will be green?

    c) None out of four will be red?

20. Selecting *with* replacement from the bag described in Exercise 18, what is the probability that

    a) Three out of three will be blue?

    b) Two out of two will be green?

    c) None out of four will be red?

21. Forty percent of the students at a given college major in business administration. Seventy percent of these are male and thirty percent female. Sixty percent of the students in the school are male. What is the probability that

    a) One student selected at random will be a BA major?

    b) One person selected at random will be a female BA major?

    c) Two students selected at random will be BA majors?

    d) Two persons selected at random will be BA majors, one male, one female?

22. What is the probability that a score chosen at random from a normally distributed population with a mean of 66 and a standard deviation of 8 will be

    a) Greater than 70?

    b) Less than 60?

    c) Between 60 and 70?

    d) In the 70s?

    e) Either equal to or less than 54 or equal to or greater than 72?

    f) Either less than 52 or between 78 and 84?

    g) Either between 56 and 64 or between 80 and 86?

23. Given the following population, what is the probability that an upperclass person favors a tax cut? The probability that a lower-class person opposes a tax cut?

Attitude Toward a Tax Cut	Social Class		Total
	Lower	Upper	
Favor	75	25	100
Oppose	25	50	75
Total	100	75	N = 175

24. A political scientist is studying all 67 grassroots political organizations in a major American city. The following table shows the clarification of the political organizations by the party allegiance and socioeconomic composition of the members.

Party	Socioeconomic Status		
	Low	Moderate	High
Republican	5	11	19
Democrat	10	12	6
Socialist	2	1	1

If one of the political organizations were chosen at random from this city, what is the probability that the members will have these characteristics?

a) high income

b) Socialist

c) Socialist of high income

d) not Republican

e) not Democrat and low income

f) not Republican and not Socialist

g) not Republican and not moderate income

25. Given the information in Exercise 24, what is the conditional probability that if an organization is selected it will have the membership characteristics of

a) Moderate income, given that it is Republican?

b) Democrat, given that it is low income?

c) Not Socialist, given high income?

26. Refer back to Table 12.4. Construct a tree diagram of the conditional probabilities when the helping response of the subject is known.

27. In another facet of the study relating physical attractiveness to helping behavior, the target was either an attractive or unattractive male and the subjects were females. The results are shown in the following table.

Helping Response	Characteristics of Target		Row Totals
	Attractive	Unattractive	
Helped	19	13	32
Did not help	22	27	49
Column totals	41	40	81

a) Prepare a joint probability table of the results.

b) Calculate the conditional probabilities of events B and $\overline{B}$ when the attractiveness status of the subject is known.

c) Construct a tree diagram of the conditional probabilities when the attractiveness status of the target person is known.

d) Construct a tree diagram of the conditional probabilities when the helping status of the subject is known.

chapter **13**

Introduction to
Statistical Inference

13.1 Why Sample?

13.2 The Concept of Sampling Distributions

13.3 Testing Statistical Hypotheses: Level of Significance

13.4 Testing Statistical Hypotheses: Null Hypothesis and Alternative Hypothesis

13.5 Testing Statistical Hypotheses: The Two Types of Error

13.6 A Final Word of Caution

13.1 Why Sample?

You are the leader of a religious denomination, and for the purpose of planning recruitment you want to know what proportion of the adults in the United States claim church membership. How would you go about getting this information?

You are a sociologist, and you want to study the differences in child-rearing practices among parents of delinquent and nondelinquent children.

You are a market researcher, and you want to know what proportion of individuals prefer certain car colors and their various combinations.

You are a park attendant, and you want to determine whether the ice is sufficiently thick to permit safe skating.

You are a gambler, and you want to determine whether a set of dice is "biased."

What do each of these problems have in common? You are asking questions about the parameter of a population to which you want to generalize your answers, but you have no hope of ever studying the *entire* population. Earlier (Section 1.2) we defined a **population** as a *complete* or theoretical set of individuals, objects, or measurements having some common observable characteristic. As has been noted, it is frequently impossible to study all of the members of a given population because the population as defined either has an infinite number of members or is so large that it defies exhaustive study. Moreover, when we refer to the *population* we are often dealing with a hypothetical entity. In some research situations the actual population may not exist (e.g., the population of all babies regardless of whether or not they have been born) or certain elements may be very difficult to locate (e.g., young black males are frequently undercounted in the census due to their high rate of geographical mobility).

Since populations can rarely be studied exhaustively, we must depend on **samples** as a basis for arriving at a hypothesis concerning various characteristics, or parameters, of the population. Note that our interest is not in descriptive statistics per se, but in making inferences from data. Thus, if we ask 100 people how they intend to vote in a forthcoming election, our primary interest is not in knowing how these 100 people will vote, but in estimating how the members of the entire voting population will cast their ballots.

Recall that in Chapter 1 we described polling a sample of registered voters in Wisconsin concerning their attitude toward the use of nuclear power as an energy source. The sample of respondents allowed us to estimate how *all* the registered voters in the state felt about the issue.

Almost all research involves the observation and the measurement of a limited number of individuals or events. These measurements are presumed to tell us something about the population. In order to understand how we are able to make inferences about a population from a sample, we need to introduce the concept of sampling distributions.

13.2 The Concept of Sampling Distributions

In actual practice inferences about the parameters of a population are made from statistics that are calculated from a sample of N observations drawn at random from this population. If we continued to draw samples of size N from this population, we should not be surprised if we found some differences among the values of the sample statistics obtained.

That is, sample statistics are not fixed values and if you draw many samples from a population their values will vary from sample to sample.

Indeed, it is this observation that has led to the concept of sampling distributions. A **sampling distribution** is a theoretical probability distribution of the possible values of some sample statistic that would occur if we were to draw all possible samples of a fixed size from a given population.

Imagine drawing simple random samples (with replacement) of $N = 50$ from the population of students at a medium-sized university. You calculate the mean age for the first sample and find that it is 20.2. Suppose you continue to draw an infinite number of samples of $N = 50$ and calculate the sample mean for each of the samples drawn. Each time you drew a sample you would record another mean so that after you drew 1000 samples you would end up with 1000 means. Each of the means would be based on averaging the ages of 50 students who were drawn in a given sample. Although the actual ages of students at the university might vary, for example, between 16 and 64, you should see that each of the means will tend to cluster around the overall mean age of the entire university student body. By treating each of the sample means as a raw score, you could draw a frequency curve of the sample mean scores as shown in Figure 13.1. The original dispersion of ages for the population has been superimposed for comparative purposes. Note that the variation of the sampling distribution of means is far smaller than that of the actual population distribution of ages, a topic that is addressed in the following chapter.

Also, realize that this exercise has been presented to demonstrate the logic behind constructing a sampling distribution. Normally, we only draw one sample from a population.

The sampling distribution is one of the most important concepts in inferential statistics. You are already familiar with several sampling distributions, although we have not previously named them as such. Recall the various sampling problems we have introduced throughout the earlier chapters in the text. In Chapter 12, Section 12.7 we started with a population of seven scores, and selected, with replacement, samples of $N = 2$. We obtained all possible combinations of these samples. We then constructed a frequency distribution and probability distribution of means drawn from that population with a fixed sample size of $N = 2$.

Recall also that in Exercise 1 at the end of Chapter 12 we constructed sampling distributions based on drawing, with replacement, all possible samples of $N = 2$ and $N = 3$ from a population of four scores (0, 3, 6, 9). Table 13.1 shows these two sampling distributions, plus the sampling distribution of the mean when $N = 4$.

Table 13.1 is not nearly so difficult as it may look. Concentrate on the situation in which $N = 2$. Here we see that if we sampled two scores, with

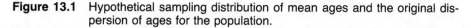

Figure 13.1 Hypothetical sampling distribution of mean ages and the original dispersion of ages for the population.

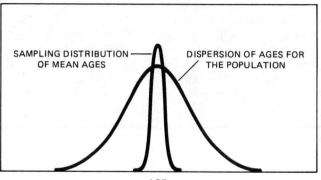

BOX 13.1

Sampling: A Matter of Survival

We tend to think of sampling procedures as activities engaged in by only a handful of professionals—pollsters, laboratory scientists, demographers, to name a few. As the following excerpt from *Winning with Statistics* makes clear, sampling followed by decision making are among the most pervasive activities of living organisms.

We have three dogs on our ranch on the outskirts of Tucson, Arizona. the baby of the three, Millie Muffin, is an eight-month-old black and white springer spaniel. Although mischief should be her middle name, she is a sheer delight. She is constantly exploring the desert flora and fauna with the indefatigable curiosity of a three-year-old human child. When spying something that moves on its own (such as a giant spider, better known as a tarantula), she leaps about two feet off the ground—ears and feathers flapping—and retreats several feet away, all the while barking like a fierce Doberman. But I know better. In reality, she is the world's greatest coward. I'll tell you how I know.

While she is prancing mindlessly about the giant saguaro, the ocotillo, the cholla, and other assorted exotic plants of the desert, I will sneak downwind of her. Then I will raise myself on the balls of my toes, stretch my arms in front of me, and shuffle my feet as I advance toward her in my best Frankenstein-monster style. When she spies me, she lets out a startled "yip," springs into the air, and begins a barking retreat. But all the while, her nose is probing the air, sniffing constantly, desperately drawing in samples in an effort to make inferences about the nature of the intruder. While observing Millie's antics, it occurred to me that the actions involved in taking samples and drawing inferences from these samples are among the most pervasive of mammalian activities. The pet dog, the family feline, the lion in the jungle, the gorilla in the rain forest, and the wife, husband, daughter, son, businessperson, doctor, lawyer, and Indian chief have this characteristic in common. They are continuously probing aspects of their environment, assessing the risks against the benefits, making probability judgments concerning alternative avenues of behavior, and pursuing those lines of activity that appear most likely to lead to desired goals. By this I do not mean to imply that all this sampling and probability assessment is conscious or deliberate. The truth of the matter is that nature has designed us all to be exquisite probability-generating machines. Without the ability to sample and thereby judge peril, or the availability of food, or the receptivity of a sexual partner, all species presently inhabiting the earth would have come from a long line of unborn ancestors.

Source: Excerpted from R. P. Runyon. *Winning with Statistics.* Reading Mass.: Addison-Wesley, 1977.

Table 13.1   Sampling distributions of means drawn from a population of four scores (0, 3, 6, 9; $\mu = 4.5$, $\sigma = 3.94$) and sample sizes $N = 2$, $N = 3$, and $N = 4$. Sampling with replacement

N = 2		N = 3		N = 4	
$\overline{X}$	$p(\overline{X})$	$\overline{X}$	$p(\overline{X})$	$\overline{X}$	$p(\overline{X})$
9.0	0.0625	9.0	0.0156	9.0	0.0039
7.5	0.1250	8.0	0.0469	8.25	0.0156
6.0	0.1875	7.0	0.0938	7.50	0.0391
4.5	0.2500	6.0	0.1562	6.75	0.0781
3.0	0.1875	5.0	0.1875	6.00	0.1211
1.5	0.1250	4.0	0.1875	5.25	0.1562
0.0	0.0625	3.0	0.1562	4.50	0.1719
		2.0	0.0938	3.75	0.1562
		1.0	0.0469	3.00	0.1211
		0.0	0.0156	2.25	0.0781
				1.50	0.0391
				0.75	0.0156
				0.00	0.0039
$\overline{X} = 4.5$		$\overline{X} = 4.5$		$\overline{X} = 4.5$	
$s_{\overline{x}} = 2.37$		$s_{\overline{x}} = 1.94$		$s_{\overline{x}} = 1.68$	

replacement, from our population, only seven possible means could result (9.0, 7.5, 6.0, 4.5, 3.0, 1.5, and 0.0). A mean of 9.0, for example, could only occur if we drew two successive 9's, added them, and divided by 2. A mean of 7.5 would result if we drew a 6 and a 9 or a 9 and a 6. Note that the probability of drawing two 9's when $N = 2$ is 0.0625. You might be wondering how we arrived at this value. Since there are only four scores in the population (0, 3, 6, 9), the probability of drawing one 9 (or one 0 or 3 or 6) is one out of four or 0.25. Recall that the multiplication rule for independent events [Eq. 12.9] states:

The probability of the simultaneous or successive occurrence of two events is the product of the separate probabilities of each event.

Therefore, the probability of a 9 and a 9 can be calculated in the following manner:

$$p(9 \text{ and } 9) = p(9)p(9)$$

$$= (0.25)(0.25)$$

$$= 0.0625$$

The probability of three successive 9's (see the middle column in which $N = 3$) is 0.0156 since the multiplication rule tells us to multiply 0.25 times 0.25 times 0.25, which yields 0.0156.

Finally, note that each of the three $p(\overline{X})$ columns sum to 1.0000, the means for the three sample sizes all equal 4.5, and the standard deviation of the sample means (s_x) becomes smaller as the sample sizes increase. This last point will become clear at the beginning of Chapter 14.

Why is the concept of a sampling distribution so important? Once you are able to describe the sampling distribution of any statistic (be it mean, standard deviation, proportion), you are in a position to entertain and test a wide variety of different hypotheses. For example, you draw four numbers at random from some population. You obtain a mean equal to 6.00. You ask, "Is this mean an ordinary event or is it an unusual or rare event?" In the absence of a frame of reference this question is meaningless. However, if we know the sampling distribution for this statistic, we would have the necessary frame of reference and the answer would be straightforward. If we were to tell you that the appropriate sampling distribution is given in Table 13.1 when $N = 4$, you would have no trouble answering the question. A mean of 6.00 would be drawn about 12% ($p = 0.1211$) of the time; and a mean of 6 or greater would occur almost 26% of the time ($p = 0.1211 + 0.0781 + 0.0391 + 0.0156 + 0.0039 = 0.2578$).

Whenever we estimate a population parameter from a sample, we will ask questions such as, "How good an estimate do I have? Can I conclude that the population parameter is identical with the sample statistic? Or is there likely to be some error? If so, how much?" To answer each of these questions, we will compare our sample results with the "expected" results. The expected results are, in turn, given by the appropriate sampling distribution. But what does the sampling distribution of a particular statistic look like? How can we ever know the form of the distribution, and thus, what are the expected results? Since the inferences we will be making imply knowledge of the *form* of the sampling distribution, it is necessary to set up certain idealized *models*. The normal curve and the **binomial distribution** are two models whose mathematical properties are known. Consequently, these two distributions are frequently used as models to describe particular sampling distributions. Thus, for example, if we know that the sampling distribution of a particular statistic takes the form of a normal distribution, we may use the known properties of the normal distribution to make inferences and predictions about the statistic. The following sections should serve to clarify these important points.

13.3 Testing Statistical Hypotheses: Level of Significance

Let us say that you have a favorite coin that you use constantly in everyday life as a basis of "either–or" decision making. For example, you may ask, "Should I study tonight for the statistics quiz, or should I relax at one of the local movie houses? Heads, I study, tails, I don't." Over a period of time you have sensed that the decision has more often gone against you than for you (in other words, you have to study more often than relax!). You begin to question the accuracy and the adequacy of the coin. Does the coin come up heads more often than tails? How might you find out?

One thing is clear. The true proportion of heads and tails characteristic of this coin can never be known. You could start tossing the coin this very minute and continue for a million years (granting a long life and a remarkably durable coin) and you would not exhaust the population of possible outcomes. In this instance the true proportion of heads and tails is unknowable because the universe, or population, is unlimited.

The fact that the *true* value is unknowable does not prevent us from trying to estimate what it is. We have already pointed out that since populations can rarely be studied exhaustively, we must depend on sample statistics to estimate population parameters.

Returning to our problem with the coin, we clearly see that in order to determine whether or not the coin is biased, we shall have to obtain a sample of the ''behavior'' of that coin and arrive at some generalization concerning its possible bias. For example, if we toss our coin ten times and obtain five heads and five tails, would we begin to suspect our coin of being biased? Of course not, since this outcome is exactly a 50–50 split, and is in agreement with the hypothesis that the coin is not biased. What if we obtained six heads and four tails? Again, this is not an unusual outcome. In fact, we can answer the question of how often, given a theoretically perfect coin, we may expect an outcome at least this much different from a 50–50 split? Looking at Figure 13.2, which represents the theoretical probability distribution of various numbers of heads when $N = 10$, we see that departures from a 50–50 split are quite common. Indeed, whenever we obtain either six or more heads, or four

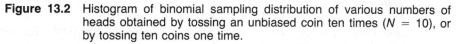

Figure 13.2 Histogram of binomial sampling distribution of various numbers of heads obtained by tossing an unbiased coin ten times ($N = 10$), or by tossing ten coins one time.

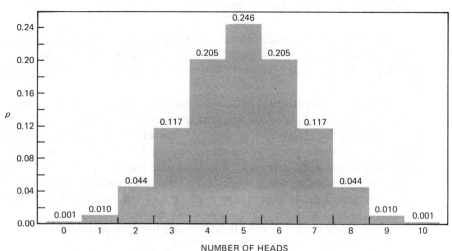

or fewer heads, we are departing from a 50–50 split. Such departures will occur fully 75.4% $(1 - 0.246 = 0.754 \times 100 = 75.4\%)$ of the time when we toss a perfect coin in a series of trials with ten tosses per trial.

What if we obtained nine heads and one tail? Clearly, we begin to suspect the honesty of the coin. Why? At what point do we change from attitudes accepting the "honesty" of the coin to attitudes rejecting its "honesty"? This question takes us to the crux of the problem of inferential statistics. We have seen that the more unusual or rare the event is, the more prone we are to look for nonchance explanations of the event. When we obtained six heads in ten tosses of our coin, we felt no necessity to find an explanation for its departure from a 50–50 split, other than to state that such a departure would occur frequently "by chance." However, when we obtained nine heads, we had an uncomfortable feeling concerning the "honesty" of the coin. Nine heads out of ten tosses is such a rare occurrence that we begin to suspect that the explanation may be found in terms of the characteristics of the coin rather than in the so-called "laws of chance." The critical question is, "Where do we draw the line that determines what inferences we make about the coin?"

The answer to this question reveals the basic nature of science: its probabilistic rather than its absolutistic orientation. In the social sciences most researchers have adopted one of the following two cutoff points as the basis for *inferring the operation of nonchance factors*.

1. When the event or one more deviant would occur 5% of the time or less, *by chance,* some researchers are willing to assert that the results are due to nonchance factors. This cutoff point is known variously as the 0.05 **significance level,** or the 5.00% significance level.

2. When the event or one more deviant would occur 1% of the time or less, *by chance,* other researchers are willing to assert that the results are due to nonchance factors. This cutoff point is known as the 0.01 **significance level,** or the 1.00% significance level.

The level of significance set by the researchers for inferring the operation of nonchance factors is known as the **alpha (α) level.** Thus, when using the 0.05 level of significance, $\alpha = 0.05$; when using the 0.01 level of significance, $\alpha = 0.01$.

In order to determine whether the results were due to nonchance factors in the present coin experiment, we need to calculate the probability of obtaining an event as *rare* as nine heads out of ten tosses. In determining the rarity of an event, we must consider the fact that the rare event can occur in both directions (e.g., nine tails and one head) and that it includes more extreme events. In other words, the probability of an event as rare as nine heads out of ten tosses or as rare as one or zero heads out of ten tosses as well is equal to

$$p(9 \text{ heads}) + p(10 \text{ heads}) + p(1 \text{ head}) + p(0 \text{ heads})$$

Since this distribution is symmetrical

$$p(9 \text{ heads}) = p(1 \text{ head}) \quad \text{and} \quad p(10 \text{ heads}) = p(0 \text{ heads})$$

Thus

$$p(9 \text{ heads}) + p(10 \text{ heads}) + p(1 \text{ head}) + p(0 \text{ heads})$$
$$= 2[p(9 \text{ heads}) + p(10 \text{ heads})]$$

These p values may be obtained from Figure 13.2 as follows.

$$p(9 \text{ heads}) = 0.010 \quad \text{and} \quad p(10 \text{ heads}) = 0.001$$

Therefore, the **two-tailed probability** of an event as rare as nine heads out of ten tosses or as rare as one or zero heads out of ten tosses is $2(0.010 + 0.001)$ = 0.022 or 2.2%.

Applying the 0.05 significance level ($\alpha = 0.05$), we would conclude that the coin was biased (i.e., the results were due to nonchance factors). However, if we employed the 0.01 significance level ($\alpha = 0.01$), we would not be able to assert that these results were due to nonchance factors.

It should be noted and strongly emphasized that you do not conduct a study, analyze the results, arrive at a probability value, and then decide upon the α-level. The α-level must be specified *prior* to the study as part of the overall strategy of designing the study.

13.4 Testing Statistical Hypotheses: Null Hypothesis and Alternative Hypothesis

At this point many students become disillusioned by the arbitrary nature of decision making in science. Let's examine the logic of statistical inference a bit further and see if we can resolve some of the doubts. Prior to the beginning of any study the researcher sets up two mutually exclusive and exhaustive hypotheses:

1. The **null hypothesis** (H_0), which specifies hypothesized values for one or more of the *population parameters*. For example, we could state a null hypothesis in which we expect there to be no difference between the incomes of male and female professors in the following manner:

$$H_0: \mu \text{ males} = \mu \text{ females}$$

2. The **alternative hypothesis** (H_1), which asserts that the *population parameter* is some value other than the one hypothesized. An alternative hypothesis to the null hypothesis just stated could be

$$H_1: \mu \text{ males} \neq \mu \text{ females}$$

where $\neq$ means "does not equal."

The alternative hypothesis is sometimes referred to as the research hypothesis. It is the hypothesis that we wish to verify and is stated in a way that anticipates the expected outcome or relationship. The null hypothesis is sometimes referred to as the hypothesis to be nullified. The researcher anticipates that it will be rejected. Thus, the preceding null hypothesis anticipates that the incomes of male and female professors will differ and the alternative hypothesis is stated in a manner that is consistent with that expectation.

In the present coin experiment these two hypotheses read as follows:

$$H_0: \text{the coin is unbiased; that is}$$

$$P = Q = \tfrac{1}{2}$$

where

$$P = \text{probability of heads}$$

$$Q = \text{probability of tails}$$

$$H_1: \text{the coin is biased; that is}$$

$$P \neq Q \neq \tfrac{1}{2}$$

The alternative hypothesis may be either **directional** or **nondirectional.** When H_1 asserts *only* that the population parameter is *different from* the one hypothesized, it is referred to as a nondirectional or two-tailed hypothesis, for example

$$P \neq Q \neq \tfrac{1}{2}$$

Very frequently in the social sciences hypotheses are **directional** or *one-tailed.* In this instance, in addition to asserting that the population parameter is different from the one hypothesized, we assert the *direction* of that difference, for example

$$P > Q \text{ or } P < Q$$

In evaluating the outcome of a study, we should use **one-tailed probability values** whenever our alternative hypothesis is directional. When the alternative hypothesis is directional, so is the null hypothesis. For example, referring back to the income of male versus female professors, if the alternative hypothesis is that μ males $>$ μ females, the corresponding null hypothesis is that μ males $\leq$ μ females. Conversely, if H_1 is μ males $<$ μ females, H_0 reads: μ males $\geq$ μ females.

13.4.1 The Notion of Indirect Proof

Careful analysis of the logic of statistical inference reveals that the null hypothesis can never be proved. For example, if we had obtained exactly five heads on ten tosses of a coin, would this prove that the coin was unbiased? The answer is a categorical "No!" A bias, if it existed, might be of such a small magnitude that we failed to detect it in ten trials. But what if we tossed the coin one hundred times and obtained fifty heads? Wouldn't this prove something? Again, the same considerations apply. No matter how many times we tossed the coin, we could never exhaust the population of possible outcomes. We can make the assertion, however, that *no basis exists for rejecting* the hypothesis that the coin is biased.

How, then, can we prove the alternative hypothesis that the coin is biased? Again, we cannot prove the alternative hypothesis directly. Think, for the moment, of the logic involved in the following problem.

Draw two lines on a paper and determine whether they are of different lengths. You compare them and say, "Well, certainly they are not equal. Therefore, they must be of different lengths." By rejecting equality (in this case, the null hypothesis) you assert that there is a difference.

Statistical logic operates in exactly the same way. We cannot prove the null hypothesis, nor can we directly prove the alternative hypothesis. However, if we can *reject* the null hypothesis, we can assert its alternative, namely, that the population parameter is some value other than the one hypothesized.* Applied to the coin problem, if we can reject the null hypothesis that $P = Q = 1/2$, we can assert the alternative, namely, that $P \neq Q \neq 1/2$. Note that the support of the alternative hypothesis is always *indirect*. We have supported it by rejecting the null hypothesis. On the other hand, since the alternative hypothesis can neither be proved nor disproved directly, we can *never prove the null hypothesis* by rejecting the alternative hypothesis. The strongest statement we are entitled to make in this respect is that we *failed to reject the null hypothesis*.

What, then, are the conditions for rejecting the null hypothesis? Simply this: When using the 0.05 level of significance, you reject the null hypothesis when a given result occurs, by chance, 5% of the time or less. When using the 0.01 level of significance, you reject the null hypothesis when a given

---

* The null hypothesis can be thought of as the hypothesis to be nullified by a statistical test.

result occurs, by chance, 1% of the time or less. Under these circumstances, of course, you *affirm* the alternative hypothesis.

In other words, one rejects the null hypothesis when the results occur, by chance, 5% of the time or less (or 1% of the time or less), *assuming that the null hypothesis is the true distribution*. That is, one assumes that the null hypothesis is true, calculates the probability on the basis of this assumption, and if the probability is small, one rejects the assumption.

For reasons stated previously, the late R. A. Fisher, eminent British statistician, has affirmed:

> In relation to any experiment we may speak of this hypothesis as the "null hypothesis," and it should be noted that the null hypothesis is never proved or established, but is possibly disproved, in the course of experimentation. *Every experiment may be said to exist only in order to give the facts a chance of disproving the null hypothesis.* *

13.5 Testing Statistical Hypotheses: The Two Types of Error

You may now ask, "But aren't we taking a chance that we will be wrong in rejecting the null hypothesis? Is it not possible that we have, in fact, obtained a statistically rare occurrence by chance?"

The answer to this question must be a simple and humble "Yes." This is precisely what we mean when we say that science is probabilistic. If there is any absolute statement that scientists are entitled to make, it is that we can never assert with complete confidence that our findings or propositions are true. There are countless examples in science in which an apparently firmly established conclusion has had to be modified in the light of further evidence.

In the coin experiment, even if all the tosses had resulted in heads, it is possible that the coin was not, in fact, biased. By chance, once in every 1024 experiments, "on the average," the coin will turn up heads ten out of ten times. When we use the 0.05 level of significance, approximately 5% of the time we will be wrong when we reject the null hypothesis and assert its alternative.

These are some of the basic facts of the reality of inductive reasoning to which the student must adjust. The student of behavior who insists on absolute certainty before speaking on an issue is a student who has been mute throughout life, and who will remain so (probably).

These same considerations have led statisticians to formulate two types of errors that may be made in statistical inference.

---

* (Italics supplied.) R. A. Fisher, *The Design of Experiments*. Edinburgh: Oliver & Boyd, 1935, p. 16.

13.5.1 Type I Error (Type α Error)

Back pain has become one of the most common disabling disorders of this century. In a number of cases trauma and aging have caused the discs (shock absorbers) between the vertebrae to lose elasticity and the gap between the vertebrae to narrow. Speculating that by surgically fusing vertebrae together, the patient might be better able to absorb shock and thereby reduce pain, spinal fusion was introduced. The initial results of this surgical procedure were so positive that the null hypothesis (H_0: Spinal fusion does not relieve pain) was rejected. More recent evidence no longer supports the view that spinal fusion is effective in relieving back pain (i.e., there have been many failures to reject H_0). It is now a relatively rare surgical procedure. As a result of the false rejection of H_0, many people underwent expensive and temporary incapacitating surgery without achieving any pain relief.

In a **type I error** we reject the null hypothesis when it is actually true. The probability of making a type I error is α. We have already pointed out that if we set our rejection point at the 0.05 level of significance, we will mistakenly reject H_0 approximately 5% of the time. It would seem, then, that in order to avoid this type of error, we should set the rejection level as low as possible. For example, if we were to set $\alpha = 0.001$, we would risk a type I error only about one time in every thousand. It should be noted that the 0.05 level is rather routinely used in the social and behavioral sciences unless there is a particular reason to be extremely conservative about making a type I error. For example, suppose we were comparing a totally new teaching method to the technique currently in use. Suppose also that the null hypothesis were really true, that is, there were *no* difference between the two methods. If a type I error were made and the null hypothesis falsely rejected, this could conceivably lead to an extremely costly and time-consuming changeover to a method that was in fact no better than the one being used. In situations such as these we might want to set a more conservative level of significance (for example $\alpha = 0.01$). To familiarize you with the use of both α-levels, we have arbitrarily employed the $\alpha = 0.01$ and $\alpha = 0.05$ levels in examples presented throughout the text. However, the lower we set α the greater the likelihood is that we will make a type II error.

13.5.2 Type II Error (Type β Error)

When DDT was first introduced into the household and on farms as an effective pesticide, there was no accumulated evidence that permitted the null hypothesis (H_0: DDT is not harmful) to be rejected. As a result of widespread use over a period of years, evidence was accumulated concerning its harmful effects on humans (cancer), domestic animals, and wildlife. Failure to reject H_0 had led to the false conclusion that DDT was not harmful (i.e., safe). Even though now banned, residual quantities still show up in water supplies, in ground

Table 13.2 The type of error made as a function of the true status of H_0 and the statistical decision made*

		True Status of H_0	
		H_0 True	H_0 False
Decision	Accept H_0	Correct $1 - \alpha$	Type II error β
	Reject H_0	Type I error α	Correct $1 - \beta$

* To illustrate, if H_0 is true (column 1) and we have rejected H_0 (row 2), we have made a Type I error. If H_0 is false (column 2) and we have rejected H_0, we have made a correct decision.

samples, and in the food chain. The decision-making error exemplified by DDT and many later pesticides and solvents is known as a type II error. As you can see, the consequences of such an error can be devastating.

In a **type II error,** we fail to reject the null hypothesis when it is actually false. Beta (β) is the probability of making a type II error. This type of error is far more common than a type I error. For example, if we apply the 0.01 level of significance as the basis of rejecting the null hypothesis and then conduct a study in which the result we obtained would have occurred by chance only 2% of the time, we cannot reject the null hypothesis.

It is clear, then, that the lower we set the rejection level, the less the likelihood is of a type I error and the greater the likelihood is of a type II error. Conversely, the higher we set the rejection level, the greater the likelihood is of a type I error and the smaller the likelihood is of a type II error.

The fact that the rejection level is set as low as it is attests to the conservatism of scientists, that is, the greater willingness on the part of the scientist to make an error in the direction of *failing* to claim a result than to make an error in the direction of *claiming* a result when he or she is wrong.

Table 13.2 summarizes the type of error made as a function of the true status of the null hypothesis and the decision we have made. We should note that type I and type II errors are sampling errors and refer to samples drawn from hypothetical populations. (See also Statistics in Action 13.1.)

Let's look at a few examples in which for illustrative purposes we supply the following information about the underlying population:

H_0, α-level, obtained p, statistical decision made, and the true status of H_0. Let's ascertain what type of error, if any, has been made.

1. H_0: $\mu_1 = \mu_2$, $\alpha = 0.05$, two-tailed test. Obtained $p = 0.03$, two-tailed value. Statistical decision: H_0 is false. Actual status of H_0: True. *Error:* Type I—rejecting a true H_0.

2. H_0: $\mu_1 = \mu_2$, $\alpha = 0.05$, two-tailed test. Obtained $p = 0.04$, two-tailed value. Statistical decision: H_0 is false. Actual status of H_0: False.
Error: No error has been made. A correct conclusion was drawn since H_0 is false and the statistical decision was that H_0 is false.

3. H_0: $\mu_1 = \mu_2$, $\alpha = 0.01$, two-tailed test. Obtained $p = 0.10$, two-tailed value. Statistical decision: fail to reject H_0. Actual status of H_0: False.
Error: Type II—failing to reject a false H_0.

4. H_0: $\mu_1 = \mu_2$, $\alpha = 0.01$, two-tailed test. Obtained $p = 0.006$, two-tailed value. Statistical decision: Reject H_0. Actual status of H_0: False.
Error: No error has been made since the statistical decision has been to reject H_0 when H_0 is actually false.

You may now ask, "In actual practice, how can we tell when we are making a type I or a type II error?" The answer is simple: We can't! If we examine once again the logic of statistical inference, we will see why. We have already stated that with rare exceptions we cannot or will not know the true parameters of a population. Without this knowledge, how can we know whether our sample statistics have approximated or have failed to approximate the true value? How can we know whether or not we have mistakenly rejected a null hypothesis? If we did know a population value, we could know whether or not we made an error. Under these circumstances, however, the need for sampling statistics is eliminated. We collect samples and draw inferences from samples only because our population values are unknowable for one reason or another. When they become known, the need for statistical inference is lost.

Is there no way, then, to know which surveys or experiments reporting significant results are accurate and which are not? The answer is a conditional "Yes." If we were to repeat the survey and obtain similar results, we would have increased confidence that we were not making a type I error. For example, if we tossed our coin in a second series of ten trials and obtained nine heads, we would feel far more confident that our coin was biased. Parenthetically, replication of studies is one of the weaker areas in social science research. The general attitude is that a study is not much good unless it is "different" and is therefore making a novel contribution. Replicating studies, when they are performed, frequently go unpublished. In consequence we may feel assured that in studies using the 0.05 significance level, approximately 1 out of every 20 that reject the null hypothesis is making a type I error.*

---

* The proportion is probably even higher, since our methods of accepting research reports for publication are heavily weighted in terms of the statistical significance of the results. Thus, if four identical studies were conducted independently, and only one obtained results that permitted rejection of the null hypothesis, *this* one would most likely be published. There is virtually no way for the general scientific public to know about the three studies that *failed* to reject the null hypothesis.

Statistics in Action 13.1

Type I and Type II Errors Applied to Decision-Making Processes, Including Medical, Psychological, Sociological, Economic, and Other Areas

Table 13.2 may be modified to exemplify an extremely broad spectrum of situations in which we must make decisions concerning one of two alternative courses of action. We may formulate two hypotheses; H_0: A given procedure will not work and H_1: A given procedure will work. If, in fact, it does not work, we have made a correct decision when we "accept" the null hypothesis. Thus, a physician who says "I will not use treatment A because it is ineffective" when the treatment is truly ineffective will have made a correct decision. But imagine that the treatment is really effective (i.e., H_0 is false) but the physician fails to reject H_0. This is analogous to a type II error. Because of this error, the patient may be denied a treatment that will cure the disorder. Thus, you see, type II errors *can* have serious consequences in the everyday world of decision making.

Let's look at another example. When considering the use of asbestos wrapping as an insulating material for hot water lines, the null hypothesis might be: H_0: Asbestos is not harmful. For years we failed to reject this hypothesis and acted as if asbestos is harmless, when, in fact, the null hypothesis was false (type II error: We failed to reject a false null hypothesis). Because of this failure to reject a false null hypothesis (i.e., H_0: Asbestos is not harmful), untold thousands of workers and others exposed to asbestos fibers are now at high risk for the development of lung cancer and other disorders of the lung. In fact, the National

Table 13.3 Type of errors and correct decisions that can be made as a function of true status of safety of substance*

	True Status of H_0	
H_0: Product Is Not Harmful	Product Is Not Harmful (H_0 True)	Product Is Harmful (H_0 False)
Fail to reject H_0 (treat as harmless)	Correct failure to reject. The product may be used without jeopardizing public health.	Incorrect failure to reject (Type II error). Harmful substance is treated as if harmless (i.e., safe). Public health is jeopardized (e.g., DDT).
Reject H_0 (treat as harmful)	Incorrect rejection (Type I error). Harmless product is treated as harmful. Public is denied a possible treatment.	Correct rejection. Product is banned. Public health is not jeopardized.

(left margin: Decision)

* H_0: Suspected substance is not harmful. H_1: Suspected substance is harmful. If we fail to reject H_0, we treat the substance as if it is not harmful (i.e., safe). If we reject H_0, we regard the substance as harmful (i.e., unsafe).

Institute of Occupational Safety and Health (NIOSH) has established exposure limits for well over 100 substances, many previously thought not to be harmful (NIOSH Recommendations for Occupational Safety and Health Standards, *Morbidity and Mortality Weekly Report, Supplement* **34**/(1S) 1985). An interesting historical note in this connection is that early in his career as a medical doctor, Sigmund Freud regarded cocaine as a miracle drug. His failure to reject a false null hypothesis (H_0: cocaine is not addictive) led to the mistaken advocacy of cocaine as a harmless way to relieve a number of disorders, including morphine addiction (cited in Dusek and Girdano, 1980).

Table 13.3 summarizes the errors that can be made as a result of accepting a false H_0 concerning the safety of a substance or incorrectly failing to reject a false H_0.

a) One of the logical problems in dealing with type I and type II errors is that the null hypothesis is usually expressed in the negative form. To illustrate, suppose that a pharmaceutical house is investigating the effectiveness of a new compound for the treatment of AIDS. The most likely null hypothesis is: H_0: The compound is ineffective. Rejection of H_0 involves a double negative. We do *not* accept the hypothesis that the compound is *in*effective. Two negatives make a positive. Thus, rejecting H_0 leads to the assertion that the compound is effective. Assuming that H_0 is true, show the consequences of a false rejection. Assuming H_0 is false, show the consequences of a failure to reject.

b) A parole board must decide whether or not to parole a previously dangerous prisoner. What is H_0? Show the consequences of the two types of decisions that can be made when H_0 is true and when H_0 is false.

c) A mental health team must decide whether the client's symptoms and complaints are "psychological" or "organic" before initiating treatment. The null hypothesis is that the symptoms are not organic. Show the consequences of falsely rejecting H_0 and failing to reject a false H_0.

ANSWERS

a) If H_0 is falsely rejected (the compound is found to be effective when it is not), the compound is likely to be used and discovered to be ineffective only after the continued deterioration and death of a number of patients. Its use may also preclude the adoption of other treatment regimes that may be effective. Many medical procedures, standard at one time, were dropped only after repeated failures, such as purging and blood letting. Also, the literature of medicine and psychology abounds with examples of charlatans who took advantage of the misfortunes of others to promote useless compounds and/or procedures as safe and effective treatments of serious disorders.

On the other hand, if the compound is truly effective, the failure to reject H_0 may lead to the false belief that the compound is ineffective. Thus, research on a promising compound may be abandoned and patients may be denied effective treatments for life-threatening disorders.

b) H_0: The prisoner is not dangerous. If H_0 is true and the prisoner is released, a correct decision has been made. If H_0 is true and a prisoner remains incarcerated (i.e., H_0 is rejected), society loses a possible productive individual (type I error). If H_0 is false and the prisoner is released, a dangerous person has been let loose in society (type II error). If H_0 is false and the prisoner is not released, a correct decision has been made.

c) If H_0 is falsely rejected (i.e., the symptoms are not organic) and the client is treated exclusively for an organic disorder, the client is unlikely to show improvement (except possibly due to a placebo effect). If H_0 is falsely accepted (i.e., the disorder really is organic), the root cause of the disorder is unlikely to be touched by psychotherapy while an effective course of therapy may be neglected.

13.6 A Final Word of Caution

There is a very fine line between a significant and a nonsignificant finding. For example, if you tested a hypothesis at the 0.05 significance level and found that the probability of the results occurring by chance was 0.06, you would not reject the null hypothesis. If a friend tested the same hypothesis at the 0.05 level using another sample from the population for which you tested your hypothesis and found the probability of the results occurring by chance to be less than 0.05 (sometimes written as $P < 0.05$), he or she would reject the null hypothesis.

Consider another example in which you hypothesize that the mean age of two groups of people does not differ. The mean age of group 1 is 36 and the mean age of group 2 is 37. You test the hypothesis at the 0.01 level of significance and conclude they differ significantly. What you have found is that a mean difference of one year is statistically significant but also possibly trivial. Significance must be interpreted within meaningful context. Had you found a mean difference of one year between two groups of preschoolers, we would be far less likely to call the difference trivial. In fact, in the latter instance, the difference probably would be considered both practically and statistically significant because of the difference one year can have on the maturational process of a preschooler.

Finally, as you study the material in the following chapters, be aware that large samples are more likely to result in a statistically significant finding than are small samples due to the influence of the sample size (N) when testing hypotheses.

Summary

In this chapter we explained that one of the basic problems of inferential statistics involves estimating population parameters from sample statistics.

In inferential statistics we are frequently called upon to compare our *obtained* values with *expected* values. The expected values are given by the appropriate sampling distribution, which is a theoretical probability distribution of the possible values of a sample statistic.

We discussed how to use sampling distributions to interpret sample statistics.

We also learned that there are two mutually exclusive and exhaustive statistical hypotheses in every study: the null hypothesis (H_0) and the alternative hypothesis (H_1).

If the outcome of a study is rare (here *rare* is defined as some arbitrary but accepted probability value), we reject the null hypothesis and assert its alternative. If the event is not rare (i.e., the probability value is greater than what we have agreed upon as being significant), we fail to reject the null hypothesis. However, in no event are we permitted to claim that we have *proved H_0*.

The researcher is faced with two types of errors in establishing a cutoff probability value that he or she will accept as significant:

Type I: rejecting the null hypothesis when it is true.

Type II: failing to reject (''accepting'') the null hypothesis when it is false.

The basic conservatism of scientists causes them to establish a low level of significance, resulting in a greater incidence of type II errors than of type I errors. Without replication of studies we have no basis for knowing when a type I error has been made, and even with replication we cannot claim knowledge of absolute truth.

Finally, and perhaps most important, we have seen that scientific knowledge is probabilistic and not absolute.

Terms to Remember

Alpha (α) level   The level of significance set by the researcher for inferring the operation of nonchance factors.

Alternative hypothesis (H_1)   A statement specifying that the population parameter is some value other than the one specified under the null hypothesis.

Binomial distribution   A model with known mathematical properties used to describe the distribution of discrete random variables.

Directional hypothesis   An alternative hypothesis that states the direction in which the population parameter differs from the one specified under H_0.

Nondirectional hypothesis   An alternative hypothesis (H_1) that states only that the population parameter is *different* from the one specified under H_0.

Null hypothesis (H_0)   A statement that specifies hypothesized values for one or more of the population parameters. Commonly, although not necessarily, involves the hypothesis of ''no difference.''

One-tailed probability value   A probability value obtained by examining only one tail of the distribution.

Population   A complete set of individuals, objects, or measurements having some common observable characteristic.

Sample   A subset of a population or universe.

Sampling distribution   A theoretical probability distribution of a statistic that would result from drawing all possible samples of a given size from some population.

Significance level   A probability value that is considered so rare in the sampling distribution specified under the null hypothesis that one is willing to assert the operation of nonchance factors. Common significance levels are 0.05, 0.01, and 0.001.

Two-tailed probability value   A probability value that takes into account both tails of the distribution.

Type I error (type α error)   The rejection of H_0 when it is actually true. The probability of a type I error is given by the α-level.

Type II error (type β error)   The probability of accepting H_0 when it is actually false. The probability of a type II error is given by β.

Exercises

1. Explain, in your own words, the nature of drawing inferences in social science. Be sure to specify the types of risks that are taken and the ways in which the researcher attempts to keep these risks within specifiable limits.

2. Give examples of studies in which

   a) A type I error would be considered more serious than a type II error.

   b) A type II error would be considered more serious than a type I error.

3. After completing a study, Nelson W. concluded, "I have proved that no difference exists between the two groups." Criticize his conclusion according to the logic of drawing inferences in science.

4. Explain what is meant by the following statement: "It can be said that the purpose of any study is to provide the occasion for rejecting the null hypothesis."

5. Identify H_0 and H_1 in the following:

    a) The population mean age is 31.

    b) The proportion of Democrats in Watanabe County is not equal to 0.50.

    c) The population mean age is not equal to 31.

    d) The proportion of Democrats in Watanabe County is equal to 0.50.

6. Suppose that you are a welfare eligibility employee responsible for approving clients for welfare. What type of error would you be making if

    a) The hypothesis that a client is qualified for welfare is erroneously accepted?

    b) The hypothesis that a client is qualified for welfare is erroneously rejected?

    c) The hypothesis that a client is qualified for welfare is correctly accepted?

    d) The hypothesis that a client is qualified for welfare is correctly rejected?

7. A public opinion analyst recommends a political campaign strategy for a candidate on the basis of hypotheses she has formulated about future trends in the candidate's popularity. What type of error is she making if she makes the following predictions under the given conditions?

    a) H_0: The candidate's popularity will remain stable.
        Fact: It goes up precipitously.

    b) H_0: The candidate's popularity will remain stable.
        Fact: It falls abruptly.

    c) H_0: The candidate's popularity will remain stable.
        Fact: It shows only minor fluctuation about a central value.

8. An investigator sets $\alpha = 0.01$ for rejection of H_0. He conducts a study in which he obtains a p value of 0.02 and fails to reject H_0. *Discuss:* Is it more likely that he is accepting a true or a false H_0?

9. *Comment:* A student has collected a mass of data to test 100 different null hypotheses. On completion of the analysis he finds that 5 of the 100 comparisons yield p values ≤ 0.05. He concludes: "Using $\alpha = 0.05$, I have found a true difference in five of the comparisons."

10. Does the null hypothesis in a one-tailed test differ from the null hypothesis in a two-tailed test? Give an example.

11. Does the alternative hypothesis in a one-tailed test differ from the alternative hypothesis in a two-tailed test? Give an example.

12. In rejecting the null hypothesis for a one-tailed test, do all deviations count equally? Explain.

13. Suppose you want to test the hypothesis that there is not an equal number of male and female executives in a given large company. The appropriate null hypothesis would be

    a) There are more female than male executives.

    b) The numbers of male and female executives are equal.

    c) There are more male than female executives.

14. Suppose a small groups expert finds a significant difference between the time it takes a group to reach a decision with three members and the time it takes to reach a decision with seven members. Although $\alpha = 0.05$ or $\alpha = 0.01$ is traditionally applied as the level of significance, this choice is arbitrary. For each of the following levels of significance, state how many times in 1000 this difference would be expected to occur by chance.

    a) 0.001   **b)** 0.01   **c)** 0.005   **d)** 0.06

    e) 0.05   **f)** 0.095   **g)** 0.004   **h)** 0.10

15. With reference to Exercise 14, the adoption of which level of significance would be most likely to result in the following statements?

    a) There is a significant difference between the decision-making times of the two groups.

    b) It cannot be concluded that there is a significant difference between the decision-making times of the two groups.

16. Refer again to Exercise 14. The adoption of which level of significance would be most likely to result in the following errors? Identify the type of each error.

    a) There is a significant difference between the decision-making times of the two groups. *Fact:* There is no difference.

    b) It cannot be concluded that there is a significant difference between the decision-making times of the two groups.

17. Refer to Table 13.2. Suppose you are working with a clinician engaged in the diagnosis of individuals seeking help for emotional disorders. Assume that a person has or does not have a disorder. Construct a table that describes the types of error that a clinician might make.

18. In view of the table you constructed in Exercise 17, what are some circumstances in which a type II error may have more serious consequences than a type I error.

In Exercises 19 through 23 H_0, α, obtained p, and true status of H_0 are given. State whether or not an error in statistical decision has been made. If so, state the type of error.

19. H_0: $P = Q$, $\alpha = 0.01$, one-tailed test. Obtained $p = 0.008$, one-tailed value (in predicted direction). Actual status of H_0: True.

20. H_0: $P = Q$, $\alpha = 0.05$, two-tailed test. Obtained $p = 0.08$, two-tailed value. Actual status of H_0: True.

21. H_0: $P = Q$, $\alpha = 0.05$, two-tailed test. Obtained $p = 0.06$, two-tailed value. Actual status of H_0: False.

22. H_0: $P = Q$, $\alpha = 0.05$, two-tailed test. Obtained $p = 0.03$, two-tailed value. Actual status of H_0: False.

23. H_0: $P = Q$, $\alpha = 0.01$, two-tailed test. Obtained $p = 0.005$, two-tailed value. Actual status of H_0: False.

24. If $\alpha = 0.05$, what is the probability of making a type I error?

chapter 14

Statistical Inference and Continuous Variables

14.1 Introduction

14.2 Sampling Distribution of the Mean

14.3 Testing Statistical Hypotheses: Population Mean and Standard Deviation Known

14.4 Estimation of Parameters: Point Estimation

14.5 Testing Statistical Hypotheses with Unknown Parameters: Student's *t*

14.6 Estimation of Parameters: Interval Estimation

14.7 Confidence Intervals and Confidence Limits

14.8 Test of Significance for Pearson's *r*: One-Sample Case

14.9 Test of Significance for Goodman and Kruskal's Gamma

14.1 Introduction

You were first introduced to the concepts of *sample, population,* and *statistical inference* in Chapter 1. In the process of studying these terms you learned that a statistic is a number that describes a characteristic of a sample and that a parameter describes a characteristic of a population. Furthermore, you learned that in many instances (but not always) the parameter is unknown and must be estimated from information about a sample drawn from the population. Statistical inference involves a number of procedures that allow us to estimate parameters from sample statistics.

Recall the example in Chapter 1 in which a poll was conducted for a U.S. Senator to estimate the percentage of a state's registered voters who approve of nuclear energy as an energy source. A simple random sample was drawn from the list of the state's registered voters, and the percentage favoring nuclear energy was computed. How confident are we that the statistic we computed from the sample of voters provides a good estimate of the population parameter? Or, how do we test the hypothesis that a sample of prisoners drawn from a prison is representative of the entire prison population from which the sample was drawn? If we find that the Pearson correlation coefficient between eductional attainment and income is $+0.65$ for those persons attending a school's ten-year reunion, can we be sure that if we contacted the population of all former graduates of the school the correlation would be $+0.65$? The statistical inference procedures to answer these and other questions are the topic of this chapter. Before we can consider these issues, however, two new terms, the

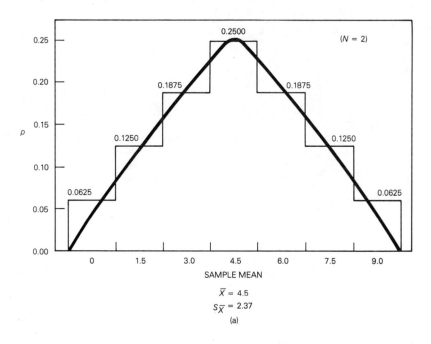

$\overline{X} = 4.5$

$S_{\overline{X}} = 2.37$

(a)

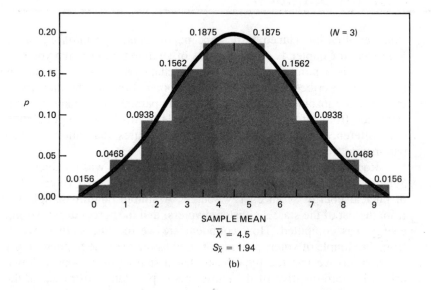

$\overline{X} = 4.5$

$S_{\overline{X}} = 1.94$

(b)

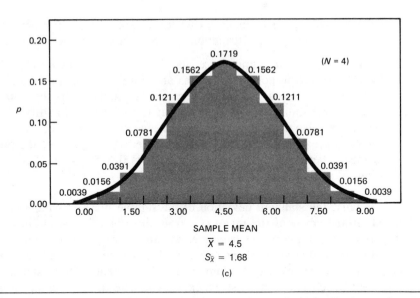

Figure 14.1 Probability histograms based on sampling distributions of means drawn, with replacement, from a population of four scores and sample sizes $N = 2$, $N = 3$, and $N = 4$.

sampling distribution of the mean and the standard error of the mean, must be presented. In Chapter 13 we illustrated the use of a sampling distribution for a discrete two-category nominal variable (the binomial distribution) and for all possible means when drawing samples of a fixed N from a population of four scores. Table 13.1 showed the frequency and probability distributions of means when all possible samples of a given size were selected from the population of four scores. Figure 14.1, which is based on Table 13.1, shows probability histograms, with superimposed curves obtained by connecting the midpoints of each bar.

Before proceeding with the discussion of sampling distributions for interval or ratio-scaled variables, examine Table 13.1 and Figure 14.1 carefully. See if you can answer the following questions:

1. How does the mean of each sampling distribution of means compare with the mean of the population from which the samples were drawn?

2. How does the variability or dispersion of the sample means change as we increase the sample size on which each sampling distribution is based?

Now compare your answers with ours:

1. The mean of the population of four scores is 4.5. The mean of each sampling distribution of means is 4.5. Thus, the mean of a sampling distribution of means is the same as the population mean from which the sample means

were drawn. This statement is true for all sizes of N. In other words, the mean of the sampling distribution does not vary with the sample size.

2. As you increase the sample size, the dispersion of sample means becomes less. A greater proportion of means are close to the population mean, and extreme deviations are rarer as N becomes larger. To verify these statements, note the probability of obtaining a mean as rare as 0 or 9 at different sample sizes. Note also that the proportion of means in the middle of the distribution becomes greater as sample size is increased. For example, the proportion of means between and including 3 and 6 is 0.6250 when $N = 2$, 0.6874 when $N = 3$, and 0.7265 when $N = 4$.

Finally, the standard deviation of the sample means—which we will call the **standard error of the mean** ($s_{\bar{x}}$) from this point forward—shows that the dispersion of sample means decreases as sample size is increased.*

In the forthcoming chapters we will calculate many different standard errors in addition to the standard error of the mean. These standard errors represent bench marks against which we evaluate differences in means, proportions, correlations, and so forth. The smaller the standard error is for a particular data set, the more precise our estimates will become. Thus, increasing sample size is one way of increasing the precision of our statistical decisions.

However, notice that the decrease in not linear. In going from $N = 1$ to $N = 2$ in Figure 14.2, the decrease in $s_{\bar{x}}$ equals $3.35 - 2.37 = 0.98$; from $N = 2$ to $N = 3$, the decrease is $2.37 - 1.94 = 0.43$; and from $N = 3$ to $N = 4$ the decrease is $1.94 - 1.68 = 0.26$. Thus, increasing the sample size is a curve of diminishing returns. A point will be reached when nonstatistical considerations (the difficulty of obtaining subjects, time, economics, and logistics) will outweigh the advantages of increasing N.

14.2 Sampling Distribution of the Mean

Let us imagine that we are conducting a sampling experiment in which we randomly draw (with replacement)[†] a sample of two scores from a population containing the values 2, 3, 4, 5, 6, 7, and 8 in which $\mu = 5.00$, and $\sigma = 0.99$ (see Table 14.1). For example, we might draw scores of 3 and 6. We calculate the sample mean and find $\bar{X} = 4.5$. Now suppose we continue to draw samples of $N = 2$ (e.g., we might draw scores of 2, 8; 3, 7; 4, 5; 5, 6; etc.) until we obtain an infinitely large number of samples. If we calculate the

---

* The relationship between the sample size and the standard error of the mean is specified by the **law of large numbers**; that is, as the sample size increases, the standard error of the mean decreases.

   Standard error of the mean is a theoretical standard deviation of sample means, of a given sample size, drawn from some specified population. When based on a known population standard deviation, $\sigma_{\bar{x}} = \sigma/\sqrt{N}$; when estimated from a single sample, $s_{\bar{x}} = s/\sqrt{N-1}$.

[†] If the population is infinite or extremely large, the difference between sampling with or without replacement is negligible.

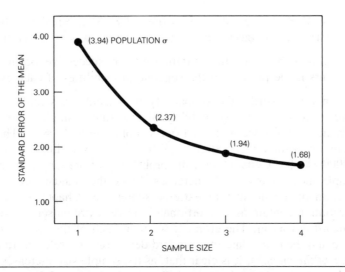

Figure 14.2 A line drawing showing the decreasing magnitude of $s_{\bar{x}}$ as the sample size increases. Shown are the population standard deviations of four scores and the standard error of the mean for the sampling distributions when $N = 2$, $N = 3$, and $N = 4$.

sample mean for each sample drawn and treat each of these sample means as a raw score, we may set up a frequency distribution of these sample means.

Let's repeat these procedures with increasingly larger sample sizes, for example, $N = 5$, $N = 15$. We now have three frequency distributions of sample means based on three different sample sizes.

Intuitively, what might we expect these distributions to look like? Since we are selecting at random from the population, we would expect the mean of the distribution of sample means to approximate the mean of the population.

How might the dispersion of these sample means compare with the variability in the original distribution of scores? In the original distribution, when $N = 1$ the probability of obtaining an extreme score such as 8 is 4/1000 or 0.004 (see Table 14.1). The probability of obtaining a sample *mean* equal to

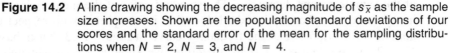

X	f	p(X)
2	4	0.004
3	54	0.054
4	242	0.242
5	400	0.400
6	242	0.242
7	54	0.054
8	4	0.004
	$N = 1000$	$\Sigma\, p(X) = 1.000$

Table 14.1 An approximately normally distributed population with $\mu = 5.00$ and $\sigma = 0.99$

8 when $N = 2$ (e.g., drawing scores of 8, 8) is equal to 0.004×0.004 or 0.000016. This is based on Eq. (12.9), which was stated earlier as:

The probability of the simultaneous or successive occurrence of two events is the product of the separate probabilities of each event.

In other words, the probability of selecting a sample with an extreme *mean* is less than the probability of selecting a single score that is equally extreme. What if we increased our sample size to $N = 4$? The probability of obtaining results this extreme $(\overline{X} = 8)$ is exceedingly small $(0.004)^4 = 0.0000000003$. Generalizing, the probability of drawing extreme values of the sample mean is less as N increases. Since the standard deviation is a direct function of the number of extreme scores (see Chapter 6), it follows that a distribution containing proportionately fewer extreme scores will have a lower standard deviation. Therefore, if we treat each of the sample means as a raw score and then calculate the standard deviation ($\sigma_{\overline{X}}$, referred to as the *standard error of the mean**), it is clear that, as the sample size increases, the variability of the sample means decreases. The standard error of the mean is interpreted in the same way that the standard deviation is interpreted with respect to the normal curve. Looking at the frequency curve in Figure 14.3 that is based on $N = 2$, we see that $\sigma_{\overline{X}} = 0.70$; therefore, we know that approximately 68% of the area under the curve lies within ± 0.70 units of the population mean ($\mu = 5$). Therefore, approximately 68% of the area lies between 4.30 $(5 - 0.70)$ and 5.70 $(5 + 0.70)$.

If the sampling experiment that was based on samples of $N = 2, 5$, and 15 was actually conducted, the frequency curves of sample means would be obtained as in Figure 14.3. There are three important lessons that may be learned from a careful examination of Figure 14.3:

1. The distribution of sample means, drawn from a normally distributed population, is bell-shaped or "normal." Indeed, it can be shown that even if the underlying distribution is skewed, the distribution of sample means will tend to be normal.

2. The mean of the sample means ($\mu_{\overline{X}}$) is equal to the mean of the population (μ) from which these samples were drawn.

3. The distribution of sample means shows less and less dispersion as we increase the size of the sample. For example, in Figure 14.3 $\sigma_{\overline{X}} = 0.70$ for the curve based on $N = 2$, $\sigma_{\overline{X}} = 0.44$ for the curve based on $N = 5$, and $\sigma_{\overline{X}} = 0.25$ for the curve based on $N = 15$. This is an extremely important point in statistical inference, about which we soon will have a great deal more to say.

---

* This notation represents the standard deviation of a sampling distribution of means. This is purely a theoretical notation since, with an infinite number of sample means, it is not possible to assign a specific value to the number of sample means involved.

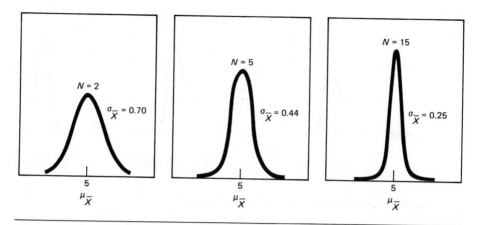

Figure 14.3 Frequency curves of sample means drawn from a population in which $\mu = 5.00$ and $\sigma = 0.99$.

If we base our estimate of the population mean on a *single* sample drawn from the population, our approximation to the parameter is likely to be closer as we increase the size of the sample. In other words, if it is true that the dispersion of sample means decreases with increasing sample size, it also follows that the mean of any single sample is more likely to be closer to the mean of the population as the sample size increases (see Case Example 14.1).

These three observations illustrate a rather startling theorem that is of fundamental importance in inferential statistics, that is, the **central limit theorem,** which states:

> If random samples of a fixed N are drawn from *any* population (regardless of the form of the population distribution), as N becomes larger, the distribution of sample means approaches normality, with the overall mean approaching μ, the variance of the sample means $\sigma_{\bar{X}}^2$ being equal to σ^2/N, and a standard error $\sigma_{\bar{X}}$ of $\sigma/\sqrt{N}$.

Stated symbolically

$$\sigma_{\bar{X}}^2 = \frac{\sigma^2}{N} \tag{14.1}$$

and

$$\sigma_{\bar{X}}^2 = \frac{\sigma}{\sqrt{N}} \tag{14.2}$$

In essence, the central limit theorem allows us to understand that if the underlying population distribution is skewed, the distribution of sample means will

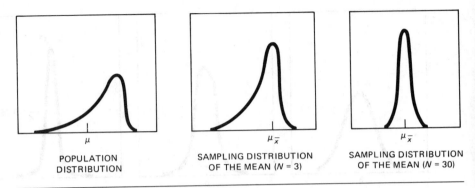

POPULATION
DISTRIBUTION

SAMPLING DISTRIBUTION
OF THE MEAN ($N = 3$)

SAMPLING DISTRIBUTION
OF THE MEAN ($N = 30$)

Figure 14.4   Effect of the central limit theorem.

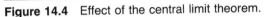

approach the form of a normal curve as the sample size increases. The effect of the central limit theorem is shown in Figure 14.4.

14.3 Testing Statistical Hypotheses: Population Mean and Standard Deviation Known

14.3.1 Finding the Probability That a Sample Mean Will Fall Within a Certain Range

Let's briefly examine some of the implications of the relationships we have just discussed.

When μ and σ are *known* for a given population, it is possible to describe the form of the distribution of sample means when N is large (regardless of the form of the original distribution). It will be a normal distribution with a mean ($\mu_{\bar{X}}$) equal to μ and a standard error ($\sigma_{\bar{X}}$) equal to $\sigma/\sqrt{N}$. It now becomes possible to determine probability values in terms of areas under the normal curve. Thus, we may use the known relationships of the normal probability curve to determine the probabilities associated with any sample mean (of a given N) randomly drawn from this population.

We have already seen (Section 7.3) that any normally distributed variable may be transformed into the normally distributed z scale. We have also seen (Section 12.6) that we may establish probability values in terms of the relationships between z scores and areas under the normal curve. That is, for any given raw score value (X) with a certain proportion of area beyond it, there is a corresponding value of z with the same proportion of area beyond it. Similarly, for any given value of a sample mean ($\bar{X}$) with a certain proportion of area beyond it, there is a corresponding value of z with the same proportion of area beyond it. Thus, assuming that the form of the distribution of sample means

A Statistical Sampling Experiment

Most of us are aware of the information processing revolution that was ushered in by the advent of the computer. Calculations that previously took hours, days, and even weeks to perform, are now completed within time frames that include microseconds and milliseconds. Moreover, as long as the data entry is accurate and the programming is flawless, the computer simply does not make errors. For this reason the computer has become an indispensable element of human endeavor, be it in business, education, or the social sciences.

What is, perhaps, less appreciated by the general public is the fact that the computer's capabilities are not limited to high-speed computation. For example, it may be used to conduct statistical experiments that illuminate some of the "shadowy corners" of statistical thinking.

In one statistical experiment the author had a computer select samples from a population and calculate the mean, variance, and standard deviation of each sample. The samples were selected from a population that was distributed in a completely uniform fashion—numbers from 1 to 85. The mean and standard deviation of the population were 43 and 24.54, respectively. Two sets of 22 samples were selected from this population—one with $N = 5$ and the other with $N = 15$. The results are shown in Table 14.2.

Table 14.2   Sample means obtained by randomly selecting 22 samples of $N = 5$ and 22 samples of $N = 15$ from a uniform population of 85 integers from 1 through 85

N = 5		N = 15	
25.4	45.6	25.07	42.27
29.2	46.0	31.07	42.40
34.2	47.0	31.40	43.00
35.4	48.8	33.00	43.60
35.6	48.8	36.67	43.60
36.2	49.0	37.40	44.07
38.6	49.2	37.67	45.07
38.8	50.6	40.00	45.73
42.6	51.6	40.80	50.07
42.8	57.8	41.50	54.13
43.6	61.8	41.60	55.93

$$\Sigma \overline{X} = 958.6 \qquad \Sigma \overline{X} = 906.05$$
$$N_s = 22 \qquad\quad N_s = 22$$
$$\overline{X}_{\overline{x}} = 43.47 \qquad \overline{X}_{\overline{x}} = 41.18$$
$$s_{\overline{x}} = 8.65 \qquad\quad s_{\overline{x}} = 7.41$$

where N_s is the number of sample means,
$\overline{X}_{\overline{x}}$ is the mean of the sample means,
and $s_{\overline{x}}$ is the standard deviation of the sample means.

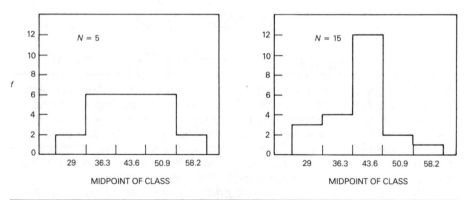

Figure 14.5 Grouped frequency histograms of sample means based on *N*s equal to 5 and 15, respectively. The samples were randomly and independently selected from a population in which the measurements are uniformly distributed.

Before looking at the table, however, try answering the following questions: Do you expect that each sample mean will equal the population mean? What about the distribution of the means of each of the 22 samples based on *N*s equal to 5 and 15, respectively? Do you expect the variability of the sample means to change in any systematic way as the sample size increases from $N = 1$ (the population distribution) to $N = 15$? What about the form of the distribution of the sample means? Does it mimic the population distribution of scores or does it tend to change with increasing sample size? Now look at Table 14.2 and Figure 14.5 and compare your answers with the results of the sampling experiment.

When examining Table 14.2 notice that:

1. Each sample mean is not equal to the population mean. However, the mean of the sample means is a pretty good approximation to the population mean. It can be shown that the means of randomly selected samples, averaged over all possible samples, will yield the population mean as the averaged value. The means are said to be **unbiased estimators** of the population mean.

2. The variability among the sample means decreases as the sample size increases. The range and standard deviation of the population were 84 and 24.54, respectively. When $N = 5$, the range and standard deviations of the sample means were 36.4 and 8.65, respectively. Finally, with $N = 15$, the range fell to 30.86, and the standard deviation declined to 7.41.

3. The form of the distribution of means also changed with increased sample size. Remember that the population distribution was absolutely flat, with all 85 values having an associated frequency of 1. Figure 14.5 presents grouped frequency histograms of the sample means. Note how nicely they illustrate the central limit theorem. With sample sizes as small as 15, the distribution of the sample means already begins to take on the classic bell-shaped form of the normal probability distribution.

Source: Based on Richard P. Runyon, "A Statistical Sampling Experiment," Chapter 7 of *Fundamentals of Statistics in the Biological, Medical, and Health Sciences.* Boston: Duxbury Press, 1985.

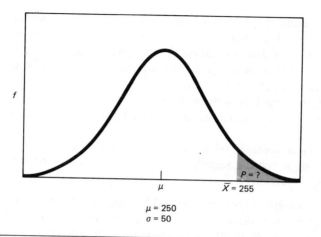

$\mu = 250$
$\sigma = 50$

Figure 14.6 The probability of $\overline{X} \geq 255$ if $\mu = 250$ and $\sigma = 50$.

is normal, we may establish probability values in terms of the relationship between z scores and areas under the normal curve.

To illustrate: Suppose we have a population of Baptist churches with a mean membership size of 250 ($\mu = 250$) and a standard deviation of 50 ($\sigma = 50$), from which we randomly draw 100 churches ($N = 100$). What is the probability that the sample mean ($\overline{X}$) will be equal to or greater than 255 members? Thus H_0: $\mu = \mu_0 = 250$. Figure 14.6 illustrates the area under the normal curve, which represents the probability that $\mu \geq 255$.

The value of z corresponding to $\overline{X} = 255$ is obtained as follows:

$$z = \frac{\overline{X} - \mu_0}{\sigma_{\overline{X}}} \qquad (14.3)$$

where μ_0 = value of the population mean under H_0:

$$\sigma_{\overline{X}} = \frac{\sigma}{\sqrt{N}} = \frac{50}{\sqrt{100}} = 5.00 \qquad \text{and} \qquad z = \frac{255 - 250}{5.00} = 1.00$$

Looking up a z of 1.00 in column C (Table A of Appendix C), we find that 0.1587 (15.87%) of the sample means fall at or above $\overline{X} = 255$. Thus, there are approximately 16 chances in 100 of obtaining a sample mean equal to or greater than 255 from this population when $N = 100$. Note that $\sigma_{\overline{X}} = 5.00$ is considerably less than $\sigma = 50$. Why?

dispersion of the whole population

14.3.2 Testing Hypotheses About the Sample Mean

Now extend this logic to a situation in which we do not know from what population a sample is drawn. We suspect that it may have been selected from the preceding population of churches with $\mu = 250$ and $\sigma = 50$, but we are not certain. We wish to test the hypothesis that our sample mean was indeed selected from this population. Let's imagine that we had obtained $\overline{X} = 263$ for $N = 100$. Is it reasonable to assume that this sample was drawn from the preceding population of churches?

Setting up this problem in formal statistical terms involves the following six steps, which are common to all hypothesis testing situations:

1. *Null hypothesis (H_0):* The mean membership size of the population (μ) from which the sample of churches was drawn equals 250; that is, $\mu = \mu_0 = 250$.

2. *Alternative hypothesis (H_1):* The mean of the population from which the sample was drawn does *not* equal 250; $\mu \neq \mu_0$. Note that H_1 is nondirectional; consequently, a two-tailed test of significance will be used.

3. *Statistical test:* The z statistic is used since σ is known.

4. *Significance level:* $\alpha = 0.01$. If the difference between the sample mean and the specified population mean is so extreme that its associated probability of occurrence under H_0 is equal to or less than 0.01, we reject H_0.

5. *Sampling distribution:* The normal probability curve.

6. *Critical region for rejection of H_0:* $|z| \geq |z_{0.01}| = 2.58.$* A **critical region** is that portion of area under the curve that includes those values of a statistic that lead to rejection of the null hypothesis.

The critical region is chosen to correspond with the selected level of significance. Thus, for $\alpha = 0.01$, two-tailed test, the critical region is bounded by those values of $z_{0.01}$ that mark off a total of 1% of the area. Referring again to column C, Table A, we find that the area beyond a z of 2.58 is approximately 0.005. We double 0.005 to account for both tails of the distribution. Figure 14.7 depicts the critical region for rejection of H_0 when $\alpha = 0.01$, two-tailed test.

Therefore, in order to reject H_0 at the 0.01 level of significance, the absolute value of the obtained z must be equal to or greater than $|z_{0.01}|$ or 2.58. Similarly, if we are to be allowed to reject H_0 at the 0.05 level of significance, the absolute value of the obtained z must be equal to or greater than $|z_{0.05}|$ or 1.96.

In the present example the value of z corresponding to $\overline{X} = 263$ is

$$z = \frac{\overline{X} - \mu_0}{\sigma_{\overline{X}}} = \frac{263 - 250}{5.00} = 2.60$$

---

* Since $z_{0.01} = \pm 2.58$, $|z| \geq |z_{0.01}|$ is equivalent to stating $z \geq 2.58$ or $z \leq -2.58$. Recall that the symbol $|\ |$ indicates the absolute value of the number, that is, without regard to sign.

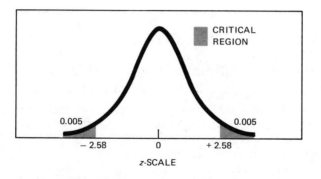

z-SCALE

Figure 14.7 Critical region for rejection of H_0 when $\alpha = 0.01$, two-tailed test.

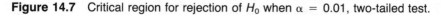

Decision Since the obtained z falls within the critical region (i.e., $2.60 > z_{0.01}$), we may reject H_0 at the 0.01 level of significance. Thus, we conclude that the sample in question ($\overline{X} = 263$) was not drawn from the population in which $\mu = 250$ and $\sigma = 50$. Having established α at the 0.01 level of significance, we know that the probability of rejecting the null hypothesis when it is actually true (and therefore making a type I error) is 1 out of 100, a rare event that is very unlikely to occur by chance.

14.4 Estimation of Parameters: Point Estimation

So far we have been concerned with testing hypotheses when the population parameters are known. However, we have taken some pains in this book to point out that population values are rarely known, particularly when the population is extremely large. Every ten years when the federal government undertakes that massive data collection effort called the census, we come close to knowing the parameters on the various questions. But knowledge of parameters is not the usual case. However, the fact that we do not know the population values does not prevent us from using the logic developed in Section 14.3.

Whenever we make inferences about population parameters from sample data, we compare our sample results with the expected results given by the appropriate sampling distribution. A hypothetical sampling distribution of sample means is associated with any sample mean. This distribution has a mean, $\mu_{\overline{X}}$, and a standard error, $\sigma_{\overline{X}}$. So far, in order to obtain the values of $\mu_{\overline{X}}$ and $\sigma_{\overline{X}}$, we have required a knowledge of μ and σ. In the absence of knowledge concerning the exact values of the parameters, we are forced to estimate μ and σ from the statistics calculated from sample data. Since in actual practice we rarely select more than one sample, our estimates are generally based on the statistics calculated from a single sample. All such estimates of population parameters involving the use of single sample values (e.g., mean age of a sample) are known as **point estimates.**

BOX 14.1

Unbiased Estimate of the Population Variance

Throughout this book we have turned to a sampling experiment whenever we wanted to illustrate a concept of fundamental importance in statistical analysis. Let's take a look at the denominator of the variance equation, and show that $N - 1$ in the denominator provides an unbiased estimate of the population variance, whereas N in the denominator underestimates the population variance.

Let's imagine the following sampling experiment. You place the following population of four scores in a hat: 1, 2, 3, 4. The mean of this population is 2.5 and the variance is 1.25. You select, with replacement, all possible samples of $N = 2$ and calculate the variance of each sample, using N and $N - 1$ in the denominator. Just as we previously placed the mean of each sample in the cell corresponding to both draws, we now place the *variance* of each sample in the appropriate cell.

First, let's do this using N in the denominator when calculating each sample variance. Use Eq. (6.3) and confirm that the variance for a sample draw of 1 and 1 is 0.00 and that the variance for a sample draw of 0 and 4 is 2.25.

Now let's construct a frequency distribution of these variances and calculate the mean variance.

The mean variance is found to be $10/16 = 0.625$. Recall that the variance of the population is 1.25. In this sampling experiment, using N in the denominator of the variance equation, the mean variance of all possible samples of $N = 2$ underestimates the population variance. Generalizing, sample variances that use N in the denominator provide a biased estimate of the population variance.

Variance of each sample when using N in the denominator ($N = 2$)

		First Draw			
		1	2	3	4
Second Draw	1	0.00	0.25	1.00	2.25
	2	0.25	0.00	0.25	1.00
	3	1.00	0.25	0.00	0.25
	4	2.25	1.00	0.25	0.00

s^2	f	fs^2
2.25	2	4.50
1.00	4	4.00
0.25	6	1.50
0.00	4	0.00
	$\Sigma f = 16$	$\Sigma fs^2 = 10.00$

Variance of each sample when using $N - 1$ in the denominator ($N = 2$)

		First Draw			
		1	2	3	4
Second Draw	1	0.00	0.50	2.00	4.50
	2	0.50	0.00	0.50	2.00
	3	2.00	0.50	0.00	0.50
	4	4.50	2.00	0.50	0.00

s^2	f	fs^2
4.50	2	9.00
2.00	4	8.00
0.50	6	3.00
0.00	4	0.00
	$\Sigma f = 16$	$\Sigma fs^2 = 20.00$

Now let's repeat the same procedures, using $N - 1$ to calculate the variance of each sample. The frequency distribution and mean of the sample variances are shown in the fourth table.

Now the mean variance is 20/16 = 1.25. Note that this is identical to the original variance of the population. Thus, using $N - 1$ in the denominator provides an unbiased estimate of the population variance since the variability of a sample tends not to be as large as that of a population. Using $N - 1$ in the denominator serves as a correction factor.

14.4.1 Estimating $\sigma_{\bar{x}}$ from Sample Data

You will recall that we previously defined the variance of a sample as

$$s^2 = \frac{\Sigma(X - \bar{X})^2}{N}$$

in Eq. (6.3). We obtained the standard deviation, s, by finding the square root of this value. These definitions are perfectly appropriate as long as we are interested only in *describing* the variability of a sample. However, when our interest shifts to *estimating* the population variance from a sample value, we find that the preceding definition is inadequate since $\Sigma(X - \bar{X})^2/N$ tends, on the average, to *underestimate* the population variance. In other words, it provides a *biased estimate* of the population variance, whereas an unbiased estimate is required.

An unbiased estimator was defined earlier as an estimate that equals, on the average, the value of the parameter. That is, when we make the statement that a statistic is an unbiased estimate of a parameter, we are saying that the mean of the distribution of an extremely large number of sample statistics drawn from a given population tends to center on the corresponding value of the parameter. We demonstrate in Box 14.1 that an unbiased estimate of the population variance may be obtained by dividing the sum of squares by $N - 1$. We will use the symbol $\hat{s}^2$ to represent a sample variance providing an *unbiased estimate of the population variance*, and $\hat{s}$ to represent a sample standard deviation based on the unbiased variance estimate. Thus

$$\text{unbiased estimate of } \sigma^2 = \hat{s}^2 = \frac{\Sigma(X - \bar{X})^2}{N - 1} \qquad (14.4)$$

and

$$\text{estimated } \sigma = \hat{s} = \sqrt{\hat{s}^2} \qquad (14.5)$$

We are now able to estimate $\sigma_{\bar{X}}^2$ and $\sigma_{\bar{X}}$ from sample data. We will use the symbols $s_{\bar{X}}^2$ and $s_{\bar{X}}$ to refer to the estimated variance and standard error of the mean, respectively. Since we do not know σ^2, we accept the unbiased variance estimate ($\hat{s}^2$) as the best estimate we have of the population variance.

Thus, the equation for determining the variance of the mean from sample data is

$$\text{estimated } \sigma_{\bar{X}}^2 = s_{\bar{X}}^2 = \frac{\hat{s}^2}{N} \qquad (14.6)$$

We estimate the standard error of the mean by finding the square root of this value:

$$\text{estimated } \sigma_{\bar{X}} = s_{\bar{X}} = \sqrt{\frac{\hat{s}^2}{N}} = \frac{\hat{s}}{\sqrt{N}} \qquad (14.7)$$

If the sample variance (not the unbiased estimate) is used, we may estimate $\sigma_{\bar{X}}$ as

$$\text{estimated } \sigma_{\bar{X}} = s_{\bar{X}} = \frac{s}{\sqrt{N-1}} = \sqrt{\frac{\Sigma(X - \bar{X})^2}{N(N-1)}} \qquad (14.8)$$

Equation (14.8) is the one most frequently used in the social sciences to estimate the standard error of the mean. We will follow this practice.

Before proceeding further, let's review some of the symbols we have been discussing. Table 14.3 shows the various symbols for the means, variances, and standard deviations depending on whether we are dealing with population parameters, unbiased population estimators, or sample statistics.

14.5 Testing Statistical Hypotheses with Unknown Parameters: Student's *t*

We previously pointed out that when the parameters of a population are known, it is possible to describe the form of the sampling distribution of sample means. It will be a normal distribution with $\sigma_{\bar{X}}$ equal to $\sigma/\sqrt{N}$. By employing the relationship between the z scale and the normal distribution, we were able to test hypotheses using

$$z = \frac{(\bar{X} - \mu_0)}{\sigma_{\bar{X}}}$$

as a test statistic. When σ is not known, we are forced to estimate its value from sample data. Consequently, estimated $\sigma_{\bar{X}}$ (i.e., $s_{\bar{X}}$) must be based on the estimated σ (i.e., $\hat{s}$); that is

$$s_{\bar{X}} = \frac{\hat{s}}{\sqrt{N}}$$

Table 14.3 Review of symbols

	Population Parameters (Theoretical)	Parameters of Sampling Distribution of Mean (Theoretical)	Unbiased Population Estimators for Sampling Distribution of Mean (Empirical)	Sample Statistics (Empirical)
Means	μ, μ_0	$\mu_{\bar{X}}$	$\bar{X}$	$\bar{X}$
Variances	σ^2	$\sigma^2_{\bar{X}}$	$\hat{s}^2$, $s^2_{\bar{X}}$	s^2
Standard deviations	σ	$\sigma_{\bar{X}}$	$\hat{s}$, $s_{\bar{X}}$	s

Now, if substituting $\hat{s}$ for σ provided a reasonably good approximation to the sampling distribution of means, we could continue to use z as our test statistic and the normal curve as the model for our sampling distribution. As a matter of fact, however, this is not the case. At the turn of the century a statistician by the name of William Gosset, who published under the pseudonym of Student, noted that the approximation of $\hat{s}$ to σ is poor, particularly for small samples. This failure of approximation is due to the fact that, with small samples, $\hat{s}$ will tend to underestimate σ more than one-half of the time. Compared to the normal distribution, the statistic

$$\frac{\bar{X} - \mu_0}{\hat{s}/\sqrt{N}}$$

will tend to be flatter in the central region and spread out more in extreme regions (see Fig. 14.8).

Gosset's major contribution to statistics consisted of his description of a distribution, or rather, a family of distributions, that permits the testing of hypotheses with samples drawn from normally distributed populations, when σ is not known. These distributions are referred to variously as the **t-distributions** or **Student's t.** The ratio used in the testing of hypotheses is known as the **t-ratio:**

$$t = \frac{\bar{X} - \mu_0}{s_{\bar{X}}} \qquad (14.9)$$

where μ_0 is the value of the population mean under H_0.

The t statistic is similar in many respects to the previously discussed z statistic [see Eq. (14.3)]. Both statistics are expressed as the deviation of a sample mean from a population mean (known or hypothesized) in terms of the standard error of the mean. By reference to the appropriate sampling distribution we may express this deviation in terms of probability. When the z statistic is used, the standard normal curve is the appropriate sampling distribution. For the t statistic there is a family of distributions that varies as a function of **degrees of freedom (df).**

The term *degrees of freedom* refers to the number of values that are free to vary after we have placed certain restrictions on our data. To illustrate, let's imagine that we have four numbers: 18, 23, 27, 32. The sum is 100 and the mean is $\overline{X} = 100/4 = 25$. Recall that if we subtract the mean from each score, we should obtain a set of four deviations that add up to zero. Thus

$$(18 - 25) + (23 - 25) + (27 - 25) + (32 - 25)$$
$$= (-7) + (-2) + 2 + 7 = 0$$

Note also that the four deviations are not independent. Once we have imposed the restriction that the deviations are taken from the mean, the values of only three deviations are free to vary. As soon as three deviations are known, the fourth is completely determined. Stated another way, the values of only three deviations are free to vary. For example, if we know three deviations to be -7, -2, and 7, we may calculate the unknown deviation by use of the equality:

$$(X_1 - \overline{X}) + (X_2 - \overline{X}) + (X_3 - \overline{X}) + (X_4 - \overline{X}) = 0$$

Therefore

$$(X_4 - \overline{X}) = 0 - [(X_1 - \overline{X}) + (X_2 - \overline{X}) + (X_3 - \overline{X})]$$

In the present example

$$(X_4 - \overline{X}) = 0 - (-7) + (-2) + 2$$
$$= 0 + 7 - 2 + 2 = 7$$

To generalize: For any given sample on which we have placed a single restriction, the number of degrees of freedom is $N - 1$. In the preceding example $N = 4$; therefore, degrees of freedom are $4 - 1 = 3$.

Note that when $s/\sqrt{N - 1}$ [Eq. (14.8)] is used to obtain $s_{\overline{X}}$, the quantity under the square root sign $(N - 1)$ is the degrees of freedom.

We noted earlier that the use of Student's t depends on the assumption that the underlying population is normally distributed. This requirement stems from a unique property of normal distributions. *Given that observations are independent and random, the sample means and sample variances are independent only when the population is normally distributed.* As we previously pointed out, two scores or statistics are independent only when the values of one do not depend on the values of the other and vice versa. Tests of significance of means, which are discussed in the following sections, demand that the means and variances be independent of one another. They cannot vary together in some systematic way—for example, with the variances becoming larger as the means become larger. If they do vary in a systematic way, the underlying population cannot be normal and tests of significance based on the assumption of normality may be invalid. It is for this reason that the assumption of normality underlies the use of **Student's *t*-ratio.**

One final note: Student's *t*-ratio is referred to as a **robust test,** meaning that statistical inferences are likely to be valid even when there are fairly large departures from normality in the population distribution. This robustness is another consequence of the central limit theorem. If we have serious doubts concerning the normality of the population distribution, it is wise to increase the *N* in each sample.

14.5.1 Characteristics of *t*-Distributions

Let's compare the characteristics of the *t*-distributions with the already familiar standard normal curve. First, both distributions are symmetrical about a mean of zero. Therefore, the proportion of area beyond a particular positive *t*-value is equal to the proportion of area below the corresponding negative *t*.

Second, the *t*-distributions are more spread out than the normal curve. Consequently, the proportion of area beyond a specific value of *t* is *greater* than the proportion of area beyond the corresponding value of *z*. However, as sample size increases, and therefore the greater the degrees of freedom are, the more the *t*-distributions resemble the standard normal curve. In order that you may see the contrast between the *t*-distributions and the normal curve, we have reproduced three curves in Figure 14.8: the sampling distributions of *t* when degrees of freedom $= 3$, degrees of freedom $= 10$, and the normal curve.

Inspection of Figure 14.8 permits several interesting observations. We have already seen that with the standard normal curve, $|z| \geq 1.96$ defines the region of rejection at the 0.05 level of significance. However, when degrees of freedom $= 3$, a $|t| \geq 1.96$ includes approximately 15% of the total area. Consequently, if we were to use the normal curve for testing hypotheses when *N* is small (therefore, degrees of freedom are small) and σ is unknown, we would be in serious danger of making a type I error, that is, rejecting H_0 when it is true. A much larger value of *t* is required to mark off the bounds of the critical region of rejection. Indeed, when degrees of freedom equal 3, the absolute value of the obtained *t* must be equal to or greater than 3.18 to reject H_0 at the 0.05 level of significance (two-tailed test). However, as degrees of freedom increase, the differences in the proportions of area under the normal curve and the Student *t*-distributions become negligible.

In contrast to our use of the normal curve, the tabled values for *t* (Table C in Appendix C) are **critical values,** that is, *those values that bound the critical rejection regions corresponding to varying levels of significance.* Thus, in using the table for the distributions of *t*, we locate the appropriate number of degrees of freedom in the left-hand column and then find the column corresponding to the chosen α. The tabled values represent the *t*-ratio required for significance. If the absolute value of our obtained *t*-ratio equals or exceeds this tabled value, we may reject H_0.

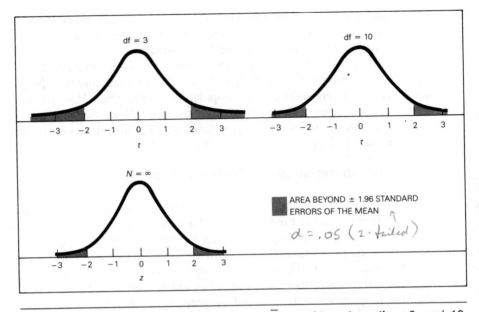

Figure 14.8 Sampling distributions of $t = (\bar{X} - \mu_0)/s_{\bar{X}}$ when df $= 3$, and 10, compared to the standard normal curve.

14.5.2 Illustrative Problem: Student's *t*

Let's now examine an example involving a small sample. A group of 17 male prisoners in federal, maximum security penitentiaries was randomly selected from the federal prison population to participate in a new rehabilitation program. The 17 prisoners had a mean score on a "dangerousness to society" index (low score = not dangerous, high score = extremely dangerous) of 84 and a standard deviation of 16. Therefore, we know that

$$\bar{X} = 84, \qquad s = 16, \qquad N = 17$$

Can we assume that the 17 prisoners who were randomly chosen to participate in the rehabilitation program are representative of a prison population in which $\mu = 78$?

Let's set up this problem in more formal statistical terms:

1. *Null hypothesis (H_0):* The mean of the population from which the sample was drawn equals 78 ($\mu = \mu_0 = 78$).

2. *Alternative hypothesis (H_1):* The mean of the population from which the sample was drawn does not equal 78 ($\mu \neq \mu_0$).

3. *Statistical test:* The Student *t*-ratio is chosen because we are dealing with a normally distributed variable in which σ is unknown.

4. *Significance level:* α = 0.05.

5. *Sampling distribution:* The sampling distribution is the Student t-distribution with df = 16. (*Note:* df = $N - 1$.)

6. *Critical region:* $|t_{0.05}| \geq 2.12$. Since H_1 is nondirectional, the critical region consists of all values of $t \geq 2.12$ and $t \leq -2.12$. In the present example the value of t corresponding to $\overline{X} = 84$ is

↖ Table C, pg. 466

$$t = \frac{\overline{X} - \mu_0}{s_{\overline{X}}} = \frac{84 - 78}{16/\sqrt{16}} = 1.50$$

where Eq. (14.8) allows us to calculate $s_{\overline{X}}$, the estimated standard error

$$s_{\overline{X}} = \frac{s}{\sqrt{N - 1}}$$

Decision   Since the obtained t does not fall within the critical region (i.e., $1.50 < t_{0.05}$), we fail to reject H_0 (see Fig. 14.9). In other words, we have statistical justification to believe that the sample of 17 prisoners is (in terms of their dangerousness to society) representative of the federal prison population; therefore, the rehabilitation program can proceed with the sample of 17 prisoners. Had our decision been that the sample was not representative, a new sample would have to be drawn and tested for representativeness before continuing with the program. Why? We wish to increase the likelihood that if the program is successful, it was not successful due to a unique sample. Once the program's success is established with a representative sample of prisoners, it should be effective for the prison population.

14.6 Estimation of Parameters: Interval Estimation

We have repeatedly pointed out that one of the basic problems in inferential statistics is the estimation of the parameters of a population from statistics calculated from a sample. This problem, in turn, involves two subproblems: (1) *point estimation* and (2) *interval estimation*.

In Section 14.4 you learned that when we estimate parameters using single sample values, these estimates are known as point estimates. A single sample value drawn from a population provides an estimate of the population parameter. But how good an estimate is it? If a population mean were known to be 100, would a sample mean of 60 constitute a good estimate? How about a sample mean of 130, 105, 98, or 99.4? Under what conditions do we consider an estimate good? Since we know that the population parameters are virtually never known and that we generally use samples to estimate these parameters,

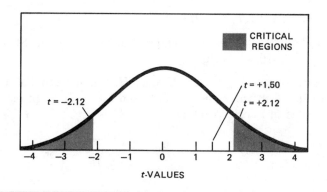

Figure 14.9 Sampling distribution of t and critical regions for a two-tailed test, $t_{0.05}$, df = 16.

is there any way to determine the amount of error we are likely to make? The answer to this question is "No." It is possible, however, not only to estimate the population parameter **(point estimation)**, but also to state a range of values that we are confident includes or encompasses the population parameter **(interval estimation)**. Moreover, we may express our confidence in terms of probabilities, and as a result social scientists generally prefer interval estimates over point estimates.

Have you ever seen a weight-guesser at a carnival who promises to guess your correct weight to within a specified number of pounds? Suppose you are that weight-guesser who is trying to estimate the weight of a man, basing the estimate on physical inspection.

Let's assume that you are unable to place him on a scale, and that you cannot ask him his weight. This problem is similar to many you have faced throughout this text. You cannot know the population value (the man's true weight), and hence you are forced to estimate it. Let's say that you have the impression that he weighs about 200 pounds. If you are asked, "How confident are you that he weighs *exactly* 200 pounds?" you would probably reply, "I doubt that he weighs exactly 200 pounds. If he does, you can credit me with a fantastically lucky guess. However, I feel reasonably confident that he weighs between 190 and 210 pounds." In doing this, you have stated the interval within which we feel confident that the true weight falls. After a moment's reflection, you might hedge slightly, "Well, he is almost certainly between 180 and 220 pounds. In any event I feel perfectly confident that his weight is included in the interval between 170 and 230 pounds." Note that the greater the size of the interval, the greater is your feeling of certainty that the true value is encompassed between these limits. Note also that in stating these confidence limits, you are, in effect, making two statements: (1) You are stating the limits that include the man's weight and (2) you are rejecting the possibility that his weight is not included in these limits. Thus, if someone asks, "Is it conceivable that our subject weighs as much as 240 pounds or as little as 160 pounds?" your reply would be negative.

14.7 Confidence Intervals and Confidence Limits

In the preceding example we were in a sense concerning ourselves with the problem of estimating *confidence limits*. In effect, we were attempting to determine the interval within which any hypotheses concerning the weight of the man might be considered tenable and outside which any hypotheses would be considered untenable. The interval within which we consider hypotheses tenable is known as the **confidence interval,** and the limits defining the interval are referred to as **confidence limits.**

Let's look at a sample problem and apply our statistical concepts to the estimation of confidence levels.

A local health systems agency is trying to decide on the feasibility of establishing a health care clinic in a particular neighborhood. In part, the decision will depend on estimates of the health care needs of the neighborhood. A limited budget does not allow assessing the needs of all the residents in the neighborhood. Consequently, we must be content with selecting a simple random sample from the neighborhood and basing our estimates on the sample. The medical team screens a simple random sample of 26 residents; each resident is assigned an overall health care needs score. We obtain the following results:

$$\overline{X} = 108, \qquad s = 15, \qquad N = 26$$

Our best estimate of the population mean (i.e., the mean health care needs score within the neighborhood) is 108. However, even though our sample statistics provide our best estimates of population values, we recognize that such estimates are subject to error. As with the weight problem, we would be very lucky if the mean of the neighborhood were actually 108. On the other hand, if we have used truly random selection procedures, we have a right to believe that our sample value is fairly close to the population mean. The critical question becomes, "Between what confidence limits do we consider as likely hypotheses concerning the value of the population mean (μ) in the neighborhood?"

We have seen that the mean of the sampling distribution of sample means ($\mu_{\overline{x}}$) is equal to the mean of the population. We have also seen that since, for any given N, we may determine how far sample means are likely to deviate from any given or hypothesized value of μ, we may determine the likelihood that a particular $\overline{X}$ could have been drawn from a population with a mean of μ_0, where μ_0 represents the value of the population mean under H_0. Now, since we do not know the value of the population mean, we are free to hypothesize *any* value we desire.

It should be clear that we could consider an unlimited number of hypotheses concerning the population mean and subsequently reject them, or fail to reject them, on the basis of the size of the *t*-ratios. This problem requires that we use a *t*-ratio due to the small sample size and unknown population parameter. Use of *z* values to estimate confidence intervals will be presented in the following example.

In the present problem let's select a number of hypothetical population means. We will use the 0.05 level of significance (two-tailed test) and test the hypothesis that $\mu_0 = 98$. The value of t corresponding to $\overline{X} = 108$ is 3.333:

$$t = \frac{\overline{X} - \mu_0}{s_{\overline{X}}} = \frac{108 - 98}{15/\sqrt{25}} = \frac{10}{3} = 3.333$$

In Table C (Appendix C) we find that $t_{0.05}$ for 25 df is 2.060. Since our obtained t is greater than this critical value, we reject the hypothesis that $\mu_0 = 98$. In other words, it is unlikely that $\overline{X} = 108$ was drawn from a population with a mean of 98.

Our next hypothesis is that $\mu_0 = 100$, which gives a t of

$$t = \frac{108 - 100}{15/\sqrt{25}} = 2.667$$

Since $2.667 > t_{0.05}$ (or 2.060), we may reject the hypothesis that the population mean is 100.

If we hypothesize $\mu_0 = 102$, the resulting t-ratio of 2.000 is less than $t_{0.05}$. Consequently, we may consider the hypothesis that $\mu_0 = 102$ is tenable. Similarly, if we obtained the appropriate t-ratios, we would find that the hypothesis $\mu_0 = 114$ is tenable, whereas hypotheses of values greater than 114 are untenable. Thus, $\overline{X} = 108$ was probably drawn from a population whose mean falls in the interval 102–114 (note that these limits, 102 and 114, represent approximate limits, that is, the closest *integers*). The hypothesis that $\overline{X} = 108$ was drawn from a population with $\mu < 102$ or $\mu > 114$ may be rejected at the 0.05 level of significance. The interval within which the population mean probably lies is called the *confidence interval*. We refer to the limits of this interval as the *confidence limits*. Since we have been using $\alpha = 0.05$, we call it the *95% confidence interval*. Similarly, if we used $\alpha = 0.01$, we could obtain the *99% confidence interval*.

Now that we have considered the hypothesis-testing approach to confidence intervals, we will calculate the exact limits of the 95% confidence interval directly. It is not necessary to perform all of these previous calculations to establish the confidence limits.

To determine the upper limit for the 95% confidence interval, we have

$$\text{upper limit } \mu_0 = \overline{X} + (t_{0.05})(s_{\overline{X}}) \tag{14.10}$$

We know that $\overline{X} = 108$ and that $s_{\overline{X}} = 15/\sqrt{25}* = 3$. Table C shows that $t_{0.05}$ with 25 degrees of freedom equals 2.060. Multiplying the critical value of t times $s_{\overline{X}}$ (the estimated standard error) provides us with the number of units we must move to the right of the mean to encompass one-half of the 95%

---

* Applying Eq. (14.8).

confidence interval. The resulting value is the upper limit of the 95% confidence interval.

Applying Eq. (14.10), we find that the upper 95% confidence limit in the preceding problem is

$$\text{upper limit } \mu_0 = 108 + (2.060)(3.0)$$
$$= 108 + 6.18 = 114.18$$

To compute the lower limit, we obtain

$$\text{lower limit } \mu_0 = \overline{X} - (t_{0.05})(s_{\overline{X}}) \qquad (14.11)$$

Similarly, using Eq. (14.11), we find that the lower confidence limit is

$$\text{lower limit } \mu_0 = 108 - (2.060)(3.0)$$
$$= 108 - 6.18 = 101.82$$

Note that to compute the lower confidence limit, we *subtracted* the same value (6.18) from the sample mean of 108 that we *added* to the sample mean when determining the upper limit. Hence, the sample mean is equidistant from the upper and lower limits.

You should also note that Eqs. (14.10) and (14.11) are derived algebraically from Eq. (14.9):

$$t_{0.05} = \frac{\overline{X} - \mu_0}{s_{\overline{X}}} \qquad \text{therefore} \qquad \mu_0 = \overline{X} + (t_{0.05})(s_{\overline{X}})$$

Having established the lower and the upper limits as 101.82 and 114.18, respectively, we may now conclude: On the basis of our obtained mean and standard deviation, which were computed from scores drawn from a population in which the true mean is unknown, we assert that the population mean probably falls within the interval that we have established.

If we wish to compute the 99% confidence interval, it is necessary to substitute $t_{0.01}$ in the preceding equation. To compute the upper limit of the 99% confidence interval, we obtain

$$108 + (2.787)(3.0) = 108 + 8.36 = 116.36$$

To compute the lower limit, we have

$$108 - (2.787)(3.0) = 108 - 8.36 = 99.64$$

Notice that the 99% confidence interval is wider than the 95% confidence interval by comparing the confidence limits in the two examples.

Some words of caution in interpreting the confidence interval. In establishing the interval within which we believe the population mean falls, we have *not* established any probability that our obtained mean is correct. In other words, we cannot claim that the chances are 95 in 100 (or 99 in 100) that the population mean is 108. Our statements are valid only with respect to the interval and not with respect to any particular value of the sample mean. In addition, since the population mean is a fixed value and does not have a distribution, our probability statements never refer to μ. The probability we assert is about the interval, that is, the probability that the interval contains μ.

Finally, when we have established the 95% confidence interval of the mean, we are not stating that the probability is 0.95 that the particular interval we have calculated contains the population mean. It should be clear that if we were to select repeated samples from a population, both the sample means and the sample standard deviations would differ from sample to sample. Consequently, our estimates of the confidence interval would also vary from sample to sample. When we have established the 95% confidence interval of the population mean, we are stating that if repeated samples of a given size are drawn from the population, 95% of the interval estimates will include the population mean. Figure 14.10 provides an illustration.

14.7.1 Confidence Intervals and Limits for Large Samples

In many instances the sample size exceeds 50 and the z distribution may be used to compute confidence intervals for a population mean. Assume we have conducted a random sample of 600 Atlanta area adolescents, and their family income averaged $15,000 with a standard deviation of $2500. We wish to compute the 95% confidence interval for the mean family income:

$$\overline{X} = \$15,000, \quad s = \$2500, \quad N = 600$$

We can compute $s_{\overline{X}}$ in the following manner using Eq. (14.8):

$$s_{\overline{X}} = \frac{s}{\sqrt{N-1}} = \frac{2500}{\sqrt{599}} = \frac{2500}{24.47} = 102.17$$

To compute the upper limit, we find that

$$\text{upper limit } \mu_0 = \overline{X} + z(s_{\overline{X}}) \qquad (14.12)$$

To compute the lower limit, we obtain

$$\text{lower limit } \mu_0 = \overline{X} - z(s_{\overline{X}}) \qquad (14.13)$$

In Table A (Appendix C) we find that the z value that includes 47.5% of the area (95/2 = 47.5) to the right (or left) of the mean is 1.96. Substituting

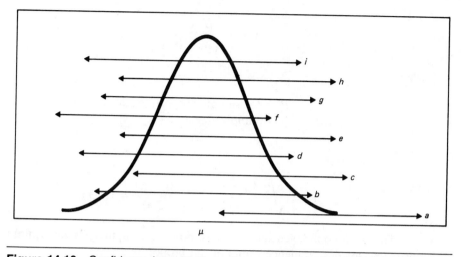

Figure 14.10 Confidence intervals based on repeated samples from a population. Interval *a* does not include μ.

this value into Eqs. (14.12) and (14.13), we can now determine the upper and lower limits of the 95% confidence interval for μ, the unknown population parameter:

$$\text{upper limit} = 15{,}000 + 1.96(102.17) = \$15{,}200.25$$
$$\text{lower limit} = 15{,}000 - 1.96(102.17) = \$14{,}799.75$$

14.7.2 Confidence Intervals and Limits for Percentages

Confidence intervals and limits can also be computed for percentages and proportions. Suppose we drew a random sample of 200 from the list of registered voters in Wisconsin that we discussed in Chapter 1 and in the introduction to this chapter in an effort to estimate the percent favoring nuclear power as an energy source. What if 56% favored nuclear energy? Hypothetically, it is possible that if we had drawn four more samples from the list of registered voters (with replacement), the following percentages of voters would favor nuclear power as an energy source: 52%, 55%, 58%, and 57%.

Our concern is that of establishing a confidence interval around the 56% value determined by the actual survey. While it *appears* that a majority of voters prefer nuclear energy, it is possible that this is not the case. To establish the confidence interval, we must first determine the **standard error of the proportion** [see Eq. (14.14)], which is an estimate of the standard deviation of the sampling distribution of proportions. Converting 56% to a proportion allows us to use Eq. (14.14) and determine the standard error of the proportion.

$$\sigma_P = \sqrt{\frac{P\,(1-P)}{N}} \qquad\qquad (14.14)$$

where

$$P = \text{the sample proportion and}$$
$$N = \text{sample size}$$

Therefore

$$\sigma_P = \sqrt{\frac{0.56(0.44)}{200}} = \sqrt{\frac{0.2464}{200}} = 0.035$$

The 95% confidence interval may now be computed by determining the upper and lower confidence limits of the proportion.

$$\begin{aligned} \text{upper limit} &= P + z(\sigma_P) \qquad\qquad (14.15)\\ &= 0.56 + 1.96(0.035)\\ &= 0.56 + 0.07\\ &= 0.63 \end{aligned}$$

$$\begin{aligned} \text{lower limit} &= P - z(\sigma_P) \qquad\qquad (14.16)\\ &= 0.56 - 1.96(0.035)\\ &= 0.56 - 0.07\\ &= 0.49 \end{aligned}$$

We now know the lower confidence limit to be 0.49 or 49% and the upper confidence limit to be 0.63 or 63%. The confidence interval therefore includes the percentages between 49 and 63%. We have *not* established that the percentage of all voters favoring nuclear energy is 56% or that the chances are 95 out of 100 that 56% favor nuclear energy. What we can say is that if we drew a large number of samples ($N = 200$) from the population, 95% of the interval estimates would include the actual population percentage. Had we increased the sample size, the standard error of the proportion would decrease, and therefore the 95% confidence interval would be narrower. Examine Eq. (14.14) and demonstrate this to yourself.

14.8 Test of Significance for Pearson's *r*: One-Sample Case

In Chapter 9 we discussed the calculation of two statistics—r_s and Pearson's *r*—commonly used to describe the extent of the relationship between two variables. If you recall, the coefficient of correlation varies between ± 1.00, with $r = 0.00$ indicating the absence of a relationship. It is easy to overlook the fact that correlation coefficients based on sample data are only estimates of the corresponding population parameter and, as such, will distribute themselves about the population value. Thus, it is quite possible that a sample drawn from a population in which the true correlation is zero may yield a high positive or negative correlation by *chance*. The null hypothesis most often investigated in the one-sample case is that the *population correlation coefficient* (ρ, pronounced "rho") is zero.

It is clear that a test of significance is called for. However, the test is complicated by the fact that the sampling distribution of ρ is usually nonnormal, particularly as ρ approaches the limiting values of ± 1.00. Consider the case in which ρ equals $+0.80$. You may determine that sample correlation coefficients drawn from this population will distribute themselves around $+0.80$ and can take on any value from -1.00 to $+1.00$. It is equally clear, however, that there is a definite restriction in the range of values that sample statistics greater than $+0.80$ can assume, whereas the range of possible values less than $+0.80$ is greater: from $r < +0.80$ to $r = -1.00$ to be precise. The result is a negatively skewed sampling distribution. The departure from normality will usually be less as the number of paired scores in the sample increases.

When the population correlation from which the sample is drawn is equal to zero, the sampling distribution is more likely to be normal. These relationships are demonstrated in Figure 14.11, which illustrates the sampling distribution of the correlation coefficient when $\rho = -0.80$, 0, and $+0.80$.

14.8.1 Testing H_0: $\rho = 0$

When testing the null hypothesis that the population correlation coefficient is zero, the following *t*-test should be used:

$$t = \frac{r\sqrt{N - 2}}{\sqrt{1 - r^2}} \qquad (14.17)$$

Figure 14.11 Illustrative sampling distributions of correlation coefficients when $\rho = -0.80$ and when $\rho = +0.80$.

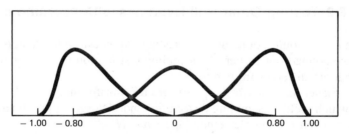

| -1.00 | -0.80 | 0 | 0.80 | 1.00 |

The number of degrees of freedom is equal to $N - 2$.

Let's look at an illustrative example. A team of social psychologists has developed a scale that purports to measure social isolation. The scores made on the scale by 15 respondents are correlated with their scores on an index revealing the degree of prejudice felt toward minority groups. They obtain a Pearson's r of 0.60. May they conclude that the obtained correlation is not likely to have been drawn from a population in which the true correlation is zero?

Let's set up this problem in formal statistical terms.

1. *Null hypothesis (H_0):* The population correlation coefficient from which this sample was drawn equals 0.00 ($\rho = 0.00$).

2. *Alternative hypothesis (H_1):* The population correlation coefficient from which the sample was drawn does *not* equal 0.00 ($\rho \neq 0.00$).

3. *Statistical test:* The t-test, with $N - 2$ degrees of freedom.

4. *Significance level:* $\alpha = 0.05$, two-tailed test.

5. *Sampling distribution:* The Student t-distribution with df $= 13$.

6. *Critical region:* $|t_{0.05}| \geq 2.160$. Since H_1 is nondirectional, the critical region consists of all values of $t \geq 2.160$ and $t \leq -2.160$.

In the present example

$$t = \frac{0.60\sqrt{13}}{0.80} = 2.70$$

Decision   Since the obtained $t > t_{0.05}$, it falls within the critical region for rejecting H_0. Thus, it may be concluded that the sample was drawn from a population in which $\rho \neq 0.00$. Having rejected the null hypothesis also allows us to conclude that the regression coefficient also differs from 0.

14.8.2 Testing Other Null Hypotheses Concerning ρ

The t-test should not be used for testing hypotheses other than $\rho = 0.00$ since, as we pointed out earlier, the sampling distribution is not normal for values of ρ that are different from zero.

Fisher has described a procedure for transforming sample r's to a statistic z_r, which yields a sampling distribution more closely approximating the normal curve, even for samples employing small N's.

The test statistic is the normal deviate, z, in which

$$z = \frac{z_r - Z_r}{\sqrt{1/(N - 3)}} \qquad (14.18)$$

where

$z_r =$ the transformed value of the sample r (see Table E), and
$Z_r =$ the transformed value of the population correlation coefficient specified under H_0

Using the same example, let's test H_0 that the population ρ from which the sample was drawn is 0.25. Recall that $r = 0.60$ and $N = 15$.

Obtaining z_r is greatly simplified by Table E, Appendix C, which shows the value of z_r, corresponding to each value of r, in steps of 0.01, between 0.00 and 0.99. Thus, referring to Table E, we see that an r of 0.60, for example, has a corresponding z_r of 0.693.

Similarly, ρ of 0.25 has a corresponding Z_r of 0.256. Substituting these values in the equation of z, we find

$$z = \frac{0.693 - 0.256}{\sqrt{1/(15 - 3)}} = \frac{0.437}{0.289} = 1.51$$

Decision At the 0.05 level, two-tailed test, $|z_{0.05}| \geq 1.96$ is required for significance. Since $z = 1.51$ is less than the critical values, we cannot reject H_0. It is quite possible that the sample was drawn from a population in which the true correlation is 0.25.

14.8.3 Test of Significance of r_s: One-Sample Case

Table F in Appendix C presents the critical values of r_s, one- and two-tailed tests, for selected values of N from 5 to 30. In Chapter 9 we demonstrated the calculation of r_s from data consisting of the social class backgrounds of 15 married couples. A correlation of 0.64 was computed. Since $N = 15$ is not listed in Table F, it is necessary to interpolate, using the critical values of $N = 14$ and 16. The critical value at the 0.05 level, two-tailed test, for $N = 14$ is 0.544; at $N = 16$ it is 0.506. By using linear interpolation, we may roughly approximate the critical value corresponding to $N = 15$.

With Table F, linear interpolation merely involves adding together the boundary values of r_s and dividing by 2. Thus

$$r_{s(0.05)} = \frac{0.544 + 0.506}{2} = 0.525$$

Since our obtained r_s of 0.64 exceeds the critical value at the 0.05 level, we may conclude that the population value of the Spearman correlation coefficient from which the sample was drawn is greater than 0.00.

14.9 Test of Significance for Goodman and Kruskal's Gamma

Gamma was discussed in Chapter 8 using an example in which the relationship between political liberalism and year in college was explored. Gamma was found to equal $+0.465$. Overall, there were 1167 concordant pairs and 426 discordant pairs. Let's test the hypothesis that in the population from which the sample was drawn, γ (the Greek letter symbolizing the parameter) is greater than 0. Therefore, our null hypothesis is H_0: $\gamma \leq 0$ and we will test it at the 0.01 level of significance with a one-tailed test using the following equation, which allows us to convert G to a z score:

$$z = (G - \gamma) \sqrt{\frac{C - D}{N(1 - G^2)}}$$

where

$$
\begin{aligned}
G &= 0.465 \\
C &= 1167 \\
D &= 426 \\
N &= 80, \text{ and} \\
\gamma &= 0 \text{ because } H_0: \gamma \leq 0
\end{aligned}
$$

Therefore

$$z = (0.465 - 0) \sqrt{\frac{1167 - 426}{80(1 - 0.216)}}$$

$$= (0.465) \sqrt{\frac{741}{62.72}}$$

$$= (0.465)(3.44)$$

$$= +1.60$$

The computed z score of 1.60 does not fall into the critical region that begins at $z = 2.33$ (see Table A in Appendix C); therefore, we must accept the null hypothesis that the association between political liberalism and year in college in the population from which the 80 students was drawn equals 0.

Summary

We have seen that if we take a number of samples from a given population, then:

1. The distribution of sample means tends to be normal.

2. The mean of these sample means ($\mu_{\bar{x}}$) is equal to the mean of the population (μ).

3. The standard error of the mean ($\sigma_{\bar{x}}$) is equal to $\sigma/\sqrt{N}$. As N increases, the variability decreases.

We used these relationships in the testing of hypotheses (e.g., $\mu = \mu_0$), when the standard deviation of a population was known, using the z statistic and the standard normal curve.

When σ is not known, we demonstrated the use of sample statistics to estimate these parameters. We used these estimates of the parameters to test hypotheses, using the Student t-ratio and the corresponding sampling distributions. We compared these t-distributions, which vary as a function of degrees of freedom (df), with the standard normal curve.

We used the t-ratio and the normal distribution as a basis for establishing confidence intervals for means and proportions.

Finally, we demonstrated the test of significance for Pearson's r, Spearman's r_s, one-sample case, and for gamma.

Terms to Remember

Central limit theorem If random samples of a fixed N are drawn from *any* population (regardless of the form of the population distribution), as N becomes larger, the distribution of sample means approaches normality, with the overall mean approaching μ, the variance of the sample means $\sigma_{\bar{x}}^2$ being equal to σ^2/N, and a standard error $\sigma_{\bar{x}}$ of $\sigma/\sqrt{N}$.

Confidence interval A confidence interval for a parameter specifies a range of values bounded by two endpoints called confidence limits. Common confidence intervals are 95% and 99%.

Confidence limits The two endpoints of a confidence interval.

Critical region The portion of the area under a curve that includes those values of a statistic that lead to rejection of the null hypothesis.

Critical values of t Those values that bound the critical rejection regions corresponding to varying levels of significance.

Degrees of freedom (df)   The number of values that are free to vary after we have placed certain restrictions upon our data.

Interval estimation   The determination of an interval within which the population parameter is presumed to fall. (Contrast *Point estimation*.)

Law of large numbers   As the sample size increases, the standard error of the mean decreases.

Point estimation   An estimate of a population parameter that involves a single sample value, selected by the criterion of "best estimate." (Contrast *Interval estimation*.)

Robust test   A statistical test from which statistical inferences are likely to be valid even when there are fairly large departures from normality in the population distribution.

Standard error of the mean   A theoretical standard deviation of sample means, of a given sample size, drawn from some specified population. When based on a known population standard deviation, $\sigma_{\bar{x}} = \sigma/\sqrt{N}$; when estimated from a single sample, $s_{\bar{x}} = s/\sqrt{N - 1}$.

Standard error of the proportion   An estimate of the standard deviation of the sampling distribution of proportions.

***t*-distributions or Student's** t Theoretical symmetrical sampling distributions with a mean of zero and a standard deviation that becomes smaller as degrees of freedom (df) increase. Used in relation to the Student t-ratio.

***t*-ratio**   A test statistic for determining the significance of a difference between means (two-sample case) or for testing the hypothesis that a given sample mean was drawn from a population with the mean specified under the null hypothesis (one-sample case). Used when population standard deviation (or standard deviations) is not known.

Unbiased estimator   An estimate that equals, on the average, the value of the corresponding parameter.

Exercises

1. Describe what happens to the distribution of sample means when you

    a) Increase the size of each sample.

    b) Increase the number of samples.

2. Explain why the standard deviation of a sample will usually underestimate the standard deviation of a population. Give an example.

3. Given that $\overline{X} = 24$ and $s = 4$ for $N = 15$, use the t-distribution to find

    a) The 95% confidence limits for μ.

    b) The 99% confidence limits for μ.

4. Given that $\overline{X} = 24$ and $s = 4$ for $N = 121$, use the t-distribution to find

    a) The 95% confidence limits for μ.

    b) The 99% confidence limits for μ.

Compare the results with Exercise 3.

5. An instructor gives his class an examination that, as he knows from years of experience, yields $\mu = 78$ and $\sigma = 7$. His present class of 22 obtains a mean of 82. Is he correct in assuming that this is a superior class? Use $\alpha = 0.01$, two-tailed test.

6. An instructor gives his class an examination that, as he knows from years of experience, yields $\mu = 78$. His present class of 22 obtains $\overline{X} = 82$ and $s = 7$. Is he correct in assuming that this is a superior class? Use $\alpha = 0.01$, two-tailed test.

7. Explain the difference between Exercises 5 and 6. What test statistic is used in each case, and why? Why is the decision different?
Generalize: What is the effect of knowing σ upon the likelihood of a type II error?

8. The Superintendent of Zody school district claims that the children in her district are brighter, on the average, than the general population of students. In order to determine the aptitude of school children in the district, a study was conducted. The results were as follows.

Test Scores
105
109
115
112
124
115
103
110
125
99

The mean of the general population of school children is 106. Set this up in formal statistical terms (i.e., H_0 , H_1, etc.) and draw the appropriate conclusions. Use a one-tailed test, $\alpha = 0.05$.

9. For a particular population with $\mu = 28.5$ and $\sigma = 5.5$, what is the probability that, in a sample of 100, $\overline{X}$ will be

   a) Equal to or less than 30.0?   **b)** Equal to or less than 28.0?

   c) Equal to or more than 29.5?   **d)** Between 28.0 and 29.0?

10. Given that $\overline{X} = 40$ for $N = 24$ from a population in which $\sigma = 8$, find

   a) The 95% confidence limits for μ.

   b) The 99% confidence limits for μ.

11. Overton University claims that because of its superior facilities and close faculty supervision, its students complete the Ph.D. program earlier than usual. They base this assertion on the fact that the national mean age for completion is 32.11, whereas the mean age of their 26 Ph.D.'s is 29.61 with $s = 6.00$. Test the validity of their assumption.

12. Using the data in the preceding exercise, find the interval within which you are confident that the true population mean (average age for Ph.D.'s at Overton University) probably falls, using the 95% confidence interval.

13. A sociologist asserts that the average length of courtship is longer before a second marriage than before a first marriage. He bases this assertion on the fact that the average for first marriages is 265 days, whereas the average for second marriages (e.g., his 626 respondents) is 268.5 days, with $s = 50$. Test the validity of his assumption.

14. Using the data in the preceding exercise, find the interval within which you are confident that the true population mean (average courtship days for a second marriage) probably falls, using the 99% confidence interval.

15. Random samples of size 2 are selected from the following finite population of scores: 1, 3, 5, 7, 9, and 11.

   a) Calculate the mean and standard deviation of the population.

   b) Construct a histogram showing the sampling distribution of means when $N = 2$. Sample *without* replacement.

   c) Construct a histogram showing the means of all possible samples that can be drawn. Sample *with* replacement.

16. Given (b) in Exercise 15, answer the following: Selecting a sample with $N = 2$, what is the probability that

   a) A mean as high as 10 will be obtained?

   b) A mean as low as 2 will be obtained?

   c) A mean as deviant as 8 will be obtained?

   d) A mean as low as 1 will be obtained?

17. Given (c) in Exercise 15, answer the following: Selecting a sample with $N = 2$, what is the probability that:

    a) A mean as high as 10 will be obtained?

    b) A mean as low as 2 will be obtained?

    c) A mean as deviant as 8 will be obtained?

    d) A mean as low as 1 will be obtained?

18. A census field supervisor ranked 25 of her workers on the length of their employment with the Census Bureau and their rate of interview completion. She correlated these ranks and obtained an $r_s = -0.397$. Assuming $\alpha = 0.05$, two-tailed test, what do you conclude?

19. As a requirement for admission to Blue Chip University, a candidate must take a standardized entrance examination. The correlation between performance on this examination and college grades is 0.43.

    a) The director of admissions claims that a better way to predict college success is by using high school averages. To test her claim, she randomly selects 52 students and correlates their college grades with their high school averages. She obtains $r = 0.54$. What do you conclude? Use $\alpha = 0.05$.

    b) The director's assistant constructs a test that he claims is better for predicting college success than the one currently used. He randomly selects 67 students and correlates their grade point averages with performance on his test. The obtained $r = 0.61$. What do you conclude? Use $\alpha = 0.05$.

20. In 1978 there were 5,206,000 families in the United States that were headed by a woman with no husband present. Of these families, 42.8% were headed by a divorced woman. If the standard error of the percentage is 0.8%, what is the 68% confidence interval? What is the 95% confidence interval? (*Source:* U.S. Bureau of the Census, *Divorce, Child Custody and Child Support*, Current Population Reports.)

21. You have conducted a survey of 420 students, and 62% have indicated that they are satisfied with the quality of the instruction they are receiving. Compute the standard error of the proportion and the 95% confidence interval. What are the confidence limits? Interpret your answer.

22. What are the statistics used to describe the distribution of a sample? The distribution of a sample statistic?

23. Is s^2 an unbiased estimate of σ^2? Why?

24. Is $\hat{s}^2$ an unbiased estimate of σ^2? Why?

25. What is a confidence interval? A confidence limit? What is their relationship?

26. Give an example to show the effect of the α level on the precision of a confidence interval.

27. How do the t-distributions differ from the normal distribution? Are they ever the same?

28. In a study of marital success and failure Bentler and Newcomb (1978) gave a personality questionnaire to 162 newly married couples. Four years later 77 couples from the original sample were located; of these, 53 were still married, while 24 had separated or divorced. Among the still-married group it was found that the correlation between the husband's and wife's score on an attractiveness scale was 0.59, and that the correlation between their scores on a generosity scale was 0.23. Among the divorced group the correlation between the ex-husband's and ex-wife's score on the attractiveness scale was 0.07, and the correlation between their scores on the generosity scale was 0.13.

    a) Using $\alpha = 0.05$, set up and test the null hypothesis that the correlation between the married couples' scores on attractiveness is equal to zero. Also, set up and test the null hypothesis that the correlation between the divorced couples' scores on attractiveness is equal to zero.

    b) Using $\alpha = 0.05$, set up and test the null hypothesis that the correlation between the married couples' scores on generosity is equal to zero. Also, set up and test the null hypothesis that the correlation between the divorced couples' scores on generosity is equal to zero.

29. Compute gamma for Exercise 1 in Chapter 8 and determine if it is significant at the 0.01 level assuming a one-tailed test.

30. Compute r_s for Exercise 18 in Chapter 9 and determine if it is significant at the 0.05 level assuming a one-tailed test.

31. Assume that the mean number of religious conversions a year per Methodist church is 50. A group of 16 Methodist ministers who attended a special seminar for increasing conversions show the following number of conversions in their churches during the year following the seminar:

Number of Conversions	
55	85
50	60
45	50
75	65
80	60
75	50
80	80
80	50

Calculate the value of t. Can you conclude that the seminar produced ministers with superior abilities to attract converts?

32. A Los Angeles criminologist found an r_s of 0.15 between the number of times 20 male prostitutes had been arrested and the number of years they had worked as prostitutes. Can she conclude that this correlation is significant? Use $\alpha = 0.05$, two-tailed test.

33. Mr. Smith stated that his training program for selling life insurance enables a company to sell more life insurance than the "average" company. The mean amount of life insurance sold by all salespeople per month is $100,000. A sample of ten people who have been through the training program show monthly selling rates (in thousands) of

Selling Rates	
$100	90
120	130
130	135
120	140
125	110

If you were a supervisor of insurance salespeople, would you adopt Mr. Smith's training program? Calculate the value of t.

chapter **15**

An Introduction to the Analysis of Variance

15.1 Multigroup Comparisons
15.2 The Concept of Sums of Squares
15.3 Obtaining Variance Estimates
15.4 Fundamental Concepts of Analysis of Variance
15.5 Assumptions Underlying Analysis of Variance
15.6 An Example Involving Three Groups
15.7 The Interpretation of *F*

15.1 Multigroup Comparisons

In Chapter 14 we were concerned with comparisons between only two groups. Yet the complexity of the phenomena that the social scientist investigates does not allow us to restrict our observations to two groups. Events in nature rarely order themselves conveniently into two groups. More commonly the questions we pose are: Which type of juvenile detention facility is more successful in terms of the recidivism rate? Do the median incomes of the residents in several neighborhoods differ significantly? Are Southern Baptists significantly more orthodox than Lutherans and Methodists? Are persons over 60 more socially isolated than the middle-aged and the young? Which of three teaching techniques is most effective?

The research design necessary to provide answers to these questions would require comparison of more than two groups. You may wonder: But why should multigroup comparisons provide any obstacles? Can we not simply compare the mean of each group with the mean of every group and obtain a Student's t-ratio for each comparison? For example, if we had four groups, A, B, C, D, could we not calculate Student's t-ratios comparing A with B, C, and D; B with C and D; and C with D?

If you will think for a moment of the errors in inference, which we have so frequently discussed, you will recall that our greatest concern has been to avoid type I errors. When we establish the region of rejection at the 0.05 level, we are, in effect, acknowledging our willingness to take the risk of being wrong as often as 5% of the time in our rejection of the null hypothesis. Now,

BOX 15.1

Comparison of Several Groups of Chronically Ill Patients on a Mental Health Index

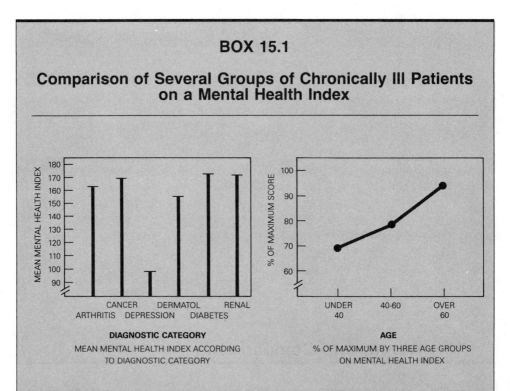

MEAN MENTAL HEALTH INDEX ACCORDING
TO DIAGNOSTIC CATEGORY

% OF MAXIMUM BY THREE AGE GROUPS
ON MENTAL HEALTH INDEX

The physical status of chronically ill patients is under almost constant supervision by care-giving professionals. But what about their psychological status— their emotional and social adjustments to a continuous state of illness? This side of their lives is often neglected in the struggle to bring about favorable changes in their physical status. The goals of one study were to obtain information on the psychological status of chronically ill patients (Cassileth et al., 1984). A Mental Health Index was obtained on a total 758 patients in the following diagnostic categories: arthritis, cancer, depression, dermatological disorder, diabetes, and renal (kidney) disorder. The Index consists of five subscales (anxiety, depression, emotional ties, general positive affect, and loss of control) and a global score—the Mental Health Index.

The accompanying bar graph shows

the mean scores obtained by the six diagnostic groups on the Mental Health Index. Since the diagnostic categories are qualitative rather than quantitative variables (that is, they differ in kind rather than "how much"), the categories are arranged alphabetically along the horizontal axis. Recall that line graphs of unordered variables are meaningless. A one-way analysis of variance is performed on these data in order to ascertain if there is an overall significant difference among the groups.

To construct the line graph, the scores of the patients in all six diagnostic categories were combined and the means obtained on the Mental Health Index by three different age groups were compared. A line graph is appropriate to display these data because age is a quantitative, ordered variable. As with the diagnostic category variable, age grouping is a single variable for which a one-way analysis of variance is the appropriate form of statistical analysis. Incidentally, the researchers found that mean scores on all six scales of the Mental Health Index improved significantly with increasing age. The older people appeared to be better able to handle the stress of chronic illness.

Source: B. Cassileth, E. Lusk, T. Strouse, D. Miller, L. Brown, P. Cross, and A. Tenaglia (1984), Psychosocial Status in Chance Illness. *New England Journal of Medicine,* **311**, 506–510.

what happens when we have numerous comparisons to make? For an extreme example, let us imagine that we have conducted a study involving the calculation of 1000 separate Student's *t*-ratios. Would we be terribly impressed if, say, 50 of the *t*'s proved to be significant at the 0.05 level? Of course not. Indeed, we would probably murmur something to the effect that, "With 1000 comparisons, we would be surprised if we don't obtain approximately 50 comparisons that are significant *by chance* (i.e., due to predictable sampling error)."

The **analysis of variance** (sometimes abbreviated ANOVA) is a technique of statistical analysis that permits us to overcome the ambiguity involved in assessing significant differences when more than two group means are compared, by allowing for a single decision at a specified level of significance. It allows us to answer the question, Is there an overall indication that the independent variable is producing differences among the means of the various groups? Although the analysis of variance may be used in the two-sample case (in which event it yields precisely the same probability values as the Student's *t*-ratio), it is most commonly used when three or more categories or groups of the independent variable are involved. The focus of this chapter is **one-way analysis of variance,** which derives its name from the fact that various groups represent different categories or levels of a *single* independent variable (sometimes referred to as an *experimental stimulus,* or *treatment variable*). (See Box 15.1.) The procedures discussed may be generalized to any number of independent variables. We will now consider the two-group situation before examining the more complex three-group situation.

15.2 The Concept of Sums of Squares

Imagine that we have conducted a study (see Table 15.1) with two groups of students concerning their attitude toward the legalization of marijuana. None of the students in group 1 has ever used marijuana, and all of the students in group 2 use it at least once a month. A high score indicates the student strongly favors legalization. We will test the hypothesis that the two groups of students have been drawn from the same population (or that there is no difference in their attitude toward legalization of marijuana).

Table 15.1 Nonuser's and user's attitude toward the legalization of marijuana.

| (Nonusers) Group 1 | | (Users) Group 2 | |
X_1	X_1^2	X_2	X_2^2
1	1	6	36
2	4	7	49
5	25	9	81
8	64	10	100
Σ 16	94	32	266

$N_1 = 4$, $\qquad \bar{X}_1 = 4 \qquad$ $N_2 = 4$, $\qquad \bar{X}_2 = 8$
$\qquad \Sigma X_{tot} = 48 \qquad N = 8 \qquad \bar{X}_{tot} = 6$

The mean for group 1 is 4; the mean for group 2 is 8. The overall mean, $\bar{X}_{tot}$, is 48/8 or 6. Now, if we were to subtract the overall mean from each score and square, we would obtain the total sum of squares (SS_{tot})

$$SS_{tot} = \Sigma(X - \bar{X}_{tot})^2 \qquad (15.1)$$

For the data in Table 15.1 the total sum of squares using Eq. (15.1) is

$$\begin{aligned} SS_{tot} &= (1 - 6)^2 + (2 - 6)^2 + (5 - 6)^2 + (8 - 6)^2 + (6 - 6)^2 \\ &+ (7 - 6)^2 + (9 - 6)^2 + (10 - 6)^2 = 25 + 16 + 1 \\ &+ 4 + 0 + 1 + 9 + 16 = 72 \end{aligned}$$

Thus, we see that the **total sum of squares** (TSS) is the sum of the squared deviations from the overall mean, and hence is a measure of the total variation in the data. We have already encountered the sum of squares in calculating the standard deviation, the variance, and the total variation of a dependent variable when studying regression analysis. The alternative raw score equation for the total sum of squares is

$$SS_{tot} = \Sigma X_{tot}^2 - \frac{(\Sigma X_{tot})^2}{N} \qquad (15.2)$$

For the data in Table 15.1 the total sum of squares is

$$SS_{tot} = 94 + 266 - \frac{(48)^2}{8}$$

$$= 360 - 288 = 72$$

The **within-group sum of squares** (SS_w) is the sum of the sum of squares obtained within each group and is a measure of the variability within the groups. Figure 15.1 shows, for example, that the scores of the students in group 1 (nonusers) and group 2 (users) vary widely about each of their re-

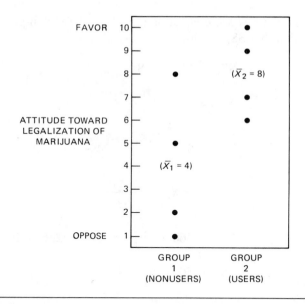

Figure 15.1 Scattergram of attitude toward legalization of marijuana scores for nonusers and users.

spective group means of 4 and 8. The source of the within-group variation includes all of the variables influencing the dependent variable (attitude toward the legalization of marijuana) other than the independent variable. Could the variability we observed in Figure 15.1 in the attitude toward marijuana legalization scores within group 1 or within group 2 have stemmed from the independent variable (nonuse versus use)? No, since everyone in group 1 was a nonuser and everyone in group 2 a user. Thus, all within-group variability must stem from variables other than the specified independent variable.

The within-group sum of squares, in this instance, measures the sum of the squared deviations of the scores in group 1 around $\overline{X}_1$ *plus* the sum of the squared deviations of the scores in group 2 around $\overline{X}_2$:

$$SS_w = SS_1 + SS_2$$

where

$$SS_1 = \Sigma(X - \overline{X}_1)^2 \text{ and}$$
$$SS_2 = \Sigma(X - \overline{X}_2)^2$$

For the data in Table 15.1 the within-group sum of squares is

$$\Sigma(X - \overline{X}_1)^2 + \Sigma(X - \overline{X}_2)^2$$
$$= (1 - 4)^2 + (2 - 4)^2 + (5 - 4)^2 + (8 - 4)^2$$
$$+ (6 - 8)^2 + (7 - 8)^2 + (9 - 8)^2 + (10 - 8)^2$$
$$= 9 + 4 + 1 + 16 + 4 + 1 + 1 + 4 = 40$$

Using the raw score equation (15.3) for the within-group sum of squares, we also find that $SS_w = 40$.

$$SS_w = SS_1 + SS_2 \tag{15.3}$$

$$SS_1 = \Sigma\, X_1^2 - \frac{(\Sigma\, X_1)^2}{N_1}$$

$$= 94 - \frac{(16)^2}{4} = 94 - 64 = 30$$

$$SS_2 = \Sigma\, X_2^2 - \frac{(\Sigma\, X_2)^2}{N_2}$$

$$= 266 - \frac{(32)^2}{4} = 266 - 256 = 10$$

$$SS_w = 30 + 10 = 40$$

The **between-group sum of squares** (SS_{bet}) is the sum of the sum of squares between each group and reflects the influence of the independent or treatment variable. It may be obtained by subtracting the overall mean from each group mean, squaring the result, multiplying by N in each group, and summing across all of the groups. Thus

$$SS_{bet} = \Sigma\, N_i(\overline{X}_i - \overline{X}_{tot})^2 \tag{15.4}$$

where N_i is the number in the ith group, and $\overline{X}_i$ is the mean of the ith group.

$$SS_{bet} = 4(4 - 6)^2 + 4(8 - 6)^2 = 32$$

The raw score equation for calculating the between-group sum of squares is

$$SS_{bet} = \Sigma\frac{(\Sigma\, X_i)^2}{N_i} - \frac{(\Sigma\, X_{tot})^2}{N} \tag{15.5}$$

and

$$SS_{bet} = \frac{(16)^2}{4} + \frac{(32)^2}{4} - \frac{(48)^2}{8}$$

$$= 64 + 256 - 288$$

$$= 320 - 288 = 32$$

It will be noted that the total sum of squares is equal to the sum of the between-group sum of squares and the within-group sum of squares. In other words

$$SS_{tot} = SS_w + SS_{bet} \qquad (15.6)$$

In this example $SS_{tot} = 72$, $SS_w = 40$, and $SS_{bet} = 32$. Thus, $72 = 40 + 32$. Therefore, we have partitioned the *total sum of squares,* which is a measure of total variation in the dependent variable into two components: the within and between sum of squares. The *within sum of squares component* is a measure of the variability of the dependent variable scores *within* each of the categories or groups of the independent variable, and hence is the variation in the dependent variable that cannot be attributed to the independent variable. The *between sum of squares component* is a measure of the variation *between* the categories or groups of the independent variable, and hence is the variation in the dependent variable that is attributable to the independent or treatment variable.

15.3 Obtaining Variance Estimates

The analysis of variance consists of obtaining two independent estimates of variance, one based on variability between groups **(between-group variance)** and the other based on the variability within groups **(within-group variance).** The significance of the difference between these two variance estimates (mean squares) is provided by Fisher's F-distributions. If the between-group variance estimate is large (i.e., the difference between means is large) relative to the within-group variance estimate, the F-ratio is large. Conversely, if the between-group variance estimate is small relative to the within-group estimate, the F-ratio will be small.

A test of our null hypothesis that the two samples were drawn from the same population (H_0: $\mu_1 = \mu_2$) requires that we create a ratio of the between- and within-group sum of squares. You may have observed, however, that both values will increase as the sample size increases. Therefore, as a "corrective" factor we control for sample size by dividing both values by their respective degrees of freedom.* This procedure allows us to arrive at variance estimates for the between- and within-group sum of squares. The *degrees of freedom of the between-group sum of squares* are the number of categories or groups (k) of the independent variable minus 1:

$$df_{bet} = k - 1 \qquad (15.7)$$

---

* The rationale for the degrees of freedom concept was presented in Section 14.5. The same rationale applies here. Degrees of freedom represent the number of values that are free to vary once we have placed certain restrictions on our data.

With two groups, $k = 2$. Therefore, df $= 2 - 1 = 1$. Thus, our between-group variance estimate for the problem at hand is

$$\hat{s}^2_{bet} = \frac{SS_{bet}}{df_{bet}} = \frac{32}{1} = 32, \qquad df = 1 \qquad (15.8)$$

The number of *degrees of freedom of the within-groups sum of squares* is the total N minus the number of categories within the independent variable. Thus

$$df_w = N - k \qquad (15.9)$$

In the present problem $df_w = 8 - 2 = 6$ and our within-group variance estimate becomes

$$\hat{s}^2_w = \frac{SS_w}{df_w} = \frac{40}{6} = 6.67, \qquad df = 6 \qquad (15.10)$$

Now all we have left to do is to calculate the F-ratio and determine whether or not our two variance estimates could have reasonably been drawn from the same population. If not, we will conclude that the significantly larger between-group variance is due to the operation of the group differences. In other words, we will conclude that the groups' differences in marijuana usage produced a significant difference in means. The **F-ratio,** in analysis of variance, is the between-group variance estimate divided by the within-group variance estimate. Symbolically

$$F = \frac{\hat{s}^2_{bet}}{\hat{s}^2_w} \qquad (15.11)$$

For this problem our F-ratio is

$$F = \frac{32}{6.67} = 4.80, \qquad df = 1, 6$$

Looking up the F-ratio under 1 and 6 degrees of freedom in Table D, Appendix C, we find that an F-ratio of 5.99 or larger is required for significance at the 0.05 level. For the present problem, then, we cannot reject the null hypothesis that there is no difference in the two groups' attitudes toward legalizing marijuana. You should note that Table D provides two-tailed values. The analysis of variance test for significance is automatically two-tailed since *any* difference among the sample means will enlarge the entire value of F, not just the difference in which the researcher is interested.

In summary, we must conclude that the nonusers and users we have studied do not differ significantly in terms of their attitudes toward the legalization of marijuana and that they were drawn from the same population.

15.4 Fundamental Concepts of Analysis of Variance

In these few pages we have examined all of the basic concepts necessary to understand simple analysis of variance. Before proceeding with an example involving three groups, let's briefly review these fundamental concepts:

1. We have seen that in a study involving two or more groups it is possible to identify two different bases for estimating the population variance: the between-group and the within-group.
    a) The between-group variance estimate reflects the magnitude of the difference between and or among the group means. The larger the difference is between means, the larger the between-group variance is.
    b) The within-group variance estimate reflects the dispersion of scores within each treatment group. It is often referred to as the *error term*.
2. The null hypothesis is that the samples were drawn from the same population, or that $\mu_1 = \mu_2 = \cdots = \mu_k$.

3. The alternative hypothesis is that the samples were not drawn from the same population; that is, $\mu_1 \neq \mu_2 \neq \cdots \neq \mu_k$.

4. The F-ratio consists of the between-group variance estimate divided by the within-group variance estimate. The within- and between-group variance estimates are known as **mean squares.** By consulting Table D of the distribution of F we can determine whether or not the null hypothesis of equal population means can reasonably be entertained. In the event of a significant F-ratio we may conclude that the group means are not all estimates of a common population mean.

5. In the two-sample case the F-ratio yields probability values identical to those of the Student's t-ratio. Indeed, in the one-degree-of-freedom situation (i.e., $k = 2$), $t = \sqrt{F}$ or $t^2 = F$. You may check this statement by calculating the Student's t-ratio for the sample problem we have just completed.

15.5 Assumptions Underlying Analysis of Variance

A fundamental assumption underlying the use of the Student's t-ratio is that the within-group population variance for all groups must be homogeneous, that is, drawn from the same population of variances. The same assumption holds true for the analysis of variance. In other words, a basic assumption underlying the analysis of variance is that the within-group variances (which, when summed together, make up $\hat{s}_w^2$) are homogeneous and is referred to as **homogeneity of variance.** As with the Student's t-ratio, there is a test for determining whether or not the hypothesis of identical variances is tenable. However, it is beyond the scope of this introductory text to delve into Bartlett's test of homogeneity of variances. Application of this test is described in Kirk (1982).

In addition, the analysis of variance requires the assumptions of normality within groups, random and independent sampling, interval scaling for the dependent variable, and nominal scaling for the independent variable(s).

15.6 An Example Involving Three Groups

Imagine we have just completed a study to assess attitudes toward welfare payments, and we have three samples of nine respondents each: Group 1 is a middle-class sample, group 2 is a sample of persons presently on welfare, and group 3 is a lower-middle-class sample. A high score indicates strong support of welfare payments. Our null hypothesis is that these samples were drawn from the same population or that the groups do not differ in their attitudes toward welfare. If we reject the null hypothesis, we would conclude that one or more of the group means is significantly different from one or both of the other group means. The results of this study are presented in Table 15.2.

The following steps are followed in a three-group analysis of variance:

Step 1. Using Eq. (15.2), we find that the total sum of squares is

$$SS_{tot} = 1216 - \frac{(158)^2}{27} = 291.41$$

Step 2. Using Eq. (15.5) for three groups, we find that the between-group sum of squares is

$$SS_{bet} = \frac{(46)^2}{9} + \frac{(78)^2}{9} + \frac{(34)^2}{9} - \frac{(158)^2}{27} = 114.96$$

Step 3. By employing Eq. (15.3) for three groups or by subtracting SS_{bet} from SS_{tot}, we obtain the within-group sum of squares:

$$SS_w = \left(292 - \frac{(46)^2}{9}\right) + \left(756 - \frac{(78)^2}{9}\right) + \left(168 - \frac{(34)^2}{9}\right) = 176.45$$

$$SS_w = SS_{tot} - SS_{bet} = 291.41 - 114.96 = 176.45$$

Table 15.2 Attitude toward welfare scores of three groups of respondents

(Middle-Class Sample) Group 1		(Welfare Sample) Group 2		(Lower-Middle-Class Sample) Group 3	
X_1	X_1^2	X_2	X_2^2	X_3	X_3^2
4	16	12	144	1	1
5	25	8	64	3	9
4	16	10	100	4	16
3	9	5	25	6	36
6	36	7	49	8	64
10	100	9	81	5	25
1	1	14	196	3	9
8	64	9	81	2	4
5	25	4	16	2	4
Σ 46	292	78	756	34	168
$N_1 = 9,$	$\bar{X}_1 = 5.11$	$N_2 = 9,$	$\bar{X}_2 = 8.67$	$N_3 = 9,$	$\bar{X}_3 = 3.78$

$$\Sigma X_{tot} = 46 + 78 + 34 = 158$$
$$\Sigma X_{tot}^2 = 292 + 756 + 168 = 1216$$
$$N = 27$$

Step 4. The between-group mean square is

$$df_{bet} = k - 1 = 2, \qquad \hat{s}_{bet}^2 = \frac{114.96}{2} = 57.48$$

Step 5. The within-group mean square is

$$df_w = N - k = 24, \qquad \hat{s}_w^2 = \frac{176.45}{24} = 7.35$$

Step 6. Using Eq. (15.11), we find that the value of F is

$$F = \frac{57.48}{7.35} = 7.82, \qquad df = 2, 24$$

To summarize these steps, we use the format shown in Table 15.3.

Table 15.3 Summary table for representing the relevant statistics in analysis of variance problems

Source of Variation	Sum of Squares	Degrees of Freedom	Mean Square*	F
Between groups	114.96	2	57.48	7.82
Within groups	176.45	24	7.35	
Total	291.41	26		

* In many texts the term *variance estimate* appears in this column.

By following the format recommended in Table 15.3, you have a final check upon your calculation of sum of squares and your assignment of degrees of freedom. Thus, $SS_{bet} + SS_w$ must equal SS_{tot}. The total degrees of freedom are found by

$$df_{tot} = N - 1 \qquad\qquad (15.12)$$

In the present example the number of degrees of freedom for the total is

$$df_{tot} = 27 - 1 = 26$$

15.7 The Interpretation of *F*

When we look up the *F* required for significance with 2 and 24 degrees of freedom, we find that an *F* of 3.40 or larger is significant at the 0.05 level. Since our *F* of 7.82 exceeds this value, we may conclude that the three-group means are not all estimates of a common population mean or that the groups' attitudes toward welfare differ. Now, do we stop at this point? After all, are we not interested in determining whether or not one of the three samples is more pro-welfare than the other two? The answer to the first question is negative, and the answer to the second is affirmative.

The truth of the matter is that our finding an overall significant *F*-ratio now permits us to investigate the following specific hypotheses, which will allow us to determine exactly which means are significantly different:

$$H_0: \mu_1 = \mu_2$$
$$H_0: \mu_1 = \mu_3$$
$$H_0: \mu_2 = \mu_3$$

In the absence of a significant *F*-ratio, any significant differences between specific comparisons would have to be regarded as representing a chance difference.

Over the past several years statisticians have developed a large number of tests that permit the researcher to investigate specific hypotheses concerning population parameters. Two broad classes of such tests exist:

1. **A priori or planned comparisons:** When comparisons are planned in advance of the investigation, an *a priori* test is appropriate. For *a priori* tests, it is not necessary that the overall *F*-ratio be significant.

2. **A posteriori comparisons:** When the comparisons are not planned in advance, an *a posteriori* test is appropriate.

In the present example we illustrate the use of an *a posteriori* test for making pairwise comparisons among means. Tukey (1953) has developed such a test, which he named the HSD (honestly significant difference) test. To use this test, the overall *F*-ratio must be significant. A difference between two means is significant at a given α-level if it equals or exceeds HSD, which is

$$HSD = q_\alpha \sqrt{\frac{\hat{s}_w^2}{N}} \qquad (15.13)$$

where

$\hat{s}_w^2$ = the within-group mean square

N = number of subjects in each group, and

q_α = tabled value for a given α-level found in Table K for df_w and k (number of means)

15.7.1 A Worked Example

Let's use the data from Section 15.5 to illustrate the application of the HSD test. We will assume α = 0.05 for testing the significance of the difference between each pair of means.

Step 1. Prepare a matrix showing the mean of each group and the differences between pairs of means. This is shown in Table 15.4.

Step 2. We must now determine the value of q. Given that the within sum of squares degrees of freedom equals 24 ($N - k = 27 - 3 = 24$), $k = 3$, and α = 0.05, we find by referring to Table K that $q_{0.05} = 3.53$.

Step 3. Find HSD by multiplying $q_{0.05}$ by $\sqrt{\hat{s}_w^2/N}$. The quantity $\hat{s}_w^2$ is found in Table 15.3 under within-group mean square. The N per group is 9. Thus

$$HSD = 3.53 \sqrt{\frac{7.35}{9}} = 3.53(0.90) = 3.18$$

Table 15.4 Differences among means

	$\overline{X}_1$ $\overline{X}_1 = 5.11$	$\overline{X}_2$ $\overline{X}_2 = 8.67$	$\overline{X}_3$ $\overline{X}_3 = 3.78$
$\overline{X}_1 = 5.11$	···	3.56	1.33
$\overline{X}_2 = 8.67$	···	···	4.89
$\overline{X}_3 = 3.78$	···	···	···

Step 4. Referring to Table 15.4, we find that the differences between $\overline{X}_1$ versus $\overline{X}_2$ and $\overline{X}_2$ versus $\overline{X}_3$ both exceed HSD = 3.18. We may therefore conclude that these differences are statistically significant at $\alpha = 0.05$. Since the group 2 mean (welfare sample) is significantly higher than the mean of the other two samples, we may conclude that the respondents' experience with welfare has influenced their attitude toward welfare in such a manner as to result in a high score relative to the other two samples.

Summary

We began this chapter with the observation that the researcher is frequently interested in conducting studies that are more extensive than the classical two-group design. However, when more than two groups are involved in a study, we increase the risk of making a type I error if we accept as significant any comparison that falls within the rejection region. In multigroup studies it is desirable to know whether or not there is an indication of an overall effect of the independent variable before we investigate specific hypotheses. The analysis of variance technique provides such a test.

In this chapter we presented an introduction to the complexities of analysis of variance. We showed that total sums of squares can be partitioned into two component sums of squares: the within-group and the between-group. These two component sums of squares provide us in turn with independent estimates of the population variance. A between-group mean square that is large, relative to the within-group mean square, suggests that the independent variable or experimental treatments are responsible for the large differences among the group means. The significance of the difference in mean squares is obtained by reference to the *F*-table (Table D, Appendix C).

When the overall *F*-ratio is found to be statistically significant, we are free to investigate specific hypotheses, employing a multiple-comparison test.

Terms to Remember

Analysis of variance A method, described initially by R. A. Fisher, for partitioning the sum of squares for experimental or survey data into known components of variation.

A posteriori comparisons Comparisons not planned in advance to investigate specific hypotheses concerning population parameters.

A priori or planned comparisons Comparisons planned in advance to investigate specific hypotheses concerning population parameters.

Between-group sum of squares (SS_{bet}) The sum of the sum of squares between each group.

***F*-ratio** The between-group mean square divided by the within-group mean square.

Homogeneity of variance   The condition that exists when two or more sample variances have been drawn from populations with equal variances.

Mean square   The sum of the squared deviations from the mean divided by degrees of freedom. Also known as the variance estimate.

One-way analysis of variance   Statistical analysis of various categories, groups, or levels of one independent (experimental) variable.

Total sum of squares (TSS)   Sum of the squared deviations from the overall mean.

Within-group sum of squares (SS_w)   The sum of the sum of squares within each group.

Exercises

1. Using the following data derived from the 10-year period 1955–1964, determine whether there is a significant difference at the 0.01 level in death rate among the various seasons. (*Note:* Assume death rates for any given year to be independent.)

Year	Winter	Spring	Summer	Fall
1955	9.8	9.0	8.8	9.4
1956	9.9	9.3	8.7	9.4
1957	9.8	9.3	8.8	10.3
1958	10.6	9.2	8.6	9.8
1959	9.9	9.4	8.7	9.4
1960	10.7	9.1	8.3	9.6
1961	9.7	9.2	8.8	9.5
1962	10.2	8.9	8.8	9.6
1963	10.9	9.3	8.7	9.5
1964	10.0	9.3	8.9	9.4

2. Conduct an HSD test, comparing the death rates of each season with every other season. Use the 0.01 level, two-tailed test for each comparison.

3. Professor Stevens negotiates contracts with ten different independent research organizations to compare the effectiveness of his marital satisfaction assessment instrument with that designed by another sociologist 10 years earlier. A significant difference (0.05 level) in favor of Professor Stevens' instrument is found in one of ten studies. He subsequently claims that independent research has demonstrated the superiority of his instrument over the instrument developed earlier. Criticize this conclusion.

4. A random sample of four interviewers associated with a large public opinion firm have completed four interviews each, and the time in minutes necessary to complete the interviews is indicated in the accompanying table. Test the null hypothesis that the interviewers require an equal amount of time to complete an interview.

Interviewer A	Interviewer B	Interviewer C	Interviewer D
28	34	29	22
19	23	24	31
30	20	33	18
25	16	21	24

5. A labor organization randomly selected three medium-sized businesses for a study of worker grievances. The number of official grievances during the past five calendar years was tabulated. Set up and test an appropriate null hypothesis that will assess the extent to which a particular business has significantly more grievances than the others. Conduct an HSD test comparing each business with every other business, using $\alpha = 0.05$.

Business A	Business B	Business C
42	52	38
36	48	44
47	43	33
43	49	35
38	51	32

6. If the F-ratio is less than 1.00, what do we conclude?

7. Determine whether there is a significant difference in the number of major work stoppages among the three geographical areas given (hypothetical data):

New England		Mid-Atlantic		Far West	
Maine	8	New York	7	Washington	9
New Hampshire	7	New Jersey	7	Oregon	7
Vermont	8	Pennsylvania	8	Nevada	6
Massachusetts	6.5	Delaware	7	California	7
Rhode Island	8	Maryland	7	Alaska	8
Connecticut	8	District of Columbia	7	Hawaii	5

8. Suppose a family stability measure were administered in four public high schools to a sample of 24 students who attend the schools. The following scores were obtained.

School A	School B	School C	School D
50	55	50	70
50	60	65	80
55	65	75	65
60	55	55	70
45	70	60	75
55	65	65	60

Note: (Low score = family instability)

Is there a significant difference in the family stability scores among the four groups of students?

9. A nutritional expert divides a sample of bicyclists into three groups. Group B is given a vitamin supplement and group C is given a diet of health foods. Group A is instructed to eat as they normally do. The expert subsequently records the number of minutes it takes each person to ride six miles.

A	B	C
15	14	13
16	13	12
14	15	11
17	16	14
15	14	11

Set up the appropriate hypothesis and conduct an analysis of variance.

10. For Exercise 9, determine which diet or diets are superior. Use $\alpha = 0.01$.

11. Banks A and B use two different forms for recording checks written. The police found that the following number of checks had bounced for 15 customers during the last 10 years.

Bank A	Bank B
4	2
8	0
3	1
0	2
3	1
5	1
3	3
4	3
0	4
5	3
2	1
4	4
6	0
2	5
0	0

Determine whether there is a significant difference between the number of checks bounced at each bank. Use $\alpha = 0.05$.

12. In 1988 three cities had the following numbers of speeches made by their top administrators.

Chicago	Houston	Cincinnati
2	9	13
16	2	39
28	1	25
2	10	9
21	13	3
2	1	0
2	12	13
19	0	27
0	1	5
4	2	1
8	7	2
6	7	4

Test the hypothesis that all three cities were drawn from the same population with respect to speeches by top administrators.

13. A graduate director in Department *A* claims that her program's students complete the doctorate more quickly than the students in three competing graduate programs. To test this claim, a statistician randomly sampled six students from each department who had completed the Ph.D. during the past 5 years. The results are in the accompanying table.

a) Is graduate director *A*'s claim supported by the data?

b) Compare the records of Departments *A* and *B*.

A	B	C	D
4.5	4.0	2.5	3.5
5.5	4.5	3.0	3.0
5.0	4.0	3.0	4.0
5.5	3.5	3.5	3.0
6.0	3.0	4.0	4.5
5.0	4.5	2.5	3.0

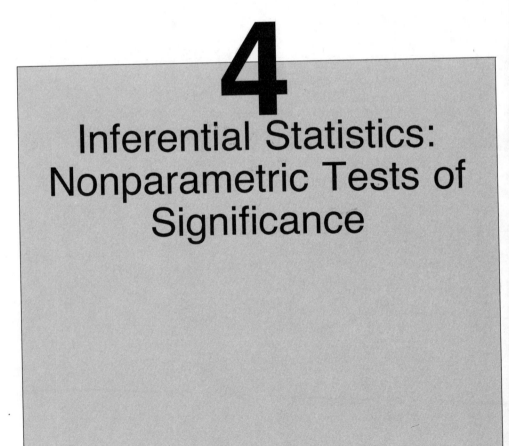

4

Inferential Statistics: Nonparametric Tests of Significance

16 Statistical Inference with Categorical Variables:
Chi Square and Related Measures
17 Statistical Inference: Ordinally Scaled
Variables

chapter 16

Statistical Inference with Categorical Variables: Chi Square and Related Measures

16.1 Introduction
16.2 The χ^2 One-Variable Case
16.3 The χ^2 Test of the Independence of Variables
16.4 Limitations in the Use of χ^2
16.5 Nominal Measures of Association Based on χ^2

16.1 Introduction

In recent years there has been a broadening in both scope and penetration of research in the social sciences. Much provocative and stimulating research has been initiated in such diverse areas as socialization, welfare rights, public opinion polling, groups processes, and social stratification. New variables have been added to the arsenal of the researcher, many of which do not lend themselves to traditional parametric statistical treatment, either because of the scales of measurement used or because of flagrant violations of the assumptions of these parametric tests.* For these reasons many new statistical techniques have been developed. In this chapter we present a few techniques from among over 40 nonparametric procedures, none of which require that we make any assumptions about the shape of the population distribution. Those presented in this chapter are appropriate for contingency tables (see Box 16.1).

Parametric techniques are usually preferable because of their greater sensitivity. This generalization is not true, however, when the underlying assumptions are seriously violated. Indeed, under certain circumstances (e.g., badly skewed distributions, particularly with small sample sizes) a nonparametric test may well be as powerful as its parametric counterpart. Consequently the

---

* Parametric statistics requires that the population from which the data have been drawn be normally distributed.

BOX 16.1

Dogs: The Best Friend of a Coronary Patient?

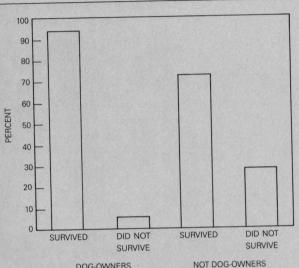

The cliché "Dog is man's best friend" is celebrated in both song and legend. Recent evidence suggests that the presence of a dog may also be therapeutic (Friedman, 1978). A group of coronary patients were studied for one year following their release from the hospital. Fifth-three of these patients owned dogs and 39 did not. One year later, 11 of the patients who did not own dogs had died, whereas only three of the dog owners succumbed.

In this study there are two nominal variables—status with respect to ownership of a pet dog and survival record after suffering a coronary heart disease. There are two values of each variable: owning vs. not owning a dog, and surviving vs. not surviving a heart condition. At the descriptive level, we could determine the percent of pet owners versus the percent of non-pet owners who survived and failed to survive at least one year following hospitalization. These results are summarized in the bar graph above.

At the inferential level, the data can be cast in the form of a 2 × 2 contin-

gency table. Reading downward, we see that fifty of fifty-three dog-owners survived at least one year. In contrast, only twenty-eight of thirty-nine non-dog-owners enjoyed a similar survival record. The appropriate test of significance—the chi squre test—permits us to ascertain whether or not dog ownership and survival are related.

2 × 2 contingency table showing number of dog-owners and number of non-dog-owners who survived at least one year following onset of a coronary disease

Survival Status	Status of Dog Ownership		
	Owners	Not Owners	Totals
Survived one year	50	28	78
Did not survive	3	11	14
Totals	53	39	92

Source: Friedman, E. "Pet Ownership and Coronary Heart Disease Patient Survival." *Circulation*, 1978, **168**, 57–58.

researcher is frequently faced with the difficult choice of a statistical test appropriate for his or her data.

16.2 The χ^2 One-Variable Case

Following a course in research methods, 86 nursing students completed a course-evaluation questionnaire that was administered to the entire class (Van Bree, 1981). One item in the questionnaire dealt with the importance of research to the nursing profession. The observed frequencies are presented in Table 16.1.

This is the type of problem for which the χ^{2}* **one-variable test** is ideally suited. In single-variable applications the χ^2 test has been described as a **"goodness-of-fit" technique:** It permits us to determine whether or not a significant difference exists between the *observed* number of cases falling into each category and the *expected* number of cases, based on the null hypothesis. In other words, it permits us to answer the question, "How well does our observed distribution fit the theoretical distribution?"

If the responses from the 86 students were randomly distributed across all five possible response categories, we would theoretically *expect* that approximately 17 students would choose each category since $86/5 = 17.2$. The observed distribution of responses that was presented in Table 16.1 will be contrasted with the expected distribution (Table 16.2). What we require, then, is a null hypothesis that allows us to specify the expected frequencies in each category, and subsequently to test this null hypothesis. The null hypothesis may be tested by

$$\chi^2 = \sum_{i=1}^{k} \frac{(f_0 - f_e)^2}{f_e} \qquad (16.1)$$

where

f_0 = the observed number in a given category

f_e = the expected number in that category, and

$\sum_{i=1}^{k}$ = directs us to sum this ratio over all k categories

In our example the null hypothesis would be that there is an equal preference for each response category; that is, $86/5 = 17.2$ is the expected frequency in each category (Table 16.2).

---

* The symbol χ^2 will be used to denote the test of significance as well as the quantity obtained from applying the test to observed frequencies, whereas the word *chi square* will refer to the theoretical chi-square distribution.

Table 16.1 Contingency table showing observed frequencies

	Student Response				
Item	Strongly Agree	Agree	Undecided	Disagree	Strongly Disagree
Research is important to nursing profession	34	41	7	3	1

Source: N. S. Van Bree. "Undergraduate Research." *Nursing Outlook*, January 1981, 39–41.

Table 16.2 Contingency table showing expected frequencies

	Student Response				
Item	Strongly Agree	Agree	Undecided	Disagree	Strongly Disagree
Research is important to the nursing profession	17.2	17.2	17.2	17.2	17.2

As is readily apparent from Eq. (16.1), if there is close agreement between the observed frequencies and expected frequencies, the resulting χ^2 will be small, leading to a failure to reject the null hypothesis. In fact, if the observed and expected values for all cells in the table are equal, χ^2 will reach its lower limit of 0.* As the discrepancy $(f_0 - f_e)$ increases, the value of χ^2 increases. The larger the χ^2 is, the more likely we are to reject the null hypothesis.

Substituting the observed and expected values into Eq. (16.1), we find χ^2 to be 82.372 as shown in Table 16.3.

In studying the Student's t-ratio (Section 14.5), we saw that the sampling distributions of t varied as a function of degrees of freedom. The same is true for χ^2. However, assignments of degrees of freedom with the Student's t-ratio are based on N, whereas for χ^2 the degrees of freedom are a function of the number of cells (k). In the one-variable case, df $= k - 1$ since the marginal total is fixed, only $k - 1$ cells are free to vary. Given that the total is 86, as soon as four cells or categories are filled, the fifth is completely determined. Thus, there are 4 degrees of freedom.

In the one-variable case df $= k - 1$. Table B, Appendix C, lists the critical values of χ^2 for various α-levels. If the obtained χ^2 value *exceeds* the critical value at a given probability level, the null hypothesis may be rejected at that level of significance. Hence, we are only concerned with the right-hand tail of the distribution as all χ^2 tests are one-tailed.

In this example $k = 5$. Therefore, df $= 4$. Employing $\alpha = 0.01$, we find that Table B indicates that a χ^2 value of 13.277 or greater is required for

---

* The upper limit of χ^2 is $N(k - 1)$ where N is the total number of cases and k the number of rows or columns in the table, whichever is smaller. For example, in a 3×3 table with 100 cases, the maximum value of χ^2 would be 200 because $100(3 - 1) = 200$.

Table 16.3 Computation of chi square

f_0	f_e	$f_0 - f_e$	$(f_0 - f_e)^2$	$(f_0 - f_e)^2/f_e$
34	17.2	16.8	282.24	16.409
41	17.2	23.8	566.44	32.933
7	17.2	−10.2	104.04	6.049
3	17.2	−14.2	201.64	11.723
1	17.2	−16.2	262.44	15.258
86	86.0		$\chi^2 =$	82.372

significance. Since our obtained value of 82.372 is greater than 13.277, we may reject the null hypothesis (see Fig. 16.1) and assert instead that each response category was not equally preferred. Incidentally, we are free to investigate any form of hypothetical distribution suggested by prior research or theoretical considerations. If we had prior reason to suspect that the distribution might be 0.25, 0.25, 0.20, 0.20, 0.10, we could investigate this H_0 by multiplying each hypothesized proportion by N in order to obtain the expected frequency in each cell.

Before proceeding, we should note that the shape of the theoretical χ^2 distribution is determined by the degrees of freedom. Figure 16.2 shows the distribution for 1, 2, and 10 degrees of freedom.

As is apparent in Figure 16.2, for all degrees of freedom the χ^2 distribution is skewed to the right, with those curves associated with large degrees of freedom reaching far to the right before approaching the horizontal axis, which designates the value of χ^2. For example, from Table B we see that the critical region for a test, given $\alpha = 0.01$ and degrees of freedom equal to 1, begins at 6.635. By following the 0.01 column down, you will see that as we deal with greater degrees of freedom (i.e., more cells), the corresponding value of χ^2 from Table B that must be exceeded to reject the null hypothesis increases until it reaches 50.892 for 30 degrees of freedom.

Figure 16.1 Sampling distributions of χ^2 for 4 degrees of freedom.

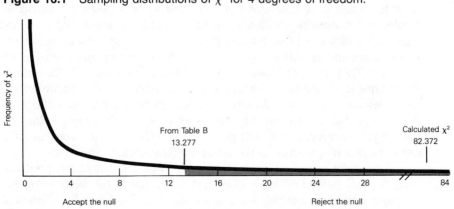

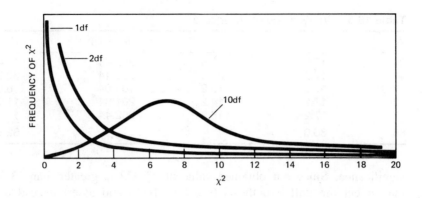

Figure 16.2 χ^2 distribution for 1, 2, and 10 degrees of freedom.

16.3 The χ^2 Test of the Independence of Variables

So far in this chapter we have been concerned with the one-variable case. In practice, we do not encounter the one-variable case very frequently when using categorical variables. More often we ask questions concerning the interrelationships between and among variables. For example, we may ask, "Is there a difference in the crime rate of children coming from different socioeconomic backgrounds? (In other words, is crime rate independent of socioeconomic background, or does it depend in part on the children's backgrounds?)" Or, "If we are conducting an opinion poll, can we determine whether there is a difference between the opinions of males and females about a given issue? (Stated another way, does the opinion on a given issue depend to any extent on the gender of the respondent?)"

There are but two examples of problems for which the χ^2 technique can be used. You could undoubtedly extend this list to include many campus activites, such as attitudes of fraternity and sorority members versus nonfraternity and nonsorority students toward certain basic issues (e.g., cheating on exams), or differences in grading practices among professors in various academic departments. All of these problems have certain characteristics in common: (1) They deal with two or more variables in which (2) the data consist of a frequency count that is tabulated and placed in the appropriate cells. These examples also share an additional and more important characteristic: (3) There is no immediately obvious way to assign expected frequency values to each category. However, as we will point out shortly, we must consequently base our expected frequencies on the observed frequencies themselves.

Let's take a look at another example. Political scientists, political sociologists, and politicians have long been interested in the relationship between religious affiliation and political party affiliation. Traditionally, Catholics have aligned themselves with the Democratic party, whereas Protestants were more likely to support Republican candidates. The following study of 550 registered voters in California will allow us to test the null hypothesis that Catholics are no more likely to affiliate with either party than are Protestants (see Table 16.4).

We will now apply a test of significance. In formal statistical terms:

1. *Null hypothesis (H_0):* There is no difference in political party affiliation between Catholics and Protestants.

2. *Alternative hypothesis (H_1):* There is a difference in political party affiliation between Catholics and Protestants.

3. *Statistical test:* Since we are assuming that religious and political affiliations are independent and the data are in terms of frequencies in discrete categories, the χ^2 test of independence is the appropriate statistical test.

4. *Significance level:* $\alpha = 0.05$.

5. *Sampling distribution:* The sampling distribution is the chi-square distribution with df $= (r - 1)(c - 1)$. Since marginal totals are fixed, the frequency of only one cell is free to vary; that is, once one cell value is known in a 2 × 2 table, the other three cell values are determined. Therefore, we have a 1-degree-of-freedom situation. The general rule for finding df in the two-variable case is $(r - 1)(c - 1)$, in which $r =$ number of rows and $c =$ number of columns. Thus, in the present example df $= (2 - 1)(2 - 1) = 1$.

6. *Critical region:* Table B in Appendix C shows that for df $= 1$, $\alpha = 0.05$, the critical region consists of all values of $\chi^2 \geq 3.841$. Thus, χ^2 is calculated from Eq. (16.1).

$$\chi^2 = \sum_{i=1}^{k} \frac{(f_0 - f_e)^2}{f_e}$$

Table 16.4   2 × 2 contingency table showing the relationship between religious and political affiliation

	Religious Affiliation		
Political Affiliation	c_1 *Catholic*	c_2 *Protestant*	Total
Democrat r_1	*a* 125	*b* 225	350
Republican r_2	*c* 75	*d* 125	200
Total	200	350	550

The main problem now is to decide on a basis for determining the expected cell frequencies. Recall from Chapter 12, Eq. (12.9), that "the probability of the simultaneous or successive occurrence of two events is the product of the separate probabilities of each event." In Table 16.4 the probability of a respondent in the total sample being Catholic is 200/550 or 0.364 and the probability of a respondent being a Democrat is 350/550 or 0.636; therefore, the joint probability of being a Catholic and a Democrat (see cell *a*) is (0.364)(0.636) or 0.2315. Multiplying 0.2315 by our total sample size of 550 results in an expected frequency in cell *a* of 127.3. You could proceed further in this manner and calculate the expected frequency for the remaining cells. However, there is a simple rule that may be followed in determining expected frequency of a given cell: You multiply the two marginal frequencies common to that cell and divide by N.

Let's again concentrate on cell *a*. The two marginal totals common to cell *a* are row 1 marginal and column 1 marginal. If the null hypothesis is correct and political affiliation is independent of religious affiliation, we would expect the same proportion of respondents who are Catholics to affiliate with the Democratic party as would those who are Protestants. Since 200 of the total sample of 550 are Catholic, we would expect that (200 × 350)/550 would be found in cell *a*. This figure comes to 127.3, a value identical to the expected frequency we calculated utilizing the more cumbersome *joint-probability method*.

Table 16.5 presents the observed data, with the expected cell frequencies within parentheses. Incidentally, you may have noted that the four expected frequencies total 550 and that the expected frequencies for a given column or row sum to the respective observed column or row marginal.

It can be seen in Table 16.5 that 125 of the 200 Catholics claimed an affiliation with the Democratic party and that 225 of the 350 Protestants were also affiliated with the Democrats. Do these data indicate that political affiliation is independent of religious affiliation? Table 16.6 summarizes the necessary calculations.

Table 16.5 Relationship between religious and political affiliation (*expected frequencies within parentheses*)

Political Affiliation	Religious Affiliation		Total
	Catholic	*Protestant*	
Democrat	*a* 125 (127.3)	*b* 225 (222.7)	350
Republican	*c* 75 (72.7)	*d* 125 (127.3)	200
Total	200	350	550

Table 16.6 Computation of chi square

Cell	f_o	f_e	$f_o - f_e$	$(f_o - f_e)^2$	$(f_o - f_e)^2/f_e$
a	125	127.3	−2.3	5.29	0.04
b	225	222.7	2.3	5.29	0.02
c	75	72.7	2.3	5.29	0.07
d	125	127.3	−2.3	5.29	0.04
	550	550.0			$\chi^2 = 0.17$

Since the χ^2 value of 0.17 is less than the value of 3.84 (1df, $\alpha = 0.05$) from Table B required for significance at the 0.05 level, we may not reject H_0. In other words, we must conclude that political party affiliation and religious affiliation are independent; that is, there is no difference in political party affiliation between Catholics and Protestants.

In research we often find that we have more than two subgroups within a nominal class. For example, we might have three categories in one scale and four in another, resulting in a 3 × 4 contingency table. The procedure for obtaining the expected frequencies is the same as the one for the 2 × 2 contingency table. Of course, the degrees of freedom will be greater than 1 (e.g., 3 × 4 contingency table, df = 6). See Case Example 16.1 for an example of a 3 × 2 table.

16.4 Limitations in the Use of χ^2

A fundamental assumption in the use of χ^2 is that each observation or frequency is independent of all other observations. Consequently, you may not make several observations on the same individual and treat each as though it were independent of all the other observations. Such an error produces what is referred to as an **inflated** N since you are counting or including some people more than once; that is, you are treating the data as though you had a greater number of independent observations than you actually have. This error is extremely serious and may easily lead to the rejection of the null hypothesis when it is in fact true.

Consider the following hypothetical example. Imagine that you are a student in a sociology course and as a class project you decide to poll the student body to determine whether male and female students differ in their opinions on some issue of contemporary significance. Each of 15 members of the class is asked to obtain replies from 10 respondents, 5 male and 5 female. The results are listed in Table 16.7 in which the expected cell frequencies are included in parentheses.

Assuming $\alpha = 0.05$, we find that the critical region consists of all the values of $\chi^2 \geq 3.84$. Since the obtained χ^2 of 10.71 > 3.84, you reject the null hypothesis of no difference in the opinions of male and female students

Table 16.7 Response to question

Response to Question	Sex Male	Sex Female	Total
Approve	30 (40)	50 (40)	80
Disapprove	45 (35)	25 (35)	70
Total	75	75	150

$$\chi^2 = 10.71$$

on the issue in question. You conclude instead that approval of the issue is dependent on the sex of the respondent.

After completing the study, you discover that a number of students were inadvertently polled as many as two or three times by different members of the class. Consequently, the frequencies within the cells are not independent since some individuals had contributed as many as two or three responses. In a reanalysis of the data, in which only one frequency per respondent was permitted, we obtained the results shown in Table 16.8.

Note that now the obtained χ^2 of 2.72 < 3.84; thus, you must accept H_0. The failure to achieve independence of responses resulted in a serious error in the original conclusion. Incidentally, you should note that the requirement of independence within a cell or condition is basic to *all* statistical tests. We have mentioned that specifically in connection with the χ^2 test because violations may be very subtle and not easily recognized.

An equally important limitation of χ^2 stems from the fact that the value of χ^2 is proportional to the sample size. For example, if the sample in Table 16.8 were doubled to 240 and the observed frequencies were increased proportionately (i.e., 56, 64, 74, and 46) χ^2 would equal 5.44 rather than 2.72. Consequently, in spite of the fact that the relationship has *not* changed, we would reject rather than accept the H_0. For this reason many social scientists prefer to avoid χ^2 when dealing with large samples because the results can be

Table 16.8 Response to question

Response to Question	Sex Male	Sex Female	Total
Approve	28 (32.5)	32 (27.5)	60
Disapprove	37 (32.5)	23 (27.5)	60
Total	65	55	120

$$\chi^2 = 2.72$$

CASE EXAMPLE 16.1

The Successful Women

Table 16.9 Relationship between FOS and educational level

Educational Level	FOS	No-FOS	Total
Less than BA	60	80	140
BA degree	60	10	70
Some graduate school	100	10	110
Column totals	220	110	320

Table 16.10 Expected cell frequencies in the study of the relationship between FOS and educational level

Educational Level	FOS	No-FOS	Total
Less than BA	96.25	43.75	140
BA degree	48.13	21.87	70
Some graduate school	75.62	34.38	110
Column totals	220.00	100.00	320

$$\chi^2 = \frac{(60 - 96.25)^2}{96.25} + \frac{(80 - 43.75)^2}{43.75} + \cdots + \frac{(10 - 34.38)^2}{34.38}$$

$$= 13.65 + 30.04 + 2.93 + 6.44 + 7.86 + 17.29$$

$$= 78.21$$

$$df = (r - 1)(c - 1) = 2$$

With the relatively recent changes in the traditional female sex roles, much attention has been directed to the possible impact of these changes on various aspects of the behavior and emotions of contemporary women. In this hypothetical study 320 women completed Horner's scale of fear of success (FOS), as well as other questionnaires aimed at tapping attitudes about sex-role traditionalism, political beliefs, and educational levels.

In one facet of the study the women were subdivided into two groups—those with fear of success (FOS) and those without fear of success (no-FOS). They were further subdivided in terms of educational level. The results are summarized in Table 16.9.

Let's test the null hypothesis that there is no difference in fear of success by educational level against the alternative hypothesis that there is a difference. We use $\alpha = 0.05$.

The expected cell frequencies are shown in Table 16.10.

The critical value at $\alpha = 0.05$ with df = 2 is 5.991. Since obtained χ^2 exceeds this value, we may reject H_0 and assert H_1. Examination of the data reveals a clear-cut tendency for fear of success to increase with increasing educational level. Note that this study is not a true experiment, but is more in the nature of a correlational investigation. Although we can conclude that there is a statistically significant increase in FOS with educational level, we cannot make a strong statement of causality. Several possibilities present themselves, one of which is that the more educated women are employed at levels that put them into competition with men, the more they may demand of themselves.

Source: Adapted from Carmen M. Caballero, Patricia Giles, and Phillip Shaver (1975), "Sex-Role Traditionalism and Fear of Success," *Sex Roles,* **1** (4), 319–326.

very misleading. Indeed, it is difficult not to reject the H_0 when the sample size is over 1000 cases!

With small N's or when the expected proportion in any cell is small, the approximation of the sample statistics to the chi-square distribution may not be very close. A rule that has been generally adopted, in the 1-degree-of-freedom situation, is that the *expected frequency* in all cells should be equal to or greater than 5. When df > 1, the expected frequency should be equal to or greater than 5 in at least 80% of the cells. When these requirements are not met, other statistical tests are available. (See Siegel and Castellan, 1988.)

When a contingency table is larger than 2 × 2, it is possible to collapse rows or columns in such a manner as to increase the frequencies within the resulting cells. Such a practice is used widely in the social sciences with the understanding that the categories that are combined logically fit together and that the procedure is not intended to increase or decrease the value of χ^2.

16.5 Nominal Measures of Association Based on χ^2

We learned in Section 16.4 that the value of χ^2 is directly proportional to the sample size. This characteristic of χ^2 plus the observation that $\chi^2 = 0$ when two variables are statistically independent led to the development of the **phi coefficient,** which is used primarily with 2 × 2 tables.

$$\phi = \sqrt{\frac{\chi^2}{N}} \qquad (16.2)$$

or

$$\phi^2 = \frac{\chi^2}{N} \qquad (16.3)$$

Table 16.11

		Sex	
Vote	Male	Female	Total
Yes	50	0	50
No	0	50	50
Total	50	50	N = 100

$$\chi^2 = \frac{(50 - 25)^2}{25} + \frac{(0 - 25)^2}{25} + \frac{(0 - 25)^2}{25} + \frac{(50 - 25)^2}{25}$$

$$= 25 + 25 + 25 + 25$$

$$= 100$$

Using Eq. (16.2) and (16.3):

$$\phi = \sqrt{\frac{100}{100}} = 1 \quad \text{and} \quad \phi^2 = \frac{100}{100} = 1$$

Table 16.12

		Sex	
Vote	Male	Female	Total
Yes	0	50	50
No	50	0	50
Total	50	50	N = 100

$$\chi^2 = \frac{(0 - 25)^2}{25} + \frac{(50 - 25)^2}{25} + \frac{(50 - 25)^2}{25} + \frac{(0 - 25)^2}{25}$$

$$= 25 + 25 + 25 + 25$$

$$= 100$$

$$\phi = \sqrt{\frac{100}{100}} = 1 \quad \text{and} \quad \phi^2 = \frac{100}{100} = 1$$

For any table in which either the number of rows or columns equals two, phi ranges from 0 when the variables are independent to 1 when the variables are perfectly related.* Phi is sometimes referred to as a measure of the degree of diagonal concentration; hence, when two diagonally opposite cells are both empty as in the following example, phi equals 1, as is demonstrated in Tables 16.11 and 16.12. As is the case with the other two measures of association to

---

* The maximum value of phi exceeds 1 when a table contains more than two rows and two columns.

Table 16.13 Educational attainment by political activism

| | Educational Attainment | | | |
	Low	Moderate	High	Total
Political Activism				
High	5	10	35	50
Moderate	15	30	5	50
Low	30	10	10	50
Total	50	50	50	N = 150

$$\chi^2 = \frac{(5 - 16.7)^2}{16.7} + \frac{(10 - 16.7)^2}{16.7} + \frac{(35 - 16.7)^2}{16.7} + \frac{(15 - 16.7)^2}{16.7}$$

$$+ \frac{(30 - 16.7)^2}{16.7} + \frac{(5 - 16.7)^2}{16.7} + \frac{(30 - 16.7)^2}{16.7} + \frac{(10 - 16.7)^2}{16.7}$$

$$+ \frac{(10 - 16.7)^2}{16.7}$$

$$= 8.2 + 2.7 + 20.1 + 0.2 + 10.6 + 8.2 + 10.6 + 2.7 + 2.7$$

$$= 66.0$$

$$C = \sqrt{\frac{\chi^2}{\chi^2 + N}} = \sqrt{\frac{66.0}{66.0 + 150}} = 0.55$$

be discussed, phi only requires nominal-level data and provides us with a measure of the strength, but not the direction, of association since the sign of phi will always be positive. By examining the percentage distribution of cases in the cells, we can, of course, determine the pattern of the relationship (See Chapter 8).

The **contingency coefficient** was developed by Karl Pearson primarily for use with square tables having more than two rows and columns, for example, 3 × 3 or 4 × 4.

$$C = \sqrt{\frac{\chi^2}{\chi^2 + N}} \qquad (16.4)$$

The contingency coefficient equals 0 when the variables are independent; however, its maximum value is always less than 1 and is determined by the number of rows and columns in the table.* C has been calculated for the data in Table 16.13.

---

* The maximum value for a square table (e.g., 2 × 2, 3 × 3, etc.) is calculated using the equation $\sqrt{(k - 1)/k}$ when k equals the number of rows or columns, whichever is less. For a 2 × 2 table, the maximum value would be $\sqrt{(2 - 1)/2} = \sqrt{1/2} = 0.707$, and for a 3 × 3 table, the maximum value would be $\sqrt{(3 - 1)/3} = 0.816$.

In this instance $C = 0.55$, and we can conclude that there is a moderately strong relationship between educational attainment and political activism since the maximum value for C with a 3×3 table is 0.816. By examining Table 16.13, we can also see that the respondents who have completed higher levels of education tend to be more politically active than those respondents who have had less education.

A disadvantage of the contingency coefficient, in addition to its interpretability when the variables are neither independent nor perfectly related, is the difficulty of comparing contingency coefficients for tables of unequal size (differing numbers of rows and columns). The fluctuation of its maximum value has led to the development of **Cramer's V,** a third measure of association for nominal-level data based on χ^2.

Cramer's V can be used with square and nonsquare tables of any size, and it ranges from 0 when the variables are independent to 1 when they are perfectly related.

$$V = \sqrt{\frac{\chi^2}{N \cdot \text{Minimum} (r - 1 \text{ or } c - 1)}} \qquad (16.5)$$

The denominator of Cramer's V is calculated by multiplying N times the smaller of the two quantities, $r - 1$ or $c - 1$. Calculating V for Table 16.13, we find it to equal 0.47 versus 0.55 for C. This example should help clarify the problems of interpreting ϕ, C, and V. They are not equivalent measures with one limited exception.*

$$V = \sqrt{\frac{66.0}{150(3 - 1)}} = \sqrt{0.220} = 0.47$$

Cramer's V is the most versatile of the three measures of association since its range is always 0 to 1 and it can be used with a table of any dimension. It does share limitations with the phi and contingency coefficients. Cramer's V does not allow for a PRE interpretation, nor does it provide an indication of the direction of relationship.

Summary

In this chapter we have discussed two tests of significance used with categorical variables, that is, the χ^2 one-variable test and the χ^2 two-variable test.

The χ^2 one-variable test has been described as a "goodness-of-fit" technique, permitting us to determine whether or not a significant difference exists between the *observed* number of cases appearing in each category and the expected number of cases specified under the null hypothesis.

---

* $V^2 = \phi^2$ in a $2 \times k$ table.

The χ^2 test of independence of variables may be used to determine whether two variables are related or independent. If the χ^2 value is significant, we may conclude that the variables are interdependent or related.

We discussed three limitations on the use of the χ^2 test. In the 1-degree-of-freedom situation, the expected frequency should equal or exceed 5 to permit the use of the χ^2 test. When df > 1, the expected frequency in 80% of the cells should equal or exceed 5. A second, and most important, restriction is that the frequency counts must be independent of one another. Failure to meet this requirement results in an error known as the inflated N and may well lead to the rejection of the null hypothesis when it is true (type I error). A third limitation is that χ^2 is directly proportional to N and hence can be misleading.

Three nominal measures of association were discussed, including the phi coefficient, the contingency coefficient, and Cramer's V.

Terms to Remember

Contingency coefficient   A nominal measure of association based on χ^2 and used primarily for square tables.

Cramer's V   A nominal measure of association based on χ^2 suitable for tables of any dimension.

Inflated N   An error produced whenever several observations are made on the same individual and treated as though they were independent observations.

One-variable test ("goodness-of-fit" technique)   A test of whether or not a significant difference exists between the *observed* number of cases falling into each category and the *expected* number of cases, based on the null hypothesis.

Phi coefficient   A nominal measure of association based on χ^2 used with 2×2 tables.

Exercises

1. The student newspaper staff polled a sample of their readers concerning satisfaction with the paper's editorial policy. The 120 student responses are summarized below. Calculate χ^2 and assume that $\alpha = 0.05$. Do the student responses differ significantly from our theoretical expectation of a random distribution?

Very Satisfied	Satisfied	Unsatisfied	Very Unsatisfied
30	65	15	10

2. Let's suppose that you are a demographer conducting research on the number of children preferred by American couples. Research 5 years ago

in 1984 indicated that 16% of the couples polled preferred no children, 65% preferred one or two children, and 19% preferred three or four children (hypothetical data). Realizing that attitudes may have changed over the past 5 years, you conduct a national study of 600 couples selected by an accepted sampling technique. The distributions for 1984 and 1989 are presented here. Using χ^2, test the null hypothesis that the preferred number of children has not changed from 1984 to 1989. Assume that the 1984 distribution is expected, the 1989 distribution is observed, and $\alpha = 0.01$.

Expected Frequencies (1984)				
	Preferred Number of Children			
	0	*1 or 2*	*3 or 4*	*Marginal Total*
Number of couples preferring	96	390	114	600

Observed Frequencies (1989)				
	Preferred Number of Children			
	0	*1 or 2*	*3 or 4*	*Marginal Total*
Number of couples preferring	120	400	80	600

3. Given the following table in which $N = 80$ and only the marginal values of shown, enter the cell values that would yield a χ^2 of 0. Calculate χ^2 and confirm its value. Calculate ϕ.

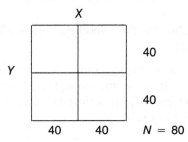

4. Calculate χ^2 for the following tables and assume $\alpha = 0.05$. Calculate ϕ. Discuss.

a)

	X	
Y	25	15
	15	25

b)

	X	
Y	30	10
	10	30

c)

	X	
Y	40	0
	0	40

5. Interviews were conducted with 70 homosexual and 110 heterosexual males concerning their fear of contracting AIDS. State an appropriate null hypothesis, assume $\alpha = 0.01$, and test the hypothesis using χ^2. Also, calculate Cramer's V and percentage down.

		Sexual Orientation		
		Homosexual Males	Heterosexual Males	
Fear of AIDS	Great	40	15	55
	Moderate	20	35	55
	Low	10	60	70
		70	110	

6. The World Series may last from four to seven games. During the period 1922 to 1979, the distribution of the number of games played per series was as follows:

Number of games	4	5	6	7
Frequency of occurrence	11	11	11	25

For these data, test the hypothesis that each number of games is equally likely to occur.

7. Suppose that a recording company is interested in a type of cover to put on an album. It sends the same record with three different covers to a store. At the end of a month it has found that the following number of albums have been sold:

Type A Cover	Type B Cover	Type C Cover
41	50	20

Is the company in a position to determine which type of cover it should use?

8. Marital status and depression has long been a topic of interest for social scientists. Given the following data, calculate χ^2, an appropriate measure of association and interpret the results if $\alpha = 0.05$.

	Marital Status		
Depression	*Married*	*Never Married*	*Formerly Married*
High	20	15	15
Moderate	26	12	10
Low	18	9	8

9. A researcher has reported that a very strong, positive relationship exists between religious affiliation and race. Critique. (*Hint:* Consider the level of measurement.)

10. Professor Stevens has the following data that do not meet the assumptions of χ^2 and must be altered. Combine categories in a defensible manner and calculate χ^2. Interpret.

	Country of Birth					
Educational Attainment	*United States*	*Germany*	*England*	*Vietnam*	*Thailand*	*Korea*
Graduate School	6	4	3	3	1	1
College	8	4	3	2	2	2
High School	9	2	5	4	3	0
Grade School	4	3	2	1	3	4

11. A study was conducted to determine if there is a relationship between socioeconomic status and attitudes toward a new urban renewal program. The results are listed in the accompanying table.

	Socioeconomic Status	
Attitude	*Lower*	*Middle*
Approve	90	60
Disapprove	200	100

Set up this study in formal statistical terms and draw the appropriate conclusion.

12. Why does $\chi^2 = 0$ when two variables are independent?

13. Discuss the ways in which ϕ, C, and V are unique with respect to each other and similar to each other.

14. In a study concerned with preferences of schools for their children 100 people in a high-income group and 200 people in a lower-income group were interviewed. The results of their choices follow.

Preference Stated	Upper-Income Group	Lower-Income Group
Private, nonreligious	36	84
Private, religious	39	51
Public	16	44
Have no preference	9	21

What conclusions would you draw from these data?

15. Evidence presented in Box 16.1 suggests that the ownership of a dog may be therapeutic. In a study of status with respect to ownership of a pet dog and survival record after suffering coronary heart disease, the following data were reported. Test the null hypothesis that ownership of a dog is unrelated to survival.

Survival Status	Status of Dog Ownership		
	Owners	Not owners	Total
Survived One Year	50	28	78
Did Not Survive	3	11	14
Total	53	39	92

16. In the preceding exercise we found a significant relationship between dog ownership and survival following coronary heart disease. Critique the conclusion, "Dog ownership leads to better survival rates of coronary victims," in the light of what we know about correlation and causation.

17. Peter Benson and his colleagues (1976) explored the effects of physical attractiveness on receiving help. In one part of the study the researchers tabulated the number of males helping when the applicant was an attractive or unattractive female. These results are presented in the table that follows.

Helping Response	Characteristics of Target		Total
	Attractive	Unattractive	
Helped	52	35	87
Did not help	62	71	133

a) What is the appropriate test of significance?

b) Conduct a test of significance using $\alpha = 0.05$.

18. The following table shows the number of female subjects helping an attractive or an unattractive male.

Helping Response	Characteristics of Target		Total
	Attractive	Unattractive	
Helped	17	13	30
Did not help	24	27	51

    a) What is the appropriate test of significance?

    b) Conduct a test of significance using $\alpha = 0.05$.

19. Infections acquired while the patient is hospitalized are a continuing problem in hospitals. One study traced the mortality rates of patients with urinary-tract infections who had a catheter inserted by medical doctors, by registered nurses, and by others. The results are shown in the following table.

Catheter Inserted By	Survived	Died	Total
Medical doctor	510	11	521
Registered nurse	542	38	580
Others	345	28	373

Source: From R. Platt, B. F. Polk, B. Murdock, and B. Rosner, "Mortality Associated with Nosocomial Urinary-Tract Infection." *New England Journal of Medicine"* (1982), **307**, 637–641.

    a) Find the percentages across. Which group experienced the highest mortality rates?

    b) What is the appropriate test of significance?

    c) Using $\alpha = 0.01$, test H_0 that mortality is independent of the professional inserting the catheter.

chapter **17**

Statistical Inference: Ordinally Scaled Variables

17.1 Introduction
17.2 Mann-Whitney *U*-Test
17.3 Nonparametric Tests Involving Correlated Samples
17.4 The Sign Test
17.5 Wilcoxon Matched-Pairs Signed-Rank Test

17.1 Introduction

In the previous chapter we pointed out that the researcher is frequently faced with a choice as to which statistical test is appropriate for the data. You will recall that this was not really a problem in relation to categorical variables because nonparametric tests alone are suitable for nominally scaled data.

In this chapter we discuss several statistical techniques that are frequently employed as alternatives to parametric tests.

Before examining them in detail, let's look at a brief summary of the situations in which their use is appropriate.

Mann-Whitney U: Used in two-group situations in which the groups are independent, that is, the respondents are not matched in any way nor are before-after measures involved. The respondents are randomly assigned to the experimental conditions. The scale of the independent measures is either ordinal or interval/ratio. If interval/ratio, the Mann-Whitney U is used as a substitute for Student's t-ratio when the validity of the assumption of normality is questionable.

Sign Test: Used in two-group correlated samples designs, before-after measures are employed or pairs of respondents are matched on some basis. Although the underlying scale of the dependent measures is ordinal, we are unwilling to assume that the scores have any precise quantitative properties.

We ignore the amount of difference between scores and concentrate only on the direction of the differences (larger than or smaller than).

Wilcoxon Matched-Pairs Signed-Rank Test: Used in matched-pairs two-group designs in which we assume the scores are quantitative and that the differences in scores achieve an ordinal level of measurement, that is, the differences in scores may legitimately be ranked from smallest to largest or vice versa.

17.2 Mann-Whitney *U*-Test

The **Mann-Whitney *U*-test** is one of the most powerful nonparametric statistical tests, since it utilizes most of the quantitative information that is inherent in the data. It is most commonly employed as an alternative to Student's *t*-ratio when the measurements fail to achieve interval scaling or when the researcher wishes to avoid the assumptions of the parametric counterpart.

Imagine that we have drawn two independent samples of N_1 and N_2 observations. The null hypothesis is that both samples are drawn from populations with the same distributions. The two-tailed alternative hypothesis, against which we test the null hypothesis, is that the parent populations from which the samples were drawn are different. Imagine further that we combine the $N_1 + N_2$ observations and assign a rank of 1 to the smallest value, a rank of 2 to the next smallest value, and continue until we have assigned ranks to all the observations. Let's refer to our two groups as E and C, respectively. If we were to count the number of times each C precedes each E in the ranks, we would expect under the null hypothesis that it would equal the number of times each E precedes a C. In other words, if there is no difference between the two groups, the order of Es preceding Cs, and vice versa, should be random. However, if the null hypothesis is not true, we would expect a bulk of the E scores or the C scores to precede their opposite number.

For example, suppose you have the hypothesis that leadership can be learned. You set up two groups, one to receive special training in leadership (E) and the other to receive no special instruction (C). Following the training, independent estimates of the leadership qualities of all the subjects are obtained. The results are

E-scores	12	18	31	45	47
C-scores	2	8	15	19	38

When using the Mann-Whitney test, we are concerned with the sampling distribution of the statistic "*U*." To find *U*, we must first rank all of the scores from the lowest to the highest, retaining the identity of each score as E or C (Table 17.1).

You will note that the number of Es preceding Cs is less than the number of Cs preceding Es. The next step is to count the number of times each E

Table 17.1

Rank	1	2	3	4	5	6	7	8	9	10
Score	2	8	12	15	18	19	31	38	45	47
Condition	C	C	E	C	E	C	E	C	E	E

precedes a C. Note that the first E (score of 12) precedes three Cs (scores of 15, 19, and 38, respectively). The second E (score of 18) precedes two Cs (scores of 19 and 38). The third E (score of 31) precedes one C (score of 38). Finally, the last two Es precede no Cs. U is the sum of the number of times each E precedes a C. Thus, in our hypothetical problem, $U = 3 + 2 + 1 + 0 + 0 = 6$. Had we concentrated on the number of times Cs precede Es we would have obtained a sum of $5 + 5 + 4 + 3 + 2 = 19$. We refer to this greater sum as U'. Under the null hypothesis U and U' should be equal. The question is whether the magnitude of the observed difference is sufficient to warrant the rejection of the null hypothesis.

The sampling distribution of U under the null hypothesis is known. Tables N_1 through N_4 show the values of U and U', which are significant at various α levels. To be significant at a given α level, the obtained U must be equal to or less than the tabled value, or the obtained U' must be equal to or *greater* than its corresponding critical value. Employing $\alpha = 0.05$, two-tailed test, we find (Table N_3) that for $N_1 = 5$ and $N_2 = 5$, either $U \leq 2$ or $U' \geq 23$ is required to reject H_0. Since our obtained U of $6 > 2$, we may not reject the null hypothesis.

Equation (17.1) may be used as a check on the calculation of U and U':

$$U = N_1 N_2 - U' \qquad (17.1)$$

The counting technique for arriving at U can become tedious, particularly with large Ns, and frequently leads to error. An alternative procedure, which provides identical results, is to *assign ranks* to the combined groups as we did before, and then to employ either of the following equations to arrive at U and/or U':

$$U = N_1 N_2 + \frac{N_1(N_1 + 1)}{2} - R_1 \qquad (17.2)$$

or

$$U' = N_1 N_2 + \frac{N_2(N_2 + 1)}{2} - R_2 \qquad (17.3)$$

where

R_1 = the sum of ranks assigned to the group with a sample size of N_1
R_2 = the sum of ranks assigned to the group with a sample size of N_2

Psychologists often conduct studies to determine the effects of a drug on the reaction time to a visual stimulus. Since reaction time and related measures (such as latency, time to traverse a runway, etc.) are commonly skewed to the right because of a restriction on the left of the distribution (i.e., no score can be less than zero) and no restrictions on the right (i.e., the score can take *any* value greater than zero), the Mann-Whitney U-test was selected in preference to Student's t-ratio. The results of the hypothetical study and the computational procedures are shown in Table 17.2.

    To check the following calculations, we should first obtain the value of U', employing Equation (17.3):

$$U' = N_1 N_2 + \frac{N_2(N_2 + 1)}{2} - 39 = 45$$

We use Equation (17.1) as a check of our calculations:

$$U = N_1 N_2 - U'$$
$$= 56 - 45 = 11$$

As a check on our calculations of the sums of the ranks, the total sum of the ranks (R_T) is given by

$$R_T = \left(\frac{N_1 + N_2}{2}\right)(N_1 + N_2 + 1) \tag{17.4}$$

In the present example $R_1 + R_2 = (15/2)(16) = 120$. In our calculations we found $R_1 = 81$ and $R_2 = 39$. Note that $R_1 + R_2 = 81 + 39 = 120$. Using $\alpha = 0.01$, two-tailed test, for $N_1 = 8$ and $N_2 = 7$, we find (in Table N_1) that a $U \leq 6$ is required to reject H_0. Since the obtained U of 11 is greater than

Table 17.2   Calculation of Mann-Whitney U using Equation (17.2) (hypothetical data)

Experimental		Control		
Time (milliseconds)	Rank	Time (milliseconds)	Rank	Computation
140	4	130	1	$U = N_1 N_2 + \dfrac{N_1(N_1 + 1)}{2} - 81$
147	6	135	2	
153	8	138	3	$= 56 + \dfrac{8(9)}{2} - 81$
160	10	144	5	
165	11	148	7	
170	13	155	9	$= 56 + 36 - 81$
171	14	168	12	
193	15			$= 11$
$R_1 = 81$		$R_2 = 39$		
$N_1 = 8$		$N_2 = 7$		

this value, we accept H_0. We do not have a valid statistical basis for asserting that the drug affected reaction time.

Tables N_1 through N_4 have been constructed so that it is not necessary to calculate both U and U'. Indeed, it is not even necessary to identify which of these statistics has been calculated. For any given N_1 and N_2, at a specific α level, the tabled values represent the upper and the lower limits of the critical region. The obtained statistic, whether it is actually U or U', must fall *outside* these limits to be significant. Thus, you need not be concerned about labeling which of the statistics you have calculated.

17.2.1 Mann-Whitney *U*-Test with Tied Ranks

A problem that often arises with data is that several scores may be exactly the same. Although the underlying dimension on which we base our measures may be continuous, our measures are, for the most part, quite crude. Even though, theoretically, there should be no ties (if we had sufficiently sensitive measuring instruments), we do in fact obtain ties quite often. The procedures for converting tied scores to ranks are the same as we used with the Spearman r_s (Section 9.6). We assign the mean of the tied ranks to each of the tied scores, with the next rank in the array receiving the rank that is normally assigned to it. Although ties within a group do not constitute a problem (U is unaffected), we do face some difficulty when ties occur between two or more observations that involve both groups. There is an equation available that corrects for the effects of ties. Unfortunately, the use of this equation is rather involved and is beyond the scope of this introductory textbook.* However, the failure to correct for ties results in a test that is more "conservative," that is, decreases the probability of a type I error (rejecting the null hypothesis when it should not be rejected). Correcting for ties is recommended only when their proportion is high and when the uncorrected U approaches our previously set level of significance.

In the event that several ties occur, we recommend that you calculate the Mann-Whitney without correcting for ties. If the uncorrected U approaches but does not achieve the α-level we have set for rejecting the null hypothesis, consult the source shown in the footnote and recalculate the Mann-Whitney U, correcting for ties.

17.2.2 Mann-Whitney *U*-Test when N_1 and/or N_2 Exceed 20

Tables N_1 through N_4 provide critical values of U for sample sizes up to and including $N_1 = 20$ and $N_2 = 20$. What test of significance should be used when either N_1 or N_2 exceeds 20? As with many other statistics, the sampling

---

* See Siegel and Castellan (1988) for corrections when a large number of ties occur.

distribution approaches the normal curve as the sample size becomes larger. As long as both Ns are approximately equal in number and one exceeds 20, the normal curve and the z-statistic may be used to evaluate the significance of the difference between ranks. The z-statistic takes the following form:

$$z = \frac{U_1 - U_E}{s_U}$$

in which U_1 is the sum of ranks of group 1, U_E is the sum expected under H_0, and s_U is the standard error of the U-statistic.

In turn

$$U_E = \frac{N_1(N_1 + N_2 + 1)}{2}$$

and

$$s_U = \sqrt{\frac{N_1 N_2 (N_1 + N_2 + 1)}{12}}$$

Imagine that an investigator has completed a study in which $N_1 = 22$ and $N_2 = 22$. The sum of the ranks of group 1 was found to be 630.* At $\alpha = 0.05$, test the null hypothesis that both groups were drawn from populations with the same mean rank. The critical value of z is ± 1.96.

$$s_U = \sqrt{\frac{(22)(22)(22 + 22 + 1)}{12}}$$

$$= \sqrt{\frac{21{,}780}{12}} = 42.60$$

The expected rank under H_0 is

$$U_E = \frac{22(22 + 22 + 1)}{2} = \frac{990}{2} = 495$$

---

* Using Equation (17.4), we find the sum of all the ranks equals $[(22 + 22)/2](22 + 22 + 1) = 44/2(45) = 990$. By subtraction, $R_2 = R_T - R_1 = 990 - 630 = 360$. Note that $U_1 - U_E$ equals $U_2 - U_E$. Thus, we could just as easily have used $z = (U_1 - U_E)/s_U$. However, *if the sample sizes differ*, U_E must be changed to

$$U_E = N_2 \frac{(N_1 + N_2 + 1)}{2}$$

in order to use U_2 in the equation for z. Both yield identical probability values and both test H_0: $\mu_1 = \mu_2$.

The test statistic z becomes

$$z = \frac{630 - 495}{42.60} = 3.17$$

Since our obtained z of 3.17 exceeds the critical value of 1.96, we may reject the null hypothesis and assert that the experimental treatment produced a significant difference between conditions.

17.3 Nonparametric Tests Involving Correlated Samples

A correlated-samples design (also known as a **matched-group design**) is one in which pairs of respondents are matched on a variable that is known to be correlated with the dependent variable. The result is a set of paired respondents in which each member of a given pair obtains approximately the same score on the matching variable. Then one member of each pair is randomly assigned to the experimental condition and the other is assigned to the control group. Thus, if we wanted to determine the effect of some drug on the ease of learning the solution to a mathematical problem, we might match individuals on the basis of IQ estimates, the amount of mathematical training, grades in statistics, or performance on other mathematics problems. Such a design has two advantages:

1. It ensures that the experimental groups are "equivalent" in initial ability.

2. It permits us to take advantage of the correlation based on initial ability and allows us in effect to remove one source of error from our measurements.

17.4 The Sign Test

Suppose that we are repeating the leadership experiment with which we introduced the chapter, employing larger samples. On the expectation that intelligence and leadership ability are correlated variables, we set up two groups, an experimental and a control, that are matched on the basis of intelligence. On completion of the leadership training course, independent observers are asked to rate the leadership qualities of each respondent on a 50-point scale. We will use the **sign test** which is a nonparametric statistical test for ordinally scaled variables, used with matched or correlated samples. The sign test simply utilizes information concerning the *direction* of the differences between pairs of scores. The results are listed in Table 17.3.

Table 17.3 Ratings of two groups of matched subjects on qualities of leadership (hypothetical data)

Matched Pair	Leadership Score Experimental	Control	Sign of Difference $(E - C)$
A	47	40	+
B	43	38	+
C	36	42	−
D	38	25	+
E	30	29	+
F	22	26	−
G	25	16	+
H	21	18	+
I	14	8	+
J	12	4	+
K	5	7	−
L	9	3	+
M	5	5	(0)

The rating scales seem to be extremely crude and we are unwilling to affirm that the scores have any precise quantitative properties. The only assumption we feel justified in making is that any existing difference between two paired scores is a valid indicator of the direction and not the magnitude of the difference.

There are 13 pairs of observations in Table 17.3. Since pair M is tied and there is consequently no indication of a difference one way or another, we drop these paired observations. Of the remaining 12 pairs, we would expect, on the basis of the null hypothesis, half the changes to be in the positive direction and half the changes to be in the negative direction. In other words, under H_0 the probability of any difference being positive is equal to the probability that it will be negative. Since we are dealing with a two-category population (positive differences and negative differences), H_0 may be expressed in precisely the same fashion as in the binomial test when $P = Q = 1/2$. That is, in the present problem, H_0: $P = Q = 1/2$. Indeed, the sign test is merely a variation of the binomial test.

Out of 12 comparisons showing a difference ($N = 12$) in the present example 9 are positive, and 3 are negative. Since $P = Q = 1/2$, we refer to Table I, under $x = 9$, $N = 12$, and find that the critical value at $\alpha = 0.05$, two-tailed test, is 10. Since x is less than the critical value, we fail to reject H_0.

The assumptions underlying the use of the sign test are that the pairs of measurements must be independent of each other and that these measurements must represent, at least, ordinal scaling.

One of the disadvantages of the sign test is that it completely eliminates any quantitative information that may be inherent in the data (e.g., $-8 = -7 = -6$, etc.). The sign test treats all plus differences as if they were the same and all minus differences as if they were the same.

Statistics in Action 17.1

Polonium-210, Smoking, and Cancer in Directly Exposed Tissue: Calculating Mann-Whitney U

The recent discovery of a radioelement in cigarettes (polonium-210) suggests the possibility that directly exposed sites (e.g., buccal cavity, pharynx, etc.) in smokers may put them at greater risk for the development of cancer at these sites. Health data for various risk groups are frequently expressed as an o/e ratio (observed to expected). Because the ratios appear to be markedly positively skewed and raise doubts concerning the normality of the population distribution, the Mann-Whitney-U is chosen over its parametric counterpart (Student's t-ratio for independent samples). However, the decision to use the Mann-Whitney U is not engraved in stone. Some researchers would use Student's t-ratio based on the robustness of the t-test.

The following table shows the observed/expected (o/e) ratios for indirectly exposed and directly exposed tissues, the conversion to ranks, and the application of the Mann-Whitney U-test. An o/e ratio greater than 1 means a higher-than-average risk.

Based on the known carcinogenic properties of radioelements, we'll use a directional test of H_0 at $\alpha = 0.01$. Since a two-tailed $\alpha = 0.02$ yields a one-tailed $\alpha = 0.01$, we'll use Table N_2 to evaluate the significance of the results.

Cancer of Indirectly Exposed Tissue	O/E Ratio	Rank	Cancer of Directly Exposed Tissue	O/E Ratio	Rank
Stomach	1.52	7	Buccal cavity	4.23	12
Intestines	1.11	3.5	Pharynx	13.14	15
Rectum	1.11	3.5	Larynx	11.75	16
Liver/biliary ducts	2.35	11	Lung and bronchus	11.29	14
Pancreas	1.79	9	Esophagus	6.5	13
Prostate	1.31	5			
Kidney	1.41	6			
Bladder	2.16	10			
Brain	1.05	1			
Malignant lymphomas	1.07	2			
Leukemias	1.61	8			
Sum of ranks		66			70

$$U = (11)(5) + \frac{11(12)}{2} - 66$$

$$= 55 + 66 - 66$$

$$= 55$$

Reference to Table N_2 shows the one-tailed critical value of U, at $\alpha = 0.01$, to be 48. Since obtained U exceeds this value, we reject H_0 and assert that directly exposed tissues are at a greater risk for the development of cancer.

a) Can we conclude that polonium-210 caused the greater risk of cancer at directly exposed sites?

b) Analyze these data with Student's t-ratio for independent samples, using $\alpha = 0.01$, one-tailed test. Compare the conclusions drawn from the two different tests of significance.

ANSWERS

a) Not necessarily. There may be other carcinogens in cigarette smoke that increase the risk of cancer in directly exposed tissue.

b) $\bar{X}_1 = 1.50$, $\bar{X}_2 = 9.38$, $t = -7.05$ with df $= 14$. Critical value $\alpha = -2.624$. Reject H_0 at $\alpha = 0.01$, one-tailed test.

Source: Based on R. T. Ravenholt. Letter to the editor. *New England Journal of Medicine* (1982), **307**, 312.

If this is the only assumption warranted by the scale of measurement employed, we have little choice but to employ the sign test. If, on the other hand, the data *do* permit us to make such quantitative statements as "a difference of $8 > 7 > 6 > \cdots$," we lose power when we employ the sign test.

17.5 Wilcoxon Matched-Pairs Signed-Rank Test

We have seen that the sign simply utilizes information concerning the direction of the differences between pairs. If the *magnitude* as well as the *direction* of these differences may be considered, a more powerful test may be employed. The **Wilcoxon matched-pairs signed-rank test** achieves greater power by utilizing the quantitative information that is inherent in the ranking of the differences.

For heuristic purposes, let's return to the data in Table 17.3, and make a different assumption about the scale of measurement employed. Suppose the rating scale is not so crude as we had imagined; that is, not only do the measurements achieve ordinal scaling, but also the differences between measures achieve ordinality. Table 17.4 reproduces these data, with an additional entry indicating the magnitude of the differences.

Note that the difference column represents differences in scores rather than in ranks. The following column represents the ranking of these differences from the smallest to largest without regard to the algebraic sign. We have placed the negative sign in parentheses so that we can keep track of the differences bearing positive and negative signs. Now, if the null hypothesis were correct, we would expect the sum of the positive and that of the negative ranks more or less to balance each other. The more the sums of the ranks are preponderantly positive or negative, the more likely we are to reject the null hypothesis.

Table 17.4 Rating of two groups of matched respondents on qualities of leadership (hypothetical data)

Matched Pair	Leadership Score		Difference	Rank of Difference	Ranks with Smaller Sum
	Experimental	*Control*			
A	47	40	+7	9	
B	43	38	+5	5	
C	36	42	−6	(−)7	−7
D	38	25	+13	12	
E	30	29	+1	1	
F	22	26	−4	(−)4	−4
G	25	16	+9	11	
H	21	18	+3	3	
I	14	8	+6	7	
J	12	4	+8	10	
K	5	7	−2	(−)2	−2
L	9	3	+6	7	
M	5	5	(0)		

$$T = -13$$

The statistic T is the sum of the ranks with the smaller sum. In this problem T is equal to -13. Table O presents the critical values of T for sample sizes up to 50 pairs. All entries are for the absolute value of T. In the present example we find that a T of 13 or less is required for significance at the 0.05 level (two-tailed test) when $N = 12$. Note that we dropped the M-pair from our calculations since, as with the sign test, a zero difference in scores cannot be considered as either a negative or a positive change. Since our obtained T was 13, we may reject the null hypothesis. We may conclude that the leadership training produced higher ratings for the experimental respondents.

You will recall that the sign test applied to these same data did not lead to the rejection of the null hypothesis. The reason should be apparent; that is, we were not taking advantage of all the information inherent in our data when we employed the sign test.

17.5.1 Assumptions Underlying Wilcoxon's Matched-Pairs Signed-Rank Test

An assumption involved in the use of the Wilcoxon signed-rank test is that the scale of measurement is at least ordinal in nature. In other words, the assumption is that the scores permit the ordering of the data into relationships of greater than and less than. However, the signed-rank test makes one additional assumption, which may rule it out of some potential applications; namely, it assumes that the differences in scores also constitute an ordinal scale. It is not always clear whether or not this assumption is valid for a given set of data. Take, for example, a personality scale purported to measure "manifest anxiety" in a testing situation. Can we validly claim that a difference between matched pairs of, say, 5 points on one part of the scale is greater than a difference of 4 points on another part of the scale? If we cannot validly make this assumption, we must employ another form of statistical analysis, even if it requires that we move to a less sensitive test of significance. Once again, our basic conservatism as scientists makes us more willing to risk a type II rather than a type I error.

Summary

In this chapter we have pointed out that the behavioral scientist does not first collect data and then "shop around" for a statistical test to determine the significance of differences between experimental conditions. *The researcher must specify in advance of the experiment* the null hypothesis, alternative hypothesis, test of significance, and the probability value that is acceptable as the basis for rejecting the null hypothesis.

We demonstrated the use of the Mann-Whitney *U*-test as an alternative to Student's *t*-ratio when the measurements fail to achieve interval scaling or when the researcher wishes to avoid the assumptions of the parametric counterpart. It is one of the most powerful of the nonparametric tests, since it utilizes most of the quantitative information that is inherent in the data.

We have seen that by taking into account correlations between respondents on a variable correlated with the dependent measure, we can increase the sensitivity of our statistical test.

The sign test accomplishes this objective by using before-after measures on the same individuals.

We have also seen that the sign test, although taking advantage of the *direction* of differences involved in ordinal measurement, fails to make use of information concerning *magnitudes* of difference.

The Wilcoxon matched-pairs signed-rank test takes advantage of both *direction* and *magnitude* implicit in ordinal measurement with correlated samples. When the assumptions underlying the test are met, the Wilcoxon paired-replicates technique is an extremely sensitive basis for obtaining probability values.

Terms to Remember

Mann-Whitney *U*-test   A powerful nonparametric statistical test commonly employed as an alternative to the Student *t*-ratio when the measurements fail to achieve interval scaling.

Matched-group design   A correlated-samples design in which pairs of respondents are matched on a variable correlated with the dependent variable. Each member of a pair receives different experimental conditions.

Sign test   A nonparametric statistical test for ordinally scaled variables, used with matched or correlated samples. The sign test simply utilizes information concerning the *direction* of the differences between pairs of scores.

Wilcoxon matched-pairs signed-rank test   A nonparametric statistical test for ordinally scaled variables used with matched or correlated samples; more powerful than the sign test since it utilizes information concerning the *magnitude* of the differences between pairs of scores.

Exercises

1. From the data presented in the accompanying table, determine whether there is a significant difference in the number of stolen bases obtained by two leagues, employing

    a) The sign test.

    b) The Wilcoxon matched-pairs test.

    c) The Mann-Whitney U-test.

    Which is the best statistical test for these data? Why?

	Number of Stolen Bases	
Team Standing	*League 1*	*League 2*
1	91	81
2	46	51
3	108	63
4	99	51
5	110	46
6	105	45
7	191	66
8	57	64
9	34	90
10	81	28

2. In a study to determine the effect of a drug on aggressiveness, group A received a drug and group B received a placebo. A test of aggressiveness was applied following the drug administration. The scores obtained were as follows (the higher the score is, the greater is the aggressiveness):

Group A	10	8	12	16	5	9	7	11	6
Group B	12	15	20	18	13	14	9	16	

    Set up this study in formal statistical terms and state the conclusion that is warranted by the statistical evidence.

3. The personnel director at a large insurance office claims that insurance agents who are trained in personal-social relations make more favorable impressions on prospective clients. To test this hypothesis, she randomly selected 22 individuals from those most recently hired and half are assigned

to the personal-social relations course. The remaining 11 individuals constitute the control group. Following the training period, all 22 individuals are observed in a simulated interview with a client, and they are rated on a 10-point scale (0–9) for their ease in establishing relationships. The higher the sore is, the better is the rating. Set up and test H_0, using the appropriate test statistic. Use $\alpha = 0.01$.

Experimental group	8	7	9	4	7	9	3	7	8	9	3
Control group	5	6	2	6	0	2	6	5	1	0	5

4. Assume that the insurance agents in Exercise 3 were matched on a variable known to be correlated with the criterion variable. Employ the appropriate test statistic to test H_0: $\alpha = 0.01$.

5. Fifteen husbands and their wives were administered an opinion scale to assess their attitudes about a particular political issue. The results were as follows (the higher the score is, the more favorable is the attitude).

Husband	Wife	Husband	Wife
37	33	32	46
46	44	35	32
59	48	39	29
17	30	37	45
41	56	36	29
36	30	45	48
29	35	40	35
38	38		

What do you conclude?

6. Suppose that during last track season there was no difference in the mean running speeds of the runners from two schools. Assume that the same people are on the teams this year.

School A trains as usual for this season. However, the coach at school B introduces bicycle riding in the training classes. During a meet the following times (in seconds) were recorded for the runners of the two schools.

A	10.2	11.1	10.5	10.0	9.7	12.0	10.7	10.9	11.5	10.4
B	9.9	10.3	11.0	10.1	9.8	9.5	10.8	10.6	9.6	9.4

Test the hypothesis that bicycle riding does not affect running speed.

7. Suppose that in Exercise 6 the people on each team had been previously matched on running speed for the 50-yard dash. The matches are as listed in Exercise 6. Using the sign test and the Wilcoxon matched-pairs signed-rank test, set up and test the null hypothesis.

8. An investigator wants to measure the effectiveness of an advertisement that promotes his brand of toothpaste. He matched subjects (all of whom had never bought his brand of toothpaste) according to the number of tubes of toothpaste they usually buy in 6 months. He then divided the sample into two groups and showed one group the advertisement. After 6 months, he found that the number of tubes of his brand of toothpaste the people bought during that time was

Advertisement group	4	4	3	1	2	0	1	0
No advertisement group	1	2	0	2	0	1	0	1

Was the advertisement effective?

9. Suppose an interviewer supervisor is interested in increasing the effectiveness of her employees. She divides 20 employees into two groups and gives a special training program to one group. Because of the complex nature of the task, there is no scale available to measure effectiveness. Therefore, she seeks the help of an efficiency expert who observes all 20 interviewers and ranks them on effectiveness, with the following results (a rank of ''1'' is most effective).

Training group	1	2	4	5	6	7	8	10	11	12
Control	3	9	13	14	15	16	17	18	19	20

What can the supervisor conclude about the effectiveness of the training program?

5
Appendixes

A

Review of
Basic
Mathematics

A Review of Basic Mathematics
B Glossary of Symbols
C Tables
D Glossary of Terms
E References

A

Review of
Basic
Mathematics

Arithmetic Operations
Algebraic Operations
Reducing Fractions to Simplest Expressions

Arithmetic Operations

You already know that addition is indicated by the sign $+$, subtraction by the sign $-$, multiplication in one of three ways, 2×4, $2(4)$, or $2 \cdot 4$, and division by a slash, $/$, an overbar, —, or the symbol $\div$. However, it is not unusual to forget the rules concerning addition, subtraction, multiplication, and division, particularly when these operations occur in a single problem.

Addition and Subtraction

When numbers are added together, the order of adding the numbers has no influence on the sum. Thus, we may add $2 + 5 + 3$ in any of the following ways:

$$2 + 5 + 3, \quad 5 + 2 + 3, \quad 2 + 3 + 5$$
$$5 + 3 + 2, \quad 3 + 2 + 5, \quad 3 + 5 + 2$$

When a series of numbers containing both positive and negative signs are added, the order of adding the numbers has no influence on the sum. It is often desirable, however, to group together the numbers preceded by positive signs, group together the numbers preceded by negative signs, add each group separately, and subtract the latter sum from the former. Thus

$$-2 + 3 + 5 - 4 + 2 + 1 - 8$$

may best be added by grouping in the following ways:

$$
\begin{array}{rl}
+3 & \\
+5 & \quad -2 \\
+2 & \quad -4 \\
\underline{+1} & \quad \underline{-8} \\
+11 & \quad -14 = -3
\end{array}
$$

Incidentally, to subtract a larger numerical value from a smaller numerical value, as in the above example $(11 - 14)$, we ignore the signs, subtract the smaller number from the larger, and affix the sign of the larger to the sum. Thus, $-14 + 11 = -3$.

Multiplication

The order in which numbers are multiplied has no effect on the product. In other words

$$2 \times 3 \times 4 = 2 \times 4 \times 3 = 3 \times 2 \times 4$$
$$= 3 \times 4 \times 2 = 4 \times 2 \times 3 = 4 \times 3 \times 2 = 24$$

When addition, subtraction, and multiplication occur in the same expression, we must develop certain procedures governing *which* operations are to be performed first.

In the expression

$$2 \times 4 + 7 \times 3 - 5$$

multiplication is performed first. Thus, the above expression is equal to

$$
\begin{array}{r}
2 \times 4 = 8 \\
7 \times 3 = 21 \\
-5 = -5
\end{array}
$$

and

$$8 + 21 - 5 = 24$$

We may *not* add first and then multiply. Thus, $2 \times 4 + 7$ is *not* equal to $2(4 + 7)$ or 22.

If a problem involves finding the product of one term multiplied by a second expression that includes two or more terms either added or subtracted, we may multiply first and then add, or add first and then multiply. Thus, the solution to the following problem becomes

$$8(6 - 4) = 8 \times 6 - 8 \times 4$$
$$= 48 - 32$$
$$= 16$$

or

$$8(6 - 4) = 8(2)$$
$$= 16$$

In most cases, however, it is more convenient to reduce the expression within the parentheses first. Thus, generally speaking, the second solution appearing above will be more frequently used.

Finally, if numbers having like signs are multiplied, the product is always positive; for example, $(+2) \times (+4) = +8$ and $(-2) \times (-4) = +8$. If numbers bearing unlike signs are multiplied, the product is always negative; for example, $(+2) \times (-4) = -8$ and $(-2) \times (+4) = -8$. The same rule applies also to division. When we obtain the quotient of two numbers of like signs, it is always positive; when the numbers differ in sign, the quotient is always negative.

Multiplication as successive addition   Many students tend to forget that multiplication is a special form of successive addition. Thus

$$15 + 15 + 15 + 15 + 15 = 5(15)$$

and

$$(15 + 15 + 15 + 15 + 15) + (16 + 16 + 16 + 16) = 5(15) + 4(16)$$

This formulation is useful in understanding the advantages of "grouping" scores into what is called a frequency distribution. In obtaining the sum of an array of scores, some of which occur a number of times, we want to multiply each score by the frequency with which it occurs and then add the products. Thus, if we were to obtain the following distribution of scores

12, 13, 13, 13, 14, 14, 14, 14, 15, 15, 15, 15,
15, 15, 15, 16, 16, 16, 17, 17, 17, 17, 18

and wanted the sum of these scores, it would be advantageous to form the following frequency distribution.

X	f	fX
12	1	12
13	3	39
14	4	56
15	7	105
16	3	48
17	4	68
18	1	18
$N = 23$		$\Sigma fX = 346$

Algebraic Operations

Transposing

To transpose a term from one side of an equation to another, you merely have to *change the sign* of the transposed term. All the following are equivalent statements:

$$a + b = c$$
$$a = c - b$$
$$b = c - a$$
$$0 = c - a - b$$
$$0 = c - (a + b)$$

Solving Equations Involving Fractions

Much of the difficulty encountered in solving equations that involve fractions can be avoided by remembering one important mathematical principle:

Equals multiplied by equals are equal.

Let's look at a few sample problems.

1. Solve the following equation for x:

$$b = \frac{a}{x}$$

In solving for x, we want to express the value of x in terms of a and b. In other words, we want our final equation to read, $x =$ _____. Note that we may multiply both sides of the equation by x/b and obtain the following:

$$b \cdot \frac{x}{\cancel{b}} = \frac{a}{\cancel{x}} \cdot \frac{\cancel{x}}{b}$$

This reduces to

$$x = \frac{a}{b}$$

2. Solve the same equation for a. Similarly, if we wanted to solve the equation in terms of a, we could multiply both sides of the equation by x. Thus

$$b \cdot x = \frac{a}{\cancel{x}} \cdot \cancel{x}$$

becomes $bx = a$, or $a = bx$.

In each of the preceding solutions you will note that the net effect of multiplying by a constant has been to rearrange the terms in the numerator and the denominator of the equations. In fact, we may state two general rules that will permit us to solve the preceding problems without having to use multiplication by equals (although multiplication by equals is implicit in the arithmetic operations):

a) A term that is in the denominator on one side of the equation may be moved to the other side of the equation by multiplying it by the numerator on that side. Thus

$$\frac{x}{a} = b$$

becomes

$$x = ab$$

b) A term in the numerator on one side of an equation may be moved to the other side of the equation by dividing the numerator on that side by it. Thus

$$ab = x$$

may become

$$a = \frac{x}{b} \qquad \text{or} \qquad b = \frac{x}{a}$$

Thus, we have seen that all of the following are equivalent statements:

$$b = \frac{a}{x}, \qquad a = bx, \qquad x = \frac{a}{b}$$

Similarly

$$\frac{\Sigma X}{N} = \bar{X}, \qquad \Sigma X = N\bar{X}, \qquad \frac{\Sigma X}{\bar{X}} = N$$

Dividing by a sum or a difference   It is true that

$$\frac{x + y}{z} = \frac{x}{z} + \frac{y}{z} \qquad \text{and} \qquad \frac{x - y}{z} = \frac{x}{z} - \frac{y}{z}$$

We cannot, however, simplify the following expressions as easily:

$$\frac{x}{y + z} \qquad \text{or} \qquad \frac{x}{y - z}$$

Thus

$$\frac{x}{y + z} \neq \frac{x}{y} + \frac{x}{z}$$

in which $\neq$ means "not equal to."

Reducing Fractions to Simplest Expressions

A corollary to the rule stating that equals multiplied by equals are equal is

Unequals multiplied by equals remain proportional.

Thus, if we were to multiply 1/4 by 8/8, the product, 8/32, is in the same proportion as 1/4. This corollary is useful in reducing the complex fractions to their simplest expression. Let's look at an example.

Example
Reduce

$$\frac{a/b}{c/d} \qquad \text{or} \qquad \frac{a}{b} \div \frac{c}{d}$$

to its simplest expression.

Note that if we multiply both the numerator and the denominator by

$$\frac{bd/1}{bd/1}$$

we obtain

$$\frac{(a/b) \cdot (bd/1)}{(c/d) \cdot (bd/1)}$$

which becomes ad/bc.

However, we could obtain the same result if we were to *invert the divisor* and multiply. Thus

$$\frac{a/b}{c/d} = \frac{a}{b} \cdot \frac{d}{c} = \frac{ad}{bc}$$

We may now formulate a general rule for dividing one fraction into another fraction. In dividing fractions, we *invert the divisor and multiply.* Thus

$$\frac{x/y}{a^2/b} \qquad \text{becomes} \qquad \frac{x}{y} \cdot \frac{b}{a^2}$$

which equals

$$\frac{bx}{a^2 y}$$

To illustrate: If $a = 5$, $b = 2$, $x = 3$, and $y = 4$, the preceding expressions become

$$\frac{3/4}{5^2/2} = \frac{3}{4} \cdot \frac{2}{5^2} = \frac{2 \cdot 3}{4 \times 5^2} = \frac{6}{100}$$

A general practice you should follow when substituting numerical values into fractional expressions is to reduce the expression to its simplest form *prior* to substitution.

Multiplication and Division of Terms Having Exponents

An exponent indicates how many times a number is to be multiplied by itself. For example, X^5 means that X is to be multiplied by itself five times, or

$$X^5 = X \cdot X \cdot X \cdot X \cdot X$$

If $X = 3$

$$X^5 = 3 \cdot 3 \cdot 3 \cdot 3 \cdot 3 = 243$$

and

$$\left(\frac{1}{X}\right)^5 = \frac{1^5}{X^5} = \frac{1 \cdot 1 \cdot 1 \cdot 1 \cdot 1}{3 \cdot 3 \cdot 3 \cdot 3 \cdot 3} = \frac{1}{243}$$

To multiply X to the ath power (X^a) times X raised to the bth power, you simply *add the exponents*, thus raising X to the $(a + b)$th power. The reason for the addition of exponents may be seen from the following illustration.

If $a = 3$ and $b = 5$, then

$$X^a \cdot X^b = X^3 X^5 = (X \cdot X \cdot X)(X \cdot X \cdot X \cdot X \cdot X)$$

which equals X^8.

Now, if $X = 5$, $a = 3$, and $b = 5$, then

$$X^a \cdot X^b = X^{a+b} = X^{3+5} = X^8 = 5^8 = 390{,}625$$

If $X = 1/6$, $a = 2$, and $b = 3$

$$X^a \cdot X^b = X^{a+b} = \left(\frac{1}{6}\right)^{2+3} = \left(\frac{1}{6}\right)^5 = \frac{1^5}{6^5} = \frac{1}{7776}$$

To divide X raised to the ath power by X raised to the bth power, you simply *subtract* the exponent in the denominator from the exponent in the numerator.* The reason for the subtraction is made clear in the following illustration:

$$\frac{X^a}{X^b} = \frac{X^5}{X^2} = \frac{X \cdot X \cdot X \cdot X \cdot X}{X \cdot X} = X^3 = 3^3 = 27$$

---

* This leads to an interesting exception to the rule that an exponent indicates the number of times a number is multiplied by itself; that is

$$\frac{X^N}{X^N} = X^{N-N} = X^0$$

however

$$\frac{X^N}{X^N} = 1; \quad \text{therefore} \quad X^0 = 1$$

Any number raised to the zero power is equal to 1.

If $X = 5/6$, $a = 4$, $b = 2$, then

$$\frac{X^a}{X^b} = X^{a-b} = X^{4-2} = X^2$$

Substituting 5/6 for X, we have

$$X^2 = \left(\frac{5}{6}\right)^2 = \frac{5^2}{6^2} = \frac{25}{36}$$

B

Glossary of
Symbols

Mathematical Operators
Greek Letters
English Letters

454

Following are definitions of the symbols that appear in the text, followed by the page number showing the first reference to the symbol.

English letters and Greek letters are listed separately in their approximate alphabetical order. Mathematical operators are also listed separately.

Symbol	Definition	Page
Mathematical operators		
$\neq$	Not equal to	133
$a < b$	a is less than b	30
$a > b$	a is greater than b	30
$\leq$	Less than or equal to	291
$\geq$	Greater than or equal to	307
$\sqrt{}$	Square root	24
X^a	X raised to the ath power	24
$|X|$	Absolute value of X	127
Σ	Sum all quantities or scores that follow	24
$\displaystyle\sum_{i=1}^{N} X_i$	Sum all quantities X_1 through X_N:	
	$$X_1 + X_2 + \cdots + X_N$$	25

Symbol	*Definition*	*Page*

Greek letters

α	Probability of a type I error, probability of rejecting H_0 when it is true	331
β	1. Probability of a type II error, probability of accepting H_0 when it is false	331
	2. Standardized multiple regression coefficient	268
χ^2	Chi square	407
ϵ	Epsilon: percentage difference in a contingency table	173
γ	Goodman and Kruskal's gamma for ordinal-level contingency data	184
λ	Lambda: an asymmetric or symmetric measure of association for nominal-level contingency table data	178
μ	Population mean	146
μ_0	Value of the population mean under H_0	354
$\mu_{\bar{X}}$	Mean of the distribution of sample means	346
ϕ	Phi coefficient	416
σ^2	Population variance	128
σ_P	Standard error of the proportion	369
σ	Population standard deviation	128
$\sigma_{\bar{X}}^2 = \dfrac{\sigma^2}{N}$	Variance of the sampling distribution of the mean	349
$\sigma_{\bar{X}} = \dfrac{\sigma}{\sqrt{N}}$	True standard error of the mean given random samples of a fixed N	348
τ_b	Kendall's tau-b for ordinal-level contingency data	190

English letters

a	Constant term in a regression equation (Y-intercept)	230
b_y	Unstandardized slope of a line relating values of Y to values of X	231
c	Number of columns in a contingency table	411
C	1. Centile: Equivalent to a percentile and is a percentage rank that divides a distribution into 100 equal parts	90
	2. Concordant pairs in a contingency table	185
	3. Contingency coefficient	418
cum f	Cumulative frequency	60

Symbol	Definition	Page
cum f_{ll}	Cumulative frequency at the lower real limit of the interval containing X	60
cum %	Cumulative percent	66
D	1. Rank on X-variable − rank on Y-variable (r_s equation)	215
	2. Score on X-variable − score on Y-variable ($X - Y$)	215
	3. Decile: a percentage rank that divides a distribution into 10 equal parts	90
	4. Discordant pairs in a contingency table	185
d_{yx}	Somer's d for ordinal-level data that incorporates tied pairs	189
df	Degrees of freedom: number of values free to vary after certain restrictions have been placed on the data	360
F	A ratio of the between-group mean square to the within-group mean square	390
f	Frequency	59
f_i	Number of cases within the interval containing X	87
f_e	Expected number in a given category	408
f_0	Observed number in a given category	408
fX	A score multiplied by its corresponding frequency	133
Gamma	Goodman and Kruskal's symmetric measure of association for ordinal-level contingency table data, sometimes written γ	184
H_0	The null hypothesis; hypothesis actually tested	327
H_1	The alternative hypothesis; hypothesis entertained if H_0 is rejected	329
i	Width of the class interval	58
k	Number of groups or categories or cells	389
k^2	Coefficient of nondetermination	242
Md_n	Median	107
M_0	Mode	109
MD	Mean deviation	125
N	1. Number of pairs	24
	2. Number in sample	24
	3. Total number of scores or quantities	24
N_s	Total number of means obtained in a sampling experiment	291
%	Percentage	39
(p)	Proportion	39

Symbol	Definition	Page
PRE	Proportional reduction in error	178
p	Probability	288
$p(A)$	Probability of event A	288
$p(B\|A)$	Probability of B given that A has occurred	297
P	**1.** Probability of the occurrence of an event	328
	2. Proportion of cases in one class in a two-category population	328
Q	**1.** Probability of the nonoccurrence of an event	328
	2. Yule's special case of gamma for 2×2 tables	184
	3. Proportion of cases in the other class of a two-category population	328
Q_1	First quartile, 25th percentile	90
Q_3	Third quartile, 75th percentile	90
r	**1.** Pearson product-moment correlation coefficient (Pearson's r)	200
	2. Number of rows in a contingency table	411
r^2	Coefficient of determination	242
r_s	Spearman rank-order correlation coefficient (Spearman's rho)	214
$r_{XY \cdot Z}$	Partial correlation coefficient	262
R	Multiple correlation coefficient	271
R_1	Sum of ranks assigned to the group with a sample size of N_1 (Mann-Whitney U)	429
R_2	Sum of ranks assigned to the group with a sample size of N_2 (Mann-Whitney U)	429
R^2	Coefficient of multiple determination	271
$1 - R^2$	Coefficient of nondetermination (k^2)	242
$s^2 = \dfrac{\Sigma(X - \overline{X})^2}{N}$	Variance of a sample	129
$s = \sqrt{\dfrac{\Sigma(X - \overline{X})^2}{N}}$	Standard deviation of a sample	129
$\hat{s}^2 = \dfrac{\Sigma(X - \overline{X})^2}{N - 1}$	Unbiased estimate of the population variance	357
$s_{\overline{X}}^2$	Estimated variance of the sampling distribution of the mean	357

	Symbol	Definition	Page
$s_{\bar{X}} = \dfrac{\hat{s}}{\sqrt{N}} = \dfrac{s}{\sqrt{N-1}}$		Estimated standard error of the mean	358
	$\hat{s}^2_{bet}$	Between-group variance estimate	390
	$\hat{s}^2_w$	Within-group variance estimate	390
	$s_{est\,y}$	Standard error of estimate when predictions are made from X to Y	240
	$\Sigma(X - \bar{X})^2$	Sum of squares, sum of the squared deviations from the mean	105
	SS_{tot}	Total sum of squares, sum of the squared deviations of each score (X) from the overall mean ($\bar{X}_{tot}$)	386
	SS_w	Within-group sum of squares, sum of the squared deviations of each score (X) from the mean of its own group ($\bar{X}_i$)	387
	SS_{bet}	Between-group sum of squares, sum of the squared deviations of each group mean ($\bar{X}_i$) from the overall mean ($\bar{X}_{tot}$), multiplied by the N in each group	388
	t	Statistic employed to test hypotheses when σ is unknown	437
	T	Sum of the ranks with the least frequent sign. Used with the Wilcoxon matched-pairs signed-rank test.	431
	T_y	Tied pairs with different X values but which share the same Y value. Used with Somer's d.	189
	U, U'	Statistics in the Mann-Whitney test	429
	V	Cramer's V	419
	X, Y	Variables; quantities or scores of variables	24
	X_i, Y_i	Specific quantities indicated by the subscript i	25
	$\bar{X}, \bar{Y}$	Arithmetic means of a sample	8
	$\bar{X}_i$	Mean of the ith group	387
$\bar{X}_{tot} = \dfrac{\Sigma X_{tot}}{N}$		Overall mean	386
	$(X - \bar{X})$	Deviation of a score from its mean	103
	ΣX^2	Sum of the squares of the raw scores	133
	$(\Sigma X)^2$	Sum of the raw scores, the quantity squared	133
	X_{ll}	Score at lower real limit of interval containing X	87

Symbol	Definition	Page
X_m	Midpoint of an interval	104
Y'	Scores predicted by regression equations (also $\hat{Y}$)	228
z	1. Deviation of a specific score from the mean, expressed in standard deviation units	146
	2. Statistic employed to test hypotheses when σ is known	150
$z_{0.01} = \pm 2.58$	Critical value of z, minimum z required to reject H_0 at the 0.01 level of significance, two-tailed test	354
$z_{0.05} = \pm 1.96$	Minimum value of z required to reject H_0 at the 0.05 level of significance, two-tailed test	354
z_y	Y' expressed in terms of a z score	234
Z	Control variable in a multivariate context	259

C

Tables

A Proportions of area under the normal curve

B Table of χ^2

C Critical values of t

D Critical values of F

D_1 Critical values of F that cut off the upper and lower 2.5% of the F-distribution

E Transformation of r to z_r

F Critical values of r_s

G Functions of r

H Binomial coefficients

I Critical values of x or $N - x$ (whichever is larger) at 0.05 and 0.01 levels when $p = Q = 1/2$

J Critical values of x for various stages of P and Q when $N \leq 49$

K Percentage points of the Studentized range

L Squares, square roots, and reciprocals of numbers from 1 to 1000

M Random digits

N_1–N_4 Critical values of U and U'

O Critical values of T

Z scores

The Use of Table A

The use of Table A requires that the raw score be transformed into a z score and that the variable be normally distributed.

The values in Table A represent the proportion of area in the standard normal curve, which has a mean of 0, a standard deviation of 1.00, and a total area also equal to 1.00.

Since the normal curve is symmetrical, it is sufficient to indicate only the areas corresponding to positive z values. Negative z values will have precisely the same proportions of area as their positive counterparts.

Column B represents the proportion of area between the mean and a given z.

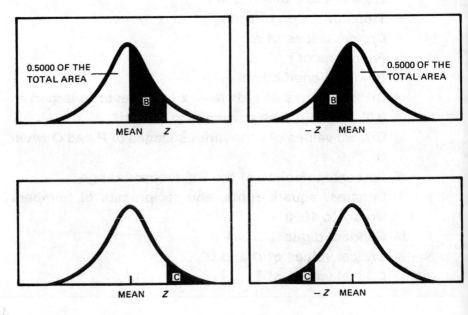

Table A Proportions of area under the normal curve

(A) z	(B) AREA BETWEEN MEAN AND z	(C) AREA BEYOND z	(A) z	(B) AREA BETWEEN MEAN AND z	(C) AREA BEYOND z	(A) z	(B) AREA BETWEEN MEAN AND z	(C) AREA BEYOND z
0.00	0.0000	0.5000	0.55	0.2088	0.2912	1.10	0.3643	0.1357
0.01	0.0040	0.4960	0.56	0.2123	0.2877	1.11	0.3665	0.1335
0.02	0.0080	0.4920	0.57	0.2157	0.2843	1.12	0.3686	0.1314
0.03	0.0120	0.4880	0.58	0.2190	0.2810	1.13	0.3708	0.1292
0.04	0.0160	0.4840	0.59	0.2224	0.2776	1.14	0.3729	0.1271
0.05	0.0199	0.4801	0.60	0.2257	0.2743	1.15	0.3749	0.1251
0.06	0.0239	0.4761	0.61	0.2291	0.2709	1.16	0.3770	0.1230
0.07	0.0279	0.4721	0.62	0.2324	0.2676	1.17	0.3790	0.1210
0.08	0.0319	0.4681	0.63	0.2357	0.2643	1.18	0.3810	0.1190
0.09	0.0359	0.4641	0.64	0.2389	0.2611	1.19	0.3830	0.1170
0.10	0.0398	0.4602	0.65	0.2422	0.2578	1.20	0.3849	0.1151
0.11	0.0438	0.4562	0.66	0.2454	0.2546	1.21	0.3869	0.1131
0.12	0.0478	0.4522	0.67	0.2486	0.2514	1.22	0.3888	0.1112
0.13	0.0517	0.4483	0.68	0.2517	0.2483	1.23	0.3907	0.1093
0.14	0.0557	0.4443	0.69	0.2549	0.2451	1.24	0.3925	0.1075
0.15	0.0596	0.4404	0.70	0.2580	0.2420	1.25	0.3944	0.1056
0.16	0.0636	0.4364	0.71	0.2611	0.2389	1.26	0.3962	0.1038
0.17	0.0675	0.4325	0.72	0.2642	0.2358	1.27	0.3980	0.1020
0.18	0.0714	0.4286	0.73	0.2673	0.2327	1.28	0.3997	0.1003
0.19	0.0753	0.4247	0.74	0.2704	0.2296	1.29	0.4015	0.0985
0.20	0.0793	0.4207	0.75	0.2734	0.2266	1.30	0.4032	0.0968
0.21	0.0832	0.4168	0.76	0.2764	0.2236	1.31	0.4049	0.0951
0.22	0.0871	0.4129	0.77	0.2794	0.2206	1.32	0.4066	0.0934
0.23	0.0910	0.4090	0.78	0.2823	0.2177	1.33	0.4082	0.0918
0.24	0.0948	0.4052	0.79	0.2852	0.2148	1.34	0.4099	0.0901
0.25	0.0987	0.4013	0.80	0.2881	0.2119	1.35	0.4115	0.0885
0.26	0.1026	0.3974	0.81	0.2910	0.2090	1.36	0.4131	0.0869
0.27	0.1064	0.3936	0.82	0.2939	0.2061	1.37	0.4147	0.0853
0.28	0.1103	0.3897	0.83	0.2967	0.2033	1.38	0.4162	0.0838
0.29	0.1141	0.3859	0.84	0.2995	0.2005	1.39	0.4177	0.0823
0.30	0.1179	0.3821	0.85	0.3023	0.1977	1.40	0.4192	0.0808
0.31	0.1217	0.3783	0.86	0.3051	0.1949	1.41	0.4207	0.0793
0.32	0.1255	0.3745	0.87	0.3078	0.1922	1.42	0.4222	0.0778
0.33	0.1293	0.3707	0.88	0.3106	0.1894	1.43	0.4236	0.0764
0.34	0.1331	0.3669	0.89	0.3133	0.1867	1.44	0.4251	0.0749
0.35	0.1368	0.3632	0.90	0.3159	0.1841	1.45	0.4265	0.0735
0.36	0.1406	0.3594	0.91	0.3186	0.1814	1.46	0.4279	0.0721
0.37	0.1443	0.3557	0.92	0.3212	0.1788	1.47	0.4292	0.0708
0.38	0.1480	0.3520	0.93	0.3238	0.1762	1.48	0.4306	0.0694
0.39	0.1517	0.3483	0.94	0.3264	0.1736	1.49	0.4319	0.0681
0.40	0.1554	0.3446	0.95	0.3289	0.1711	1.50	0.4332	0.0668
0.41	0.1591	0.3409	0.96	0.3315	0.1685	1.51	0.4345	0.0655
0.42	0.1628	0.3372	0.97	0.3340	0.1660	1.52	0.4357	0.0643
0.43	0.1664	0.3336	0.98	0.3365	0.1635	1.53	0.4370	0.0630
0.44	0.1700	0.3300	0.99	0.3389	0.1611	1.54	0.4382	0.0618
0.45	0.1736	0.3264	1.00	0.3413	0.1587	1.55	0.4394	0.0606
0.46	0.1772	0.3228	1.01	0.3438	0.1562	1.56	0.4406	0.0594
0.47	0.1808	0.3192	1.02	0.3461	0.1539	1.57	0.4418	0.0582
0.48	0.1844	0.3156	1.03	0.3485	0.1515	1.58	0.4429	0.0571
0.49	0.1879	0.3121	1.04	0.3508	0.1492	1.59	0.4441	0.0559
0.50	0.1915	0.3085	1.05	0.3531	0.1469	1.60	0.4452	0.0548
0.51	0.1950	0.3050	1.06	0.3554	0.1446	1.61	0.4463	0.0537
0.52	0.1985	0.3015	1.07	0.3577	0.1423	1.62	0.4474	0.0526
0.53	0.2019	0.2981	1.08	0.3599	0.1401	1.63	0.4484	0.0516
0.54	0.2054	0.2946	1.09	0.3621	0.1379	1.64	0.4495	0.0505

Table A (continued)

(A) z	(B) AREA BETWEEN MEAN AND z	(C) AREA BEYOND z	(A) z	(B) AREA BETWEEN MEAN AND z	(C) AREA BEYOND z	(A) z	(B) AREA BETWEEN MEAN AND z	(C) AREA BEYOND z
1.65	0.4505	0.0495	2.22	0.4868	0.0132	2.79	0.4974	0.0026
1.66	0.4515	0.0485	2.23	0.4871	0.0129	2.80	0.4974	0.0026
1.67	0.4525	0.0475	2.24	0.4875	0.0125	2.81	0.4975	0.0025
1.68	0.4535	0.0465	2.25	0.4878	0.0122	2.82	0.4976	0.0024
1.69	0.4545	0.0455	2.26	0.4881	0.0119	2.83	0.4977	0.0023
1.70	0.4554	0.0446	2.27	0.4884	0.0116	2.84	0.4977	0.0023
1.71	0.4564	0.0436	2.28	0.4887	0.0113	2.85	0.4978	0.0022
1.72	0.4573	0.0427	2.29	0.4890	0.0110	2.86	0.4979	0.0021
1.73	0.4582	0.0418	2.30	0.4893	0.0107	2.87	0.4979	0.0021
1.74	0.4591	0.0409	2.31	0.4896	0.0104	2.88	0.4980	0.0020
1.75	0.4599	0.0401	2.32	0.4898	0.0102	2.89	0.4981	0.0019
1.76	0.4608	0.0392	2.33	0.4901	0.0099	2.90	0.4981	0.0019
1.77	0.4616	0.0384	2.34	0.4904	0.0096	2.91	0.4982	0.0018
1.78	0.4625	0.0375	2.35	0.4906	0.0094	2.92	0.4982	0.0018
1.79	0.4633	0.0367	2.36	0.4909	0.0091	2.93	0.4983	0.0017
1.80	0.4641	0.0359	2.37	0.4911	0.0089	2.94	0.4984	0.0016
1.81	0.4649	0.0351	2.38	0.4913	0.0087	2.95	0.4984	0.0016
1.82	0.4656	0.0344	2.39	0.4916	0.0084	2.96	0.4985	0.0015
1.83	0.4664	0.0336	2.40	0.4918	0.0082	2.97	0.4985	0.0015
1.84	0.4671	0.0329	2.41	0.4920	0.0080	2.98	0.4986	0.0014
1.85	0.4678	0.0322	2.42	0.4922	0.0078	2.99	0.4986	0.0014
1.86	0.4686	0.0314	2.43	0.4925	0.0075	3.00	0.4987	0.0013
1.87	0.4693	0.0307	2.44	0.4927	0.0073	3.01	0.4987	0.0013
1.88	0.4699	0.0301	2.45	0.4929	0.0071	3.02	0.4987	0.0013
1.89	0.4706	0.0294	2.46	0.4931	0.0069	3.03	0.4988	0.0012
1.90	0.4713	0.0287	2.47	0.4932	0.0068	3.04	0.4988	0.0012
1.91	0.4719	0.0281	2.48	0.4934	0.0066	3.05	0.4989	0.0011
1.92	0.4726	0.0274	2.49	0.4936	0.0064	3.06	0.4989	0.0011
1.93	0.4732	0.0268	2.50	0.4938	0.0062	3.07	0.4989	0.0011
1.94	0.4738	0.0262	2.51	0.4940	0.0060	3.08	0.4990	0.0010
1.95	0.4744	0.0256	2.52	0.4941	0.0059	3.09	0.4990	0.0010
1.96	0.4750	0.0250	2.53	0.4943	0.0057	3.10	0.4990	0.0010
1.97	0.4756	0.0244	2.54	0.4945	0.0055	3.11	0.4991	0.0009
1.98	0.4761	0.0239	2.55	0.4946	0.0054	3.12	0.4991	0.0009
1.99	0.4767	0.0233	2.56	0.4948	0.0052	3.13	0.4991	0.0009
2.00	0.4772	0.0228	2.57	0.4949	0.0051	3.14	0.4992	0.0008
2.01	0.4778	0.0222	2.58	0.4951	0.0049	3.15	0.4992	0.0008
2.02	0.4783	0.0217	2.59	0.4952	0.0048	3.16	0.4992	0.0008
2.03	0.4788	0.0212	2.60	0.4953	0.0047	3.17	0.4992	0.0008
2.04	0.4793	0.0207	2.61	0.4955	0.0045	3.18	0.4993	0.0007
2.05	0.4798	0.0202	2.62	0.4956	0.0044	3.19	0.4993	0.0007
2.06	0.4803	0.0197	2.63	0.4957	0.0043	3.20	0.4993	0.0007
2.07	0.4808	0.0192	2.64	0.4959	0.0041	3.21	0.4993	0.0007
2.08	0.4812	0.0188	2.65	0.4960	0.0040	3.22	0.4994	0.0006
2.09	0.4817	0.0183	2.66	0.4961	0.0039	3.23	0.4994	0.0006
2.10	0.4821	0.0179	2.67	0.4962	0.0038	3.24	0.4994	0.0006
2.11	0.4826	0.0174	2.68	0.4963	0.0037	3.25	0.4994	0.0006
2.12	0.4830	0.0170	2.69	0.4964	0.0036	3.30	0.4995	0.0005
2.13	0.4834	0.0166	2.70	0.4965	0.0035	3.35	0.4996	0.0004
2.14	0.4838	0.0162	2.71	0.4966	0.0034	3.40	0.4997	0.0003
2.15	0.4842	0.0158	2.72	0.4967	0.0033	3.45	0.4997	0.0003
2.16	0.4846	0.0154	2.73	0.4968	0.0032	3.50	0.4998	0.0002
2.17	0.4850	0.0150	2.74	0.4969	0.0031	3.60	0.4998	0.0002
2.18	0.4854	0.0146	2.75	0.4970	0.0030	3.70	0.4999	0.0001
2.19	0.4857	0.0143	2.76	0.4971	0.0029	3.80	0.4999	0.0001
2.20	0.4861	0.0139	2.77	0.4972	0.0028	3.90	0.49995	0.00005
2.21	0.4864	0.0136	2.78	0.4973	0.0027	4.00	0.49997	0.00003

Tabled values are two-tailed.

Table B   Table of χ^2

DEGREES OF FREEDOM df	0.10	0.05	0.02	0.01
1	2.706	3.841	5.412	6.635
2	4.605	5.991	7.824	9.210
3	6.251	7.815	9.837	11.341
4	7.779	9.488	11.668	13.277
5	9.236	11.070	13.388	15.086
6	10.645	12.592	15.033	16.812
7	12.017	14.067	16.622	18.475
8	13.362	15.507	18.168	20.090
9	14.684	16.919	19.679	21.666
10	15.987	18.307	21.161	23.209
11	17.275	19.675	22.618	24.725
12	18.549	21.026	24.054	26.217
13	19.812	22.362	25.472	27.688
14	21.064	23.685	26.873	29.141
15	22.307	24.996	28.259	30.578
16	23.542	26.296	29.633	32.000
17	24.769	27.587	30.995	33.409
18	25.989	28.869	32.346	34.805
19	27.204	30.144	33.687	36.191
20	28.412	31.410	35.020	37.566
21	29.615	32.671	36.343	38.932
22	30.813	33.924	37.659	40.289
23	32.007	35.172	38.968	41.638
24	33.196	36.415	40.270	42.980
25	34.382	37.652	41.566	44.314
26	35.563	38.885	42.856	45.642
27	36.741	40.113	44.140	46.963
28	37.916	41.337	45.419	48.278
29	39.087	42.557	46.693	49.588
30	40.256	43.773	47.962	50.892

For any given df, Table C shows the values of *t* corresponding to various levels of probability. Obtained *t* is significant at a given level if it is equal to or *greater than* the value shown in the table.

Table C Critical values of *t*

	LEVEL OF SIGNIFICANCE FOR ONE-TAILED TEST					
	0.10	0.05	0.025	0.01	0.005	0.0005
	LEVEL OF SIGNIFICANCE FOR TWO-TAILED TEST					
df	0.20	0.10	0.05	0.02	0.01	0.001
1	3.078	6.314	12.706	31.821	63.657	636.619
2	1.886	2.920	4.303	6.965	9.925	31.598
3	1.638	2.353	3.182	4.541	5.841	12.941
4	1.533	2.132	2.776	3.747	4.604	8.610
5	1.476	2.015	2.571	3.365	4.032	6.859
6	1.440	1.943	2.447	3.143	3.707	5.959
7	1.415	1.895	2.365	2.998	3.499	5.405
8	1.397	1.860	2.306	2.896	3.355	5.041
9	1.383	1.833	2.262	2.821	3.250	4.781
10	1.372	1.812	2.228	2.764	3.169	4.587
11	1.363	1.796	2.201	2.718	3.106	4.437
12	1.356	1.782	2.179	2.681	3.055	4.318
13	1.350	1.771	2.160	2.650	3.012	4.221
14	1.345	1.761	2.145	2.624	2.977	4.140
15	1.341	1.753	2.131	2.602	2.947	4.073
16	1.337	1.746	2.120	2.583	2.921	4.015
17	1.333	1.740	2.110	2.567	2.898	3.965
18	1.330	1.734	2.101	2.552	2.878	3.922
19	1.328	1.729	2.093	2.539	2.861	3.883
20	1.325	1.725	2.086	2.528	2.845	3.850
21	1.323	1.721	2.080	2.518	2.831	3.819
22	1.321	1.717	2.074	2.508	2.819	3.792
23	1.319	1.714	2.069	2.500	2.807	3.767
24	1.318	1.711	2.064	2.492	2.797	3.745
25	1.316	1.708	2.060	2.485	2.787	3.725
26	1.315	1.706	2.056	2.479	2.779	3.707
27	1.314	1.703	2.052	2.473	2.771	3.690
28	1.313	1.701	2.048	2.467	2.763	3.674
29	1.311	1.699	2.045	2.462	2.756	3.659
30	1.310	1.697	2.042	2.457	2.750	3.646
40	1.303	1.684	2.021	2.423	2.704	3.551
60	1.296	1.671	2.000	2.390	2.660	3.460
120	1.289	1.658	1.980	2.358	2.617	3.373
∞	1.282	1.645	1.960	2.326	2.576	3.291

Note: Table C is taken from Table III (page 46) of Fisher and Yates *Statistical Tables for Biological, Agricultural and Medical Research*, published by Longman Group Ltd., London (previously published by Oliver and Boyd, Edinburgh), and by permission of the authors and publishers.

The obtained F is significant at a given level if it is equal to or *greater than* the value shown in Table D. 0.05 (light row) and 0.01 (dark row) values for the distribution of F.

The values shown are the right tail of the distribution obtained by dividing the larger variance estimate by the smaller variance estimate. To find the complementary left or lower tail for a given df and α-level, reverse the degrees of freedom and find the reciprocal of that value in the F-table. For example, the value cutting off the top 5% of the area for df 7 and 12 is 2.85. To find the cutoff point of the bottom 5% of the area, find the tabled value at the $\alpha = 0.05$ level for 12 and 7 df. This is found to be 3.57. The reciprocal is $1/3.57 = 0.28$. Thus, 5% of the area falls *at or below an* $F = 0.28$.

Table D   Critical values of *F*

DEGREES OF FREEDOM FOR NUMERATOR

Each cell shows the critical value for the 0.05 level (upper) and the 0.01 level (lower, bold).

df (denom.)	∞	500	200	100	75	50	40	30	24	20	16	14	12	11	10	9	8	7	6	5	4	3	2	1
1	254 / 6366	254 / 6361	254 / 6352	253 / 6334	253 / 6323	252 / 6302	251 / 6286	250 / 6258	249 / 6234	248 / 6208	246 / 6169	245 / 6142	244 / 6106	243 / 6082	242 / 6056	241 / 6022	239 / 5981	237 / 5928	234 / 5859	230 / 5764	225 / 5625	216 / 5403	200 / 4999	161 / 4052
2	19.50 / 99.50	19.50 / 99.50	19.49 / 99.49	19.49 / 99.49	19.48 / 99.49	19.47 / 99.48	19.47 / 99.48	19.46 / 99.47	19.45 / 99.46	19.44 / 99.45	19.43 / 99.44	19.42 / 99.43	19.41 / 99.42	19.40 / 99.41	19.39 / 99.40	19.38 / 99.38	19.37 / 99.36	19.36 / 99.34	19.33 / 99.33	19.30 / 99.30	19.25 / 99.25	19.16 / 99.17	19.00 / 99.01	18.51 / 98.49
3	8.53 / 26.12	8.54 / 26.14	8.54 / 26.18	8.56 / 26.23	8.57 / 26.27	8.58 / 26.30	8.60 / 26.41	8.62 / 26.50	8.64 / 26.60	8.66 / 26.69	8.69 / 26.83	8.71 / 26.92	8.74 / 27.05	8.76 / 27.13	8.78 / 27.23	8.81 / 27.34	8.84 / 27.49	8.88 / 27.67	8.94 / 27.91	9.01 / 28.24	9.12 / 28.71	9.28 / 29.46	9.55 / 30.81	10.13 / 34.12
4	5.63 / 13.46	5.64 / 13.48	5.65 / 13.52	5.66 / 13.57	5.68 / 13.61	5.70 / 13.69	5.71 / 13.74	5.74 / 13.83	5.77 / 13.93	5.80 / 14.02	5.84 / 14.15	5.87 / 14.24	5.91 / 14.37	5.93 / 14.45	5.96 / 14.54	6.00 / 14.66	6.04 / 14.80	6.09 / 14.98	6.16 / 15.21	6.26 / 15.52	6.39 / 15.98	6.59 / 16.69	6.94 / 18.00	7.71 / 21.20
5	4.36 / 9.02	4.37 / 9.04	4.38 / 9.07	4.40 / 9.13	4.42 / 9.17	4.44 / 9.24	4.46 / 9.29	4.50 / 9.38	4.53 / 9.47	4.56 / 9.55	4.60 / 9.68	4.64 / 9.77	4.68 / 9.89	4.70 / 9.96	4.74 / 10.05	4.78 / 10.15	4.82 / 10.27	4.88 / 10.45	4.95 / 10.67	5.05 / 10.97	5.19 / 11.39	5.41 / 12.06	5.79 / 13.27	6.61 / 16.26
6	3.67 / 6.88	3.68 / 6.90	3.69 / 6.94	3.71 / 6.99	3.72 / 7.02	3.75 / 7.09	3.77 / 7.14	3.81 / 7.23	3.84 / 7.31	3.87 / 7.39	3.92 / 7.52	3.96 / 7.60	4.00 / 7.72	4.03 / 7.79	4.06 / 7.87	4.10 / 7.98	4.15 / 8.10	4.21 / 8.26	4.28 / 8.47	4.39 / 8.75	4.53 / 9.15	4.76 / 9.78	5.14 / 10.92	5.99 / 13.74
7	3.23 / 5.65	3.24 / 5.67	3.25 / 5.70	3.28 / 5.75	3.29 / 5.78	3.32 / 5.85	3.34 / 5.90	3.38 / 5.98	3.41 / 6.07	3.44 / 6.15	3.49 / 6.27	3.52 / 6.35	3.57 / 6.47	3.60 / 6.54	3.63 / 6.62	3.68 / 6.71	3.73 / 6.84	3.79 / 7.00	3.87 / 7.19	3.97 / 7.46	4.12 / 7.85	4.35 / 8.45	4.74 / 9.55	5.59 / 12.25
8	2.93 / 4.86	2.94 / 4.88	2.96 / 4.91	2.98 / 4.96	3.00 / 5.00	3.03 / 5.06	3.05 / 5.11	3.08 / 5.20	3.12 / 5.28	3.15 / 5.36	3.20 / 5.48	3.23 / 5.56	3.28 / 5.67	3.31 / 5.74	3.34 / 5.82	3.39 / 5.91	3.44 / 6.03	3.50 / 6.19	3.58 / 6.37	3.69 / 6.63	3.84 / 7.01	4.07 / 7.59	4.46 / 8.65	5.32 / 11.26
9	2.71 / 4.31	2.72 / 4.33	2.73 / 4.36	2.76 / 4.41	2.77 / 4.45	2.80 / 4.51	2.82 / 4.56	2.86 / 4.64	2.90 / 4.73	2.93 / 4.80	2.98 / 4.92	3.02 / 5.00	3.07 / 5.11	3.10 / 5.18	3.13 / 5.26	3.18 / 5.35	3.23 / 5.47	3.29 / 5.62	3.37 / 5.80	3.48 / 6.06	3.63 / 6.42	3.86 / 6.99	4.26 / 8.02	5.12 / 10.56
10	2.54 / 3.91	2.55 / 3.93	2.56 / 3.96	2.59 / 4.01	2.61 / 4.05	2.64 / 4.12	2.67 / 4.17	2.70 / 4.25	2.74 / 4.33	2.77 / 4.41	2.82 / 4.52	2.86 / 4.60	2.91 / 4.71	2.94 / 4.78	2.97 / 4.85	3.02 / 4.95	3.07 / 5.06	3.14 / 5.21	3.22 / 5.39	3.33 / 5.64	3.48 / 5.99	3.71 / 6.55	4.10 / 7.56	4.96 / 10.04
11	2.40 / 3.60	2.41 / 3.62	2.42 / 3.66	2.45 / 3.70	2.47 / 3.74	2.50 / 3.80	2.53 / 3.86	2.57 / 3.94	2.61 / 4.02	2.65 / 4.10	2.70 / 4.21	2.74 / 4.29	2.79 / 4.40	2.82 / 4.46	2.86 / 4.54	2.90 / 4.63	2.95 / 4.74	3.01 / 4.88	3.09 / 5.07	3.20 / 5.32	3.36 / 5.67	3.59 / 6.22	3.98 / 7.20	4.84 / 9.65
12	2.30 / 3.36	2.31 / 3.38	2.32 / 3.41	2.35 / 3.46	2.36 / 3.49	2.40 / 3.56	2.42 / 3.61	2.46 / 3.70	2.50 / 3.78	2.54 / 3.86	2.60 / 3.98	2.64 / 4.05	2.69 / 4.16	2.72 / 4.22	2.76 / 4.30	2.80 / 4.39	2.85 / 4.50	2.92 / 4.65	3.00 / 4.82	3.11 / 5.06	3.26 / 5.41	3.49 / 5.95	3.88 / 6.93	4.75 / 9.33
13	2.21 / 3.16	2.22 / 3.18	2.24 / 3.21	2.26 / 3.27	2.28 / 3.30	2.32 / 3.37	2.34 / 3.42	2.38 / 3.51	2.42 / 3.59	2.46 / 3.67	2.51 / 3.78	2.55 / 3.85	2.60 / 3.96	2.63 / 4.02	2.67 / 4.10	2.72 / 4.19	2.77 / 4.30	2.84 / 4.44	2.92 / 4.62	3.02 / 4.86	3.18 / 5.20	3.41 / 5.74	3.80 / 6.70	4.67 / 9.07
14	2.13 / 3.00	2.14 / 3.02	2.16 / 3.06	2.19 / 3.11	2.21 / 3.14	2.24 / 3.21	2.27 / 3.26	2.31 / 3.34	2.35 / 3.43	2.39 / 3.51	2.44 / 3.62	2.48 / 3.70	2.53 / 3.80	2.56 / 3.86	2.60 / 3.94	2.65 / 4.03	2.70 / 4.14	2.77 / 4.28	2.85 / 4.46	2.96 / 4.69	3.11 / 5.03	3.34 / 5.56	3.74 / 6.51	4.60 / 8.86
15	2.07 / 2.87	2.08 / 2.89	2.10 / 2.92	2.12 / 2.97	2.15 / 3.00	2.18 / 3.07	2.21 / 3.12	2.25 / 3.20	2.29 / 3.29	2.33 / 3.36	2.39 / 3.48	2.43 / 3.56	2.48 / 3.67	2.51 / 3.73	2.55 / 3.80	2.59 / 3.89	2.64 / 4.00	2.70 / 4.14	2.79 / 4.32	2.90 / 4.56	3.06 / 4.89	3.29 / 5.42	3.68 / 6.36	4.54 / 8.68

DEGREES OF FREEDOM FOR DENOMINATOR

Table D   (*continued*)

DEGREES OF FREEDOM FOR NUMERATOR

df denom	1	2	3	4	5	6	7	8	9	10	11	12	14	16	20	24	30	40	50	75	100	200	500	∞
16	4.49 / 8.53	3.63 / 6.23	3.24 / 5.29	3.01 / 4.77	2.85 / 4.44	2.74 / 4.20	2.66 / 4.03	2.59 / 3.89	2.54 / 3.78	2.49 / 3.69	2.45 / 3.61	2.42 / 3.55	2.37 / 3.45	2.33 / 3.37	2.28 / 3.25	2.24 / 3.18	2.20 / 3.10	2.16 / 3.01	2.13 / 2.96	2.09 / 2.89	2.07 / 2.86	2.04 / 2.80	2.02 / 2.77	2.01 / 2.75
17	4.45 / 8.40	3.59 / 6.11	3.20 / 5.18	2.96 / 4.67	2.81 / 4.34	2.70 / 4.10	2.62 / 3.93	2.55 / 3.79	2.50 / 3.68	2.45 / 3.59	2.41 / 3.52	2.38 / 3.45	2.33 / 3.35	2.29 / 3.27	2.23 / 3.16	2.19 / 3.08	2.15 / 3.00	2.11 / 2.92	2.08 / 2.86	2.04 / 2.79	2.02 / 2.76	1.99 / 2.70	1.97 / 2.67	1.96 / 2.65
18	4.41 / 8.28	3.55 / 6.01	3.16 / 5.09	2.93 / 4.58	2.77 / 4.25	2.66 / 4.01	2.58 / 3.85	2.51 / 3.71	2.46 / 3.60	2.41 / 3.51	2.37 / 3.44	2.34 / 3.37	2.29 / 3.27	2.25 / 3.19	2.19 / 3.07	2.15 / 3.00	2.11 / 2.91	2.07 / 2.83	2.04 / 2.78	2.00 / 2.71	1.98 / 2.68	1.95 / 2.62	1.93 / 2.59	1.92 / 2.57
19	4.38 / 8.18	3.52 / 5.93	3.13 / 5.01	2.90 / 4.50	2.74 / 4.17	2.63 / 3.94	2.55 / 3.77	2.48 / 3.63	2.43 / 3.52	2.38 / 3.43	2.34 / 3.36	2.31 / 3.30	2.26 / 3.19	2.21 / 3.12	2.15 / 3.00	2.11 / 2.92	2.07 / 2.84	2.02 / 2.76	2.00 / 2.70	1.96 / 2.63	1.94 / 2.60	1.91 / 2.54	1.90 / 2.51	1.88 / 2.49
20	4.35 / 8.10	3.49 / 5.85	3.10 / 4.94	2.87 / 4.43	2.71 / 4.10	2.60 / 3.87	2.52 / 3.71	2.45 / 3.56	2.40 / 3.45	2.35 / 3.37	2.31 / 3.30	2.28 / 3.23	2.23 / 3.13	2.18 / 3.05	2.12 / 2.94	2.08 / 2.86	2.04 / 2.77	1.99 / 2.69	1.96 / 2.63	1.92 / 2.56	1.90 / 2.53	1.87 / 2.47	1.85 / 2.44	1.84 / 2.42
21	4.32 / 8.02	3.47 / 5.78	3.07 / 4.87	2.84 / 4.37	2.68 / 4.04	2.57 / 3.81	2.49 / 3.65	2.42 / 3.51	2.37 / 3.40	2.32 / 3.31	2.28 / 3.24	2.25 / 3.17	2.20 / 3.07	2.15 / 2.99	2.09 / 2.88	2.05 / 2.80	2.00 / 2.72	1.96 / 2.63	1.93 / 2.58	1.89 / 2.51	1.87 / 2.47	1.84 / 2.42	1.82 / 2.38	1.81 / 2.36
22	4.30 / 7.94	3.44 / 5.72	3.05 / 4.82	2.82 / 4.31	2.66 / 3.99	2.55 / 3.76	2.47 / 3.59	2.40 / 3.45	2.35 / 3.35	2.30 / 3.26	2.26 / 3.18	2.23 / 3.12	2.18 / 3.02	2.13 / 2.94	2.07 / 2.83	2.03 / 2.75	1.98 / 2.67	1.93 / 2.58	1.91 / 2.53	1.87 / 2.46	1.84 / 2.42	1.81 / 2.37	1.80 / 2.33	1.78 / 2.31
23	4.28 / 7.88	3.42 / 5.66	3.03 / 4.76	2.80 / 4.26	2.64 / 3.94	2.53 / 3.71	2.45 / 3.54	2.38 / 3.41	2.32 / 3.30	2.28 / 3.21	2.24 / 3.14	2.20 / 3.07	2.14 / 2.97	2.10 / 2.89	2.04 / 2.78	2.00 / 2.70	1.96 / 2.62	1.91 / 2.53	1.88 / 2.48	1.84 / 2.41	1.82 / 2.37	1.79 / 2.32	1.77 / 2.28	1.76 / 2.26
24	4.26 / 7.82	3.40 / 5.61	3.01 / 4.72	2.78 / 4.22	2.62 / 3.90	2.51 / 3.67	2.43 / 3.50	2.36 / 3.36	2.30 / 3.25	2.26 / 3.17	2.22 / 3.09	2.18 / 3.03	2.13 / 2.93	2.09 / 2.85	2.02 / 2.74	1.98 / 2.66	1.94 / 2.58	1.89 / 2.49	1.86 / 2.44	1.82 / 2.36	1.80 / 2.33	1.76 / 2.27	1.74 / 2.23	1.73 / 2.21
25	4.24 / 7.77	3.38 / 5.57	2.99 / 4.68	2.76 / 4.18	2.60 / 3.86	2.49 / 3.63	2.41 / 3.46	2.34 / 3.32	2.28 / 3.21	2.24 / 3.13	2.20 / 3.05	2.16 / 2.99	2.11 / 2.89	2.06 / 2.81	2.00 / 2.70	1.96 / 2.62	1.92 / 2.54	1.87 / 2.45	1.84 / 2.40	1.80 / 2.32	1.77 / 2.29	1.74 / 2.23	1.72 / 2.19	1.71 / 2.17
26	4.22 / 7.72	3.37 / 5.53	2.98 / 4.64	2.74 / 4.14	2.59 / 3.82	2.47 / 3.59	2.39 / 3.42	2.32 / 3.29	2.27 / 3.17	2.22 / 3.09	2.18 / 3.02	2.15 / 2.96	2.10 / 2.86	2.05 / 2.77	1.99 / 2.66	1.95 / 2.58	1.90 / 2.50	1.85 / 2.41	1.82 / 2.36	1.78 / 2.28	1.76 / 2.25	1.72 / 2.19	1.70 / 2.15	1.69 / 2.13
27	4.21 / 7.68	3.35 / 5.49	2.96 / 4.60	2.73 / 4.11	2.57 / 3.79	2.46 / 3.56	2.37 / 3.39	2.30 / 3.26	2.25 / 3.14	2.20 / 3.06	2.16 / 2.98	2.13 / 2.93	2.08 / 2.83	2.03 / 2.74	1.97 / 2.63	1.93 / 2.55	1.88 / 2.47	1.84 / 2.38	1.80 / 2.33	1.76 / 2.25	1.74 / 2.21	1.71 / 2.16	1.68 / 2.12	1.67 / 2.10
28	4.20 / 7.64	3.34 / 5.45	2.95 / 4.57	2.71 / 4.07	2.56 / 3.76	2.44 / 3.53	2.36 / 3.36	2.29 / 3.23	2.24 / 3.11	2.19 / 3.03	2.15 / 2.95	2.12 / 2.90	2.06 / 2.80	2.02 / 2.71	1.96 / 2.60	1.91 / 2.52	1.87 / 2.44	1.81 / 2.35	1.78 / 2.30	1.75 / 2.22	1.72 / 2.18	1.69 / 2.13	1.67 / 2.09	1.65 / 2.06
29	4.18 / 7.60	3.33 / 5.42	2.93 / 4.54	2.70 / 4.04	2.54 / 3.73	2.43 / 3.50	2.35 / 3.33	2.28 / 3.20	2.22 / 3.08	2.18 / 3.00	2.14 / 2.92	2.10 / 2.87	2.05 / 2.77	2.00 / 2.68	1.94 / 2.57	1.90 / 2.49	1.85 / 2.41	1.80 / 2.32	1.77 / 2.27	1.73 / 2.19	1.71 / 2.15	1.68 / 2.10	1.65 / 2.06	1.64 / 2.03
30	4.17 / 7.56	3.32 / 5.39	2.92 / 4.51	2.69 / 4.02	2.53 / 3.70	2.42 / 3.47	2.34 / 3.30	2.27 / 3.17	2.21 / 3.06	2.16 / 2.98	2.12 / 2.90	2.09 / 2.84	2.04 / 2.74	1.99 / 2.66	1.93 / 2.55	1.89 / 2.47	1.84 / 2.38	1.79 / 2.29	1.76 / 2.24	1.72 / 2.16	1.69 / 2.13	1.66 / 2.07	1.64 / 2.03	1.62 / 2.01

DEGREES OF FREEDOM FOR DENOMINATOR

Table D (*continued*)   0.05 (light row) and 0.01 (dark row) values for the distribution of *F*

DEGREES OF FREEDOM FOR NUMERATOR

df (denom.)		1	2	3	4	5	6	7	8	9	10	11	12	14	16	20	24	30	40	50	75	100	200	500	∞
32	.05	4.15	3.30	2.90	2.67	2.51	2.40	2.32	2.25	2.19	2.14	2.10	2.07	2.02	1.97	1.91	1.86	1.82	1.76	1.74	1.69	1.67	1.64	1.61	1.59
	.01	7.50	5.34	4.46	3.97	3.66	3.42	3.25	3.12	3.01	2.94	2.86	2.80	2.70	2.62	2.51	2.42	2.34	2.25	2.20	2.12	2.08	2.02	1.98	1.96
34	.05	4.13	3.28	2.88	2.65	2.49	2.38	2.30	2.23	2.17	2.12	2.08	2.05	2.00	1.95	1.89	1.84	1.80	1.74	1.71	1.67	1.64	1.61	1.59	1.57
	.01	7.44	5.29	4.42	3.93	3.61	3.38	3.21	3.08	2.97	2.89	2.82	2.76	2.66	2.58	2.47	2.38	2.30	2.21	2.15	2.08	2.04	1.98	1.94	1.91
36	.05	4.11	3.26	2.86	2.63	2.48	2.36	2.28	2.21	2.15	2.10	2.06	2.03	1.98	1.93	1.87	1.82	1.78	1.72	1.69	1.65	1.62	1.59	1.56	1.55
	.01	7.39	5.25	4.38	3.89	3.58	3.35	3.18	3.04	2.94	2.86	2.78	2.72	2.62	2.54	2.43	2.35	2.26	2.17	2.12	2.04	2.00	1.94	1.90	1.87
38	.05	4.10	3.25	2.85	2.62	2.46	2.35	2.26	2.19	2.14	2.09	2.05	2.02	1.96	1.92	1.85	1.80	1.76	1.71	1.67	1.63	1.60	1.57	1.54	1.53
	.01	7.35	5.21	4.34	3.86	3.54	3.32	3.15	3.02	2.91	2.82	2.75	2.69	2.59	2.51	2.40	2.32	2.22	2.14	2.08	2.00	1.97	1.90	1.86	1.84
40	.05	4.08	3.23	2.84	2.61	2.45	2.34	2.25	2.18	2.12	2.07	2.04	2.00	1.95	1.90	1.84	1.79	1.74	1.69	1.66	1.61	1.59	1.55	1.53	1.51
	.01	7.31	5.18	4.31	3.83	3.51	3.29	3.12	2.99	2.88	2.80	2.73	2.66	2.56	2.49	2.37	2.29	2.20	2.11	2.05	1.97	1.94	1.88	1.84	1.81
42	.05	4.07	3.22	2.83	2.59	2.44	2.32	2.24	2.17	2.11	2.06	2.02	1.99	1.94	1.89	1.82	1.78	1.73	1.68	1.64	1.60	1.57	1.54	1.51	1.49
	.01	7.27	5.15	4.29	3.80	3.49	3.26	3.10	2.96	2.86	2.77	2.70	2.64	2.54	2.46	2.35	2.26	2.17	2.08	2.02	1.94	1.91	1.85	1.80	1.78
44	.05	4.06	3.21	2.82	2.58	2.43	2.31	2.23	2.16	2.10	2.05	2.01	1.98	1.92	1.88	1.81	1.76	1.72	1.66	1.63	1.58	1.56	1.52	1.50	1.48
	.01	7.24	5.12	4.26	3.78	3.46	3.24	3.07	2.94	2.84	2.75	2.68	2.62	2.52	2.44	2.32	2.24	2.15	2.06	2.00	1.92	1.88	1.82	1.78	1.75
46	.05	4.05	3.20	2.81	2.57	2.42	2.30	2.22	2.14	2.09	2.04	2.00	1.97	1.91	1.87	1.80	1.75	1.71	1.65	1.62	1.57	1.54	1.51	1.48	1.46
	.01	7.21	5.10	4.24	3.76	3.44	3.22	3.05	2.92	2.82	2.73	2.66	2.60	2.50	2.42	2.30	2.22	2.13	2.04	1.98	1.90	1.86	1.80	1.76	1.72
48	.05	4.04	3.19	2.80	2.56	2.41	2.30	2.21	2.14	2.08	2.03	1.99	1.96	1.90	1.86	1.79	1.74	1.70	1.64	1.61	1.56	1.53	1.50	1.47	1.45
	.01	7.19	5.08	4.22	3.74	3.42	3.20	3.04	2.90	2.80	2.71	2.64	2.58	2.48	2.40	2.28	2.20	2.11	2.02	1.96	1.88	1.84	1.78	1.73	1.70
50	.05	4.03	3.18	2.79	2.56	2.40	2.29	2.20	2.13	2.07	2.02	1.98	1.95	1.90	1.85	1.78	1.74	1.69	1.63	1.60	1.55	1.52	1.48	1.46	1.44
	.01	7.17	5.06	4.20	3.72	3.41	3.18	3.02	2.88	2.78	2.70	2.62	2.56	2.46	2.39	2.26	2.18	2.10	2.00	1.94	1.86	1.82	1.76	1.71	1.68
55	.05	4.02	3.17	2.78	2.54	2.38	2.27	2.18	2.11	2.05	2.00	1.97	1.93	1.88	1.83	1.76	1.72	1.67	1.61	1.58	1.52	1.50	1.46	1.43	1.41
	.01	7.12	5.01	4.16	3.68	3.37	3.15	2.98	2.85	2.75	2.66	2.59	2.53	2.43	2.35	2.23	2.15	2.06	1.96	1.90	1.82	1.78	1.71	1.66	1.64
60	.05	4.00	3.15	2.76	2.52	2.37	2.25	2.17	2.10	2.04	1.99	1.95	1.92	1.86	1.81	1.75	1.70	1.65	1.59	1.56	1.50	1.48	1.44	1.41	1.39
	.01	7.08	4.98	4.13	3.65	3.34	3.12	2.95	2.82	2.72	2.63	2.56	2.50	2.40	2.32	2.20	2.12	2.03	1.93	1.87	1.79	1.74	1.68	1.63	1.60
65	.05	3.99	3.14	2.75	2.51	2.36	2.24	2.15	2.08	2.02	1.98	1.94	1.90	1.85	1.80	1.73	1.68	1.63	1.57	1.54	1.49	1.46	1.42	1.39	1.37
	.01	7.04	4.95	4.10	3.62	3.31	3.09	2.93	2.79	2.70	2.61	2.54	2.47	2.37	2.30	2.18	2.09	2.00	1.90	1.84	1.76	1.71	1.64	1.60	1.56
70	.05	3.98	3.13	2.74	2.50	2.35	2.22	2.14	2.07	2.01	1.97	1.93	1.89	1.84	1.79	1.72	1.67	1.62	1.56	1.53	1.47	1.45	1.40	1.37	1.35
	.01	7.01	4.92	4.08	3.60	3.29	3.07	2.91	2.77	2.67	2.59	2.51	2.45	2.35	2.28	2.15	2.07	1.98	1.88	1.82	1.74	1.69	1.62	1.56	1.53
80	.05	3.96	3.11	2.72	2.48	2.33	2.21	2.12	2.05	1.99	1.95	1.91	1.88	1.82	1.77	1.70	1.65	1.60	1.54	1.51	1.45	1.42	1.38	1.35	1.32
	.01	6.96	4.88	4.04	3.56	3.25	3.04	2.87	2.74	2.64	2.55	2.48	2.41	2.32	2.24	2.11	2.03	1.94	1.84	1.78	1.70	1.65	1.57	1.52	1.49

DEGREES OF FREEDOM FOR DENOMINATOR

Table D   (*continued*)

DEGREES OF FREEDOM FOR NUMERATOR

df (denom)	1	2	3	4	5	6	7	8	9	10	11	12	14	16	20	24	30	40	50	75	100	200	500	∞
100	3.94 / 6.90	3.09 / 4.82	2.70 / 3.98	2.46 / 3.51	2.30 / 3.20	2.19 / 2.99	2.10 / 2.82	2.03 / 2.69	1.97 / 2.59	1.92 / 2.51	1.88 / 2.43	1.85 / 2.36	1.79 / 2.26	1.75 / 2.19	1.68 / 2.06	1.63 / 1.98	1.57 / 1.89	1.51 / 1.79	1.48 / 1.73	1.42 / 1.64	1.39 / 1.59	1.34 / 1.51	1.30 / 1.46	1.28 / 1.43
125	3.92 / 6.84	3.07 / 4.78	2.68 / 3.94	2.44 / 3.47	2.29 / 3.17	2.17 / 2.95	2.08 / 2.79	2.01 / 2.65	1.95 / 2.56	1.90 / 2.47	1.86 / 2.40	1.83 / 2.33	1.77 / 2.23	1.72 / 2.15	1.65 / 2.03	1.60 / 1.94	1.55 / 1.85	1.49 / 1.75	1.45 / 1.68	1.39 / 1.59	1.36 / 1.54	1.31 / 1.46	1.27 / 1.40	1.25 / 1.37
150	3.91 / 6.81	3.06 / 4.75	2.67 / 3.91	2.43 / 3.44	2.27 / 3.13	2.16 / 2.92	2.07 / 2.76	2.00 / 2.62	1.94 / 2.53	1.89 / 2.44	1.85 / 2.37	1.82 / 2.30	1.76 / 2.20	1.71 / 2.12	1.64 / 2.00	1.59 / 1.91	1.54 / 1.83	1.47 / 1.72	1.44 / 1.66	1.37 / 1.56	1.34 / 1.51	1.29 / 1.43	1.25 / 1.37	1.22 / 1.33
200	3.89 / 6.76	3.04 / 4.71	2.65 / 3.88	2.41 / 3.41	2.26 / 3.11	2.14 / 2.90	2.05 / 2.73	1.98 / 2.60	1.92 / 2.50	1.87 / 2.41	1.83 / 2.34	1.80 / 2.28	1.74 / 2.17	1.69 / 2.09	1.62 / 1.97	1.57 / 1.88	1.52 / 1.79	1.45 / 1.69	1.42 / 1.62	1.35 / 1.53	1.32 / 1.48	1.26 / 1.39	1.22 / 1.33	1.19 / 1.28
400	3.86 / 6.70	3.02 / 4.66	2.62 / 3.83	2.39 / 3.36	2.23 / 3.06	2.12 / 2.85	2.03 / 2.69	1.96 / 2.55	1.90 / 2.46	1.85 / 2.37	1.81 / 2.29	1.78 / 2.23	1.72 / 2.12	1.67 / 2.04	1.60 / 1.92	1.54 / 1.84	1.49 / 1.74	1.42 / 1.64	1.38 / 1.57	1.32 / 1.47	1.28 / 1.42	1.22 / 1.32	1.16 / 1.24	1.13 / 1.19
1000	3.85 / 6.66	3.00 / 4.62	2.61 / 3.80	2.38 / 3.34	2.22 / 3.04	2.10 / 2.82	2.02 / 2.66	1.95 / 2.53	1.89 / 2.43	1.84 / 2.34	1.80 / 2.26	1.76 / 2.20	1.70 / 2.09	1.65 / 2.01	1.58 / 1.89	1.53 / 1.81	1.47 / 1.71	1.41 / 1.61	1.36 / 1.54	1.30 / 1.44	1.26 / 1.38	1.19 / 1.28	1.13 / 1.19	1.08 / 1.11
∞	3.84 / 6.64	2.99 / 4.60	2.60 / 3.78	2.37 / 3.32	2.21 / 3.02	2.09 / 2.80	2.01 / 2.64	1.94 / 2.51	1.88 / 2.41	1.83 / 2.32	1.79 / 2.24	1.75 / 2.18	1.69 / 2.07	1.64 / 1.99	1.57 / 1.87	1.52 / 1.79	1.46 / 1.69	1.40 / 1.59	1.35 / 1.52	1.28 / 1.41	1.24 / 1.36	1.17 / 1.25	1.11 / 1.15	1.00 / 1.00

DEGREES OF FREEDOM FOR DENOMINATOR

A difference in variances is significant at $\alpha = 0.05$ with df_1 and df_2 if it *equals* or *exceeds* the upper value in each cell or is *less than or equal to* the lower value in that cell; for example, if $\hat{s}_1^2 = 8.69$, df $= 12$ and $\hat{s}_2^2 = 2.63$, df $= 9$, $F = 3.30$. The critical values at df_{12} and df_9 are 0.291 and 3.87. Since obtained F is between these values, we fail to reject the hypothesis of homogeneity of variances. (*Note:* Had we calculated F with $\hat{s}_1^2$ in the denominator, the critical lower and upper values at 9 and 12 df would have been 0.259 and 3.44.)

Table D₁   Critical values of F that cut off the upper and lower 2.5% of the F distributions

df	1	2	3	4	5	6	7	8	9	10	11	12	15	20	24	30	40	50	60	100	200	500
1	.002	.026	.057	.082	.100	.113	.124	.132	.139	.144	.149	.153	.161	.170	.175	.180	.184	.187	.189	.193	.196	.198
	648	800	864	900	922	937	948	957	963	969	973	977	985	993	997	1000	1010	1010	1010	1010	1020	1020
2	.001	.026	.062	.094	.119	.138	.153	.165	.175	.183	.190	.196	.210	.224	.232	.239	.247	.251	.255	.261	.266	.269
	38.5	39.0	39.2	39.2	39.3	39.3	39.4	39.4	39.4	39.4	39.4	39.4	39.4	39.4	39.5	39.5	39.5	39.5	39.5	39.5	39.5	39.5
3	.001	.026	.065	.100	.129	.152	.170	.185	.197	.207	.216	.224	.241	.259	.269	.279	.289	.295	.299	.308	.314	.318
	17.4	16.0	15.4	15.1	14.9	14.7	14.6	14.5	14.5	14.4	14.4	14.3	14.3	14.2	14.1	14.1	14.0	14.0	14.0	14.0	13.9	13.9
4	.001	.026	.066	.104	.135	.161	.181	.198	.212	.224	.234	.243	.263	.284	.296	.308	.320	.327	.332	.342	.351	.356
	12.2	10.6	9.98	9.60	9.36	9.20	9.07	8.98	8.90	8.84	8.79	8.75	8.66	8.56	8.51	8.46	8.41	8.38	8.36	8.32	8.29	8.27
5	.001	.025	.067	.107	.140	.167	.189	.208	.223	.236	.248	.257	.280	.304	.317	.330	.344	.353	.359	.370	.380	.386
	10.0	8.43	7.76	7.39	7.15	6.98	6.85	6.76	6.68	6.62	6.57	6.52	6.43	6.33	6.28	6.23	6.18	6.14	6.12	6.08	6.05	6.03
6	.001	.025	.068	.109	.143	.172	.195	.215	.231	.246	.258	.268	.293	.320	.334	.349	.364	.375	.381	.394	.405	.415
	8.81	7.26	6.60	6.23	5.99	5.82	5.70	5.60	5.52	5.46	5.41	5.37	5.27	5.17	5.12	5.07	5.01	4.98	4.96	4.92	4.88	4.86
7	.001	.025	.068	.110	.146	.176	.200	.221	.238	.253	.266	.277	.304	.333	.348	.364	.381	.392	.399	.413	.426	.433
	8.07	6.54	5.89	5.52	5.29	5.12	4.99	4.90	4.82	4.76	4.71	4.67	4.57	4.47	4.42	4.36	4.31	4.28	4.25	4.21	4.18	4.16
8	.001	.025	.069	.111	.148	.179	.204	.226	.244	.259	.273	.285	.313	.343	.360	.377	.395	.407	.415	.431	.442	.450
	7.57	6.06	5.42	5.05	4.82	4.65	4.53	4.43	4.36	4.30	4.24	4.20	4.10	4.00	3.95	3.89	3.84	3.81	3.78	3.74	3.70	3.68
9	.001	.025	.069	.112	.150	.181	.207	.230	.248	.265	.279	.291	.320	.352	.370	.388	.408	.420	.428	.446	.459	.467
	7.21	5.71	5.08	4.72	4.48	4.32	4.20	4.10	4.03	3.96	3.91	3.87	3.77	3.67	3.61	3.56	3.51	3.47	3.45	3.40	3.37	3.35
10	.001	.025	.069	.113	.151	.183	.210	.233	.252	.269	.283	.296	.327	.360	.379	.398	.419	.431	.441	.459	.474	.483
	6.94	5.46	4.83	4.47	4.24	4.07	3.95	3.85	3.78	3.72	3.66	3.62	3.52	3.42	3.37	3.31	3.26	3.22	3.20	3.15	3.12	3.09

Table D₁ (continued)

11	.001	.025	.069	.114	.152	.185	.212	.236	.256	.273	.288	.301	.332	.368	.386	.407	.429	.442	.450	.472	.485	.495
	6.72	5.26	4.63	4.28	4.04	3.88	3.76	3.66	3.59	3.53	3.47	3.43	3.33	3.23	3.17	3.12	3.06	3.03	3.00	2.96	2.92	2.90
12	.001	.025	.070	.114	.153	.186	.214	.238	.259	.276	.292	.305	.337	.374	.394	.416	.437	.450	.461	.481	.498	.508
	6.55	5.10	4.47	4.12	3.89	3.73	3.61	3.51	3.44	3.37	3.32	3.28	3.18	3.07	3.02	2.96	2.91	2.87	2.85	2.80	2.76	2.74
15	.001	.025	.070	.116	.156	.190	.219	.244	.265	.284	.300	.315	.349	.389	.410	.433	.458	.474	.485	.508	.526	.538
	6.20	4.76	4.15	3.80	3.58	3.41	3.29	3.20	3.12	3.06	3.01	2.96	2.86	2.76	2.70	2.64	2.59	2.55	2.52	2.47	2.44	2.41
20	.001	.025	.071	.117	.158	.193	.224	.250	.273	.292	.310	.325	.363	.406	.430	.456	.484	.503	.514	.541	.562	.575
	5.87	4.46	3.86	3.51	3.29	3.13	3.01	2.91	2.84	2.77	2.72	2.68	2.57	2.46	2.41	2.35	2.29	2.25	2.22	2.17	2.13	2.10
24	.001	.025	.071	.117	.159	.195	.227	.253	.277	.297	.315	.331	.370	.415	.441	.468	.498	.518	.531	.562	.585	.599
	5.72	4.32	3.72	3.38	3.15	2.99	2.87	2.78	2.70	2.64	2.59	2.54	2.44	2.33	2.27	2.21	2.15	2.11	2.08	2.02	1.98	1.95
30	.001	.025	.071	.118	.161	.197	.229	.257	.281	.302	.321	.337	.378	.426	.453	.482	.515	.535	.551	.585	.610	.625
	5.57	4.18	3.59	3.25	3.03	2.87	2.75	2.65	2.57	2.51	2.46	2.41	2.31	2.20	2.14	2.07	2.01	1.97	1.94	1.88	1.84	1.81
40	.001	.025	.071	.119	.162	.199	.232	.260	.285	.307	.327	.344	.387	.437	.466	.498	.533	.556	.573	.610	.641	.662
	5.42	4.05	3.46	3.13	2.90	2.74	2.62	2.53	2.45	2.39	2.33	2.29	2.18	2.07	2.01	1.94	1.88	1.83	1.80	1.74	1.69	1.66
60	.001	.025	.071	.120	.163	.202	.235	.264	.290	.313	.333	.351	.396	.450	.481	.515	.555	.581	.600	.641	.680	.704
	5.29	3.93	3.34	3.01	2.79	2.63	2.51	2.41	2.33	2.27	2.22	2.17	2.06	1.94	1.88	1.82	1.74	1.70	1.67	1.60	1.54	1.51
120	.001	.025	.072	.120	.165	.204	.238	.268	.295	.318	.340	.359	.406	.464	.498	.536	.580	.611	.633	.684	.729	.762
	5.15	3.80	3.23	2.89	2.67	2.52	2.39	2.30	2.22	2.16	2.10	2.05	1.95	1.82	1.76	1.69	1.61	1.56	1.53	1.45	1.39	1.34

Table E Transformation of r to z_r

r	z_r	r	z_r	r	z_r
.01	.010	.34	.354	.67	.811
.02	.020	.35	.366	.68	.829
.03	.030	.36	.377	.69	.848
.04	.040	.37	.389	.70	.867
.05	.050	.38	.400	.71	.887
.06	.060	.39	.412	.72	.908
.07	.070	.40	.424	.73	.929
.08	.080	.41	.436	.74	.950
.09	.090	.42	.448	.75	.973
.10	.100	.43	.460	.76	.996
.11	.110	.44	.472	.77	1.020
.12	.121	.45	.485	.78	1.045
.13	.131	.46	.497	.79	1.071
.14	.141	.47	.510	.80	1.099
.15	.151	.48	.523	.81	1.127
.16	.161	.49	.536	.82	1.157
.17	.172	.50	.549	.83	1.188
.18	.181	.51	.563	.84	1.221
.19	.192	.52	.577	.85	1.256
.20	.203	.53	.590	.86	1.293
.21	.214	.54	.604	.87	1.333
.22	.224	.55	.618	.88	1.376
.23	.234	.56	.633	.89	1.422
.24	.245	.57	.648	.90	1.472
.25	.256	.58	.663	.91	1.528
.26	.266	.59	.678	.92	1.589
.27	.277	.60	.693	.93	1.658
.28	.288	.61	.709	.94	1.738
.29	.299	.62	.725	.95	1.832
.30	.309	.63	.741	.96	1.946
.31	.321	.64	.758	.97	2.092
.32	.332	.65	.775	.98	2.298
.33	.343	.66	.793	.99	2.647

A given value of r_s is statistically significant if it equals or exceeds the tabled value at the designated α-level at a given N. To interpolate, sum the critical values above and below the N of interest and divide by 2. Thus, the critical value at $\alpha = 0.05$, two-tailed test, when $N = 21$, is $(0.450 + 0.428)/2 = 0.439$.

Table F Critical values of r_s

	LEVEL OF SIGNIFICANCE FOR ONE-TAILED TEST			
	.05	.025	.01	.005
	LEVEL OF SIGNIFICANCE FOR TWO-TAILED TEST			
N^*	.10	.05	.02	.01
5	.900	1.000	1.000	--
6	.829	.886	.943	1.000
7	.714	.786	.893	.929
8	.643	.738	.833	.881
9	.600	.683	.783	.833
10	.564	.648	.746	.794
12	.506	.591	.712	.777
14	.456	.544	.645	.715
16	.425	.506	.601	.665
18	.399	.475	.564	.625
20	.377	.450	.534	.591
22	.359	.428	.508	.562
24	.343	.409	.485	.537
26	.329	.392	.465	.515
28	.317	.377	.448	.496
30	.306	.364	.432	.478

$^*N$ = number of pairs

Table G Functions of r

r	$\sqrt{r}$	r^2	$\sqrt{r - r^2}$	$\sqrt{1 - r}$	$1 - r^2$	$\sqrt{1 - r^2}$	$100(1 - k)$	r
						k	% EFF.	
1.00	1.0000	1.0000	0.0000	0.0000	0.0000	0.0000	100.00	1.00
.99	.9950	.9801	.0995	.1000	.0199	.1411	85.89	.99
.98	.9899	.9604	.1400	.1414	.0396	.1990	80.10	.98
.97	.9849	.9409	.1706	.1732	.0591	.2431	75.69	.97
.96	.9798	.9216	.1960	.2000	.0784	.2800	72.00	.96
.95	.9747	.9025	.2179	.2236	.0975	.3122	68.78	.95
.94	.9695	.8836	.2375	.2449	.1164	.3412	65.88	.94
.93	.9644	.8649	.2551	.2646	.1351	.3676	63.24	.93
.92	.9592	.8464	.2713	.2828	.1536	.3919	60.81	.92
.91	.9539	.8281	.2862	.3000	.1719	.4146	58.54	.91
.90	.9487	.8100	.3000	.3162	.1900	.4359	56.41	.90
.89	.9434	.7921	.3129	.3317	.2079	.4560	54.40	.89
.88	.9381	.7744	.3250	.3464	.2256	.4750	52.50	.88
.87	.9327	.7569	.3363	.3606	.2431	.4931	50.69	.87
.86	.9274	.7396	.3470	.3742	.2604	.5103	48.97	.86
.85	.9220	.7225	.3571	.3873	.2775	.5268	47.32	.85
.84	.9165	.7056	.3666	.4000	.2944	.5426	45.74	.84
.83	.9110	.6889	.3756	.4123	.3111	.5578	44.22	.83
.82	.9055	.6724	.3842	.4243	.3276	.5724	42.76	.82
.81	.9000	.6561	.3923	.4359	.3439	.5864	41.36	.81
.80	.8944	.6400	.4000	.4472	.3600	.6000	40.00	.80
.79	.8888	.6241	.4073	.4583	.3759	.6131	38.69	.79
.78	.8832	.6084	.4142	.4690	.3916	.6258	37.42	.78
.77	.8775	.5929	.4208	.4796	.4071	.6380	36.20	.77
.76	.8718	.5776	.4271	.4899	.4224	.6499	35.01	.76
.75	.8660	.5625	.4330	.5000	.4375	.6614	33.86	.75
.74	.8602	.5476	.4386	.5099	.4524	.6726	32.74	.74
.73	.8544	.5329	.4440	.5196	.4671	.6834	31.66	.73
.72	.8485	.5184	.4490	.5292	.4816	.6940	30.60	.72
.71	.8426	.5041	.4538	.5385	.4959	.7042	29.58	.71
.70	.8367	.4900	.4583	.5477	.5100	.7141	28.59	.70
.69	.8307	.4761	.4625	.5568	.5239	.7238	27.62	.69
.68	.8246	.4624	.4665	.5657	.5376	.7332	26.68	.68
.67	.8185	.4489	.4702	.5745	.5511	.7424	25.76	.67
.66	.8124	.4356	.4737	.5831	.5644	.7513	24.87	.66
.65	.8062	.4225	.4770	.5916	.5775	.7599	24.01	.65
.64	.8000	.4096	.4800	.6000	.5904	.7684	23.16	.64
.63	.7937	.3969	.4828	.6083	.6031	.7766	22.34	.63
.62	.7874	.3844	.4854	.6164	.6156	.7846	21.54	.62
.61	.7810	.3721	.4877	.6245	.6279	.7924	20.76	.61
.60	.7746	.3600	.4899	.6325	.6400	.8000	20.00	.60
.59	.7681	.3481	.4918	.6403	.6519	.8074	19.26	.59
.58	.7616	.3364	.4936	.6481	.6636	.8146	18.54	.58
.57	.7550	.3249	.4951	.6557	.6751	.8216	17.84	.57
.56	.7483	.3136	.4964	.6633	.6864	.8285	17.15	.56
.55	.7416	.3025	.4975	.6708	.6975	.8352	16.48	.55
.54	.7348	.2916	.4984	.6782	.7084	.8417	15.83	.54
.53	.7280	.2809	.4991	.6856	.7191	.8480	15.20	.53
.52	.7211	.2704	.4996	.6928	.7296	.8542	14.58	.52
.51	.7141	.2601	.4999	.7000	.7399	.8602	13.98	.51
.50	.7071	.2500	.5000	.7071	.7500	.8660	13.40	.50

Table G (*continued*)

r	$\sqrt{r}$	r^2	$\sqrt{r - r^2}$	$\sqrt{1 - r}$	$1 - r^2$	$\sqrt{1 - r^2}$ k	100(1 - k) % EFF.	r
.50	.7071	.2500	.5000	.7071	.7500	.8660	13.40	.50
.49	.7000	.2401	.4999	.7141	.7599	.8717	12.83	.49
.48	.6928	.2304	.4996	.7211	.7696	.8773	12.27	.48
.47	.6856	.2209	.4991	.7280	.7791	.8827	11.73	.47
.46	.6782	.2116	.4984	.7348	.7884	.8879	11.21	.46
.45	.6708	.2025	.4975	.7416	.7975	.8930	10.70	.45
.44	.6633	.1936	.4964	.7483	.8064	.8980	10.20	.44
.43	.6557	.1849	.4951	.7550	.8151	.9028	9.72	.43
.42	.6481	.1764	.4936	.7616	.8236	.9075	9.25	.42
.41	.6403	.1681	.4918	.7681	.8319	.9121	8.79	.41
.40	.6325	.1600	.4899	.7746	.8400	.9165	8.35	.40
.39	.6245	.1521	.4877	.7810	.8479	.9208	7.92	.39
.38	.6164	.1444	.4854	.7874	.8556	.9250	7.50	.38
.37	.6083	.1369	.4828	.7937	.8631	.9290	7.10	.37
.36	.6000	.1296	.4800	.8000	.8704	.9330	6.70	.36
.35	.5916	.1225	.4770	.8062	.8775	.9367	6.33	.35
.34	.5831	.1156	.4737	.8124	.8844	.9404	5.96	.34
.33	.5745	.1089	.4702	.8185	.8911	.9440	5.60	.33
.32	.5657	.1024	.4665	.8246	.8976	.9474	5.25	.32
.31	.5568	.0961	.4625	.8307	.9039	.9507	4.93	.31
.30	.5477	.0900	.4583	.8367	.9100	.9539	4.61	.30
.29	.5385	.0841	.4538	.8426	.9159	.9570	4.30	.29
.28	.5292	.0784	.4490	.8485	.9216	.9600	4.00	.28
.27	.5196	.0729	.4440	.8544	.9271	.9629	3.71	.27
.26	.5099	.0676	.4386	.8602	.9324	.9656	3.44	.26
.25	.5000	.0625	.4330	.8660	.9375	.9682	3.18	.25
.24	.4899	.0576	.4271	.8718	.9424	.9708	2.92	.24
.23	.4796	.0529	.4208	.8775	.9471	.9732	2.68	.23
.22	.4690	.0484	.4142	.8832	.9516	.9755	2.45	.22
.21	.4583	.0441	.4073	.8888	.9559	.9777	2.23	.21
.20	.4472	.0400	.4000	.8944	.9600	.9798	2.02	.20
.19	.4359	.0361	.3923	.9000	.9639	.9818	1.82	.19
.18	.4243	.0324	.3842	.9055	.9676	.9837	1.63	.18
.17	.4123	.0289	.3756	.9110	.9711	.9854	1.46	.17
.16	.4000	.0256	.3666	.9165	.9744	.9871	1.29	.16
.15	.3873	.0225	.3571	.9220	.9775	.9887	1.13	.15
.14	.3742	.0196	.3470	.9274	.9804	.9902	.98	.14
.13	.3606	.0169	.3363	.9327	.9831	.9915	.85	.13
.12	.3464	.0144	.3250	.9381	.9856	.9928	.72	.12
.11	.3317	.0121	.3129	.9434	.9879	.9939	.61	.11
.10	.3162	.0100	.3000	.9487	.9900	.9950	.50	.10
.09	.3000	.0081	.2862	.9539	.9919	.9959	.41	.09
.08	.2828	.0064	.2713	.9592	.9936	.9968	.32	.08
.07	.2646	.0049	.2551	.9644	.9951	.9975	.25	.07
.06	.2449	.0036	.2375	.9695	.9964	.9982	.18	.06
.05	.2236	.0025	.2179	.9747	.9975	.9987	.13	.05
.04	.2000	.0016	.1960	.9798	.9984	.9992	.08	.04
.03	.1732	.0009	.1706	.9849	.9991	.9995	.05	.03
.02	.1414	.0004	.1400	.9899	.9996	.9998	.02	.02
.01	.1000	.0001	.0995	.9950	.9999	.9999	.01	.01
.00	.0000	.0000	.0000	1.0000	1.0000	1.0000	.00	.00

Table H Binomial coefficients

N	$\binom{N}{0}$	$\binom{N}{1}$	$\binom{N}{2}$	$\binom{N}{3}$	$\binom{N}{4}$	$\binom{N}{5}$	$\binom{N}{6}$	$\binom{N}{7}$	$\binom{N}{8}$	$\binom{N}{9}$	$\binom{N}{10}$
0	1										
1	1	1									
2	1	2	1								
3	1	3	3	1							
4	1	4	6	4	1						
5	1	5	10	10	5	1					
6	1	6	15	20	15	6	1				
7	1	7	21	35	35	21	7	1			
8	1	8	28	56	70	56	28	8	1		
9	1	9	36	84	126	126	84	36	9	1	
10	1	10	45	120	210	252	210	120	45	10	1
11	1	11	55	165	330	462	462	330	165	55	11
12	1	12	66	220	495	792	924	792	495	220	66
13	1	13	78	286	715	1287	1716	1716	1287	715	286
14	1	14	91	364	1001	2002	3003	3432	3003	2002	1001
15	1	15	105	455	1365	3003	5005	6435	6435	5005	3003
16	1	16	120	560	1820	4368	8008	11440	12870	11440	8008
17	1	17	136	680	2380	6188	12376	19448	24310	24310	19448
18	1	18	153	816	3060	8568	18564	31824	43758	48620	43758
19	1	19	171	969	3876	11628	27132	50388	75582	92378	92378
20	1	20	190	1140	4845	15504	38760	77520	125970	167960	184756

In Table I x is the frequency in the P category, and $N - x$ is the frequency in the Q category. The obtained x or $N - x$ must be *equal to* or *greater than* the value shown for significance at the chosen level. Dashes indicate that no decision is possible for N at the given α-level.

Table I   Critical values of x or $N - x$ (whichever is larger) at 0.05 and 0.01 levels when $P = Q = 1/2$

| | ONE-TAILED TEST | | TWO-TAILED TEST | |
N	0.05	0.01	0.05	0.01
5	5	—	—	—
6	6	—	6	—
7	7	7	7	—
8	7	8	8	—
9	8	9	8	9
10	9	10	9	10
11	9	10	10	11
12	10	11	10	11
13	10	12	11	12
14	11	12	12	13
15	12	13	12	13
16	12	14	13	14
17	13	14	13	15
18	13	15	14	15
19	14	15	15	16
20	15	16	15	17
21	15	17	16	17
22	16	17	17	18
23	16	18	17	19
24	17	19	18	19
25	18	19	18	20
26	18	20	19	20
27	19	20	20	21
28	19	21	20	22
29	20	22	21	22
30	20	22	21	23
31	21	23	22	24
32	22	24	23	24
33	22	24	23	25
34	23	25	24	25
35	23	25	24	26
36	24	26	25	27
37	24	27	25	27
38	25	27	26	28
39	26	28	27	28
40	26	28	27	29
41	27	29	28	30
42	27	29	28	30
43	28	30	29	31
44	28	31	29	31
45	29	31	30	32
46	30	32	31	33
47	30	32	31	33
48	31	33	32	34
49	31	34	32	35
50	32	34	33	35

Table J was prepared to expedite decision making when dealing with binomial populations in which $P \neq Q$. *Example:* A researcher has conducted 12 independent repetitions of the same study, using $\alpha = 0.01$. Four of these studies achieved statistical significance. Is this result (4 out of 12 statistically significant outcomes) itself statistically significant, or is it within chance expectations? Looking in the column headed .01 opposite $N = 12$, we find that two or more differences significant at $\alpha = .01$ is in itself significant at $\alpha = .01$. Thus, the researcher may conclude that the overall results of his or her investigations justify rejecting H_0.

A given value of x is significant at a given α-level if it equals or exceeds the critical value shown in the table. All values shown are one-tailed. Since the binomial is not symmetrical when $P \neq Q \neq 1/2$, there is no straightforward way to obtain two-tailed values.

Table J   Critical values of *x* at $\alpha = 0.05$ (lightface) and $\alpha = 0.01$ (boldface) at varying values of *P* and *Q* for *N*'s equal to 2 through 49

N	.01	.02	.03	.04	.05	.06	.07	.08	.09	.10	.11	.12	.13	.14	.15	.16	.17	.18	.19	.20	.21	.22	.23	.24	.25
Q	.99	.98	.97	.96	.95	.94	.93	.92	.91	.90	.89	.88	.87	.86	.85	.84	.83	.82	.81	.80	.79	.78	.77	.76	.75
2	1	1	2	2	2	2	2	2	2	2	2	2	2	2	2	2	2	2	2	2	2	2	—	—	—
	1	**2**	**2**	**2**	**2**	**2**	**2**	**2**	**2**	**2**	—	—	—	—	—	—	—	—	—	—	—	—	—	—	—
3	1	2	2	2	2	2	2	2	2	2	2	2	2	3	3	3	3	3	3	3	3	3	3	3	3
	2	**2**	**2**	**2**	**2**	**3**	**3**	**3**	**3**	**3**	**3**	**3**	**3**	**3**	**3**	**3**	**3**	**3**	**3**	**3**	**3**	**3**	—	—	—
4	1	2	2	2	2	2	2	2	2	3	3	3	3	3	3	3	3	3	3	3	3	3	3	3	4
	2	**2**	**2**	**2**	**3**	**3**	**3**	**3**	**3**	**3**	**3**	**3**	**3**	**3**	**4**	**4**	**4**	**4**	**4**	**4**	**4**	**4**	**4**	**4**	**4**
5	1	2	2	2	2	2	2	3	3	3	3	3	3	3	3	3	3	3	4	4	4	4	4	4	4
	2	**2**	**2**	**3**	**3**	**3**	**3**	**3**	**3**	**3**	**4**	**4**	**4**	**4**	**4**	**4**	**4**	**4**	**4**	**4**	**4**	**4**	**5**	**5**	**5**
6	2	2	2	2	2	3	3	3	3	3	3	3	3	3	3	4	4	4	4	4	4	4	4	5	5
	2	**2**	**3**	**3**	**3**	**3**	**3**	**3**	**4**	**4**	**4**	**4**	**4**	**4**	**4**	**4**	**5**	**5**	**5**	**5**	**5**	**5**	**5**	**5**	**5**
7	2	2	2	2	2	3	3	3	3	3	3	3	4	4	4	4	4	4	4	4	4	5	5	5	5
	2	**2**	**3**	**3**	**3**	**3**	**3**	**4**	**4**	**4**	**4**	**4**	**4**	**4**	**5**	**5**	**5**	**5**	**5**	**5**	**6**	**6**	**6**	**6**	**6**
8	2	2	2	2	3	3	3	3	3	3	3	4	4	4	4	4	4	4	4	5	5	5	5	5	5
	2	**3**	**3**	**3**	**3**	**3**	**4**	**4**	**4**	**4**	**4**	**4**	**5**	**5**	**5**	**5**	**5**	**5**	**5**	**6**	**6**	**6**	**6**	**6**	**6**
9	2	2	2	2	3	3	3	3	3	4	4	4	4	4	4	4	5	5	5	5	5	5	5	5	5
	2	**3**	**3**	**3**	**3**	**4**	**4**	**4**	**4**	**4**	**5**	**5**	**5**	**5**	**5**	**5**	**6**	**6**	**6**	**6**	**6**	**6**	**6**	**6**	**6**
10	2	2	2	3	3	3	3	3	4	4	4	4	4	4	4	5	5	5	5	5	5	5	6	6	6
	2	**3**	**3**	**3**	**4**	**4**	**4**	**4**	**4**	**5**	**5**	**5**	**5**	**5**	**5**	**6**	**6**	**6**	**6**	**6**	**6**	**7**	**7**	**7**	**7**
11	2	2	2	3	3	3	3	4	4	4	4	4	4	5	5	5	5	5	5	6	6	6	6	6	6
	2	**3**	**3**	**3**	**4**	**4**	**4**	**4**	**5**	**5**	**5**	**5**	**5**	**6**	**6**	**6**	**6**	**6**	**6**	**7**	**7**	**7**	**7**	**7**	**7**
12	2	2	2	3	3	3	3	4	4	4	4	4	5	5	5	5	5	5	6	6	6	6	6	6	7
	2	**3**	**3**	**4**	**4**	**4**	**4**	**5**	**5**	**5**	**5**	**6**	**6**	**6**	**6**	**6**	**7**	**7**	**7**	**7**	**7**	**7**	**7**	**8**	**8**
13	2	2	3	3	3	3	4	4	4	4	4	5	5	5	5	5	6	6	6	6	6	6	7	7	7
	2	**3**	**3**	**4**	**4**	**4**	**5**	**5**	**5**	**5**	**5**	**6**	**6**	**6**	**6**	**6**	**7**	**7**	**7**	**7**	**7**	**7**	**8**	**8**	**8**
14	2	2	3	3	3	3	4	4	4	4	5	5	5	5	5	6	6	6	6	6	7	7	7	7	7
	2	**3**	**3**	**4**	**4**	**4**	**5**	**5**	**5**	**5**	**6**	**6**	**6**	**6**	**7**	**7**	**7**	**7**	**7**	**8**	**8**	**8**	**8**	**8**	**9**
15	2	2	3	3	3	4	4	4	4	5	5	5	5	6	6	6	6	6	7	7	7	7	7	7	8
	2	**3**	**3**	**4**	**4**	**5**	**5**	**5**	**5**	**6**	**6**	**6**	**6**	**7**	**7**	**7**	**7**	**8**	**8**	**8**	**8**	**8**	**9**	**9**	**9**

Table J (continued)

.26/.74	.27/.73	.28/.72	.29/.71	.30/.70	.31/.69	.32/.68	.33/.67	.34/.66	.35/.65	.36/.64	.37/.63	.38/.62	.39/.61	.40/.60	.41/.59	.42/.58	.43/.57	.44/.56	.45/.55	.46/.54	.47/.53	.48/.52	.49/.51	.50/.50
—	—	—	—	—	—	—	—	—	—	—	—	—	—	—	—	—	—	—	—	—	—	—	—	—
3	3	3	3	3	3	3	3	3	3	3	—	—	—	—	—	—	—	—	—	—	—	—	—	—
—	—	—	—	—	—	—	—	—	—	—	—	—	—	—	—	—	—	—	—	—	—	—	—	—
4	4	4	4	4	4	4	4	4	4	4	4	4	4	4	4	4	4	4	4	4	—	—	—	—
4	4	4	4	4	4	—	—	—	—	—	—	—	—	—	—	—	—	—	—	—	—	—	—	—
4	4	4	4	4	4	4	4	4	5	5	5	5	5	5	5	5	5	5	5	5	5	5	5	5
5	5	5	5	5	5	5	5	5	5	5	5	5	5	5	5	—	—	—	—	—	—	—	—	—
5	5	5	5	5	5	5	5	5	5	5	5	5	5	5	6	6	6	6	6	6	6	6	6	6
5	5	5	5	5	5	5	5	5	5	6	6	6	6	6	6	—	—	—	—	—	—	—	—	—
5	5	5	5	5	5	5	5	5	6	6	6	6	6	6	6	6	6	6	6	6	6	7	7	7
6	6	6	6	6	6	6	6	6	6	7	7	7	7	7	7	7	7	7	7	7	7	7	7	7
5	5	5	6	6	6	6	6	6	6	6	6	6	6	6	6	7	7	7	7	7	7	7	7	7
6	6	6	6	7	7	7	7	7	7	7	7	7	7	7	7	8	8	8	8	8	8	8	8	8
6	6	6	6	6	6	6	6	6	7	7	7	7	7	7	7	7	7	7	8	8	8	8	8	8
7	7	7	7	7	7	7	7	7	8	8	8	8	8	8	8	8	8	8	9	9	9	9	9	9
6	6	6	6	6	7	7	7	7	7	7	7	7	7	8	8	8	8	8	8	8	8	8	8	9
7	7	7	7	8	8	8	8	8	8	8	8	9	9	9	9	9	9	9	9	9	9	9	9	10
6	6	7	7	7	7	7	7	7	8	8	8	8	8	8	8	8	9	9	9	9	9	9	9	9
7	8	8	8	8	8	8	8	9	9	9	9	9	9	9	9	9	10	10	10	10	10	10	10	10
7	7	7	7	7	7	8	8	8	8	8	8	8	8	9	9	9	9	9	9	9	9	10	10	10
8	8	8	8	8	9	9	9	9	9	9	9	10	10	10	10	10	10	10	10	11	11	11	11	11
7	7	7	8	8	8	8	8	8	8	9	9	9	9	9	9	9	10	10	10	10	10	10	10	10
8	8	9	9	9	9	9	9	10	10	10	10	10	10	10	10	11	11	11	11	11	11	11	11	12
7	8	8	8	8	8	8	9	9	9	9	9	9	9	10	10	10	10	10	10	11	11	11	11	11
9	9	9	9	9	10	10	10	10	10	10	10	11	11	11	11	11	11	11	12	12	12	12	12	12
8	8	8	8	9	9	9	9	9	9	10	10	10	10	10	10	10	11	11	11	11	11	11	12	12
9	9	9	10	10	10	10	10	10	11	11	11	11	11	11	12	12	12	12	12	12	12	13	13	13

Table J (*continued*)

N	P:	.01	.02	.03	.04	.05	.06	.07	.08	.09	.10	.11	.12	.13	.14	.15	.16	.17	.18	.19	.20	.21	.22	.23	.24	.25
	Q:	.99	.98	.97	.96	.95	.94	.93	.92	.91	.90	.89	.88	.87	.86	.85	.84	.83	.82	.81	.80	.79	.78	.77	.76	.75
16		2	2	3	3	3	4	4	4	4	5	5	5	5	6	6	6	6	7	7	7	7	7	8	8	8
		3	3	4	4	4	5	5	5	6	6	6	6	7	7	7	7	8	8	8	8	8	9	9	9	9
17		2	2	3	3	4	4	4	4	5	5	5	5	6	6	6	6	7	7	7	7	7	8	8	8	8
		3	3	4	4	4	5	5	5	6	6	6	7	7	7	7	8	8	8	8	9	9	9	9	9	10
18		2	2	3	3	4	4	4	5	5	5	5	6	6	6	6	6	7	7	7	7	8	8	8	8	9
		3	3	4	4	5	5	5	6	6	6	7	7	7	7	8	8	8	8	9	9	9	9	10	10	10
19		2	3	3	3	4	4	4	5	5	5	6	6	6	6	7	7	7	7	8	8	8	8	9	9	9
		3	3	4	4	5	5	5	6	6	6	7	7	7	8	8	8	8	9	9	9	9	10	10	10	10
20		2	3	3	3	4	4	4	5	5	5	6	6	6	7	7	7	7	8	8	8	8	9	9	9	9
		3	3	4	4	5	5	6	6	6	7	7	7	8	8	8	8	9	9	9	9	10	10	10	10	11
21		2	3	3	3	4	4	5	5	5	5	6	6	6	6	7	7	7	8	8	8	8	9	9	9	10
		3	3	4	4	5	5	6	6	6	7	7	7	8	8	8	9	9	9	10	10	10	10	11	11	11
22		2	3	3	4	4	4	5	5	5	6	6	6	7	7	7	8	8	8	8	9	9	9	9	10	10
		3	3	4	5	5	5	6	6	7	7	7	8	8	8	9	9	9	10	10	10	10	11	11	11	11
23		2	3	3	4	4	4	5	5	6	6	6	6	7	7	7	8	8	8	9	9	9	9	10	10	10
		3	4	4	5	5	6	6	6	7	7	7	8	8	9	9	9	9	10	10	10	11	11	11	12	12
24		2	3	3	4	4	5	5	5	6	6	6	7	7	7	8	8	8	9	9	9	9	10	10	10	11
		3	4	4	5	5	6	6	7	7	7	8	8	8	9	9	9	10	10	10	11	11	11	12	12	12
25		2	3	3	4	4	5	5	5	6	6	6	7	7	8	8	8	8	9	9	9	10	10	10	11	11
		3	4	4	5	5	6	6	7	7	7	8	8	9	9	9	10	10	10	11	11	11	12	12	12	13
26		2	3	3	4	4	5	5	6	6	6	7	7	7	8	8	8	9	9	9	10	10	10	11	11	11
		3	4	4	5	5	6	6	7	7	8	8	8	9	10	10	10	11	11	11	12	12	12	13	13	13
27		2	3	3	4	4	5	5	6	6	6	7	7	8	8	8	9	9	9	10	10	10	11	11	11	12
		3	4	4	5	6	6	6	7	7	8	8	9	9	9	10	10	11	11	11	12	12	12	13	13	13
28		2	3	4	4	4	5	5	6	6	7	7	7	8	8	8	9	9	10	10	10	11	11	11	12	12
		3	4	4	5	6	6	7	7	8	8	8	9	9	10	10	10	11	11	12	12	12	13	13	13	14
29		2	3	4	4	5	5	5	6	6	7	7	8	8	8	9	9	9	10	10	10	11	11	11	12	12
		3	4	5	5	6	6	7	7	8	8	9	9	9	10	10	11	11	11	12	12	12	13	13	14	14
30		2	3	4	4	5	5	6	6	6	7	7	8	8	9	9	9	10	10	10	11	11	11	12	12	13
		3	4	5	5	6	6	7	7	8	8	9	9	10	10	10	11	11	12	12	12	13	13	14	14	14
31		2	3	4	4	5	5	6	6	7	7	7	8	8	9	9	9	10	10	11	11	11	12	12	12	13
		3	4	5	5	6	6	7	7	8	8	9	9	10	10	11	11	12	12	12	13	13	14	14	14	15
32		2	3	4	4	5	5	6	6	7	7	8	8	8	9	9	10	10	10	11	11	12	12	12	13	13
		3	4	5	5	6	7	7	8	8	9	9	10	10	10	11	11	12	12	13	13	14	14	15	15	15
33		2	3	4	4	5	5	6	6	7	7	8	8	9	9	9	10	10	11	11	11	12	12	13	13	13
		3	4	5	5	6	7	7	8	8	9	9	10	10	11	11	12	12	12	13	13	14	14	15	15	15
34		2	3	4	4	5	6	6	7	7	7	8	8	9	9	10	10	11	11	11	12	12	13	13	13	14
		3	4	5	6	6	7	7	8	8	9	9	10	10	11	11	12	12	13	13	14	14	14	15	15	16
35		2	3	4	5	6	6	6	7	7	8	8	9	9	9	10	11	11	12	12	13	13	14	14	14	14
		3	4	5	6	6	7	7	8	9	9	10	10	11	11	12	12	13	13	13	14	14	15	15	16	16
36		3	3	4	5	5	6	6	7	7	8	8	9	9	10	10	11	11	11	12	12	13	13	14	14	14
		3	4	5	6	6	7	8	8	9	9	10	10	11	11	12	12	13	13	14	14	15	15	15	16	16
37		3	3	4	5	5	6	6	7	7	8	8	9	9	10	10	11	11	12	12	13	13	13	14	14	15
		3	4	5	6	6	7	8	8	9	9	10	11	11	12	12	13	13	13	14	14	15	15	16	16	17

Table J (*continued*)

.26	.27	.28	.29	.30	.31	.32	.33	.34	.35	.36	.37	.38	.39	.40	.41	.42	.43	.44	.45	.46	.47	.48	.49	.50
.74	.73	.72	.71	.70	.69	.68	.67	.66	.65	.64	.63	.62	.61	.60	.59	.58	.57	.56	.55	.54	.53	.52	.51	.50
8	8	9	9	9	9	9	9	10	10	10	10	10	10	11	11	11	11	11	11	12	12	12	12	12
9	**10**	**10**	**10**	**10**	**10**	**11**	**11**	**11**	**11**	**11**	**11**	**12**	**12**	**12**	**12**	**12**	**12**	**13**	**13**	**13**	**14**	**14**	**14**	**14**
8	9	9	9	9	9	10	10	10	10	10	11	11	11	11	11	12	12	12	12	12	13	13	13	13
10	**10**	**10**	**10**	**11**	**11**	**11**	**11**	**11**	**12**	**12**	**12**	**13**	**13**	**13**	**13**	**13**	**13**	**14**	**14**	**14**	**14**	**14**	**14**	**14**
9	9	9	9	10	10	10	10	10	11	11	11	11	11	12	12	12	12	12	13	13	13	13	13	13
10	**10**	**11**	**11**	**11**	**11**	**12**	**12**	**12**	**12**	**12**	**13**	**13**	**13**	**13**	**13**	**13**	**14**	**14**	**14**	**14**	**14**	**14**	**15**	**15**
9	9	10	10	10	10	10	11	11	11	11	12	12	12	12	12	13	13	13	13	13	14	14	14	14
11	**11**	**11**	**11**	**12**	**12**	**12**	**12**	**12**	**13**	**13**	**13**	**13**	**13**	**14**	**14**	**14**	**14**	**15**	**15**	**15**	**15**	**15**	**15**	**15**
10	10	10	10	10	11	11	11	11	12	12	12	12	13	13	13	13	14	14	14	14	14	14	15	15
11	**12**	**12**	**12**	**12**	**13**	**13**	**13**	**13**	**14**	**14**	**14**	**14**	**15**	**15**	**15**	**15**	**16**	**16**	**16**	**16**	**16**	**17**	**17**	
10	10	11	11	11	11	12	12	12	12	13	13	13	13	14	14	14	15	15	15	15	15	16	16	
12	**12**	**12**	**13**	**13**	**13**	**13**	**14**	**14**	**14**	**14**	**15**	**15**	**15**	**15**	**16**	**16**	**16**	**17**	**17**	**17**	**17**	**18**	**18**	**18**
11	11	11	12	12	12	13	13	13	13	14	14	14	14	15	15	15	16	16	16	16	17	17	17	
13	**13**	**13**	**13**	**14**	**14**	**14**	**14**	**15**	**15**	**15**	**15**	**16**	**16**	**16**	**16**	**17**	**17**	**17**	**17**	**18**	**18**	**18**	**18**	**19**
11	12	12	12	12	13	13	13	13	14	14	15	15	15	15	16	16	16	16	17	17	17	17	18	
13	**13**	**13**	**14**	**14**	**14**	**15**	**15**	**15**	**15**	**16**	**16**	**16**	**17**	**17**	**17**	**17**	**18**	**18**	**18**	**18**	**19**	**19**	**19**	**19**
12	12	12	13	13	13	14	14	14	15	15	15	16	16	16	16	17	17	17	17	18	18	18	18	19
14	**14**	**14**	**15**	**15**	**15**	**15**	**16**	**16**	**16**	**17**	**17**	**17**	**18**	**18**	**18**	**18**	**19**	**19**	**19**	**19**	**20**	**20**	**20**	**20**
12	13	13	13	13	14	14	14	15	15	15	16	16	16	16	17	17	17	18	18	18	18	19	19	19
14	**14**	**15**	**15**	**15**	**16**	**16**	**16**	**17**	**17**	**17**	**17**	**18**	**18**	**18**	**19**	**19**	**19**	**19**	**20**	**20**	**20**	**21**	**21**	**21**
13	13	14	14	14	14	15	15	15	16	16	16	17	17	17	17	18	18	18	19	19	19	20	20	20
14	**15**	**15**	**15**	**16**	**16**	**17**	**17**	**17**	**18**	**18**	**18**	**18**	**19**	**19**	**19**	**20**	**20**	**20**	**21**	**21**	**21**	**21**	**21**	**22**
13	13	14	14	14	15	15	15	16	16	16	17	17	17	17	18	18	18	19	19	19	20	20	20	20
15	**15**	**15**	**16**	**16**	**16**	**17**	**17**	**17**	**18**	**18**	**19**	**19**	**19**	**20**	**20**	**20**	**21**	**21**	**21**	**21**	**22**	**22**	**22**	
13	14	14	14	15	15	15	16	16	16	17	17	17	18	18	18	19	19	19	20	20	20	20	21	21
15	**15**	**16**	**16**	**16**	**17**	**17**	**17**	**18**	**18**	**19**	**19**	**19**	**19**	**20**	**20**	**20**	**21**	**21**	**21**	**22**	**22**	**22**	**23**	**23**
14	14	14	15	15	15	16	16	16	17	17	17	18	18	18	19	19	20	20	20	21	21	21	21	22
15	**16**	**16**	**16**	**17**	**17**	**18**	**18**	**18**	**19**	**19**	**20**	**20**	**20**	**21**	**21**	**21**	**22**	**22**	**22**	**22**	**23**	**23**	**24**	
14	14	15	15	15	16	16	16	17	17	17	18	18	19	19	19	20	20	20	21	21	21	22	22	22
16	**16**	**16**	**17**	**17**	**18**	**18**	**18**	**19**	**19**	**19**	**20**	**20**	**20**	**21**	**21**	**21**	**22**	**22**	**22**	**23**	**23**	**23**	**24**	**24**
14	15	15	15	16	16	16	17	17	18	18	18	19	19	19	20	20	20	21	21	21	22	22	22	23
16	**16**	**17**	**17**	**17**	**18**	**18**	**19**	**19**	**20**	**20**	**20**	**21**	**21**	**21**	**22**	**22**	**22**	**23**	**23**	**23**	**24**	**24**	**24**	**25**
14	15	15	16	16	16	17	17	18	18	18	19	19	19	20	20	21	21	21	22	22	22	23	23	23
16	**17**	**17**	**18**	**18**	**18**	**19**	**19**	**20**	**20**	**20**	**21**	**21**	**21**	**22**	**22**	**23**	**23**	**23**	**24**	**24**	**24**	**25**	**25**	**25**
15	15	16	16	16	17	17	18	18	18	19	19	20	20	20	21	21	21	22	22	22	23	23	24	24
17	**17**	**18**	**18**	**18**	**19**	**19**	**20**	**20**	**20**	**21**	**21**	**22**	**22**	**22**	**23**	**23**	**23**	**24**	**24**	**25**	**25**	**25**	**26**	**26**
15	16	16	16	17	17	18	18	18	19	19	20	20	20	21	21	22	22	22	23	23	23	24	24	24
17	**18**	**18**	**18**	**19**	**19**	**20**	**20**	**20**	**21**	**21**	**22**	**22**	**22**	**23**	**23**	**24**	**24**	**24**	**25**	**25**	**25**	**26**	**26**	**27**

Table J (*continued*)

N	P .01 / Q .99	.02 / .98	.03 / .97	.04 / .96	.05 / .95	.06 / .94	.07 / .93	.08 / .92	.09 / .91	.10 / .90	.11 / .89	.12 / .88	.13 / .87	.14 / .86	.15 / .85	.16 / .84	.17 / .83	.18 / .82	.19 / .81	.20 / .80	.21 / .79	.22 / .78	.23 / .77	.24 / .76	.25 / .75
38	3	3	4	5	5	6	6	7	8	8	9	9	10	10	10	11	11	12	12	13	13	14	14	15	15
	3	4	5	6	7	7	8	8	9	10	10	11	11	12	12	13	13	14	14	15	15	16	16	17	17
39	3	3	4	5	5	6	6	7	8	8	9	9	10	10	11	11	12	12	13	13	14	14	14	15	15
	3	4	5	6	7	7	8	9	9	10	10	11	11	12	12	13	13	14	14	15	15	16	16	17	17
40	3	3	4	5	5	6	7	7	8	8	9	9	10	10	11	11	12	12	13	13	14	14	15	15	15
	3	4	5	6	7	7	8	9	9	10	10	11	12	12	13	13	14	14	15	15	16	16	17	17	18
41	3	3	4	5	6	6	7	7	8	8	9	10	10	11	11	12	12	13	13	14	14	15	15	15	16
	3	4	5	6	7	8	8	9	9	10	11	11	12	12	13	13	14	14	15	16	16	17	17	18	18
42	3	4	4	5	6	6	7	7	8	9	9	10	10	11	11	12	12	13	13	14	14	15	15	16	16
	3	4	5	6	7	8	8	9	10	10	11	11	12	12	13	14	14	15	15	16	16	17	17	18	18
43	3	4	4	5	6	6	7	8	8	9	9	10	10	11	11	12	13	13	14	14	15	15	16	16	17
	3	5	5	6	7	8	8	9	10	10	11	12	12	13	13	14	14	15	16	16	17	17	18	18	19
44	3	4	4	5	6	6	7	8	8	9	9	10	11	11	12	12	13	13	14	14	15	15	16	16	17
	3	5	5	6	7	8	8	9	10	11	11	12	12	13	14	14	15	15	16	16	17	17	18	18	19
45	3	4	4	5	6	7	7	8	8	9	10	10	11	11	12	12	13	13	14	15	15	16	16	17	17
	4	5	6	7	8	8	9	9	10	11	11	12	13	13	14	14	15	15	16	17	17	18	18	19	19
46	3	4	4	5	6	7	7	8	9	9	10	10	11	11	12	13	13	14	14	15	15	16	16	17	17
	4	5	6	6	7	8	9	9	10	11	11	12	13	13	14	15	15	16	16	17	17	18	19	19	20
47	3	4	5	5	6	7	7	8	9	9	10	10	11	12	12	13	13	14	15	15	16	16	17	17	18
	4	5	6	7	7	8	9	10	10	11	12	12	13	14	14	15	15	16	17	17	18	18	19	19	20
48	3	4	5	5	6	7	7	8	9	9	10	11	11	12	12	13	14	14	15	15	16	16	17	18	18
	4	5	6	7	7	8	9	10	10	11	12	12	13	14	14	15	16	16	17	17	18	18	19	20	20
49	3	4	5	5	6	7	8	8	9	10	10	11	11	12	13	13	14	14	15	16	16	17	17	18	18
	4	5	6	7	8	8	9	10	11	11	12	13	13	14	15	15	16	16	17	18	18	19	19	20	21

Table J (continued)

| .26 | .27 | .28 | .29 | .30 | .31 | .32 | .33 | .34 | .35 | .36 | .37 | .38 | .39 | .40 | .41 | .42 | .43 | .44 | .45 | .46 | .47 | .48 | .49 | .50 |
.74	.73	.72	.71	.70	.69	.68	.67	.66	.65	.64	.63	.62	.61	.60	.59	.58	.57	.56	.55	.54	.53	.52	.51	.50
15	16	16	17	17	18	18	18	19	19	20	20	20	21	21	22	22	22	23	23	24	24	24	25	25
17	**18**	**18**	**19**	**19**	**20**	**20**	**20**	**21**	**21**	**22**	**22**	**23**	**23**	**23**	**24**	**24**	**24**	**25**	**25**	**26**	**26**	**26**	**27**	**27**
16	16	17	17	17	18	18	19	19	20	20	20	21	21	22	22	22	23	23	24	24	24	25	25	26
18	**18**	**19**	**19**	**20**	**20**	**20**	**21**	**21**	**22**	**22**	**23**	**23**	**23**	**24**	**24**	**25**	**25**	**25**	**26**	**26**	**27**	**27**	**27**	**28**
16	17	17	17	18	18	19	19	20	20	20	21	21	22	22	23	23	23	24	24	25	25	25	26	26
18	**19**	**19**	**20**	**20**	**21**	**21**	**22**	**22**	**23**	**23**	**23**	**24**	**24**	**25**	**25**	**26**	**26**	**26**	**27**	**27**	**28**	**28**	**28**	**29**
17	17	18	18	19	19	19	20	20	21	21	22	22	23	23	23	24	24	25	25	26	26	26	27	27
19	**19**	**20**	**20**	**21**	**21**	**22**	**22**	**23**	**23**	**23**	**24**	**24**	**25**	**25**	**26**	**26**	**27**	**27**	**28**	**28**	**28**	**29**	**29**	**29**
17	18	18	18	19	19	20	20	21	21	22	22	23	23	24	24	24	25	25	26	26	27	27	27	28
19	**20**	**20**	**21**	**21**	**22**	**22**	**23**	**23**	**23**	**24**	**24**	**25**	**25**	**26**	**26**	**27**	**27**	**28**	**28**	**28**	**29**	**29**	**30**	**30**
17	18	18	19	19	20	20	21	21	22	22	23	23	24	24	24	25	25	26	26	27	27	28	28	28
19	**20**	**21**	**21**	**21**	**22**	**22**	**23**	**23**	**24**	**24**	**25**	**25**	**26**	**26**	**27**	**27**	**28**	**28**	**28**	**29**	**29**	**30**	**30**	**31**
18	18	19	19	20	20	21	21	22	22	23	23	24	24	24	25	25	26	26	27	27	28	28	29	29
20	**20**	**21**	**21**	**22**	**22**	**23**	**23**	**24**	**24**	**25**	**25**	**26**	**26**	**27**	**27**	**28**	**28**	**29**	**29**	**29**	**30**	**30**	**31**	**31**
18	18	19	20	20	21	21	22	22	22	23	23	24	24	25	25	26	26	27	27	28	28	29	29	30
20	**21**	**21**	**22**	**22**	**23**	**23**	**24**	**24**	**25**	**25**	**26**	**26**	**27**	**27**	**28**	**28**	**29**	**29**	**30**	**30**	**30**	**31**	**31**	**32**
18	19	19	20	20	21	21	22	22	23	23	24	24	25	25	26	26	27	27	28	28	29	29	30	30
21	**21**	**22**	**22**	**23**	**23**	**24**	**24**	**25**	**25**	**26**	**26**	**27**	**27**	**28**	**28**	**29**	**29**	**30**	**30**	**31**	**31**	**31**	**32**	**32**
19	19	20	20	21	22	22	23	23	24	24	25	25	26	26	27	27	28	28	29	29	30	30	31	31
21	**21**	**22**	**22**	**23**	**24**	**24**	**25**	**25**	**26**	**26**	**27**	**27**	**28**	**28**	**29**	**29**	**30**	**30**	**31**	**31**	**32**	**32**	**33**	**33**
19	19	20	21	21	22	22	23	23	24	24	25	25	26	26	27	27	28	28	29	29	30	30	31	31
21	**22**	**22**	**23**	**23**	**24**	**24**	**25**	**26**	**26**	**27**	**27**	**28**	**28**	**29**	**29**	**30**	**30**	**31**	**31**	**32**	**32**	**33**	**33**	**34**

Table K Percentage points of the Studentized range

Error df	a	K = NUMBER OF MEANS OR NUMBER OF STEPS BETWEEN ORDERED MEANS									
		2	3	4	5	6	7	8	9	10	11
5	.05	3.64	4.60	5.22	5.67	6.03	6.33	6.58	6.80	6.99	7.17
	.01	5.70	6.98	7.80	8.42	8.91	9.32	9.67	9.97	10.24	10.48
6	.05	3.46	4.34	4.90	5.30	5.63	5.90	6.12	6.32	6.49	6.65
	.01	5.24	6.33	7.03	7.56	7.97	8.32	8.61	8.87	9.10	9.30
7	.05	3.34	4.16	4.68	5.06	5.36	5.61	5.82	6.00	6.16	6.30
	.01	4.95	5.92	6.54	7.01	7.37	7.68	7.94	8.17	8.37	8.55
8	.05	3.26	4.04	4.53	4.89	5.17	5.40	5.60	5.77	5.92	6.05
	.01	4.75	5.64	6.20	6.62	6.96	7.24	7.47	7.68	7.86	8.03
9	.05	3.20	3.95	4.41	4.76	5.02	5.24	5.43	5.59	5.74	5.87
	.01	4.60	5.43	5.96	6.35	6.66	6.91	7.13	7.33	7.49	7.65
10	.05	3.15	3.88	4.33	4.65	4.91	5.12	5.30	5.46	5.60	5.72
	.01	4.48	5.27	5.77	6.14	6.43	6.67	6.87	7.05	7.21	7.36
11	.05	3.11	3.82	4.26	4.57	4.82	5.03	5.20	5.35	5.49	5.61
	.01	4.39	5.15	5.62	5.97	6.25	6.48	6.67	6.84	6.99	7.13
12	.05	3.08	3.77	4.20	4.51	4.75	4.95	5.12	5.27	5.39	5.51
	.01	4.32	5.05	5.50	5.84	6.10	6.32	6.51	6.67	6.81	6.94
13	.05	3.06	3.73	4.15	4.45	4.69	4.88	5.05	5.19	5.32	5.43
	.01	4.26	4.96	5.40	5.73	5.98	6.19	6.37	6.53	6.67	6.79
14	.05	3.03	3.70	4.11	4.41	4.64	4.83	4.99	5.13	5.25	5.36
	.01	4.21	4.89	5.32	5.63	5.88	6.08	6.26	6.41	6.54	6.66
15	.05	3.01	3.67	4.08	4.37	4.59	4.78	4.94	5.08	5.20	5.31
	.01	4.17	4.84	5.25	5.56	5.80	5.99	6.16	6.31	6.44	6.55
16	.05	3.00	3.65	4.05	4.33	4.56	4.74	4.90	5.03	5.15	5.26
	.01	4.13	4.79	5.19	5.49	5.72	5.92	6.08	6.22	6.35	6.46
17	.05	2.98	3.63	4.02	4.30	4.52	4.70	4.86	4.99	5.11	5.21
	.01	4.10	4.74	5.14	5.43	5.66	5.85	6.01	6.15	6.27	6.38
18	.05	2.97	3.61	4.00	4.28	4.49	4.67	4.82	4.96	5.07	5.17
	.01	4.07	4.70	5.09	5.38	5.60	5.79	5.94	6.08	6.20	6.31
19	.05	2.96	3.59	3.98	4.25	4.47	4.65	4.79	4.92	5.04	5.14
	.01	4.05	4.67	5.05	5.33	5.55	5.73	5.89	6.02	6.14	6.25
20	.05	2.95	3.58	3.96	4.23	4.45	4.62	4.77	4.90	5.01	5.11
	.01	4.02	4.64	5.02	5.29	5.51	5.69	5.84	5.97	6.09	6.19
24	.05	2.92	3.53	3.90	4.17	4.37	4.54	4.68	4.81	4.92	5.01
	.01	3.96	4.55	4.91	5.17	5.37	5.54	5.69	5.81	5.92	6.02
30	.05	2.89	3.49	3.85	4.10	4.30	4.46	4.60	4.72	4.82	4.92
	.01	3.89	4.45	4.80	5.05	5.24	5.40	5.54	5.65	5.76	5.85
40	.05	2.86	3.44	3.79	4.04	4.23	4.39	4.52	4.63	4.73	4.82
	.01	3.82	4.37	4.70	4.93	5.11	5.26	5.39	5.50	5.60	5.69
60	.05	2.83	3.40	3.74	3.98	4.16	4.31	4.44	4.55	4.65	4.73
	.01	3.76	4.28	4.59	4.82	4.99	5.13	5.25	5.36	5.45	5.53
120	.05	2.80	3.36	3.68	3.92	4.10	4.24	4.36	4.47	4.56	4.64
	.01	3.70	4.20	4.50	4.71	4.87	5.01	5.12	5.21	5.30	5.37
∞	.05	2.77	3.31	3.63	3.86	4.03	4.17	4.29	4.39	4.47	4.55
	.01	3.64	4.12	4.40	4.60	4.76	4.88	4.99	5.08	5.16	5.23

Table L **489**

Table L Squares, square roots, and reciprocals of numbers from 1 to 1000

N	N²	√N	1/N	N	N²	√N	1/N	N	N²	√N	1/N
1	1	1.0000	1.000000	61	3721	7.8102	.016393	121	14641	11.0000	.00826446
2	4	1.4142	.500000	62	3844	7.8740	.016129	122	14884	11.0454	.00819672
3	9	1.7321	.333333	63	3969	7.9373	.015873	123	15129	11.0905	.00813008
4	16	2.0000	.250000	64	4096	8.0000	.015625	124	15376	11.1355	.00800452
5	25	2.2361	.200000	65	4225	8.0623	.015385	125	15625	11.1803	.00800000
6	36	2.4495	.166667	66	4356	8.1240	.015152	126	15876	11.2250	.00793651
7	49	2.6458	.142857	67	4489	8.1854	.014925	127	16129	11.2694	.00787402
8	64	2.8284	.125000	68	4624	8.2462	.014706	128	16384	11.3137	.00781250
9	81	3.0000	.111111	69	4761	8.3066	.014493	129	16641	11.3578	.00775194
10	100	3.1623	.100000	70	4900	8.3666	.014286	130	16900	11.4018	.00769231
11	121	3.3166	.090909	71	5041	8.4261	.014085	131	17161	11.4455	.00763359
12	144	3.4641	.083333	72	5184	8.4853	.013889	132	17424	11.4891	.00757576
13	169	3.6056	.076923	73	5329	8.5440	.013699	133	17689	11.5326	.00751880
14	196	3.7417	.071429	74	5476	8.6023	.013514	134	17956	11.5758	.00746269
15	225	3.8730	.066667	75	5625	8.6603	.013333	135	18225	11.6190	.00740741
16	256	4.0000	.062500	76	5776	8.7178	.013158	136	18496	11.6619	.00735294
17	289	4.1231	.058824	77	5929	8.7750	.012987	137	18769	11.7047	.00729927
18	324	4.2426	.055556	78	6084	8.8318	.012821	138	19044	11.7473	.00724638
19	361	4.3589	.052632	79	6241	8.8882	.012658	139	19321	11.7898	.00719424
20	400	4.4721	.050000	80	6400	8.9443	.012500	140	19600	11.8322	.00714286
21	441	4.5826	.047619	81	6561	9.0000	.012346	141	19881	11.8743	.00709220
22	484	4.6904	.045455	82	6724	9.0554	.012195	142	20164	11.9164	.00704225
23	529	4.7958	.043478	83	6889	9.1104	.012048	143	20449	11.9583	.00699301
24	576	4.8990	.041667	84	7056	9.1652	.011905	144	20736	12.0000	.00694444
25	625	5.0000	.040000	85	7225	9.2195	.011765	145	21025	12.0416	.00689655
26	676	5.0990	.038462	86	7396	9.2736	.011628	146	21316	12.0830	.00684932
27	729	5.1962	.037037	87	7569	9.3274	.011494	147	21609	12.1244	.00680272
28	784	5.2915	.035714	88	7744	9.3808	.011364	148	21904	12.1655	.00675676
29	841	5.3852	.034483	89	7921	9.4340	.011236	149	22201	12.2066	.00671141
30	900	5.4772	.033333	90	8100	9.4868	.011111	150	22500	12.2474	.00666667
31	961	5.5678	.032258	91	8281	9.5394	.010989	151	22801	12.2882	.00662252
32	1024	5.6569	.031250	92	8464	9.5917	.010870	152	23104	12.3288	.00657895
33	1089	5.7446	.030303	93	8649	9.6437	.010753	153	23409	12.3693	.00653595
34	1156	5.8310	.029412	94	8836	9.6954	.010638	154	23716	12.4097	.00649351
35	1225	5.9161	.028571	95	9025	9.7468	.010526	155	24025	12.4499	.00645161
36	1296	6.0000	.027778	96	9216	9.7980	.010417	156	24336	12.4900	.00641026
37	1369	6.0828	.027027	97	9409	9.8489	.010309	157	24649	12.5300	.00636943
38	1444	6.1644	.026316	98	9604	9.8995	.010204	158	24964	12.5698	.00632911
39	1521	6.2450	.025641	99	9801	9.9499	.010101	159	25281	12.6095	.00628931
40	1600	6.3246	.025000	100	10000	10.0000	.010000	160	25600	12.6491	.00625000
41	1681	6.4031	.024390	101	10201	10.0499	.00990099	161	25921	12.6886	.00621118
42	1764	6.4807	.023810	102	10404	10.0995	.00980392	162	26244	12.7279	.00617284
43	1849	6.5574	.023256	103	10609	10.1489	.00970874	163	26569	12.7671	.00613497
44	1936	6.6332	.022727	104	10816	10.1980	.00961538	164	26896	12.8062	.00609756
45	2025	6.7082	.022222	105	11025	10.2470	.00952381	165	27225	12.8452	.00606061
46	2116	6.7823	.021739	106	11236	10.2956	.00943396	166	27556	12.8841	.00602410
47	2209	6.8557	.021277	107	11449	10.3441	.00934579	167	27889	12.9228	.00598802
48	2304	6.9282	.020833	108	11664	10.3923	.00925926	168	28224	12.9615	.00595238
49	2401	7.0000	.020408	109	11881	10.4403	.00917431	169	28561	13.0000	.00591716
50	2500	7.0711	.020000	110	12100	10.4881	.00909091	170	28900	13.0384	.00588235
51	2601	7.1414	.019608	111	12321	10.5357	.00900901	171	29241	13.0767	.00584795
52	2704	7.2111	.019231	112	12544	10.5830	.00892857	172	29584	13.1149	.00581395
53	2809	7.2801	.018868	113	12769	10.6301	.00884956	173	29929	13.1529	.00578035
54	2916	7.3485	.018519	114	12996	10.6771	.00877193	174	30276	13.1909	.00574713
55	3025	7.4162	.018182	115	13225	10.7238	.00869565	175	30625	13.2288	.00571429
56	3136	7.4833	.017857	116	13456	10.7703	.00862069	176	30976	13.2665	.00568182
57	3249	7.5498	.017544	117	13689	10.8167	.00854701	177	31329	13.3041	.00564972
58	3364	7.6158	.017241	118	13924	10.8628	.00847458	178	31684	13.3417	.00561798
59	3481	7.6811	.016949	119	14161	10.9087	.00840336	179	32041	13.3791	.00558659
60	3600	7.7460	.016667	120	14400	10.9545	.00833333	180	32400	13.4164	.00555556

Table L (continued)

N	N²	√N	1/N	N	N²	√N	1/N	N	N²	√N	1/N
181	32761	13.4536	.00552486	241	58081	15.5242	.00414938	301	90601	17.3494	.00332226
182	33124	13.4907	.00549451	242	58564	15.5563	.00413223	302	91204	17.3781	.00331126
183	33489	13.5277	.00546448	243	59049	15.5885	.00411523	303	91809	17.4069	.00330033
184	33856	13.5647	.00543478	244	59536	15.6205	.00409836	304	92416	17.4356	.00328047
185	34225	13.6015	.00540541	245	60025	15.6525	.00408163	305	93025	17.4642	.00328947
186	34596	13.6382	.00537634	246	60516	15.6844	.00406504	306	93636	17.4929	.00326797
187	34969	13.6748	.00534759	247	61009	15.7162	.00404858	307	94249	17.5214	.00325733
188	35344	13.7113	.00531915	248	61504	15.7480	.00403226	308	94864	17.5499	.00324675
189	35721	13.7477	.00529101	249	62001	15.7797	.00401606	309	95481	17.5784	.00323625
190	36100	13.7840	.00526316	250	62500	15.8114	.00400000	310	96100	17.6068	.00322581
191	36481	13.8203	.00523560	251	63001	15.8430	.00398406	311	96721	17.6352	.00321543
192	36864	13.8564	.00520833	252	63504	15.8745	.00396825	312	97344	17.6635	.00320513
193	37249	13.8924	.00518135	253	64009	15.9060	.00395257	313	97969	17.6918	.00319489
194	37636	13.9284	.00515464	254	64516	15.9374	.00393701	314	98596	17.7200	.00318471
195	38025	13.9642	.00512821	255	65025	15.9687	.00392157	315	99225	17.7482	.00317460
196	38416	14.0000	.00510204	256	65536	16.0000	.00390625	316	99856	17.7764	.00316456
197	38809	14.0357	.00507614	257	66049	16.0312	.00389105	317	100489	17.8045	.00315457
198	39204	14.0712	.00505051	258	66564	16.0624	.00387597	318	101124	17.8326	.00314466
199	39601	14.1067	.00502513	259	67081	16.0935	.00386100	319	101761	17.8606	.00313480
200	40000	14.1421	.00500000	260	67600	16.1245	.00384615	320	102400	17.8885	.00312500
201	40401	14.1774	.00497512	261	68121	16.1555	.00383142	321	103041	17.9165	.00311526
202	40804	14.2127	.00495050	262	68644	16.1864	.00381679	322	103684	17.9444	.00310559
203	41209	14.2478	.00492611	263	69169	16.2173	.00380228	323	104329	17.9722	.00309598
204	41616	14.2829	.00490196	264	69696	16.2481	.00378788	324	104976	18.0000	.00308642
205	42025	14.3178	.00487805	265	70225	16.2788	.00377358	325	105625	18.0278	.00307692
206	42436	14.3527	.00485437	266	70756	16.3095	.00375940	326	106276	18.0555	.00306748
207	42849	14.3875	.00483092	267	71289	16.3401	.00374532	327	106929	18.0831	.00305810
208	43264	14.4222	.00480769	268	71824	16.3707	.00373134	328	107584	18.1108	.00304878
209	43681	14.4568	.00478469	269	72361	16.4012	.00371747	329	108241	18.1384	.00303951
210	44100	14.4914	.00476190	270	72900	16.4317	.00370370	330	108900	18.1659	.00303030
211	44521	14.5258	.00473934	271	73441	16.4621	.00369004	331	109561	18.1934	.00302115
212	44944	14.5602	.00471698	272	73984	16.4924	.00367647	332	110224	18.2209	.00301205
213	45369	14.5945	.00469484	273	74529	16.5227	.00366300	333	110889	18.2483	.00300300
214	45796	14.6287	.00467290	274	75076	16.5529	.00364964	334	111556	18.2757	.00299401
215	46225	14.6629	.00465116	275	75625	16.5831	.00363636	335	112225	18.3030	.00298507
216	46656	14.6969	.00462963	276	76176	16.6132	.00362319	336	112896	18.3303	.00297619
217	47089	14.7309	.00460829	277	76729	16.6433	.00361011	337	113569	18.3576	.00296736
218	47524	14.7648	.00458716	278	77284	16.6733	.00359712	338	114244	18.3848	.00295858
219	47961	14.7986	.00456621	279	77841	16.7033	.00358423	339	114921	18.4120	.00294985
220	48400	14.8324	.00454545	280	78400	16.7332	.00357143	340	115600	18.4391	.00294118
221	48841	14.8661	.00452489	281	78961	16.7631	.00355872	341	116281	18.4662	.00293255
222	49284	14.8997	.00450450	282	79524	16.7929	.00354610	342	116964	18.4932	.00292398
223	49729	14.9332	.00448430	283	80089	16.8226	.00353357	343	117649	18.5203	.00291545
224	50176	14.9666	.00446429	284	80656	16.8523	.00352113	344	118336	18.5472	.00290698
225	50625	15.0000	.00444444	285	81225	16.8819	.00350877	345	119025	18.5742	.00289855
226	51076	15.0333	.00442478	286	81796	16.9115	.00349650	346	119716	18.6011	.00289017
227	51529	15.0665	.00440529	287	82369	16.9411	.00348432	347	120409	18.6279	.00288184
228	51984	15.0997	.00438596	288	82944	16.9706	.00347222	348	121104	18.6548	.00287356
229	52441	15.1327	.00436681	289	83521	17.0000	.00346021	349	121801	18.6815	.00286533
230	52900	15.1658	.00434783	290	84100	17.0294	.00344828	350	122500	18.7083	.00285714
231	53361	15.1987	.00432900	291	84681	17.0587	.00343643	351	123201	18.7350	.00284900
232	53824	15.2315	.00431034	292	85264	17.0880	.00342466	352	123904	18.7617	.00284091
233	54289	15.2643	.00429185	293	85849	17.1172	.00341297	353	124609	18.7883	.00283286
234	54756	15.2971	.00427350	294	86436	17.1464	.00340136	354	125316	18.8149	.00282486
235	55225	15.3297	.00425532	295	87025	17.1756	.00338983	355	126025	18.8414	.00281690
236	55696	15.3623	.00423729	296	87616	17.2047	.00337838	356	126736	18.8680	.00280899
237	56169	15.3948	.00421941	297	88209	17.2337	.00336700	357	127449	18.8944	.00280112
238	56644	15.4272	.00420168	298	88804	17.2627	.00335570	358	128164	18.9209	.00279330
239	57121	15.4596	.00418410	299	89401	17.2916	.00334448	359	128881	18.9473	.00278552
240	57600	15.4919	.00416667	300	90000	17.3205	.00333333	360	129600	18.9737	.00277778

Table L   **491**

Table L   (*continued*)

N	N²	√N	1/N	N	N²	√N	1/N	N	N²	√N	1/N
361	130321	19.0000	.00277008	421	177241	20.5183	.00237530	481	231361	21.9317	.00207900
362	131044	19.0263	.00276243	422	178084	20.5426	.00236967	482	232324	21.9545	.00207469
363	131769	19.0526	.00275482	423	178929	20.5670	.00236407	483	233289	21.9773	.00207039
364	132496	19.0788	.00274725	424	179776	20.5913	.00235849	484	234256	22.0000	.00206612
365	133225	19.1050	.00273973	425	180625	20.6155	.00235294	485	235225	22.0227	.00206186
366	133956	19.1311	.00273224	426	181476	20.6398	.00234742	486	236196	22.0454	.00205761
367	134689	19.1572	.00272480	427	182329	20.6640	.00234192	487	237169	22.0681	.00205339
368	135424	19.1833	.00271739	428	183184	20.6882	.00233645	488	238144	22.0907	.00204918
369	136161	19.2094	.00271003	429	184041	20.7123	.00233100	489	239121	22.1133	.00204499
370	136900	19.2354	.00270270	430	184900	20.7364	.00232558	490	240100	22.1359	.00204082
371	137641	19.2614	.00269542	431	185761	20.7605	.00232019	491	241081	22.1585	.00203666
372	138384	19.2873	.00268817	432	186624	20.7846	.00231481	492	242064	22.1811	.00203252
373	139129	19.3132	.00268097	433	187489	20.8087	.00230947	493	243049	22.2036	.00202840
374	139876	19.3391	.00267380	434	188356	20.8327	.00230415	494	244036	22.2261	.00202429
375	140625	19.3649	.00266667	435	189225	20.8567	.00229885	495	245025	22.2486	.00202020
376	141376	19.3907	.00265957	436	190096	20.8806	.00229358	496	246016	22.2711	.00201613
377	142129	19.4165	.00265252	437	190969	20.9045	.00228833	497	247009	22.2935	.00201207
378	142884	19.4422	.00264550	438	191844	20.9284	.00228311	498	248004	22.3159	.00200803
379	143641	19.4679	.00263852	439	192721	20.9523	.00227790	499	249001	22.3383	.00200401
380	144400	19.4936	.00263158	440	193600	20.9762	.00227273	500	250000	22.3607	.00200000
381	145161	19.5192	.00262467	441	194481	21.0000	.00226757	501	251001	22.3830	.00199601
382	145924	19.5448	.00261780	442	195364	21.0238	.00226244	502	252004	22.4054	.00199203
383	146689	19.5704	.00261097	443	196249	21.0476	.00225734	503	253009	22.4277	.00198807
384	147456	19.5959	.00260417	444	197136	21.0713	.00225225	504	254016	22.4499	.00198413
385	148225	19.6214	.00259740	445	198025	21.0950	.00224719	505	255025	22.4722	.00198020
386	148996	19.6469	.00259067	446	198916	21.1187	.00224215	506	256036	22.4944	.00197628
387	149769	19.6723	.00258398	447	199809	21.1424	.00223714	507	257049	22.5167	.00197239
388	150544	19.6977	.00257732	448	200704	21.1660	.00223214	508	258064	22.5389	.00196850
389	151321	19.7231	.00257069	449	201601	21.1896	.00222717	509	259081	22.5610	.00196464
390	152100	19.7484	.00256410	450	202500	21.2132	.00222222	510	260100	22.5832	.00196078
391	152881	19.7737	.00255754	451	203401	21.2368	.00221729	511	261121	22.6053	.00195695
392	153664	19.7990	.00255102	452	204304	21.2603	.00221239	512	262144	22.6274	.00195312
393	154449	19.8242	.00254453	453	205209	21.2838	.00220751	513	263169	22.6495	.00194932
394	155236	19.8494	.00253807	454	206116	21.3073	.00220264	514	264196	22.6716	.00194553
395	156025	19.8746	.00253165	455	207025	21.3307	.00219870	515	265225	22.6936	.00194175
396	156816	19.8997	.00252525	456	207936	21.3542	.00219298	516	266256	22.7156	.00193798
397	157609	19.9249	.00251889	457	208849	21.3776	.00218818	517	267289	22.7376	.00193423
398	158404	19.9499	.00251256	458	209764	21.4009	.00218341	518	268324	22.7596	.00193050
399	159201	19.9750	.00250627	459	210681	21.4243	.00217865	519	269361	22.7816	.00192678
400	160000	20.0000	.00250000	460	211600	21.4476	.00217391	520	270400	22.8035	.00192308
401	160801	20.0250	.00249377	461	212521	21.4709	.00216920	521	271441	22.8254	.00191939
402	161604	20.0499	.00248756	462	213444	21.4942	.00216450	522	272484	22.8473	.00191571
403	162409	20.0749	.00248139	463	214369	21.5174	.00215983	523	273529	22.8692	.00191205
404	163216	20.0998	.00247525	464	215296	21.5407	.00215517	524	274576	22.8910	.00190840
405	164025	20.1246	.00246914	465	216225	21.5639	.00215054	525	275625	22.9129	.00190476
406	164836	20.1494	.00246305	466	217156	21.5870	.00214592	526	276676	22.9347	.00190114
407	165649	20.1742	.00245700	467	218089	21.6102	.00214133	527	277729	22.9565	.00189753
408	166464	20.1990	.00245098	468	219024	21.6333	.00213675	528	278784	22.9783	.00189394
409	167281	20.2237	.00244499	469	219961	21.6564	.00213220	529	279841	23.0000	.00189036
410	168100	20.2485	.00243902	470	220900	21.6795	.00212766	530	280900	23.0217	.00188679
411	168921	20.2731	.00243309	471	221841	21.7025	.00212314	531	281961	23.0434	.00188324
412	169744	20.2978	.00242718	472	222784	21.7256	.00211864	532	283024	23.0651	.00187970
413	170569	20.3224	.00242131	473	223729	21.7486	.00211416	533	284089	23.0868	.00187617
414	171396	20.3470	.00241546	474	224676	21.7715	.00210970	534	285156	23.1084	.00187266
415	172225	20.3715	.00240964	475	225625	21.7945	.00210526	535	286225	23.1301	.00186916
416	173056	20.3961	.00240385	476	226576	21.8174	.00210084	536	287296	23.1517	.00186567
417	173889	20.4206	.00239808	477	227529	21.8403	.00209644	537	288369	23.1733	.00186220
418	174724	20.4450	.00239234	478	228484	21.8632	.00209205	538	289444	23.1948	.00185874
419	175561	20.4695	.00238663	479	229441	21.8861	.00208768	539	290521	23.2164	.00185529
420	176400	20.4939	.00238095	480	230400	21.9089	.00208333	540	291600	23.2379	.00185185

Table L (*continued*)

N	N²	√N̄	1/N	N	N²	√N̄	1/N	N	N²	√N̄	1/N
541	292681	23.2594	.00184843	601	361201	24.5153	.00166389	661	436921	25.7099	.00151286
542	293764	23.2809	.00184502	602	302404	24.5357	.00166113	662	438244	25.7294	.00151057
543	294849	23.3024	.00184162	603	363609	24.5561	.00165837	663	439569	25.7488	.00150830
544	295936	23.3238	.00183824	604	364816	24.5764	.00165563	664	440896	25.7682	.00150602
545	297025	23.3452	.00183486	605	366025	24.5967	.00165289	665	442225	25.7876	.00150376
546	298116	23.3666	.00183150	606	367236	24.6171	.00165017	666	443556	25.8070	.00150150
547	299209	23.3880	.00182815	607	368449	24.6374	.00164745	667	444889	25.8263	.00149925
548	300304	23.4094	.00182482	608	369664	24.6577	.00164474	668	446224	25.8457	.00149701
549	301401	23.4307	.00182149	609	370881	24.6779	.00164204	669	447561	25.8650	.00149477
550	302500	23.4521	.00181818	610	372100	24.6982	.00163934	670	448900	25.8844	.00149254
551	303601	23.4734	.00181488	611	373321	24.7184	.00163666	671	450241	25.9037	.00149031
552	304704	23.4947	.00181159	612	374544	24.7386	.00163399	672	451584	25.9230	.00148810
553	305809	23.5160	.00180832	613	375769	24.7588	.00163132	673	452929	25.9422	.00148588
554	306916	23.5372	.00180505	614	376996	24.7790	.00162866	674	454276	25.9615	.00148368
555	308025	23.5584	.00180180	615	378225	24.7992	.00162602	675	455625	25.9808	.00148148
556	309136	23.5797	.00179856	616	379456	24.8193	.00162338	676	456976	26.0000	.00147929
557	310249	23.6008	.00179533	617	380689	24.8395	.00162075	677	458329	26.0192	.00147710
558	311364	23.6220	.00179211	618	381924	24.8596	.00161812	678	459684	26.0384	.00147493
559	312481	23.6432	.00178891	619	383161	24.8797	.00161551	679	461041	26.0576	.00147275
560	313600	23.6643	.00178571	620	384400	24.8998	.00161290	680	462400	26.0768	.00147059
561	314721	23.6854	.00178253	621	385641	24.9199	.00161031	681	463761	26.0960	.00146843
562	315844	23.7065	.00177936	622	386884	24.9399	.00160772	682	465124	26.1151	.00146628
563	316969	23.7276	.00177620	623	388129	24.9600	.00160514	683	466489	26.1343	.00146413
564	318096	23.7487	.00177305	624	389376	24.9800	.00160256	684	467856	26.1534	.00146199
565	319225	23.7697	.00176991	625	390625	25.0000	.00160000	685	469225	26.1725	.00145985
566	320356	23.7908	.00176678	626	391876	25.0200	.00159744	686	470596	26.1916	.00145773
567	321489	23.8118	.00176367	627	393129	25.0400	.00159490	687	471969	26.2107	.00145560
568	322624	23.8328	.00176056	628	394384	25.0599	.00159236	688	473344	26.2298	.00145349
569	323761	23.8537	.00175747	629	395641	25.0799	.00158983	689	474721	26.2488	.00145138
570	324900	23.8747	.00175439	630	396900	25.0998	.00158730	690	476100	26.2679	.00144928
571	326041	23.8956	.00175131	631	398161	25.1197	.00158479	691	477481	26.2869	.00144718
572	327184	23.9165	.00174825	632	399424	25.1396	.00158228	692	478864	26.3059	.00144509
573	328329	23.9374	.00174520	633	400689	25.1595	.00157978	693	480249	26.3249	.00144300
574	329476	23.9583	.00174216	634	401956	25.1794	.00157729	694	481636	26.3439	.00144092
575	330625	23.9792	.00173913	635	403225	25.1992	.00157480	695	483025	26.3629	.00143885
576	331776	24.0000	.00173611	636	404496	25.2190	.00157233	696	484416	26.3818	.00143678
577	332929	24.0208	.00173310	637	405769	25.2389	.00156986	697	485809	26.4008	.00143472
578	334084	24.0416	.00173010	638	407044	25.2587	.00156740	698	487204	26.4197	.00143266
579	335241	24.0624	.00172712	639	408321	25.2784	.00156495	699	488601	26.4386	.00143062
580	336400	24.0832	.00172414	640	409600	25.2982	.00156250	700	490000	26.4575	.00142857
581	337561	24.1039	.00172117	641	410881	25.3180	.00156006	701	491401	26.4764	.00142653
582	338724	24.1247	.00171821	642	412164	25.3377	.00155763	702	492804	26.4953	.00142450
583	339889	24.1454	.00171527	643	413449	25.3574	.00155521	703	494209	26.5141	.00142248
584	341056	24.1661	.00171233	644	414736	25.3772	.00155280	704	495616	26.5330	.00142045
585	342225	24.1868	.00170940	645	416025	25.3969	.00155039	705	497025	26.5518	.00141844
586	343396	24.2074	.00170648	646	417316	25.4165	.00154799	706	498436	26.5707	.00141643
587	344569	24.2281	.00170358	647	418609	25.4362	.00154560	707	499849	26.5895	.00141443
588	345744	24.2487	.00170068	648	419904	25.4558	.00154321	708	501264	26.6083	.00141243
589	346921	24.2693	.00169779	649	421201	25.4755	.00154083	709	502681	26.6271	.00141044
590	348100	24.2899	.00169492	650	422500	25.4951	.00153846	710	504100	26.6458	.00140845
591	349281	24.3105	.00169205	651	423801	25.5147	.00153610	711	505521	26.6646	.00140647
592	350464	24.3311	.00168919	652	425104	25.5343	.00153374	712	506944	26.6833	.00140449
593	351649	24.3516	.00168634	653	426409	25.5539	.00153139	713	508369	26.7021	.00140252
594	352836	24.3721	.00168350	654	427716	25.5734	.00152905	714	509796	26.7208	.00140056
595	354025	24.3926	.00168067	655	429025	25.5930	.00152672	715	511225	26.7395	.00139860
596	355216	24.4131	.00167785	656	430336	25.6125	.00152439	716	512656	26.7582	.00139665
597	356409	24.4336	.00167504	657	431649	25.6320	.00152207	717	514089	26.7769	.00139470
598	357604	24.4540	.00167224	658	432964	25.6515	.00151976	718	515524	26.7955	.00139276
599	358801	24.4745	.00166945	659	434281	25.6710	.00151745	719	516961	26.8142	.00139082
600	360000	24.4949	.00166667	660	435600	25.6905	.00151515	720	518400	26.8328	.00138889

Table L   **493**

Table L (continued)

N	N²	√N	1/N	N	N²	√N	1/N	N	N²	√N	1/N
721	519841	26.8514	.00138696	781	609961	27.9464	.00128041	841	707281	29.0000	.00118906
722	521284	26.8701	.00138504	782	611524	27.9643	.00127877	842	708964	29.0172	.00118765
723	522729	26.8887	.00138313	783	613089	27.9821	.00127714	843	710649	29.0345	.00118624
724	524176	26.9072	.00138122	784	614656	28.0000	.00127551	844	712336	29.0517	.00118483
725	525625	26.9258	.00137931	785	616225	28.0179	.00127389	845	714025	29.0689	.00118343
726	527076	26.9444	.00137741	786	617796	28.0357	.00127226	846	715716	29.0861	.00118203
727	528529	26.9629	.00137552	787	619369	28.0535	.00127065	847	717409	29.1033	.00118064
728	529984	26.9815	.00137363	788	620944	28.0713	.00126904	848	719104	29.1204	.00117925
729	531441	27.0000	.00137174	789	622521	28.0891	.00126743	849	720801	29.1376	.00117786
730	532900	27.0185	.00136986	790	624100	28.1069	.00126582	850	722500	29.1548	.00117647
731	534361	27.0370	.00136799	791	625681	28.1247	.00126422	851	724201	29.1719	.00117509
732	535824	27.0555	.00136612	792	627264	28.1425	.00126263	852	725904	29.1890	.00117371
733	537289	27.0740	.00136426	793	628849	28.1603	.00126103	853	727609	29.2062	.00117233
734	538756	27.0924	.00136240	794	630436	28.1780	.00125945	854	729316	29.2233	.00117096
735	540225	27.1109	.00136054	795	632025	28.1957	.00125786	855	731025	29.2404	.00116959
736	541696	27.1293	.00135870	796	633616	28.2135	.00125628	856	732736	29.2575	.00116822
737	543169	27.1477	.00135685	797	635209	28.2312	.00125471	857	734449	29.2746	.00116686
738	544644	27.1662	.00135501	798	636804	28.2489	.00125313	858	736164	29.2916	.00116550
739	546121	27.1846	.00135318	799	638401	28.2666	.00125156	859	737881	29.3087	.00116414
740	547600	27.2029	.00135135	800	640000	28.2843	.00125000	860	739600	29.3258	.00116279
741	549081	27.2213	.00134953	801	641601	28.3019	.00124844	861	741321	29.3428	.00116144
742	550564	27.2397	.00134771	802	643204	28.3196	.00124688	862	743044	29.3598	.00116009
743	552049	27.2580	.00134590	803	644809	28.3373	.00124533	863	744769	29.3769	.00115875
744	553536	27.2764	.00134409	804	646416	28.3549	.00124378	864	746496	29.3939	.00115741
745	555025	27.2947	.00134228	805	648025	28.3725	.00124224	865	748225	29.4109	.00115607
746	556516	27.3130	.00134048	806	649636	28.3901	.00124069	866	749956	29.4279	.00115473
747	558009	27.3313	.00133869	807	651249	28.4077	.00123916	867	751689	29.4449	.00115340
748	559504	27.3496	.00133690	808	652864	28.4253	.00123762	868	753424	29.4618	.00115207
749	561001	27.3679	.00133511	809	654481	28.4429	.00123609	869	755161	29.4788	.00115075
750	562500	27.3861	.00133333	810	656100	28.4605	.00123457	870	756900	29.4958	.00114943
751	564001	27.4044	.00133156	811	657721	28.4781	.00123305	871	758641	29.5127	.00114811
752	565504	27.4226	.00132979	812	659344	28.4956	.00123153	872	760384	29.5296	.00114679
753	567009	27.4408	.00132802	813	660969	28.5132	.00123001	873	762129	29.5466	.00114548
754	568516	27.4591	.00132626	814	662596	28.5307	.00122850	874	763876	29.5635	.00114416
755	570025	27.4773	.00132450	815	664225	28.5482	.00122699	875	765625	29.5804	.00114286
756	571536	27.4955	.00132275	816	665856	28.5657	.00122549	876	767376	29.5973	.00114155
757	573049	27.5136	.00132100	817	667489	28.5832	.00122399	877	769129	29.6142	.00114025
758	574564	27.5318	.00131926	818	669124	28.6007	.00122249	878	770884	29.6311	.00113895
759	576081	27.5500	.00131752	819	670761	28.6182	.00122100	879	772641	29.6479	.00113766
760	577600	27.5681	.00131579	820	672400	28.6356	.00121951	880	774400	29.6848	.00113636
761	579121	27.5862	.00131406	821	674041	28.6531	.00121803	881	776161	29.6816	.00113507
762	580644	27.6043	.00131234	822	675684	28.6705	.00121655	882	777924	29.6985	.00113379
763	582169	27.6225	.00131062	823	677329	28.6880	.00121507	883	779689	29.7153	.00113250
764	583696	27.6405	.00130890	824	678976	28.7054	.00121359	884	781456	29.7321	.00113122
765	585225	27.6586	.00130719	825	680625	28.7228	.00121212	885	783225	29.7489	.00112994
766	586756	27.6767	.00130548	826	682276	28.7402	.00121065	886	784996	29.7658	.00112867
767	588289	27.6948	.00130378	827	683929	28.7576	.00120919	887	786769	29.7825	.00112740
768	589824	27.7128	.00130208	828	685584	28.7750	.00120773	888	788544	29.7993	.00112613
769	591361	27.7308	.00130039	829	687241	28.7924	.00120627	889	790321	29.8161	.00112486
770	592900	27.7489	.00129870	830	688900	28.8097	.00120482	890	792100	29.8329	.00112360
771	594441	27.7669	.00129702	831	690561	28.8271	.00120337	891	793881	29.8496	.00112233
772	595984	27.7849	.00129534	832	692224	28.8444	.00120192	892	795664	29.8664	.00112108
773	597529	27.8029	.00129366	833	693889	28.8617	.00120048	893	797449	29.8831	.00111982
774	599076	27.8209	.00129199	834	695556	28.8791	.00119904	894	799236	29.8998	.00111857
775	600625	27.8388	.00129032	835	697225	28.8964	.00119760	895	801025	29.9166	.00111732
776	602176	27.8568	.00128866	836	698896	28.9137	.00119617	896	802816	29.9333	.00111607
777	603729	27.8747	.00128700	837	700569	28.9310	.00119474	897	804609	29.9500	.00111483
778	605284	27.8927	.00128535	838	702244	28.9482	.00119332	898	806404	29.9666	.00111359
779	606841	27.9106	.00128370	839	703921	28.9655	.00119190	899	808201	29.9833	.00111235
780	608400	27.9285	.00128205	840	705600	28.9828	.00119048	900	810000	30.0000	.00111111

Table L *(continued)*

N	N²	√N	1/N	N	N²	√N	1/N	N	N²	√N	1/N
901	811801	30.0167	.00110988	936	876096	30.5941	.00106838	971	942841	31.1609	.00102987
902	813604	30.0333	.00110865	937	877969	30.6105	.00106724	972	944784	31.1769	.00102881
903	815409	30.0500	.00110742	938	879844	30.6268	.00106610	973	946729	31.1929	.00102775
904	817216	30.0666	.00110619	939	881721	30.6431	.00106496	974	948676	31.2090	.00102669
905	819025	30.0832	.00110497	940	883600	30.6594	.00106383	975	950625	31.2250	.00102564
906	820836	30.0998	.00110375	941	885481	30.6757	.00106270	976	952576	31.2410	.00102459
907	822649	30.1164	.00110254	942	887364	30.6920	.00106157	977	954529	31.2570	.00102354
908	824464	30.1330	.00110132	943	889249	30.7083	.00106045	978	956484	31.2730	.00102249
909	826281	30.1496	.00110011	944	891136	30.7246	.00105932	979	958441	31.2890	.00102145
910	828100	30.1662	.00109890	945	893025	30.7409	.00105820	980	960400	31.3050	.00102041
911	829921	30.1828	.00109769	946	894916	30.7571	.00105708	981	962361	31.3209	.00101937
912	831744	30.1993	.00109649	947	896809	30.7734	.00105597	982	964324	31.3369	.00101833
913	833569	30.2159	.00109529	948	898704	30.7896	.00105485	983	966289	31.3528	.00101729
914	835396	30.2324	.00109409	949	900601	30.8058	.00105374	984	968256	31.3688	.00101626
915	837225	30.2490	.00109290	950	902500	30.8221	.00105263	985	970225	31.3847	.00101523
916	839056	30.2655	.00109170	951	904401	30.8383	.00105152	986	972196	31.4006	.00101420
917	840889	30.2820	.00109051	952	906304	30.8545	.00105042	987	974169	31.4166	.00101317
918	842724	30.2985	.00108932	953	908209	30.8707	.00104932	988	976144	31.4325	.00101215
919	844561	30.3150	.00108814	954	910116	30.8869	.00104822	989	978121	31.4484	.00101112
920	846400	30.3315	.00108696	955	912025	30.9031	.00104712	990	980100	31.4643	.00101010
921	848241	30.3480	.00108578	956	913936	30.9192	.00104603	991	982081	31.4802	.00100908
922	850084	30.3645	.00108460	957	915849	30.9354	.00104493	992	984064	31.4960	.00100806
923	851929	30.3809	.00108342	958	917764	30.9516	.00104384	993	986049	31.5119	.00100705
924	853776	30.3974	.00108225	959	919681	30.9677	.00104275	994	988036	31.5278	.00100604
925	855625	30.4138	.00108108	960	921600	30.9839	.00104167	995	990025	31.5436	.00100503
926	857476	30.4302	.00107991	961	923521	31.0000	.00104058	996	992016	31.5595	.00100402
927	859329	30.4467	.00107875	962	925444	31.0161	.00103950	997	994009	31.5753	.00103842
928	861184	30.4631	.00107759	963	927369	31.0322	.00103842	998	996004	31.5911	.00100200
929	863041	30.4795	.00107643	964	929296	31.0483	.00103734	999	998001	31.6070	.00100100
930	864900	30.4959	.00107527	965	931225	31.0644	.00103627	1000	1000000	31.6228	.00100000
931	866761	30.5123	.00107411	966	933156	31.0805	.00103520				
932	868624	30.5287	.00107296	967	935089	31.0966	.00103413				
933	870489	30.5450	.00107181	968	937024	31.1127	.00103306				
934	872356	30.5614	.00107066	969	938961	31.1288	.00103199				
935	874225	30.5778	.00106952	970	940900	31.1448	.00103093				

Table M Random digits

ROW NUMBER											
00000	10097	32533	76520	13586	34673	54876	80959	09117	39292	74945
00001	37542	04805	64894	74296	24805	24037	20636	10402	00822	91665
00002	08422	68953	19645	09303	23209	02560	15953	34764	35080	33606
00003	99019	02529	09376	70715	38311	31165	88676	74397	04436	27659
00004	12807	99970	80157	36147	64032	36653	98951	16877	12171	76833
00005	66065	74717	34072	76850	36697	36170	65813	39885	11199	29170
00006	31060	10805	45571	82406	35303	42614	86799	07439	23403	09732
00007	85269	77602	02051	65692	68665	74818	73053	85247	18623	88579
00008	63573	32135	05325	47048	90553	57548	28468	28709	83491	25624
00009	73796	45753	03529	64778	35808	34282	60935	20344	35273	88435
00010	98520	17767	14905	68607	22109	40558	60970	93433	50500	73998
00011	11805	05431	39808	27732	50725	68248	29405	24201	52775	67851
00012	83452	99634	06288	98033	13746	70078	18475	40610	68711	77817
00013	88685	40200	86507	58401	36766	67951	90364	76493	29609	11062
00014	99594	67348	87517	64969	91826	08928	93785	61368	23478	34113
00015	65481	17674	17468	50950	58047	76974	73039	57186	40218	16544
00016	80124	35635	17727	08015	45318	22374	21115	78253	14385	53763
00017	74350	99817	77402	77214	43236	00210	45521	64237	96286	02655
00018	69916	26803	66252	29148	36936	87203	76621	13990	94400	56418
00019	09893	20505	14225	68514	46427	56788	96297	78822	54382	14598
00020	91499	14523	68479	27686	46162	83554	94750	89923	37089	20048
00021	80336	94598	26940	36858	70297	34135	53140	33340	42050	82341
00022	44104	81949	85157	47954	32979	26575	57600	40881	22222	06413
00023	12550	73742	11100	02040	12860	74697	96644	89439	28707	25815
00024	63606	49329	16505	34484	40219	52563	43651	77082	07207	31790
00025	61196	90446	26457	47774	51924	33729	65394	59593	42582	60527
00026	15474	45266	95270	79953	59367	83848	82396	10118	33211	59466
00027	94557	28573	67897	54387	54622	44431	91190	42592	92927	45973
00028	42481	16213	97344	08721	16868	48767	03071	12059	25701	46670
00029	23523	78317	73208	89837	68935	91416	26252	29663	05522	82562
00030	04493	52494	75246	33824	45862	51025	61962	79335	65337	12472
00031	00549	97654	64051	88159	96119	63896	54692	82391	23287	29529
00032	35963	15307	26898	09354	33351	35462	77974	50024	90103	39333
00033	59808	08391	45427	26842	83609	49700	13021	24892	78565	20106
00034	46058	85236	01390	92286	77281	44077	93910	83647	70617	42941
00035	32179	00597	87379	25241	05567	07007	86743	17157	85394	11838
00036	69234	61406	20117	45204	15956	60000	18743	92423	97118	96338
00037	19565	41430	01758	75379	40419	21585	66674	36806	84962	85207
00038	45155	14938	19476	07246	43667	94543	59047	90033	20826	69541
00039	94864	31994	36168	10851	34888	81553	01540	35456	05014	51176
00040	98086	24826	45240	28404	44999	08896	39094	73407	35441	31880
00041	33185	16232	41941	50949	89435	48581	88695	41994	37548	73043
00042	80951	00406	96382	70774	20151	23387	25016	25298	94624	61171
00043	79752	49140	71961	28296	69861	02591	74852	20539	00387	59579
00044	18633	32537	98145	06571	31010	24674	05455	61427	77938	91936
00045	74029	43902	77557	32270	97790	17119	52527	58021	80814	51748
00046	54178	45611	80993	37143	05335	12969	56127	19255	36040	90324
00047	11664	49883	52079	84827	59381	71539	09973	33440	88461	23356
00048	48324	77928	31249	64710	02295	36870	32307	57546	15020	09994
00049	69074	94138	87637	91976	35584	04401	10518	21615	01848	76938
00050	09188	20097	32825	39527	04220	86304	83389	87374	64278	58044
00051	90045	85497	51981	50654	94938	81997	91870	76150	68476	64659
00052	73189	50207	47677	26269	62290	64464	27124	67018	41361	82760
00053	75768	76490	20971	87749	90429	12272	95375	05871	93823	43178
00054	54016	44056	66281	31003	00682	27398	20714	53295	07706	17813
00055	08358	69910	78542	42785	13661	58873	04618	97553	31223	08420
00056	28306	03264	81333	10591	40510	07893	32604	60475	94119	01840
00057	53840	86233	81594	13628	51215	90290	28466	68795	77762	20791
00058	91757	53741	61613	62669	50263	90212	55781	76514	83483	47055
00059	89415	92694	00397	58391	12607	17646	48949	72306	94541	37408

Table M (*continued*)

ROW NUMBER										
00060	77513	03820	86864	29901	68414	82774	51908	13980	72893	55507
00061	19502	37174	69979	20288	55210	29773	74287	75251	65344	67415
00062	21818	59313	93278	81757	05686	73156	07082	85046	31853	38452
00063	51474	66499	68107	23621	94049	91345	42836	09191	08007	45449
00064	99559	68331	62535	24170	69777	12830	74819	78142	43860	72834
00065	33713	48007	93584	72869	51926	64721	58303	29822	93174	93972
00066	85274	86893	11303	22970	28834	34137	73515	90400	71148	43643
00067	84133	89640	44035	52166	73852	70091	61222	60561	62327	18423
00068	56732	16234	17395	96131	10123	91622	85496	57560	81604	18880
00069	65138	56806	87648	85261	34313	65861	45875	21069	85644	47277
00070	38001	02176	81719	11711	71602	92937	74219	64049	65584	49698
00071	37402	96397	01304	77586	56271	10086	47324	62605	40030	37438
00072	97125	40348	87083	31417	21815	39250	75237	62047	15501	29578
00073	21826	41134	47143	34072	64638	85902	49139	06441	03856	54552
00074	73135	42742	95719	09035	85794	74296	08789	88156	64691	19202
00075	07638	77929	03061	18072	96207	44156	23821	99538	04713	66994
00076	60528	83441	07954	19814	59175	20695	05533	52139	61212	06455
00077	83596	35655	06958	92983	05128	09719	77433	53783	92301	50498
00078	10850	62746	99599	10507	13499	06319	53075	71839	06410	19362
00079	39820	98952	43622	63147	64421	80814	43800	09351	31024	73167
00080	59580	06478	75569	78800	88835	54486	23768	06156	04111	08408
00081	38508	07341	23793	48763	90822	97022	17719	04207	95954	49953
00082	30692	70668	94688	16127	56196	80091	82067	63400	05462	69200
00083	65443	95659	18238	27437	49632	24041	08337	65676	96299	90836
00084	27267	50264	13192	72294	07477	44606	17985	48911	97341	30358
00085	91307	06991	19072	24210	36699	53728	28825	35793	28976	66252
00086	68434	94688	84473	13622	62126	98408	12843	82590	09815	93146
00087	48908	15877	54745	24591	35700	04754	83824	52692	54130	55160
00088	06913	45197	42672	78601	11883	09528	63011	98901	14974	40344
00089	10455	16019	14210	33712	91342	37821	88325	80851	43667	70883
00090	12883	97343	65027	61184	04285	01392	17974	15077	90712	26769
00091	21778	30976	38807	36961	31649	42096	63281	02023	08816	47449
00092	19523	59515	65122	59659	86283	68258	69572	13798	16435	91529
00093	67245	52670	35583	16563	79246	86686	76463	34222	26655	90802
00094	60584	47377	07500	37992	45134	26529	26760	83637	41326	44344
00095	53853	41377	36066	94850	58838	73859	49364	73331	96240	43642
00096	24637	38736	74384	89342	52623	07992	12369	18601	03742	83873
00097	83080	12451	38992	22815	07759	51777	97377	27585	51972	37867
00098	16444	24334	36151	99073	27493	70939	85130	32552	54846	54759
00099	60790	18157	57178	65762	11161	78576	45819	52979	65130	04860
00100	03991	10461	93716	16894	66083	24653	84609	58232	88618	19161
00101	38555	95554	32886	59780	08355	60860	29735	47762	71299	23853
00102	17546	73704	92052	46215	55121	29281	59076	07936	27954	58909
00103	32643	52861	95819	06831	00911	98936	76355	93779	80863	00514
00104	69572	68777	39510	35905	14060	40619	29549	69616	33564	60780
00105	24122	66591	27699	06494	14845	46672	61958	77100	90899	75754
00106	61196	30231	92962	61773	41839	55382	17267	70943	78038	70267
00107	30532	21704	10274	12202	39685	23309	10061	68829	55986	66485
00108	03788	97599	75867	20717	74416	53166	35208	33374	87539	08823
00109	48228	63379	85783	47619	53152	67433	35663	52972	16818	60311
00110	60365	94653	35075	33949	42614	29297	01918	28316	98953	73231
00111	83799	42402	56623	34442	34994	41374	70071	14736	09958	18065
00112	32960	07405	36409	83232	99385	41600	11133	07586	15917	06253
00113	19322	53845	57620	52606	66497	68646	78138	66559	19640	99413
00114	11220	94747	07399	37408	48509	23929	27482	45476	85244	35159
00115	31751	57260	68980	05339	15470	48355	88651	22596	03152	19121
00116	88492	99382	14454	04504	20094	98977	74843	93413	22109	78508
00117	30934	47744	07481	83828	73788	06533	28597	20405	94205	20380
00118	22888	48893	27499	98748	60530	45128	74022	84617	82037	10268
00119	78212	16993	35902	91386	44372	15486	65741	14014	87481	37220

Table M (continued)

ROW NUMBER										
00120	41849	84547	46850	52326	34677	58300	74910	64345	19325	81549
00121	46352	33049	69248	93460	45305	07521	61318	31855	14413	70951
00122	11087	96294	14013	31792	59747	67277	76503	34513	39663	77544
00123	52701	08337	56303	97315	16520	69676	11654	99893	02181	68161
00124	57275	36898	81304	48595	68652	27376	92852	55866	88448	03584
00125	20857	73156	70284	24326	79375	95220	01159	63267	10622	48391
00126	15633	84924	90415	93614	33521	26665	55823	47641	86225	31704
00127	92694	48297	39904	02115	59589	49067	66821	41575	49767	04037
00128	77613	19019	88152	00080	20554	91409	96277	48257	50816	97616
00129	38688	32486	45134	63545	59404	72059	43947	51680	43852	59693
00130	25163	01889	70014	15021	41290	67312	71857	15957	68971	11403
00131	65251	07629	37239	33295	05870	01119	92784	26340	18477	65622
00132	36815	43625	18637	37509	82444	99005	04921	73701	14707	93997
00133	64397	11692	05327	82162	20247	81759	45197	25332	83745	22567
00134	04515	25624	95096	67946	48460	85558	15191	18782	16930	33361
00135	83761	60873	43253	84145	60833	25983	01291	41349	20368	07126
00136	14387	06345	80854	09279	43529	06318	38384	74761	41196	37480
00137	51321	92246	80088	77074	88722	56736	66164	49431	66919	31678
00138	72472	00008	80890	18002	94813	31900	54155	83436	35352	54131
00139	05466	55306	93128	18464	74457	90561	72848	11834	79982	68416
00140	39528	72484	82474	25593	48545	35247	18619	13674	18611	19241
00141	81616	18711	53342	44276	75122	11724	74627	73707	58319	15997
00142	07586	16120	82641	22820	92904	13141	32392	19763	61199	67940
00143	90767	04235	13574	17200	69902	63742	78464	22501	18627	90872
00144	40188	28193	29593	88627	94972	11598	62095	36787	00441	58997
00145	34414	82157	86887	55087	19152	00023	12302	80783	32624	68691
00146	63439	75363	44989	16822	36024	00867	76378	41605	65961	73488
00147	67049	09070	93399	45547	94458	74284	05041	49807	20288	34060
00148	79495	04146	52162	90286	54158	34243	46978	35482	59362	95938
00149	91704	30552	04737	21031	75051	93029	47665	64382	99782	93478
00150	94015	46874	32444	48277	59820	96163	64654	25843	41145	42820
00151	74108	88222	88570	74015	25704	91035	01755	14750	48968	38603
00152	62880	87873	95160	59221	22304	90314	72877	17334	39283	04149
00153	11748	12102	80580	41867	17710	59621	06554	07850	73950	79552
00154	17944	05600	60478	03343	25852	58905	57216	39618	49856	99326
00155	66067	42792	95043	52680	46780	56487	09971	59481	37006	22186
00156	54244	91030	45547	70818	59849	96169	61459	21647	87417	17198
00157	30945	57589	31732	57260	47670	07654	46376	25366	94746	49580
00158	69170	37403	86995	90307	94304	71803	26825	05511	12459	91314
00159	08345	88975	35841	85771	08105	59987	87112	21476	14713	71181
00160	27767	43584	85301	88977	29490	69714	73035	41207	74699	09310
00161	13025	14338	54066	15243	47724	66733	47431	43905	31048	56699
00162	80217	36292	98525	24335	24432	24896	43277	58874	11466	16082
00163	10875	62004	90391	61105	57411	06368	53856	30743	08670	84741
00164	54127	57326	26629	19087	24472	88779	30540	27886	61732	75454
00165	60311	42824	37301	42678	45990	43242	17374	52003	70707	70214
00166	49739	71484	92003	98086	76668	73209	59202	11973	02902	33250
00167	78626	51594	16453	94614	39014	97066	83012	09832	25571	77628
00168	66692	13986	99837	00582	81232	44987	09504	96412	90193	79568
00169	44071	28091	07362	97703	76447	42537	98524	97831	65704	09514
00170	41468	85149	49554	17994	14924	39650	95294	00556	70481	06905
00171	94559	37559	49678	53119	70312	05682	66986	34099	74474	20740
00172	41615	70360	64114	58660	90850	64618	80620	51790	11436	38072
00173	50273	93113	41794	86861	24781	89683	55411	85667	77535	99892
00174	41396	80504	90670	08289	40902	05069	95083	06783	28102	57816
00175	25807	24260	71529	78920	72682	07385	90726	57166	98884	08583
00176	06170	97965	88302	98041	21443	41808	68984	83620	89747	98882
00177	60808	54444	74412	81105	01176	28838	36421	16489	18059	51061
00178	80940	44893	10408	36222	80582	71944	92638	40333	67054	16067
00179	19516	90120	46759	71643	13177	55292	21036	82808	77501	97427

Table M (*continued*)

ROW NUMBER										
00180	49386	54480	23604	23554	21785	41101	91178	10174	29420	90438
00181	06312	88940	15995	69321	47458	64809	98189	81851	29651	84215
00182	60942	00307	11897	92674	40405	68032	96717	54244	10701	41393
00183	92329	98932	78284	46347	71209	92061	39448	93136	25722	08564
00184	77936	63574	31384	51924	85561	29671	58137	17820	22751	36518
00185	38101	77756	11657	13897	95889	57067	47648	13885	70669	93406
00186	39641	69457	91339	22502	92613	89719	11947	56203	19324	20504
00187	84054	40455	99396	63680	67667	60631	69181	96845	38525	11600
00188	47468	03577	57649	63266	24700	71594	14004	23153	69249	05747
00189	43321	31370	28977	23896	76479	68562	62342	07589	08899	05985
00190	64281	61826	18555	64937	13173	33365	78851	16499	87064	13075
00191	66847	70495	32350	02985	86716	38746	26313	77463	55387	72681
00192	72461	33230	21529	53424	92581	02262	78438	66276	18396	73538
00193	21032	91050	13058	16218	12470	56500	15292	76139	59526	52113
00194	95362	67011	06651	16136	01016	00857	55018	56374	35824	71708
00195	49712	97380	10404	55452	34030	60726	75211	10271	36633	68424
00196	58275	61764	97586	54716	50259	46345	87195	46092	26787	60939
00197	89514	11788	68224	23417	73959	76145	30342	40277	11049	72049
00198	15472	50669	48139	36732	46874	37088	63465	09819	58869	35220
00199	12120	86124	51247	44302	60883	52109	21437	36786	49226	77837

Table N₁ Critical values of U and U' for a one-tailed test at $\alpha = 0.005$ or a two-tailed test at $\alpha = 0.01$

To be significant for any given N_1 and N_2: Obtained U must be equal to or *less than* the value shown in the table. Obtained U' must be equal to or *greater than* the value shown in the table. *Example:* If $\alpha = 0.01$, two-tailed test, $N_1 = 13$, $N_2 = 15$, and obtained $U = 150$, we cannot reject H_0 since obtained U is within the upper (153) and lower (42) critical values.

Each cell shows the top number (U critical) over the bottom number (U').

$N_2 \backslash N_1$	1	2	3	4	5	6	7	8	9	10	11	12	13	14	15	16	17	18	19	20
1	--	--	--	--	--	--	--	--	--	--	--	--	--	--	--	--	--	--	--	--
2	--	--	--	--	--	--	--	--	--	--	--	--	--	--	--	--	--	--	0/38	0/40
3	--	--	--	--	--	--	--	--	0/27	0/30	0/33	1/35	1/38	1/41	2/43	2/46	2/49	2/52	3/54	3/57
4	--	--	--	--	--	0/24	0/28	1/31	1/35	2/38	2/42	3/45	3/49	4/52	5/55	5/59	6/62	6/66	7/69	8/72
5	--	--	--	--	0/25	1/29	1/34	2/38	3/42	4/46	5/50	6/54	7/58	7/63	8/67	9/71	10/75	11/79	12/83	13/87
6	--	--	--	0/24	1/29	2/34	3/39	4/44	5/49	6/54	7/59	9/63	10/68	11/73	12/78	13/83	15/87	16/92	17/97	18/102
7	--	--	--	0/28	1/34	3/39	4/45	6/50	7/56	9/61	10/67	12/72	13/78	15/83	16/89	18/94	19/100	21/105	22/111	24/116
8	--	--	--	1/31	2/38	4/44	6/50	7/57	9/63	11/69	13/75	15/81	17/87	18/94	20/100	22/106	24/112	26/118	28/124	30/130
9	--	--	0/27	1/35	3/42	5/49	7/56	9/63	11/70	13/77	16/83	18/90	20/97	22/104	24/111	27/117	29/124	31/131	33/138	36/144
10	--	--	0/30	2/38	4/46	6/54	9/61	11/69	13/77	16/84	18/92	21/99	24/106	26/114	29/121	31/129	34/136	37/143	39/151	42/158
11	--	--	0/33	2/42	5/50	7/59	10/67	13/75	16/83	18/92	21/100	24/108	27/116	30/124	33/132	36/140	39/148	42/156	45/164	48/172
12	--	--	1/35	3/45	6/54	9/63	12/72	15/81	18/90	21/99	24/108	27/117	31/125	34/134	37/143	41/151	44/160	47/169	51/177	54/186
13	--	--	1/38	3/49	7/58	10/68	13/78	17/87	20/97	24/106	27/116	31/125	34/125	38/144	42/153	45/163	49/172	53/181	56/191	60/200
14	--	--	1/41	4/52	7/63	11/73	15/83	18/94	22/104	26/114	30/124	34/134	38/144	42/154	46/164	50/174	54/184	58/194	63/203	67/213
15	--	--	2/43	5/55	8/67	12/78	16/89	20/100	24/111	29/121	33/132	37/143	42/153	46/164	51/174	55/185	60/195	64/206	69/216	73/227
16	--	--	2/46	5/59	9/71	13/83	18/94	22/106	27/117	31/129	36/140	41/151	45/163	50/174	55/185	60/196	65/207	70/218	74/230	79/241
17	--	--	2/49	6/62	10/75	15/87	19/100	24/112	29/124	34/148	39/148	44/160	49/172	54/184	60/195	65/207	70/219	75/231	81/242	86/254
18	--	--	2/52	6/66	11/79	16/92	21/105	26/118	31/131	37/143	42/156	47/169	53/181	58/194	64/206	70/218	75/231	81/243	87/255	92/268
19	--	0/38	3/54	7/69	12/83	17/97	22/111	28/124	33/138	39/151	45/164	51/177	56/191	63/203	69/216	74/230	81/242	87/255	93/268	99/281
20	--	0/40	3/57	8/72	13/87	18/102	24/116	30/130	36/144	42/158	48/172	54/186	60/200	67/213	73/227	79/241	86/254	92/268	99/281	105/295

(Dashes in the body of the table indicate that no decision is possible at the stated level of significance.)

Table N₂ Critical values of U and U' for a one-tailed test at $\alpha = 0.001$ or a two-tailed test at $\alpha = 0.02$

To be significant for any given N_1 and N_2: Obtained U must be equal to or *less than* the value shown in the table. Obtained U' must be equal to or *greater than* the value shown in the table.

N_2 \ N_1	1	2	3	4	5	6	7	8	9	10	11	12	13	14	15	16	17	18	19	20
1	--	--	--	--	--	--	--	--	--	--	--	--	--	--	--	--	--	--	--	--
2	--	--	--	--	--	--	--	--	--	--	--	--	0/26	0/28	0/30	0/32	0/34	0/36	1/37	1/39
3	--	--	--	--	--	--	0/21	0/24	1/26	1/29	1/32	2/34	2/37	2/40	3/42	3/45	4/47	4/50	4/52	5/55
4	--	--	--	--	0/20	1/23	1/27	2/30	3/33	3/37	4/40	5/43	5/47	6/50	7/53	7/57	8/60	9/63	9/67	10/70
5	--	--	--	0/20	1/24	2/28	3/32	4/36	5/40	6/44	7/48	8/52	9/56	10/60	11/64	12/68	13/72	14/76	15/80	16/84
6	--	--	--	1/23	2/28	3/33	4/38	6/42	7/47	8/52	9/57	11/61	12/66	13/71	15/75	16/80	18/84	19/89	20/94	22/98
7	--	--	0/21	1/27	3/32	4/38	6/43	7/49	9/54	11/59	12/65	14/70	16/75	17/81	19/86	21/91	23/96	24/102	26/107	28/112
8	--	--	0/24	2/30	4/36	6/42	7/49	9/55	11/61	13/67	15/73	17/79	20/84	22/90	24/96	26/102	28/108	30/114	32/120	34/126
9	--	--	1/26	3/33	5/40	7/47	9/54	11/61	14/67	16/74	18/81	21/87	23/94	26/100	28/107	31/113	33/120	36/126	38/133	40/140
10	--	--	1/29	3/37	6/44	8/52	11/59	13/67	16/74	19/81	22/88	24/96	27/103	30/110	33/117	36/124	38/132	41/139	44/146	47/153
11	--	--	1/32	4/40	7/48	9/57	12/65	15/73	18/81	22/88	25/96	28/104	31/112	34/120	37/128	41/135	44/143	47/151	50/159	53/167
12	--	--	2/34	5/43	8/52	11/61	14/70	17/79	21/87	24/96	28/104	31/113	35/121	38/130	42/138	46/146	49/155	53/163	56/172	60/180
13	--	0/26	2/37	5/47	9/56	12/66	16/75	20/84	23/94	27/103	31/112	35/121	39/130	43/139	47/148	51/157	55/166	59/175	63/184	67/193
14	--	0/28	2/40	6/50	10/60	13/71	17/81	22/90	26/100	30/110	34/120	38/130	43/139	47/149	51/159	56/168	60/178	65/187	69/197	73/207
15	--	0/30	3/42	7/53	11/64	15/75	19/86	24/96	28/107	33/117	37/128	42/138	47/148	51/159	56/169	61/179	66/189	70/200	75/210	80/220
16	--	0/32	3/45	7/57	12/68	16/80	21/91	26/102	31/113	36/124	41/135	46/146	51/157	56/168	61/179	66/190	71/201	76/212	82/222	87/233
17	--	0/34	4/47	8/60	13/72	18/84	23/96	28/108	33/120	38/132	44/143	49/155	55/166	60/178	66/189	71/201	77/212	82/224	88/234	93/247
18	--	0/36	4/50	9/63	14/76	19/89	24/102	30/114	36/126	41/139	47/151	53/163	59/175	65/187	70/200	76/212	82/224	88/236	94/248	100/260
19	--	1/37	4/53	9/67	15/80	20/94	26/107	32/120	38/133	44/146	50/159	56/172	63/184	69/197	75/210	82/222	88/235	94/248	101/260	107/273
20	--	1/39	5/55	10/70	16/84	22/98	28/112	34/126	40/140	47/153	53/167	60/180	67/193	73/207	80/220	87/233	93/247	100/260	107/273	114/286

(Dashes in the body of the table indicate that no decision is possible at the stated level of significance.)

Table N₃ Critical values of U and U' for a one-tailed test at $\alpha = 0.025$ or a two-tailed test at $\alpha = 0.05$

To be significant for any given N_1 and N_2: Obtained U must be equal to or *less than* the value shown in the table. Obtained U' must be equal to or *or greater than* the value shown in the table.

Each cell is shown as U / U'.

N_2 \ N_1	1	2	3	4	5	6	7	8	9	10	11	12	13	14	15	16	17	18	19	20
1	--	--	--	--	--	--	--	--	--	--	--	--	--	--	--	--	--	--	--	--
2	--	--	--	--	--	--	--	0/16	0/18	0/20	0/22	1/23	1/25	1/27	1/29	1/31	2/32	2/34	2/36	2/38
3	--	--	--	--	0/15	1/17	1/20	2/22	2/25	3/27	3/30	4/32	4/35	5/37	5/40	6/42	6/45	7/47	7/50	8/52
4	--	--	--	0/16	1/19	2/22	3/25	4/28	4/32	5/35	6/38	7/41	8/44	9/47	10/50	11/53	11/57	12/60	13/63	13/67
5	--	--	0/15	1/19	2/23	3/27	5/30	6/34	7/38	8/42	9/46	11/49	12/53	13/57	14/61	15/65	17/68	18/72	19/76	20/80
6	--	--	1/17	2/22	3/27	5/31	6/36	8/40	10/44	11/49	13/53	14/58	16/62	17/67	19/71	21/75	22/80	24/84	25/89	27/93
7	--	--	1/20	3/25	5/30	6/36	8/41	10/46	12/51	14/56	16/61	18/66	20/71	22/76	24/81	26/86	28/91	30/96	32/101	34/106
8	--	0/16	2/22	4/28	6/34	8/40	10/46	13/51	15/57	17/63	19/69	22/74	24/80	26/86	29/91	31/97	34/102	36/108	38/114	41/119
9	--	0/18	2/25	4/32	7/38	10/44	12/51	15/57	17/64	20/70	23/76	26/82	28/89	31/95	34/101	37/107	39/114	42/120	45/126	48/132
10	--	0/20	3/27	5/35	8/42	11/49	14/56	17/63	20/70	23/77	26/84	29/91	33/97	36/104	39/111	42/118	45/125	48/132	52/138	55/145
11	--	0/22	3/30	6/38	9/46	13/53	16/61	19/69	23/76	26/84	30/91	33/99	37/106	40/114	44/121	47/129	51/136	55/143	58/151	62/158
12	--	1/23	4/32	7/41	11/49	14/58	18/66	22/74	26/82	29/91	33/99	37/107	41/115	45/123	49/131	53/139	57/147	61/155	65/163	69/171
13	--	1/25	4/35	8/44	12/53	16/62	20/71	24/80	28/89	33/97	37/106	41/115	45/124	50/132	54/141	59/149	63/158	67/167	72/175	76/184
14	--	1/27	5/37	9/47	13/57	17/67	22/76	26/86	31/95	36/104	40/114	45/123	50/132	55/141	59/151	64/160	67/171	74/178	78/188	83/197
15	--	1/29	5/40	10/50	14/61	19/71	24/81	29/91	34/101	39/111	44/121	49/131	54/141	59/151	64/161	70/170	75/180	80/190	85/200	90/210
16	--	1/31	6/42	11/53	15/65	21/75	26/86	31/97	37/107	42/118	47/129	53/139	59/149	64/160	70/170	75/181	81/191	86/202	92/212	98/222
17	--	2/32	6/45	11/57	17/68	22/80	28/91	34/102	39/114	45/125	51/136	57/147	63/158	67/171	75/180	81/191	87/202	93/213	99/224	105/235
18	--	2/34	7/47	12/60	18/72	24/84	30/96	36/108	42/120	48/132	55/143	61/155	67/167	74/178	80/190	86/202	93/213	99/225	106/236	112/248
19	--	2/36	7/50	13/63	19/76	25/89	32/101	38/114	45/126	52/138	58/151	65/163	72/175	78/188	85/200	92/212	99/224	106/236	113/248	119/261
20	--	2/38	8/52	13/67	20/80	27/93	34/106	41/119	48/132	55/145	62/158	69/171	76/184	83/197	90/210	98/222	105/235	112/248	119/261	127/273

(Dashes in the body of the table indicate that no decision is possible at the stated level of significance.)

Table N$_4$ Critical values of U and U' for a one-tailed test at $\alpha = 0.05$ or a two-tailed test at $\alpha = 0.10$

To be significant for any given N_1 and N_2: Obtained U must be equal to or *less than* the value shown in the table. Obtained U' must be equal to or *greater than* the value shown in the table.

Each cell shows the U value (upper) over the U' value (lower), written here as $U\,/\,U'$.

N_2\N_1	1	2	3	4	5	6	7	8	9	10	11	12	13	14	15	16	17	18	19	20
1	--	--	--	--	--	--	--	--	--	--	--	--	--	--	--	--	--	--	0/19	0/20
2	--	--	--	--	0/10	0/12	0/14	1/15	1/17	1/19	1/21	2/22	2/24	2/26	3/27	3/29	3/31	4/32	4/34	4/36
3	--	--	0/9	0/12	1/14	2/16	2/19	3/21	3/24	4/26	5/28	5/31	6/33	7/35	7/38	8/40	9/42	9/45	10/47	11/49
4	--	--	0/12	1/15	2/18	3/21	4/24	5/27	6/30	7/33	8/36	9/39	10/42	11/45	12/48	14/50	15/53	16/56	17/59	18/62
5	--	0/10	1/14	2/18	4/21	5/25	6/29	8/32	9/36	11/39	12/43	13/47	15/50	16/54	18/57	19/61	20/65	22/68	23/72	25/75
6	--	0/12	2/16	3/21	5/25	7/29	8/34	10/38	12/42	14/46	16/50	17/55	19/59	21/63	23/67	25/71	26/76	28/80	30/84	32/88
7	--	0/14	2/19	4/24	6/29	8/34	11/38	13/43	15/48	17/53	19/58	21/63	24/67	26/72	28/77	30/82	33/86	35/91	37/96	39/101
8	--	1/15	3/21	5/27	8/32	10/38	13/43	15/49	18/54	20/60	23/65	26/70	28/76	31/81	33/87	36/92	39/97	41/103	44/108	47/113
9	--	1/17	3/24	6/30	9/36	12/42	15/48	18/54	21/60	24/66	27/72	30/78	33/84	36/90	39/96	42/102	45/108	48/114	51/120	54/126
10	--	1/19	4/26	7/33	11/39	14/46	17/53	20/60	24/66	27/73	31/79	34/86	37/93	41/99	44/106	48/112	51/119	55/125	58/132	62/138
11	--	1/21	5/28	8/36	12/43	16/50	19/58	23/65	27/72	31/79	34/87	38/94	42/101	46/108	50/115	54/122	57/130	61/137	65/144	69/151
12	--	2/22	5/31	9/39	13/47	17/55	21/63	26/70	30/78	34/86	38/94	42/102	47/109	51/117	55/125	60/132	64/140	68/148	72/156	77/163
13	--	2/24	6/33	10/42	15/50	19/59	24/67	28/76	33/84	37/93	42/101	47/109	51/118	56/126	61/134	65/143	70/151	75/159	80/167	84/176
14	--	2/26	7/35	11/45	16/54	21/63	26/72	31/81	36/90	41/99	46/108	51/117	56/126	61/135	66/144	71/153	77/161	82/170	87/179	92/188
15	--	3/27	7/38	12/48	18/57	23/67	28/77	33/87	39/96	44/106	50/115	55/125	61/134	66/144	72/153	77/163	83/172	88/182	94/191	100/200
16	--	3/29	8/40	14/50	19/61	25/71	30/82	36/92	42/102	48/112	54/122	60/132	65/143	71/153	77/163	83/173	89/183	95/193	101/203	107/213
17	--	3/31	9/42	15/53	20/65	26/76	33/86	39/97	45/108	51/119	57/130	64/140	70/151	77/161	83/172	89/183	96/193	102/204	109/214	115/225
18	--	4/32	9/45	16/56	22/68	28/80	35/91	41/103	48/114	55/123	61/137	68/148	75/159	82/170	88/182	95/193	102/204	109/215	116/226	123/237
19	0/19	4/34	10/47	17/59	23/72	30/84	37/96	44/108	51/120	58/132	65/144	72/156	80/167	87/179	94/191	101/203	109/214	116/226	123/238	130/250
20	0/20	4/36	11/49	18/62	25/75	32/88	39/101	47/113	54/126	62/138	69/151	77/163	84/176	92/188	100/200	107/213	115/225	123/237	130/250	138/262

(Dashes in the body of the table indicate that no decision is possible at the stated level of significance.)

502

Table O Critical values of T

The symbol T denotes the smaller sum of ranks associated with differences that are all of the same sign. For any given N (number of ranked differences), the obtained T is significant at a given level if it is equal to or *less than* the value shown in the table. All entries are for the *absolute* value of T.

	Level of significance for one-tailed test					Level of significance for one-tailed test			
	.05	.025	.01	.005		.05	.025	.01	.005
	Level of significance for two-tailed test					Level of significance for two-tailed test			
N	.10	.05	.02	.01	N	.10	.05	.02	.01
5	0	--	--	--	28	130	116	101	91
6	2	0	--	--	29	140	126	110	100
7	3	2	0	--	30	151	137	120	109
8	5	3	1	0	31	163	147	130	118
9	8	5	3	1	32	175	159	140	128
10	10	8	5	3	33	187	170	151	138
11	13	10	7	5	34	200	182	162	148
12	17	13	9	7	35	213	195	173	159
13	21	17	12	9	36	227	208	185	171
14	25	21	15	12	37	241	221	198	182
15	30	25	19	15	38	256	235	211	194
16	35	29	23	19	39	271	249	224	207
17	41	34	27	23	40	286	264	238	220
18	47	40	32	27	41	302	279	252	233
19	53	46	37	32	42	319	294	266	247
20	60	52	43	37	43	336	310	281	261
21	67	58	49	42	44	353	327	296	276
22	75	65	55	48	45	371	343	312	291
23	83	73	62	54	46	389	361	328	307
24	91	81	69	61	47	407	378	345	322
25	100	89	76	68	48	426	396	362	339
26	110	98	84	75	49	446	415	379	355
27	119	107	92	83	50	466	434	397	373

Slight discrepancies will be found between the critical values appearing in the table above and in Table 2 of the 1964 revision of F. Wilcoxon and R. A. Wilcox, *Some Rapid Approximate Statistical Procedures*, New York: Lederle Laboratories. The disparity reflects the latter's policy of selecting the critical value nearest a given significance level, occasionally overstepping that level. For example, for $N = 8$,

the probability of a T of 3 = 0.0390 (two-tail),

and

the probability of a T of 4 = 0.0546 (two-tail).

Wilcoxon and Wilcox selects a T of 4 as the critical value at the 0.05 level of significance (two-tail), whereas Table J reflects a more conservative policy by setting a T of 3 as the critical value at this level.

Acknowledgments

We are grateful to the following authors and publishers for permission to adapt from the following tables.

Table B   R. A. Fisher, *Statistical Methods for Research Workers* 14th ed. Reprinted with permission of Macmillan Publishing Company, Inc. Copyright © 1970, University of Adelaide.

Table C   Table III of R. A. Fisher and F. Yates, *Statistical Tables for Biological, Agricultural, and Medical Research*. 6th ed. London: Longman Group Ltd., 1974. (Previously published by Oliver and Boyd, Ltd., Edinburgh.)

Table D and Table D$_1$ G. W. Snedecor and William G. Cochran, *Statistical Methods,* 7th edition, Ames, Iowa: Iowa State University Press © 1980. Reprinted by permission.

Table E   Q. McNemar, Table B of *Psychological Statistics*. New York: John Wiley and Sons, Inc., 1962.

Table F   E. G. Olds, The 5 percent significance levels of sums of squares of rank differences and a correction. *Ann. Math. Statist*. **20,** 117–118, 1949. E. G. Olds, Distribution of sums of squares of rank differences for small numbers of individuals. *Ann. Math. Statist*. **9,** 133–148, 1938.

Table G   W. V. Bingham, Table XVII of *Aptitudes and Aptitude Testing*. New York: Harper and Row, 1937.

Table H   S. Siegel, *Nonparametric Statistics*. New York: McGraw-Hill, 1956.

Table I   R. P. Runyon, Table A of *Nonparametric Statistics,* Reading, Mass.: Addison-Wesley Publishing Co., 1977.

Table J   R. P. Runyon, Table B of *Nonparametric Statistics,* Reading, Mass.: Addison-Wesley Publishing Co., 1977.

Table K   E. S. Pearson and H. O. Hartley, *Biometrika Tables for Statisticians,* Vol. 1, 2nd ed. New York: Cambridge, 1958.

Table L   A. L. Edwards, *Statistical Analysis,* 3rd ed. New York: Holt, Rinehart and Winston, Inc., 1969.
J. W. Dunlap and A. K. Kurtz, *Handbook of Statistical Nomographs, Tables, and Formulas*. New York: World Book Company, 1932.

Table M   RAND Corporation, *A Million Random Digits,* Glencoe, Ill.: Free Press of Glencoe, 1955.

Table N   H. B. Mann and D. R. Whitney (1947), "On a Test of Whether One of Two Random Variables Is Stochastically Larger Than the Other," *Ann. Math. Statist*., **18,** 52–54.
D. Auble (1953), "Extended Tables for the Mann-Whitney Statistic," *Bulletin of the Institute of Educational Research at Indiana University,* **1** (2).

504

Table O   F. Wilcoxon, S. Katti, and R. A. Wilcox, *Critical Values and Probability Levels for the Wilcoxon Rank Sum Test and the Wilcoxon Signed Rank Test*. New York: American Cyanamid Co., 1963.
F. Wilcoxon and R. A. Wilcox, *Some Rapid Approximate Statistical Procedures*. New York: Lederle Laboratories, 1964.

D

Glossary of Terms

From
Abscissa (*X*-axis)
to
Within-group sum of squares (SS_w)

Abscissa (X-axis)   Horizontal axis of a graph.

Absolute value of a number   The value of a number without regard to sign.

Addition rule   If A and B are mutually exclusive events, the probability of obtaining *either of them* is equal to the probability of A plus the probability of B. Symbolically

$$p(A \text{ or } B) = p(A) + p(B)$$

Alpha (α) level   The level of significance set by the researcher for inferring the operation of nonchance factors.

Alternative hypothesis (H_1)   A statement specifying that the population parameter is some value other than the one specified under the null hypothesis.

Analysis of variance   A method, described initially by R. A. Fisher, for partitioning the sum of squares for experimental or survey data into known components of variation.

A posteriori comparisons   Comparisons not planned in advance to investigate specific hypotheses concerning population parameters.

A priori* or *planned comparisons　Comparisons planned in advance to investigate specific hypotheses concerning population parameters.

Array　An arrangement of data according to their magnitude from the smallest to the largest value.

Asymmetric measure of association　A measure of the one-way effect of one variable upon another.

Bar graph　A form of graph that uses bars to indicate the frequency of occurrence of observations within each nominal or ordinal category.

Between-group sum of squares (SS_{bet})　The sum of the sum of squares between each group.

Bias　In sampling, when selections favor certain events or certain collections of events.

Binomial distribution　A model with known mathematical properties used to describe the distributions of discrete random variables.

Centile　A percentage rank that divides a distribution into 100 equal parts. Same as a percentile.

Central limit theorem　If random samples of a fixed N are drawn from *any* population (regardless of the form of the population distribution), as N becomes larger, the distribution of sample means approaches normality, with the overall mean approaching μ, the variance of the sample means $\sigma_{\bar{X}}^2$ being equal to σ^2/N, and a standard error of $\sigma_{\bar{X}}$ of $\sigma/\sqrt{N}$.

Coefficient of determination (r^2)　The ratio of the explained variation to the total variation.

Coefficient of multiple determination (R^2)　A measure of the proportion of total variation in a dependent variable that is explained jointly by two or more independent variables.

Coefficient of Nondetermination ($1 - r^2$)　The proportion of variation not explained in terms of the correlation between the two variables.

Concordant pair　Two cases are ranked similarly on two variables.

Conditional distribution　The distribution of the categories of one variable under the differing conditions or categories of another.

Conditional probability　The probability of an event given that another event has occurred. Represented symbolically as $p(A|B)$, the probability of A given that B has occurred.

Conditional table　A contingency table that summarizes the relationship between two variables for categories or conditions of one or the other.

Confidence interval   A confidence interval for a parameter specifies a range of values bounded by two endpoints called confidence limits. Common confidence intervals are 95% and 99%.

Confidence limits   The two endpoints of a confidence interval.

Contingency coefficient   A nominal measure of association based on χ^2 and used primarily for square tables.

Contingency table   A table showing the joint distribution of two variables.

Continuous scales   Scales in which the variables can assume an unlimited number of intermediate values.

Control variable   A variable whose subgroups or categories are used in a conditional table to examine the relationship between two variables. Same as a test variable.

Correlation coefficient   A measure that expresses the extent to which two variables are related.

Correlation matrix   A summary of the statistical relationships between all possible pairs of variables.

Covariation   The extent to which two variables vary together.

Cramer's V   A nominal measure of association based on χ^2 suitable for tables of any dimension.

Critical region   The portion of the area under a curve that includes those values of a statistic that lead to rejection of the null hypothesis.

Critical values of t   Those values that bound the critical rejection regions corresponding to varying levels of significance.

Cumulative frequency   The number of cases (frequencies) at and below a given point.

Cumulative frequency curve (Ogive)   A curve that shows the number of cases below the upper real limit of an interval.

Cumulative frequency distribution   A distribution that shows the cumulative frequency at and below the upper real limit of the corresponding class interval.

Cumulative percentage   The percentage of cases (frequencies) at and below a given point.

Cumulative percentage distribution   A distribution that shows the cumulative percentage at and below the upper real limit of the corresponding class interval.

Cumulative proportion   The proportion of cases (frequencies) at and below a given point.

Cumulative proportion distribution   A distribution that shows the cumulative proportion at and below the upper real limit of the corresponding class interval.

Data   Numbers or measurements that are collected as a result of observations, interviews, etc.

Decile   A percentage rank that divides a distribution into ten equal parts.

Degrees of freedom (df)   The number of values that are free to vary after we have placed certain restrictions on our data.

Dependent variable   The variable that is being predicted. Also referred to as the criterion variable.

Descriptive statistics   Procedures used to organize and present data in a convenient, usable, summary form.

Deviation   The distance and direction of a score from a reference point.

Directional hypothesis   An alternative hypothesis that states the direction in which the population parameter differs from the one specified under H_0.

Discordant pair   Two cases are ranked on the opposite order on two variables.

Discrete scales (Discontinuous scales)   Scales in which the variables have equality of counting units.

Dispersion   The spread or variability of scores about the measure of central tendency.

Element   A single member of a population.

Epsilon (ϵ)   The percentage difference within a category of the dependent variable between the two extreme categories of the independent variable.

Exhaustive   Two or more events are said to be exhaustive if they exhaust all possible outcomes. Symbolically

$$p(A \text{ or } B \text{ or } . . .) = 1.00$$

Explained variation   Variation of predicted scores about the mean of the distribution. Same as the regression sum of squares.

F-ratio   The between-group mean square divided by the within-group mean square.

Finite population   A population whose elements or members can be listed.

Frequency curve (Frequency polygon)   A form of graph, representing a frequency distribution, in which a continuous line is used to indicate the frequency of the corresponding scores.

Gamma (γ)   A symmetric measure of association for ordinal-level data based on pair-by-pair comparison with a PRE interpretation.

Grouped frequency distribution   A frequency distribution in which the values of the variable have been grouped into class intervals.

Histogram   A form of bar graph used with interval- or ratio-scaled frequency distribution.

Homogeneity of variance   The condition that exists when two or more sample variances have been drawn from populations with equal variances.

Independence   The condition that exists when the occurrence of a given event will not affect the probability of the occurrence of another event. Symbolically

$$p(A|B) = p(A) \quad \text{and} \quad p(B|A) = p(B)$$

Independent variable   The predictor variable. Referred to as the experimental variable in an experiment.

Inferential or inductive statistics   Procedures used to arrive at broader generalizations or inferences from sample data to populations.

Infinite population   A population whose elements or members cannot be listed.

Inflated N   An error produced whenever several observations are made on the same individual and treated as though they were independent observations.

Interquartile range   A measure of variability obtained by subtracting the score at the 1st quartile from the score at the 3rd quartile.

Interval estimation   The determination of an interval within which the population parameter is presumed to fall.

Interval scale   Scale in which exact distances can be known between categories. The zero point in this scale is arbitrary, and arithmetic operations are permitted.

Intervening variable   A variable that causally links two other variables.

Joint (or successive) occurrence   The occurrence of two events simultaneously. Such events cannot be mutually exclusive.

Kendall's tau-b   A symmetric measure of association for ordinal-level data.

Lambda (λ)   An asymmetric or symmetric measure of association for nominal-level data.

Law of large numbers   As the sample size increases, the standard error of the mean decreases.

Leptokurtic distribution   A bell-shaped distribution characterized by a piling up of scores in the center of the distribution.

Mann-Whitney U-Test   A powerful nonparametric statistical test commonly used as an alternative to the Student *t*-ratio when the measurements fail to achieve interval scaling.

Marginals   The column and row totals of a contingency table.

Matched-group design   A correlated-samples design in which pairs of individuals are matched on a variable correlated with the dependent variable. Each member of a pair receives different experimental conditions.

Mean   Sum of the scores or values of a variable divided by their number.

Mean deviation (average deviation)   Sum of the deviation of each score from the mean, without regard to sign, divided by the number of scores.

Mean square   The sum of the squared deviations from the mean divided by degrees of freedom. Also known as the variance estimate.

Measurement   The assignment of numbers to objects or events according to sets of predetermined (or arbitrary) rules.

Measure of central tendency   Index of central location used in the description of frequency distributions.

Median   The score in a distribution of scores, above and below which one-half of the frequencies fall.

Mesokurtic distribution   A bell-shaped distribution; ''ideal'' form of normal curve.

Mode   The score that occurs with the greatest frequency.

Multiple correlation coefficient (R)   A measure of the linear relationship between a dependent variable and the combined effects of two or more independent variables.

Multiple regression coefficient   A measure of the influence of an independent variable on a dependent variable when the effects of all other independent variables in the multiple regression equation have been held constant.

Multiplication rule   Given two events A and B, the probability of obtaining both A and B jointly is the product of the probability of obtaining one of these events times the conditional probability of obtaining one event, given that the other event has occurred. Symbolically

$$p(A \text{ and } B) = p(A)p(B|A) = p(B)p(A|B)$$

Multivariate statistical technique   A statistical technique used to determine the nature of the relationships between three or more variables.

Mutually exclusive   Events A and B are said to be mutually exclusive if both cannot occur simultaneously. Symbolically, for mutually exclusive events

$$p(A \text{ and } B) = 0.00$$

Negatively skewed distribution   A distribution that has relatively fewer frequencies at the low end of the horizontal axis.

Negative relationship   Variables are said to be negatively related when high scores on one variable tend to be associated with low scores on the other variable. Conversely, low scores on one variable tend to be associated with high scores on the other.

Nominal numbers   Numbers used to name.

Nominal scale   Scales in which the categories are homogeneous, mutually exclusive, and unordered.

Nondirectional hypothesis   An alternative hypothesis (H_1) that states only that the population parameter is *different* from the one specified under H_0.

Nonindependence   The condition that exists when the occurrence of a given event affects the probability of the occurrence of another event.

Normal curve   A frequency curve with a characteristic bell-shaped form.

Null hypothesis (H_0)   A statement that specifies hypothesized values for one or more of the population parameters. Commonly, although not necessarily, involves the hypothesis of "no difference."

Ogive   A cumulative frequency curve that shows the number of cases below the upper real limit of an interval.

One-tailed probability value   Probability values obtained by examining only one tail of the distribution.

One-variable test ("goodness-of-fit" technique)   A test of whether or not a significant difference exists between the *observed* number of cases falling into each category and the *expected* number of cases, based on the null hypothesis.

One-way analysis of variance   A statistical analysis of various categories, groups, or levels of one independent (experimental) variable.

Order of a conditional table   The order of a table is the number of control or test variables that are included.

Order of a partial correlation coefficient   The order of a partial correlation coefficient indicates the number of control or test variables.

Ordinal numbers   Numbers used to represent position or order in a series.

Ordinal scale   A scale in which the classes can be rank ordered, that is, expressed in terms of the algebra of inequalities (e.g., $a < b$ or $a > b$).

Ordinate (Y-axis)   Vertical axis of a graph.

Pair-by-pair comparison   An approach to prediction for ordinal-level data in contingency form.

Parameter   Any characteristic of a finite population that can be estimated and is measurable or of an infinite population that can be estimated.

Partial correlation coefficient   A measure of the linear relationship between two interval-level variables controlling for one or more other interval-level variables.

Partial table   A contingency table that summarizes the relationship between two variables for categories or conditions of one or more other variables. Same as a conditional table.

Pearson's r (product-moment correlation coefficient)   A correlation coefficient used with interval- or ratio-scaled variables.

Percentage   A proportion that has been multiplied by 100.

Percentage difference   Differences in percentages normally measured between the two extreme categories of the independent variable within a category of the dependent variable. Also referred to as epsilon (ϵ).

Percentile rank   The number that represents the percentage of cases in a distribution that had scores at or lower than the one cited.

Percentiles   Numbers that divide a distribution into 100 equal parts. Same as a centile.

Perfect relationship   A relationship in which knowledge of the independent variable allows a perfect prediction of the dependent variable, or vice versa.

Phi coefficient   A nominal measure of association based on χ^2 used with 2×2 tables.

Platykurtic distribution   A frequency distribution characterized by a flattening in the central position.

Point estimation   An estimate of a population parameter that involves a single sample value, selected by the criterion of "best estimate."

Population   A complete set of individuals, objects, or measurements having some common observable characteristic.

Positively skewed distribution   A distribution that has relatively fewer frequencies at the high end of the horizontal axis.

Positive relationship   High scores on one variable tend to be associated with high scores on the other variable, and conversely, low scores on one variable tend to be associated with low scores on the other variable.

Post hoc fallacy   Faulty causal inferences from correlational data.

Probability   A theory concerned with possible outcomes of studies. Symbolically

$$p(A) = \frac{\text{number of outcomes in which } A \text{ occurs}}{\text{total number of outcomes}}$$

Proportion   A value calculated by dividing the quantity in one category by the total of all the components.

Proportional reduction in error (PRE)   A ratio of the prediction errors without information about the independent variable to the prediction errors having information about the independent variable.

Quartile   A percentage rank that divides a distribution into four equal parts.

Random sample   Samples selected in such a way that each sample of a given size has precisely the same probability of being selected.

Range   A measure of dispersion; the scale distance between the largest and the smallest score.

Rate   A ratio of the occurrences in a group category to the total number of elements in the group with which we are concerned.

Ratio   The number of cases in one category divided by the number of cases in another category.

Ratio scale   Same as interval scale, except that there is a true zero point.

Regression line (line of "best fit")   A straight line that makes the squared deviations around it minimal.

Regression sum of squares   Variation of predicted scores about the mean of the distribution. Same as the explained variation.

Research design   The plan for collecting data.

Residual   The size and direction of the error in prediction or the vertical distance from the observed data coordinate to the regression line.

Residual sum of squares   Variation of scores around the regression line. Same as the unexplained variation.

Residual variance   Variance around the regression line.

Restricted range   A truncated range on one or both variables resulting in a deceptively low correlation between these variables.

Robust test A statistical test from which statistical inferences are likely to be valid even when there are fairly large departures from normality in the population distribution.

Sample A subset or part of a population.

Sampling distribution A theoretical probability distribution of a statistic that would result from drawing all possible samples of a given size from some population.

Scatter diagram A graphic device used to summarize visually the relationship between two variables.

Significance level A probability value that is considered so rare in the sampling distribution specified under the null hypothesis that one is willing to assert the operation of nonchance factors. Common significance levels are 0.05 and 0.01, and 0.001.

Sign test A nonparametric statistical test for ordinally scaled variables, used with matched or correlated samples. The sign test simply utilizes information concerning the *direction* of the differences between pairs of scores.

Simple random sampling A method of selecting samples so that each sample of a given size in a population has an equal chance of being selected.

Skewed distribution A distribution that departs from symmetry and tails off at one end.

Somer's d An asymmetrical measure of association for ordinal-level data that incorporates tied ranks.

Spearman's rho (r_s) A measure of association for ordinal-level data that provides a measure of the extent to which two sets of ranks are in agreement or disagreement.

Spurious relationship Exists when the zero-order relationship between an independent and dependent variable disappears or becomes significantly weaker with the introduction of a control variable.

Standard deviation A measure of dispersion defined as the square root of the sum of the squared deviations from the mean, divided by N. Also can be defined as the square root of the variance.

Standard error of estimate Standard deviation of scores around the regression line.

Standard error of the mean A theoretical standard deviation of sample means, of a given sample size, drawn from some specified population. When based on a known population standard deviation, $\sigma_{\bar{X}} = \sigma/\sqrt{N}$; when estimated from a single sample, $s_{\bar{X}} = s/\sqrt{N-1}$.

Standard error of the proportion   An estimate of the standard deviation of the sampling distribution of proportions.

Standard normal distribution   A frequency distribution that has a mean of 0, a standard deviation of 1, and a total area equal to 1.00.

Standard score (z)   A score that represents the deviation of a specific score from the mean, expressed in standard deviation units.

Statistic   A number that describes a characteristic of a sample.

Statistical elaboration   The process of introducing a control variable to determine whether a bivariate relationship remains the same or varies under the different categories or conditions of the control variable.

Statistics   A collection of numerical facts expressed in summarizing statements; method of dealing with data: a tool for collecting, organizing, and analyzing numerical facts or observations that are collected in accordance with a systematic plan.

Symmetric measure of association   A measure of the mutual association between two variables.

t-distributions or Student's t   Theoretical symmetrical sampling distributions with a mean of zero and a standard deviation that becomes smaller as degrees of freedom (df) increase. Used in relation to the Student t-ratio.

t-ratio   A test statistic for determining the significance of a difference between means (two-sample case) or for testing the hypothesis that a given sample mean was drawn from a population with the mean specified under the null hypothesis (one-sample case). Used when population standard deviation (or standard deviations) is not known.

Test variable   A variable whose subgroups or categories are used in a conditional table to examine the relationship between two variables. Same as a control variable.

Tied pair   Two cases are ranked similarly on one or both of two variables.

Total sum of squares   Variation of scores around the sample mean. Same as the total variation.

Total variation   Variation of scores around the sample mean. Same as the total sum of squares.

True limits of a number   The true limits of a value of a continuous variable are equal to that number plus or minus one-half of the unit of measurement.

Two-tailed probability value   Probability values that take into account both tails of the distribution.

Type I error (***type α error***)   The rejection of H_0 when it is actually true. The probability of a type I error is given by the α-level.

Type II error (***type β error***)   The probability of accepting H_0 when it is actually false. The probability of a type II error is given by β.

Unbiased estimator   An estimate that equals, on the average, the value of the corresponding parameter.

Unexplained variation   Variation of scores around the regression line. Same as the residual sum of squares.

Ungrouped frequency distribution   A frequency distribution shows the number of times each score occurs when the values of a variable are arranged in order according to their magnitudes.

Variable   Any characteristic of a person, group, or environment that can vary or denotes a difference.

Variance   The sum of the squared deviations from the mean, divided by N.

Weighted mean   The sum of the mean of each group multiplied by its respective weight (the N in each group), divided by the sum of the weights (total N).

Wilcoxon matched-pairs signed-rank test   A nonparametric statistical test for ordinally scaled variables used with matched or correlated samples; more powerful than the sign test since it utilizes information concerning the *magnitude* of the differences between pairs of scores.

Within-group sum of squares (***SS_w***)   A sum of the sum of squares within each group.

E

References

From
American Bar Foundation
to
World Population Data Sheet of the Population Reference Bureau, Inc.

American Bar Foundation (1985), Chicago, Ill.: *The Lawyer Statistical Report: A Statistical Profile of the U.S. Legal Profession in the 1980s.*

Anas, N., V. Namasthoni, and M. Ginsburg (1981) Criteria for hospitalizing children who have ingested products containing hydrocarbons. *Journal of the American Medical Association* 246:840–843.

Auble, D. (1953) Extended tables for the Mann–Whitney statistic. *Bulletin of the Institute of Educational Research at Indiana University,* 1(2).

Benson, P. L., S. A. Karabenick, and R. M. Lerner (1976) Pretty pleases: The effects of physical attractiveness, race, and sex on receiving help. *Journal of Experimental Social Psychology* 12:409–415.

Berenson, W. M., K. W. Elifson, and T. Tollerson, III (1976) Preachers in politics: A study of political activism among the black ministry. *Journal of Black Studies* 6:373–383.

Bingham, W. V. (1937) *Aptitudes and Aptitude Testing.* New York: Harper and Bros.

Blalock, H. M. (1979) *Social Statistics* (Revised 2nd ed.). New York: McGraw-Hill Book Co.

Bureau of the Census, *The Social and Economic Status of the Black Population in the United States: An Historical View,* 1790–1978, Series P-23, No. 80, Current Population Reports.

Caballero, C. M., P. Giles, and P. Shaver (1975) Sex-role traditionalism and fear of success. *Sex Roles* 1:319–326.

Cassileth, B., E. Lusk, T. Strouse, D. Miller, L. Brown, P. Cross, and A. Tenaglia (1984) Psychological status in chance illness. *New England Journal of Medicine* 311:506–510.

Centers for Disease Control (1986) Homicide Surveillance: High-Risk Racial and Ethnic Groups—Blacks and Hispanics, 1970 to 1983.

Centers for Disease Control (1986) Acquired immunodeficiency syndrome—Europe. *Morbidity and Mortality Weekly Report* 35:35–46.

Cowens, E. L. (1982) Help is where you find it. *American Psychologist* 37:385–395.

Digest of Educational Statistics, 1977–1978, National Center for Education Statistics.

Dunlap, J. W., and A. K. Kurtz (1932) *Handbook of Statistical Nomographs, Tables, and Formulas.* New York: World Book Company.

Dusek, D., and D. A. Girdano (1980) *Drugs, A Factual Account* (3rd ed.). Reading, Mass.: Addison-Wesley.

Edwards, A. L. (1969) *Statistical Analysis* (3rd ed.). New York: Holt, Rinehart and Winston, Inc.

Elifson, K. W., D. M. Petersen, and C. K. Hadaway (1983) Religion and delinquency: A contextual analysis. *Criminology* 21:505–527.

Fisher, R. A. (1950) *Statistical Methods for Research Workers.* Edinburgh: Oliver and Boyd, Ltd.

Fisher R. A. and F. Yates, *Statistical Tables for Biological, Agricultural, and Medical Research,* 6th ed. London: Longman Group Ltd., 1974. (Previously published by Oliver and Boyd, Ltd., Edinburgh.)

Freeman, S., M. R. Walker, R. Borden, and B. Latane (1975) Diffusion of responsibility and restaurant tipping. Cheaper by the bunch. *Personality and Social Psychology Bulletin* 1:584–587.

Friedman, E. (1978) Pet ownership and coronary heart disease patient survival. *Circulation* 168:57–58.

Gerard, H. B., R. A. Wilhelmy, and E. S. Conolley (1968) Conformity and group size. *Journal of Personality and Social Psychology* 8:79–82.

Henkel, R. E. (1975) Part–whole correlations and the treatment of ordinal and quasi-interval data as interval data. *Pacific Sociological Review* 18:3–26.

Huff, D. (1954) *How to Lie with Statistics*. New York: W. W. Norton and Co., Inc.

Kirk, R. E. (1982) *Experimental Design: Procedures for the Behavioral Sciences* (2nd ed.). Belmont, Calif.: Brooks/Cole.

Labovitz, S. (1970) The assignment of numbers to rank order categories. *American Sociological Review* 35:515–524.

Langan, P. A., and C. A. Innes (1985) The risk of violent crime. *Bureau of Justice Statistics Special Report,* NCJ-97119.

Latané, B. (1981) The psychology of social impact. *American Psychologist* 36:342–356.

Mann, H. B., and D. R. Whitney (1947) On a test of whether one of two random variables is stochastically larger than the other. *Annals of Mathematical Statistics* 18:52–54.

Manstead, A. S. R., H. L. Wagner, and C. J. MacDonald (1983) A contrast effect in judgments of own emotional state. *Motivation and Emotion* 7:279–289.

Milgram, S., L. Bickman, and L. Berkowitz (1969) Note on the drawing power of crowds. *Journal of Personality and Social Psychology* 13:79–82.

Meyer, G. E., and K. Hilterbrand (1984) Does it pay to be "Bashful"?: The seven dwarfs and long-term memory. *American Journal of Psychology* 97:47–55.

McNemar, Q. (1962) *Psychological Statistics*. New York: John Wiley and Sons, Inc.

NIOSH Recommendations for Occupational Safety and Health Standards (1985) *Morbidity and Mortality Weekly Report,* Supplement, 34/No. 1S.

Olds, E. G. (1949) The 5 percent significance levels of sums of squares of rank differences and a correction. *Annals of Mathematical Statistics* 20:117–118.

Pearson, E. S., and H. O. Hartley (1958) *Biometrika Tables for Statisticians* (Vol. 1, 2nd ed.). New York: Cambridge University Press.

Platt, R., B. F. Polk, B. Murdock, and B. Rosner (1982) Mortality associated with nosocomial urinary-tract infection. *New England Journal of Medicine* 307:637–641.

Rand Corporation (1955) *A Million Random Digits*. Glencoe, Ill.: The Free Press of Glencoe.

Ravenholt, R. T. (1982) Letter to the editor. *New England Journal of Medicine* 307:312.

Runyon, R. P. (1977) *Non-Parametric Statistics*. Reading, Mass.: Addison-Wesley Publishing Co.

Runyon, R. P. (1977) *Winning with Statistics*. Reading, Mass.: Addison-Wesley.

Runyon, R. P. (1985) A Statistical Sampling Experiment, Ch. 7 of *Fundamentals of Statistics in the Biological, Medical, and Health Sciences*. Boston: Duxbury Press.

Seiden, R. H. (1966) Campus tragedy: A story of student suicide. *Journal of Abnormal Social Psychology* 71:389–399.

Siegel, S., and N. J. Castellan, Jr. (1988) *Nonparametric Statistics* (2nd ed.). New York: McGraw-Hill Book Co.

Snedecor, G. W., and W. G. Cochran (1956) *Statistical Methods* (6th ed.). Ames, Iowa: Iowa State University Press.

Social Security Administration, *Social Security Bulletin,* May 1979, 42.

Statistical Abstract of the United States, 1986.

Thorton, B. (1977) Toward a linear prediction model of marital happiness. *Personality and Social Psychology Bulletin* 3:674–676.

Tukey, J. W. (1953) The problem of multiple comparisons. Ditto: Princeton University, 396 pp.

U.S. Bureau of the Census (1985) Special Demographic Analysis, CDS-85-1, *Education in the United States: 1940–1983.*

U.S. Bureau of Prisons, *Statistical Report,* annual.

U.S. Center for Health Statistics, *Vital Statistics of the United States,* annual.

U.S. Department of Defense, *Selected Manpower Statistics* (1984), annual.

U.S. Department of Labor, Bureau of Labor Statistics (1977), *U.S. Working Women: A Data Book.*

U.S. Federal Bureau of Investigation, *Crime in the United States,* annual.

U.S. Immigration and Naturalization Service, annual report.

U.S. National Center for Health Statistics, *Vital Statistics of the United States,* annual.

Van Bree, N. S. (1981) Undergraduate research. *Nursing Outlook* January:39–41.

Wilcoxon, F., S. Katti, and R. A. Wilcox (1963) *Critical Values and Probability Levels for the Wilcoxon Rank Sum Test and the Wilcoxon Signed Rank Test*. New York: American Cyanamid Co.

Wilcoxon, F., and R. A. Wilcox (1964) *Some Rapid Approximate Statistical Procedures.* New York: Lederle Laboratories.

World Health Organization, *World Health Statistics,* annual.

World Population Data Sheet of the Population Reference Bureau, Inc.

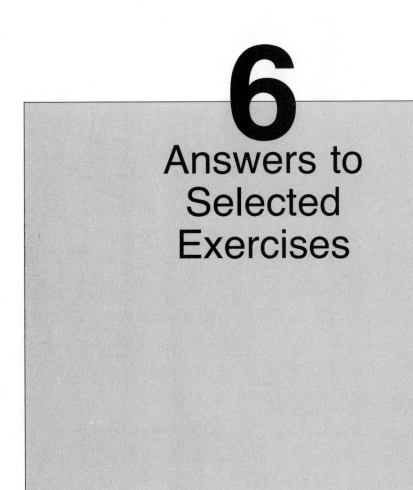

6

Answers to Selected Exercises

Answers to
Selected
Exercises

From
Chapter 1
to
Chapter 17

In problems involving many steps, you may occasionally find a discrepancy between the answers you obtained and those shown here. Where the discrepancies are small, they are probably due to rounding errors. These disparities are more common today because of the wide differences in methods used; that is, varying degrees of sophistication among calculators, adding machines, and hand calculations.

Chapter 1

2. **a)** constant   **b)** variable   **c)** constant   **d)** variable
   e) constant   **f)** variable   **g)** constant   **h)** variable
   i) constant

3. **a)** No
   b) nuclear accident, oil price increase, new information on health risks, interviewer error, major support by believable and prominent persons, etc.

5. finite—school superintendents in a state; infinite—all past, present, and future heroin addicts, stars, and roaches

6. U.S. Senators, astronauts

7. population

10. **a)** data **b)** data

13. For example, did you exclude men, women, or anyone else?

14. You might wish to poll *all* the students if they were voting on a student activity fee increase.

15. **a)** Single women, public officials and personalities, the very rich, and those persons not in the current directory due to change of address, etc. are among those who tend to have unlisted numbers and hence would be underrepresented.
b) Random digit dialing procedures would provide a more representative sample because all persons with active telephone numbers would have a chance of being included in the sample.

16. **a)** wardens **b)** prisons **c)** counties **d)** female students

17. It would be impossible because no comprehensive list of residents is available in any major American city.

18. **a)** descriptive **b)** inferential **c)** descriptive
d) descriptive **e)** inferential

19. These are not statistics; they are data. Statistics that may be calculated from these data include proportion or percentage of passes completed by each team, proportion or percentage of yards gained on the ground or in the air, proportion or percentage of time of possession. (See Chapter 2 for a discussion of proportions and percentages.)

20. **a)** statistic **b)** inference from statistics **c)** data
d) data **e)** inference from statistics

Chapter 2

1. **a)** 12.65 **b)** 4.00 **c)** 1.26 **d)** 0.40 **e)** 0.13

2. $a = 5$ **3.** $y = 22$ **4.** $\Sigma X = 1200$

5. $N = 4$ **6.** $N = 40$ **7.** $s^2 = 20$

8. **a)** 25 **b)** 60 **c)** 37 **d)** 31 **e)** 60 **f)** 44

9. **a)** $\sum_{i=1}^{3} X_i$ **b)** $\sum_{i=1}^{N} X_i$ **c)** $\sum_{i=3}^{6} X_i^2$ **d)** $\sum_{i=4}^{N} X_i^2$

10.
$$\sum_{i=1}^{N} X_i^2 = 4^2 + 5^2 + 7^2 + 9^2 + 10^2 + 11^2 + 14^2 = 588$$

$$\left(\sum_{i=1}^{N} X_i\right)^2 = (4 + 5 + 7 + 9 + 10 + 11 + 14)^2$$

$$= 60^2 = 3600$$

$$588 \neq 3600$$

11. **a)** nominal   **b)** ordinal   **c)** nominal
     d) ordinal   **e)** ratio

12. **a)** ordinal   **b)** nominal   **c)** ratio   **d)** ratio
     e) ratio   **f)** nominal   **g)** nominal

13. **a)** discrete   **b)** discrete   **c)** continuous   **d)** continuous

14. **a)** -0.5 to $+0.5$ **b)** 0.45 to 0.55   **c)** 0.95 to 1.05
     d) 0.485 to 0.495   **e)** -4.5 to -5.5 **f)** -4.45 to -4.55

15. **a)** 100.00   **b)** 46.41   **c)** 2.96   **d)** 0.01
     e) 16.46   **f)** 1.05   **g)** 86.21   **h)** 10.00

16. 6:7 or 0.86:1

17.

	Black and White Males	Black and White Females	Total
1980	18,766	5,075	23,841
1981	18,253	4,950	23,203
1982	16,990	4,922	21,912

a) Using these figures, which were calculated using the original data, the male:female ratio can be calculated by year.

1980 $\dfrac{18,766}{5075} = 3.70$, therefore, the male:female ratio is 3.70:1

1981 $\dfrac{18,253}{4950} = 3.69$, therefore, the male:female ratio is 3.69:1

1982 $\dfrac{16,990}{4922} = 3.45$, therefore, the male:female ratio is 3.45:1

b) The calculations below are based on the original data and show the male:female ratio by race and year.

	Whites	**Blacks**
1980	$\dfrac{10381}{3177} = 3.27$, therefore, 3.27:1	$\dfrac{8385}{1898} = 4.42$, therefore, 4.42:1
1981	$\dfrac{9941}{3125} = 3.18$, therefore, 3.18:1	$\dfrac{8312}{1825} = 4.55$, therefore, 4.55:1
1982	$\dfrac{9260}{3179} = 2.91$, therefore, 2.91:1	$\dfrac{7730}{1743} = 4.43$, therefore, 4.43:1

18. 90.45

19. 26.88 million are less than 15 and 12.22 million are over 64.

$$\frac{26.88 + 12.22}{83.10} \times 100 = 47.05$$

20.

		Proportion	Percentage
Anne Arundel County	389,000	0.173	17.3%
Baltimore County	673,000	0.300	30.0%
Carroll County	105,000	0.047	4.7%
Harford County	151,000	0.067	6.7%
Howard County	136,000	0.061	6.1%
Queen Anne's County	28,000	0.012	1.2%
Baltimore City	764,000	0.340	34.0%

22. a)

	Proportion*	Percentage*
Too little	0.77	77
About right	0.21	21
Too much	0.02	2
No opinion	0.01	1

b)

	Proportion	Percentage
Too little	0.71	71
About right	0.24	24
Too much	0.03	3
No opinion	0.02	2

c)

	Proportion	Percentage
Too little	0.83	83
About right	0.13	13
Too much	0.02	2
No opinion	0.02	2

d)

	Proportion*	Percentage*
Too little	0.25	25
About right	0.28	28
Too much	0.43	43
No opinion	0.03	3

* The slight disparity from 1.00 and 100 is due to rounding.

The majority of the respondents appear to want more information about earthquakes and how to prepare for them. Thus, the results appear to contradict the view that Californians would prefer not thinking about earthquakes.

23.　time 1 $= 38 + 25 = 63$
　　time 2 $= 38$

Eq. (2.3)　$\dfrac{38 - 63}{63} \times 100 = -39.68\%$

24.　$\dfrac{t_2 - t_1}{t_1} \times 100 = 25\%$　　and　　$t_1 = 150$, therefore, $t_2 = 187.5$

25.　**a)** -25.2%　　**b)** 74.83%

28.

	(a)	(b)
Year	Percentage of Male* Homicide Victims	Percentage of Female* Homicide Victims
1978	17.91	18.51
1979	19.93	19.83
1980	21.58	20.91
1981	21.00	20.44
1982	19.58	20.32

* The slight disparity from 100.00 is due to rounding.

c) 77.44%　　**d)** 21.92%

29. a)

Business administration	20.00%
Education	75.00%
Humanities	57.14%
Science	28.57%
Social science	50.00%

b) 38.10   **c)** 13.33   **d)** 58.33 Males
    4.76   20.00   41.67 Females
 14.29   26.67
 23.81   13.33
 19.05   26.67

30.

Year	% Males	% Females
1950	51.31	48.69
1955	51.24	48.76
1960	51.20	48.80
1965	51.25	48.75
1970	51.33	48.67
1975	51.30	48.70
1980	51.29	48.71

32. $\dfrac{192}{1,902,000} \times 1000 = 0.101$ per 1000

33.

	Population per Lawyer	Lawyers per 1000
Alaska	297	3.37
Arkansas	717	1.39
California	365	2.74
D.C.	25	39.91
Georgia	493	2.03
Illinois	352	2.84
New York	280	3.57

Chapter 3

1.

	True Limits	Width	Midpoint
a)	7.5–12.5	5	10
b)	5.5–7.5	2	6.5
c)	(−0.5)–(+2.5)	3	1
d)	4.5–14.5	10	9.5
e)	(−8.5)–(−1.5)	7	−5
f)	2.45–3.55	1.1	3
g)	1.495–1.755	0.26	1.625
h)	(−3.5)–(+3.5)	7	0

2.

	Width	Apparent Limits	True Limits	Midpoint
i)	7	0–6	0.5–6.5	3
ii)	1	29	28.5–29.5	29
iii)	2	18–19	17.5–19.5	18.5
iv)	4	(-30)–(-27)	(-30.5)–(-26.5)	-28.5
v)	0.01	0.30	0.295–0.305	0.30
vi)	0.006	0.206–0.211	0.2055–0.2115	0.2085

3.

Class Intervals	True Limits	Midpoint	f	Cumulative f	Cumulative %
40–44	39.5–44.5	42	1	1	2.5
45–49	44.5–49.5	47	1	2	5.0
50–54	49.5–54.5	52	1	3	7.5
55–59	54.5–59.5	57	0	3	7.5
60–64	59.5–64.5	62	3	6	15.0
65–69	64.5–69.5	67	3	9	22.5
70–74	69.5–74.5	72	4	13	32.5
75–79	74.5–79.5	77	11	24	60.0
80–84	79.5–84.5	82	8	32	80.0
85–89	84.5–89.5	87	4	36	90.0
90–94	89.5–94.5	92	3	39	97.5
95–99	94.5–99.5	97	1	40	100.0

4. **b)** $i = 3$

Class Intervals	f	Class Intervals	f
40–42	1	70–72	3
43–45	0	73–75	2
46–48	1	76–78	8
49–51	0	79–81	6
52–54	1	82–84	4
55–57	0	85–87	3
58–60	1	88–90	1
61–63	2	91–93	2
64–66	1	94–96	1
67–69	2	97–99	1

c) $i = 10$

Class Intervals	f
40–49	2
50–59	1
60–69	6
70–79	15
80–89	12
90–99	4

d) $i = 20$

Class Intervals	f
40–59	3
60–79	21
80–99	16

6.   **a)** 5   **b)** 0.5–5.5   **c)** 3
                               5.5–10.5   8
                               10.5–15.5   13

8.

Class Intervals	f
5–9	1
10–14	2
15–19	3
20–24	4
25–29	5
30–34	6
35–39	8
40–44	6
45–49	5
50–54	4
55–59	3
60–64	2
65–69	1

9.

Class Intervals	f
3–7	1
8–12	0
13–17	5
18–22	0
23–27	9
28–32	0
33–37	14
38–42	0
43–47	11
48–52	0
53–57	7
58–62	0
63–67	3

10.

Class Intervals	f
4–5	1
6–7	0
8–9	0
10–11	0
12–13	1
14–15	2
16–17	2
18–19	0
20–21	0
22–23	2
24–25	3
26–27	4
28–29	0
30–31	0
32–33	3
34–35	4
36–37	7
38–39	0
40–41	0
42–43	2
44–45	7
46–47	2
48–49	0
50–51	0
52–53	2
54–55	3
56–57	2
58–59	0
60–61	0
62–63	1
64–65	1
66–67	1

11.

Class Intervals	f
0–9	1
10–19	5
20–29	9
30–39	14
40–49	11
50–59	7
60–69	3

12. a) height, age, I.Q.

b) relationship between personal freedom and age in Japan

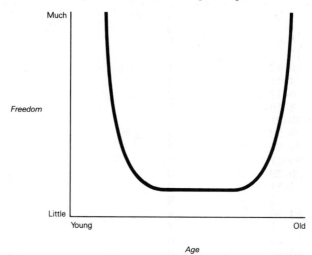

c) family income distribution in the United States
d) family income distribution in a wealthy county
e) relationship between freedom and length of prison sentence

13.

Class Interval	f	cum f	%	cum %
0–2	0	0	0.0	0.0
3–5	17	17	34.0	34.0
6–8	15	32	30.0	64.0
9–11	8	40	16.0	80.0
12–14	4	44	8.0	88.0
15–17	3	47	6.0	94.0
18–20	1	48	2.0	96.0
21–23	1	49	2.0	98.0
24–26	0	49	0.0	98.0
27–29	1	50	2.0	100.0

14.

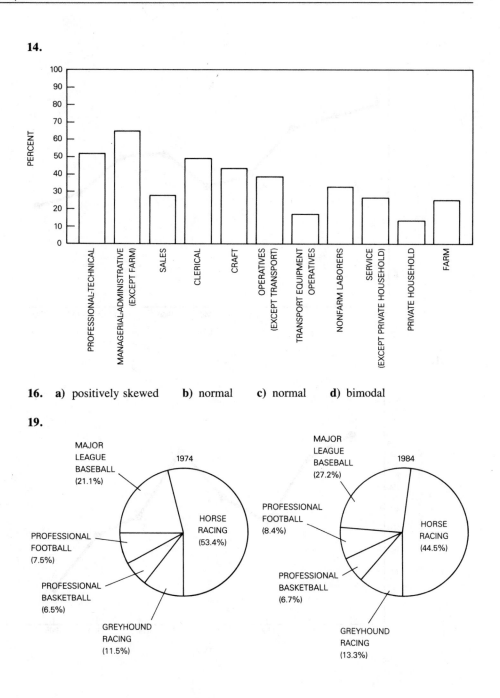

16. **a)** positively skewed   **b)** normal   **c)** normal   **d)** bimodal

19.

20.

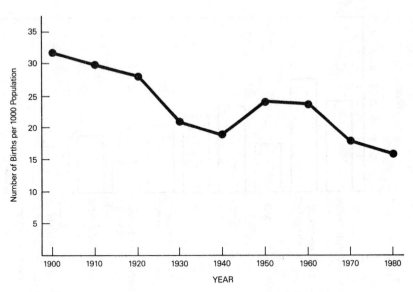

21.

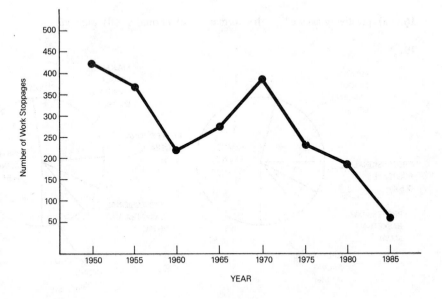

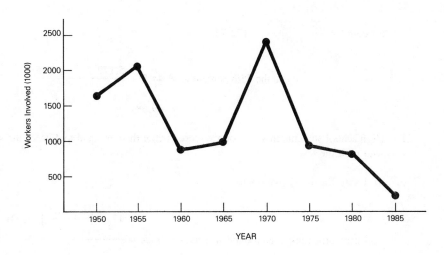

Chapter 4

2. **a)** Using Eq. (4.2), we obtain

$$\text{percentile rank of } 1 = 0 + \frac{\left(\dfrac{1 - (-0.5)}{5}\right)(18.8)}{230.3} \times 100$$

$$= 0.02449 \times 100$$

$$= 2.45$$

b) 18.84   **c)** 55.65

4. **a)** First, calculate the cum f of the score at the 25th percentile.

$$\text{cum} f = \frac{\text{percentile rank} \times N}{100}$$

$$= \frac{25 \times 230.3}{100} = 57.57$$

Second, calculate the age at the 25th percentile.

$$\text{score at a given percentile} = X_{ll} + \frac{i(\text{cum} f - \text{cum} f_{ll})}{f_i}$$

$$= 14.5 + \frac{5(57.57 - 51.7)}{18} \doteq 16.13$$

b) 30.64

c) $\text{cum} f = \dfrac{75 \times 230.3}{100} = 172.72$

$$\text{age at the 75th percentile} = 44.5 + \dfrac{5(172.72 - 161.5)}{11.5}$$

$$= 49.38$$

5. High school students in your county scored better than or equal to 42% of the students who took the test.

6. **a)** Using Eq. (4.2), we obtain

$$\text{percentile rank of an inmate arrested six times} = \dfrac{17 + \left(\dfrac{6 - 5.5}{3}\right)(15.0)}{50} \times 100$$

$$= 39.0$$

b) $Q_1 = C_{25}$, therefore, using Eq. (4.3), we get

$$\text{cum} f = \dfrac{25 \times 50}{100} = 12.5$$

Using Eq. (4.4), we have

$$\text{score at the 25th percentile} = 2.5 + \dfrac{3(12.5 - 0)}{17}$$

$$= 4.7 \text{ arrests}$$

$$\text{score at } Q_3 \text{ or the 75th percentile} = 10.6 \text{ arrests}$$

$$\text{score at } Q_2 \text{ or the 50th percentile} = 7.1 \text{ arrests}$$

7.

Interval	f	cum f	%	cum %
0–2	12	12	33.3	33.3
3–5	10	22	27.8	61.1
6–8	9	31	25.0	86.1
9–11	5	36	13.9	100.0

a) We wish to find the score corresponding to a percentile rank of 75 (Q_3).

$$\text{cum} f = \dfrac{75 \times 36}{100} = 27$$

Using Eq. (4.4), we obtain

$$\text{score at the 75th percentile} = 5.5 + \frac{3(27 - 22)}{9}$$

$$= 7.17$$

Therefore, any score above 7.17 would be above the 3rd quartile.

b and c) The score at the 50th percentile or 50th centile is 4.30.
d) The score at the 9th decile or 90th percentile is 9.34.

8. b) 480 and 560　　　**c)** 500
d) His chances are not good since he scored a 500 and a score of 520 is necessary to be at the 72nd percentile.

10. a) $\text{cum} f = \dfrac{10 \times 110}{100} = 11$

$$\text{score at the 10th percentile} = 14.5 + \frac{5(11 - 7)}{5}$$

$$= 18.5$$

b) 41.0　　　**c)** 45.7

12. a) i) 24th percentile　　　ii) 70th percentile
iii) cannot be calculated since the class is open-ended.

Chapter 5

1. a) $\overline{X} = 5.0$;　median $= 5.5$;　mode $= 8$　　　**2.** (c)
b) $\overline{X} = 5.0$;　median $= 5.0$;　mode $= 5.0$
c) $\overline{X} = 17.5$;　median $= 3.83$;　mode $= 4$

3. The median and mode can be computed. Some statisticians would contend the mean should not be computed because the data are measured at the ordinal level.

4. All measures of central tendency will be multiplied by 100.

5. $\overline{X} = 39.91$, Mode 42 (midpoint of the class interval 40–44)

6. $\overline{X} = 5.0$; median unchanged; mode unchanged.

7. a) negative skew　　　**b)** positive skew
c) no evidence of skew　　　**d)** no evidence of skew

8. 7(c) is symmetrical and 7(d) is bimodal.

9. $\bar{X} = 5.0$ **a)** $\bar{X} = 7.0$ **b)** $\bar{X} = 3.0$ **c)** $\bar{X} = 26.7$
  d) $\bar{X} = 10$ **e)** $\bar{X} = 2.5$

11. The distribution is symmetrical.

13. a) 71.9 **b)**

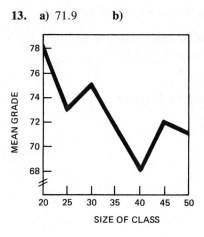

14. raise median: (c)
raise mean: (b)

15. The mean is most affected by a skewed distribution.

17. 3.04

18. $\bar{X} = 13.95$

19. $\bar{X} = 3.11$, median $= 3.00$, mode $= 3.00$.

20. a)

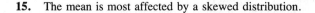

Age	Sex	Attitude Toward Pornography
mean = 39.1		mean = 29.7
median = 36		median = 27
mode = 21	mode = F	mode = 24

b) Eight of the 10 respondents are females. The sampling procedures should be reviewed to ensure that females are not oversampled.

21.

1950	$\overline{X}$ = 4004.7
1955	$\overline{X}$ = 5661.2
1960	$\overline{X}$ = 4036.0
1965	$\overline{X}$ = 3727.6
1970	$\overline{X}$ = 6477.7
1975	$\overline{X}$ = 4106.4
1980	$\overline{X}$ = 4251.3
1985	$\overline{X}$ = 6000.0

23.   b)

	Means f	Medians f
1	1	4
2	4	3
3	7	6
4	11	9
5	6	5
6	1	3

d) Drawing from means: **i)** $\frac{1}{30}$ **ii)** $\frac{1}{30}$ **iii)** $\frac{2}{30}$
      Drawing from medians: **i)** $\frac{3}{30}$ **ii)** $\frac{4}{30}$ **iii)** $\frac{7}{30}$

Chapter 6

1. $s^2 = 1.66$; $s = 1.29$ **a)** no change   **b)** increase

2. s for sentence = 46.7; s for time served = 16.2

4. mean = 746.7;   standard deviation = 703.9;   variance = 495,488.9

5. All scores have the same value.

6. a) 3.52   **b)** 2.31   **c)** 5.89   **d)** 0

7. The standard deviation is very skewed to the right. Extreme deviations increase the size of the standard deviation.

8. a) 10   **b)** 8   **c)** 20   **d)** 0

9. s for males = 0.78
     s for females = 0.73

10. $s = 5.06$; $s^2 = 25.64$

11. $s = 1.65$; $s^2 = 2.72$

12. political science, $\overline{X} = 28,429$; $s = 1591$; range $= 5000$
history, $\overline{X} = 38,429$; $s = 6184$; range $= 17,000$
sociology, $\overline{X} = 32,571$; $s = 2555$; range $= 7000$

14. Class II had the most variability and Class I had the least.

15. The class in which the lecturer was present achieved the highest mean final examination score. It is quite possible that a few individual students in the experimental group achieved a higher score on the final examination than anyone in the control group.

16. neighborhood A; $s = 4.34$; $\overline{X} = 36.3$ (most homogeneous)
neighborhood B; $s = 8.36$; $\overline{X} = 83.2$ (most affluent)
neighborhood C; $s = 17.74$; $\overline{X} = 37.5$ (most heterogeneous)
neighborhood D; $s = 5.33$; $\overline{X} = 14.8$ (least affluent)

17. range $= 41$; $\overline{X} = 13.95$; $s = 10.6$; $s^2 = 112.4$

18. $s = 11.43$; $s^2 = 130.75$

19. all cities $s = 26.5$; $\overline{X} = 33.0$
nine cities without Juneau $s = 13.4$; $\overline{X} = 25.2$
nine cities without Atlanta $s = 25.7$; $\overline{X} = 36.4$

21. a)

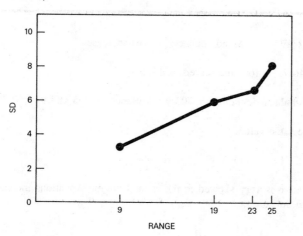

Chapter 7

1. **a)** 0.94   **b)** -0.40 **c)** 0.00   **d)** -1.32 **e)** 2.23   **f)** -2.53

2. **a)** 0.4798   **b)** 0.4713   **c)** 0.0987
   d) 0.1554   **e)** 0.4505   **f)** 0.4750

3. **a)** 0.0202   **b)** 0.0287   **c)** 0.4013
   d) 0.3446   **e)** 0.0495   **f)** 0.0250

4. **a)** i)   0.3413; 341   ii)   0.4772; 477
       iii) 0.1915; 192   iv) 0.4938; 494
   b) i)   0.1587; 159   ii)   0.0228; 23   iii)   0.6915; 692
       iv) 0.9938; 994   v)   0.5000; 500
   c) i)   0.1359; 136   ii)   0.8351; 835
       iii) 0.6687; 669   iv) 0.3023; 302

5. **a)** arithmetic: $z = 1.21$;   verbal comprehension: $z = 0.77$;   geography: $z = -0.29$
   b) arithmetic; geography   **c)** 0.1131, 0.2206, 0.6141
   d) We must assume the data are normally distributed.
   e) 62.53

6. **a)** 40.13; 57.93   **b)** 60.26

7. a, b, c, and e

8. **a)** $z = -0.67$ **b)** $z = 0.67$
       $X = 63.96$ $X = 80.04$
   c) $z = 1.28$ **d)** $z = 0.67$
       $X = 87.36$ 25.14% score above
   e) $z = -0.5$ **f)** $z = 0.67$ and $z = 0.67$
       30.85% score below $63.96 - 80.04$

9. $\mu = 72$, $\sigma = 8$:
   a) 66.64   **b)** 77.36
   c) 82.24   **d)** $z = 1.00$
   e) $z = -0.75$ 15.87% score above
       22.66% score below   **f)** $66.64 - 77.36$
   g) below 58.88,   **h)** below 51.36,
       above 85.12   above 92.64

9. $\mu = 72$, $\sigma = 4$:
   a) 69.32   **b)** 74.68
   c) 77.12   **d)** $z = 2.00$
   e) $z = -1.5$ 2.28% score above
       6.68% score below   **f)** $69.32 - 74.68$
   g) below 65.44,   **h)** below 61.68,
       above 78.56   above 82.32

9. $\mu = 72$, $\sigma = 2$:
   a) 70.66
   c) 74.56
   e) $z = -3.00$
      0.13% score below
   g) below 68.72,
      above 75.28

   b) 73.34
   d) $z = 4.00$
      0.003% score above
   f) 70.66 − 73.34
   h) below 66.84,
      above 77.16

10. test 2, test 1

11. No, z scores merely reflect the form of the distributions from which they were derived. Normally distributed variables will yield normally distributed z scores.

12. a) assume $z = 1.28$, 17.24 years
    b) Assume $z = 1.00$, 16.40 years
    c) 71.58 ministers

13. Assume $z = 1.27$, Her percentile rank is 89.80

14.

X	z Score	Percentile Rank
270	−2.35	0.94%
780	2.65	99.60%
500	−0.10	46.02%
410	−0.98	16.35%
565	0.54	70.54%

15. a) 780
    d) 270; 410
    b) 780
    e) 98.66%
    c) 565; 780
    f) assume $z = 1.96$; 310, 710

16. a) 3.55
    b) 0.67
    c) −0.20
    d) −1.60

17. a) $\overline{X} = 5.42$
       $s = 1.68$
    b) yes
    c) assume $z = -0.67$, 4.29 days
    d) 4 days or less
       $z = -0.85$, proportion $= 0.1977$
       7 days or more
       $z = +0.94$, proportion $= 0.6736$

18. The normal distribution includes a family of bell-shaped curves of which the standard normal distribution ($\mu = 0$, $\sigma = 1.0$) is one.

19. The smaller the standard deviation is, the smaller the deviations of scores about the mean are. When the mean is used to predict a given score, the error will be, on the average, small when the standard deviation is small. In the limiting case, when $s = 0.00$, all of the scores are identical. There is no error in prediction.

Chapter 8

1. Percentaging down

	Low	Moderate	High
High	0.0	25.0	50.0
Moderate	60.0	50.0	33.3
Low	40.0	25.0	16.7
Total	100.0	100.0	100.0

Percentaging across

	Low	Moderate	High	Total
High	0.0	25.0	75.0	100.0
Moderate	42.9	28.6	28.6	100.1*
Low	50.0	25.0	25.0	100.0

* Does not sum to 100.0 because of rounding.

Percentaging on the total

	Low	Moderate	High	Total
High	0.0	6.7	20.0	
Moderate	20.0	13.3	13.3	
Low	13.3	6.7	6.7	
				100.0

2. Either variable could serve as the independent variable. One could contend that high school grades would influence drug use or vice versa. If you assume that grade point average is the independent variable, you would percentage down and compare across.

3. $C = 975$ gamma $= 0.560$, Somer's $d_{yx} = 0.378$, tau-$b = 0.384$
$D = 275$
$T_y = 600$
$T_x = 550$

4. lambda $= 0.125$

5. gamma $= -0.538$ Somer's $d = -0.375$ tau-$b = -0.374$
$C = 133$
$D = 443$
$T_y = 251$
$T_x = 255$

6.

Reason For Not Seeking Work	Sex	
	Male	*Female*
In School	51.1 (693)	24.0 (681)
Ill or Disabled	24.0 (326)	13.9 (394)
Keeping House	2.4 (32)	43.2 (1226)
Thinks Cannot Get a Job	22.5 (305)	19.0 (540)
Total	100.0 (1356)	100.1* (2841)

$N = 4197$
lambda = 0.193

* Does not add to 100.0 because of rounding.

10.

Racial Composition of Marriage Partners	Year		
	1970	*1977*	*1984*
Husband Black, Wife White	13.2 (41)	22.6 (95)	14.6 (111)
Wife Black, Husband White	7.7 (24)	7.1 (30)	8.4 (64)
Husband Black, Wife Other	2.6 (8)	4.8 (20)	2.2 (17)
Wife Black, Husband Other	1.3 (4)	0.5 (2)	0.8 (6)
Husband White, Wife Other	44.8 (139)	42.0 (177)	44.6 (340)
Wife White, Husband Other	30.3 (94)	23.0 (97)	29.4 (224)
Total	99.9* (310)	100.0 (421)	100.0 (762)

* Does not add to 100.0 because of rounding.

12. lambda = 0.125   **15. a)** lambda = 0.222

Chapter 9

1. $r = 0.48$

2.

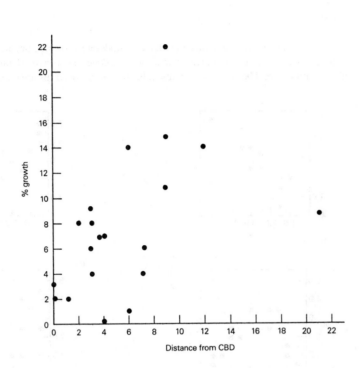

3. **a)** $r = 0.89$
b) Reversing the scoring of fear of crime results in the following scores: 14, 9, 10, 2, 3 and $r = -0.89$

5. **a)** nonlinear relationship and/or restricted range   **b)** restricted range
c) restricted range

6. $r = 0.83$ **7.** $r = 0.00$; $r_s = 0.50$

9. Strongest is -0.89;   weakest is $+0.32$;   negative is -0.89

10.

	1.	2.	3.	4.
1. age	1.00			
2. education	−0.61	1.00		
3. income	−0.30	0.93	1.00	
4. family size	0.66	−0.83	−0.65	1.00

11. The correlation between age and attitude toward the police ($r = -0.14$) tells us that age has a weak, negative relationship with attitude toward the police in that older black ministers are slightly more likely to hold a negative attitude toward the police than are younger black ministers. The correlation between church size and minister's education ($r = 0.41$) indicates that well-educated ministers tend to serve larger churches than do less-educated ministers.

12. $r = 0.76$

13. $r = -0.76$ indicates that two variables have a moderately strong, negative relationship; whereas, $r = +0.76$ indicates that two variables have a moderately strong, positive relationship. The two coefficients indicate the relationships are equally strong.

14. **a)**   **b)**

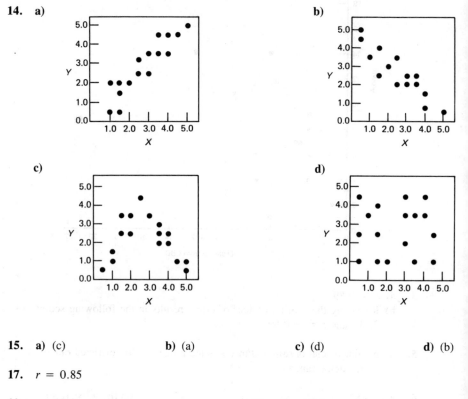

         c)   **d)**

15. **a)** (c)   **b)** (a)   **c)** (d)   **d)** (b)

17. $r = 0.85$

20. $r = 0.91$ **22.** $r = 0.80$

23. Nonlinear relationships give rise to artificially low Pearson's r correlation coefficients.

24. If the range is markedly restricted (truncated range), Pearson's r will be artificially low.

25. Reversing the scoring of a variable included in a correlation matrix will reverse the sign of its correlation with all other variables in the matrix.

26. **a)** Pearson's r or Spearman's rho may be computed.
         b) The following matrix is based on Pearson's r.

	1.	2.	3.
1. Order of recall	1.00		
2. Recalled %	−0.92	1.00	
3. Recognized %	−0.69	0.57	1.00

Chapter 10

1. $Y' = 5.7 - 0.9X$

2.

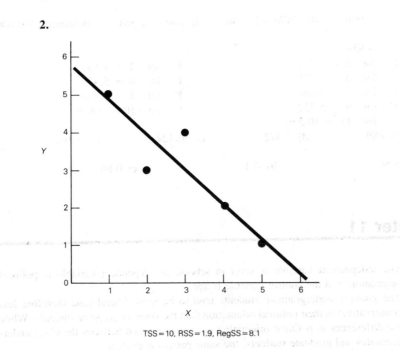

TSS = 10, RSS = 1.9, RegSS = 8.1

3. TSS $= 10$; RSS $= 1.9$; RegSS $= 8.1$
   $r = -0.9$; $r^2 = +0.81$

4.

X	Y	Y'	Y – Y'
1	5	4.8	+0.2
2	3	3.9	−0.9
3	4	3.0	+1.0
4	2	2.1	−0.1
5	1	1.2	−0.2

5. $r^2 = 0.25$; $1 - r^2 = 0.75$

6. **a)** 1.72 **b)** 118.48 **c)** $s_{\text{est } y} = 0.39$

7. **a)** 1.59 **b)** $s_{\text{est } y} = 0.47$ **c)** 0.13

9. **a)** $a = -51.081$, $b_y = 2.442$ **c)** $r = 0.995$; $r^2 = 0.989$

11. **a)** 33.35 **b)** 46.82

12. a) If group size equals 15, the predicted group cohesiveness score is 3.61.
   b) 57.75%

13. a) $r = -0.84$ **b)** 3.78

16. b) $r = 0.966$ **d)** Chile: 429.858   Ireland: 831.364   Belgium: 1390.606

17. a) $r = 0.958$
   b) Y' for 3 = 3.222 Y' for 4 = 4.139
         Y' for 5 = 5.055 Y' for 6 = 5.972
         Y' for 7 = 6.889 Y' for 8 = 7.806
         Y' for 9 = 8.722 Y' for 10 = 9.639
         Y' for 11 = 10.556
   c) 54.889   **d)** 4.473   **e)** 50.424   **f)** 0.919

18. a) 5.56   **b)** 4.16   **c)** 0.86

Chapter 11

4. a) The independent variable is level in school; the dependent variable is political orientation; and the control variable is age.
   b) The younger undergraduate students tend to be more liberal (and therefore less conservative) in their political orientation than the younger graduate students. While the differences in political orientation are not so marked between the older undergraduates and graduate students, the same pattern is evident.

   c)

Political Orientation	Age		
	Young	Old	
Liberal	45.0 (45)	55.0 (55)	The older students tend to be slightly more liberal than the younger students.
Conservative	55.0 (55)	45.0 (45)	
Total	100.0 (100)	100.0 (100)	

6. $r_{21.3} = -0.278$

8. The partial correlation coefficient is a "weighted average" of the correlation between two variables across all categories of the control variable and would be misleading if the association were not uniform across all categories of the control variable.

9. $r_{xy \cdot z} = 0.750$

11. The equation is in unstandardized form because the Y-intercept (1.1) is shown and not equal to 0.

12.

Employee	Y'	Residual*
1	4.84	1.16
2	6.71	−1.71
3	4.97	2.03
4	9.53	−0.53
5	19.00	2.00

* The sum of the five residuals does not equal 0 because the scores of other employees included in the study are not provided.

13. **a)** The model predicts that the math achievement scores of the white students are better than those of the black students because the coefficient of multiple determination is 0.52 for the white students and 0.14 for the black students.

b) Family socioeconomic status (SES) is the most important predictor variable for both black and white students. For white students cumulative grade point average and teacher's ability are the least important predictors, and for the black students reading test scores and percentage of white students in class are least important.

c) A standardized regression coefficient allows for an assessment of the relative importance of the independent variables as predictors of the dependent variable. The coefficient of 0.17 indicates that if teacher's ability increases one standard deviation unit, the math achievement scores of the white students increase 0.17 standard deviation units when the remaining independent variables are controlled. The coefficient of 0.34 indicates that if teacher's ability increases one standard deviation unit, the math achievement scores of the black students increase 0.34 standard deviation units when the remaining independent variables are controlled. Thus, the teacher's ability is more important for black students than for white students when the other independent variables have been controlled.

14. **a)** Unstandardized equation

$$Y' = 2.11 - 2.01X_1 + 0.93X_2 - 2.46X_3 - 0.55X_4 + 1.00X_5 - 0.74X_6 - 0.11X_7$$

Standardized equation

$$Y' = -0.20X_1 + 0.12X_2 - 0.12X_3 - 0.11X_4 + 0.10X_5 - 0.09X_6 + 0.01X_7$$

b) The unstandardized coefficient of −0.55 associated with grade point average indicates that if a student's grade point average increases one unit, his or her delinquency score will decrease 0.55 units when the remaining independent variables are statistically controlled. The standardized coefficient of −0.11 associated with grade point average indicates that as one's grade point average increases one standard deviation unit, his or her delinquency score will decrease 0.11 standard deviation units when the remaining independent variables are statistically controlled.

c) The Y-intercept tells us that the multi-dimensional structure (hyperstructure) characterizing the multiple regression equation crosses the Y-axis at $+2.11$. The Y-intercept for a standardized equation always equals 0; therefore, it is not shown here.

d) The dependent variable is the weighted delinquency scale and the seven independent variables are shown in Table 11.6.

e) The independent variables have jointly explained 0.17 or 17%. The unexplained proportion of variance is 0.83.

f) Friends smoke marijuana is the best predictor because its standardized regression coefficient is largest, whereas importance of religion is the poorest predictor.

Chapter 12

1. a)

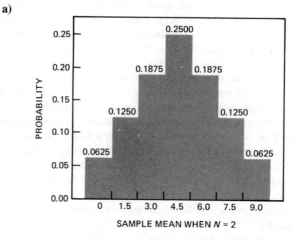

b)

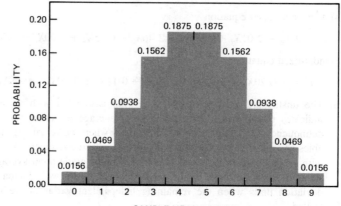

2. An extreme deviation is rarer as sample size increases.

3. **a)** 0.0625; 0.0156 **b)** 0.1250; 0.0312
   c) 0.3750; 0.3125 **d)** 0.7500; 0.6250

4. **a)** 0.6250 **b)** 0.1875 **c)** 0.2500

5. **a)** 0.6874 **b)** 0.3750 **c)** 0.1407

6. (a) and (b) **c)** Mean = 0.00; Standard deviation = 1.63

$\overline{X}$	f	$p(\overline{X})$
4	1	0.0123
3	4	0.0494
2	10	0.1235
1	16	0.1975
0	19	0.2346
−1	16	0.1975
−2	10	0.1235
−3	4	0.0494
−4	1	0.0123
$N_{\overline{X}} = 81$		$\Sigma\, p(\overline{X}) = 1.0000$

7. **a)** 0.2346 **b)** 0.6296 **c)** 0.0123 **d)** 0.0246
   e) 0.0617 **f)** 0.0617 **g)** 0.1234 **h)** 0.8766

8. **a)** 0.1250 **b)** 0.1250 **c)** 0.3750 **d)** 0.5000

9. **a)** 0.0192 **b)** 0.0769 **c)** 0.3077 **d)** 0.4231

10. Problem 1: **a)** 7 to 1 against **b)** 7 to 1 against
   Problem 2: **a)** 51 to 1 against **b)** 12 to 1 against

11. **a)** 0.1667 **b)** 0.1667 **c)** 0.2778 **d)** 0.5000

12. **a)** 0.0046 **b)** 0.0278 **c)** 0.0139
   d) 0.0556 **e)** 0.5787

13. **a)** 0.0129 **b)** 0.4135 **c)** 0.0100

14. **a)** 0.0156 **b)** 0.4219 **c)** 0.0123

15. **a)** 0.0838 **b)** 126.40 **c)** <68.64 and >131.36 **d)** 0.4648
   e) i) 0.0070 ii) 0.2160 iii) 0.03895

16. (b) **17.** **a)** $p = 0.20$ **b)** $p = 0.04$ **c)** $p = 0.80$ **d)** $p = 0.64$

18. **a)** $\frac{1}{3}$ **b)** $\frac{1}{2}$ **c)** $\frac{1}{6}$ **d)** 0

19. **a)** $\frac{1}{11}$ **b)** $\frac{1}{66}$ **c)** $\frac{14}{99}$

20. **a)** $\frac{1}{8}$ **b)** $\frac{1}{36}$ **c)** $\frac{16}{81}$

21. **a)** 0.40   **b)** 0.12   **c)** 0.16   **d)** 2(0.0336) = 0.0672

22. **a)** $p = 0.3085$ **b)** $p = 0.2266$ **c)** $p = 0.4649$
        d) $p = 0.2564$ **e)** $p = 0.2934$ **f)** $p = 0.0947$ **g)** $p = 0.3296$

23. 0.33, 0.33

26.

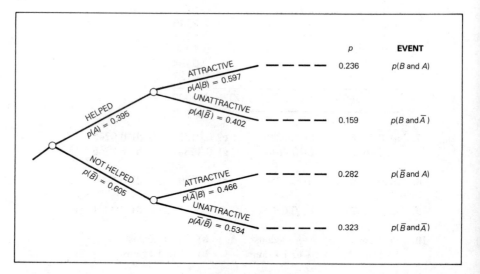

27. **a)**

Helping Response	Attractive (A)	Unattractive ($\overline{A}$)	Marginal Probability
Helped (B)	0.235	0.160	0.395
Did not help ($\overline{B}$)	0.271	0.333	0.605
Marginal probability	0.506	0.494	1.000

b) $p(B|A) = 0.464$, $p(B|\overline{A}) = 0.324$, $p(\overline{B}|A) = 0.536$, $p(\overline{B}|\overline{A}) = 0.674$

Chapter 13

2. **a)** In the event a critical theoretical issue is involved, the commission of a type I error might lead to a false conclusion concerning the validity of the theory.
    b) In many studies in which the toxic effects of new drugs are being studied the null hypothesis is that the drug has no adverse effects. In the event of a type II error a toxic drug might be mistakenly introduced into the market.

3. The null hypothesis cannot be proved. Failure to reject the null hypothesis does not constitute proof that the null hypothesis is correct.

4. All studies involve two statistical hypotheses: the null hypothesis and the alternative hypothesis. One designs the study so that the rejection of the null hypothesis leads to affirmation of the alternative hypothesis.

5. **a)** H_0 **b)** H_1 **c)** H_1 **d)** H_0

6. **a)** type II **b)** type I **c)** no error **d)** no error

7. **a)** type II **b)** type II **c)** no error

8. It is more likely that he is accepting a false H_0 since the probability that the observed event occurred by chance is still quite low ($p = 0.02$).

9. By chance, one would expect five differences to be statistically significant at the 0.05 level.

10. No

11. Yes

12. No. The only deviations that count are those in the direction specified under H_1.

13. (b)

15. **a)** (h) **b)** (a)

18. Failure to detect a potentially serious condition in a client (e.g., suicidal tendency) may lead to the false conclusion that nothing should be done to intervene in the client's behalf. Similarly, failure to detect possible unfavorable reactions to a treatment (e.g., thalidomide) may lead to the certification of the treatment as safe.

19. On the basis of the data, we would reject H_0. However, since H_0 is true, we have made a type I or type α error.

20. On the basis of the data, we would fail to reject H_0. Since H_0 is true, we have made the correct decision.

21. We fail to reject H_0. Since H_0 is false, we have failed to reject a false H_0. Therefore, we have made a type II or type β error.

22. We reject H_0. Since H_0 is false, we have made a correct decision.

23. We reject H_0. Since H_0 is false, we have made a correct decision.

24. The probability of making a type I error is equal to α. In the present case $\alpha = 0.05$.

Chapter 14

1. **a)** As sample size increases, the dispersion of sample means decreases.
   b) As you increase the number of samples, you are more likely to obtain extreme values of the sample mean. For example, suppose the probability of obtaining a sample mean of a given value is 0.01. If the number of samples drawn is 10, you probably will not obtain any sample means with that value. However, if you draw as many as 1000 samples, you would expect to obtain approximately 10 sample means with values so extreme that the probability of their occurrence is 0.01.

2. Suppose we have a population in which the mean = 100 and the standard deviation = 10. The probability of obtaining scores as extreme as 80 or less or 120 or more (± 2 standard deviations) is 0.0456, or less than five in a hundred. The probability of obtaining scores even more extreme (e.g., 50, 60, 70, or 130, 140, 150) is even lower. Thus, we would expect very few (if any) of these extreme scores to occur in a given sample. Since the value of the standard deviation is a direct function of the number of extreme scores, the standard deviation of a sample will usually underestimate the standard deviation of the population.

3. **a)** 21.71–26.29   **b)** 20.82–27.18

4. **a)** 23.28–24.72   **b)** 23.05–24.95

5. Reject H_0; $z = 2.68$ in which $z_{0.01} = \pm 2.58$

6. Accept H_0; $t = 2.618$ in which $t_{0.01} = \pm 2.831$, df $= 21$

7. In Exercise 5 the value of the population standard deviation is known; thus, we may employ the z-statistic and determine probability values in terms of areas under the normal curve. In Exercise 6 the value of the population standard deviation is not known and must be estimated from the sample data. Thus, the test statistic is the t-ratio.

    Since the t-distributions are more spread out than the normal curve, the proportion of area beyond a specific value of t is greater than the proportion of area beyond the corresponding value of z. Thus, a larger value of t is required to mark off the bounds of the critical region of rejection. In Exercise 5 the absolute value of the obtained z must equal or exceed 2.58. In Exercise 6 the absolute value of the obtained t must equal or exceed 2.83.

To generalize: The probability of making a type II error is less when we know the population standard deviation.

8. Reject H_0; $t = 2.134$ in which $t_{0.05} = 1.833$ (one-tailed test), df $= 9$

9. **a)** $z = 2.73, p = 0.9968$ **b)** $z = -0.91, p = 0.1814$
    c) $z = 1.82, p = 0.0344$ **d)** $p = 0.6372$

10. **a)** $36.80 - 43.20$ **b)** $35.79 - 44.21$

11. $t = 2.083$;   df $= 25$

12. 27.14–32.08 **13.** $t = 1.75$, df $= 625$

14. 263.34–273.66 **15.** **a)** $\mu = 6.0$, $\sigma = 3.42$

16. **a)** $p = \dfrac{1}{15}$ **b)** $p = \dfrac{1}{15}$ **c)** $p = \dfrac{8}{15}$ **d)** $p = 0$

17. **a)** $p = \dfrac{1}{12}$ **b)** $p = \dfrac{1}{12}$ **c)** $p = \dfrac{5}{9}$ **d)** $p = \dfrac{1}{36}$

18. The critical value of r_s for $N = 25$ ($\alpha = 0.05$, two-tailed test) may be obtained by interpolating: 0.409 for $N = 24$, 0.392 for $N = 26$; thus, the critical value for $N = 25$ is 0.400. Since the absolute value of the obtained r_s is less than the critical value, we accept H_0.

19. **a)** $z = 1.01$ **b)** $z = 1.99$

22. The statistics used to describe the distribution of a sample are $\overline{X}$ (the mean) and s (the standard deviation). The statistics used to describe the distribution of a sample statistic are the mean ($\mu_{\overline{X}}$) and the standard error of the mean ($\sigma_{\overline{X}}$).

23. s^2 is not an unbiased estimate of σ^2. When we use N in the denominator of the variance equation, we underestimate the population variance.

24. $\hat{s}^2$ is an unbiased estimate of σ^2 since $N - 1$ is used in the denominator of the equation.

26. Using the example in Section 14.7 of the text, we find the 99% confidence interval:

upper limit $\mu_0 = 108 + (2.787)(3.0) = 116.36$
lower limit $\mu_0 = 108 - (2.787)(3.0) = 99.64$

Thus, the 99% confidence limits are 99.64–116.36 as compared to the 95% confidence limits: 101.82–114.18.

27. The t-distributions are more spread out than the normal curve. Thus, the proportion of area beyond a specific value of t is greater than the proportion of area beyond the corresponding value of z. As df increases, the t-distributions more closely resemble the normal curve.

28. **a)** Married couples: $t = 5.219$;   df $= 51$; $p < 0.05$
       Divorced couples: $t = 0.329$;   df $= 22$;   not significant
   b) Married couples: $t = 1.688$;   df $= 51$;   not significant
       Divorced couples: $t = 0.615$;   df $= 22$;   not significant

31. $t = 4.28$

32. $r_{s(0.05)} = 0.450$

33. $t = 4$

Chapter 15

1. $F = 47.02$;   reject H_0.

2. All comparisons are significant at 0.01 level. It is clear that death rates are lowest in summer, next to lowest in spring, next to highest in fall, and highest in winter.

3. When we use the 0.05 level, one out of every 20 comparisons will be significant *by chance*. Thus, a significant difference at the 0.05 level in one of ten studies can be attributed to chance.

4. $F = 0.30$;   df $= 3, 12$

5. $F = 10.43$;   df $= 2, 12$; HSD $= 7.16$

6. If the F-ratio is less than 1.00, we conclude that the groups probably come from the same population.

7.

Source of Variation	Sum of Squares	Degrees of Freedom	Mean Square	F
Between groups	1.083	2	0.5415	0.6228
Within groups	13.042	15	0.8695	
Total	14.125	17		

8.

Source of Variation	Sum of Squares	Degrees of Freedom	Mean Square	F
Between groups	919.793	3	306.598	6.43
Within groups	954.167	20	47.708	
Total	1873.96	23		

9.

Source of Variation	Sum of Squares	Degrees of Freedom	Mean Square	F
Between groups	26.80	2	13.4	9.37
Within groups	17.20	12	1.43	
Total	44.00	14		

10. All comparisons are significant at 0.01 level. It is clear that group C is superior, next group B, followed by group A.

13. a)

Source of Variation	Sum of Squares	Degrees of Freedom	Mean Square	F
Between groups	15.8645	3	5.288	15.57
Within groups	6.7917	20	0.3396	
Total	22.6562	23		

Chapter 16

1. $\chi^2 = 68.19$; df $= 3$; all expected cell values equal 27.5.

2.

f_0	f_e	$f_0 - f_e$	$(f - f_e)^2$	$(f_0 - f_e)^2/f_e$
120	96	24	576	6.00
400	390	10	100	0.26
80	114	−34	1156	10.14
600	600			$\chi^2 = 16.40$

In this example $k = 3$; therefore, df $= 2$. Assuming $\alpha = 0.01$, we find that Table B indicates that a χ^2 value of 9.21 or greater is required for significance. Since our calculated value of 16.40 is greater than 9.21, we may reject the null hypothesis and assert that the preferred number of children has changed over the past 5 years.

3.

20	20	40	$\chi^2 = 0$; phi $= 0$
20	20	40	
40	40		

4. a) $\chi^2 = 5$; phi $= 0.25$ **b)** $\chi^2 = 20$; phi $= 0.50$ **c)** $\chi^2 = 80$; phi $= 1.00$

5. $\chi^2 = 44.46;\quad V = 0.50$

| | | **Sexual Orientation** | |
		Homosexual Males	Heterosexual Males
	Great	57.1	13.6
Fear of AIDS	Moderate	28.6	31.8
	Low	14.3	54.5
		100.0	99.9*

* Due to rounding.

6. $\chi^2 = 10.14;\quad df = 3$

8. $\chi^2 = 2.29;\quad df = 4$

9. Race and religious affiliation are nominal-level variables, and hence it is not possible to specify the direction of the relationship between the variables.

11. $\chi^2 = 1.94;\quad df = 1$

14. $\chi^2 = 6.00;\quad df = 3$

15. $\chi^2 = 8.87;\quad df = 1$

16. The research merely demonstrated that the two variables are related. Since the ownership of dogs was not randomly assigned to the coronary victims, we do not know whether the dog-owners differ in other systematic ways from those who do not own dogs. For example, dog-owners may differ from nonowners in personality characteristics, dietary habits, family ties, etc. They may also exercise more (walking their dogs).

17. **a)** The χ^2 test of independence   **b)** $\chi^2 = 3.645$. The obtained χ^2 falls short of the critical value of 3.841 at $\alpha = 0.05;\quad df = 1$.

19. **a)** MDs: 97.9% survived, 2.1% died;   RNs: 93.4% survived, 6.6% died; Others: 92.5% survived, 7.5% died
b) Chi square test of independence.
c) Obtained $\chi^2 = 16.186$;   critical value at $\alpha = 0.01$ level $= 9.210$; $df = 2$. Reject H_0. The mortality rate is related to the care-giver who inserts the catheter.

Chapter 17

1. **a)** sign test $N = 10$, $x = 7$ **b)** $N = 10$, $T = 10$ **c)** $U = 23$, $U' = 77$

3. $U = 18$, $U' = 103$ **5.** $T = 48$

7. sign test $N = 10$, $x = 6$;   Wilcoxon $T = -12$

9. $U' = 89$, $U = 11$

Index

A posteriori comparisons, 394
A priori comparisons, 394
Absolute values, 127
Addition rule, 291
Alpha (α) level, 326
Analysis of variance (ANOVA):
  assumptions in, 391–392
  interpretation of F in, 394–396
  multigroup comparisons in, 383–385
  sample of, 392–394
  sums of squares in, 385–389
  variance estimates in, 389–390
Arithmetic mean:
  calculation of, 99–103
  median and mode compared with, 110–114
  properties of, 103–106
  skewness and, 114–115
  standard normal distribution and, 149–150
  weighted, 106–107
Arrays, 104
Association, measures of, 11, 177
  based on chi-square (χ^2), 416–419
  correlations, 199–201
  Goodman's and Kruskal's gamma, 184–189
    test of significance of, 374–375
  Kendall's tau-b (τ_b), 190–191
  lambda (λ), 178–180
    interpretation and limitations of, 181–182
  ordinal, 182–183
    pair-by-pair comparisons, 183–184
  Somer's d, 189–190
Asymmetric measures of association, 177
Average deviation, 125–128

Averages (*see* Central tendency, measures of;
  Mean)

Bar graphs, 62
  histograms and, 64
Beta (β), 332
Beta weights, 268n
Between-group sum of squares (SS_{bet}), 388–389
  degrees of freedom for, 389
Between-group variances, 389, 391
Biased sampling, 285–286
Binomial distribution, 287, 324
  tables of, 479, 481–487
Bivariate contingency table, 168–170

Carlyle, Thomas, 23
Causality, 14–15
  correlation and, 243–245
  in multivariate analysis, 257
  spurious relationships and, 259
Centiles, 90
Central limit theorem, 349
Central tendency, measures of, 97
  arithmetic mean as
    calculation of, 99–103
    properties of, 103–106
    weighted mean, 106–107
  comparisons of, 110–112

567

Central tendency *(Cont.)*:
  frequency distributions and, 98–99
  median as, 107–109
  mode as, 109–110
  skewness and, 114–115
Chi-square (χ^2):
  limitations in use of, 413–416
  nominal measures of association based on, 416–419
  one-variable case of, 407–409
  table of, 465
  to test independence of variable, 410–413
Class intervals, 56–59
  labeling, 173
  open-ended, 112
  unequal, 65
Coefficients:
  contingency, 418–419
  of correlation, 199
    interpreting, 208–212
  of multiple regression, 267, 271–272
  of nondetermination, 242, 271*n*
  of partial correlation, 259–262
    computational equation for, 262–263
  phi (ϕ), 416–418
Computers:
  random numbers generated by, 286
  sampling by, 351
Concordant pairs, 183
  Goodman's and Kruskal's gamma for, 187
Conditional distributions, 170
Conditional probability, 297–298
Conditional tables, 255
  order of, 257
Confidence intervals and limits, 365–368
  for large samples, 368–369
  for percentages, 369–370
Contingency coefficient, 418–419
Contingency tables:
  bivariate, 168–170
  measures of association for, 177
  percentaging, 170–172
Continuous variables, 33–35
  probability and, 302–303
Control variables, 255–257, 259
Correlated samples, 433
Correlation, 14, 199–201
  causation and, 243–245
  correlation matrices, 206–208
  interpreting coefficients of, 208–212
  multiple regression, 264–265
    coefficient of, 271–272
    example of, 266–271
    graphs of, 265–266
  partial, 258–259, 263
    coefficient of, 259–262
    computational equation for, 262–263
  Pearson's *r* for
    mean deviation method for calculating, 201–203
    raw score method for calculating, 203–204

Correlation *(Cont.)*:
  test of significance of, 370–374
  z scores and, 204–206
  Spearman's rho (r_s) for, 214–216
Correlation coefficients, 199
  interpreting, 208–212
  population (ρ), 371
Correlation matrices, 206–208
Cramer's *V*, 419
Critical regions:
  in chi-square (χ^2) tests, 411
  in testing hypotheses, 354
Critical values:
  in *t*-distribution, 361
Cumulative frequencies, 59–60
Cumulative frequency curves (ogives), 66–69
  obtaining percentile rank from, 84–85
Cumulative frequency distributions, 59–60
Cumulative percent distributions, 60
Cumulative percentages, 59–60
  percentile ranks and, 84–85

Data, 7
  collection of, 6, 13
  cumulative frequencies and percentage distributions of, 59–60
  graphing of, 60–61
  misuse of, 61–62
  grouping of, 55–56
    class intervals for, 56–59
Deciles, 90
Degrees of freedom (df), 360
  in analysis of variance, 389, 390
  for chi-square (χ^2), 408
Dependency ratio, 38
Dependent variables, 167–168
  in contingency tables, 172
  in multiple regression, 265–267
    coefficient of, 271–272
  predicting from independent variable, 231–233
  in scatter diagrams, 200
Descriptive statistics, 6, 10–12
Deviation from mean, 103–104
  standard scores and, 145–146
Discontinuous (discrete) variables, 33–34
Discordant pairs, 183
  Goodman's and Kruskal's gamma for, 185–186
Discrete variables, 33–34
Dispersion, measures of, 123–124
  interquartile range as, 125
  mean deviation as, 125–128
  range as, 124–125
  variance and standard deviation as, 128–129
    errors in, 132–133
    interpretation of, 134
    mean deviation method of calculation of, 129–131
    raw score method of calculation of, 131–132

Distributions:
  binomial, 287, 324
  conditional, 170
  cumulative frequencies and percentages, 59–60
  F, 389
  frequency distributions
    class intervals for, 56–59
    graphs of, 63–73
    ungrouped, 55–56
  sampling distributions, 320–324
    of means, 346–350
  standard normal distribution, 148–150
    raw scores transformed into, 150–152
  t, 359–361

Elements, in populations, 7–8
Empirical probabilities, 289
Epsilon (ε), 173, 178
Errors:
  in calculation of standard deviation, 132–133
  in causation, 243–245
  gambler's fallacy as, 284
  of measurement, 35
  proportional reduction in, 178, 181
  standard deviation as estimate of, 158
  standard error of estimate, 238–240
  type I and II, 330–336
  in use of chi-square (χ^2), 413
Estimates:
  of error, standard deviation as, 158
  interval estimation, 363–365
  point estimation, 355–358
  standard error of, 238–240
  of variance, 389–390
Explained variation, 241
Exponents, 24–25

F-distributions, 389
  table of, 467–474
Finite populations, 7
First-order tables, 257
Fisher, R. A., 372
F-ratio, 390, 391
  interpretation of, 394–396
Frequency curves (frequency polygons), 65–66
  forms of, 69–71
Frequency distributions, 98–99
  binomial distribution, 287
  bivariate contingency table and, 168–170
  class intervals for, 56–59
  cumulative, 59–60
  graphs of
    forms of, 69–71
    frequency curves of, 65–66
    histograms, 63–65
    ogives (cumulative frequency curves) of, 66–69

Frequency distributions *(Cont.):*
  pictographs, pie charts, and trend charts, 72–73
  grouped
    mean calculated from, 103
    median calculated from, 107–108
  ungrouped, 55–56
    mean calculated from, 102
    standard deviation calculated from, 129–132

Gambler's fallacy, 284
Goodman's and Kruskal's gamma, 184–187
  interpretation and limitations of, 188–189
  test of significance of, 374–375
"Goodness-of-fit" technique, 407
Gosset, William ("Student"), 359
Graphs, 60–61
  bar graphs, 62
  frequency curves, 65–66
    forms of, 69–71
  histograms, 63–65
    mode shown in, 110
  misuse of, 61–62
  of multiple regression analysis, 265–266
  ogives (cumulative frequency curves), 66–69
    obtaining percentile rank from, 84–85
  pictographs, pie charts, and trend charts, 72–73
  scatter diagrams, 200
Grouped frequency distributions, 58
  mean calculated from, 103
  median calculated from, 107–108

Histograms, 63–65
  mode shown in, 110
Homogeneity of variance, 392
Huff, D., 244
Hypothesis testing:
  about sample mean, 353–355
  indirect proofs in, 329–330
  with known population mean and standard deviation, 350–353
  null and alternative hypotheses in, 327–329
  significance levels in, 324–327
  type I and II errors in, 330–336
  with unknown parameters, Student's *t,* 358–361

Independence:
  chi-square (χ^2) test of, 410–413
  in probability, 284, 286, 298
Independent variables, 167–168
  in contingency tables, 170–172
  control variables as, 259
  lambda (λ) and, 178–180
    interpretation and limitations of, 181–182

Independent variables *(Cont.)*:
  in multiple regression, 264–267
    coefficient of, 271–272
  one-way analysis of variance of, 385
  predicting dependent variable from, 231–233
  in scatter diagrams, 200
  in strength of relationships, 173
Indeterminant values, 111–112
Indirect proof, 329–330
Inductive statistics, 6–7, 12–13
Inferential statistics, 6–7, 12–13, 343–346
  cautions regarding, 336
Infinite populations, 7
Intelligence quotients (I.Q.s), 32
Interaction, between variables, 264
Interquartile range, 125
Interval estimation, 363–365
Interval scales, 32–33
  frequency curves, 65–66
    forms of, 69–71
  histograms, 63–65
    mode shown in, 110
  labeling, 173
  ogives (cumulative frequency curves), 66–69
    obtaining percentile rank from, 84–85
Intervening variables, 258

Joint probability, 296
Joint-probability method, 412

Kendall's tau-*b* (τb), 184, 190–191

Lambda (λ), 178–180
  interpretation and limitations of, 181–182
Large numbers, law of, 346*n*
Least-squares rule, 105
Leptokurtic distributions, 69
Limits, 35
  of class intervals, 59
Linear regression:
  equation for, 228–231
  mean deviation and raw score methods of computing, 234–235
  predicting dependent variable from independent variable in, 231–233
  regression lines, 235–238
  sample problem in, 233–234

Mann-Whitney *U*-test, 427–431
  with *N* greater than 20, 431–433
  tables for, 499–503
  with tied ranks, 431
Marginal probability, 296–297

Marginals, 170
Matched pairs, Wilcoxon signed-rank test of, 436–438
Matched-group design, 433
Mathematical notation, 24
Mathematical operators, 25
Mathematics, 23
  numbers and scales in, 27–28
    interval and ratio scales, 32–33, 63–69
    nominal scales, 28–29, 62–63
    ordinal scales, 29–31, 63
  proportions, percentages, and rates in, 38–43
  of ratios, 37–38
  of rounding, 35–37
  summation rules in, 24–25
  variables in, 33–35
Mean:
  calculation of, 99–103
  median and mode compared with, 110–111
  properties of, 103–106
  sampling distribution of, 346–350
  skewness and, 114–115
  standard error of, 346
  standard normal distribution and, 149–150
  weighted, 106–107
Mean deviation, 125–128
  calculating linear regression from, 234–235
  Pearson's *r* calculated from, 201–203
  variance and standard deviation calculated from, 129–131
Mean squares, 391
Measurement, 28
  errors of, 35
Median, 107–109
  mean and mode compared with, 110–114
  skewness and, 114–115
Mesokurtic distributions, 69
Misuse of statistics, 15–16
  of graphic techniques, 61–62
  of measures of central tendency, 989
  post hoc fallacy in, 244–245
Mode, 109–110
  mean and median compared with, 110–114
  skewness and, 114–115
Mu (μ), 148
Multigroup comparisons, 383–385
Multiple regression analysis, 264–265
  coefficient of, 271–272
  example of, 266–271
  graphs of, 265–266
Multiplication rule, 295–298
  for independent events, 298–299
  for nonindependent events, 299–302
Multivariate data analysis, 253–255
  multiple regression analysis in, 264–271
    coefficient of, 271–272
  multivariate contingency table for, 255–258
  partial correlation in, 258–259
    coefficient of, 259–262
    computational equation for, 262–263
Mutually exclusive events, 291–294

Negative relationships, 176, 201
Nominal numbers, 27–28
Nominal scales, 28–29
Nominally-scaled variables, 62–63
  lambda (λ) to measure association between, 178–180
    interpretation and limitations of, 181–182
  measures of association based on chi-square (χ^2) for, 416–419
Nonparametric statistical methods, 405–407
  chi-square (χ^2)
    limitations in use of, 413–416
    nominal measures of association based on, 416–419
    one-variable case of, 407–409
    to test independence of variable, 410–413
  for ordinally-scaled variables, 427–428
    for correlated samples, 433
    Mann-Whitney U-test, 428–433
    sign test, 433–436
    Wilcoxon matched-pairs signed rank test, 436–438
Normal curve, 69–70, 287
  probability and, 303–305
  tables of areas under, 462–464
Normal distribution, 148–150
  raw scores transformed into, 150–152
  standard deviation and, 134
Notation, mathematical, 24
Null hypotheses, 327
  reasons to reject, 329–330
  in testing hypotheses, 354
  type I and II errors in testing of, 331–333
Numbers:
  absolute values of, 127
  large, law of, 346n
  random, 286
    table of, 495–498
  rounding, 35–37
  table of squares, square roots and reciprocals of, 489–494
  true limits of, 35
  types of, 27–28

Ogives (cumulative frequency curves), 66–69
  obtaining percentile rank from, 84–85
One-tailed tests:
  p values for, 305–307
  probability values in, 328–329
One-variable test, 407–409
One-way analysis of variance, 385
Open-ended classes, 112
Operators, mathematical, 25
Order of conditional tables, 257
Ordinal numbers, 27–28
Ordinal scales, 29–31
  labeling, 173
Ordinally-scaled variables, 63
  inferential statistics for, 427–428

Ordinally-scaled variables *(Cont.)*:
  Mann-Whitney U-test, 428–433
  nonparametric tests, 433
  sign test, 433–436
  Wilcoxon matched-pairs signed-rank test, 436–438
  measures of association between, 182–183
  pair-by-pair comparisons, 183–184

Pair-by-pair comparisons, 182–184
  Goodman's and Kruskal's gamma for, 184–189
    test of significance of, 374–375
  Kendall's tau-b (τ_b) for, 190–191
  Somer's d for, 189–190
  Wilcoxon matched-pairs signed-rank test of, 436–438
Parameters, 8
  interval estimation of, 363–365
  point estimation of, 355–358
  unknown, Student's t for testing, 358–361
Parametric statistics, 405
Partial correlation, 258–259, 263
  coefficient of, 259–262
  computational equation for, 262–263
Partial tables, 255
Pearson, Karl, 418
Pearson's r, 200–210
  calculation of
    mean deviation method of, 201–203
    raw score method of, 203–204
  interpreting, 208–212
  tables for, 476
    functions of, 477–478
    transformation of z into, 475
  test of significance of, 370–374
  z scores and, 204–206
Percentages, 39–40
  for contingency tables, 170–172
  cumulative distributions of, 59–60
  probabilities expressed as, 291
Percentile ranks, 83–90, 143
Percentiles, 83–84
  centiles, deciles and quartiles, 90
  confidence intervals and limits for, 369–370
  cumulative, and percentile ranks, 83–90
  interquartile range of, 125
Perfect relationships, 177
Phi coefficient (ϕ), 416–418
Pictographs, 72–73
Pie charts, 73
Platykurtic distributions, 69
Point estimation, 355–358, 364
Populations, 7, 319–320
  correlation coefficient (ρ) of, 371
  estimates of variance in, 356–357
  null and alternative hypotheses on, 327–329
  sampling distribution of mean for, 349
  sampling distributions and, 320–324
Positive relationships, 173, 201

Post hoc fallacy, 244–245
Prediction, 225–228
  causation and, 243–245
  linear regression and, 228–238
Probability, 283–285
  approaches to
    classical, 288
    empirical, 288–290
    subjective, 290
  continuous variables in, 302–303
  formal properties of, 290–291
  multiplication rule in, 295–298
    for independent events, 298–299
    for nonindependent events, 299–302
  mutually exclusive events in, 291–294
  normal-curve model in, 303–305
  one- and two-tailed p values of, 305–307
  randomness in, 285–288
  significance levels and, 324–327
Proof, indirect, 329–330
Proportional reduction in error (PRE), 178, 181
Proportions, 38–39
  probabilities as, 288, 291
  standard errors of, 369

Quartiles, 90

r (see Pearson's r)
Random number tables, 286, 495–498
Random samples, 8, 55, 285
Randomness, 285–288
Range, 124–125
  restriction on, 211
  of sample means, 350–353
Ranks:
  Mann-Whitney U-test of, 429, 431
  in ordinal scales, 30
    measures of association in, 182–184
  percentile ranks, 83–90, 143
  Spearman's rho (r_s) for, 214–216
  Wilcoxon matched-pairs signed-rank test of,
    436–438
Rates, 40–43
Ratio scales, 32–33
  graphs of, 63–69
Ratios, 37–38
Raw scores:
  calculating linear regression from, 234–235
  calculating standard deviation from, 131–132
  Pearson's r calculated from, 203–204
  transforming into z scores, 150–152
Reciprocals, table of, 489–494
Rectangular distributions, 70
Regression, 226–227
  linear
    equation for, 228–231

Regression (Cont.):
  mean deviation and raw score methods of
    computing, 234–235
  predicting dependent variable from indepen-
    dent variable in, 231–233
  regression lines in, 235–238
  multiple, 264–265
    coefficient of, 271–272
    example of, 266–271
    graphs of, 265–266
  standard error of estimate in, 238–240
Regression lines, 232
  constructing, 235–238
  standard error of estimate and, 238–240
Regression planes, 266
Regression sum of squares (RegSS), 241
Relationships:
  causality in, 14–15, 243–245
  existence, direction, and strength of, 172–177
  interpreting correlation coefficients of, 208–212
  linear, 228–231
  measures of association as, 11
  in ordinal scales, 30
  Pearson's r, 201
    test of significance of, 370–374
  in research design, 14
  spurious, 259
Research design, 6
  dependent and independent variables in, 167–
    168
Residual sum of squares (RSS), 241
Residual variance, 238–240
Rho (ρ), 371–374
Robustness, 361
Rounding, 35–37

Sample mean:
  testing hypotheses about, 353–355
  testing range of, 350–353
Sampling and samples, 8, 319–320
  confidence intervals and limits for, 368–369
  law of large numbers in, 346n
  random samples in, 285–286
Sampling distributions, 320–324, 345
  of means, 346–350
  in testing hypotheses, 354
Scales:
  interval and ratio, 32–33
    frequency curves, 65–66, 69–71
    histograms, 63–65
    ogives (cumulative frequency curves) of, 66–
      69
  labeling, 173
  nominal, 28–29, 62–63
    lambda (λ) to measure association in, 178–
      182
    measures of association based on chi-square
      (χ^2) for, 416–419
  ordinal, 29–31, 63
    measures of association in, 182–184

Scatter diagrams, 200
Sex ratios, 37
Sigma (Σ), 24
Sigma (σ), 148
Sign test, 427–428, 433–436
Significance, tests of:
  of Goodman's and Kruskal's gamma, 374–375
  of Student's *t*, 370–374
Significance levels, 324–327
  caution regarding, 336
  in testing hypotheses, 354
  type II errors and, 332
Skewed distributions, 71
  mean, median, and mode in, 114–115
Slope, 230
Somer's *d*, 184, 189–190
Spurious relationships, 259
Square roots, table of, 489–494
Squares, table of, 489–494
Standard deviations, 128–129
  errors in calculation of, 132–133
  as estimate of error and precision, 158
  estimated from sample data, 357–358
  interpretation of, 134
  interpreting, 159–160
  mean deviation method of calculation of, 129–131
  raw score method of calculation of, 131–132
  standard error of mean as, 346
  standard normal distribution and, 149–150
  z scores and, 146–148
Standard errors:
  of estimate, 238–240
  of mean, 346, 348
  of proportions, 369
Standard normal distribution, 148–150
  raw scores transformed into, 150–152
Standard scores, 143–148
Standardized path coefficients, 268*n*
Statistical control, 260
Statistical elaboration, 257
Statistical inference (*see* Inferential statistics)
Statistics, 3–7
  definition of, 8–9
  descriptive, 10–12
  inferential, 12–13
  mathematics in, 23
  (*See also* Inferential statistics)
Student's *t*, 358–361
  assumptions in, 391–392
  confidence intervals and limits for, 365–366
  sample problem using, 362–363
  table of, 466
Student's *t*-ratio, 361
Sum of squares, 105, 129
  in analysis of variance, 385–389
  regression (RegSS), 241
  residual (RSS), 241
  total (TSS), 240–241
Summation rules, 24–25
Symmetric measures of association, 177

t distribution, 359–361
Test variables, 255–257
Tied pairs, 183
Total sum of squares (TSS), 240–241, 386, 389
Total variation, 240–241
t-ratio, 359
Treatment variables, 385
Trend charts, 73
True limits, 35
  of class intervals, 59
Truncated ranges, 211
Two-tailed tests:
  p values for, 305–307
  significance levels in, 327
Type I errors, 331, 383–385
Type II errors, 331–334

U-distributions, 70–71
Ungrouped frequency distributions, 55–56
  mean calculated from, 102
  standard deviation calculated from
    mean deviation method for, 129–131
    raw score method for, 131–132

Values:
  absolute, 127
  indeterminant, 111–112
  of variables, 28
Variables, 7, 28
  analysis of variance of, 385
  causation in relationships between, 243–245
  chi-square (χ^2) tests
    of independence, 410–413
    limitations in use of, 413–416
    nominal measures of association based on, 416–419
    one-variable, 407–409
  continuous and discrete, 33–35
    probability and, 302–303
  correlations between, 199–201
    correlation matrices for, 206–208
    interpreting, 208–212
    partial, 258–263
    Pearson's *r* for, 201–206
    Spearman's rho (r_s), 214–216
  dependent and independent, 167–168
    in contingency tables, 170–172
    predicting values of, 231–233
  indeterminant values of, 111–112
  interaction between, 264
  interval- and ratio-scales of
    frequency curves, 65–66, 69–71
    histograms of, 63–65
    ogives (cumulative frequency curves) of, 66–69
  in multiple regression, 264–265
    coefficient of, 271–272

Variables *(Cont.)*:
 multivariate analysis of, 254–255
  multiple regression analysis in, 264–272
  multivariate contingency table for, 255–258
 nominally-scaled, 62–63
  lambda (λ) to measure association between, 178–182
  measures of association based on chi-square (χ^2) for, 416–419
 ordinal, 32
  measures of association between, 182–184
 ordinally-scaled, 63
  inferential statistics for, 427–428
  Mann-Whitney U-test for, 428–433
  nonparametric tests for, 433
  sign test for, 433–436
  Wilcoxon matched-pairs signed-rank test, 436–438
Variance, 128–129
 estimates of, 389–390
 mean deviation method of calculation of, 129–131
 of populations
  biased estimates of, 357
  unbiased estimates of, 356–357
 residual, 238–240
 (See also Analysis of variance)

Variation:
 explained and unexplained, 240–242
 multivariate analysis of, 258

Weighted mean, 106–107
Wells, H. G., 15
Wilcoxon matched-pairs signed-rank test, 428, 436–438
Within-group sum of squares (SS$_w$), 386–389
 degrees of freedom for, 390
Within-group variances, 389, 391

Yule's Q, 184n

z scores, 144, 146–148
 Pearson's r and, 204–206
 for sample mean, 350
 sample r's transformed into, 372–373
 t distribution and, 359–360
 tables of, 462–464
  transformation of r into, 475
 transforming raw scores into, 150–152
Zero point, in ratio scales, 32
Zero-order tables, 257

List of Equations *(Continued)*

NUMBER	EQUATION	PAGE
(10.9)	$s_{\text{est } y} = \sqrt{\dfrac{\Sigma(Y - Y')^2}{N}}$	240
(10.11)	$\underset{\substack{\text{Total} \\ \text{variation}}}{\Sigma(Y - \overline{Y})^2} = \underset{\substack{\text{Unexplained} \\ \text{variation}}}{\Sigma(Y - Y')^2} + \underset{\substack{\text{Explained} \\ \text{variation}}}{\Sigma(Y' - \overline{Y})^2}$	241
(10.12)	$r^2 = \dfrac{\text{explained variation}}{\text{total variation}} = \dfrac{\Sigma(Y' - \overline{Y})^2}{\Sigma(Y - \overline{Y})^2}$	242
(11.1)	$r_{XY.Z} = \dfrac{r_{XY} - r_{XZ}\,r_{YZ}}{\sqrt{(1 - r_{XZ}^2)(1 - r_{YZ}^2)}}$	262
(11.2)	$Y' = a + b_1 X_1 + b_2 X_2$	265
(12.4)	$p(A \text{ or } B) = p(A) + p(B)$, when A and B are *mutually exclusive*	293
(12.6)	$P + Q = 1.00$, when the events are *mutually exclusive* and *exhaustive*	294
(12.9)	$p(A \text{ and } B) = p(A)p(B)$, when the events are *independent*	299
(12.10)	$p(A \text{ and } B) = p(A)p(B|A) = p(B)p(A|B)$	300
(14.3)	$z = \dfrac{\overline{X} - \mu_0}{\sigma_{\overline{X}}}$	353
(14.8)	$\text{estimated } \sigma_{\overline{X}} = s_{\overline{X}} = \dfrac{s}{\sqrt{N - 1}} = \sqrt{\dfrac{\Sigma(X - \overline{X})^2}{N(N - 1)}}$	358
(14.9)	$t = \dfrac{\overline{X} - \mu_0}{s_{\overline{X}}}$	359
(14.10)	$\text{upper limit } \mu_0 = \overline{X} + (t_{0.05})(s_{\overline{X}})$	366
(14.11)	$\text{lower limit } \mu_0 = \overline{X} - (t_{0.05})(s_{\overline{X}})$	367
(14.14)	$\sigma_P = \sqrt{\dfrac{P(1 - P)}{N}}$	370
(15.2)	$SS_{\text{tot}} = \Sigma X_{\text{tot}}^2 - \dfrac{(\Sigma X_{\text{tot}})^2}{N}$	386